上海市统计局·编
SHANGHAI MUNICIPAL STATISTICS BUREAU

上海统计年鉴 2008

SHANGHAI STATISTICAL YEARBOOK

中国统计出版社
China Statistics Press

《上海统计年鉴—2008》编辑委员 EDITORIAL BOARD

编者说明

一、《上海统计年鉴——2008》是一本信息高度密集的资料工具书。本书收录了2007年上海的经济和社会等各方面的统计数据,以及重要年份和改革开放以来的主要统计数据。

二、全书内容分为24个篇目,即:1. 行政区划和自然地理;2. 综合;3. 人口和劳动力;4. 国民经济核算;5. 财政收支;6. 固定资产投资;7. 对外经济贸易和旅游;8. 价格水平;9. 人民生活;10. 城市建设;11. 农业;12. 工业;13. 建筑业;14. 交通运输、邮政和信息传输;15. 批发和零售;16. 金融业;17. 房地产业;18. 科学技术;19. 环境保护治理;20. 教育;21. 卫生、社会保障和社会福利业;22. 文化和体育;23. 法律、公证和其他;24. 浦东新区。为便于读者正确地使用资料,各篇目还附有主要统计指标解释。

三、本年鉴数据主要是由我局通过年报调查收集,不作特别说明。凡是由专业部门提供的数据均在表式的注释中说明了数据来源。

四、资料中所使用的度量衡单位均采用国际统一标准计量单位。

五、本年鉴总量指标计算所采用的价格均为现行价格。

六、本年鉴部分数据合计数或相对数由于单位取舍不同产生的计算误差均未作机械调整。

七、本年鉴表中的符号使用说明:

“…”表示数据不足本表最小计量单位数;

“空格”表示该项统计数据不详或无该项数据;

“#”表示其中的主要项。

八、《上海统计年鉴》公开出版以来,受到了国内外广大读者的关心和支持,对本年鉴的内容和编辑工作提出了许多宝贵的意见,对此我们深表谢意。限于我们的水平,本年鉴还存在一些不足之处,欢迎读者继续给予批评和指正,帮助我们进一步改进年鉴的编辑工作,以期更好地为广大读者服务。

EDITOR'S NOTE

Ⅰ. Shanghai Statistical Yearbook 2008 contains comprehensive statistics of Shanghai's social and economic development in 2007 and selected data of some important years and of the period since China adopted the policy of reform and opening to the outside world.

Ⅱ. The book is composed of 24 parts viz. 1. Administrative Division and Physical Geography; 2. General Survey; 3. Porpulation and Labor Force; 4. National Economic Accounting; 5. Fiscal Revenue and Expenditure; 6. Investment in Fixed Assets; 7. Foreign Economic Relations, Trade and Tourism; 8. Prices; 9. Living Standards; 10. Urban Construction; 11. Agriculture; 12. Industry; 13. Construction; 14. Transportation, Posts and Information Transmission; 15. Wholesale and Retail; 16. Finance; 17. Real Estate; 18. Science and Technology; 19. Environment Protection and Treatment; 20. Education; 21. Health, Social Security and Social Welfare; 22. Culture, Sports; 23. Laws, Notary and others; 24. Pudong New Area. In order to make readers using materials correctly, explanations of major statistical indicators are attached after every chapter.

Ⅲ. Main part of the data in this yearbook are investigated and collected by Municipal Statistical Bureau, we haven't mentioned especially. As to the data provided by professional bureaus, we especially mentioned the source of data in the notes after the tables.

Ⅳ. The international standard unit of measurement is applied in this book.

Ⅴ. The prices used for gross indicators' calculating in this yearbook are current prices.

Ⅵ. Statistical discrepancies in this book due to rounding are not adjusted.

Ⅶ. Marks in this book: … means not large enough to be rounded into the least unit of measurement; Blank space means data are not available; # indicates major item in a category.

Ⅷ. Previous editions of Shanghai Statistical Yearbook have won wide acclaim among the readers. In order to excel, we welcome all candid comments and criticism from our readers.

目录
CONTENTS

第一篇 CHAPTER 1 行政区划和自然地理 ADMINISTRATIVE DIVISION AND PHYSICAL GEOGRAPHY

第二篇 CHAPTER 2 综合 GENERAL SURVEY

目录
CONTENTS

第三篇 CHAPTER 3 人口和劳动力 POPULATION AND LABOUR FORCE

第四篇 CHAPTER 4 国民经济核算 NATIONAL ECONOMIC ACCOUNTING

目录
CONTENTS

第五篇 CHAPTER 5 财政收支 FISCAL REVENUE AND EXPENDITURE

第六篇 CHAPTER 6 固定资产投资 INVESTMENT IN FIXED ASSETS

目录
CONTENTS

第七篇 CHAPTER 7 对外经济贸易和旅游 FOREIGN ECONOMIC RELATIONS, TRADE AND TOURISM

第八篇 CHAPTER 8 价格水平 PRICES

目录
CONTENTS

第九篇 CHAPTER 9 人民生活 LIVING STANDARDS

目录
CONTENTS

第十一篇 CHAPTER 11 农业 AGRICULTURE

目录
CONTENTS

第十二篇 CHAPTER 12 工业 INDUSTRY

第十三篇 CHAPTER 13 建筑业 CONSTRUCTION

目录
CONTENTS

第十四篇 CHAPTER 14 交通运输、邮政和信息传输 TRANSPORTATION, POSTS AND INFORMATION TRANSMISSION

第十五篇 CHAPTER 15 批发和零售 WHOLESALE AND RETAIL

目录
CONTENTS

第十六篇 CHAPTER 16 金融业 FINANCE

目录
CONTENTS

第十七篇 CHAPTER 17 房地产业 REAL ESTATE

第十八篇 CHAPTER 18 科学技术 SCIENCE AND TECHNOLOGY

目录
CONTENTS

第十九篇 CHAPTER 19 环境保护治理 ENVIRONMENT PROTECTION AND TREATMENT

第二十篇 CHAPTER 20 教 育 EDUCATION

目录
CONTENTS

第二十一篇 CHAPTER 21 卫生、社会保障和社会福利业 HEALTH,SOCIAL SECURITY AND SOCIAL WELFARE

目录

CONTENTS

第二十二篇 CHAPTER 22 文化和体育 CULTURE,SPORTS

目录 CONTENTS

第二十三篇 CHAPTER 23 法律、公证和其他 LAWS,NOTARY AND OTHERS

第二十四篇 CHAPTER 24 浦东新区 PUDONG NEW AREA

第一篇

CHAPTER 1

行政区划和自然地理

ADMINISTRATIVE DIVISION
AND PHYSICAL GEOGRAPHY

表1.1 行政区划（2007）
ADMINISTRATIVE DIVISION

单位：个（unit）

地区	District	镇 Towns	乡 Township	街道办事处 Urban Sub-district Office	居民委员会 Neighbourhood Committees	村民委员会 Village Committees
全　市	**Total**	**107**	**3**	**101**	**3 525**	**1 830**
浦东新区	Pudong New Area	11		12	601	233
黄浦区	Huangpu			6	120	
卢湾区	Luwan			4	74	
徐汇区	Xuhui	1		12	298	10
长宁区	Changning	1		9	174	5
静安区	Jing'an			5	74	
普陀区	Putuo	3		6	228	8
闸北区	Zhabei	1		8	212	1
虹口区	Hongkou			10	239	
杨浦区	Yangpu	1		11	306	
宝山区	Baoshan	9		3	261	113
闵行区	Minhang	9		3	331	161
嘉定区	Jiading	8		3	110	160
金山区	Jinshan	9		1	77	131
松江区	Songjiang	11		4	134	115
青浦区	Qingpu	8		3	70	184
南汇区	Nanhui	14		1	76	185
奉贤区	Fengxian	8			82	252
崇明县	Chongming	13	3		58	272

注：本表由市民政局提供。
Note: The figures on the table are provided by Shanghai Civil Affairs Bureau.

自然状况(2007)
NATURAL CONDITIONS

位　置:

上海,简称沪。位于北纬 31 度 14 分,东经 121 度 29 分。它北界长江,东濒东海,南临杭州湾,西接江苏、浙江两省。

上海地处长江三角洲东缘,位于我国南北海岸的中心,长江由此入海,交通便利,腹地广阔,地理位置优越,是一个良好的江海港口。

Location:

Shanghai, or "Hu" alternatively, located at 31° 14 ′ north latitude and 121°29 ′ east longtitude, with the Yangtze River to the north, the East China Sea to the east, the Hangzhou Bay to the south, Jiangsu and Zhejiang Provinces to the west.

The city situates on the eastern fringe of the Yangtze River Delta, which is in the centre of the coastline from north to south. Located at the mouth of the Yangtze River, Shanghai enjoys convenienn communications and a favourable geographical location with a good harbour and a vast hinterland.

地　势:

全境除西南部有少数残丘外,全为坦荡低平的长江三角洲冲击平原的一部分,平均高度海拔 4 米左右。

Topography:

Shanghai averages about 4 metres above the sea level, whose territory is a part of the broad flat alluvial plain of the Yangtze River Delta with few remnant hills in the southwest.

面　积:

全市面积 6 340. 5 平方公里,其中陆地面积 6 218. 65 平方公里,水面面积 121. 85 平方公里,南北长约 120 公里,东西宽约 100 公里。

Area:

Covering an area of 6 340. 5 square kilometres, land area of 6 218. 65 square kilometres and water area of 121. 85 square kilometres. The city is about 100 kilometres wide from east to west and 120 kilometres long from north to south.

河　流:

上海地区天然河港密布,多属太湖流域,主要河流有黄浦江及其支流吴淞江(苏州河)。

River:

Shanghai is thick with natural rivers and branch streams mostly in the Taihu drainge area. The main waterways are the Huangpu River and its branch Wusong River (or Suzhou Creek).

气 候:

上海地区属亚热带季风气候,四季分明。

Climate:

Shanghai has a subtropical monsoon climate with four distinct seasons.

岛 屿:

上海的崇明岛是我国的第三大岛,由长江挟带下来的泥沙冲积而成。此外,上海所属的岛屿还有长兴岛、横沙岛等。

Islands:

Chongming island in Shanghai is the third largest island in China, which is an alluvial island formed with soil carried by the Yangtze River. Other islands under Shanghai administration are Changxing Island and Hengsha Island etc.

河流名称 River		长度(公里) Length(km)	宽度(米) Width(m)	深度(米) Depth(m)
黄浦江	Huangpu River	80	400 左右(or so)	7~9
苏州河	Suzhou Creek	125	70~80	
#在本市境内	In Shanghai Territory	53.1		

岛屿名称 Island		面 积(平方公里) Area(sq. km)
崇明岛	Chongming Island	1 041.21
长兴岛	Changxing Island	74.14
横沙岛	Hengsha Island	45.92

指 标 Indicators		2007	指 标 Indicators		2007
平均气温(℃)	Annual Average Temperature(℃)	18.5	蒸发量(毫米)	Evaporation (mm)	813.8
极端最高气温(℃)	Utmost Highest Air Temperature(℃)	39.6	降水量(毫米)	Precipitation(mm)	1 208.8
极端最低气温(℃)	Utmost Lowest Air Temperature(℃)	-1.1	降雨日(天)	Annual Rainy Days(day)	126
日照时间(小时)	Annual Sunshine Time (h)	1 416.6	无霜期(天)	Frost-free Period(day)	331
			晴天天数(天)	Sunshine Days(day)	72

表 1.2　各月主要气象指标(2007)
MAIN CLIMATE INDICATORS

月　份 Month		平均气温(℃) Annual Average Temperature (℃)	极端最高气温(℃) Utmost Highest Air Temperature(℃)	极端最低气温(℃) Utmost Lcwest Air Temperature(℃)	日照时数(小时) Annual Sunshine Hours(h)
1 月	Jan.	5.9	12.7	-0.7	90.8
2 月	Feb.	9.8	23.4	-1.1	129.9
3 月	Mar.	12.1	28.4	0.8	123.9
4 月	Apr.	15.9	28.9	7.2	171.4
5 月	May.	22.9	32.6	14.7	179.7
6 月	Jun.	25.0	36.4	19.2	64.8
7 月	Jul.	30.4	39.6	24.0	135.4
8 月	Aug.	29.7	39.5	24.0	210.4
9 月	Sep.	25.4	32.6	20.2	109.5
10 月	Oct.	20.6	31.1	12.6	11.9
11 月	Nov.	14.2	22.0	6.8	127.2
12 月	Dec.	9.8	16.9	2.1	61.7

注：资料由上海市气象局提供。
Note: Data are provided by Shanghai Meteorological Bureau.

表 1.2 续表 continued

月　份 Month		降水量(毫米) Precipitation (mm)	降雨日(天) Annual Rainy Days (day)	蒸发量(毫米) Evaporation (mm)	晴天天数(天) Sunshine Days (day)
1 月	Jan.	46.2	12	23.9	5
2 月	Feb.	70.8	9	36.0	7
3 月	Mar.	104.0	11	51.9	7
4 月	Apr.	89.6	11	80.3	11
5 月	May.	27.5	5	111.6	12
6 月	Jun.	196.0	17	75.3	
7 月	Jul.	124.6	14	123.4	3
8 月	Aug.	180.2	11	121.7	13
9 月	Sep.	191.9	14	64.9	4
10 月	Oct.	124.0	5	58.3	2
11 月	Nov.	15.0	5	42.1	8
12 月	Dec.	39.0	12	24.4	

上／海／统／计／年／鉴

主要统计指标解释

行政区划

指国家对行政区域的划分。根据宪法规定，我国的行政区域划分如下：(1)全国分为省、自治区、直辖市；(2)省、自治区分为自治州、县、自治县、市；(3)自治州分为县、自治县、市；(4)县、自治县分为乡、民族乡、镇；(5)直辖市和较大的市分为区、县；(6)国家在必要时设立的特别行政区。

气　候

指地球与大气之间长期能量交换与质量交换所形成的一种自然环境状态，它是多种因素综合作用的结果。气候既是人类生活和生产的环境要素之一，又是供给人类生活和生产的重要资源。气温、降水、湿度等气象要素的多年平均值是用来描述一个地区气候状况的主要参数，而各种气象要素某年、某月的平均值(或总量)则可以反映出该时期天气气候状况的重要特征。

气　温

指空气的温度，一般以摄氏度(℃)为单位表示。气象观测的温度表是放在离地面约1.5米处通风良好的百叶箱里测量的，因此，通常说的气温指的是离地面1.5米处百叶箱中的温度。其统计计算方法为:

月平均气温是将全月各日的平均气温相加，除以该月的天数而得。

年平均气温是将12个月的月平均气温累加后除以12而得。

降水量

指从天空降落到地面的液态或固态(经融化后)水，未经蒸发、渗透、流失而在地面上积聚的深度。其统计计算方法为:

月降水量是将全月各日的降水量累加而得。

年降水量是将12个月的月降水量累加而得。

日照时数

指太阳实际照射地面的时间。其统计方法与降水量相同。

SHANGHAI STATISTICAL YEARBOOK

EXPLANATORY NOTES TO MAJOR STATISTICAL INDICATORS

□ Divisions of Administrative Areas

Divisions of Administrative Areas refer to the division of administrative areas by the state. The Constitution of the People's Republic of China stipulates that the administrative areas in China are divided as: 1) The whole country is divided into provinces, autonomous regions and municipalities directly under the central government; 2) Provinces and autonomous regions are divided into autonomous prefectures, counties, autonomous counties and cities; 3) Autonomous prefectures are divided into counties, autonomous counties and cities; 4) Counties and autonomous counties are divided into townships, nationality townships and towns; 5) Municipalities and large cities are divided into districts and counties, 6) The state shall, when necessary, establish special administrative regions.

□ Climate

Climate refers to the natural environmental status formed by the long-term exchange of energy and mass between the earth and the air, and is the results of interaction of many factors. Climate is both one of the environment factors and the important resources for the living and production activities of the human being. The average values across several years of meteorological factors such as temperature, rainfall and humidity are used as important parameters to describe the climate of a region, while the average values (or total values) of a given year or month of meteorological factors reflect the key characteristics of climate for that period of time.

□ Temperature

Temperature refers to the air temperature. It often uses centigrade as the unit. The thermometry used for weather observation is put in a breezy shutter, which is 1.5 meters high from the ground. Therefore, the commonly used temperature refers to the temperature in the breezy shutter 1.5 meters away from the ground. The calculation method is as follows:

Monthly average temperature is the summation of average daily temperature of one month divided by the actual days of that particular month. Annual average temperature is the summation of monthly average of a year divided by 12 months.

□ Volume of Precipitation

Volume of Precipitation refers to the deepness of liquid state or solid state (thawed) water falling from the sky to the ground that has not been evaporated, infiltrated or run off. The calculation method is as follows:

Monthly precipitation is the summation of daily precipitation of a month.

Annual precipitation is the summation of 12 months precipitation of a year.

□ Sunshine Hours

Sunshine Hours refer to the actual hours of sun irradiating the earth. The calculation method is the same as that of the precipitation.

第二篇

CHAPTER 2

综　　合

GENERAL SURVEY

表 2.1　主要年份社会经济主要指标
MAJOR SOCIAL AND ECONOMIC INDICATORS IN MAIN YEARS

指　标	Indicators	1990	2000	2006	2007
人口与就业	**Population and Employment**				
人　口	**Population**				
年末户籍人口(万人)	Year-end Population(10 000 persons)	1 283.35	1 321.63	1 368.08	1 378.86
#非农业人口	Non-agricultural Population	864.46	986.16	1 173.30	1 196.94
就　业	**Employment**				
从业人员(万人)	Employees(10 000 persons)	787.72	745.24	885.51	909.08
职工人数(万人)	Staff and Workers(10 000 persons)	508.10	390.14	500.94	522.67
城镇登记失业率(%)	Registered Unemployment Rate in Urban Areas(%)	1.5	3.5	4.4	4.3
宏观经济	**Macro Economy**				
国民经济核算	**Domestic Economic Accounts**				
上海市生产总值(亿元)	Gross Domestic Product(100 million yuan)	781.66	4 771.17	10 366.37	12 188.85
第一产业	Primary Industry	34.24	76.68	93.80	101.84
第二产业	Secondary Industry	505.70	2 207.63	5 028.37	5 678.51
#工　业	Industry	469.83	1 998.96	4 670.11	5 298.08
第三产业	Tertiary Industry	241.82	2 486.86	5 244.20	6 408.50
人均生产总值(元)	Per Capita Gross Domestic Product(yuan)				
按户籍人口计算	Calculated by Registered Population	6 107	36 217	75 990	88 745
按常住人口计算	Calculated by Resident Population	6 107	29 671	57 695	66 367
固定资产投资	**Investment in Fixed Assets**				
全社会固定资产投资总额(亿元)	Total Investment in Fixed Assets(100 million yuan)	227.08	1 869.67	3 925.09	4 458.61
#房地产投资	Investment in Real Estate	8.16	566.17	1 275.59	1 307.53
财　政	**Public Finance**				
全市财政收入(亿元)	Fiscal Revenue(100 million yuan)	284.36	1 752.69	4 798.93	7 310.26
#地方财政收入	Local Fiscal Revenue	166.99	497.96	1 600.37	2 102.63
地方财政支出(亿元)	Local Fiscal Expenditure(100 million yuan)	75.56	622.84	1 813.80	2 201.92
价　格	**Price**				
居民消费价格指数(上年=100)	Consumer Price Index(preceding=100)	106.3	102.5	101.2	103.2
商品零售价格指数(上年=100)	Retail Price Index(preceding=100)	104.8	96.4	100.2	102.4

注：从业人员为在岗从业人员。
Note: Employees refer to working employees.

表 2.1 续表 1 continued

	指　标 Indicators	1990	2000	2006	2007
外商直接投资	**Foreign Direct Investment**				
签订合同项目(个)	Number of Contracts(unit)	203	1 814	4 061	4 206
签订合同金额(亿美元)	Contractual Foreign Investment(100 million USD)	2.14	63.90	145.74	148.69
实际到位金额(亿美元)	Foreign Investment Actually Absorbed(100 million USD)	1.77	31.60	71.07	79.20
产　业	**Industries**				
农　业	**Agriculture**				
农业总产值(亿元)	Gross Output Value of Agriculture(100 million yuan)	68.16	216.50	237.01	255.98
主要农副产品产量(万吨)	Output of Major Farm and Sideline Products(10 000 tons)				
粮　食	Grain	244.36	174.00	111.30	109.20
棉　花	Cotton	1.22	0.12	0.20	0.25
油菜籽	Rapeseed	18.17	15.71	4.91	3.28
牛　奶	Milk	22.68	25.95	22.09	22.04
蔬　菜	Vegetables	186.79	377.00	418.76	413.49
猪　肉	Pork	23.32	25.96	15.20	15.15
水产品	Aquatic Products	27.36	28.87	38.75	37.02
工　业	**Industry**				
工业总产值(亿元)	Gross Output Value of Industry(100 million yuan)	1 642.75	7 002.98	19 631.23	23 108.63
轻工业	Light Industry	846.63	2 903.40	4 747.28	5 318.85
重工业	Heavy Industry	796.12	4 119.59	14 883.94	17 789.78
主要工业产品产量	Output of Major Industrial Products				
钢　材(万吨)	Steel Products(10 000 tons)	609.59	1 544.46	2 129.78	2 144.16
发电量(亿千瓦·时)	Electric Generation(100 million kwh)	284.1	553.09	710.96	737.80
程控交换机(万线)	Program Controlled Exchanges(10 000 lines)	95.23	1 091.64	553.53	447.54
微型电子计算机(万部)	Micro-Computers(10 000 units)	0.77	42.04	2 670.09	4 478.78
移动通信设备(万部)	Mobile Communication Equipments(10 000 units)		1.60	174.16	307.46
集成电路(亿块)	Semi-conductor IC (100 million units)	0.12	23.93	64.05	89.11
汽　车(万辆)	Motor Vehicles(10 000 vehicles)	2.81	25.29	65.28	82.12
#轿　车	Cars	2.46	25.15	64.47	81.15
金属切削机床(万台)	Metal-cutting Machines(10 000 units)	1.38	2.23	1.34	1.44
民用钢质船舶(万总吨)	Civil Steel Ships(10 000 syn-tons)	39.07	118.81	295.48	303.24
建筑业	**Construction**				
总产值(亿元)	Gross Output Value(100 million yuan)	75.62	631.64	2 285.38	2 524.18
全员劳动生产率(元/人)(按总产值计算)	Overall Labor Productivity(yuan/person)(In Term of Output Value)	18 569	109 244	208 368	228 710

表2.1 续表2 continued

指标	Indicators	1990	2000	2006	2007
交通运输、邮政业和信息传输	**Transportation, Post and Information Transmission**				
货物运输量(万吨)	Freight Transportation Volume(10 000 tons)	22 848	47 954	72 617	78 108
旅客发送量(万人次)	Passenger Departures(10 000 person-times)	3 835	6 893	9 619	10 371
港口货物吞吐量(万吨)	Port Cargo throughput(10 000 tons)	13 959	20 440	53 748	56 145
国际标准集装箱吞吐量(万TEU)	International Container Throughput Capacity(10 000TEU)	45.60	561.20	2 171.90	2 615.20
邮电业务总量(亿元)	Revenue from Post and Telecommunications Services (100 million yuan)	10.23	171.70	555.00	715.48
年末固定电话用户(万户)	Year-end Installed Telephone Subscribers (10 000 households)	46	549	1 112	1 022
数字数据用户(万户)	Digital and Data Users(10 000 households)			1.8	1.7
批发和零售	**Wholesale and Retail**				
社会消费品零售总额(亿元)	Retail Sales of Consumer Goods(100 million yuan)	333.86	1 865.28	3 360.41	3 847.79
批发零售业商品销售总额(亿元)	Total Sales of Wholesale and Retail (100 million yuan)	1 305.41	7 474.81	15 504.05	20 400.79
对外经济贸易	**Foreign Trade**				
口岸进出口总额(亿美元)	Total Value of Port Imports and Exports(100 million USD)	172.89	1 093.11	4 287.54	5 209.09
进口额	Imports	86.27	477.39	1 621.89	1 924.29
出口额	Exports	86.62	615.72	2 665.65	3 284.80
外贸进出口总额(亿美元)	Total Value of Foreign Imports and Exports(100 million USD)	74.31	547.10	2 274.89	2 829.73
进口额	Imports	21.10	293.56	1 139.16	1 390.45
出口额	Exports	53.21	253.54	1 135.73	1 439.28
国际旅游	**International Tourism**				
上海入境境外旅游者人数(万人次)	Number of Overseas Tourists (10 000 person-times)	89.30	181.40	605.67	665.59
国际旅游(外汇)收入(亿美元)	Foreign Exchange Earnings from International Tourism(100 million USD)	2.31	16.13	39.61	47.37
金融保险	**Finance and Insurance**				
金融机构存款余额(亿元)	Total Saving Deposits of Financial Institutions(100 million yuan)	851.51	9 349.83	26 454.88	30 315.53
金融机构贷款余额(亿元)	Total Loan Balance of Financial Institutions(100 million yuan)	1 106.80	7 254.26	18 603.92	21 709.95
保险费收入(亿元)	Premium Income(100 million yuan)	8.99	127.23	407.04	482.64
保险赔款及给付支出(亿元)	Indemnity Payments(100 million yuan)	2.22	36.44	91.31	139.82
教育、科技、文化	**Education, Science&Technology and Culture**				
教　育	**Education**				
在校学生数(万人)	Students Enrollment(10 000 persons)				
高等学校	Institutions of Higher Education	12.13	22.68	46.63	48.49
普通中学	Regular Secondary Schools	48.31	79.54	71.17	65.60
小　学	Primary Schools	110.19	78.86	53.37	53.33
每万人拥有大学生(人)	Number of College and University Students Per 10 000 Persons(person)	94	172	341	352

表2.1 续表3 continued

指　标	Indicators	1990	2000	2006	2007
科　技	**Science and Technology**				
科技成果(项)	Achievements in Science and Technology(item)	2 092	1 102	1 953	2 396
研究与试验发展经费支出(亿元)	Research and Development Expenditures (100 million yuan)	10.13	76.73	258.84	307.50
研究与试验发展经费支出相当于上海市生产总值比例(%)	R&D Expenditure as Percentage of Gross Domestic Product(%)	1.30	1.61	2.50	2.52
文　化	**Culture**				
出版数量	Number of Publications				
图　书(亿册、张)	Books(100 million copies)	2.98	2.54	2.54	2.40
期　刊(亿册)	Periodicals(100 million copies)	1.73	1.85	1.83	1.83
报　纸(亿份)	Newspapers(100 million copies)	16.16	16.77	17.89	17.04
故事影片产量(部)	Feature Films Produced(film)	16	10	9	9
家庭、生活、环境	**Family, Living and Environment**				
家　庭	**Household**				
家庭总户数(万户)	Total Households(10 000 households)	415.28	475.73	499.54	503.29
平均每户家庭人口(人)	Average Persons per Household(person)	3.1	2.8	2.7	2.7
婚　姻	**Marriages and Divorces**				
准予登记结婚(万对)	Marriage Registration Permitted(10 000 couples)	10.77	9.31	16.56	12.01
离婚人数(万人)	Divorce(10 000 persons)	3.27	6.36	9.43	9.38
离婚率(‰)	Divorce Rate(‰)	1.37	2.42	3.45	3.41
住　宅	**Housing**				
市区人均居住面积(平方米)	Per Capita Net Floor Space of Urban Residents(sq · m)	6.6	11.8	16.0	16.5
农村居民人均居住面积(平方米)	Per Capita Net Floor Space of Rural Residents(sq · m)	37.08	53.58	59.99	61.22
生　活	**Living**				
城市居民人均可支配收入(元)	Per Capita Annual Disposable Income of Urban Households(yuan)	2 182	11 718	20 668	23 623
城市居民人均消费支出(元)	Per Capita Annual Consumption Expenditures of Urban Households(yuan)	1 936	8 868	14 762	17 255
农村居民人均可支配收入(元)	Per Capita Annual Disposable Income of Rural Households(yuan)	1 665	5 565	9 213	10 222
农村居民人均生活消费支出(元)	Per Capita Annual Consumption Expenditure of Rural Households(yuan)	1 262	4 138	8 006	8 845
城乡居民储蓄存款余额(亿元)	Saving Deposits of Urban and Rural Households(100 million yuan)	252.16	2 627.07	9 480.28	9 326.45

注：根据国家对离婚率计算方法调整的要求，本年鉴的离婚率计算方法相应作了调整，分子为离婚对数，分母为年平均人口数。

Note: According to the adjustment of Calculate Method of Divorce Rate, the calculate method of divorce rate has been adjusted, which the molecule is the divorced couples and the denominator is the yearly average population.

表 2.1 续表 4 continued

指　标	Indicators	1990	2000	2006	2007
工　资	**Wages**				
职工工资总额(亿元)	Total Wages of Staff and Workers(100 million yuan)	146.78	614.53	1 475.93	1 802.17
职工平均工资(元)	Average Wages of Staff and Workers(yuan)	2 917	15 420	29 569	34 707
卫　生	**Health Care**				
医　院(个)	Quantity of Hospitals(unit)	462	459	505	288
医　生(万人)	Doctors(10 000 persons)	5.82	4.99	4.55	4.88
医院床位数(万张)	Quantity of Hospital Beds(10 000 beds)	6.21	7.31	9.28	7.54
每万人拥有医生(人)	Quantity of Doctors Per 10 000 Persons(person)	45	38	33	35
城市建设	**Urban Construction**				
城市基础设施投资额(亿元)	Investment in Urban Infrastructure(100 million yuan)	47.22	449.90	1 125.54	1 466.33
自来水售水量(亿立方米)	Sales Volume of Tap Water(100 million cu. m)	12.25	19.75	23.30	23.90
用电量(亿千瓦时)	Electric Power Consumption(100 million kwh)	264.74	559.42	990.15	1 072.38
煤气销售总量(亿立方米)	Total Sales Volume(100 million cu. m)	12.15	18.40	19.22	18.50
年末出租车运营总数(辆)	Year-end Operating Taxi Vehicles(vehicle)	11 298	42 943	48 022	48 614
运营公交车辆数(辆)	Total Number of Public Buses(vehicle)	6 264	17 939	17 284	16 944
道路长度(公里)	Length of Roads(km)	1 631	6 641	14 619	15 458
城市人均公共绿地面积(平方米)	Public Green Areas Per Capita(sq. m)	1.02	4.60	11.50	12.01
城市绿化覆盖率(%)	Coverage Rate of Urban Green Areas(%)	12.4	22.2	37.3	37.6
森林覆盖率(%)	Coverage Rate of Forest(%)	5.5	9.2	11.6	11.6
环境保护投资相当于上海市生产总值比例(%)	Environment Protection Investment as Percentage of Gross Domestic Product(%)		3.10	3.00	3.00
环境空气质量优良率(%)	Rate of Good Ambient Air Quality(%)		80.8	88.8	89.9
火灾、交通事故	**Fires and Traffic Accidents**				
火灾发生数(起)	Quantity of Fires(unit)	2 146	5 164	4 526	4 233
火灾损失额(万元)	Loss of Fires(10 000 yuan)	1 868	1 919	2 292	2 650
交通事故发生数(万起)	Quantity of Traffic Accidents(10 000 unit)	0.76	4.13	0.66	0.40
交通事故损失额(万元)	Loss of Traffic Accidents(10 000 yuan)	1 345	20 391	3 292	1 943

①本表总量指标中的价值量指标均按当年价格计算。
②1990、2000 年邮电业务总量按 1990 年不变价格计算,2006、2007 年按 2000 年不变价格计算。
③1990 年农村居民年人均可支配收入为农村居民年人均纯收入。
❶The data in value terms in the table are calculated at current prices.
❷Figures of in 1990 and 2000 were calculated at constant prices of 1990, and those figures in 2005 were calculated at constant prices of 2000 Revenue Post and Telecommunication Services.
❸1990, Per Captia Annual Disposable Income of Rural Households referred to per capia annual net income of rural residents. (Same as follows).

表 2.2　主要年份社会经济主要指标发展速度
GROWTH RATE OF MAJOR SOCIAL AND ECONOMIC INDICATORS IN MAIN YEARS

单位:%

指　标	Indicators	2007年比下列各年增长 Indicatars' Growth Rate Between Years Below and Year 2007		
		1990	2000	2006
年末户籍人口	Yea-end Registered Population	7.4	4.3	0.8
上海市生产总值	Gross Domestic Product	6.2 倍	1.2 倍	14.3
第一产业	Primary Industry	22.3	-3.4	2.0
第二产业	Secondary Industry	6.1 倍	1.3 倍	11.5
第三产业	Tertiary Industry	7.3 倍	1.2 倍	17.1
全市财政收入	Fiscal Revenue	25 倍	3.2 倍	52.3
#地方财政收入	Local Fiscal Revenue	12 倍	3.2 倍	31.4
地方财政支出	Local Fiscal Expenditure	28 倍	2.5 倍	21.4
直接吸收外资	Foreign Direct Investment			
签订合同项目	Number of Contracts	20 倍	1.3 倍	3.6
签订合同金额	Contractual Foreign Investment	68 倍	1.3 倍	2.0
实际到位金额	Foreign Investment Actually Absorbed	44 倍	1.5 倍	11.4
农业总产值	Gross Output Value of Agriculture	50.5	-4.9	1.5
工业总产值	Gross Output Value of Industry	12 倍	2.2 倍	15.7
轻工业	Light Industry	5.8 倍	1.1 倍	9.9
重工业	Heavy Industry	18 倍	2.8 倍	17.5
货物运输量	Freight Transportation Volume	2.4 倍	62.9	7.6
旅客发送量	Passenger Departures	1.7 倍	50.5	7.8
港口货物吞吐量	Port Cargo Throughput	3.0 倍	1.7 倍	4.5
社会消费品零售总额	Retail Sales of Consumer Goods	11 倍	1.1 倍	14.5
口岸进出口总额	Total Value of Port Imports and Exports	29 倍	3.8 倍	21.5
进口额	Imports	21 倍	3.0 倍	18.6
出口额	Exports	37 倍	4.3 倍	23.2
外贸进出口总额	Total Value of Foreign Imports and Exports	37 倍	4.2 倍	24.4
进口额	Imports	65 倍	3.7 倍	22.1
出口额	Exports	26 倍	4.7 倍	26.7
城市居民家庭人均可支配收入	Per Capita Annual Disposable Income of Urban Households	9.8 倍	1.0 倍	14.3
城市居民家庭人均消费支出	Per Capita Annual Consumption Expenditures of Urban Households	7.9 倍	94.6	16.9
农村居民家庭人均可支配收入	Per Capita Annual Disposable Income of Rural Households	5.1 倍	83.7	11.0
农村居民家庭人均生活消费支出	Per Capita Annual Consumption Expenditures of Rural Households	6.0 倍	1.1 倍	10.5
全社会固定资产投资总额	Total Investment in Fixed Assets	19 倍	1.4 倍	13.6
城市基础设施投资额	Investment in Urban Infrastructure	30 倍	2.3 倍	30.3
医　生	Doctors	-16.2	-2.2	7.3
高等学校在校学生	Student Enrollment of Institutions of Higher Education	3.0 倍	1.1 倍	4.0

注：本表速度指标中，上海市生产总值及三次产业、工业总产值、农业总产值均按可比价格计算。
Note: The Growth Rates of the Following indicators are calculated at comparable prices: Gross Domestic Product, three industries, gross output value of agriculture and Gross Output Value of Industry.

表 2.2 续表 continued

单位:%

指 标	Indicators	平均每年增长 Indicators' Average Annual Growth Rate 1991～2007	2001～2007
年末户籍人口	Year-end Registered Population	0.4	0.6
上海市生产总值	Gross Domestic Product	12.3	12.2
第一产业	Primary Industry	1.2	-0.5
第二产业	Secondary Industry	12.3	12.9
第三产业	Tertiary Industry	13.2	11.9
全社会固定资产投资总额	Total Investment in Fixed Assets	21.3	10.3
全市财政收入	Fiscal Revenue	21.0	22.6
#地方财政收入	Local Fiscal Revenue	16.1	22.8
地方财政支出	Local Fiscal Expenditure	21.9	19.8
农业总产值	Gross Output Value of Agriculture	2.4	-0.7
工业总产值	Gross Output Value of Industry	16.3	17.9
轻工业	Light Industry	11.9	11.2
重工业	Heavy Industry	18.9	21.2
货物运输量	Freight Transportation Volume	7.5	7.2
旅客发送量	Passenger Departures	6.0	6.0
港口货物吞吐量	Port Cargo Throughput	8.5	15.5
社会消费品零售总额	Retail Sales of Consumer Goods	15.5	10.9
口岸进出口总额	Total Value of Port Imports and Exports	22.2	25.0
进口额	Imports	20.0	22.0
出口额	Exports	23.8	27.0
外贸进出口总额	Total Value of Foreign Imports and Exports	23.9	26.5
进口额	Imports	27.9	24.9
出口额	Exports	21.4	28.2
城市居民家庭人均可支配收入	Per Capita Annual Disposable Income of Urban Households	15.0	10.5
城市居民家庭人均消费支出	Per Capita Annual Consumption Expenditures of Urban Households	13.7	10.0
农村居民家庭人均可支配收入	Per Capita Annual Disposable Income of Rural Households	11.3	9.1
农村居民家庭人均生活消费支出	Per Capita Consumption Expenditure of Rural Households	12.1	11.5
医 生	Doctors	-1.0	-0.3
高等学校在校学生	Student Enrollment of Institutions of Higher Education	8.5	11.5
城市基础设施投资额	Investment in Urban Infrastructure	23.7	15.5

表 2.3　主要年份社会经济发展结构指标
STRUCTURAL INDICATORS OF SOCIAL AND ECONOMIC DEVELOPMENT IN MAIN YEARS

单位:%

指　标	Indicators	1990	2000	2006	2007
农业非农业人口结构	Structure of Agriculture and Non-agriculture	100	100	100	100
农　业	Agriculture	32.6	25.4	14.2	13.2
非农业	Non-agriculture	67.4	74.6	85.8	86.8
人口性别结构	Structure of Sex	100	100	100	100
男	Male	50.4	50.4	50.2	50.1
女	Female	49.6	49.6	49.8	49.9
从业人员产业结构	Industrial Structure of Employees	100	100	100	100
第一产业	Primary Industry	11.1	10.8	6.3	5.9
第二产业	Secondary Industry	59.3	44.3	37.0	37.7
第三产业	Tertiary Industry	29.6	44.9	56.7	56.4
上海市生产总值产业结构	Industrial Structure of GDP	100	100	100	100
第一产业	Primary Industry	4.4	1.6	0.9	0.8
第二产业	Secondary Industry	64.7	46.3	48.5	46.6
第三产业	Tertiary Industry	30.9	52.1	50.6	52.6
上海市生产总值所有制结构	Ownership Structure of GDP	100	100	100	100
公有制经济	Public State-owned	95.4	71.4	55.9	54.9
国有经济	State-owned	71.2	55.0	47.9	47.7
集体经济	Collective-owned	24.2	16.4	8.0	7.2
非公有制经济	Non-state-owned	4.6	28.6	44.1	45.1
全社会固定资产投资所有制结构	Ownership Structure of Total Investment	100	100	100	100
国有经济	State-owned	84.7	44.4	37.2	39.9
非国有经济	Non-State-owned	15.3	55.6	62.8	60.1
地方财政收入结构	Structure of Local Fiscal Revenue	100	100	100	100
#增值税	Value-added Tax		18.8	16.9	14.9
营业税	Business Tax		30.9	34.9	34.0
企业所得税	Enterprise Income Tax		20.7	16.9	20.2
个人所得税	Personal Income Tax		12.1	8.2	8.1
外商直接投资实际吸收外资结构	Foreign Direct Investment Structure of Foreign Investment Actually Absorbed	100	100	100	100
#合资企业	Joint Ventures	61.0	40.9	22.3	21.6
合作企业	Coopratїve Enterprises	37.9	9.5	2.6	2.0
独资企业	Sole-foreign Enterprises	1.1	49.6	75.1	76.3
农业总产值结构	Structure of Gross Output Value of Agriculture	100	100	100	100
#种植业	Planting	42.7	41.5	50.6	49.5
牧　业	Animal Husbandry	44.4	40.3	19.5	22.7
渔　业	Fishery	11.8	17.5	23.3	21.2
工业总产值结构	Structure of Gross Output Value of Industry	100	100	100	100
轻工业	Light Industry	51.5	41.3	24.2	23.0
重工业	Heavy Industry	48.5	58.7	75.8	77.0

表 2.3 续表 continued

指标	Indicators	1990	2000	2006	2007
货物运输总量结构	Structure of Freight Transportation	100	100	100	100
铁 路	Railways	5.5	2.2	1.7	1.5
公 路	Roadways	38.2	59.1	46.5	45.6
水 运	Waterways	56.3	38.5	51.4	52.5
民用航空	Civil Aviation	…	0.2	0.4	0.4
社会消费品零售总额结构	Structure of Retail Sales of Consumer Goods	100	100	100	100
吃	Food	42.6	39.8	39.5	39.6
穿	Clothing	15.7	13.4	12.7	12.4
用	Articles	41.1	46.0	46.6	46.7
烧	Fuels	0.6	0.8	1.2	1.3
出口商品结构	Structure of Exports		100	100	100
初级产品	Primary Goods		3.4	2.4	2.2
工业制成品	Manufactured Goods		96.6	97.6	97.8
进口商品结构	Structure of Imports		100	100	100
初级产品	Primary Goods		11.9	10.7	11.3
工业制成品	Manufactured Goods		88.1	89.3	88.7
中资金融机构人民币存款结构	Structure of RMB Saving Deposit in Chinese Financial Instituation	100	100	100	100
#企业存款	Enterprise Deposits	43.1	56.9	49.1	50.2
储蓄存款	Saving Deposits	41.1	32.5	37.1	32.2
中资金融机构人民币贷款结构	Structure of RMB Loans in Chinese Financial Instituation	100	100	100	100
#短期贷款	Short Term Loans	75.2	72.9	31.5	34.3
中长期贷款	Medium and Long Term Loans	14.8	18.0	60.5	61.2
在校学生结构	Structure of Students Enrollment	100	100	100	100
大学生	University and College Students	7.1	12.5	26.9	29.0
中学生	Secondary Students	28.3	43.9	41.8	39.2
小学生	Primary Students	64.6	43.6	31.3	31.8
城市居民消费结构	Consumption Structure of Urban Households	100	100	100	100
#食 品	Food	56.5	44.5	35.6	35.5
衣 着	Clothing	10.8	6.4	6.9	7.7
家庭设备、用品及服务	Household Facilities, Articles and Services	10.1	7.7	5.9	5.6
交通和通信	Transportation and Communications	3.0	8.6	15.8	18.3
教育文化娱乐服务	Cultural, Education and Recreation Services	11.9	14.5	16.5	15.4
居 住	Residence	4.6	9.0	9.7	8.2
农村居民消费结构	Consumption Structure of Rural Households	100	100	100	100
#食 品	Food	46.4	44.0	37.8	36.8
衣 着	Clothing	8.5	4.9	5.2	5.4
家庭设备、用品及服务	Household Facilities, Articles and Services	10.2	5.4	6.0	5.1
交通和通信	Transportation and Communications	0.5	6.7	9.7	10.0
文教娱乐用品及服务	Culture, Education ,Recreation Articles and Services	4.7	13.5	11.5	9.7
居 住	Residence	21.6	17.5	20.7	23.7
卫生机构数结构	Structure of Health Care Institutions	100	100	100	100
#医 院	Hospitals	6.0	10.4	20.0	10.9
卫生技术人员结构	Structure of Medical Professionals	100	100	100	100
#医 生	Doctors	49.2	46.6	41.7	39.9
护师、护士	Senior and Junior Nurses	27.6	34.4	38.7	38.2

表 2.4　各时期社会经济主要指标
MAJOR SOCIAL AND ECONOMIC INDICATORS OF EACH FIVE-YEAR PLAN PERIOD

时　期 Period		上海市生产总值（亿元）Gross Domestic Product (100 million yuan)	其中 of which 第一产业 Primary Industry	第二产业 Secondary Industry	第三产业 Tertiary Industry	全市财政收入（亿元）Total Fiscal Revenue (100 million yuan)	地方财政收入（亿元）Local Fiscal Revenue (100 million yuan)
"一五"时期	"First Five-Year Plan" Period	293.26	12.56	163.89	116.81	177.51	14.93
"二五"时期	"Second Five-Year Plan" Period	568.99	21.03	412.70	135.26	430.23	304.28
	1963～1965	304.94	17.28	220.81	66.85	224.52	172.51
"三五"时期	"Third Five-Year Plan" Period	657.06	37.64	487.88	131.54	466.76	374.19
"四五"时期	"Fourth Five-Year Plan" Period	918.76	42.75	708.84	167.17	680.97	633.79
"五五"时期	"Fifth Five-Year Plan" Period	1 309.61	49.26	1 004.23	256.12	886.60	797.56
"六五"时期	"Sixth Five-Year Plan" Period	1 871.24	74.20	1 349.98	447.06	1 089.20	846.92
"七五"时期	"Seventh Five-Year Plan" Period	3 162.79	132.52	2 105.23	925.04	1 342.38	846.96
"八五"时期	"Eighth Five-Year Plan" Period	8 017.61	213.47	4 698.27	3 105.87	2 422.69	1 006.06
"九五"时期	"Ninth Five-Year Plan" Period	19 157.33	365.76	9 434.90	9 356.67	6 233.99	1 962.85
"十五"时期	"Tenth Five-Year Plan" Period	34 872.39	402.49	16 579.69	17 890.21	14 714.28	4 792.93
"十一五"时期前两年							
	2006	10 366.37	93.80	5 028.37	5 244.20	4 798.93	1 600.37
	2007	12 188.85	101.84	5 678.51	6 408.50	7 310.26	2 102.63
	1953～2007	93 699.12	1 574.52	47 873.30	44 251.30	40 778.32	15 389.61

表 2.4 续表 continued

时　期 Period		地方财政支出（亿元）Local Fiscal Expenditure (100 million yuan)	工业总产值（亿元）Gross Output Value of Industry (100 million yuan)	全社会固定资产投资总额（亿元）Total Investment in Fixed Assets (100 million yuan)	外贸出口商品总额（亿美元）Total Exports Value of Foreign Trade (100 million USD)	社会消费品零售总额（亿元）Retail Sales of Consumer Goods (100 million yuan)
"一五"时期	"First Five-Year Plan" Period	12.25	512.03	19.29	17.46	121.02
"二五"时期	"Second Five-Year Plan" Period	60.79	1 069.50	55.60	31.00	145.82
	1963～1965	19.28	596.63	20.29	20.12	79.50
"三五"时期	"Third Five-Year Plan" Period	39.41	1 334.94	34.77	43.08	153.86
"四五"时期	"Fourth Five-Year Plan" Period	86.78	1 894.01	95.79	92.86	200.62
"五五"时期	"Fifth Five-Year Plan" Period	111.30	2 550.91	151.44	150.33	302.07
"六五"时期	"Sixth Five-Year Plan" Period	138.52	3 509.15	412.74	180.08	576.32
"七五"时期	"Seventh Five-Year Plan" Period	327.68	6 498.13	1 020.34	226.96	1 383.16
"八五"时期	"Eighth Five-Year Plan" Period	775.11	17 308.90	3 994.67	403.31	3 408.52
"九五"时期	"Ninth Five-Year Plan" Period	2 421.50	29 776.04	9 620.86	880.57	7 874.26
"十五"时期	"Tenth Five-Year Plan" Period	5 762.87	59 716.74	13 261.11	2 724.27	12 254.59
"十一五"时期前两年						
	2006	1 813.80	19 631.23	3 925.09	1 135.73	3 360.41
	2007	2 201.92	23 108.63	4 458.61	1 439.28	3 847.79
	1953～2007	13 771.21	167 506.84	37 070.61	7 345.09	33 707.94

表2.5 各时期社会经济主要指标平均增长率
GROWTH RATE OF MAJOR SOCIAL AND ECONOMIC INDICATORS OF EACH FIVE-YEAR PLAN PERIOD

单位:%

时期 Period	上海市生产总值 Gross Domestic Product	其中 of which 第一产业 Primary Industry	第二产业 Secondary Industry	第三产业 Tertiary Industry	全市财政收入 Total Fiscal Revenue	地方财政收入 Local Fiscal Revenue
"一五"时期"First Five-Year Plan" Period	13.8	3.3	18.4	8.3	18.9	12.6
"二五"时期"Second Five-Year Plan" Period	1.6	1.3	4.1	-3.1	6.2	57.2
1963～1965	17.0	11.6	21.8	5.6	10.5	12.3
"三五"时期"Third Five-Year Plan" Period	8.7	3.3	9.7	5.7	6.5	9.7
"四五"时期"Fourth Five-Year Plan" Period	6.6	-1.6	7.1	6.2	5.2	6.4
"五五"时期"Fifth Five-Year Plan" Period	8.4	0.9	8.6	8.6	6.2	5.1
"六五"时期"Sixth Five-Year Plan" Period	9.1	4.3	8.3	12.3	5.8	1.1
"七五"时期"Seventh Five-Year Plan" Period	5.7	1.2	5.0	8.0	1.5	-1.6
"八五"时期"Eighth Five-Year Plan" Period	13.1	1.4	13.9	12.8	19.8	6.0
"九五"时期"Ninth Five-Year Plan" Period	11.5	3.4	9.7	15.5	20.1	17.0
"十五"时期"Tenth Five-Year Plan" Period	11.9	-1.3	13.3	10.9	18.5	23.6
"十一五"时期前两年						
2006～2007	13.1	1.4	11.9	14.5	33.6	21.1
1953～2007	9.5	2.1	10.5	8.5	11.4	13.0

表2.5 续表 continued

单位:%

时期 Period		地方财政支出 Local Fiscal Expenditure	工业总产值 Gross Output Value of Industry	全社会固定资产投资总额 Total Investment in Fixed Assets	外贸出口商品总额 Total Exports Value of Foreign Trade	社会消费品零售总额 Retail Sales of Consumer Goods
"一五"时期	"First Five-Year Plan" Period	12.3	14.5	23.1	30.6	5.6
"二五"时期	"Second Five-Year Plan" Period	0.6	4.9	26.5	4.2	1.2
	1963～1965	25.2	18.8	31.4	11.4	-0.1
"三五"时期	"Third Five-Year Plan" Period	11.2	10.2	-3.6	2.5	3.3
"四五"时期	"Fourth Five-Year Plan" Period	15.5	7.5	19.4	20.7	8.4
"五五"时期	"Fifth Five-Year Plan" Period	-6.3	7.6	-2.4	14.0	11.0
"六五"时期	"Sixth Five-Year Plan" Period	19.2	7.7	20.6	-4.7	16.6
"七五"时期	"Seventh Five-Year Plan" Period	10.4	5.9	18.7	9.6	14.0
"八五"时期	"Eighth Five-Year Plan" Period	28.8	18.0	45.4	16.8	25.8
"九五"时期	"Ninth Five-Year Plan" Period	18.4	12.3	6.2	17.0	12.2
"十五"时期	"Tenth Five-Year Plan" Period	21.7	19.2	11.9	29.0	9.8
"十一五"时期前两年						
	2006～2007	15.2	14.8	11.8	20.6	13.8
	1953～2007	13.5	11.2	15.1	13.8	10.1

表2.6　国民经济主要指标比上年增长(1978～2007)
GROWTH RATE OF MAJOR NATIONAL ECONOMIC INDICATORS OVER PRECEDING YEAR

单位:%

年　份 Year	上海市 生产总值 Gross Domestic Product	全　市 财政收入 Fiscal Revenue	地　方 财政收入 Local Fiscal Revenue	地　方 财政支出 Local Fiscal Expenditure	工　业 总产值 Gross Output Value of Industry	全社会固定资产 投资总额 Total Investment in Fixed Assets
1978	15.8	19.2	14.6	51.4	12.1	55.1
1979	7.4	1.1	2.1	4.0	8.6	27.5
1980	8.4	3.2	1.2	-29.1	6.5	27.7
1981	5.6	2.9	-0.2	-0.6	3.7	20.2
1982	7.2	-1.9	-3.6	8.5	4.7	30.7
1983	7.8	1.8	-6.9	8.3	7.0	6.4
1984	11.6	5.6	4.8	35.4	9.9	21.5
1985	13.4	22.3	12.4	51.9	13.5	28.5
1986	4.4	-2.3	-2.6	28.2	5.5	23.9
1987	7.5	-6.3	-5.8	-8.9	6.7	26.8
1988	10.1	8.4	-4.3	22.3	10.5	31.7
1989	3.0	13.6	3.3	11.3	3.0	-12.4
1990	3.5	-4.3	0.1	3.1	4.0	5.7
1991	7.1	14.2	5.1	13.9	14.1	13.7
1992	14.8	4.8	5.7	10.4	20.2	38.4
1993	15.1	29.2	30.6	36.1	20.0	83.0
1994	14.5	40.1	-27.7	52.3	18.2	71.8
1995	14.3	14.1	29.6	36.0	17.4	42.6
1996	13.1	24.4	26.9	27.9	15.5	21.9
1997	12.8	22.6	22.1	25.2	14.5	1.3
1998	10.3	7.0	11.3	12.1	7.8	-0.6
1999	10.4	21.3	10.1	13.7	10.5	-5.5
2000	11.0	26.0	15.3	14.0	13.5	0.7
2001	10.5	13.9	24.6	16.6	16.4	6.7
2002	11.3	25.6	44.5	40.9	14.6	9.6
2003	12.3	28.5	32.5	25.6	31.4	12.1
2004	14.2	27.0	24.5	26.6	20.3	25.8
2005	11.1	13.9	20.7	19.0	13.9	14.8
2006	12.0	17.2	11.6	9.2	13.9	10.8
2007	14.3	52.3	31.4	21.4	15.7	13.6

表 2.6 续表 continued

单位:%

年 份 Year	外贸进出口总额 Total Value of Foreign Import and Export	出口总额 Export	社会消费品零售总额 Retail Sales of Consumer Goods	直接吸收外资合同金额 Contracted Foreign Direct Investment	直接吸收外资实际到位金额 Actually Absorbed Foreign Direct Investment	港口货物吞吐量 Cargo Handled at Ports	城市居民家庭人均可支配收入 Per Capita Annual Disposable Income of Urban Households
1978	30.4	30.3	9.8			30.6	
1979	28.2	27.0	26.2			5.0	
1980	16.2	16.1	17.8			1.6	
1981	-7.9	-10.8	10.3	1.0 倍	…	-1.7	
1982	-6.2	-5.3	1.2	1.8 倍	…	7.7	3.5
1983	6.3	1.2	12.1	1.8 倍	2.7 倍	2.4	4.8
1984	6.3	-1.7	22.9	3.1 倍	1.5 倍	9.5	20.7
1985	17.6	-6.3	40.1	56.4	1.2 倍	12.2	28.9
1986	0.6	6.6	13.5	-68.9	58.1	11.6	20.3
1987	15.2	16.1	14.4	35.8	1.2 倍	1.8	11.1
1988	20.8	10.7	31.3	28.7	71.7	3.8	19.9
1989	8.3	9.3	12.0	6.6	15.9	9.6	14.6
1990	-5.3	5.7	0.7	20.9	-58.1	-4.4	10.4
1991	8.2	7.9	14.4	30.4	-1.1	5.2	13.9
1992	21.3	14.2	21.7	5.7 倍	6.2 倍	11.0	21.1
1993	30.5	12.6	34.3	1.0 倍	84.1	8.0	42.1
1994	24.6	23.0	23.5	42.3	39.4	-5.8	37.2
1995	19.9	27.5	25.9	0.2	0.6	-0.1	22.2
1996	17.0	14.3	19.7	8.4	45.1	-1.0	13.8
1997	11.2	11.2	14.1	-8.4	2.0		3.4
1998	26.6	8.4	11.0	9.9	-24.3	-0.1	4.0
1999	23.2	17.7	8.1	-29.8	-16.2	13.7	24.6
2000	41.7	35.0	8.3	55.7	3.7	9.7	7.2
2001	11.3	9.0	8.1	15.4	39.0	8.1	9.9
2002	19.3	16.0	9.3	43.4	14.5	19.4	11.5
2003	54.7	51.2	9.1	23.5	30.1	19.8	12.2
2004	42.4	51.6	10.5	12.6	11.8	19.8	12.2
2005	16.5	23.4	11.9	18.3	4.7	16.9	11.8
2006	22.1	25.2	13.0	5.4	3.8	21.3	10.8
2007	24.4	26.7	14.5	2.0	11.4	4.5	14.3

表 2.7 上海社会经济主要指标占全国比重(2007)
PERCENTAGE OF THE NATIONAL TOTAL OF SHANGHAI'S MAJOR SOCIAL AND ECONOMIC INDICATORS

指　标	Indicators	全　国 Country	上　海 Shanghai	上海占全国比重(%) Percentage of the National Total(%)
土地面积(万平方公里)	Land Area(10 000 sq. km)	960	0.62	0.1
生产总值(亿元)	Gross Domestic Product(100 million yuan)	249 530	12 188.85	4.9
第一产业	Primary Industry	28 095	101.84	0.4
第二产业	Secondary Industry	121 381	5 678.51	4.7
#工　业	Industry	107 367	5 298.08	4.9
第三产业	Tertiary Industry	100 054	6 408.50	6.4
财政收入(亿元)	Total Fiscal Revenue(100 million yuan)	51 304	7 310.26	14.2
港口货物吞吐量(亿吨)	Port Cargo Handled at Seaports(100 millions tons)	38.8	5.6	14.4
国际标准集装箱吞吐量(万 TEU)	International Container Throughput Capacity(10 000 TEU)	11 179	2 615	23.4
邮电业务总量(亿元)	Revenue of Post and Telecommunication (100 million yuan)	19 759	715.48	3.6
全社会固定资产投资总额(亿元)	Total Investment in Fixed Assets(100 million yuan)	137 239	4 458.61	3.2
社会消费品零售总额(亿元)	Retail Sales of Consumer Goods(100 million yuan)	89 210	3 847.79	4.3
口岸进出口商品总额(亿美元)	Total Port Exports and Imports(100 million USD)	21 738	5 209.09	24.0
进口额	Imports	9 558	1 924.29	20.1
出口额	Exports	12 180	3 284.80	27.0
外商直接投资实际到位金额(亿美元)	Foreign Direct Investment Actually Absorbed (100 million USD)	835.2	79.20	9.5
国际旅游入境人数(万人次)	Number of International Tourists(10 000 person-times)	13 187	665.59	5.0
研究与试验发展经费支出(亿元)	Research and Development Expenditure (100 million yuan)	3 664	307.5	8.4
图书出版量(亿册/张)	Books Published(100 million copies/signatures)	66	2.40	3.6
期刊出版量(亿册)	Periodicals Published(100 million copies)	29	1.83	6.3
报纸出版量(亿份)	Newspapers Published(100 million copies)	439	17.04	3.9
医　生(万人)	Doctors(10 000 persons)	204	4.88	2.4
医院床位数(万张)	Beds in Hospitals(10 000 beds)	328	7.54	2.3

表 2.8 主要年份人大情况
BASIC STATISTIC OF SHANGHAI MUNICIPAL PEOPLE'S CONGRESS IN MAIN YEARS

类 别	Types	2000	2006	2007
全国人大代表人数(人)	Quantity of National Congress(Person)	68	66	64
#女 性	Female	17	17	17
全国人大代表提出议案(件)	Proposals Offered by National Congress Representations(Case)		57	32
市人大代表人数(人)	Quantity of Municipal CongressRepresentatives(Person)	865	869	859
#女 性	Female	203	208	242
市人大常委人数(人)	Quantity of Municipal Standing Committee(Person)	65	64	56
#女 性	Female	13	11	9
市人大代表提出议案(件)	Proposals Offered by Municipal CongressRepresentatives(Case)		58	49
区县人大代表人数(人)	Quantity of District Level Congress Representatives(Person)	4 944	4 961	4 934
#女 性	Female	1 451	1 561	1 557
区县人大常委人数(人)	Quantity of District Level Standing Committee(Person)	432	416	421
#女 性	Female	67	87	98
区县人大代表提出议案(件)	Proposals Offered by District Level Congress Representatives(Case)		150	254

注：本表数据由市人大代表工作委员会提供。
Note: Data in this table are provided by Shanghai Committee of People's Congress.

表 2.9 主要年份政协情况
BASIC STATISTICS ON SHANGHAI MUNICIPAL PEOPLE'S POLITICAL CONSULTATIVE CONFERENCE IN MAIN YEARS

类 别	Types	2000	2006	2007
全国政协委员人数(人)	Quantity of National Commissary(person)	104	113	113
#女 性	Female	20	26	26
全国政协委员提出议案(件)	Proposals Offered by National Commissary(Case)		282	85
市政协委员人数(人)	Quantity of Municipal Commissary(person)	729	791	789
#女 性	Female	120	144	144
市政协常委人数(人)	Quantity of Municipal Standing Committee(person)	121	131	131
#女 性	Female	20	18	18
市政协委员提出议案(件)	Proposals Offered by Municipal Commissary(Case)	1 197	962	1 093
区县政协委员人数(人)	Quantity of District Level Commissary(person)	4 802	5 004	5 079
#女 性	Female	1 230	1 310	1 410
区县政协常委人数(人)	Quantity of District Level Standing Committee(person)	707	691	719
#女 性	Female	174	160	168
区县政协委员提出议案(件)	Offering Proposals Offered by District Level Commissary(Case)		3 480	3 748

注：本表数据由市政协提供。
Note: Data in this table are provided by Shanghai Municipal People's Political Consultative Conference.

上 / 海 / 统 / 计 / 年 / 鉴

主要统计指标解释

登记注册类型

登记注册类型是以工商行政管理机关登记注册的具有法人资格的各类企业为划分对象。产业活动单位和行政机关、事业单位、社会团体及其他经济组织参照执行。

国有企业指企业全部资产归国家所有，并按《中华人民共和国企业法人登记管理条例》规定登记注册的非公司制的经济组织。不包括有限责任公司中的国有独资公司。

集体企业指企业资产归集体所有，并按《中华人民共和国企业法人登记管理条例》规定登记注册的经济组织。

股份合作企业指以合作制为基础，由企业职工共同出资入股，吸收一定比例的社会资产投资组建，实行自主经营，自负盈亏，共同劳动，民主管理，按劳动分配与按股分红相结合的一种集体经济组织。

联营企业指两个及两个以上相同或不同所有制性质的企业法人或事业单位法人，按自愿、平等、互利的原则，共同投资组成的经济组织。联营企业包括国有联营企业、集体联营企业、国有与集体联营企业和其他联营企业。

有限责任公司指根据《中华人民共和国公司登记管理条例》规定登记注册，由2个以上，50个以下的股东共同出资，每个股东以其所认缴的出资额对公司承担有限责任，公司以其全部资产对其债务承担责任的经济组织。有限责任公司包括国有独资公司以及其他有限责任公司。

股份有限公司指根据《中华人民共和国公司登记管理条例》规定登记注册，其全部注册资本由等额股份构成并通过发行股票筹集资本，股东以其认购的股份对公司承担有限责任，公司以其全部资产对其债务承担责任的经济组织。

私营企业指由自然人投资设立或由自然人控股，以雇佣劳动为基础的营利性经济组织。包括按照《公司法》、《合伙企业法》、《私营企业暂行条列》规定登记注册的私营有限责任公司、私营股份有限公司、私营合伙企业和私营独资企业。

港澳台商投资合资经营企业指港澳台地区投资者与内地的企业依照《中华人民共和国中外合资经营企业法》及有关法律的规定，按合同规定的比例投资设立、分享利润和分担风险的企业。

港澳台商投资合作经营企业指港澳台地区投资者与内地企业依照《中华人民共和国中外合作经营企业法》及有关法律的规定，依照合作合同的约定进行投资或提供条件设立、分享利润和分担风险的企业。

港澳台商独资经营企业指依照《中华人民共和国外资企业法》及有关法律的规定，在内地由港澳台商地区投资者全额投资设立的企业。

港澳台商投资股份有限公司指根据国家有关规定，经外经贸部依法批准设立，其中港、澳、台商的股本占公司注册资本的比例达25%以上的股份有限公司。凡其中港、澳、台商的股本占公司注册资本的比例小于25%的，属于内资企业中股份有限公司。

中外合资经营企业指外国企业或外国人与中国内地企业依照《中华人民共和国中外合资经营企业法》及有关法律的规定，按合同规定的比例投资设立、分享利润和分担风险的企业。

中外合作经营企业指外国企业或外国人与中国内地企业依照《中华人民共和国中外合作经营企业法》及有关法律的规定，依照合作合同的约定进行投资或提供条件设立、分享利润和分担风险的企业。

外资企业指依照《中华人民共和国外资企业法》及有关法律的规定，在中国内地由外国投资者全额投资设立的企业。

外商投资股份有限公司指根据国家有关规定，经外经贸部依法批准设立，其中外资的股本占公司注册资本的比例达25%以上的股份有限公司。凡其中外资股本占公司注册资本的比例小于25%的，属于内资企业中的股份有限公司。

国民经济行业分类

《国民经济行业分类》国家标准于1984年首次发布，1994年对其进行了第一次修订，2002年为第二次修订。

本年鉴的行业分类使用2002年修订的行业分类标准。

2002年新行业分类标准按照国际通行的经济活动同质性原则划分行业，进一步打破了部门管理界限，对原标准中不符合这一原则的分类进行了调整；根据我国社会经济活动的发展状况，重点加强了第三产业的分类，新增了大量服务业方面的活动类别；对新标准的每一个行业小类，全部与国际标准产业分类的最细一层分类建立了对应关系。新修订的国民经济行业分类主要目的之一

主要统计指标解释

是与联合国的《全部经济活动的国际标准产业分类》接轨，准确反映一定时期内国民经济行业的构成状况。

各个计划时期

表内所用各个“时期”代表的年份如下：恢复时期为1950到1952年；第一个五年计划时期（简称“一五”时期）为1953到1957年；第二个五年计划时期（简称“二五”时期）为1958到1962年；第三个五年计划时期（简称“三五”时期）为1966到1970年；第四个五年计划时期（简称“四五”时期）为1971到1975年；第五个五年计划时期（简称“五五”时期）为1976到1980年；第六个五年计划时期（简称“六五”时期）为1981到1985年；第七个五年计划时期（简称“七五”时期）为1986到1990年；第八个五年计划时期（简称“八五”时期）为1991到1995年；第九个五年计划时期（简称“九五”时期）为1996到2000年；第十个五年计划时期（简称“十五”时期）为2001到2005年；第十一个五年计划时期（简称“十一五”时期）为2006到2010年。

可比价格

指在不同时期的价值指标对比时，扣除了价格变动的因素，以确切反映物量的变化。按可比价格计算有两种方法：一种是直接用产品产量乘某一年的不变价格计算；另一种是用价格指数换算。

不变价格

指以同类产品某年的平均价格作为固定价格，用于计算各年的产品价值。按不变价格计算的产品价值消除了价格变动因素，不同时期对比可以反映生产的发展速度。新中国成立后，随着工农业产品价格水平的变化，国家统计局先后五次制定了全国统一的工业产品不变价格和农业产品不变价格。从1952年到1957年使用1952年工(农)业产品不变价格，从1957年到1970年使用1957年不变价格，从1971年到1980年使用1970年不变价格，从1981年到1990年使用1980年不变价格，从1991年到2000年使用1990年不变价格，从2001年开始使用2000年不变价格。

指　数

指数是一种表明社会经济现象动态的相对数。运用指数可以测定不能直接相加和直接对比的社会经济现象的总动态；可以分析社会经济现象总变动中各因素变动的影响程度；可以研究总平均指标变动中各组标志水平和总体结构变动的作用。它是在把各个年份的产值换算成可比价格的基础上，根据定基数等于相应各个环比指数的连乘积这个换算关系计算出来的。

本年鉴所列的上海市生产总值、工业总产值、农业总产值等指标增长速度，就是分别使用上海市生产总值指数、工业总产值指数、农业总产值指数直接计算的。

平均每年增长速度

在我国计算平均增长速度有两种方法。一种是习惯上经常使用的“水平法”，又称几何平均法，是以间隔期最后一年的水平同基期水平对比来计算平均每年增长（或下降）速度；另一种是“累计法”，又称代数平均法或方程法，是以间隔期内各年水平的总和同基期水平对比来计算平均每年增长(或下降)速度。

在一般正常情况下，两种方法计算的平均每年增长速度比较接近。但在经济发展不平衡，出现大起大落时，两种方法计算的结果差别较大。

本年鉴内所列的平均每年增长速度，除固定资产投资、直接吸收外资是用“累计法”计算以外，其余均用“水平法”计算。从某年到某年平均增长速度的年份，均不包括基期年在内。如1953-2006年平均增长速度是以1952年为基期计算的，余类推。

恩格尔系数

恩格尔系数是家庭或个人食品支出总额占全部消费支出总额的比重，是国际上通行的衡量一个国家和地区人民生活水平状况的重要指标。家庭生活越贫困，其消费支出中用于食品支出的比重就越高，恩格尔系数就越大；反之，恩格尔系数就越小。

国有企业

指企业全部资产归国家所有，并按《中华人民共和国企业法人登记管理条例》规定登记注册的非公司制的经济组织。不包括有限责任公司中的国有独资公司。

集体企业

集体企业指企业资产归集体所有，并按《中华人民共和国企业法人登记管理条例》规定登记注册的经济组织。

SHANGHAI STATISTICAL YEARBOOK

EXPLANATORY NOTES TO MAJOR STATISTICAL INDICATORS

□ Registration Categories

Registration Categories are used to classify all kinds of enterprises that have the legal person status and have registered with the industrial and commercial administrations. The classification of business units, administrative and public institutions, social organizations and other economical bodies may refer to it.

The state-owned enterprises are economic organizations whose assets are solely owned by the state and whose registrations are made according to "Regulations of the People's Republic of China for Controlling the Registration of Enterprises as Legal Persons" excluding the state-owned liability limited companies.

The collective-owned enterprises are economic organizations whose assets are owned by collecting and whose registration are made according to "Regulations of the People's Republic of China for Controlling the Registration of Enterprises as Legal Persons."

Share-holding cooperative enterprises are a kind of collective economic organizations based on a cooperative system. In addition to the shares bought by their workers and staff, the enterprises also absorb a certain percentage of social capital. They enjoy the autonomy in operation and are responsible for their own losses and profits. The share-holders work together, conduct democratic management, and combine labor-based distribution with share-based dividents.

Joint-owned enterprises refer to economic organizations set up with joint investment from legal persons of two or more enterprises of different ownerships or institutions according to principle of voluntary participation, equality and mutual benefit. They include state-owned joint operation enterprises, collective joint operation enterprises, state-collective joint operation enterprises and other types of joint operation enterprises.

A company with limited liability is a company registered in accordance with the "Regulations of the People's Republic of China on Administration of Company Registration." Its investment comes from more than 2 and less than 50 shareholders. Each shareholder assumes limited liability for the company according to his subscription to capital stock. The company assumes liabilities for its debts according to all its assets. Such economic organizations include solely state-invested companies and other types of companies with limited liability.

A share-holding company with limited liability refers to economic organizations registered in accordance with the "Regulations of the People's Republic of China on Administration of Company Registration." All its registered capital is composed of shares of equal value and its capital is collected through share issuing. The shareholders bear limited liability for the company according to the amount of shares they have bought from the company and the company assumes liabilities for its debts according all its assets.

A private enterprise refers to profit-making economic organizations set up with investment from natural persons or with controlling interest in the hands of natural persons who employ laborers for operation. Such enterprises include private companies with limited liability, private joint stock companies limited, private partnership enterprises and solely individual-invested enterprises, which are registered according to the "Company Law," "Partnership Enterprises Law" and "Interim Regulations of Private Enterprises."

The joint ventures with investment from Hong Kong, Macao and Taiwan refer to those established according to the "Law of the People's Republic of China on Chinese-foreign Joint Ventures" and regulations stipulated in relevant laws, by investors from those regions and the Chinese mainland enterprises with contracted share of investment and sharing profits and ventures between the parties.

Cooperative businesses with investment from Hong Kong, Macao and Taiwan refer to enterprises jointly set up by investors from Hong Kong, Macao and Taiwan and mainland enterprises according to the "Law of the People's Republic of China on Chinese-foreign Contractural Joint Ventures" and other relevant regulations. They invest or provide conditions for establishment, decide profit distribution, and share risks according to provisions prescribed in the cooperative venture contracts.

Solely Hong Kong, Macao and Taiwan Funded enterprises refer to enterprises set up on the mainland according to the "Law of the People's Republic of China on Foreign Capital Enterprises and solely invested by investors from Hong Kong, Macao and Taiwan."

A share-holding company with limited liability with investment from Hong Kong, Macao and Taiwan refers to any joint stock company limited that is set up according relevant state regulations

EXPLANATORY NOTES TO MAJOR STATISTICAL INDICATORS

and is approved by the Ministry of Foreign Economic Relations and Trade. The investment from Hong Kong, Macao and Taiwan investors must account more than 25 percent of the company's total capital. If such investment is less than 25 percent, it shall be classified as a joint stock company limited invested by domestic investors.

A Sino-foreign joint venture refers to any enterprise that is jointly set up by foreign enterprises or foreigners with Chinese enterprises in accordance with the "Law of the People's Republic of China on Joint Ventures with Chinese and Foreign Investment." The investors shall put in investment, share profits and risks according to the contract on the joint venture.

Sino-foreign cooperative Businesses refers to the enterprises set up by foreign enterprises or foreigners with Chinese enterprises as their partners, in line with "The Sino-foreign Cooperative Ventures Law of the People's Republic of China" and other relevant laws and regulations. The partners of the cooperative ventures will invest, take profits and share risks according to the requirements of stipulated in the contract.

A Solely Foreign-Funded enterprise refers to any enterprise that is set up on the Chinese mainland according to the "Law of the People's Republic of China on Foreign-Capital Enterprises" and with all its investment coming from foreign investors.

The foreign-invested joint stock company limited refers to any joint stock company limited that is set up according to relevant state regulations and is approved by the Ministry of Foreign Economic Relations and Trade. The foreign investment must account more than 25 percent of the company's total capital. If such investment is less than 25 percent, it shall be classified as a joint stock company limited invested by Chinese investors.

□ Classification of the Sectors of the National Economy

Classification of the Sectors of the National Economy was first published in 1984 and revisions were made into it in 1994 and 2002 respectively.

This Yearbook follows standards in the 2002 version of the Classification of the Sectors of the National Economy.

In the 2002 version, economic sectors are classified in accordance with the international categories of the economic activities, abolishing in definition between different administrative departments. Given the development of China's social and economic activities, more detailed classification is made of the service sector. The further breakdown of each economic sector in the latest version is geared to the most specific categorization in international practice. The latest version aims at, among others, an objective and precise presentation of the composition of the national economy in a certain period.

□ Various Planning Periods

The conventional division of time period in this statistical yearbook is as follows: Rehabilitation Period, 1950-1952; The First Five-Year Plan period (cited as first-five period), 1953-1957; The Second Five-Year Plan period (cited as second-five period), 1958-1962; The Third Five-Year Plan period (cited as third-five period), 1966-1970; The Fourth Five-Year Plan period (cited as fourth-five period), 1971-1975; The Fifth Five-Year Plan period (cited as fifth-five period), 1976-1980; The Sixth Five-Year Plan period (cited as sixth-five period), 1981-1985; The Seventh Five-Year Plan period (cited as seventh-five period), 1986-1990; The Eight Five-Year Plan period (cited as eighth-five period), 1991-1995; The Ninth Five-Year Plan period (cited as ninth-five period), 1996-2000; The Tenth Five-Year Plan period (cited as tenth-five period), 2001-2005; The eleventh Five-Year Plan period (cited as eleventh-five period),2006-2010.

□ Comparable Prices

Comparable Prices are applied when comparing indicators over time to reflect accurately the changes in real term. Two methods are used for calculating comparable prices: 1. output by constant price of certain year; 2. output in current prices divided by relevant price index.

□ Constant Price

Constant Price refers to the average price of a given product in certain year, which is used for comparison of output value over time. As the output value at constant prices removes the factor of price changes, it reflects the trend of production development over time. Since 1949, with the changes in general price level, National Bureau of Statistics has issued nationally unified constant prices five times: the 1952 constant prices for 1949-1957; the 1957 constant prices for 1957-1971; the 1970 constant prices for 1971-1981; the 1980 constant prices for 1981-1990; the 1990 constant prices for 1991-2000; and the 2000 constant prices have been used since 2001.

□ Index

Index refers to the relative figures indicating social and eco-

EXPLANATORY NOTES TO MAJOR STATISTICAL INDICATORS

nomic phenomena and developments. Index is used to evaluate the overall development of social and economic phenomena which can not be determined by simple addition or direct comparison. It is also used to analyze the outcome of various changes in the general phenomenon movement of social and economic development, and to study the level of each sub-index in the changes of general average index and the role of the changes of the overall structure. It is calculated at the comparable prices conversed from the output value of each year, using the formula of index number with fixed base period equal to the continuous product of its relative chain index.

The increases of Shanghai Gross Domestic Product, industrial output value and agricultural output value compared with the previous year, which are listed in this yearbook, are calculated according to Shanghai GDP index, industrial output value index and agricultural output value index.

□ Average Annual Growth Rate

Two methods for calculating Average Annual Growth Rate are applied in China, one is often called "level approach" or geometry average, which is derived by comparing the growth rate for the last year of the interval with that of the beginning year; the other is called "accumulating approach" or algebraic average or equation method, which is calculated by comparing the total growth rate of each year for the interval with that of base year.

Usually the results calculated by the two methods are fairly close, but they differ sharply when imbalance occurred in economic development with striking fluctuations in growth.

The Average Annual Growth Rates listed in this statistical yearbook are calculated by "level approach" except for the growth rate of investment in fixed assets and foreign capital absorbed. The base years are not listed when the years are listed for average annual growth rates for instance, the average annual growth rate of 1953-2006 is calculated with the base year 1952, and the analogy of this is also for the rest.

□ Engel Coefficient

Engel Coefficient refers to the proportion of food expenditure in the family's total consumption. It is an international standard to evaluate the living standard in a country or region. The poorer a family is, the higher the proportion of food expenditure is in the family's total consumption, hence the higher E. C. is and vice versa.

□ State-owned Enterprises

State-owned Enterprises refer to non-corporation economic units where the entire assets are owned by the state and which have registered in accordance with the Regulation of the People's Republic of China on the Management of Registration of Corporate Enterprises. Excluded from this category are sole state-funded corporations in the limited liability corporations.

□ Collective-owned Enterprises

Collective-owned Enterprises refer to economic units where the assets are owned collectively and which have registered in accordance with the Regulation of the People's Republic of China on the Management of Registration of Corporate Enterprises.

第三篇

CHAPTER 3

人口和劳动力

POPULATION AND
LABOUR FORCE

表 3.1 主要年份常住人口
RESIDENT POPULATION IN MAIN YEARS

单位：万人(10 000 persons)

指 标	Indicators	2000	2006	2007
年末常住人口	Year-end Resident Population	1 608	1 815.08	1 858.08
户籍人口	Year-end Registered Population	1 309	1 347.82	1 358.86
外来人口(半年以上人口)	Year-end Floating Population (Above Half Year)	299	467.26	499.22

注：本表户籍人口不包括离开上海、外出(市外)半年以上本市户籍人口。
Note: Registered population in this table does not include those outside of Shanghai for over half year.

表 3.2 主要年份户籍人口
REGISTERED POPULATION IN MAIN YEARS

单位：万人(10 000 persons)

指 标	Indicators	2000	2006	2007
年末户籍人口	Year-end Registered Population	1 321.63	1 368.08	1 378.86
农业人口	Agriculture	335.47	194.78	181.92
非农业人口	Non-agriculture	986.16	1 173.30	1 196.94

表 3.3 主要年份外来人口
FLOATING POPULATION IN MAIN YEARS

单位：万人(10 000 persons)

指 标	Indicators	2000	2006	2007
外来人口总量	Floating Population	387	627.01	660.30
半年以下流动人口	Below Half Year	88	159.75	161.08
半年及以上常住人口	Above Half Year	299	467.26	499.22

表3.4 户籍人口、户数、人口密度和平均期望寿命(1978～2007)
TOTAL HOUSEHOLDS, REGISTERED POPULATION, DENSITY OF POPULATION AND LIFE EXPECTANCY

年份 Year	总户数(万户) Total Households (10 000 households)	年末户籍人口(万人) Year-end Registered Population (10 000 persons)	按性别分 Grouped by Sex		按农业非农业分 Grouped by Agriculture and Non-agriculture	
			男性 Male	女性 Female	农业 Agriculture	非农业 Non-agriculture
1978	291.69	1 098.28	542.70	555.58	453.05	645.23
1979	296.71	1 132.14	560.40	571.74	444.76	687.38
1980	303.87	1 146.52	569.30	577.22	444.09	702.43
1981	314.56	1 162.84	578.76	584.08	447.76	715.08
1982	321.71	1 180.51	588.82	591.69	449.20	731.31
1983	330.60	1 194.01	596.67	597.34	448.15	745.86
1984	340.78	1 204.78	602.59	602.19	444.03	760.75
1985	351.72	1 216.69	609.70	606.99	440.32	776.37
1986	364.92	1 232.33	618.88	613.45	429.77	802.56
1987	380.19	1 249.51	628.78	620.73	427.20	822.31
1988	394.95	1 262.42	635.82	626.60	423.49	838.93
1989	406.82	1 276.45	643.51	632.94	420.61	855.84
1990	415.28	1 283.35	647.13	636.22	418.89	864.46
1991	425.84	1 287.20	649.03	638.17	417.32	869.88
1992	431.67	1 289.37	649.97	639.40	413.82	875.55
1993	438.69	1 294.74	652.92	641.82	401.28	893.46
1994	444.38	1 298.81	655.14	643.67	388.32	910.49
1995	450.76	1 301.37	656.48	644.89	379.67	921.70
1996	457.49	1 304.43	657.86	646.57	372.29	932.14
1997	461.40	1 305.46	657.93	647.53	362.43	943.03
1998	465.72	1 306.58	658.22	648.36	352.93	953.65
1999	470.11	1 313.12	661.19	651.93	343.49	969.63
2000	475.73	1 321.63	665.51	656.12	335.47	986.16
2001	478.92	1 327.14	668.32	658.82	328.07	999.07
2002	481.77	1 334.23	672.05	662.18	315.42	1 018.81
2003	486.06	1 341.77	675.47	666.30	300.38	1 041.39
2004	490.58	1 352.39	680.38	672.01	254.79	1 097.60
2005	496.69	1 360.26	683.51	676.75	211.32	1 148.94
2006	499.54	1 368.08	686.66	681.42	194.78	1 173.30
2007	503.29	1 378.86	691.08	687.78	181.92	1 196.94

注：户数和年末户籍人口由市公安局提供，平均期望寿命由市卫生局提供。

Note: The figures of household and year-end population are provided by Municipal Public Security Bureau, and the figures of life expendency are provided by Shanghai Municipal Health Bureau.

表 3.4 续表 continued

年份 Year	非农业人口占总人口比重(%) Percentage of Non-agriculture Population in Total(%)	平均每户人口(人) Average Persons Per Household (person)	人口密度(人/平方公里) Density of Population (person/sq・km)	平均期望寿命(岁) Life Expectancy (year)	其中 of which 男性 Male	 女性 Female
1978	58.7	3.8	1 776	73.35	70.69	74.78
1979	60.7	3.8	1 830	73.14	70.64	75.48
1980	61.3	3.8	1 854	73.33	71.25	75.36
1981	61.5	3.7	1 880	73.38	71.28	75.47
1982	61.9	3.7	1 908	74.04	71.77	76.25
1983	62.5	3.6	1 930	73.23	71.15	75.26
1984	63.1	3.5	1 948	73.90	71.73	76.17
1985	63.8	3.5	1 967	74.27	72.14	76.37
1986	65.1	3.4	1 944	74.71	72.54	76.85
1987	65.8	3.3	1 971	74.46	72.32	76.60
1988	66.5	3.2	1 991	74.63	72.50	76.77
1989	67.0	3.1	2 013	74.98	72.85	77.12
1990	67.4	3.1	2 024	75.46	73.16	77.74
1991	67.6	3.0	2 030	75.79	73.58	77.95
1992	67.9	3.0	2 034	75.97	74.04	77.91
1993	69.0	3.0	2 042	75.97	74.04	77.91
1994	70.1	2.9	2 048	76.26	74.29	78.23
1995	70.8	2.9	2 052	76.03	74.11	77.97
1996	71.5	2.9	2 057	76.11	74.07	78.21
1997	72.2	2.8	2 059	77.20	75.18	79.21
1998	73.0	2.8	2 061	77.03	75.06	79.02
1999	73.8	2.8	2 071	78.44	76.38	80.53
2000	74.6	2.8	2 084	78.77	76.71	80.81
2001	75.3	2.8	2 093	79.66	77.47	81.83
2002	76.4	2.8	2 104	79.52	77.36	81.63
2003	77.6	2.8	2 116	79.80	77.78	81.81
2004	81.2	2.8	2 133	80.29	78.08	82.48
2005	84.5	2.7	2 145	80.13	77.89	82.36
2006	85.8	2.7	2 158	80.97	78.64	83.29
2007	86.8	2.7	2 175	81.08	78.87	83.29

表3.5 各区、县土地面积、户籍人口、户数及人口密度(2007)
LAND AREA, HOUSEHOLDS, REGISTERED POPULATION AND DENSITY OF POPULATION IN DISTRICTS AND COUNTIES

地区	District	土地面积(平方公里) Land Area (sq. km)	户数(万户) Total Households (10 000 households)	年末户籍人口(万人) Year-end Registered Population (10 000 persons)	平均每户人口(人) Average Persons Per Household (person)	人口密度(人/平方公里) Density of Population (person/sq·km)
全市	**Total**	**6 340.50**	**503.29**	**1 378.86**	**2.7**	**2 175**
浦东新区	PudongNewArea	532.75	71.35	191.16	2.7	3 588
黄浦区	Huangpu	12.41	19.17	60.56	3.2	48 799
卢湾区	Luwan	8.05	10.63	31.15	2.9	38 696
徐汇区	Xuhui	54.76	32.05	89.18	2.8	16 286
长宁区	Changning	38.30	21.28	61.13	2.9	15 961
静安区	Jing'an	7.62	10.55	30.99	2.9	40 669
普陀区	Putuo	54.83	31.99	86.29	2.7	15 738
闸北区	Zhabei	29.26	25.29	69.51	2.7	23 756
虹口区	Hongkou	23.48	27.95	78.96	2.8	33 629
杨浦区	Yangpu	60.73	37.78	107.71	2.9	17 736
宝山区	Baoshan	270.99	32.04	83.06	2.6	3 065
闵行区	Minhang	370.75	34.21	88.58	2.6	2 389
嘉定区	Jiading	464.20	18.56	53.79	2.9	1 159
金山区	Jinshan	586.05	17.50	52.10	3.0	889
松江区	Songjiang	605.64	17.89	54.27	3.0	896
青浦区	Qingpu	670.14	15.49	45.74	3.0	683
南汇区	Nanhui	677.66	29.47	73.40	2.5	1 083
奉贤区	Fengxian	687.39	20.94	51.57	2.5	750
崇明县	Chongming	1 185.49	29.15	69.71	2.4	588

注：土地面积由市民政局提供，户数、年末户籍人口由市公安局提供。
Note: The figures of land area are provided by Shanghai Civil Affairs Bureau. The figures of total households and year-end registered population are provided by Shanghai Municipal Public Security Bureau.

表 3.6 各区、县土地面积、常住人口及人口密度（2007）
LAND AREA, RESIDENT POPULATION AND DENSITY OF POPULATION IN DISTRICTS AND COUNTIES

地 区	District	土地面积（平方公里）Land Area (sq. km)	年末常住人口（万人）Year-end Resident Population (10 000 persons)	其中 of which 外来人口 Floating People	人口密度（人/平方公里）Density of Population (person/sq·km)
全 市	**Total**	**6 340.50**	**1 858.08**	**499.22**	**2 930**
浦东新区	Pudong New Area	532.75	305.36	98.34	5 732
黄 浦 区	Huangpu	12.41	52.19	7.99	42 055
卢 湾 区	Luwan	8.05	26.80	3.50	33 292
徐 汇 区	Xuhui	54.76	96.59	13.51	17 639
长 宁 区	Changning	38.30	65.02	9.66	16 977
静 安 区	Jing'an	7.62	25.21	2.91	33 084
普 陀 区	Putuo	54.83	113.40	23.77	20 682
闸 北 区	Zhabei	29.26	74.39	9.97	25 424
虹 口 区	Hongkou	23.48	78.17	10.08	33 292
杨 浦 区	Yangpu	60.73	117.51	12.02	19 350
宝 山 区	Baoshan	270.99	133.21	34.52	4 916
闵 行 区	Minhang	370.75	189.56	79.17	5 113
嘉 定 区	Jiading	464.20	99.90	43.57	2 152
金 山 区	Jinshan	586.05	66.78	14.94	1 139
松 江 区	Songjiang	605.64	98.86	44.00	1 632
青 浦 区	Qingpu	670.14	77.76	31.88	1 160
南 汇 区	Nanhui	677.66	96.75	24.90	1 428
奉 贤 区	Fengxian	687.39	74.89	26.25	1 089
崇 明 县	Chongming	1 185.49	65.73	8.24	554

注：土地面积由市民政局提供。
Note: The figures of land area are provided by Shanghai Civil Affairs Bureau.

表 3.7 主要年份户籍人口出生率、死亡率、自然增长率
BIRTH RATE, DEATH RATE AND NATURAL GROWTH RATE OF REGISTERED POPULATION IN MAIN YEARS

年 份 Year	出 生 Birth		死 亡 Death		自然增长 Natural Growth	
	人 数（万人）Population (10 000 persons)	出生率（‰）Birth Rate (‰)	人 数（万人）Population (10 000 persons)	死亡率（‰）Death Rate (‰)	人 数（万人）Population (10 000 persons)	自然增长率（‰）Natural Growth Rate(‰)
1990	13.12	10.25	8.63	6.74	4.49	3.51
1995	7.11	5.47	9.79	7.53	-2.68	-2.06
1996	6.79	5.21	9.77	7.50	-2.98	-2.29
1997	6.42	4.92	9.57	7.33	-3.15	-2.41
1998	6.17	4.73	10.13	7.75	-3.96	-3.03
1999	6.56	5.01	9.54	7.28	-2.98	-2.27
2000	6.95	5.27	9.45	7.17	-2.50	-1.90
2001	5.76	4.34	9.34	7.05	-3.58	-2.71
2002	6.20	4.66	9.67	7.27	-3.47	-2.61
2003	5.73	4.28	10.07	7.52	-4.34	-3.24
2004	8.09	6.00	9.65	7.16	-1.56	-1.16
2005	8.25	6.08	10.23	7.54	-1.98	-1.46
2006	8.12	5.95	9.80	7.19	-1.68	-1.24
2007	10.08	7.34	10.22	7.44	-0.14	-0.10

表 3.8 主要年份户籍人口迁移
MIGRATION IN MAIN YEARS

年 份 Year	迁 入 Inflows		迁 出 Outflows		机械增长 Mechanical Increase	
	人 口（万人）Population (10 000 persons)	迁入率（‰）Rate of Inflows (‰)	人 口（万人）Population (10 000 persons)	迁出率（‰）Rate of Outflows (‰)	人 口（万人）Population (10 000 persons)	增长率（‰）Growth Rate (‰)
1990	12.18	9.52	10.72	8.38	1.46	1.14
1995	13.12	10.09	6.47	4.98	6.65	5.11
1996	13.01	9.99	6.41	4.92	6.60	5.07
1997	11.47	8.79	5.72	4.38	5.75	4.41
1998	11.73	8.98	5.04	3.86	6.69	5.12
1999	14.06	10.73	5.08	3.88	8.98	6.85
2000	15.16	11.51	5.32	4.04	9.84	7.47
2001	14.63	11.05	5.56	4.20	9.07	6.85
2002	15.41	11.58	4.38	3.29	11.03	8.29
2003	14.92	11.15	3.69	2.76	11.23	8.39
2004	13.93	10.34	2.74	2.03	11.19	8.31
2005	12.96	9.55	3.46	2.55	9.50	7.00
2006	12.86	9.43	3.50	2.57	9.36	6.86
2007	14.69	10.70	3.95	2.88	10.74	7.82

注：本页数据由市公安局提供。
Note: Data on this page are provided by Shanghai Municipal Public Security Bureau.

表3.9 各区、县户籍人口迁移(2007)
MIGRATION IN DISTRICTS AND COUNTIES

地 区 District		迁 入(人) Inflows(person)		迁 出(人) Outflows(person)	
		市内迁入 From Inside of the City	市外迁入 From Outside of the City	迁往市内 To the Inside of the City	迁往市外 To the Outside of the City
全 市	**Total**	**9 175**	**146 918**	**9 189**	**39 472**
浦东新区	Pudong New Area	686	23 101	294	4 812
黄 浦 区	Huangpu	88	5 633	78	472
卢 湾 区	Luwan	33	3 143	17	407
徐 汇 区	Xuhui	248	13 491	99	4 303
长 宁 区	Changning	78	6 952	51	1 564
静 安 区	Jing'an	32	1 859	18	339
普 陀 区	Putuo	245	6 242	142	2 492
闸 北 区	Zhabei	303	6 617	133	964
虹 口 区	Hongkou	327	5 950	151	1 322
杨 浦 区	Yangpu	506	21 966	326	12 920
宝 山 区	Baoshan	2 449	10 246	1 753	1 375
闵 行 区	Minhang	562	16 365	184	2 673
嘉 定 区	Jiading	83	3 630	26	442
金 山 区	Jinshan	27	1 395	20	824
松 江 区	Songjiang	62	9 826	26	2 811
青 浦 区	Qingpu	12	2 026	20	443
南 汇 区	Nanhui	50	3 476	23	517
奉 贤 区	Fengxian	55	2 947	12	409
崇 明 县	Chongming	3 329	2 053	5 816	383

注：本表数据由市公安局提供。
Note: This table is provided by Shanghai Municipal Public Security Bureau.

表 3.10　各区、县户籍人口自然变动情况（2007）
NATURAL CHANGES OF REGISTERED POPULATION IN DISTRICTS AND COUNTIES

地　区 District		出　生 Birth		死　亡 Death		自然增长 Natural Growth	
		人　数（万人）Population (10 000 persons)	出生率（‰）Birth Rate (‰)	人　数（万人）Population (10 000 persons)	死亡率（‰）Death Rate (‰)	人　数（万人）Population (10 000 persons)	自然增长率（‰）Natural Growth Rate(‰)
全　市	**Total**	**10.08**	**7.34**	**10.22**	**7.44**	**-0.14**	**-0.10**
浦东新区	Pudong New Area	1.67	8.82	1.37	7.24	0.30	1.58
黄 浦 区	Huangpu	0.42	7.01	0.52	8.63	-0.10	-1.62
卢 湾 区	Luwan	0.19	6.02	0.28	8.85	-0.09	-2.83
徐 汇 区	Xuhui	0.57	6.43	0.63	7.12	-0.06	-0.69
长 宁 区	Changning	0.37	6.11	0.43	7.02	-0.06	-0.91
静 安 区	Jing'an	0.20	6.30	0.26	8.46	-0.06	-2.16
普 陀 区	Putuo	0.60	6.90	0.68	7.89	-0.08	-0.99
闸 北 区	Zhabei	0.46	6.51	0.56	8.01	-0.10	-1.50
虹 口 区	Hongkou	0.51	6.45	0.64	8.11	-0.13	-1.66
杨 浦 区	Yangpu	0.59	5.51	0.80	7.44	-0.21	-1.93
宝 山 区	Baoshan	0.63	7.66	0.60	7.35	0.03	0.31
闵 行 区	Minhang	1.01	11.62	0.62	7.12	0.39	4.50
嘉 定 区	Jiading	0.43	7.95	0.41	7.60	0.02	0.35
金 山 区	Jinshan	0.33	6.37	0.35	6.78	-0.02	-0.41
松 江 区	Songjiang	0.40	7.49	0.34	6.32	0.06	1.17
青 浦 区	Qingpu	0.32	6.96	0.32	6.91	…	0.05
南 汇 区	Nanhui	0.61	8.30	0.46	6.30	0.15	2.00
奉 贤 区	Fengxian	0.34	6.64	0.35	6.73	-0.01	-0.09
崇 明 县	Chongming	0.43	6.20	0.60	8.57	-0.17	-2.37

注：本表数据由市公安局提供。
Note: This table is provided by Shanghai Municipal Public Security Bureau.

表 3.11　各区、县户籍人口年龄构成(2007)
AGE STRUCTURE OF POPULATION IN DISTRICTS AND COUNTIES

单位:万人(10 000 persons)

地　区	District	合　计 Total	17 岁及以下 17 and below	18～34 岁 18～34	35～59 岁 35～59	60 岁及以上 60 and above
全　市	**Total**	**1 378.86**	**149.95**	**334.08**	**608.00**	**286.83**
浦东新区	Pudong New Area	191.16	21.65	47.40	83.77	38.34
黄浦区	Huangpu	60.56	5.80	14.90	26.90	12.96
卢湾区	Luwan	31.15	2.72	7.63	13.46	7.34
徐汇区	Xuhui	89.18	9.54	22.55	37.21	19.88
长宁区	Changning	61.13	5.57	17.56	25.12	12.88
静安区	Jing'an	30.99	3.07	7.31	13.16	7.45
普陀区	Putuo	86.29	8.00	20.86	39.13	18.30
闸北区	Zhabei	69.51	6.71	16.51	31.74	14.55
虹口区	Hongkou	78.96	7.66	18.54	35.29	17.47
杨浦区	Yangpu	107.71	9.46	29.52	46.76	21.97
宝山区	Baoshan	83.06	9.20	19.27	37.99	16.60
闵行区	Minhang	88.58	10.88	22.65	37.48	17.57
嘉定区	Jiading	53.79	6.19	12.08	23.77	11.75
金山区	Jinshan	52.10	6.65	11.07	24.35	10.03
松江区	Songjiang	54.27	6.95	13.65	23.25	10.42
青浦区	Qingpu	45.74	5.81	9.84	20.96	9.13
南汇区	Nanhui	73.40	9.71	17.49	32.44	13.76
奉贤区	Fengxian	51.57	6.55	11.58	23.34	10.10
崇明县	Chongming	69.71	7.83	13.67	31.88	16.33

注：本表数据由市公安局提供。
Note：This table is provided by Shanghai Municipal Public Security Bureau.

表3.12 各区、县户籍老年人口年龄构成(2007)
AGE STRUCTURE OF AGING POPULATION IN DISTRICTS AND COUNTIES

单位:万人(10 000 persons)

地 区	District	合 计 Total	60～64岁 60～64	65～79岁 65～79	80岁及以上 80 and above
全 市	**Total**	**286.83**	**75.65**	**160.94**	**50.24**
浦东新区	Pudong New Area	38.34	10.40	21.28	6.66
黄 浦 区	Huangpu	12.96	2.91	7.08	2.97
卢 湾 区	Luwan	7.34	1.69	4.01	1.64
徐 汇 区	Xuhui	19.88	4.91	11.40	3.58
长 宁 区	Changning	12.88	3.01	7.60	2.27
静 安 区	Jing'an	7.45	1.79	4.01	1.65
普 陀 区	Putuo	18.30	4.45	10.51	3.34
闸 北 区	Zhabei	14.55	3.42	8.34	2.79
虹 口 区	Hongkou	17.47	4.22	9.76	3.49
杨 浦 区	Yangpu	21.97	5.21	12.82	3.94
宝 山 区	Baoshan	16.60	4.76	9.13	2.71
闵 行 区	Minhang	17.57	4.91	9.91	2.75
嘉 定 区	Jiading	11.75	3.34	6.53	1.88
金 山 区	Jinshan	10.03	3.04	5.60	1.39
松 江 区	Songjiang	10.42	3.04	5.81	1.57
青 浦 区	Qingpu	9.13	2.62	5.20	1.31
南 汇 区	Nanhui	13.76	4.14	7.46	2.16
奉 贤 区	Fengxian	10.10	3.13	5.53	1.44
崇 明 县	Chongming	16.33	4.67	8.96	2.70

表3.13 各区、县计划生育基本情况(2007)
FAMILY PLANNING IN DISTRICTS AND COUNTIES

地 区 District		出生人数(万人) Birth (10 000 persons)	已婚育龄妇女人数(万人) Married Women at Childbearing Age (10 000 persons)	领独生子女证人数(万人) Married Couples with One-child Certificate (10 000 persons)	采取避孕措施人数(万人) Married People Adopting Contraception (10 000 persons)	计划生育率(%) Family Planning Rate (%)	领证率(%) Coverage of One-child Certificate (%)	避孕率(%) Comprehensive Contraception Rate (%)
全 市	**Total**	**10.08**	**219.14**	**69.78**	**186.82**	**99.3**	**31.9**	**85.3**
浦东新区	Pudong New Area	1.67	28.73	10.06	25.03	99.7	35.0	87.1
黄 浦 区	Huangpu	0.42	8.25	2.34	6.68	97.8	28.4	81.0
卢 湾 区	Luwan	0.19	4.38	1.33	3.50	99.2	30.3	79.7
徐 汇 区	Xuhui	0.57	13.26	4.06	10.99	98.9	30.6	82.9
长 宁 区	Changning	0.37	8.28	2.45	6.64	98.8	29.6	80.3
静 安 区	Jing'an	0.20	3.75	1.11	3.02	99.5	29.7	80.6
普 陀 区	Putuo	0.60	11.86	4.19	9.28	99.3	35.3	78.2
闸 北 区	Zhabei	0.46	9.80	2.80	8.04	99.1	28.6	82.1
虹 口 区	Hongkou	0.51	10.03	3.07	8.12	99.1	30.6	81.0
杨 浦 区	Yangpu	0.59	14.50	4.16	11.67	99.5	28.7	80.5
宝 山 区	Baoshan	0.63	12.49	3.83	11.23	99.1	30.7	89.8
闵 行 区	Minhang	1.01	13.63	3.97	11.47	99.8	29.2	84.2
嘉 定 区	Jiading	0.43	9.97	3.28	8.61	99.3	32.9	86.4
金 山 区	Jinshan	0.33	10.73	3.34	9.36	99.7	31.1	87.2
松 江 区	Songjiang	0.40	9.93	3.49	8.93	99.7	35.2	89.9
青 浦 区	Qingpu	0.32	9.91	3.09	8.88	97.4	31.2	89.6
南 汇 区	Nanhui	0.61	15.66	5.74	13.99	99.5	36.7	89.3
奉 贤 区	Fengxian	0.34	9.94	3.27	8.68	99.6	32.9	87.3
崇 明 县	Chongming	0.43	14.04	4.20	12.70	99.9	29.9	90.5

注：本表由市人口和计划生育委员会提供。
Note: This table is provided by Shanghai Municipal Committee of Population and Family Planning.

表 3.14 主要年份婚姻情况
MARRIAGE STATISTICS IN MAIN YEARS

年份 Year	准予登记结婚（万对） Marriage Registration Permitted (10 000 couples)	初婚（万人） First Marriage (10 000 persons)	再婚（万人） Remarriage (10 000 persons)	其中 of which 女性 Female	离婚人数（万人） Divorce (10 000 persons)	其中 of which 民政部门批准 Approved by the Civil Administration	其中 of which 法院调判 Mediated by the Court
1980	16.82	33.07	0.57		0.66	0.18	0.48
1985	18.24	35.47	1.01	0.48	1.39	0.46	0.93
1990	10.77	19.49	2.04	1.06	3.27	1.45	1.82
1995	8.40	14.61	2.19	1.09	4.54	1.97	2.57
1996	8.96	14.98	2.31	1.24	4.93	2.14	2.79
1997	8.84	15.12	2.57	1.27	5.46	2.38	3.08
1998	8.57	14.48	2.67	1.28	5.92	2.85	3.07
1999	9.05	15.07	2.46	1.24	6.24	3.39	2.85
2000	9.31	15.08	2.89	1.45	6.36	3.52	2.84
2001	9.30	15.23	2.68	1.40	6.29	3.36	2.93
2002	9.10	14.60	3.05	1.40	5.92	3.08	2.84
2003	10.82	17.20	3.97	2.31	6.60	3.97	2.63
2004	12.49	20.27	4.18	2.05	7.26	5.35	1.91
2005	10.27	16.44	4.09	2.05	7.86	6.21	1.65
2006	16.56	27.29	5.83	2.93	9.43	7.55	1.88
2007	12.01	18.10	5.93	2.95	9.38	7.49	1.88

表 3.15 涉外婚姻情况（1985～2007）
CHINESE-FOREIGN MARRIAGE

年份 Year	涉外婚姻（对） Chinese-Foreign Marriage (couple)	在涉外婚姻中的国内公民（人） In Chinese-Foreign Marriage Chinese Citizens (person)	在国内公民中 Among the Chinese Citizens 男性 Male	在国内公民中 Among the Chinese Citizens 女性 Female
1985	826	824	91	733
1986	794	793	73	720
1987	773	767	95	672
1988	802	800	92	708
1989	963	961	90	871
1990	1 345	1 345	136	1 209
1995	3 033	3 030	274	2 756
1996	3 107	3 105	307	2 798
1997	2 839	2 838	298	2 540
1998	2 926	2 923	293	2 630
1999	2 872	2 869	343	2 526
2000	3 187	3 182	374	2 808
2001	3 447	3 438	399	3 039
2002	2 705	2 690	67	2 623
2003	2 418	2 418	367	2 051
2004	2 636	2 623	417	2 206
2005	2 407	2 385	372	2 013
2006	2 943	2 943	540	2 403
2007	2 495	2 483	109	2 374

注：本页数据由市民政局提供。
Note: Data on this page are provided by Shanghai Civil Affairs Bureau.

表 3.16 在沪外国常住人口(2005～2007)
RESIDENT FOREIGNERS IN SHANGHAI

单位:人(person)

类 别	Types	2005	2006	2007
总 计	**Total**	**100 011**	**119 876**	**133 340**
居留许可外国人	**Residence Permitted Foreigners**	**95 384**	**115 326**	**129 475**
按国别(地区)分	Grouped by Country and Region			
#日 本	Japan	27 812	29 326	31 025
韩 国	Republic of Korea	14 047	17 020	18 600
马来西亚	Malaysia	3 480	4 097	4 594
新加坡	Singapore	5 547	6 336	7 001
德 国	Germany	4 591	5 636	6 333
英 国	United Kingdom	2 904	3 725	4 228
加拿大	Canada	4 279	4 572	5 376
美 国	United States	14 329	15 877	18 152
澳大利亚	Australia	3 729	3 927	4 478
法 国	France	4 181	5 437	6 203
按类别分	By Types			
#留学人员及家属	Overseas Students and Relatives	10 224	12 555	13 368
驻华机构代表及家属	Delegate and Relatives of Institutions Stationed in China	9 769	11 281	11 589
外资企业工作人员及家属	Employees and Relatives at Foreign Ventures	60 137	76 873	87 271
外国专家及家属	Foreign Experts and Relatives	4 586	4 942	5 753
永久居留外国人	Permanent Resident Foreigners		295	435
半年以上长期签证外国人	Long-term Vise Foreigners Above Half Year		4 255	3 430

注：本表由市公安局出入境管理局提供。
Note: The figures of this table are provided by Bureau of Exit-Entry Administration Shanghai Municipal Public Security Bureau.

表 3.17 主要年份从业人员和职工人数
NUMBER OF EMPLOYEES AND STAFF AND WORKERS IN MAIN YEARS

单位:万人(10 000 persons)

类 别	Types	2000	2006	2007
从业人员	**Employees**	**745.24**	**885.51**	**909.08**
国 有	State-owned	180.99	138.92	140.74
集 体	Collective-owned	282.18	214.77	196.67
港澳台及外商投资企业	Enterprises with Investment from Hongkong, Macao, Taiwan and Foreign Countries	51.77	92.41	123.78
其 他	Others	230.41	439.41	447.89
#有限责任公司	Companies With Limited Liability	25.77	47.39	47.69
股份有限公司	Share-holding Companies with Limited Liabilities	22.34	33.74	35.84
城镇私营	Urban Privately Run Businesses	58.23	240.76	244.60
城镇个体	Urban Self-employed Businesses	9.27	21.18	22.16
非正规就业及自由职业	Free Labor Jobs	19.90	51.44	56.49
职工人数	**Staff and Workers**	**390.14**	**500.94**	**522.67**
国 有	State-owned	229.24	146.38	141.90
集 体	Collective-owned	47.45	18.11	16.45
港澳台及外商投资企业	Enterprises with Overseas Investment	54.97	75.60	102.55
其 他	Others	58.48	260.85	261.77
#有限责任公司	Companies With Limited Liability	27.99	42.95	42.47
股份有限公司	Share-holding Companies with Limited Liabilities	21.86	30.34	31.68

①本表从业人员是指在本市工作并由本市支付工资或其他形式的劳动报酬的从业人员。
②2006 年起职工人数中包括 120 人以上的私营企业职工。
❶Employees is this table refer to the employees work in shanghai and get wage or other kind of compensation in shanghai.
❷Quantity of workers in 2006～2007 includes those work for private enterprises over 120 persons.

表3.18 各行业从业人员(2007)
EMPLOYEES IN DIFFERENT SECTORS

单位:万人(10 000 persons)

行业	Sector	从业人员 Employees	按登记注册类型分 Classified According to the Categories of Registration			
			国有 State-owned Units	集体 Collective-owned Units	港澳台及外商投资单位 Units with Investment from Hong Kong, Macao, Taiwan and Foreign Countries	其他 Other Ownership Units
总计	**Total**	**909.08**	**140.74**	**196.67**	**123.78**	**447.89**
一、按产业分	**Grouped by Industry**					
第一产业	Primary Industry	53.71	0.70	51.88	0.02	1.11
第二产业	Secondary Industry	342.75	26.59	93.46	104.01	118.69
第三产业	Tertiary Industry	512.62	113.45	51.33	19.75	328.09
二、按行业分	**Grouped by Sector**					
农、林、牧、渔业	Farming, Forestry, Animal Husbandry and Fishery	53.71	0.70	51.88	0.02	1.11
采矿业	Mining	0.08	0.06			0.02
制造业	Manufacturing	295.07	16.84	83.45	103.15	91.63
电力、燃气及水的生产和供应业	Power, Gas and Water Production and Supply	5.46	3.98	0.06	0.31	1.11
建筑业	Construction	42.14	5.70	9.95	0.55	25.94
交通运输、仓储和邮政业	Transportation, Warehousing and Post Industries	49.74	12.75	8.69	2.38	25.92
信息传输、计算机服务和软件业	Information Transmission, Computer Servcie and Software Industries	10.95	1.53	1.24	2.82	5.36
#信息传输	Information Transmission	2.82	1.33	0.03	1.05	0.41
批发和零售业	Retail and Wholesale	132.01	3.50	3.53	3.51	121.47
住宿和餐饮业	Hoteling and Catering	24.81	1.86	1.51	3.31	18.13
金融业	Finance Industry	21.61	4.34	2.29	1.61	13.37
房地产业	Real Estate	31.48	2.95	12.83	2.93	12.77
租赁和商务服务业	Leasing and Business Service Industries	52.28	7.86	4.90	1.81	37.71
科学研究、技术服务和地质勘查业	Scientific Research, Technical Service and Geological Prospecting	17.55	13.76	2.08	0.39	1.32
水利、环境和公共设施管理业	Water Conservancy, Environment and Public Facility Management	6.96	4.01	1.97	0.15	0.83
#公共设施管理业	Public Facility Management	1.55	0.90	0.07	0.14	0.44
居民服务和其他服务业	Resident Service and Other Services	89.43	1.23	2.87	0.38	84.95
教育	Education	28.11	24.90	2.10	0.10	1.01
卫生、社会保障和社会福利业	Health, Social Security and Welfare	18.20	13.43	3.48	0.03	1.26
文化、体育和娱乐业	Culture, Sports and Entertainment	10.14	3.58	2.24	0.32	4.00
公共管理和社会组织	Public Administration and Social Organizations	19.35	17.75	1.60		

表3.19 各行业职工人数(2007)
STAFF AND WORKERS IN DIFFERENT SECTORS

单位:万人(10 000 persons)

行业	Sector	职工人数 Staff and Workers	按登记注册类型分 Classified According to the Categories of Registration			
			国有单位 State-owned Units	集体单位 Collective-owned Units	港澳台及外商投资单位 Units with Investment from Hong Kong, Macao, Taiwan and Foreign Countries	其他单位 Other Ownership Units
总计	**Total**	**522.67**	**141.90**	**16.45**	**102.55**	**261.77**
一、按产业分	**Grouped by Industry**					
第一产业	Primary Industry	1.65	0.46	0.07	0.02	1.10
第二产业	Secondary Industry	247.70	36.06	4.70	87.61	119.33
第三产业	Tertiary Industry	273.32	105.38	11.68	14.92	141.34
二、按行业分	**Grouped by Sector**					
农、林、牧、渔业	Farming, Forestry, Animal Husbandry and Fishery	1.65	0.46	0.07	0.02	1.10
采矿业	Mining	0.06	0.04			0.02
制造业	Manufacturing	218.47	27.69	4.30	86.95	99.53
电力、燃气及水的生产和供应业	Power, Gas and Water Production and Supply	5.27	3.85	0.07	0.31	1.04
建筑业	Construction	23.90	4.48	0.33	0.35	18.74
交通运输、仓储和邮政业	Transportation, Warehousing and Post Industries	35.39	11.56	0.86	2.19	20.78
信息传输、计算机服务和软件业	Information Transmission, Computer Servcie and Software Industries	8.13	1.58	0.04	2.22	4.30
#信息传输	Information Transmission	2.53	1.38	0.03	0.51	0.61
批发和零售业	Retail and Wholesale	52.45	5.93	2.87	2.99	40.66
住宿和餐饮业	Hotel and Cateries	10.59	1.66	0.21	1.58	7.15
金融业	Financial Industry	16.96	3.85		1.25	11.86
房地产业	Real Estate	10.27	1.92	0.18	1.95	6.22
租赁和商务服务业	Leasing and Business Service Industries	40.48	6.87	4.29	1.59	27.74
科学研究、技术服务和地质勘查业	Scientific Research, Technology Service and Geological Prospecting	14.68	13.17	0.17	0.35	0.99
水利、环境和公共设施管理业	Water Conservancy, Environment and Public Facility Management	4.23	3.15	0.31	0.15	0.63
#公共设施管理业	Public Facility Management	1.28	0.71	0.08	0.13	0.36
居民服务和其他服务业	Resident Service and Other Service	19.33	1.59	0.47	0.33	16.94
教育	Education	23.51	22.69	0.19	0.07	0.56
卫生、社会保障和社会福利业	Health, Social Security and Welfare	14.50	11.56	1.76	0.02	1.16
文化、体育和娱乐业	Culture, Sports and Entertainment	5.91	3.17	0.14	0.23	2.37
公共管理和社会组织	Public Administration and Social Organizations	16.88	16.69	0.20		

表 3.20 各行业在岗职工人数(2007)
WORKING STAFF AND WORKERS IN DIFFERENT SECTORS

单位:万人(10 000 persons)

行业	Sector	职工人数 Staff and Workers	按登记注册类型分 Classified According to the Categories of Registration: 国有单位 State-owned Units	集体单位 Collective-owned Units	港澳台及外商投资单位 Units with Investment from Hong Kong, Macao, Taiwan and Foreign Countries	其他单位 Other Ownership Units
总计	**Total**	**475.52**	**116.56**	**9.72**	**99.82**	**249.42**
一、按产业分	**Grouped by Industry**					
第一产业	Primary Industry	1.44	0.39	0.06	0.02	0.97
第二产业	Secondary Industry	222.79	21.48	1.99	85.33	113.99
第三产业	Tertiary Industry	251.29	94.69	7.67	14.47	134.46
二、按行业分	**Grouped by Sector**					
农、林、牧、渔业	Farming, Forestry, Animal Husbandry and Fishery	1.44	0.39	0.06	0.02	0.97
采矿业	Mining	0.05	0.03			0.02
制造业	Manufacturing	195.23	14.12	1.67	84.68	94.76
电力、燃气及水的生产和供应业	Power, Gas and Water Production and Supply	5.18	3.78	0.06	0.31	1.04
建筑业	Construction	22.32	3.54	0.25	0.35	18.17
交通运输、仓储和邮政业	Transportation, Warehousing and Post Industries	31.87	10.19	0.56	2.09	19.03
信息传输、计算机服务和软件业	Information Transmission, Computer Servcie and Software Industries	7.97	1.51	0.03	2.15	4.28
#信息传输	Information Transmission	2.43	1.31	0.03	0.50	0.60
批发和零售业	Retail and Wholesale	46.40	2.87	1.28	2.95	39.30
住宿和餐饮业	Hotel and Cateries	9.68	1.28	0.12	1.58	6.71
金融业	Financial Industry	16.53	3.62		1.23	11.68
房地产业	Real Estate	9.33	1.59	0.16	1.75	5.83
租赁和商务服务业	Leasing and Business Service Industries	34.60	4.97	2.69	1.58	25.36
科学研究、技术服务和地质勘查业	Scientific Research, Technology Service and Geological Prospecting	14.18	12.73	0.13	0.35	0.96
水利、环境和公共设施管理业	Water Conservancy, Environment and Public Facility Management	3.79	2.81	0.29	0.14	0.55
#公共设施管理业	Public Facility Management	1.22	0.68	0.06	0.13	0.35
居民服务和其他服务业	Resident Service and Other Service	17.95	0.62	0.31	0.33	16.68
教育	Education	22.77	22.02	0.14	0.06	0.55
卫生、社会保障和社会福利业	Health, Social Security and Welfare	13.94	11.09	1.66	0.02	1.16
文化、体育和娱乐业	Culture, Sports and Entertainment	5.59	2.89	0.11	0.23	2.36
公共管理和社会组织	Public Administration and Social Organizations	16.68	16.49	0.18		

注:本表包括120人以上的私营企业职工。
Note: Data in this table includes those of employees work for private enterprises over 120 persons.

表3.21 各行业在岗女职工人数(2007)
WORKING FEMALE STAFF AND WORKERS IN VARIOUS SECTORS

单位:万人(10 000 persons)

行业	Sector	在岗女职工人数 Working Female Staff and Workers	按登记注册类型分 Classified According to the Categories of Registration			
			国有单位 State-owned Units	集体单位 Collective-owned Units	港澳台及外商投资单位 Units with Investment from Hong Kong, Macao,Taiwan and Foreign Countries	其他单位 Other Ownership Units
总计	**Total**	**200.88**	**45.70**	**3.92**	**47.62**	**103.64**
一、按产业分	**Grouped by Industry**					
第一产业	Primary Industry	0.49	0.10	0.01	0.01	0.37
第二产业	Secondary Industry	94.00	5.01	0.63	41.48	46.88
第三产业	Tertiary Industry	106.39	40.59	3.28	6.13	56.39
二、按行业分	**Grouped by Sector**					
农、林、牧、渔业	Farming, Forestry, Animal Husbandry and Fishery	0.49	0.10	0.01	0.01	0.37
采矿业	Mining	0.02	0.01			0.01
制造业	Manufacturing	85.19	3.44	0.57	41.29	39.88
电力、燃气及水的生产和供应业	Power, Gas and Water Production and Supply	1.27	0.93	0.02	0.11	0.21
建筑业	Construction	7.53	0.64	0.03	0.09	6.78
交通运输、仓储和邮政业	Transportation, Warehousing and Post Industries	7.78	1.98	0.19	0.65	4.96
信息传输、计算机服务和软件业	Information Transmission, Computer Servcie and Software Industries	3.19	0.48	0.01	0.87	1.84
#信息传输	Information Transmission	0.88	0.42	0.01	0.22	0.24
批发和零售业	Retail and Wholesale	20.52	0.99	0.45	1.38	17.70
住宿和餐饮业	Hotel and Cateries	4.23	0.53	0.04	0.75	2.91
金融业	Financial Industry	8.25	1.83		0.71	5.71
房地产业	Real Estate	3.46	0.48	0.03	0.64	2.31
租赁和商务服务业	Leasing and Business Service Industries	13.67	0.83	0.91	0.76	11.16
科学研究、技术服务和地质勘查业	Scientific Research, Technology Service and Geological Prospecting	6.00	5.52	0.05	0.12	0.31
水利、环境和公共设施管理业	Water Conservancy, Environment and Public Facility Management	1.16	0.83	0.12	0.06	0.15
#公共设施管理业	Public Facility Management	0.38	0.20	0.03	0.06	0.10
居民服务和其他服务业	Resident Service and Other Service Industries	7.78	0.20	0.17	0.02	7.39
教育	Education	13.76	13.31	0.10	0.03	0.32
卫生、社会保障和社会福利业	Health, Social Security and Welfare	9.09	7.43	1.09	0.02	0.55
文化、体育和娱乐业	Culture, Sports and Entertainment	2.36	1.11	0.04	0.13	1.07
公共管理和社会组织	Public Administration and Social Organizations	5.14	5.07	0.07		

注:本表包括120人以上的私营企业职工。
Note: Data in this table includes those of employees work for private enterprises over 120 persons.

表 3.22 主要年份城镇新就业人数
NUMBER OF NEW URBAN EMPLOYEES IN MAIN YEARS

单位：万人（10 000 persons）

指 标	Indicators	1990	2000	2006	2007
总 计	**Total**	**14.17**	**49.74**	**68.99**	**70.75**
按主要来源分	**Grouped by Source of Employment**				
城镇劳动力	Urban Labour Force	4.55	39.14	46.98	37.60
农村劳动力	Rural Labour Force	2.51	1.76	11.15	14.84
大学、中专、技校毕业生	Graduates from Universities, Secondary Technical Schools and Worker Training Schools	5.76	4.09	7.47	10.38
其 他	Others	1.35	4.75	3.39	7.93
按安置去向分	**Grouped by Employment Assignment**				
国有经济单位	State-owned Units	11.46	7.40	10.09	10.92
城镇集体经济单位	Urban Collective-owned Units	1.46	1.42	0.88	0.85
其他经济单位	Other Ownership Units	0.76	8.60	29.25	45.23
其他劳动者	Others	0.49	32.32	28.77	13.75

表 3.23 主要年份城镇登记失业人数和城镇登记失业率
NUMBER OF URBAN REGISTERED UNEMPLOYED AND URBAN REGISTERED UNEMPLOYMENT RATE IN MAIN YEARS

单位：万人（10 000 persons）

指 标	Indicators	1990	2000	2006	2007
城镇登记失业人数（万人）	Registered Urban Unemployment (10 000 persons)	7.70	20.08	27.82	26.78
区	District	6.62	18.86	27.06	26.09
县	County	1.08	1.22	0.76	0.69
城镇登记失业率（%）	Registered Urban Unemployment Rate (%)	1.5	3.5	4.4	4.3

注：本表由市劳动和社会保障局提供。
Note: This table is provided by Shanghai Municipal Labour and Social Security Bureau.

表 3.24 主要年份新增就业岗位
NEWLY ADDED WORKING POST IN MAIN YEARS

单位：万人（10 000 persons）

指 标	Indicators	2003	2006	2007
新增就业岗位（万个）	Newly Added Working Post (10 000 units)	46.2	66.3	70.3
#农村富余劳动力实现非农就业	Non-agricultural Working Post Gained by Surplus Rural Labor Force	12.5	13.7	15.1

注：本表由市劳动和社会保障局提供。
Note: This table is provided by Shanghai Municipal Labour and Social Security Bureau.

表 3.25 主要年份离休、退休及退职职工人数
NUMBER OF RETIRED AND RESIGNED PERSONS IN MAIN YEARS

单位：万人（10 000 persons）

指 标	Indicators	1990	2000	2006	2007
总 计	**Total**	**159.14**	**234.23**	**294.69**	**309.99**
国有单位	State-owned Units	113.65	165.55	166.73	169.32
离 休	Retired Veteran Cadres	3.85	3.39	2.36	2.18
退 休	Retired	108.54	161.03	159.82	162.58
退 职	Resigned	1.26	1.13	4.55	4.56
集体单位	Collective-owned Units	44.18	50.22	46.91	46.60
离 休	Retired Veteran Cadres	0.40	0.10	0.06	0.05
退 休	Retired	42.02	48.40	44.96	44.66
退 职	Resigned	1.76	1.72	1.89	1.89
其他单位	Other Ownership Units	1.31	18.46	81.05	94.07
离 休	Retired Veteran Cadres	0.01	0.21	0.66	0.71
退 休	Retired	1.22	18.05	77.56	89.84
退 职	Resigned	0.08	0.20	2.83	3.52

表 3.26 在岗职工人数变动（2007）
CHANGES IN THE NUMBER OF WORKING STAFF AND WORKERS

单位：万人（10 000 persons）

指 标	Indicators	合 计 Total	按登记注册类型划分 Classified According to the Categories of Registration		
			国有单位 State-owned Units	集体单位 Collective-owned Units	其他单位 Other Ownership Units
增加人数	**Increase of Staff and Workers**	**78.81**	**16.58**	**1.67**	**60.56**
从农村招收	Recruited from Rural Areas	14.84	0.61	0.21	14.02
从城镇招收	Recruited from Urban Areas	23.84	6.56	0.38	16.90
录用的复员转业军人	Demobilized Soldiers	0.39	0.13	0.06	0.20
录用的大、中专、技工学校毕业生	Graduates from Colleges, Secondary Technical Schools and Worker Training Schools	10.38	2.97	0.10	7.31
调入人数	Number Transferred in	8.78	3.87	0.45	4.46
#市外调入	From Outside Areas	0.61	0.11		0.50
其 他	Others	20.58	2.44	0.47	17.67
减少人数	**Decrease of Staff and Workers**	**69.91**	**16.80**	**1.93**	**51.18**
离休、退休、退职	Retired and Resigned	7.61	3.65	0.47	3.49
开除、除名、辞退	Expelled and Discharged	2.06	0.12	0.02	1.92
终止、解除合同	Contract Terminated	40.37	7.56	0.62	32.19
死 亡	Death	0.21	0.10	0.02	0.09
调出人数	Number Transferred Out	7.39	3.17	0.45	3.77
#调往市外	To Outside Areas	0.36	0.04		0.32
其 他	Others	12.27	2.20	0.35	9.72

表 3.27 在岗长期职工和临时职工人数(2007)
NUMBER OF PERMANENT AND TEMPORARY WORKING STAFF AND WORKERS

单位:万人(10 000 persons)

行 业	Sector	合 计 Total	其中 of which 在岗长期职工 Permanent Working Staff and Workers	在岗临时职工 Temporary Working Staff and Workers
总 计	**Total**	**475.52**	**414.86**	**60.66**
农、林、牧、渔业	Farming, Forestry, Animal Husbandry and Fishery	1.44	1.21	0.23
采矿业	Mining	0.05	0.05	
制造业	Manufacturing	195.23	169.07	26.16
电力、燃气及水的生产和供应业	Power, Gas and Water Production and Supply	5.18	5.18	
建筑业	Construction	22.33	18.05	4.28
交通运输、仓储和邮政业	Transportation, Warehousing and Post Industries	31.88	29.67	2.21
信息传输、计算机服务和软件业	Information Transmission, Computer Servcie and Software Industries	7.97	6.85	1.12
#信息传输	Information Transmission	2.43	2.34	0.10
批发和零售业	Retail and Wholesale Industries	46.41	36.91	9.50
住宿和餐饮业	Hotel and Cateries	9.68	8.10	1.58
金融业	Financial Industry	16.53	16.15	0.38
房地产业	Real Estate	9.34	8.06	1.28
租赁和商务服务业	Leasing and Business Service Industries	34.60	27.56	7.04
科学研究、技术服务和地质勘查业	Scientific Research, Technology Service and Geological Prospecting	14.18	14.16	0.02
水利、环境和公共设施管理业	Water Conservancy, Environment and Public Facility Management	3.79	3.71	0.08
#公共设施管理业	Public Facility Management	1.22	1.22	
居民服务和其他服务业	Community Service and Other Service Industries	17.94	13.14	4.80
教 育	Education	22.77	22.66	0.11
卫生、社会保障和社会福利业	Health, Social Security and Welfare Industries	13.94	13.30	0.64
文化、体育和娱乐业	Culture, Sports and Entertainment	5.59	4.93	0.66
公共管理和社会组织	Public Administration and Social Organizations	16.67	16.10	0.57

表 3.28 主要年份离岗职工人数
NUMBER OF LAID-OFF EMPLOYEES IN MAIN YEARS

单位:万人(10 000 persons)

指 标	Indicators	2000	2005	2006
总 计	**Total**	**83.11**	**54.49**	**47.15**
国有单位	State-owned Units	48.25	29.71	25.34
集体单位	Collective-owned Units	20.87	8.03	6.74
其他单位	Other Ownership Units	13.99	16.75	15.07

表3.29 主要年份职业介绍所
EMPLOYMENT AGENCIES IN MAIN YEARS

指 标	Indicators	2000	2006	2007
机构数(个)	**Number of Institutions(unit)**	**465**	**493**	**488**
#劳动保障部门	Run by Labor Insurance Departments	346	266	269
其他组织办	Run by Other Organs	110	92	86
公民个人办	Run by Individuals	9	135	133
职工人数(人)	Staff and Workers (person)	2 807	4 673	4 564
登记招聘人数(万人次)	Number of Vacancies Registered (10 000 person times)	54.09	168.36	168.43
登记求职人数(万人次)	Number of Registered People Seeking a Job(10 000 person times)	54.69	149.13	150.37
#女　性	Females	25.45	61.26	62.56
#失业人员	Unemployed	29.86	85.44	86.25
#获得职业资格人员	Personnel with Job Qualifications		24.37	25.39
职业指导人数(万人次)	**Number of People Receiving Career Training(10 000 person times)**	**55.58**	**110.38**	**110.53**
介绍成功人数(万人次)	**Number of People that Got a Job through Employment Agencies(10 000 person times)**	**28.59**	**59.48**	**59.52**
#女　性	Females	13.87	28.62	29.15
#失业人员	Unemployed	14.33	38.11	38.24
#获得职业资格人员	Personnel with Job Qualifications		16.57	16.61

注：本表由市劳动和社会保障局提供。
Note: The figures of this table are provided by Shanghai Municipal Labour and Social Security Bureau.

表3.30 主要年份人才市场
HUMAN RESOURCE MARKET IN MAIN YEARS

指 标	Indicators	2000	2006	2007
挂牌人才市场数(个)	Number of Human Resource Markets with Registration(unit)	24	30	28
人才流动机构数(个)	Number of Human Resource Exchange Organizations(unit)	105	608	638
人才流动机构人数(人)	Number of Persons in Human Resource Exchange Organization(person)	746	7 078	12 658
举办人才交流大会次数(次)	Number of Human Resource Exchange Meetings(time)	662	1 998	1 714
参加人才交流大会人数(万人)	Number of Persons Attending Human Resource Exchange Meetings(10 000 persons)	134.11	249.81	411.05

注：本表由市人事局提供。
Note: Data in this table are provided by Shanghai Municipal Personel Bureau.

上 / 海 / 统 / 计 / 年 / 鉴

主要统计指标解释

人　口

人口数为每年12月31日的年末总人口。根据统计口径的不同,分为户籍人口和常住人口。户籍人口是指在公安部门办理了户籍登记的人口。常住人口是指实际上经常居住在一个地方(住所)的人口,一般都以在其住所居住半年以上者为常住人口。

出生率

出生率(又称粗出生率)指在一定时期内(通常为一年)一定地区的出生人数与同期平均人数(或期中人数)之比,一般用千分率表示。计算公式:

$$出生率=\frac{年出生人数}{年平均人数}\times 1000‰$$

出生人数是指活产婴儿,即胎儿脱离母体时(不管怀孕月数),有过呼吸或其他生命现象。年平均人数是年初、年底人口数的平均数,也可用年中人口数代替。

死亡率

死亡率(又称粗死亡率)指在一定时期内(通常为一年)一定地区的死亡人数与同期平均人数(或期中人数)之比,一般用千分率表示。计算公式:

$$死亡率=\frac{年死亡人数}{年平均人数}\times 1000‰$$

自然增长率

指在一定时期内(通常为一年)人口自然增加数(出生人数减死亡人数)与该时期内平均人数(或期中人数)之比,一般用千分率表示。计算公式:

$$人口自然增长率=\frac{本年出生人数-本年死亡人数}{年平均人数}\times 1000‰$$

$$自然增长率=出生率-死亡率$$

平均期望寿命

指在一定年龄组的死亡率水平下,该年龄组人群日后平均可能继续生存的年(岁)数。通常所说的平均期望寿命是指刚出生的一批人平均一生可能存活的年数。

从业人员

指从事一定社会劳动并取得劳动报酬或经营收入的人员,包括在岗职工、再就业的离退休人员、私营业主、个体户主、私营和个体从业人员、乡镇企业从业人员、农村从业人员、其他从业人员(包括民办教师、宗教职业者、现役军人等)。这一指标反映了一定时期内全部劳动力资源的实际利用情况,是研究我国基本国情国力的重要指标。

各单位的从业人员指在各级国家机关、政党机关、社会团体及企业、事业单位中工作,取得工资或其他形式的劳动报酬的全部人员。包括在岗职工、再就业的离退休人员、民办教师以及在各单位中工作的外方人员和港澳台方人员、兼职人员、借用的外单位人员和第二职业者。不包括离开本单位仍保留劳动关系的职工。各单位的就业人员反映了各单位实际参加生产或工作的全部劳动力。

职　工

指在国有、城镇集体、联营、股份制、外商和港、澳、台投资、其他单位及其附属机构工作,并由其支付工资的各类人员。不包括下列人员:(1)乡镇企业就业人员;(2)私营企业就业人员;(3)城镇个体劳动者;(4)离休、退休、退职人员;(5)再就业的离、退休人员;(6)民办教师;(7)在城镇单位中工作的外方及港、澳、台人员;(8)其他按有关规定不列入职工统计范围的人员。(1998年及以后的数据均为在岗职工数据,其他相关指标如职工工资总额,职工平均工资等指标也从1998年按此口径进行了相应调整)。

城镇登记失业人员

指有非农业户口,在一定的劳动年龄内(16岁以上及男50岁以下、女45岁以下),有劳动能力,无业而要求就业,并在当地就业服务机构进行求职登记的人员。

城镇登记失业率

指城镇登记失业人员同城镇单位就业人员、城镇私营企业及个体就业人员(扣除使用的农村劳动力、聘用的离退休人员、港澳台及外方人员)和城镇登记失业人员、城镇单位中的不在岗职工之和的比。计算公式为:

主要统计指标解释

城镇登记失业率 = 城镇登记失业人员 / （城镇单位就业人员 − 使用的农村劳动力 − 聘用的离退休人员 − 聘用的港澳台及外方人员）+ 不在岗职工 + 城镇私营企业及个体就业人员 + 城镇登记失业人员 × 100%

在岗职工

指在本单位工作并由单位支付工资的人员，以及有工作岗位，但由于学习、病伤产假等原因暂未工作，仍由单位支付工资的人员。

SHANGHAI STATISTICAL YEARBOOK

EXPLANATORY NOTES TO MAJOR STATISTICAL INDICATORS

□ Population

Population refers to the total population by December 31 every year. According to different statistical approaches, there are two definitions of population named as population with registered residence and population with permanent residence. The former refers to the population with registration in the police while the latter refers to the population that actually reside in a place (residence) permanently ,usually longer than half a year.

□ Birth Rate

Birth Rate (or gross birth rate) means the ratio of the number of births in a certain period (usually a year) to the average population in the same period (or mid-year figure). It is usually calculated in terms of permillage and its calculating formula is:

$$\text{Birth Rate} = \frac{\text{Number of Births}}{\text{Average Number of Population}} \times 1000‰$$

Number of Births refers to live births, when babies have showed any vital phenomena regardless of the length of pregnancy. Average Number of Population is the average of the number of population at the beginning of the year and, at the end of the year and sometimes is substituted for with mid-year population.

□ Death Rate

Death Rate (or Gross Death Rate) refers to the ratio of number of deaths to the average population (or mid-year population) during a certain period of time (usually a year), which is often presented as permillage. Its calculating formula is :

$$\text{Death Rate} = \frac{\text{Number of Deaths}}{\text{Average Number of Population}} \times 1000‰$$

□ Natural Growth Rate of Population

Natural Growth Rate of Population refers to the ratio of natural increase in population (number of births minus number of deaths) in a certain period of time (usually a year) to the average population (or mid-year population) of the same period, which is often presented as permillage. The following formula are applied:

Number of Births-Number of Deaths

$$\text{Natural Growth Rate of Population} = \frac{\text{Number of Births} - \text{Number of Deaths}}{\text{Average Number of Population}} \times 1000‰$$

Natural Growth Rate of Population = Birth Rate—Death Rate

□ Average Life Expectancy

Average Life Expectancy refers to the average age that an age group may possibly live at a certain mortality rate of the group, in the common knowledge, the average age that a group of new-borns may possibly live.

□ Employees

Employees refer to the persons who are engaged in social working and receive remuneration payment or earn business income, including total staff and workers, re-employed retirees, employers of private enterprises, self-employ ed workers, employees in private enterprises and individual economy, employees in township enterprises, employed persons in the rural areas , and other employed persons (including teachers in the schools run by the local people, people engaged in religious profession and t he servicemen, etc.). This indicator reflects the actual utilization of total labour force during a certain period of time and is often used for the research on China's economic situation and national power. Employees in Various Units refer to all the persons working in government agencies of various levels, political and party organizations, social organizations, enterprises and institutions, and receiving wages or other forms of payment. They include fully-employed staff and workers, re-employed retirees, teachers in schools run by the local people, foreigners and Chinese compatriots from Hong Kong, Macao, and Taiwan working in various units, part -time employees, employees of other units working temporarily at current post s, and employees holding the second job, but exclude staff and workers who have left their working units while keeping their labor contract (employment relation) unchanged. This indicator reflects the total number of laborers actually engaged in production or other operations in various units.

□ Staff and Workers

Staff and Workers refer to persons working in, and receive payment from units of state ownership, collective ownership, joint ownership, share holding ownership, foreign ownership, and ownership by entrepreneurship from Hong Kong, Macao, and Taiwan, and other types of ownership and their affiliated units. They do not

EXPLANATORY NOTES TO MAJOR STATISTICAL INDICATORS

include 1) persons employed in township enterprises, 2) persons employed in private enterprises, 3) urban self–employed persons, 4) retirees, 5) re–employed retirees, 6) teachers in the schools run by the local people, 7) foreigners and persons from Hong Kong, Macao and Taiwan who work in urban units, and 8) other persons not to be included by relevant regulations. (Data of 1998 and afterward refer to fully employed staff and workers. Other related statistics such as total wages and average wage are adjusted since 1998 accordingly).

□ Registered Urban Unemployment

Registered Urban Unemployment refers to those non–agricultural population within working age (16–50 years for male and 16–45 years for females),who are able and willing to work but unemployed and have registered for job in local employment service agencies.

□ Registered Urban Unemployment Rate

Registered Urban Unemployment Rate refers to the ratio of the number of the registered unemployed to the sum of the number of persons employed in various units (minus the rural labour force, retirees, and Hong Kong, Macao, Taiwan and foreign employees they employ) laid–off workers in urban units, urban self–employed individuals and the registered urban unemployed persons . The formula is as follows:

Registered Urban Unemployment Rate = Number of Registered Urban Unemployed Persons ÷ (Number of Persons Employed in Urban Units – rural labour force employed– retirees employed – Hong Kong, Macao, Taiwan and foreign employees + laid–off workers + Self–employed Individuals in Urban Areas + Number of Registered Urban Unemployed Persons) × 100%.

□ Fully Employed Staff and Workers

Fully Employed Staff and Workers refer to persons who work in, and receive wages from their working units, as well as persons who have their work posts, but are temporarily absent from work for reasons of study or on sick, injury or maternal leave and still receive wages from their working units.

第四篇

CHAPTER 4

国民经济核算

NATIONAL ECONOMIC ACCOUNTING

表 4.1　上海市生产总值(1978～2007)
GROSS DOMESTIC PRODUCT

年　份 Year	上海市生产总值(亿元) Gross Domestic Product (100 million yuan)	其中 of which 第一产业 Primary Industry	第二产业 Secondary Industry	其中 of which 工　业 Industry	建筑业 Construction	第三产业 Tertiary Industry	人均生产总值(元) Per Capita Gross Domestic Product (yuan)
1978	272.81	11.00	211.05	207.47	3.58	50.76	2 497
1979	286.43	11.39	221.21	216.62	4.59	53.83	2 568
1980	311.89	10.10	236.10	230.87	5.23	65.69	2 737
1981	324.76	10.58	244.34	237.12	7.22	69.84	2 813
1982	337.07	13.31	249.32	240.75	8.57	74.44	2 877
1983	351.81	13.52	255.32	246.26	9.06	82.97	2 963
1984	390.85	17.26	275.37	263.19	12.18	98.22	3 259
1985	466.75	19.53	325.63	311.12	14.51	121.59	3 855
1986	490.83	19.69	336.02	318.89	17.13	135.12	4 008
1987	545.46	21.60	364.38	336.54	27.84	159.48	4 396
1988	648.30	27.36	433.05	399.53	33.52	187.89	5 162
1989	696.54	29.63	466.18	432.92	33.26	200.73	5 487
1990	781.66	34.24	505.60	469.83	35.77	241.82	6 107
1991	893.77	34.06	550.64	514.79	35.85	309.07	6 954
1992	1 114.32	34.16	677.39	636.68	40.71	402.77	8 650
1993	1 519.23	37.82	902.38	846.71	55.67	579.03	10 729
1994	1 990.86	47.61	1 148.45	1 074.37	74.08	794.80	13 807
1995	2 499.43	59.82	1 419.41	1 308.20	111.21	1 020.20	17 022
1996	2 957.55	68.72	1 596.72	1 452.79	143.93	1 292.11	19 779
1997	3 438.79	72.03	1 774.02	1 598.91	175.11	1 592.74	22 583
1998	3 801.09	73.84	1 871.89	1 670.19	201.70	1 855.36	24 513
1999	4 188.73	74.49	1 984.64	1 787.98	196.66	2 129.60	26 527
2000	4 771.17	76.68	2 207.63	1 998.96	208.67	2 486.86	29 671
2001	5 210.12	78.00	2 403.18	2 166.74	236.44	2 728.94	32 201
2002	5 741.03	79.68	2 622.45	2 368.02	254.43	3 038.90	35 329
2003	6 694.23	81.02	3 209.02	2 941.24	267.78	3 404.19	39 128
2004	8 072.83	83.45	3 892.12	3 593.25	298.87	4 097.26	46 338
2005	9 164.10	90.26	4 452.92	4 129.52	323.40	4 620.92	51 529
2006	10 366.37	93.80	5 028.37	4 670.11	358.26	5 244.20	57 695
2007	12 188.85	101.84	5 678.51	5 298.08	380.43	6 408.50	66 367

注：1978 年～1992 年的人均生产总值按户籍人口计算，1993 年以后按半年以上常住人口计算。
Note：Per Capita Gross Domestic Product from 1978 to 1992 were calculated by registered population, and resident population above half year after 1993.

表4.2 上海市生产总值指数(以1978年为100，1978～2007)
INDEX OF GROSS DOMESTIC PRODUCT (1978 = 100)

年份 Year	上海市生产总值 Gross Domestic Product	其中 of which 第一产业 Primary Industry	第二产业 Secondary Industry	其中 of which 工业 Industry	建筑业 Construction	第三产业 Tertiary Industry	人均生产总值 Per Capita Gross Domestic Product
1978	100	100	100	100	100	100	100
1979	107.4	99.3	108.6	108.8	97.8	103.1	105.2
1980	116.4	98.7	115.1	115.4	99.4	126.0	111.7
1981	122.9	99.0	120.7	120.1	138.4	137.2	116.4
1982	131.7	124.9	126.3	125.1	164.3	155.6	122.9
1983	142.0	124.9	135.8	134.5	178.9	170.8	130.8
1984	158.5	156.4	149.4	147.5	213.4	195.9	144.5
1985	179.7	121.7	171.7	169.6	237.1	224.7	162.4
1986	187.6	121.5	178.6	175.9	264.8	238.2	167.5
1987	201.7	118.2	191.8	187.9	323.9	259.4	177.7
1988	222.1	123.6	209.8	205.4	363.1	292.1	193.4
1989	228.8	124.0	213.2	209.3	347.1	312.8	197.1
1990	236.8	129.3	219.2	215.0	364.8	329.4	202.3
1991	253.6	129.8	234.3	233.9	296.6	357.7	215.8
1992	291.1	130.3	274.6	275.3	319.4	400.6	247.3
1993	335.1	126.8	320.5	321.8	363.5	455.5	283.9
1994	383.7	130.5	366.0	367.5	414.8	529.3	319.1
1995	438.6	138.9	420.2	420.1	518.5	601.8	358.0
1996	496.1	145.8	466.8	463.8	647.6	710.7	397.4
1997	559.6	151.9	516.3	511.1	757.0	837.9	440.3
1998	617.2	155.2	558.6	551.0	869.0	961.9	476.8
1999	681.4	158.5	608.9	603.9	863.8	1 090.8	516.4
2000	756.4	163.9	668.6	665.5	889.7	1 238.1	562.9
2001	835.8	168.8	748.8	746.0	986.7	1 354.5	618.1
2002	930.2	173.9	839.4	840.7	1 049.8	1 502.1	685.5
2003	1 044.6	177.9	974.5	988.7	1 063.4	1 637.3	730.7
2004	1 192.9	169.0	1 119.7	1 147.9	1 071.9	1 868.2	819.8
2005	1 325.3	154.0	1 248.5	1 283.4	1 149.1	2 075.6	891.9
2006	1 484.3	155.2	1 402.1	1 442.5	1 270.9	2 324.7	979.3
2007	1 696.6	158.3	1 563.3	1 620.0	1 290.0	2 722.2	1 094.8

表 4.3 上海市生产总值比上年增长(1978～2007)
GROWTH RATE OF GROSS DOMESTIC PRODUCT RAISED PRECEDING YEAR

单位:%

年 份 Year	上海市生产总值 Gross Domestic Product	其中 of which					人均生产总值 Per Capita Gross Domestic Product
		第一产业 Primary Industry	第二产业 Secondary Industry	其中 of which		第三产业 Tertiary Industry	
				工业 Industry	建筑业 Construction		
1978	15.8	27.0	16.6	15.8	89.8	10.6	14.9
1979	7.4	-0.7	8.6	8.8	-2.2	3.1	5.2
1980	8.4	-0.6	6.0	6.1	1.6	22.2	6.1
1981	5.6	0.3	4.9	4.1	39.2	8.9	4.2
1982	7.2	26.2	4.6	4.2	18.7	13.4	5.6
1983	7.8	平	7.5	7.5	8.9	9.8	6.4
1984	11.6	25.2	10.0	9.7	19.3	14.7	10.5
1985	13.4	-22.2	14.9	15.0	11.1	14.7	12.3
1986	4.4	-0.2	4.0	3.7	11.7	6.0	3.2
1987	7.5	-2.7	7.4	6.8	22.3	8.9	6.1
1988	10.1	4.6	9.4	9.3	12.1	12.6	8.8
1989	3.0	0.3	1.6	1.9	-4.4	7.1	1.9
1990	3.5	4.3	2.8	2.7	5.1	5.3	2.7
1991	7.1	0.4	6.9	8.8	-18.7	8.6	6.7
1992	14.8	0.4	17.2	17.7	7.7	12.0	14.6
1993	15.1	-2.7	16.7	16.9	13.8	13.7	14.8
1994	14.5	2.9	14.2	14.2	14.1	16.2	12.4
1995	14.3	6.4	14.8	14.3	25.0	13.7	12.2
1996	13.1	5.0	11.1	10.4	24.9	18.1	11.0
1997	12.8	4.2	10.6	10.2	16.9	17.9	10.8
1998	10.3	2.2	8.2	7.8	14.8	14.8	8.3
1999	10.4	2.1	9.0	9.6	-0.6	13.4	8.3
2000	11.0	3.4	9.8	10.2	3.0	13.5	9.0
2001	10.5	3.0	12.0	12.1	10.9	9.4	9.8
2002	11.3	3.0	12.1	12.7	6.4	10.9	10.9
2003	12.3	2.3	16.1	17.6	1.3	9.0	6.6
2004	14.2	-5.0	14.9	16.1	0.8	14.1	12.2
2005	11.1	-8.9	11.5	11.8	7.2	11.1	8.8
2006	12.0	0.8	12.3	12.4	10.6	12.0	9.8
2007	14.3	2.0	11.5	12.3	1.5	17.1	11.8

表 4.4 上海市生产总值构成(1978～2007)
STRUCTURE OF GROSS DOMESTIC PRODUCT

单位:%

年 份 Year	上海市生产总值 Gross Domestic Product	其中 of which 第一产业 Primary Industry	第二产业 Secondary Industry	其中 of which 工业 Industry	建筑业 Construction	第三产业 Tertiary Industry
1978	100	4.0	77.4	76.1	1.3	18.6
1979	100	4.0	77.2	75.6	1.6	18.8
1980	100	3.2	75.7	74.0	1.7	21.1
1981	100	3.3	75.2	73.0	2.2	21.5
1982	100	3.9	74.0	71.4	2.6	22.1
1983	100	3.8	72.6	70.0	2.6	23.6
1984	100	4.4	70.5	67.4	3.1	25.1
1985	100	4.2	69.8	66.7	3.1	26.0
1986	100	4.0	68.5	65.0	3.5	27.5
1987	100	4.0	66.8	61.7	5.1	29.2
1988	100	4.2	66.8	61.6	5.2	29.0
1989	100	4.3	66.9	62.1	4.8	28.8
1990	100	4.4	64.7	60.1	4.6	30.9
1991	100	3.8	61.6	57.6	4.0	34.6
1992	100	3.1	60.8	57.1	3.7	36.1
1993	100	2.5	59.4	55.7	3.7	38.1
1994	100	2.4	57.7	54.0	3.7	39.9
1995	100	2.4	56.8	52.3	4.5	40.8
1996	100	2.3	54.0	49.1	4.9	43.7
1997	100	2.1	51.6	46.5	5.1	46.3
1998	100	1.9	49.3	44.0	5.3	48.8
1999	100	1.8	47.4	42.7	4.7	50.8
2000	100	1.6	46.3	41.9	4.4	52.1
2001	100	1.5	46.1	41.6	4.5	52.4
2002	100	1.4	45.7	41.3	4.4	52.9
2003	100	1.2	47.9	43.9	4.0	50.9
2004	100	1.0	48.2	44.5	3.7	50.8
2005	100	1.0	48.6	45.1	3.5	50.4
2006	100	0.9	48.5	45.0	3.5	50.6
2007	100	0.8	46.6	43.5	3.1	52.6

表 4.5　主要年份上海市生产总值(按三次产业分)
GROSS DOMESTIC PRODUCT (CLASSIFIED BY THREE INDUSTRIES) IN MAIN YEARS

单位:亿元(100 million yuan)

指　标	Indicators	2001	2006	2007
上海市生产总值	**Gross Domestic Product**	**5 210.12**	**10 366.37**	**12 188.85**
第一产业	Primary Industry	78.00	93.80	101.84
第二产业	Secondary Industry	2 403.18	5 028.37	5 678.51
工　业	Industry	2 166.74	4 670.11	5 298.08
建筑业	Construction	236.44	358.26	380.43
第三产业	Tertiary Industry	2 728.94	5 244.20	6 408.5
交通运输、仓储和邮政业	Transportation, Warehousing and Post	345.99	669.01	723.13
#交通运输业	Transportation	305.25	595.19	636.23
仓储业	Warehousing	21.43	50.20	58.23
信息传输、计算机服务和软件业	Information Transmission, Computer Servcie and Software Industries	176.72	421.31	500.65
批发和零售业	Retail and Wholesale Industries	555.06	929.16	1 077.76
住宿和餐饮业	Hoteling and Catering	104.30	194.08	219.36
金融业	Financial Industry	529.26	825.20	1 209.08
房地产业	Real Estate Industry	328.59	688.10	806.79
租赁和商务服务业	Leasehold and Business in Services	136.97	332.98	475.3
科学研究、技术服务和地质勘查业	Scientific Research, Technology Service and Geological Prospecting	114.91	234.12	269.74
水利、环境和公共设施管理业	Water Conservancy, Environment and Public Facility Management Industries	32.59	56.45	56.11
居民服务和其他服务业	Community Service and Other Service Industries	46.16	113.81	139.62
教　育	Education	136.53	312.62	364.5
卫生、社会保障和社会福利业	Health, Social Security and Welfare Industries	72.27	162.16	186.15
文化、体育和娱乐业	Culture, Sports and Entertainment	43.96	88.31	99.54
公共管理和社会组织	Public Administration and Social Organizations	105.63	216.89	280.77

表 4.6 主要年份上海市生产总值指数(按三次产业分，以上年为100)
INDEX OF GROSS DOMESTIC PRODUCT IN MAIN YEARS(CLASSIFIED BY THREE INDUSTRIES, PRECEDING YEAR = 100)

	指 标 Indicators	2001	2006	2007
上海市生产总值	**Gross Domestic Product**	**110.5**	**112.0**	**114.3**
第一产业	Primary Industry	103.0	100.8	102
第二产业	Secondary Industry	112.0	112.3	111.5
工 业	Industry	112.1	112.4	112.3
建筑业	Construction	110.9	110.6	101.5
第三产业	Tertiary Industry	109.4	112.0	117.1
交通运输、仓储和邮政业	Transportation, Warehousing and Post	108.9	111.3	108.6
#交通运输业	Transportation	109.0	111.7	107.5
信息传输、计算机服务和软件业	Information Transmission, Computer Servcie and Software Industries	118.1	117.3	117.4
批发和零售业	Retail and Wholesale Industries	115.7	110.2	111.9
住宿和餐饮业	Hoteling and Catering	107.8	115.4	109.1
金融业	Financial Industry	90.9	121.3	134.3
房地产业	Real Estate Industry	120.4	100.8	110.8
租赁和商务服务业	Leasehold and Business in Services	129.5	112.2	128.5
科学研究、技术服务和地质勘查业	Scientific Research, Technological Service and Geological Prospecting	109.9	107.3	114.2
水利、环境和公共设施管理业	Water Conservancy, Environment and Public Facility Management Industries	123.9	103.2	96.3
居民服务和其他服务业	Community Service and Other Services Industries	118.8	135.3	117.2
教 育	Education	114.4	113.1	115.4
卫生、社会保障和社会福利业	Health, Social Security and Welfare Industries	114.0	109.4	113.7
文化、体育和娱乐业	Culture, Sports and Entertainment	113.8	112.0	112.7
公共管理和社会组织	Public Administration and Social Organizations	114.5	114.1	123.3

表 4.7 上海市生产总值收入法项目(1978～2007)
STRUCTURE OF GROSS DOMESTIC PRODUCT(BY INCOME ITEM)

单位:亿元(100 million yuan)

年 份 Year	上海市生产总 值 Gross Domestic Product	劳动者报酬 Compensation of Employees	生产税净额 Net Taxes on Production	固定资产折旧 Depreciation of Fixed Assets	营业盈余 Operating Surplus
1978	272.81	62.03	45.53	10.60	154.65
1979	286.43	68.15	45.61	11.13	161.54
1980	311.89	74.47	49.49	13.05	174.88
1981	324.76	78.99	54.52	14.70	176.55
1982	337.07	85.00	57.09	16.30	178.68
1983	351.81	90.36	57.51	18.73	185.21
1984	390.85	108.79	68.74	20.81	192.51
1985	466.75	125.99	87.36	26.16	227.24
1986	490.83	141.95	86.31	33.42	229.15
1987	545.46	163.88	98.61	40.73	242.24
1988	648.30	197.69	126.95	71.85	251.81
1989	696.54	223.35	136.01	79.79	257.39
1990	781.66	244.03	149.35	92.93	295.35
1991	893.77	302.94	170.42	126.62	293.79
1992	1 114.32	397.72	207.40	160.36	348.84
1993	1 519.23	563.59	257.30	159.93	538.41
1994	1 990.86	692.40	356.32	245.26	696.88
1995	2 499.43	901.83	430.67	339.77	827.16
1996	2 957.55	1 065.85	576.01	376.70	938.99
1997	3 438.79	1 195.63	716.02	425.04	1 102.10
1998	3 801.09	1 341.22	809.04	514.85	1 135.98
1999	4 188.73	1 518.26	902.10	615.28	1 153.09
2000	4 771.17	1 724.29	1 124.30	679.43	1 243.15
2001	5 210.12	1 934.27	1 184.62	769.59	1 321.64
2002	5 741.03	2 205.79	1 219.35	850.69	1 465.20
2003	6 694.23	2 452.32	1 265.89	975.24	2 000.78
2004	8 072.83	2 771.77	1 313.83	1 265.16	2 722.07
2005	9 164.10	3 279.30	1 418.96	1 501.79	2 964.05
2006	10 366.37	3 756.56	1 623.36	1 730.51	3 255.94
2007	12 188.85	4 261.73	2 072.56	1 951.84	3 902.72

表4.8　上海市生产总值收入法构成(1978～2007)
STRUCTURE OF GROSS DOMESTIC PRODUCT(BY INCOME ITEM)

单位:%

年　份 Year	上海市生产总　值 Gross Domestic Product	劳动者报酬 Compensation of Employees	生产税净额 Net Taxes on Production	固定资产折旧 Depreciation of Fixed Assets	营业盈余 Operating Surplus
1978	100	22.7	16.7	3.9	56.7
1979	100	23.8	15.9	3.9	56.4
1980	100	23.9	15.8	4.2	56.1
1981	100	24.3	16.8	4.5	54.4
1982	100	25.2	17.0	4.8	53.0
1983	100	25.7	16.4	5.3	52.6
1984	100	27.8	17.6	5.3	49.3
1985	100	27.0	18.7	5.6	48.7
1986	100	28.9	17.6	6.8	46.7
1987	100	30.0	18.1	7.5	44.4
1988	100	30.5	19.6	11.1	38.8
1989	100	32.1	19.5	11.5	36.9
1990	100	31.2	19.1	11.9	37.8
1991	100	33.9	19.1	14.1	32.9
1992	100	35.7	18.6	14.4	31.3
1993	100	37.1	16.9	10.5	35.5
1994	100	34.8	17.9	12.3	35.0
1995	100	36.1	17.2	13.6	33.1
1996	100	36.0	19.5	12.7	31.8
1997	100	34.8	20.8	12.4	32.0
1998	100	35.3	21.3	13.5	29.9
1999	100	36.3	21.5	14.7	27.5
2000	100	36.1	23.6	14.2	26.1
2001	100	37.1	22.7	14.8	25.4
2002	100	38.4	21.3	14.8	25.5
2003	100	36.6	18.9	14.6	29.9
2004	100	34.3	16.3	15.7	33.7
2005	100	35.7	15.5	16.4	32.4
2006	100	36.2	15.7	16.7	31.4
2007	100	35.0	17.0	16.0	32.0

表4.9 主要年份上海市生产总值(按所有制分)
GROSS DOMESTIC PRODUCT IN MAIN YEARS(BY OWNERSHIP)

年份 Year	上海市生产总值 Gross Domestic Product	其中 of which				
		公有制经济 Public-owned	其中 of which		非公有制经济 Non-public-owned	其中 of which
			国有经济 State-owned	集体经济 Collective-owned		#私营和个体 Private
绝对值(亿元)	Absolute Volume (100 million yuan)					
1978	272.81	270.10	235.22	34.88	2.71	2.71
1990	781.66	746.03	556.87	189.16	35.63	15.52
1995	2 499.43	2 047.57	1 489.06	558.51	451.86	134.53
1996	2 957.55	2 302.16	1 677.56	624.60	655.39	205.19
1997	3 438.79	2 648.19	1 953.84	694.35	790.60	265.43
1998	3 801.09	2 860.45	2 118.64	741.81	940.64	320.27
1999	4 188.73	3 063.77	2 297.74	766.03	1 124.96	410.30
2000	4 771.17	3 409.97	2 626.33	783.64	1 361.20	539.35
2001	5 210.12	3 554.56	2 773.76	780.80	1 655.56	744.37
2002	5 741.03	3 703.46	2 888.57	814.89	2 037.57	968.12
2003	6 694.23	4 171.16	3 360.21	810.95	2 523.07	1 165.95
2004	8 072.83	4 810.32	4 069.95	740.37	3 262.51	1 496.11
2005	9 164.10	5 277.62	4 488.60	789.02	3 886.48	1 777.01
2006	10 366.37	5 791.89	4 967.55	824.34	4 574.48	2 069.58
2007	12 188.85	6 686.49	5 808.73	877.76	5 502.36	2 521.84
构　成(%)	Composition(%)					
1978	100	99.0	86.2	12.8	1.0	
1990	100	95.4	71.2	24.2	4.6	2.0
1995	100	81.9	59.6	22.3	18.1	5.4
1996	100	77.8	56.7	21.1	22.2	6.9
1997	100	77.0	56.8	20.2	23.0	7.7
1998	100	75.2	55.7	19.5	24.8	8.4
1999	100	73.2	54.9	18.3	26.8	9.8
2000	100	71.4	55.0	16.4	28.6	11.3
2001	100	68.2	53.2	15.0	31.8	14.3
2002	100	64.5	50.3	14.2	35.5	16.9
2003	100	62.3	50.2	12.1	37.7	17.4
2004	100	59.6	50.4	9.2	40.4	18.5
2005	100	57.6	49.0	8.6	42.4	19.4
2006	100	55.9	47.9	8.0	44.1	20.0
2007	100	54.9	47.7	7.2	45.1	20.7

表 4.10 主要年份非公有制经济增加值(按产业分)
ADDED VALUE OF NON-PUBLIC-OWNED IN MAIN YEARS(GROWPED BY INDUSTRY)

单位:亿元(100 million yuan)

年 份 Year	非公经济增加值 Added Value of Non-public-owned	其中 of which			
		第一产业 Primary Industry	第二产业 Secondary Industry	其中 of which 工业 Industry	第三产业 Tertiary Industry
1978	2.71	1.64	0.67	0.40	0.40
1990	35.63	9.01	15.22	13.74	11.40
1995	451.86	13.29	285.73	274.64	152.84
1996	655.39	14.31	424.30	407.69	216.78
1997	790.60	13.42	503.69	470.23	273.49
1998	940.64	13.25	561.66	518.25	365.72
1999	1 124.96	13.56	635.83	585.76	475.57
2000	1 361.20	14.25	773.50	715.18	573.45
2001	1 655.56	14.77	924.21	857.62	716.58
2002	2 037.57	14.34	1 085.12	1 004.78	938.11
2003	2 523.07	13.04	1 459.67	1 378.21	1 050.36
2004	3 262.51	10.44	1 921.74	1 757.96	1 330.33
2005	3 886.48	11.12	2 305.75	2 137.26	1 569.61
2006	4 574.48	11.41	2 723.54	2 541.34	1 839.53
2007	5 502.36	11.98	3 193.71	3 006.04	2 296.67

表 4.11 上海市生产总值分配(1990～2007)
STRUCTURE OF GROSS DOMESTIC PRODUCT BY DISTRIBUTION

单位:亿元(100 million yuan)

年 份 Year	上海市生产总值 Gross Domestic Product	政府所得 State-owned	企业所得 Collective-owned	个人所得 Personal-owned
1990	781.66	252.74	201.99	326.93
1991	893.77	283.08	240.30	370.39
1992	1 114.32	296.98	352.54	464.80
1993	1 519.23	360.66	537.82	620.75
1994	1 990.86	505.14	657.24	828.48
1995	2 499.43	590.96	872.16	1 036.31
1996	2 957.55	725.27	980.04	1 252.24
1997	3 438.79	1 000.07	1 059.09	1 379.63
1998	3 801.09	1 100.75	1 175.22	1 525.12
1999	4 188.73	1 217.92	1 286.23	1 684.58
2000	4 771.17	1 483.36	1 448.83	1 838.98
2001	5 210.12	1 625.56	1 587.93	1 996.63
2002	5 741.03	1 798.64	1 739.11	2 203.28
2003	6 694.23	2 195.62	2 008.80	2 489.81
2004	8 072.83	2 659.12	2 423.58	2 990.13
2005	9 164.10	3 018.63	2 672.07	3 473.40
2006	10 366.37	3 447.83	3 013.79	3 904.75
2007	12 188.85	4 145.23	3 742.68	4 300.94

表 4.12 主要年份上海市生产总值(支出法)
GROSS DOMESTIC PRODUCT IN MAIN YEARS(BY EXPENDITURE APPROACH)

年份 Year	上海市生产总值(亿元) Gross Domestic Product (100 million yuan)	其中 of which				上海市生产总值构成(%) Composition of GDP(%)		可供投资率(%) Available Investment Rate(%)
		货物和服务净流出 Net Outflows of Goods and Services	本市使用的生产总值 Gross Domestic Product Used	其中 of which				
				最终消费 Final Consumption	资本形成总额 Gross Capital Formation	#最终消费 Final Consumption	#资本形成总额 Gross Capital Formation	
1978	272.81	165.79	107.02	59.06	47.96	21.6	17.6	78.4
1980	311.89	164.13	147.76	81.24	66.52	26.0	21.3	74.0
1981	324.76	158.35	166.41	89.73	76.68	27.6	23.6	72.4
1982	337.07	153.90	183.17	92.90	90.27	27.6	26.8	72.4
1983	351.81	178.76	173.05	101.19	71.86	28.8	20.4	71.2
1984	390.85	171.97	218.88	117.25	101.63	30.0	26.0	70.0
1985	466.75	122.47	344.28	155.15	189.13	33.2	40.5	66.8
1986	490.83	80.97	409.86	181.74	228.12	37.0	46.5	63.0
1987	545.46	103.70	441.76	200.74	241.02	36.8	44.2	63.2
1988	648.30	57.32	590.98	255.42	335.56	39.4	51.8	60.6
1989	696.54	46.24	650.30	298.62	351.68	42.9	50.5	57.1
1990	781.66	91.87	689.79	358.45	331.34	45.9	42.4	54.1
1991	893.77	167.68	726.09	386.06	340.03	43.2	38.0	56.8
1992	1 114.32	150.12	964.20	476.57	487.63	42.8	43.8	57.2
1993	1 519.23	75.60	1 443.63	699.52	744.11	46.0	49.0	54.0
1994	1 990.86	-90.46	2 081.32	919.83	1 161.49	46.2	58.3	53.8
1995	2 499.43	-218.64	2 718.07	1 150.35	1 567.72	46.0	62.7	54.0
1996	2 957.55	-348.05	3 305.60	1 348.76	1 956.84	45.6	66.2	54.4
1997	3 438.79	-210.99	3 649.78	1 600.83	2 048.95	46.6	59.6	53.4
1998	3 801.09	32.25	3 768.84	1 758.09	2 010.75	46.3	52.9	53.7
1999	4 188.73	259.37	3 929.36	1 959.12	1 970.24	46.8	47.0	53.2
2000	4 771.17	356.93	4 414.24	2 244.52	2 169.72	47.0	45.5	53.0
2001	5 210.12	377.21	4 832.91	2 476.20	2 356.71	47.5	45.2	52.5
2002	5 741.03	418.68	5 322.35	2 791.06	2 531.29	48.6	44.1	51.4
2003	6 694.23	399.96	6 294.27	3 217.59	3 076.68	48.1	46.0	51.9
2004	8 072.83	457.99	7 614.84	3 832.59	3 782.25	47.5	46.9	52.5
2005	9 164.10	558.25	8 605.85	4 418.99	4 186.86	48.2	45.7	51.8
2006	10 366.37	523.75	9 842.62	5 079.76	4 762.86	49.0	45.9	51.0
2007	12 188.85	604.05	11 584.8	6 016.31	5 568.49	49.4	45.7	50.6

表 4.13 主要年份六大支柱产业增加值
VALUE ADDED OF SIX PILLAR INDUSTRIES IN MAIN YEARS

指 标	Indicators	2000	2006	2007
增加值(亿元)	**Value Added (100 million yuan)**	**1 919.10**	**4 691.05**	**5 753.06**
信息产业	Information Industry	338.18	1 337.89	1 632.82
金融业	Financial Industry	602.95	825.20	1 209.08
商贸流通业	Trading and Circulation Industry	431.43	929.16	1 077.76
汽车制造业	Auto Manufacturing	166.05	359.52	439.00
成套设备制造业	Whole-set Equipment Manufacturing Industry	129.73	572.76	617.00
房地产业	Real Estate Industry	263.35	688.10	806.79
增加值占上海市生产总值比重(%)	**Ratio of Value Added to GDP(%)**	**40.2**	**45.3**	**47.2**
信息产业	Information Industry	7.1	12.9	13.4
金融业	Financial Industry	12.6	8.0	9.9
商贸流通业	Trading and Circulation Industry	9.0	9.0	8.8
汽车制造业	Auto Manufacturing	3.5	3.5	3.6
成套设备制造业	Whole-set Equipment Manufacturing Industry	2.7	5.5	5.1
房地产业	Real Estate Industry	5.5	6.6	6.6

①信息产业增加值含有与其他行业的交叉重复因素，本表中"六大支柱产业增加值占上海市生产总值的比重"已经扣除重复计算因素。
②商贸流通业中不包括餐饮业增加值。
❶The ratio of value added from six pillar industries to GDP has excluded some overlapping factors.
❷Trading and circulation industry does not include the catering industry.

表 4.14 主要年份信息产业增加值
VALUE ADDED OF INFORMATION INDUSTRY IN MAIN YEARS

指 标	Indicators	2000	2006	2007
增加值(亿元)	**Value Added(100 million yuan)**	**338.18**	**1 337.89**	**1 632.82**
信息产品制造业	Information Products Manufacturing	195.82	813.43	1 038.00
信息产品销售业	Information Products Distribution	12.59	24.91	29.39
信息服务业	Information Services	129.77	499.55	565.43
增加值指数(以 1998 年为 100)	**Index of Value Added(1998 = 100)**	**163.2**	**580.7**	**675.9**
信息产品制造业	Information Products Manufacturing	201.1	746.5	866.7
信息产品销售业	Information Products Distribution	126.8	268.2	308.4
信息服务业	Information Services	128.1	442.4	517.2
结 构(%)	**Composition(%)**	**100**	**100**	**100.0**
信息产品制造业	Information Products Manufacturing	57.9	60.8	63.6
信息产品销售业	Information Products Distribution	3.7	1.9	1.8
信息服务业	Information Services	38.4	37.3	34.6
信息产业增加值占上海市生产总值比重(%)	**Ratio of Value Added of Information Industry to GDP(%)**	**7.1**	**12.9**	**13.4**

表 4.15　旅游产业增加值(2004～2007)
VALUE ADDED OF TOURISM INDUSTRY

指　标	Indicators	2004	2005	2006	2007
增加值(亿元)	**Value Added(100 million yuan)**	**498.09**	**584.26**	**695.06**	**858.09**
一、按行业分	**Grouped by Sectors**				
旅行社服务业	Travel Agency	8.34	9.02	10.43	11.30
旅游宾(旅)馆业	Hotel	79.68	91.78	122.47	159.42
旅游运输业	Travel Transportation	103.36	120.86	136.88	144.71
邮电通信业	Post and Telecommunication	18.95	25.21	27.80	30.24
旅游商业	Tourism Commerce	73.63	96.17	107.17	156.72
餐饮业	Catering	58.59	68.92	83.93	106.83
城市交通业	Urban Traffic	39.43	45.96	59.39	75.90
园林文化业	Gardening	76.54	92.42	103.84	118.06
金融保险业	Finance Banking and Insurance	6.80	7.61	8.07	8.80
其他服务业	Other Services	32.77	26.31	35.08	46.11
二、按境内、外分	**Grouped by Domestic and Overseas**				
境　内	Domestic	384.48	469.94	555.05	680.39
境　外	Overseas	88.28	114.32	140.01	177.70
旅游产业增加值占上海市生产总值比重(%)	**Ratio of Value Added of Tourism Industry to GDP(%)**	**5.9**	**6.4**	**6.7**	**7.0**

表 4.16　文化产业增加值(2004～2007)
VALUE ADDED OF CULTURE INDUSTRY

指　标	Indicators	2004	2005	2006	2007
总　计(亿元)	**Total(100 million yuan)**	**441.40**	**509.23**	**581.38**	**683.75**
文化服务业	**Culture Service**	**268.83**	**307.82**	**358.08**	**437.30**
#出版发行和版权服务	Issue & Copyright Service	38.69	42.08	49.07	54.19
广播、电视、电影服务	Broadcasting, Television & Film Service	19.05	24.17	29.31	31.85
文化艺术服务	Art Service	13.83	17.71	19.31	20.59
网络文化服务	Net Culture Service	47.25	58.19	69.33	84.67
文化休闲娱乐服务	Entertainment Service	74.09	82.26	99.33	125.83
文化相关产业	**Culture Relative Service**	**172.57**	**201.41**	**223.30**	**246.45**
文化用品、设备及相关文化产品生产	Production of Stationery, Equipment & Relative Product	124.71	148.48	164.17	182.49
文化用品、设备及相关文化产品销售	Sales of Stationery, Equipment & Relative Product	47.86	52.93	59.13	63.96
文化产业增加值占上海市生产总值比重(%)	**Ratio of Value Added of Culture Industry to GDP(%)**	**5.47**	**5.56**	**5.61**	**5.61**

表 4.17 最终消费及构成(1978～2007) FINAL CONSUMPTION AND COMPOSITION

年份 Year	最终消费(亿元) Final Consumption (100 million yuan)					最终消费构成(%) Composition of Final Consumption (%)	
	合计 Total	居民消费 Household Consumption	其中 of which 农村居民 Rural Residents	城镇居民 Urban Residents	政府消费 Government Consumption	居民消费 Household Consumption	政府消费 Government Consumption
1978	59.06	48.25	12.82	35.43	10.81	81.7	18.3
1979	71.34	58.80	17.02	41.78	12.54	82.4	17.6
1980	81.24	66.31	19.43	46.88	14.93	81.6	18.4
1981	89.73	73.69	23.25	50.44	16.04	82.1	17.9
1982	92.90	75.02	26.41	48.61	17.88	80.8	19.2
1983	101.19	81.64	26.91	54.73	19.55	80.7	19.3
1984	117.25	94.56	31.10	63.46	22.69	80.6	19.4
1985	155.15	124.78	38.35	86.43	30.37	80.4	19.6
1986	181.74	145.73	42.49	103.24	36.01	80.2	19.8
1987	200.74	161.09	47.23	113.86	39.65	80.2	19.8
1988	255.42	211.04	55.97	155.07	44.38	82.6	17.4
1989	298.62	244.60	61.15	183.45	54.02	81.9	18.1
1990	358.45	284.79	66.15	218.64	73.66	79.5	20.5
1991	386.06	311.09	72.17	238.92	74.97	80.6	19.4
1992	476.57	366.09	84.86	281.23	110.48	76.8	23.2
1993	699.52	555.45	110.30	445.15	144.07	79.4	20.6
1994	919.83	732.71	130.08	602.63	187.12	79.7	20.3
1995	1 150.35	926.54	152.90	773.64	223.81	80.5	19.5
1996	1 348.76	1 080.79	168.13	912.66	267.97	80.1	19.9
1997	1 600.83	1 262.12	176.50	1 085.62	338.71	78.8	21.2
1998	1 758.09	1 379.41	178.52	1 200.89	378.68	78.5	21.5
1999	1 959.12	1 528.95	176.73	1 352.22	430.17	78.0	22.0
2000	2 244.52	1 756.27	176.79	1 579.48	488.25	78.2	21.8
2001	2 476.20	1 910.44	181.22	1 729.22	565.76	77.2	22.8
2002	2 791.06	2 134.79	185.58	1 949.21	656.27	76.5	23.5
2003	3 217.59	2 437.44	187.78	2 249.66	780.15	75.8	24.2
2004	3 832.59	2 869.26	186.78	2 682.48	963.33	74.9	25.1
2005	4 418.99	3 271.64	184.02	3 087.62	1 147.35	74.0	26.0
2006	5 079.76	3 763.15	202.19	3 560.96	1 316.61	74.1	25.9
2007	6 016.31	4 455.52	233.16	4 222.36	1 560.79	74.1	25.9

表 4.18 居民消费水平及指数(1978～2007)
HOUSEHOLD CONSUMPTION LEVEL AND INDEX

年份 Year	居民消费水平(元/人) Household Consumption Level(yuan/person)			指数(以1978年为100) Index(1978=100)		
	全市 Total	其中 of which		全市 Total	其中 of which	
		农村居民 Rural Households	城镇居民 Urban Households		农村居民 Rural Households	城镇居民 Urban Households
1978	442	283	555	100.0	100.0	100.0
1979	527	379	627	117.2	129.1	111.6
1980	582	437	675	123.1	141.9	114.2
1981	638	521	712	133.1	167.2	118.7
1982	640	589	672	133.5	168.9	118.6
1983	688	600	741	142.8	192.9	122.9
1984	788	697	842	160.8	219.5	137.2
1985	1 031	938	1 078	182.0	252.2	153.1
1986	1 190	1 058	1 254	197.7	266.6	167.6
1987	1 298	1 102	1 401	199.9	257.5	173.3
1988	1 680	1 316	1 867	220.3	269.9	194.3
1989	1 927	1 449	2 165	221.4	271.5	194.7
1990	2 225	1 576	2 542	216.1	249.5	193.7
1991	2 420	1 726	2 755	234.3	283.9	206.7
1992	2 842	2 042	3 222	249.5	306.0	219.1
1993	3 923	2 737	4 394	287.4	311.8	255.9
1994	5 081	3 371	5 706	325.3	357.0	286.1
1995	6 310	4 120	7 050	379.3	402.7	333.3
1996	7 228	4 680	8 033	416.5	438.1	364.0
1997	8 289	5 086	9 234	449.0	462.2	391.3
1998	8 896	5 344	9 871	480.4	480.7	417.5
1999	9 683	5 497	10 753	515.9	495.1	448.0
2000	10 922	5 705	12 168	557.7	509.0	484.3
2001	11 807	6 052	13 114	604.5	543.6	523.0
2002	13 137	6 464	14 569	673.4	580.6	582.1
2003	14 247	6 914	15 631	721.9	616.0	617.0
2004	16 470	7 715	17 883	815.0	671.4	689.8
2005	18 396	9 157	19 573	896.5	778.8	743.6
2006	20 944	10 136	22 294	1 005.9	846.6	835.1
2007	24 260	11 235	25 919	1 119.6	894.0	933.6

注：1993 年以前为年平均户籍人口数，1993 年起为年平均常住人口数。
Note: Data in this table refer to yealy average registered population before 1993, and yearly average resident population after 1993.

表 4.19 资本形成总额和指数(1978 ~ 2007)
GROSS CAPITAL FORMATION AND INDEX

年 份 Year	资本形成总额(亿元) Gross Capital Formation(100 million yuan)			资本形成总额指数(以 1978 年为 100) Index of Gross Capital Formation (1978 = 100)		
	合 计 Total	固定资本形成总额 Fixed Capital Formation	存 货 增 加 Inventory Change	总指数 Indices	固定资本形成总额 Fixed Capital Formation	存 货 增 加 Inventory Change
1978	47.96	31.69	16.27	100	100	100
1979	43.61	39.05	4.56	90	120	37
1980	66.52	45.57	20.95	134.6	133.5	136.7
1981	76.68	55.10	21.58	156.4	164.4	138.1
1982	90.27	70.49	19.78	178.8	210.5	107.6
1983	71.86	74.51	-2.65	150.7	223.7	-12.5
1984	101.63	90.70	10.93	210.0	262.7	91.9
1985	189.13	116.70	72.43	387.6	308.1	564.0
1986	228.12	144.41	83.71	431.8	352.5	607.4
1987	241.02	183.79	57.23	380.0	415.9	298.8
1988	335.56	236.92	98.64	449.2	474.1	392.1
1989	351.68	232.22	119.46	423.1	419.6	429.7
1990	331.34	248.46	82.88	338.1	430.5	131.1
1991	340.03	276.08	63.95	334.0	447.7	109.0
1992	487.63	382.01	105.62	435.2	561.5	162.1
1993	744.11	624.31	119.80	530.1	731.0	154.5
1994	1 161.49	996.48	165.01	726.8	1 019.1	196.1
1995	1 567.72	1 380.85	186.87	950.6	1 373.7	218.8
1996	1 956.84	1 711.46	245.38	1 158.8	1 660.8	279.5
1997	2 048.95	1 795.83	253.12	1 175.0	1 700.6	268.3
1998	2 010.75	1 804.81	205.94	1 129.2	1 695.5	201.2
1999	1 970.24	1 801.59	168.65	1 098.7	1 683.7	164.0
2000	2 169.72	1 933.01	236.71	1 152.5	1 746.0	191.0
2001	2 356.71	2 099.99	256.72	1 263.2	1 906.6	216.1
2002	2 531.29	2 366.10	165.19	1 387.0	2 192.6	148.9
2003	3 076.68	2 643.07	433.61	1 588.1	2 365.8	299.4
2004	3 782.25	3 239.04	543.21	1 804.1	2 680.5	347.3
2005	4 186.86	3 743.42	443.44	1 962.8	3 023.6	282.0
2006	4 762.86	4 272.85	490.01	2 186.6	3 383.4	302.6
2007	5 568.49	5 041.4	527.09	2 529.9	3 948.4	322.3

表4.20 经营性固定资产原价年末数(1978～2007)
ORIGINAL VALUE OF OPERATING FIXED ASSETS(YEAR-END)

单位:亿元(100 million yuan)

年份 Year	合计 Total	其中 of which				
		第一产业 Primary Industry	第二产业 Secondary Industry	其中 of which		第三产业 Tertiary Industry
				工业 Industry	建筑业 Construction	
1978	298.53	8.03	205.17	197.68	7.49	85.33
1979	321.52	10.56	213.94	205.94	8.00	97.02
1980	355.16	11.81	225.55	216.16	9.39	117.80
1981	388.93	10.04	249.08	237.37	11.71	129.81
1982	413.23	9.56	271.76	255.57	16.19	131.91
1983	448.41	10.88	298.22	280.77	17.45	139.31
1984	493.76	11.47	327.20	309.22	17.98	155.09
1985	569.97	12.09	377.06	355.61	21.45	180.82
1986	726.95	13.25	496.56	472.68	23.88	217.14
1987	868.91	14.73	576.61	548.62	27.99	277.57
1988	975.78	15.78	656.35	629.34	27.01	303.65
1989	1 106.60	20.04	755.02	723.02	32.00	331.54
1990	1 263.17	22.80	866.64	827.01	39.63	373.73
1991	1 656.84	24.03	1 067.81	1 026.08	41.73	565.00
1992	2 011.38	26.29	1 279.04	1 236.56	42.48	706.05
1993	2 486.40	31.36	1 581.16	1 537.56	43.60	873.88
1994	3 536.83	47.58	2 330.14	2 271.38	58.76	1 159.11
1995	4 756.42	59.48	2 915.53	2 810.27	105.26	1 781.41
1996	5 827.13	69.64	3 393.66	3 263.77	129.89	2 363.83
1997	6 915.42	80.87	3 879.13	3 721.96	157.17	2 955.42
1998	8 392.45	82.93	4 573.10	4 406.50	166.60	3 736.42
1999	9 991.27	91.22	5 311.01	5 137.11	173.90	4 589.04
2000	11 684.90	104.25	5 940.30	5 749.23	191.07	5 640.35
2001	12 667.45	112.71	6 451.78	6 249.24	202.54	6 102.96
2002	13 839.09	118.78	6 937.81	6 596.13	341.68	6 782.50
2003	15 639.55	127.33	7 614.96	7 197.71	417.25	7 897.26
2004	18 896.30	152.61	9 183.79	8 717.45	466.34	9 559.90
2005	21 843.13	162.19	10 963.19	10 445.07	518.12	10 717.75
2006	24 069.59	164.44	12 335.84	11 752.39	583.45	11 569.31
2007	26 075.14	169.77	13 433.65	12 801.20	632.45	12 471.72

表 4.21 存货年末数(1978 ~ 2007)
YEAR-END INVENTORY

单位:亿元(100 million yuan)

年 份 Year	合 计 Total	其中 of which 第一产业 Primary Industry	第二产业 Secondary Industry	其中 of which 工 业 Industry	建筑业 Construction	第三产业 Tertiary Industry
1978	264.20	3.00	108.10	106.69	1.41	153.10
1979	267.45	2.05	112.27	107.60	4.67	153.13
1980	288.41	1.99	117.84	112.92	4.92	168.58
1981	310.09	3.22	125.21	120.27	4.94	181.66
1982	316.31	2.98	126.04	120.73	5.31	187.29
1983	305.04	2.79	129.03	123.82	5.21	173.22
1984	332.15	2.08	151.59	144.79	6.80	178.48
1985	412.20	2.87	206.32	194.62	11.70	203.01
1986	512.61	3.84	272.77	251.55	21.22	236.00
1987	577.18	4.50	299.99	281.86	18.13	272.69
1988	688.13	5.94	364.38	341.53	22.85	317.81
1989	834.92	6.84	451.30	424.89	26.41	376.78
1990	908.98	7.70	522.20	490.51	31.69	379.08
1991	994.92	8.43	632.74	602.03	30.71	353.75
1992	1 096.19	8.59	704.17	673.86	30.31	383.43
1993	1 269.30	10.46	852.01	789.73	62.28	406.83
1994	1 417.12	14.85	911.57	879.26	32.31	490.70
1995	1 528.21	21.74	1 066.51	1 029.50	37.01	439.96
1996	1 726.41	25.48	1 196.31	1 153.02	43.29	504.62
1997	1 874.05	31.98	1 276.86	1 227.71	49.15	565.21
1998	1 876.73	32.81	1 231.86	1 189.80	42.06	612.06
1999	1 965.43	33.46	1 290.14	1 244.17	45.97	641.83
2000	2 093.40	34.20	1 392.88	1 343.70	49.18	666.32
2001	2 156.65	34.53	1 425.91	1 374.52	51.39	696.21
2002	2 201.73	35.22	1 440.11	1 386.15	53.96	726.40
2003	2 512.05	35.06	1 711.72	1 654.75	56.97	765.27
2004	3 719.86	35.81	2 278.35	2 218.54	59.81	1 405.70
2005	4 032.85	36.53	2 501.82	2 441.09	60.73	1 494.50
2006	4 361.72	37.26	2 713.94	2 652.00	61.94	1 610.52
2007	5 063.79	34.19	3 314.71	3 251.47	63.24	1 714.89

表 4.22 每百元增加值占用的资产总额(1978～2007)
TOTAL ASSETS PER 100 YUAN WORTH OF VALUE ADDED

单位:元(yuan)

年份 Year	合计 Total	其中 of which				
		第一产业 Primary Industry	第二产业 Secondary Industry	其中 of which		第三产业 Tertiary Industry
				工业 Industry	建筑业 Construction	
1978	196.80	99.59	141.67	140.09	233.24	447.09
1979	201.05	103.78	144.54	142.62	234.97	453.82
1980	197.59	130.74	141.80	139.17	257.93	408.38
1981	206.70	127.88	146.86	144.80	214.40	428.01
1982	211.91	96.92	154.84	152.43	222.58	423.61
1983	210.77	96.93	161.57	158.55	243.71	380.69
1984	202.04	78.86	164.51	163.11	194.74	328.91
1985	193.69	72.99	163.09	161.39	199.62	295.01
1986	226.32	81.39	201.29	199.83	228.40	309.71
1987	246.19	84.08	225.85	230.99	163.83	314.58
1988	239.86	74.84	219.07	225.44	143.17	311.81
1989	258.81	82.02	238.87	244.71	162.76	331.24
1990	263.14	83.79	256.64	262.37	181.34	302.11
1991	269.86	92.43	280.52	286.11	200.50	270.41
1992	258.42	98.56	271.91	277.89	178.37	249.30
1993	225.88	101.41	244.71	250.25	160.47	204.67
1994	218.74	109.48	247.07	254.93	132.93	184.35
1995	224.82	120.07	254.46	267.17	104.91	189.72
1996	233.94	128.31	268.43	284.16	109.59	196.96
1997	237.63	144.37	274.47	292.65	108.36	200.82
1998	250.70	154.79	292.56	315.47	102.87	212.28
1999	265.30	161.37	312.56	334.94	108.95	224.91
2000	269.69	171.58	315.60	337.03	110.25	231.97
2001	274.49	183.14	316.48	339.61	104.51	240.12
2002	268.81	189.03	309.93	329.52	127.65	235.42
2003	255.39	195.25	275.86	286.18	162.42	237.52
2004	252.50	210.19	267.06	275.36	167.36	239.52
2005	264.58	214.46	279.89	288.44	170.84	250.79
2006	261.94	213.44	283.54	292.18	170.86	242.10
2007	244.36	199.17	279.99	287.43	176.26	213.52

表 4.23　每百元增加值占用的存货(1978～2007)
INVENTORY PER 100 YUAN WORTH OF VALUE ADDED

单位:元(yuan)

年 份 Year	合 计 Total	其 中 of which				
		第一产业 Primary Industry	第二产业 Secondary Industry	其 中 of which		第三产业 Tertiary Industry
				工 业 Industry	建筑业 Construction	
1978	93.85	27.18	50.70	51.04	30.73	287.71
1979	92.81	22.17	49.81	49.46	66.23	284.44
1980	89.11	20.00	48.73	47.76	91.68	244.87
1981	92.14	24.62	49.74	49.17	68.28	250.74
1982	92.92	23.29	50.39	50.05	59.80	247.82
1983	88.31	21.34	49.95	49.65	58.06	217.25
1984	81.51	14.11	50.95	51.03	49.30	179.04
1985	79.74	12.67	54.96	54.55	63.75	156.88
1986	94.21	17.04	71.29	69.96	96.09	162.45
1987	99.90	19.31	78.59	79.25	70.67	159.48
1988	97.59	19.08	76.71	78.02	61.13	157.14
1989	109.33	21.57	87.49	88.52	74.05	173.02
1990	111.55	21.23	96.27	97.42	81.21	156.29
1991	106.51	23.68	104.87	106.12	87.03	118.55
1992	93.83	24.91	98.68	100.20	74.94	91.51
1993	77.85	25.19	86.23	86.43	83.16	68.24
1994	67.47	26.58	76.78	77.67	63.84	56.46
1995	58.92	30.58	69.68	72.95	31.17	45.61
1996	55.02	34.36	70.86	75.11	27.90	36.55
1997	52.35	39.89	69.71	74.45	26.39	33.58
1998	49.34	43.87	67.01	72.37	22.61	31.73
1999	45.86	44.48	63.54	68.06	22.38	29.44
2000	42.53	44.12	60.77	64.73	22.80	26.30
2001	40.79	44.06	58.65	62.73	21.27	24.96
2002	37.96	43.77	54.64	58.29	20.70	23.41
2003	35.21	43.37	49.11	51.69	20.71	21.91
2004	38.60	42.46	51.26	53.90	19.54	26.49
2005	42.30	40.07	53.67	56.42	18.64	31.38
2006	40.49	39.33	51.86	54.53	17.12	29.60
2007	38.66	35.08	53.08	55.71	16.45	25.95

表4.24 每百元增加值占用的固定资产(1978~2007)
FIXED ASSETS PER 100 YUAN WORTH OF VALUE ADDED

单位:元(yuan)

年份 Year	合计 Total	其中 of which				
		第一产业 Primary Industry	第二产业 Secondary Industry	其中 of which 工业 Industry	其中 of which 建筑业 Construction	第三产业 Tertiary Industry
1978	102.95	72.41	90.97	89.05	202.51	159.39
1979	108.24	81.61	94.73	93.16	168.74	169.38
1980	108.48	110.74	93.07	91.42	166.25	163.51
1981	114.56	103.26	97.12	95.63	146.12	177.27
1982	118.99	73.63	104.45	102.38	162.78	175.79
1983	122.46	75.59	111.62	108.90	185.65	163.44
1984	120.53	64.75	113.56	112.08	145.44	149.87
1985	113.95	60.32	108.14	106.84	135.87	138.13
1986	132.11	64.35	130.00	129.87	132.31	147.26
1987	146.29	64.77	147.26	151.74	93.16	155.10
1988	142.27	55.76	142.36	147.42	82.04	154.67
1989	149.48	60.45	151.38	156.19	88.71	158.22
1990	151.59	62.56	160.37	164.96	100.13	145.83
1991	163.35	68.75	175.65	179.99	113.47	151.86
1992	164.59	73.65	173.23	177.69	103.43	157.79
1993	148.03	76.22	158.48	163.82	77.31	136.43
1994	151.27	82.90	170.29	177.26	69.06	127.89
1995	165.90	89.49	184.78	194.22	73.74	144.11
1996	178.92	93.95	197.57	209.05	81.69	160.41
1997	185.28	104.48	204.76	218.20	81.97	167.24
1998	201.36	110.92	225.55	243.10	80.26	180.55
1999	219.44	116.89	249.02	266.88	86.57	195.47
2000	227.16	127.46	254.83	272.30	87.45	205.67
2001	233.70	139.08	257.83	276.88	83.24	215.16
2002	230.85	145.26	255.29	271.23	106.95	212.01
2003	220.18	151.88	226.75	234.49	141.71	215.61
2004	213.90	167.73	215.80	221.46	147.82	213.03
2005	222.28	174.39	226.22	232.02	152.20	219.41
2006	221.45	174.11	231.68	237.65	153.74	212.49
2007	205.70	164.09	226.90	231.72	159.81	187.57

表 4.25 全员劳动生产率(1978～2007)
OVERALL LABOUR PRODUCTIVITY IN MAIN YEARS

单位:元/人(yuan/person)

年 份 Year	合 计 Total	第一产业 Primary Industry	第二产业 Secondary Industry	第三产业 Tertiary Industry
1978	3 960	455	7 001	3 488
1979	4 060	490	6 931	3 500
1980	4 322	462	6 886	4 096
1981	4 386	508	6 697	4 177
1982	4 452	667	6 532	4 234
1983	4 590	729	6 431	4 510
1984	5 080	1 055	6 641	5 140
1985	6 041	1 408	7 493	6 098
1986	6 299	1 653	7 444	6 473
1987	6 944	2 019	7 913	7 314
1988	8 205	2 796	9 301	8 288
1989	8 833	3 258	10 011	8 655
1990	9 940	3 892	10 863	10 382
1991	11 272	4 011	11 737	12 940
1992	13 885	4 270	14 382	16 013
1993	19 060	4 957	19 485	22 473
1994	25 308	6 327	25 626	30 192
1995	31 634	7 791	32 503	36 878
1996	37 269	8 717	37 813	44 181
1997	43 497	8 895	44 461	51 279
1998	47 816	9 071	49 227	55 670
1999	52 130	9 191	52 397	61 961
2000	58 443	9 754	59 909	67 345
2001	62 876	10 003	64 470	72 215
2002	67 818	10 297	69 207	77 877
2003	75 665	10 523	81 186	82 534
2004	88 893	12 409	100 507	90 326
2005	98 762	14 744	114 500	96 716
2006	108 623	16 898	126 979	104 294
2007	125 792	19 428	140 613	124 993

表4.26 固定资产产出率(1978~2007)
OUTPUT RATE OF FIXED ASSETS

单位:%

年份 Year	合计 Total	其中 of which 第一产业 Primary Industry	第二产业 Secondary Industry	其中 of which 工业 Industry	第三产业 Tertiary Industry
1978	97.1	138.1	109.9	112.3	62.7
1979	92.4	122.5	105.6	107.3	59.0
1980	92.2	90.3	107.4	109.4	61.2
1981	87.3	96.8	103.0	104.6	56.4
1982	84.0	135.8	95.7	97.7	56.9
1983	81.7	132.3	89.6	91.8	61.2
1984	83.0	154.5	88.1	89.2	66.7
1985	87.8	165.8	92.5	93.6	72.4
1986	75.7	155.4	76.9	77.0	67.9
1987	68.4	154.4	67.9	65.9	64.5
1988	70.3	179.4	70.2	67.8	64.7
1989	66.9	165.4	66.1	64.0	63.2
1990	66.0	159.9	62.4	60.6	68.6
1991	61.2	145.5	56.9	55.6	65.8
1992	60.8	135.8	57.7	56.3	63.4
1993	67.6	131.2	63.1	61.0	73.3
1994	66.1	120.6	58.7	56.4	78.2
1995	60.3	111.8	54.1	51.5	69.4
1996	55.9	106.4	50.6	47.8	62.3
1997	54.0	95.7	48.8	45.8	59.9
1998	49.7	90.2	44.3	41.1	55.5
1999	45.6	85.6	40.2	37.5	51.2
2000	44.0	78.5	39.2	36.7	48.6
2001	42.8	71.9	38.8	36.1	46.5
2002	43.3	68.8	39.2	36.9	47.2
2003	45.4	65.8	44.1	42.6	46.4
2004	46.8	59.6	46.3	45.2	46.9
2005	45.0	57.3	44.2	43.1	45.6
2006	45.2	57.4	43.2	42.1	47.1
2007	48.6	60.9	44.1	43.2	53.3

上/海/统/计/年/鉴

主要统计指标解释

■ 生产总值(原国内生产总值)

指按市场价格计算的一个地区所有常住（驻)单位在一定时期内生产活动的最终成果。生产总值有三种表现形态,即价值形态、收入形态和产品形态。从价值形态看,它是所有常住单位在一定时期内所生产的全部货物和服务价值超过同期投入的全部非固定资产货物和服务价值的差额,即所有常住(驻)单位的增加值之和;从收入形态看,它是所有常住(驻)单位在一定时期内所创造并分配给常住(驻)单位和非常住(驻)单位的初次(分配)收入之和;从产品形态看,它是所有常住单位在一定时期内最终使用的货物和服务减去进口货物和服务。在实际核算中,生产总值有三种计算方法,(其三种表现形态体现为三种计算方法,)即生产法、收入法和支出法。三种方法分别从不同的方面反映生产总值及其构成。根据国务院和国家统计局有关我国 GDP 核算和数据发布制度的规定,上海国内生产总值自 2004 年起更名为“上海市生产总值”,简称“上海市 GDP”。

■ 三次产业

根据社会生产活动历史发展的顺序对产业结构的划分，产品直接取自自然界的部门称为第一产业，对初级产品进行再加工的部门称为第二产业,为生产和消费提供各种服务的部门称为第三产业。

第一产业:农林牧渔业(包括农业、林业、畜牧业、渔业和农林牧渔服务业)。

第二产业:包括采矿业、制造业、电力、燃气及水的生产和供应业、建筑业。

第三产业:除第一、第二产业以外的其他各业。

■ 劳动者报酬

指劳动者因从事生产活动所获得的全部报酬。包括劳动者获得的各种形式的工资、奖金和津贴，既包括货币形式的,也包括实物形式的,还包括劳动者所享受的公费医疗和医药卫生费、上下班交通补贴、单位支付的社会保险费、住房公积金等。对于个体经济来说,其所有者所获得的劳动报酬和经营利润不易区分，这两部分统一作为劳动者报酬处理。

■ 生产税净额

指生产税减生产补贴后的余额。生产税指政府对生产单位从事生产、销售和经营活动以及因从事生产活动使用某些生产要素(如固定资产、土地、劳动力)所征收的各种税、附加费和规费。生产补贴与生产税相反,指政府对生产单位的单方面转移支出,因此视为负生产税,包括政策亏损补贴、价格补贴等。

■ 固定资产折旧

指一定时期内为弥补固定资产损耗按照规定的固定资产折旧率提取的固定资产折旧,或按国民经济核算统一规定的折旧率虚拟计算的固定资产折旧。它反映了固定资产在当期生产中的转移价值。各类企业和企业化管理的事业单位的固定资产折旧是指实际计提的折旧费;不计提折旧的政府机关、非企业化管理的事业单位和居民住房的固定资产折旧是按照统一规定的折旧率和固定资产原值计算的虚拟折旧。原则上,固定资产折旧应按固定资产当期的重置价值计算,但是目前我国尚不具备对全社会固定资产进行重估价的基础,所以暂时只能采用上述办法。

■ 营业盈余

指常住单位创造的增加值扣除劳动者报酬、生产税净额和固定资产折旧后的余额。它相当于企业的营业利润加上生产补贴，但要扣除从利润中开支的工资和福利等。

■ 支出法生产总值

是从最终使用的角度反映一个国家(或地区)一定时期内生产活动最终成果的一种方法,包括最终消费、资本形成总额及货物和服务净出口三部分。计算公式为:

支出法生产总值 = 最终消费 + 资本形成总额 + 货物和服务净出口

■ 最终消费

指常住单位在一定时期内对于货物和服务的全部最终消费支出,也就是常住单位为满足物质、文化和精神生活的需要，从本国经济领土和国外购买的货物和服务的支出;不包括非常住单位在本国经济领土内的消费支出。最终消费分为居民消费和政府消费。

主要统计指标解释

■ 居民消费

指常住住户在一定时期内对货物和服务的全部最终消费支出。居民消费按市场价格计算，即按居民支付的购买者价格计算。购买者价格是购买者取得货物所支付的价格，包括购买者支付的运输和商业费用。居民消费除了直接以货币形式购买货物和服务的消费之外，还包括以其他方式获得的货物和服务的消费支出，即所谓的虚拟消费支出。居民虚拟消费支出包括以下几种类型：单位以实物报酬及实物转移的形式提供给劳动者的货物和服务；住户生产并由本住户消费了的货物和服务，其中的服务仅指住户的自有住房服务；金融机构提供的金融媒介服务；保险公司提供的保险服务。

■ 政府消费

指一定时期内政府部门为全社会提供公共服务的消费支出和免费或以较低价格向住户提供的货物和服务的净支出。前者等于政府服务的产出价值减去政府单位所获得的经营收入的价值，政府服务的产出价值等于它的经常性业务支出加上固定资产折旧；后者等于政府部门免费或以较低价格向住户提供的货物和服务的市场价值减去向住户收取的价值。

■ 资本形成总额

指常住单位在一定时期内获得的，并减去处置的固定资产，加上存货的变动，包括固定资本形成总额和存货增加。

■ 固定资本形成总额

指生产者在一定时期内获得的固定资产减处置的固定资产的价值总额。固定资产是通过生产活动生产出来的，且其使用年限在一年以上、单位价值在规定标准以上的资产，不包括自然资产。可分为有形固定资本形成总额和无形固定资本形成总额。有形固定资本形成总额包括一定时期内完成的建筑工程、安装工程和设备工器具购置(减处置)价值，以及土地改良、新增役、种、奶、毛、娱乐用牲畜和新增经济林木价值。无形固定资本形成总额包括矿藏的勘探、计算机软件等获得减处置。

■ 存货增加

指常住单位在一定时期内存货实物量变动的市场价值，即期末价值减期初价值的差额，再扣除当期由于价格变动而产生的持有收益。存货增加可以是正值，也可以是负值，正值表示存货上升，负值表示存货下降。存货包括生产单位购进的原材料、燃料和储备物资等存货，以及生产单位生产的产成品、在制品和半成品等存货。

■ 货物和服务净流出

指货物和服务流出减货物和服务流入的差额。流出包括常住单位向非常住单位出售或无偿转让的各种货物和服务的价值；流入包括常住单位从非常住单位购买或无偿得到的各种货物和服务的价值。地区核算净流出，除包括本地区对外贸易及国外非贸易往来的净出口额，还包括地区间货物和服务流出减流入后的净额。

■ 信息产业

是指与电子信息相关联的各种活动的集合，包括信息产品的制造、销售和信息服务等活动。由于信息产业增加值是依据若干行业的有关资料进行跨行业核算的，因此不宜将其与上海市生产总值中其他行业的增加值进行加总，否则会造成重复计算。

■ 旅游产业

指本市与旅游相关的各行业，为境内外旅游者提供旅游服务的产业。这些服务包括：旅行社服务、交通运输服务、住宿服务、电讯服务、娱乐服务、餐饮服务、商品零售服务等。由于旅游产业增加值是依据相关行业的有关资料进行跨行业核算的，因此不宜将其与上海市生产总值中其他行业的增加值进行加总，否则会造成重复计算。

■ 全员劳动生产率

表示全社会从业人员在一定时期内平均每人创造的生产总值(增加值)，这是衡量现有劳动力资源生产效率的重要指标。其中平均从业人数包括非正式登记的从业人员。

全员劳动生产率 = 全市生产总值 / 年均从业人数

■ 固定资产产出率

在一定时期内生产总值(增加值)与经营性固定资产原价的比例，即单位经营性固定资产原价所提供的生产总值(增加值)，表示经营性固定资产的投资效益，是反映固定资产产出效率的重要指标。

固定资产产出率 = 全市生产总值 / 经营性固定资产原价年均数

SHANGHAI STATISTICAL YEARBOOK

EXPLANATORY NOTES TO MAJOR STATISTICAL INDICATORS

□ Gross Regional Product(former Gross Domestic Product)

Gross Regional Product refers to the final products at market prices by (of) all resident units of a region during a certain period of time. Gross product is expressed in three different forms, i.e value, income, and products respectively. The form of value added refers to the total value of all products and services produced by all resident units during a certain period of time minus the total value of inputs of non–fixed–assets products and services or the summation of the value added of all resident units; the form of income includes all the income items produced by all resident units and distributed primarily to all resident and non–resident units; the form of product refers to all final goods and services minus imports of goods and services. In the practice of national accounting, it is calculated by three approaches, i.e. product approach, income approach, and expenditure approach, respectively, to reflect Gross Product and its composition of different aspects. According to the regulations of GDP national accounting and data release issued by the State Council and National Bureau of Statistics, since 2004 Shanghai Gross Domestic Product has been renamed as Shanghai Gross Product Value, for short Shanghai GDP.

□ Three Industries

Three Industries have been classified according to the historical sequence of development. Primary industry refers to extraction of natural resources; secondary industry involves processing of primary products; and tertiary industry provides services of various kinds for production and consumption.

Primary industry: Agriculture, forestry, animal husbandry and fishery.(including farming, forestry, animal husbandry, fishery industry and service industry for farming, forestry, animal husbandry and fishery).

Secondary industry: Mining, manufacturing, power, steam and water production and supply and construction.

Tertiary industry: All other industries not included in primary or secondary industries.

□ Labourers Remuneration

Labourers Remuneration refers to the whole payment of various forms earned by the labourers from the productive activities they are engaged in. It includes wages, bonuses and allowances the labourers earned in monetary form and in kind. It also includes the free medical services provided to the labourers and the medicine expenses, traffic subsidies and social insurance, housing fund paid by the employers. As the individual economy is concerned, since the labourers remuneration is not easily distinguished from the operating profit, both are treated as labourers remuneration.

□ Net Taxes on Production

Net Taxes on Production refers to the difference of the taxes on production minus the subsidies on production. The taxes on production refers to the various taxes, extra charges and fees levied on the production units on their production, sale and business activities as well as on the use of some factors of production, such as fixed assets, land and labour force in the production activities they are engaged in. In contrast to the taxes on production, the subsidies on production refer to the unilateral government transfer to the production units and are therefore regarded as negative taxes on production. They include subsidies on the loss due to implementation of government policies, price subsidies, etc.

□ Depreciation of Fixed Assets

Depreciation of Fixed Assets refers to the depreciation of fixed assets of a given period, drawn in accordance with the stipulated depreciation rate for the purpose of compensating the wear loss of the fixed assets or the depreciation of fixed assets calculated in a fictitious way in accordance with the stipulated unified depreciation rate in the national economic accounting system. It reflects the value of transfer of the fixed assets in the production of the current period. The depreciation of fixed assets in various enterprises and institutions managed as enterprises refers to the depreciation expenses actually drawn. In government agencies and institutions not managed as enterprises which do not draw the depreciation expenses, as well as for the houses of residents, the depreciation of fixed assets is the imputed depreciation, which is calculated in accordance with the stipulated unified depreciation rate. In principle, the depreciation of fixed assets should be calculated on the basis of the re–purchased value of the fixed assets. However, there is no actual condition to re–evaluate all the fixed assets in China. Therefore, the above–mentioned methods are

EXPLANATORY NOTES TO MAJOR STATISTICAL INDICATORS

temporarily adopted at present.

□ Operating Surplus

Operating Surplus refers to the balance of the value added created by the resident units deducting the labourers remuneration, net taxes on production and the depreciation of fixed assets. It is equivalent to the business profit of the enterprises plus subsidies on production, but the wages and welfare expenses paid from the profits should be deducted.

□ GDP by Expenditure Approach

GDP by Expenditure Approach refers to the method of measuring the final results of production activities of a country (region) during a given period from the perspective of final use. It includes final consumption, total capital formation and net export of goods and services, i.e.:

GDP by expenditure approach = final consumption + total capital formation + net export of goods and services

□ Final Consumption

Final Consumption refers to the total expenditure of resident units on final consumption of goods and services in a certain period, namely the expenditure of the resident units for purchases of goods and services from domestic economic territory and abroad to meet the requirements of material, cultural and spiritual life. It excludes the expenditure of non-resident units on consumption in the economic territory of the country. The final consumption is classified into household consumption and government consumption.

□ Household Consumption

Household Consumption refers to the total expenditure of resident households on the final consumption of goods and services in a certain period of time. The households consumption is calculated at market prices, namely the purchasers prices which the households pay; the purchasers prices of goods are the prices the households pay when they obtain the goods, including the transport and commercial expenses paid by the households. In addition to the consumption of goods and services bought by the households directly with money, the expenditure on goods and services obtained by the households in other ways, i.e. the so-called imputed expenditure on consumption, is also included in the households consumption. The imputation expenditure of the households on consumption includes the following types: (a) the goods and services provided to the households by the units in the form of payment in kind and transfer in kind; (b) the goods and services produced and consumed by the households themselves, in which the services refer only to the services provided by the residential buildings owned by the households; (c) the services of financial intermediary provided by the financial institutions; (d) the insurance services provided by the insurance companies.

□ Government Consumption

Government Consumption refers to the expenditure on the consumption of the public services provided by the government to the whole society and the net expenditure on the goods and services provided by the government to the households at free charge or lower prices in a certain period of time. The former equals to the output value of the government services minus the value of operating income obtained by the government departments. (The output value of the government services equals to its current operating expenditure plus depreciation of fixed assets). The latter equals to the market value of the goods and services provided by the government free of charge or at low prices to the households minus the value received by the government from the households.

□ Total Capital Formation

Total Capital Formation refers to the fixed assets acquired minus those disposed and the change in inventory, including the total fixed capital assets formation and the increase in inventory.

□ Total Fixed Capital Formation

Total Fixed Capital Formation refers to the value of fixed assets acquired minus those disposed of during a given period. Fixed assets are the assets produced through production activities with specified unit value which could be used for over one year, excluding natural assets. Total fixed capital formation can be categorized into total tangible capital formation and total intangible capital formation. The total tangible capital formation include the value of the construction projects, installation projects completed and the equipment, apparatus and instruments purchased as well as the value of land improved, the value of draught animals, breeding stock, animals for milk, wool and for recreational purpose, and the newly increased forest with economic value during a given period. The total intangible capital formation includes the prospecting of minerals, the acquisition of computer software minus the disposal of them.

EXPLANATORY NOTES TO MAJOR STATISTICAL INDICATORS

□ Increase in Inventory

Increase in Inventory refers to the market value of the change in inventory of resident units during a given period, i.e. the difference of value between the beginning and the end of the period minus the current gains due to the change in prices. The increase in inventory can be positive or negative. A positive value indicates the increase in inventory while a negative value indicates the decrease in stock. The inventory includes the raw materials, fuels and reserve materials purchased by the production units as well as the inventory of finished products, semi–finished products, work–in–progress, etc.

□ Net Outflow of Goods and Services

Net Outflow of Goods and Service refers to difference of outflow of goods and service minus inflow of goods and service. The outflow includes the value of various goods and service sold or gratuitously transferred by resident unit to non–resident unit, and the inflow includes the value of various goods and service sold or gratuitously transferred by non–resident unit to resident unit. The net outflow of district, include the net outflow of foreign trade or non–trade of local district, and also the difference of outflow minus inflow of goods and service between domestic districts.

□ Information Industry

Information Industry refers to the aggregation of all kinds of activities related to electronic information, including manufactory and distribution of information–related products and information service. As accounted by referring to relevant documents of several industries, the value added of the information industry shall not be counted together with that of other industries in the Shanghai GDP to avoid repetitive computation.

□ Tourism Industry

Tourism Industry refers to those tourism–related industries that provide tourism services to domestic and overseas tourists, including: travel agency service, transportation service, hostelling service, telecommunication service, entertainment service, catering service and retailing service, etc.. As accounted by referring to relevant cross–industry data of several industries, the value added of the tourism industry shall not be counted together with that of other industries in the Shanghai GDP to avoid repetitive computation.

□ Whole–society Labor Productivity

Whole–society Labor Productivity refers to the output value (or added value) per capita created by whole–society labors during a certain period. It's an important indicator to evaluate the production efficiency of labors in existence. Of which, the Average Quantity of Employees includes the informality registered employees.

Whole–society Labor Productivity = GDP / Yearly Average Quantity of Employees

□ Fixed Assets Output Rate

Fixed Assets Output Rate refers to the ratio between output value (or added value) and original value of operating fixed assets, viz. output value (or added value) provided by operating fixed assets per unit. It shows the invest benefit of operating fixed assets, and is an important indicator to reflect the output efficiency of fixed assets.

Fixed Assets Output Rate = GDP / Yearly Average Original Value of Operating Fixed Assets

第五篇

CHAPTER 5

财政收支

FISCAL REVENUE AND EXPENDITURE

表5.1　财政收入(1978～2007)
FISCAL REVENUES

单位:亿元 (100 million yuan)

年　份 Year	全市财政收　入 Fiscal Revenue	其　中　of which #中央财政收　入 Central Fiscal Revenue	#地方财政收　入 Local Fiscal Revenue	在地方财政收入中　of Local Fiscal Revenue 税收收入 Taxes	亏损补贴 Loss Subsidies	地方附加收入 Local Additional Revenue	地方财政支　出 Local Fiscal Expenditure
1978	190.67	21.45	169.22			2.38	26.01
1979	192.75	20.06	172.69			2.53	27.06
1980	198.85	24.12	174.73			2.68	19.18
1981	204.52	30.17	174.35			2.82	19.06
1982	200.69	32.70	167.99			2.91	20.68
1983	204.34	47.95	156.39			2.69	22.39
1984	215.79	51.83	163.96			2.86	30.32
1985	263.86	79.63	184.23			2.64	46.07
1986	257.72	78.26	179.46			3.36	59.08
1987	241.36	72.39	168.97			3.84	53.85
1988	261.69	100.07	161.62			4.15	65.88
1989	297.25	130.37	166.88			3.87	73.31
1990	284.36	114.33	166.99	183.31	-28.74	4.26	75.56
1991	324.66	149.13	175.53	182.88	-25.26	4.54	86.05
1992	340.10	154.54	185.56	188.61	-24.81	6.71	94.99
1993	439.53	197.19	242.34	252.99	-33.59	6.09	129.26
1994	615.91	440.58	175.33	196.60	-42.07	5.71	196.98
1995	702.46	475.16	227.30	240.06	-44.95	7.69	267.89
1996	873.76	585.26	288.49	308.26	-45.50	8.03	342.66
1997	1 070.95	718.62	352.33	369.23	-45.88	9.95	428.92
1998	1 146.00	751.49	392.22	406.73	-45.94	11.53	480.70
1999	1 390.58	952.36	431.85	427.23	-44.85	11.90	546.38
2000	1 752.69	1 246.47	497.96	484.00	-37.23	12.73	622.84
2001	1 995.62	1 371.49	620.24	589.91	-36.23	10.79	726.38
2002	2 202.25	1 479.06	719.79	657.70	-35.52	10.84	877.84
2003	2 828.87	1 926.51	899.29	796.87	-36.19	13.06	1 102.64
2004	3 591.73	2 400.46	1 119.72	1 036.23	-27.51	13.52	1 395.69
2005	4 095.81	2 651.81	1 433.90	1 238.40	-17.99	16.50	1 660.32
2006	4 798.93	3 157.02	1 600.37	1 393.97	-4.84	24.29	1 813.80
2007	7 310.26	5 207.63	2 102.63	1 975.48	-8.30	28.15	2 201.92

注：本表数据由市财政局提供。
Note: Data in the table are provided by Shanghai Municipal Financial Bureau.

表 5.2 主要年份地方财政收入
LOCAL FISCAL REVENUE IN MAIN YEARS

指 标	Indicators	2000	2006	2007
地方财政收入(亿元)	**Local Fiscal Revenue (100 million yuan)**	**497.96**	**1 600.37**	**2 102.63**
#增值税	Value-added Tax	93.55	270.21	313.42
营业税	Business Tax	153.81	558.67	714.60
企业所得税	Enterprise Income Tax	103.03	270.63	425.63
证券交易印花税	Stamp Tax of Stock Transaction	28.04	3.46	39.93
城市维护建设税	City Maintenance Tax	22.01	52.97	65.53
个人所得税	Personal Income Tax	60.24	131.07	169.44
房产税	Real Estate Tax	13.24	42.68	42.83
#市级财政收入	Fiscal Revenue at Municipal Level	215.81	782.65	1 083.05
区县级财政收入	Fiscal Revenue at District (County) Level	282.15	817.71	1 019.58
地方财政收入构成(%)	**Compostion of Local Fiscal Revenue(%)**	**100**	**100**	**100**
#增值税	Value-added Tax	18.8	16.9	14.9
营业税	Business Tax	30.9	34.9	34.0
企业所得税	Enterprise Income Tax	20.7	16.9	20.2
证券交易印花税	Stamp Tax of Stock Transaction	5.6	0.2	1.9
城市维护建设税	City Maintenance Tax	4.4	3.3	3.1
个人所得税	Personal Income Tax	12.1	8.2	8.1
房产税	Real Estate Tax	2.7	2.7	2.0
#市级财政收入	Fiscal Revenue at Municipal Level	43.3	48.9	51.5
区县级财政收入	Fiscal Revenue at District (County) Level	56.7	51.1	48.5

注：本表数据由市财政局提供。
Note: Date in the table are provided by Shanghai Municipal Financical Bureau.

表5.3 主要年份各区、县级财政收支
FISICAL REVENUE AND EXPENDITURES OF DISTRICTS AND COUNTIES IN MAIN YEARS

单位:亿元 (100 million yuan)

地区	District	地方财政收入 Local Fiscal Revenue			地方财政支出 Local Fiscal Expenditure		
		2000	2006	2007	2000	2006	2007
总 计	**Total**	**225.74**	**817.71**	**1 019.58**	**261.45**	**1 205.16**	**1 431.63**
浦东新区	Pudong New Area	56.41	178.31	260.80	69.70	222.58	287.24
黄浦区	Huangpu	21.91	42.55	45.96	22.80	59.78	64.18
卢湾区	Luwan	11.37	26.84	33.50	11.32	35.04	42.07
徐汇区	Xuhui	15.40	48.30	64.02	19.10	61.32	77.87
长宁区	Changning	13.74	39.78	46.09	14.80	51.62	58.63
静安区	Jing'an	11.00	34.62	40.68	11.27	43.29	49.42
普陀区	Putuo	12.70	35.02	36.98	14.56	51.94	56.50
闸北区	Zhabei	11.89	26.67	30.10	13.95	42.15	47.81
虹口区	Hongkou	14.20	33.63	35.35	16.35	48.79	56.06
杨浦区	Yangpu	11.52	29.80	35.34	14.70	49.85	58.46
宝山区	Baoshan	16.17	45.10	52.15	17.60	70.80	79.25
闵行区	Minhang	18.98	68.30	85.66	20.65	85.75	102.07
嘉定区	Jiading	13.33	42.68	50.52	16.12	72.66	79.44
金山区	Jinshan	8.16	21.64	22.82	13.61	44.77	47.69
松江区	Songjiang	12.12	39.22	54.00	13.34	65.53	80.97
青浦区	Qingpu	13.24	34.19	39.73	15.36	59.90	66.92
南汇区	Nanhui	8.12	33.53	41.44	9.75	57.02	68.27
奉贤区	Fengxian	6.53	22.56	25.94	8.04	42.79	49.00
崇明县	Chongming	5.36	14.97	18.52	8.13	39.56	59.78

注：本表数据由市财政局提供。
Note: Date in the table are provided by Shanghai Municipal Financial Bureau.

表5.4 地方财政支出(2006~2007)
LOCAL FISCAL EXPENDITURES

指 标	Indicators	2006	2007
地方财政支出(亿元)	**Local Fiscal Expenditure (100 million yuan)**	**1 813.80**	**2 201.92**
#一般公共服务	Common Public Service	168.94	182.61
公共安全	Public Security	121.83	134.33
教 育	Education	235.17	283.33
社会保障和就业	Social Security and Jobs	174.78	274.22
城乡社区事务	Urban and Country Community Affairs	291.16	385.85
工业商业金融等事务	Industrial, Commercial and Financial Affairs	264.35	290.75
#市级财政支出	Fiscal Expenditure at Municipal Level	608.64	770.29
区县级财政支出	Fiscal Expenditure at District (County) Level	1 205.16	1 431.63
地方财政支出(%)	**Local Fiscal Expenditure (%)**	**100**	**100**
#一般公共服务	Common Public Service	9.3	8.3
公共安全	Public Security	6.7	6.1
教 育	Education	13.0	12.9
社会保障和就业	Social Security and Jobs	9.6	12.5
城乡社区事务	Urban and Country Community Affairs	16.1	17.5
工业商业金融等事务	Industrial, Commercial and Financial Affairs	14.6	13.2
#市级财政支出	Fiscal Expenditure at Municipal Level	33.6	35.0
区县级财政支出	Fiscal Expenditure at District (County) Level	66.4	65.0

注：本表数据由市财政局提供。
Note: Date in the table are provided by Shanghai Municipal Financial Bureau.

表5.5 主要年份税收收入
TAXATION IN MAIN YEARS

单位:亿元(100 million yuan)

指 标	Indicators	2000	2006	2007
税收收入	**Taxation**	**1 479.21**	**4 141.85**	**6 470.53**
#国内增值税	Domestic Value Added Tax	380.21	1 082.94	1 255.27
国内消费税	Domestic Excise	69.71	154.60	181.12
海关代征	Custom Taxation	313.04	986.79	1 220.84
营业税	Business Tax	171.42	558.71	714.64
企业所得税	Enterprise Income Tax	142.47	511.79	801.19
涉外企业所得税	Foreign Enterprise Income Tax	43.89	214.04	310.25
个人所得税	Personal Income Tax	67.79	327.54	423.52
证券交易印花税	Stamp Tax of Stock Transaction	245.49	115.71	1 330.99

注：本表数据由市税务局提供。
Note: Date in the table are provided by Shanghai Local Taxation Bureau.

上 / 海 / 统 / 计 / 年 / 鉴

主要统计指标解释

财政收入

指国家财政参与社会产品分配所取得的收入，是实现国家职能的财力保证。财政收入所包括的内容几经变化，目前主要包括：

(1)各项税收：包括增值税、营业税、消费税、土地增值税、城市维护建设税、资源税、城市土地使用税、企业所得税、个人所得税、关税、证券交易印花税、车辆购置税、农牧业税和耕地占用税等。

(2)专项收入：包括排污费收入、城市水资源费收入、矿产资源补偿费收入、教育费附加收入等。

(3)其他收入：包括利息收入、基本建设贷款归还收入、基本建设收入、捐赠收入等。

(4)国有企业亏损补贴：此项为负收入，冲减财政收入。主要包括对工业企业、商业企业、粮食企业的补贴。

中央财政收入和地方财政收入

指按现行分税制财政体制划分的中央本级收入和地方本级收入。1994 年实行分税制财政体制以后，属于中央财政的收入主要包括关税、海关代征消费税和增值税，消费税，企业所得税中央部分，铁道部门、各银行总行、各保险总公司等集中缴纳的营业税、利润和城市维护建设税，车辆购置税，船舶吨税，增值税的 75%部分，证券交易印花税 97%部分，个人所得税中央部分，海洋石油资源税。属于地方财政的收入主要包括营业税，企业所得税地方部分，城镇土地使用税，固定资产投资方向调节税，城市维护建设税，房产税，车船使用税，印花税，耕地占用税，契税，土地增值税、国有土地有偿使用收入，增值税 25%部分，证券交易印花税 3%部分和除海洋石油资源税以外的其他资源税。

地方财政支出

根据政府在经济和社会活动中的不同职责，划分中央和地方政府的责权，按照政府的责权划分确定的支出。中央财政支出包括国防支出，武装警察部队支出，中央级行政管理费和各项事业费，重点建设支出以及中央政府调整国民经济结构、协调地区发展、实施宏观调控的支出。地方财政支出主要包括一般公共服务，公共安全，教育，科学技术，文化体育与传媒，社会保障和就业，医疗卫生，环境保护，城乡社区事务，农林水事务，交通运输，工业商业金融等事务等。

SHANGHAI STATISTICAL YEARBOOK

EXPLANATORY NOTES TO MAJOR STATISTICAL INDICATORS

□ Fiscal Revenue

Fiscal Revenue refers to the revenue of the government finance by means of participating in the distribution of the social products, which is the financial resources for ensuring the government to function. The contents of fiscal revenue have been changed several times. Now it includes the following main items:

(1) Various tax revenues, including value added tax, business tax, consumption tax, land value added tax, tax on city maintenance and construction, resources tax, tax on use of urban land, enterprise income tax, personal income tax, tariff, stamp tax on security transactions, tax on purchase of motor vehicles, tax on agriculture and animal husbandry and tax on occupancy of cultivated land, etc.

(2) Special revenues, including revenues from the fee on sewage treatment, fee on urban water resources, fee for the compensation of mineral resources and extra-charges for education, etc.

(3) Other revenues, including revenue from interest, revenue from the repayment of capital construction loan, revenue from capital construction projects, and donations and grants.

(4) Subsidies for the losses of the state-owned enterprises. This is an item of negative revenue, consisting of subsidies to industrial, commercial and grain purchasing and supply enterprises.

□ Central Fiscal Revenue and Local Fiscal Revenue

Central Fiscal Revenue and Local Fiscal Revenue: refer to the revenue of the central government and that of the local governments as defined by the decentralized taxation system starting from 1994. In accordance with this system, the revenue of the central government includes tariff, consumption tax and value added tax levied by the customs, consumption tax, part of the enterprises income tax for central government, business tax, profits and the tax on town maintenance and construction of railways, head offices of banks, head office of insurance company, which are handed over to the government in a centralized way, tax on purchasing motor vehicles, tonnage tax of ships, 75% of the value added tax, 97% of the tax on stock dealing (stamp tax), proportion of the personal income tax (other that interest income tax) to be shared by the central government, and tax on ocean petroleum resources. The revenue of the local governments includes business tax, part of the enterprises income tax for local government, tax on the use of urban land, tax on the adjustment of the investment in fixed assets, tax on town maintenance and construction, tax on real estates, tax on the use of vehicles and ships, stamp tax, tax on the occupancy of cultivated land, contract tax, value-added tax on land, income from charges on use of state-owned land, 25% of the value added tax, 3% of the tax on stock dealing (stamp tax) and tax on resources other than the ocean petroleum resources.

□ Fiscal Expenditure of Local Government

According to the different responsibility of government in the economic and social activities, the government has been divided into central government and local government, and the expenditure of them has been divided accordingly. Fiscal expenditure of central government includes the expenditures on national defense, armed police, administrative and operating activities of central government. And also on the basic construction and central government's adjusting national economic structure, harmonizing district development and economic macro-controlling. Fiscal expenditure of local government includes the expenditure on local administrative and operating activities, public security, education, science and technology, culture, sports and communication, social security and employment, health care, community affairs in districts and counties, affairs of agriculture, forest and water, transport, industrial affairs, business affairs and financial affairs.

第六篇

CHAPTER 6

固定资产投资

INVESTMENT IN FIXED ASSETS

表 6.1　全社会固定资产投资总额(按管理渠道分)(1978～2007)
TOTAL INVESTMENT IN FIXED ASSETS(GROUPED BY ADMINISTRATIVE CHANNELS)

单位:亿元(100 million yuan)

年　份 Year	合　计 Total	其　中 of which						
		基本建设 Capital Construction	更新改造 Technical Update and Transformation	其他投资 Other Investment	房地产开发 Investment in Real Estate	农村集体 Rural Collective	城镇私人建房 Urban Private Home Construction	农村私人建房 Rural Private Home Construction
1978	27.91	14.46	5.60	3.77		2.96	0.09	0.79
1979	35.58	21.13	7.69	3.26		2.17	0.14	0.94
1980	45.43	25.73	11.30	3.24		3.01	0.17	1.41
1981	54.60	30.80	11.18	3.02		4.65	0.20	3.97
1982	71.34	43.63	14.41	3.58		4.06	0.29	4.32
1983	75.94	43.01	17.44	4.56		4.95	0.25	4.48
1984	92.30	47.42	22.56	5.82		7.07	0.24	7.28
1985	118.56	57.05	35.61	3.26		7.04	0.20	12.00
1986	146.93	71.37	46.83	4.26		9.80	0.18	10.30
1987	186.30	92.10	57.39	4.02	0.97	13.84	0.53	12.66
1988	245.27	115.55	76.95	4.55	1.68	22.19	0.66	16.90
1989	214.76	111.76	61.88	3.42	1.85	16.94	0.64	14.32
1990	227.08	108.54	71.77	3.77	8.16	14.38	0.59	15.96
1991	258.30	108.90	95.21	3.91	7.59	23.62	0.70	14.17
1992	357.38	129.60	126.84	6.52	12.71	55.42	0.55	17.00
1993	653.91	273.64	220.30	9.91	22.04	104.82	2.13	5.33
1994	1 123.29	511.24	304.01	13.99	117.43	141.23	1.21	10.40
1995	1 601.79	551.86	389.20	16.33	466.20	139.57	0.72	13.10
1996	1 952.05	651.28	415.73	12.43	657.79	158.32	1.09	20.00
1997	1 977.59	762.00	386.24	7.43	614.23	166.16	1.09	16.80
1998	1 964.83	844.15	365.01	13.44	577.12	137.40	1.41	12.76
1999	1 856.72	786.81	393.59	9.88	514.83	134.33	1.23	5.54
2000	1 869.67	703.50	396.26	21.21	566.17	161.61	1.50	10.36
2001	1 994.73	712.49	436.84	30.70	630.73	173.13	1.06	9.28
2002	2 187.06	784.13	422.58	54.93	748.89	167.92	1.13	6.87
2003	2 452.11	927.29	388.01	57.01	901.24	170.00	2.07	6.49
2004	3 084.66	1 721.56			1 175.46	180.82	0.95	5.86
2005	3 542.55	1 984.61			1 246.86	304.00		7.08
2006	3 925.09	2 246.93			1 275.59	396.60		5.96
2007	4 458.61	2 775.81			1 307.53	370.06		5.21

注:2004 年起,全社会投资由城镇投资和农村投资两部分组成。其中城镇投资包括建设改造投资和房地产开发投资,农村投资包括农村集体和农村私人建房。

Note: Since 2004, total investment in fix assets was composed of urban investment and rural investment. Urban investment includes construction rebuild investment and real estate investment, and rural investment includes rural collective investment and rural private home construction.

表6.2 全社会固定资产投资总额(按经济类型分)(1978～2007)
TOTAL INVESTMENT IN FIXED ASSETS (GROUPED BY ECONOMIC TYPES)

单位:亿元(100 million yuan)

年 份 Year	合 计 Total	其 中 of which #国 有 经 济 State-owned	#集 体 经 济 Collective-owned	#股份制 经 济 Shareholding	#外商、港澳台 经 济 Hong Kong, Macao, Taiwan and Foreign Funded
1978	27.91	23.83	3.20		
1979	35.58	32.08	2.42		
1980	45.43	40.27	3.58		
1981	54.60	45.00	5.43		
1982	71.34	61.62	5.11		
1983	75.94	65.01	6.20		
1984	92.30	75.80	8.98		
1985	118.56	95.92	10.44		
1986	146.93	122.46	13.99		
1987	186.30	154.45	18.65		
1988	245.27	198.68	29.03		
1989	214.76	178.81	21.00		
1990	227.08	192.24	18.29		
1991	258.30	215.61	27.82		
1992	357.38	275.67	64.16		
1993	653.91	419.22	124.18	32.83	61.61
1994	1 123.29	721.37	189.75	76.99	101.78
1995	1 601.79	935.92	247.11	150.17	208.30
1996	1 952.05	1 048.27	239.47	165.57	340.18
1997	1 977.59	1 148.69	257.10	118.80	367.50
1998	1 964.83	1 087.94	208.84	203.81	405.17
1999	1 856.72	986.82	227.19	268.68	325.58
2000	1 869.67	829.98	156.34	421.53	319.05
2001	1 994.73	760.58	136.81	580.75	362.25
2002	2 187.06	742.72	101.33	631.70	369.96
2003	2 452.11	811.85	116.63	647.27	468.20
2004	3 084.66	955.12	146.58	667.52	851.39
2005	3 542.55	1 240.27	131.07	916.27	640.31
2006	3 925.09	1 460.09	159.31	910.31	725.85
2007	4 458.61	1 779.43	121.51	1 169.49	711.35

表6.3 主要年份全社会固定资产投资主要指标
MAJOR INDICATORS OF TOTAL INVESTMENT IN FIXED ASSETS IN MAIN YEARS

单位:亿元(100 million yuan)

指标	Indicators	1990	2000	2006	2007
投资总额	**Total Investment**	**227.08**	**1 869.67**	**3 925.09**	**4 458.61**
按隶属关系分	**Grouped by Administrative Relationship**				
中央项目	Central Government Projects	75.49	257.67	532.93	720.91
地方项目	Local Projects	151.59	1 612.00	3 392.16	3 737.70
按构成分	**Grouped by Use of Funds**				
建筑安装工程	Construction and Installation	127.63	882.91	2 114.01	2 418.61
设备、工具、器具购置	Purchase of Equipment and Instruments	79.51	482.47	762.24	941.22
其他费用	Others	19.94	504.29	1 048.84	1 098.78
按建设性质分	**Grouped by Type of Construction**				
#新　建	New Construction	78.01	730.76	1 801.45	2 005.41
改　建	Reconstruction	70.48	216.40	261.04	326.09
扩　建	Expansion	47.50	216.71	415.33	510.84
单纯建造生活设施	Construction of Living Facilities	24.00	39.02	13.03	193.66
按产业分	**Grouped by Type of Industry**				
第一产业	Primary Industry	3.20	7.87	14.29	8.37
第二产业	Secondary Industry	133.00	615.94	1 212.71	1 397.57
第三产业	Tertiary Industry	90.88	1 245.86	2 698.09	3 052.67
#住　宅	Residential Housing	42.94	443.90	854.15	853.13
按经济类型分	**Grouped by Economic Types**				
国有经济	State-owned		829.98	1 460.09	1 779.43
非国有经济	Non-state-owned		1 039.69	2 465.00	2 679.18
集体经济	Collective-owned		156.34	159.31	121.51
私营经济	Private		83.29	626.93	644.71
联营经济	Joint Owned		41.20	21.36	15.67
股份制经济	Shareholding		421.53	910.31	1 169.49
外商经济	Foreign Funded		222.86	547.48	522.15
港澳台经济	Hong Kong, Macao and Taiwan Funded		96.19	178.37	189.21
其他经济	Others		18.28	21.24	16.45
新增固定资产	**Newly Increased Fixed Assets**	**222.99**	**1 493.35**	**2 680.85**	**2 466.68**
固定资产交付使用率(%)	Rate of Fixed Assets Transfered and in Use(%)	98.2	79.9	68.3	55.3
房屋建筑面积(万平方米)	**Floor Space of Buildings (10 000 sq. m)**				
施工面积	Floor Space Under Construction	3 801.46	8 636.31	14 596.49	14 979.37
#住　宅	Residential Housing	2 269.06	4 804.12	8 085.28	7 789.91
竣工面积	Floor Space Completed	2 138.44	3 266.52	4 901.46	5 068.46
#住　宅	Residential Housing	1 339.02	1 724.02	2 746.80	2 843.62

注：从2000年起，固定资产投资统计起点为50万元以上(含50万元)项目，按建设性质分中不包括房地产开发投资。
Note: Since 2000, the statistics that have been collected are about projects of fixed assets investment each involving 500,000 yuan and more. In "Type of Construction" the investment in real estate development is excluded.

表6.4 建设改造投资主要指标(2007)
MAJOR INDICATORS OF INVESTMENT FOR CONSTRUCTION AND TRANSFORMATION

单位:亿元(100 million yuan)

指 标	Indicators	全 市 Total	#地 方 Local Projects
投资总额	**Total Investment**	**2 775.81**	**2 063.50**
按建设性质分	**Grouped by Type of Construction**		
#新 建	New Construction	1 767.51	1 542.38
改 建	Reconstruction	287.66	162.08
扩 建	Expansion	449.58	236.55
单纯建造生活设施	Construction of Living Facilities	173.75	104.32
按产业分	**Grouped by Type of Industry**		
第一产业	Primary Industry	3.65	3.65
第二产业	Secondary Industry	1 124.86	692.82
第三产业	Tertiary Industry	1 647.30	1 367.03
#住 宅	Residential Housing	11.09	1.39
按行业分	**Grouped by Economic Sectors**		
#工 业	Industry	1 122.70	690.67
交通运输、仓储和邮政业	Transportation, Storage and Post Industries	861.11	733.32
信息传输、计算机服务和软件业	Information Transmission,Computer Servcie and Software Industries	111.20	12.68
批发和零售业	Retail and Wholesale	20.96	20.96
住宿和餐饮业	Hotel and Eateries	23.95	23.93
金融业	Financial Industry	5.21	4.78
房地产业	Real Estate Industry	140.97	140.96
租赁和商务服务业	Leasing and Business Service	13.56	13.53
科学研究、技术服务和地质勘查业	Scientific Research,Technology Service and Geological Prospecting	23.19	16.73
水利、环境和公共设施管理业	Water Conservancy,Environment and Public Facility Management	310.74	308.79
居民服务和其他服务业	Residents Service and Other Service	2.34	2.34
教 育	Education	65.71	21.52
卫生、社会保障和社会福利业	Health,Social Security and Welfare	20.58	20.50
文化、体育和娱乐业	Culture,Sports and Entertainment	27.70	26.91
公共管理和社会组织	Public Administration and Social Organizations	20.08	20.08
新增固定资产	**Newly Increased Fixed Assets**	**1 136.35**	**722.46**
固定资产交付使用率(%)	Rate of Fixed Assets Transfered and in Use(%)	49.9	35.0
房屋建筑面积(万平方米)	**Floor Space of Buildings (10 000 sq. m)**		
施工面积	Floor Space Under Construction	2 687.78	2 306.71
#住 宅	Residential Housing	101.97	36.21
竣工面积	Floor Space Completed	940.37	751.84
#住 宅	Residential Housing	56.73	16.99

注：本表不包括农村投资。
Note: Data of this table exclude rural investment.

表6.5 地方固定资产投资主要指标(2005～2007)
MAJOR INDICATORS OF LOCAL INVESTMENT IN FIXED ASSETS

单位:亿元(100 million yuan)

指 标	Indicators	2005	2006	2007
投资总额	**Total Investment**	**3 122.13**	**3 392.16**	**3 737.70**
按构成分	**Grouped by Use of Funds**			
建筑安装工程	Construction and Installation	1 912.76	1 885.98	2 107.82
设备、工具、器具购置	Purchase of Equipment and Instruments	412.84	500.45	577.25
其他费用	Others	796.53	1 005.75	1 052.63
按建设性质分	**Grouped by Type of Construction**			
#新 建	New Construction	1 412.19	1 589.97	1 778.90
改 建	Reconstruction	165.23	164.56	200.43
扩 建	Expansion	199.12	238.86	297.17
单纯建造生活设施	Construction of Living Facilities	9.85	13.03	124.24
按产业分	**Grouped by Type of Industry**			
第一产业	Primary Industry	5.50	14.25	8.23
第二产业	Secondary Industry	800.47	906.15	963.69
第三产业	Tertiary Industry	2 316.16	2 471.76	2 765.77
#住 宅	Residential Housing	932.36	846.59	840.80
按行业分	**Grouped by Sectors**			
#工 业	Industry	797.70	903.72	960.99
交通运输、仓储和邮政业	Transportation, Storage, Postal and Telecommunications	381.35	575.26	747.99
信息传输、计算机服务和软件业	Information Transmission, Computer Servcie and Software Industries	10.82	13.92	12.68
批发和零售业	Wholesale and Retail	38.57	46.98	48.54
住宿和餐饮业	Hotel and Eateries	33.67	26.52	30.51
金融业	Finance	0.99	5.81	4.78
房地产业	Real Estate	1 370.42	1 387.94	1 450.65
租赁和商务服务业	Leasing and Business Service	18.03	9.88	13.94
科学研究、技术服务和地质勘查业	Scientific Research, Technology Service and Geological Prospecting	12.76	20.18	17.61
水利、环境和公共设施管理业	Water Conservancy, Environment and Public Facility Management	318.06	288.35	332.17
居民服务和其他服务业	Residents Service and Other Service	1.99	2.48	4.68
教 育	Education	33.22	30.45	29.67
卫生、社会保障和社会福利业	Health, Social Security and Welfare	18.26	25.31	22.91
文化、体育和娱乐业	Culture, Sports and Entertainment	61.69	11.81	28.52
公共管理和社会组织	Public Administration and Social Organizations	16.33	26.86	21.12
新增固定资产	**Newly Increased Fixed Assets**	**2 033.39**	**2 378.04**	**2 050.85**
固定资产交付使用率(%)	Rate of Fixed Assets Transfered and in Use(%)	65.1	70.1	54.9
房屋建筑面积(万平方米)	**Floor Space of Buildings (10 000 sq. m)**			
施工面积	Floor Space Under Construction	14 087.25	14 139.18	14 542.25
#住 宅	Residential Housing	8 205.07	8 033.03	7 702.34
竣工面积	Floor Space Completed	4 697.36	4 796.34	4 870.85
#住 宅	Residential Housing	2 803.00	2 739.15	2 800.96

表6.6 工业各行业建设改造投资主要指标(2007)
MAIN INDICATORS OF INVESTMENT FOR CONSTRUCTION AND TRANSFORMATION BY INDUSTRIAL SECTORS

行　业	Sectors	施工项目(个) Projects Under Construction (unit)	全部建成投产项目(个) Projects Completed and Put into Production (unit)	建成投产率(%) Rate of Projects Completed and Put into Use(%)	建设改造投资额(亿元) Construction and Transformation Investment (100 million yuan)
总　计	**Total**	**3 689**	**2 088**	**76.7**	**1 394.86**
采矿业	**Excavation**	**20**	**16**	**25.0**	**17.20**
石油和天然气开采业	Petroleum and Natural Gas Exploiting	3			14.80
非金属矿采选业	Nonmetal Minerals Mining	17	16	6.3	1.76
其他采矿业	Other Excavation				0.65
制造业	**Manufacturing**	**2 757**	**1 349**	**104.4**	**1 152.12**
农副食品加工业	Farm and Sideline Products Processing	18	10	80.0	5.12
食品制造业	Food Manufacturing	28	9	211.1	14.96
饮料制造业	Beverage Manufacturing	18	10	80.0	3.88
烟草制品业	Tabacco Manufacturing	20	2	900.0	3.45
纺织业	Textile	57	29	96.6	12.46
纺织服装、鞋、帽制造业	Garments, Shoes and Accessories Manufacturing	97	61	59.0	15.46
皮革、毛皮、羽毛(绒)及其他制品业	Leather, Fur, and Wool Products Manufacturing	24	12	100.0	3.70
木材加工及木、竹、藤、棕、草制品业	Timber Processing and Timber, Bamboo, Rattan, Coir and Straw Products Manufacturing	20	14	42.9	3.02
家具制造业	Furniture Manufacturing	17	11	54.5	3.63
造纸及纸制品业	Paper-making and Paper Products Manufacturing	17	11	54.5	4.76
印刷业和记录媒介的复制	Printing and Record Duplicating	21	13	61.5	6.00
文教体育用品制造业	Stationary, Education and Sports Goods Manufacturing	27	21	28.6	4.57
石油加工、炼焦及核燃料加工业	Oil Processing, Coking and Nuclear Fuel Processing	17	10	70.0	29.87
化学原料及化学制品制造业	Raw Chemical Materials and Chemical Products Manufacturing	142	68	108.8	107.02
医药制造业	Medicine Manufacturing	31	11	181.8	6.65
化学纤维制造业	Chemical Fiber Manufacturing	14	8	75.0	2.81
橡胶制品业	Rubber Products Manufacturing	19	15	26.7	5.14
塑料制品业	Plastic Products Manufacturing	76	41	85.4	19.05
非金属矿物制品业	Nonmetal Mineral Products	49	30	63.3	11.66
黑色金属冶炼及压延加工业	Smelting and Pressing of Ferrous Metals	359	185	94.1	268.77
有色金属冶炼及压延加工业	Smelting and Pressing of Nonferrous Metals	29	15	93.3	10.80
金属制品业	Metal Products Manufacturing	136	69	97.1	37.54
通用设备制造业	General Equipment Manufacturing	709	336	111.0	97.49
专用设备制造业	Special Purpose Equipment Manufacturing	137	63	117.5	39.94
交通运输设备制造业	Transportation Equipment Manufacturing	174	63	176.2	143.72
电气机械及器材制造业	Electric Machinery Equipments and Manufacturing	155	84	84.5	43.37
通信设备、计算机及其他电子设备制造业	Communications Equipment, Computer and Other Electronic Equipment Manufacturing	105	44	138.6	180.18
仪器仪表及文化、办公用机械制造业	Instruments, Meters, Culture and Office Equipments Manufacturing	23	15	53.3	4.18
工艺品及其他制造业	Artworks and Other Manufacturing	217	89	143.8	61.96
废弃资源和废旧材料回收加工业	Waste Resources and Materials Recycling and Processing	1			0.98
电力、燃气及水的生产和供应业	**Power, Gas, Water Production and Supply**	**912**	**723**	**26.1**	**225.53**
电力、热力的生产和供应业	Power and Heat Production and Supply	652	527	23.7	164.63
燃气生产和供应业	Gas Production and Supply	132	125	5.6	10.78
水的生产和供应业	Water Production and Supply	128	71	80.3	50.12

表6.7 主要年份新增固定资产
NEWLY INCREASED FIXED ASSETS IN MAIN YEARS

年 份 Year	新增固定资产 (亿元) Newly Increased Fixed Assets (100 million yuan)	其 中 of which #房地产开发 Investment in Real Estate Development	固定资产交付使用率(%) Rate of Fixed Assets Transferred and in Use(%)
1978	17.46	62.6	
1980	23.71	52.2	
1985	75.64	63.8	
1990	222.99	4.97	98.2
1995	826.94	127.08	51.6
1996	1 199.10	318.58	61.4
1997	1 316.43	427.19	66.6
1998	1 534.90	508.32	78.1
1999	1 858.70	427.66	100.1
2000	1 493.35	477.39	79.9
2001	1 178.24	519.20	59.1
2002	1 207.33	536.22	55.2
2003	1 618.45	812.56	66.0
2004	2 122.14	825.23	68.8
2005	2 547.02	1 054.02	71.9
2006	2 680.85	1 058.94	68.3
2007	2 466.68	1 048.47	55.3

表6.8 主要年份固定资产投资资金来源
CAPITAL SOURCES OF INVESTMENT IN FIXED ASSETS IN MAIN YEARS

单位:亿元(100 million yuan)

指 标	Indicators	1990	2000	2006	2007
资金来源合计	**Total Capital Sources**	**261.46**	**2 061.66**	**5 746.69**	**6 281.70**
上年末结余资金	Balance at End of Previous Year	28.85	241.05	794.67	764.26
本年资金来源小计	Sub-total Capital Source of this Year	232.61	1 820.61	4 952.02	5 517.44
国家预算内资金	State Budgetary Funds	14.39	48.30	74.33	98.03
国内贷款	Domestic Loans	62.52	379.21	1 162.17	1 296.92
债 券	Bonds		4.85		18.79
利用外资	Foreign Investment	35.46	161.83	271.2	262.41
#外商直接投资	Foreign Direct Investment		73.71	210.46	201.98
自筹资金	Self-Financed Capital	94.13	905.46	2 265.02	2 364.93
#市自筹	Self-Financed by Municipal Government	32.12	72.63	102.39	83.03
企、事业单位自筹	Self-Financed by Enterprises and Institutions	57.13	509.93	1 964.7	2 059.20
其他资金	Other Capital	26.11	320.96	1 179.3	1 476.36
本年各项应付投资款	Investment Due to Pay of this Year		310.42	785.85	1 080.00
#工程款	Project Funds		76.52	348.98	383.87

表6.9 市重大项目完成情况(2007)
PROGRESS OF CITY'S MAJOR PROJECTS

单位:亿元(100 million yuan)

项　目	Item	本年完成投资额 Investment in 2007
世博园区场馆及配套项目	World Expo Site Pavilion and Related Facilities Item	11.19
世博园区主要基础设施项目	World Expo Site Main Infrastructure Item	12.14
轨道交通7号线工程	Rail Transport No.7	35.21
轨道交通8号线杨浦一期工程	Rail Transport No.8, Yangpu First Phase Project	29.04
西藏南路越江工程	South Xizang Road Tunnel Project	6.05
打浦路隧道复线	Dapu Road Tunnel (Multiple line)	2.06
宝钢集团浦钢搬迁工程	Pu Steel's Movement of Bao Steel	73.40
中船长兴基地及市政配套项目	Changxing Ship Building Base and Municipal Related Facilities	49.48
轨道交通6号线	Rail Transport No.6	29.70
轨道交通9号线一期工程	Rail Transport No.9, First Phase Project	21.48
轨道交通9号线二期(首段)工程	Rail Transport No.9, Second Phase Project(First Section)	18.81
轨道交通10号线	Rail Transport No.10	33.20
轨道交通11号线(北段)	Rail Transport No.11(North Section)	24.35
轨道交通2号线东延伸段	Rail Transport No.2 East Extension Project	12.00
罗店中心镇公共交通配套工程	Luodian Center Town Public Traffic Ralated Project	3.07
浦江镇公共交通配套工程	Pujiang Town Public Transportation Related Facilities	12.17
世博园区专用交通联络线工程	World Expo Site Accommodation Road Project	4.56
军工路越江工程	Jungong Road Tunnel Project	7.15
新建路越江工程	Xinjian Road Tunnel Project	26.37
人民路越江工程	Renmin Road Tunnel Project	25.30
上中路越江工程	Shangzhong Road Tunnel Project	2.44
河南路改建工程	Henan Road Rebuild Project	2.05
外滩东西通道	The Bund East and West Tunnel	2.75
浦东国际机场扩建工程	Pudong International Airport Extension Project	56.02
虹桥综合交通枢纽基础设施	Hongqiao Synthetical Traffic Hinge Layout, Land Prophase	81.66
罗泾港区二期工程	Luojing Port Area, second phase	9.82
上海港国际客运中心工程	Shanghai Yangtze River Bridge and Tunnel Project	7.72
苏州河环境综合整治三期工程	Suzhou Creek Environment Renovation Project, third phase	0.90
辰山植物园	Chenshan Arboretum	2.43
竹园污水处理厂升级改造工程	Zhuyuan Sewage Plant Improvement and Reconstruction Project	0.43
白龙港污水处理厂升级改造及扩容	Bailong Port Savage Plant Reconstruction and Expansion Project	6.51
液化天然气(LNG)项目	LNG Item	12.72

表 6.9 续表 continued

单位:亿元(100 million yuan)

项　目	Item	本年完成投资额 Investment in 2006
外高桥电厂三期工程	Waigaoqiao Electric Power Plant, Third Phase Project	52.22
500KV 静安输电变电	500KV Jingan Transmission Project	2.00
A14 上海长江桥隧工程	A14 Shanghai Yangtze River Bridge and Tunnel Project	35.35
A11 沪宁高速公路拓宽	A11 Huning Speedway Widen Project	7.61
A15 浦东机场高速公路	A15 (Pudong Airport Expressway)	15.23
A16 苏沪高速公路	A16 Suhu Speedway	1.50
闵浦二桥	Minpu Second Bridge	1.09
大芦线航道整治一期工程	Dalu Channel Regulation Project, first phase	3.02
赵家沟航道整治工程	Zhaojiagou Channel Regulation Project	1.72
郊区污水管网	Suburban Sewage Drainpipe Net	11.35
青草沙水源地	Qingcao Sandlot Water Source Base	2.63
上海光源工程	SSRF	4.79
纳米技术及应用国家工程研究中心	National Engineering Research Center for Nanotechnology	0.77
上海地面交通工具风洞中心项目	Shanghai Ground Vehicle Wind Tunnel Item	1.47
上海汽车工程研究院自主品牌	Shanghai Automotive Engineering Academy, R&D of Own Brands	1.31
上海化工区聚碳酸酯(PC)	Shanghai Chemical District PC	5.82
临港重型装备制造基础建设项目	Lin Port Heavy Equipment Product Base, Land Prophase	15.62
4.5 代 TFT-LCD 生产线项目	4.5 Edition TFT-LCD Product Line Item	23.84
12 英寸集成电路生产线项目	12 Inch IC Product Line Item	31.64
外高桥粮食储备库及码头设施项目	Waigaoqiao Foodstuff Storage and Dock Establishment	4.58
社区文化活动中心	Community Cultural Center	3.54
残疾人综合设施特奥竞赛训练基地	Synthetical Establishment for Handicapped and Training Base for Special Olympic Games	1.13
重大赛事场馆改造	Gymnasium Transformation for Special Olympic Games	3.22
文化广场改造	Cultural Square Transformation	1.60
上海市直升机工程	Shanghai Helicopter Project	0.69
音乐学院改扩建	Shanghai Conservatory of Music, Extension Project	1.16
交通大学闵行校区二期工程	Jiaotong University, Minhang Campus Second Phase Project	2.99
上海水产大学临港新校区一期	Shanghai Maritime University, Lingang Campus First Phase Project	6.00
上海应用技术学院奉贤校区一期	Shanghai Institute of Technology, Fengxian Campus First Phase Project	3.84

上 / 海 / 统 / 计 / 年 / 鉴

主要统计指标解释

全社会固定资产投资

固定资产投资是国民经济再生产活动的一个重要部分。固定资产投资额是以货币形式表现的在一定时期内建造和购置固定资产的工作量以及与此有关的费用总称。它是反映固定资产投资规模、结构和发展速度的综合性指标。按照现行国家统计制度,全社会固定资产投资包括建设改造、房地产开发、城乡集体经济单位、城乡私人建房和其他经济单位投资。

从 1997 年起,固定资产投资统计起点为 50 万元(含 50 万元)以上项目。

房地产开发投资

指各种登记注册类型的房地产开发公司、商品房建设公司及其他房地产开发法人单位和附属于其他法人单位实际从事房地产开发或经营活动的单位统一开发的包括统代建、拆迁还建的住宅、厂房、仓库、饭店、宾馆、度假村、写字楼、办公楼等房屋建筑物和配套的服务设施,土地开发工程(如道路、给水、排水、供电、供热、通讯、平整场地等基础设施工程)的投资;不包括单纯的土地交易活动。

固定资产投资按国民经济行业分

固定资产投资按国民经济行业分是根据建设项目建成投产后的主要产品或主要用途及社会经济活动性质来确定国民经济行业。一般情况下,一个建设项目或一个企业、事业单位只能属于一种国民经济行业。

固定资产投资按隶属关系分

固定资产投资按隶属关系分是按建设单位或企业、事业、行政单位的主管上级机关确定的。

(1)中央:是指中共中央、人大常委会和国务院各部、委、局、总公司以及直属机构直接领导的建设项目和企业、事业、行政单位。这些单位的固定资产投资计划由国务院各部门直接编制和下达,建设中所需物资、主要设备以及建设中的问题都由中央有关部门安排和解决。

(2)地方:是由省(自治区、直辖市)、地区(州、盟、省辖市)、县(旗、县级市)三级政府及业务主管部门直接领导和管理的建设项目、企业、事业、行政单位。地方项目还包括不隶属以上各级政府及主管部门的建设项目和企业、事业单位,如外商投资企业和无主管部门的企业等。

固定资产投资按构成分

固定资产投资按构成分是按其工作内容和实现方式来划分的,主要分为建筑安装工程,设备、工具、器具购置,其他费用三个部分。

(1)建筑安装工程(建筑安装工作量):指各种房屋、建筑物的建造工程和各种设备、装置的安装工程。包括各种房屋建造工程;各种用途设备基础和各种工业窑炉的砌筑工程及金属结构工程;为施工而进行的各种准备工作和临时工程以及完工后的清理工作等;铁路、道路的铺设,矿井的开凿及石油管道的架设等;水利工程;防空地下建筑等特殊工程;列入房屋工程预算内的暖气、卫生、通风、照明、煤气等设备的价值及装设油饰工程;列入建筑工程预算内的各种管道(蒸汽、压缩空气、石油、给排水等管道)、电力、电讯电缆导线等的敷设工程;以及各种机械设备的安装工程;为测定安装工程质量,对设备进行的试运工作;房地产开发单位进行的商品房屋开发建设工程、土地开发工程。

在安装工程中,不包括被安装设备本身的价值。

(2)设备、工具、器具购置:指建设单位或企、事业单位购置或自制的,达到固定资产标准的设备、工具、器具的价值。新建单位及扩建单位的新建车间,按照设计或计划要求购置或自制的全部设备、工具、器具,不论是否达到固定资产标准均计入"设备、工具、器具购置"中。

(3)其他费用:指在固定资产建造和购置过程中发生的,除上述几项内容以外的各种应分摊计入固定资产的费用。

固定资产投资的资金来源

固定资产投资的资金来源是根据固定资产投资的资金来源不同,分为国家预算内资金、国内贷款、债券、利用外资、自筹资金和其他资金来源。

(1)国家预算内资金:指中央财政和地方财政中由国家统筹安排的基本建设拨款和更新改造拨款,以及中央财政安排的专项拨款中用于基本建设的资金和基本建设拨款改贷款的资金等。

(2)国内贷款:指报告期内企、事业单位向银行及非银行金融机构借入的用于固定资产投资的各种国内借

主要统计指标解释

款。包括银行利用自有资金及吸收的存款发放的贷款、上级主管部门拨入的国内贷款、国家专项贷款(包括煤代油贷款、劳改煤矿专项贷款等)、地方财政专项资金安排的贷款、国内储备贷款、周转贷款等。

(3)债券:

(4)利用外资:指报告期内收到的用于固定资产投资的国外资金,包括统借统还、自借自还的国外贷款,中外合资项目中的外资,以及对外发行债券和股票等。国家统借统还的外资指由我国政府出面同外国政府、团体或金融组织签订贷款协议、并负责偿还本息的国外贷款。

(5)自筹资金:指建设单位报告期内收到的,用于进行固定资产投资的上级主管部门、地方和企、事业单位自筹资金。

(6)其他资金来源:指报告期内收到的除以上各种拨款、借款、自筹资金以外其他用于固定资产投资的资金。

固定资产投资按建设性质分

建设项目的性质一般分为新建、改建、扩建和单纯建造生活设施。

(1)新建:一般指从无到有"平地起家"开始建设的企业、事业和行政单位或独立的工程。现有企业、事业、行政单位一般不属于新建。但如有的单位原有基础很小,经过建设后新增的固定资产价值超过该企、事业、行政单位原有固定资产价值(原值)三倍以上的也应作为新建。

(2)改建:指现有企业、事业单位,对原有设施进行技术改造或更新(包括相应配套的辅助性生产、生活福利设施)的建设项目。现有企业、事业单位为适应市场变化的需要,而改变企业的主要产品种类(如军工企业转产民用品等)的建设项目,应作为改建。原有产品生产作业线由于各工序(车间)之间能力不平衡,为填平补齐充分发挥原有生产能力而增建不增加本企业主要产品设计能力的车间,也应作为改建。

(3)扩建:指在厂内或其他地点,为扩大原有产品的生产能力(或效益)或增加新的产品生产能力,而增建主要的生产车间(或主要工程)、分厂、独立的生产线。行政、事业单位在原单位增建业务用房(如学校增建教学用房、医院增建门诊部、病房等)也作为扩建。

现有企、事业单位为扩大原有主要产品生产能力或增加新的产品生产能力,增建一个或几个主要生产车间(或主要工程)、分厂,同时进行一些更新改造工程的,也应作为扩建。

(4)单纯建造生活设施:

新增固定资产

新增固定资产又称交付使用的固定资产,是指已经完成建造和购置过程,并已交付生产或使用单位的固定资产价值。新增固定资产是表示固定资产投资成果的价值量指标,也是反映建设进度、计算固定资产投资效果的必要数据。

固定资产交付使用率

指一定时期新增固定资产与同期完成投资额的比率。该指标是反映固定资产动用速度,衡量建设过程中宏观投资效果的综合指标。由于新增固定资产是较长时期内形成的结果,而投资额则是当年完成的,因此,该指标一般适宜于反映较长时期内固定资产的动用情况。

施工项目

指报告期内进行过建筑或安装施工活动的项目。凡是报告期内施过工的建设项目,不论施工时间长短,均作为施工项目统计。施工项目个数可以反映一定时期固定资产投资的实际规模,与同期建成投产的建设项目个数相比,可以从建设速度的角度反映固定资产投资的效果。根据建设项目施工活动的不同性质,施工项目又分为:本年正式施工项目、本年收尾项目和以前年度全部停缓建项目。

全部建成投产项目

工业项目指设计文件规定形成生产能力的主体工程及其相应配套的辅助设施全部建成,经负荷试运转,证明具备生产设计规定合格产品的条件,并经过验收鉴定合格或达到竣工验收标准,与生产性工程配套的生活福利设施可以满足近期正常生产的需要,正式移交生产的建设项目。非工业项目指设计文件规定的主体工程和相应的配套工程全部建成,能够发挥设计规定的全部效益,经验收鉴定合格或达到竣工验收标准,正式移交使用的建设项目。

建成投产率

指一定时期内全部建成投产项目个数与同期施工项目个数的比率。该指标是从建设单位建设速度的角度反映投资效果的指标。

SHANGHAI STATISTICAL YEARBOOK

EXPLANATORY NOTES TO MAJOR STATISTICAL INDICATORS

□ Total Investment in Fixed Assets

Investment in Fixed Assets constitutes an important portion of the national economic reproduction. Fixed assets investment is a general term for both the work volume of production and purchase of fixed assets and relevant expenditure, in the form of currency, during a certain period. It is a comprehensive indicator of scale, structure and development speed of fixed assets investment. As stipulated in the current national statistics regulations, the social fixed assets investment includes the investment into infrastructure and reformation, real estate development, urban and rural collective economic bodies, private house construction in urban and rural areas and other economic bodies.

From 1997, the fixed assets items only include those with investment of 0.5 million yuan and above.

□ Investment in Real Estate Development

Investment in Real Estate Development refers to the investment by the real estate development companies, commercial buildings construction companies and other real estate development units of various types of ownership in the construction of house buildings, such as residential buildings, factory buildings, warehouses, hotels, guesthouses, holiday villages, office buildings, and the complementary service facilities and land development projects, such as roads, water supply, water drainage, power supply, heating, telecommunications, land leveling and other projects of infrastructure. It excludes the activities in pure land transactions.

□ Investment in Fixed Assets by Sector

Investment in Fixed Assets by Sector refers to determining the classification of construction projects by the major products or the purpose of the projects when they are put into production or use, and by the nature of their social economic activities. In general, one project or one enterprise or institution can only be classified into one sector.

□ Investment in Fixed Assets by Administrative Relationship

Investment in Fixed Assets by Jurisdiction of Management refers to the classification of investment by the competent authorities under which investment is made by construction units, enterprises, institutions or administrative units.

(1) Central investment refers to the investment in projects or by enterprises, institutions or administrative units which are under the direct leadership and management of the CPC Central Committee, the NPC Standing Committee, the State Council and of the national commissions, ministries, agencies and state-owned large corporations. Various ministries and departments of the State Council prepare and implement plans for investment in fixed assets by those departments, and arrange and ensure the supply of materials and key equipment required for the projects.

(2) Local investment refers to the investment in projects or by enterprises, institutions or administrative units which are under the direct leadership and management of departments under the provincial, prefecture and county governments. Also included are projects by foreign-invested enterprises and enterprises without competent managing authorities.

□ Investment in Fixed Assets by Use of Funds

Investment in Fixed Assets by Structure is classified by their contents. It is mainly classified into 3 categories, i.e. construction and installation, purchase of equipment and instrument, and other expenses.

(1) Construction and installation (work volume of construction and installation) refers to the construction of various houses and buildings and installation of various kinds of equipment and instruments. They include construction of various houses; equipment foundations, industrial kilns and stoves, and metal structure work; preparation works for project construction, and clearing up works post project construction; pavement of railways and roads, drilling of mines and putting up of oil pipes; construction of projects of water conservancy; construction of underground air-raid shelters and construction of other special projects; value of equipment for heating, sanitation, ventilation, lighting, gas, painting, etc. that are covered by the budget of housing projects; laying out of various pipelines (for steam, compressed air, petroleum, tap water and sewage) and lines for electric power and for communications; installation of various machinery equipment, testing operation for pre-testing the quality of installation projects, and land and other development work conducted by real estate developers

EXPLANATORY NOTES TO MAJOR STATISTICAL INDICATORS

for commercial housing. The value of equipment installed is not included in the value of installation projects.

(2) Purchase of equipment and instruments refers to the total value of equipment, tools, and instruments purchased or self-produced which come up to standards for fixed assets by the construction units or investing enterprises or institutions. Equipment, tools and instruments purchased or self-produced for new workshops by newly established or expanded units are categorized as "purchase of equipment and instruments" no matter whether they come up to the standards for fixed assets.

(3) Other expenses refer to expenses occurring during the construction or purchase of fixed assets other than those mentioned above.

□ Sources of Capital for Investment in Fixed Assets

Sources of capital for Investment in Fixed Assets include state budgetary appropriation, domestic loans, foreign investment, self-raised funds, and others.

(1)State budgetary appropriation refers to appropriation in the budget of the central and local governments earmarked for capital construction and for innovation projects, and the special appropriation from the budget of the central government for capital construction and for the transfer fund to banks to be issued as loans for capital construction projects.

(2)Domestic loans refer to various funds borrowed by enterprises and institutions from banks and non-bank financial institutions during the reference period for the purpose of investment in fixed assets, including loans issued by banks from their self-owned funds and deposit, loans appropriated by higher responsible authorities, special loans by government (including loan for replacing petroleum with coal, special loan for reform-through-labour coal mines), loans arranged by local government from special funds, domestic reserve loan, and working loan, etc..

(3)Bond

(4) Foreign Investment refers to foreign funds received during the reference period for the purpose of investment in fixed assets, including foreign funds borrowed and managed by the government, by individual units, foreign fund in joint venture program, and issue of bonds and stocks at the international financial markets. The foreign funds borrowed and managed by the government refer to foreign loans borrowed by the government from foreign governments, organizations, or financial institutions under official agreements signed by both parties, under which government is responsible for the repayment of both the principal and interests of the foreign loans.

(5)Self-raised funds refer to funds received by construction enterprises from their higher responsible authorities, local governments, or raised by enterprises or institutions themselves for the purpose of investment in fixed assets during the reference period.

(6) Others refer to funds received during the reference period which are not included in the above-mentioned sources.

□ Investment in Fixed Assets by Type of Construction

The construction projects in general can be classified, by the type of construction, into new construction, expansion, reconstruction and construction of living facilities.

(1) New construction in general refers to newly constructed enterprises, institutions, administrative agencies or independent projects from scratch. Construction in the existing enterprises, institutions or agencies is not considered as new construction. In case the assets of the existing unit is quite small, and the value of newly added fixed assets exceeds the original value of assets by three times, the expansion will be considered as new construction.

(2) Reconstruction refers to construction projects by existing enterprises or institutions in innovation or technical transformation of the old facilities (including auxiliary production equipment and welfare facilities). Also considered as reconstruction is the construction of new workshops by the existing enterprises or institutions to change the variety of products to meet the market demand (such as the production of civil products by defence industries), or to bring the designed production capacity into full play through a more balanced production process on production lines.

(3) Expansion refers to construction of new major production workshop, branch factory or independent production line within a factory or in other locations, for the purpose of increasing the production capacity (or improving efficiency) of the original products. Newly constructed houses for the operation of institutions and administrative organizations (such as the newly constructed buildings for teaching in schools, buildings for clinics or wards in hospitals, etc.) are also classified as expansion.

Also included in the expansion are investments by existing enterprises or institutions in building major production line (s) or branch factory (ies) along with some work on innovation, for the purpose of expending the production capacity of original products or producing new products.

EXPLANATORY NOTES TO MAJOR STATISTICAL INDICATORS

☐ Newly Increased Fixed Assets

Newly Increased Fixed Assets, also called fixed assets put into operation, refers to the value of fixed assets that has been put into production or handed over to the production units after the completion of the process of construction and purchase. The newly increased fixed asset is an value indicator of the result of investment. It is also the necessary data for reflecting the construction process and the result of investment in fixed assets.

☐ Rate of Fixed Assets Transferred and in Use

Rate of Projects of Fixed Assets Completed and Put into Operation refers to the ratio of the newly increased fixed assets to the total investment made in the same period. This is a comprehensive indicator reflecting the speed of the employment of fixed assets and the investment efficiency at the macro-level. As the newly increase fixed assets is the result of a long period while the investment is completed in the current year, this indicator is expected to be used to reflect the employment of fixed assets over a long period of time.

☐ Projects under Construction

Projects under Construction refer to projects with construction and installation activities undertaken in the reference period. All projects that have construction activities undertaken during the reference period are reported as projects under construction irrespective of the length of construction work. The number of projects under construction can reflect the actual size of investment in fixed assets during a given period, and when compared with the number of projects completed and put into use during the same period, it demonstrates the results of investment in fixed assets. Depending on the nature of construction activities, projects under construction can also be classified into projects under construction in current year, winding-up projects in current year and stopped or suspended projects in previous years (with preservation work in current year).

☐ Projects Completed and Put into Use

Projects Completed and Put into Use refers to the major projects and accessory facilities completed which result in forming production capacity and have been checked and accepted while the living and welfare facilities have been completed and can ensure normal production and formally put into production. Non-industrial projects refer to the major projects and accessory facilities completed which possess the designed capacity and have been checked, accepted and formally put into production.

☐ Rate of Projects Completed and Put into Use

Rate of Construction Projects Completed and Put into Use refers to the ratio of the number of construction projects completed and put into use in certain period of time to the number of projects under construction in the same period. This reflects the investment efficiency from the perspective of the speed of projects construction.

第七篇

CHAPTER 7

对外经济贸易和旅游

FOREIGN ECONOMIC RELATIONS, TRADE AND TOURISM

表 7.1 主要年份口岸出口商品总额
TOTAL VALUE OF PORT EXPORTS IN MAIN YEARS

单位:亿美元 (100 million USD)

年 份 Year	出口商品总额 Total Value of Port Exports	其中 of which				
		#一般贸易 Ordinary Trade	#来料加工装配贸易 Processing and Assembly Trade with Customers' Materials	#进料加工贸易 Processing Trade with Imported Materials	#对外承包工程货物 Construction Projects in Foreign Countries	#出料加工贸易 Outward Processing Trade
1985	49.08	47.04	0.73	1.05		
1990	86.62	51.39	3.20	30.67	0.41	0.45
1995	256.07	149.16	14.31	90.12	0.63	0.06
1996	272.13	146.05	25.42	97.69	1.01	
1997	334.51	178.93	37.17	115.17	0.71	
1998	374.58	199.24	44.13	127.55	0.79	
1999	442.88	234.43	55.08	149.68	0.59	
2000	615.72	341.02	64.21	205.13	1.25	
2001	680.07	380.43	61.09	228.43	1.26	0.13
2002	818.03	473.13	66.88	266.72	1.44	0.13
2003	1 123.06	618.90	78.81	408.79	1.18	0.12
2004	1 612.68	824.92	126.99	623.27	3.18	0.14
2005	2 124.30	1 057.68	195.83	813.26	6.37	0.16
2006	2 665.65	1 319.56	212.77	1 058.07	9.45	0.14
2007	3 284.80	1 659.44	228.77	1 273.71	20.55	0.17

表 7.2 主要年份口岸进口商品总额
TOTAL VALUE OF PORT IMPORTS IN MAIN YEARS

单位:亿美元 (100 million USD)

年 份 Year	进口商品总额 Total Value of Port Imports	其中 of which				
		#一般贸易 Oridinary Trade	#来料加工装配贸易 Processing and Assembly Trade with Customers' Materials	#进料加工贸易 Processing Trade with Imported Materials	#外商投资企业进口设备 Imported Equipment of Foreign Funded Enterprise	#租赁贸易 Leasing Trade
1985	99.65	93.45	0.43	5.03		
1990	86.27	51.79	2.40	19.70	6.11	
1995	225.30	93.79	13.49	65.96	45.16	0.11
1996	256.57	85.64	20.48	69.33	70.09	3.10
1997	252.32	83.02	27.64	79.79	45.86	3.65
1998	261.80	93.24	29.63	80.37	40.52	2.63
1999	318.63	137.56	35.72	82.84	30.36	4.55
2000	477.39	212.65	44.87	125.13	40.26	2.47
2001	524.81	245.94	47.38	123.39	47.46	2.45
2002	606.98	267.66	48.12	160.91	54.95	1.89
2003	888.95	377.21	54.47	243.24	66.32	2.36
2004	1 213.07	472.16	89.47	338.57	99.72	4.70
2005	1 382.48	502.49	133.69	409.30	74.76	7.85
2006	1 621.89	574.40	122.52	497.41	73.72	23.74
2007	1 924.29	719.30	154.88	528.03	75.22	24.46

注：本页数据由上海海关提供。
Note: Data on this page are provided by Shanghai Custom.

表 7.3 按国别(地区)分的口岸出口商品总额(2003~2007)
TOTAL VALUE OF PORT EXPORTS BY COUNTRIES AND REGIONS

单位:亿美元 (100 million USD)

国别(地区)	Country (Region)	2003	2004	2005	2006	2007
总　计	**Total**	**1 123.06**	**1 612.68**	**2 124.30**	**2 665.65**	**3 284.80**
亚　洲	**Asia**	**498.54**	**708.74**	**898.90**	**1 086.64**	**1 307.46**
#中国香港	Hong Kong, China	78.26	119.92	160.72	184.74	207.43
中国台湾	Taiwan, China	28.68	46.96	59.81	77.40	92.18
日　本	Japan	194.47	253.42	298.78	334.85	367.58
韩　国	Republic of Korea	38.90	57.78	78.66	103.98	124.37
新加坡	Singapore	25.50	38.46	48.69	65.67	78.79
马来西亚	Malaysia	18.36	28.63	38.27	46.73	59.86
泰　国	Thailand	10.29	16.48	22.39	28.24	34.97
菲律宾	Philippines	11.44	16.64	16.58	19.67	23.45
巴基斯坦	Pakistan	5.53	7.08	8.07	10.21	12.14
科威特	Kuwait	1.08	1.24	1.40	1.81	3.29
沙特阿拉伯	Saudi Arabia	4.77	7.06	8.84	11.45	16.88
阿拉伯联合酋长国	United Arab Emirates	12.95	17.43	23.24	27.96	36.11
非　洲	**Africa**	**32.61**	**42.08**	**53.42**	**73.16**	**89.32**
#埃　及	Egypt	3.29	4.64	5.89	8.23	10.44
苏　丹	Sudan	0.88	1.11	2.35	3.09	4.58
欧　洲	**Europe**	**252.54**	**369.86**	**505.52**	**632.46**	**846.67**
#德　国	Germany	50.15	74.97	99.69	122.30	156.33
法　国	France	31.22	41.29	44.84	53.57	89.21
意大利	Italy	23.89	30.71	42.81	55.87	70.79
荷　兰	Netherlands	29.78	47.65	75.62	91.16	112.13
英　国	United Kingdoms	30.15	45.13	59.10	75.54	94.67
瑞　典	Sweden	5.09	7.16	9.42	10.78	14.86
俄罗斯	Russia	7.86	14.01	18.6	22.95	37.41
美　洲	**America**	**313.18**	**454.84**	**618.05**	**812.55**	**963.14**
#美　国	United States	251.04	361.53	501.11	646.99	749.33
加拿大	Canada	18.72	29.48	42.58	54.39	63.39
巴　西	Brazil	6.62	11.33	14.61	23.94	33.01
智　利	Chile	4.45	5.81	7.26	10.18	13.25
大洋洲及太平洋岛屿	**Oceanic and Pacific Island**	**26.19**	**37.15**	**48.41**	**60.84**	**78.21**
#澳大利亚	Australia	22.71	32.55	41.94	52.71	66.43
新西兰	New Zealand	2.99	4.12	5.50	6.40	8.51
其　他	**Others**		**0.01**			

①本表数据由上海海关提供。
②其他为无国别数(以下同)。
❶Data in this table are provided by Shanghai Custom.
❷Others refer to regions without sovereignty (Same as follows).

表7.4 按国别(地区)分的口岸进口商品总额(2003～2007)
TOTAL VALUE OF PORT IMPORTS BY COUNTRIES AND REGIONS

单位:亿美元(100 million USD)

国别(地区)	Country (Region)	2003	2004	2005	2006	2007
总 计	**Total**	**888.95**	**1 213.07**	**1 382.48**	**1 621.89**	**1 924.29**
亚 洲	**Asia**	**525.25**	**742.55**	**873.45**	**1 020.51**	**1 164.38**
#中国香港	Hong Kong, China	23.86	17.67	17.41	14.23	19.89
中国台湾	Taiwan, China	92.02	132.90	155.56	181.37	189.15
日 本	Japan	189.00	254.70	267.91	311.91	361.20
韩 国	Republic of Korea	83.31	130.02	163.95	176.27	209.77
新加坡	Singapore	25.62	34.00	44.30	39.77	38.95
马来西亚	Malaysia	26.65	37.22	43.88	52.00	54.19
泰 国	Thailand	20.22	29.78	36.53	41.99	50.08
菲律宾	Philippines	16.25	25.43	36.08	53.29	82.06
巴基斯坦	Pakistan	0.90	1.11	2.15	1.48	1.49
科威特	Kuwait	0.21	0.16	0.23	0.27	0.43
沙特阿拉伯	Saudi Arabia	2.37	2.97	4.01	3.72	4.55
阿拉伯联合酋长国	United Arab Emirates	0.68	0.80	0.95	0.99	1.04
非 洲	**Africa**	**7.06**	**11.60**	**13.76**	**16.30**	**18.31**
#埃 及	Egypt	0.33	0.40	0.44	0.40	0.52
南 非	South Africa	4.13	5.71	6.62	8.09	9.09
欧 洲	**Europe**	**205.93**	**253.55**	**264.89**	**320.15**	**406.63**
#德 国	Germany	88.43	103.97	103.93	125.93	164.44
法 国	France	24.99	29.13	28.81	40.31	45.31
意大利	Italy	16.53	20.55	23.91	29.56	34.05
荷 兰	Netherlands	6.22	8.94	8.17	9.12	10.00
英 国	United Kingdoms	10.18	13.71	15.62	20.30	25.48
瑞 典	Sweden	10.04	13.67	11.94	13.08	16.09
俄罗斯	Russia	4.68	5.53	8.3	8.55	11.54
美 洲	**America**	**137.91**	**186.14**	**202.70**	**234.63**	**298.01**
#美 国	United States	93.33	128.21	139.52	170.62	193.90
加拿大	Canada	12.69	15.70	14.89	16.57	23.15
巴 西	Brazil	10.18	10.69	13.08	12.34	17.25
智 利	Chile	12.00	18.63	18.42	16.70	41.02
大洋洲及太平洋岛屿	**Oceanic and Pacific Island**	**12.69**	**18.86**	**27.50**	**30.13**	**36.75**
#澳大利亚	Australia	10.31	16.03	23.79	25.15	31.95
新西兰	New Zealand	2.37	2.46	3.04	3.70	4.54
其 他	**Others**	**0.11**	**0.37**	**0.18**	**0.17**	**0.21**

注：本表数据由上海海关提供。
Note: Data in this table are provided by Shanghai Custom.

表7.5 主要年份外贸进出口商品总额
TOTAL VALUE OF FOREIGN TRADE IMPORTS AND EXPORTS IN MAIN YEARS

年份 Year	外贸进出口商品总额(亿美元) Total Value of Foreign Trade Imports and Exports (100 million USD)	外贸进口商品总额(亿美元) Total Value of Foreign Trade Imports (100 million USD)	外贸出口商品总额(亿美元) Total Value of Foreign Trade Exports (100 million USD)	外贸进出口差额(亿美元) Balance (100 million USD)	外贸进出口相当于生产总值的比例(%) Foreign Trade Imports and Export as Percentage of Gross Domestic Product(%)	外贸出口相当于生产总值的比例(%) Foreign Trade Export as Percentage of Gross Domestic Product(%)
1978	30.26	1.33	28.93	27.60	19.1	18.2
1980	45.06	2.40	42.66	40.26	21.5	20.4
1985	51.74	18.13	33.61	15.48	35.5	23.0
1990	74.31	21.10	53.21	32.11	47.0	33.6
1995	190.25	74.48	115.77	41.29	63.6	38.7
1996	222.63	90.25	132.38	42.13	62.6	37.2
1997	247.64	100.40	147.24	46.84	59.7	35.5
1998	313.44	153.88	159.56	5.68	68.3	34.8
1999	386.04	198.19	187.85	-10.34	76.3	37.1
2000	547.10	293.56	253.54	-40.02	94.9	44.0
2001	608.98	332.70	276.28	-56.42	96.7	43.9
2002	726.64	406.09	320.55	-85.54	104.8	46.2
2003	1 123.97	639.15	484.82	-154.33	139.0	59.9
2004	1 600.26	865.06	735.20	-129.86	164.1	75.4
2005	1 863.65	956.23	907.42	-48.81	166.6	81.1
2006	2 274.89	1 139.16	1 135.73	-3.43	174.9	87.3
2007	2 829.73	1 390.45	1 439.28	48.83	176.5	89.8

注：1999 年以前外贸进口、出口商品总额为外经贸委统计口径，1999 年以后为海关统计的上海企业进口、出口总额。
Note: Before 1999, the figures of Shanghai's foreign trade imports and exports were based on statistics from Shanghai Foreign Trade and Economic Cooperation Commission. Since 1999, the figures representing imports and exports are made by Shanghai enterprises through Shanghai Custom and other Customs in China.

表7.6 主要年份外贸出口商品总额
TOTAL VALUE OF FOREIGN TRADE EXPORTS IN MAIN YEARS

单位:亿美元 (100 million USD)

指标	Indicators	1990	2000	2005	2006	2007
出口总额	**Total Value of Exports**	**53.21**	**253.54**	**907.42**	**1 135.73**	**1 439.28**
按企业性质分	**Grouped by Different Enterprises**					
#国有企业	State-owned Enterprises	50.21	106.78	206.85	248.74	285.98
外商投资企业	Foreign-funded Enterprises	2.99	142.61	615.93	759.35	978.15
按贸易方式分	**Grouped by Trade**					
#一般贸易	Ordinary Trade	29.03	101.72	339.11	433.04	539.27
加工贸易	Processing Trade	24.07	147.83	518.84	637.69	796.75
按产品类别分	**Grouped by Different Products**					
#机电产品	Electrical and Mechanical Products	12.68	121.43	602.47	754.15	985.54
#高新技术产品	High-tech Products			362.53	442.81	580.92

注：本页数据由上海海关提供。
Note: Data on this page are provided by Shanghai Custom.

表7.7 主要年份按国别(地区)分的外贸出口商品总额
TOTAL VALUE OF FOREIGN TRADE EXPORTS BY COUNTRIES AND REGIONS IN MAIN YEARS

单位:亿美元 (100 million USD)

国别(地区)	Country (Region)	1978	1990	2000	2005	2006	2007
总　计	**Total**	**28.93**	**53.21**	**253.54**	**907.42**	**1 135.73**	**1 439.28**
亚　洲	**Asia**	**13.63**	**25.57**	**129.10**	**383.99**	**469.15**	**579.10**
#中国香港	Hong Kong, China	5.78	10.64	23.02	85.66	102.02	125.08
中国台湾	Taiwan, China		0.24	5.67	25.71	35.56	44.61
日　本	Japan	2.69	7.59	60.81	133.56	151.71	170.53
韩　国	Republic of Korea			10.59	30.38	38.67	49.17
新加坡	Singapore	0.98	1.82	7.88	22.32	29.88	39.68
马来西亚	Malaysia	0.38	0.39	2.59	20.54	22.95	28.83
泰　国	Thailand	0.11	0.78	2.48	9.11	11.50	14.68
巴基斯坦	Pakistan	0.21	0.33	0.55	2.30	2.92	3.16
科威特	Kuwait	0.58	0.58	0.20	0.73	0.90	1.51
沙特阿拉伯	Saudi Arabia	0.21	0.66	1.14	2.86	3.72	6.14
阿拉伯联合酋长国	United Arab Emirates	0.37	0.90	1.79	7.83	9.14	12.13
非　洲	**Africa**	**2.89**	**1.38**	**5.63**	**13.92**	**19.48**	**23.64**
#埃　及	Egypt	0.25	0.13	0.44	1.67	2.53	2.07
苏　丹	Sudan	0.20	0.01	0.22	0.74	0.57	0.62
阿尔及利亚	Algeria			0.09	0.45	0.70	1.03
摩洛哥	Morocco	0.27	0.13	0.20	0.56	0.70	1.04
欧　洲	**Europe**	**9.37**	**15.52**	**45.62**	**216.28**	**278.10**	**375.10**
#德　国	Germany	1.93	2.54	9.48	42.48	55.90	68.25
法　国	France	0.80	0.85	4.50	20.91	26.09	52.10
意大利	Italy	0.73	1.27	4.98	12.71	19.11	22.92
荷　兰	Netherlands	0.25	0.74	6.16	35.07	40.26	53.88
比利时	Belgium	0.11	0.30	2.95	11.75	14.65	16.39
英　国	United Kingdoms	1.19	1.15	7.07	24.70	32.35	41.41
俄罗斯	Russia	0.69	1.74	0.37	4.64	7.18	11.94
美　洲	**America**	**2.24**	**9.57**	**67.82**	**272.00**	**340.61**	**423.34**
#美　国	United States	1.03	7.45	56.25	227.39	282.74	346.11
加拿大	Canada	0.46	0.92	4.04	18.74	22.04	26.22
巴　西	Brazil		0.03	1.06	5.41	7.05	11.17
古　巴	Cuba			0.07	0.48	0.53	0.67
大洋洲及太平洋岛屿	**Oceanic and Pacific Island**	**0.80**	**1.17**	**5.37**	**21.23**	**28.39**	**38.10**
#澳大利亚	Australia	0.67	1.02	4.74	18.43	24.73	32.20

注：本表数据由上海海关提供。
Note: Data in this table are provided by Shanghai Custom.

表7.8 主要年份按国别(地区)分的外贸进口商品总额
TOTAL VALUE OF FOREIGN TRADE IMPORTS BY COUNTRIES AND REGIONS IN MAIN YEARS

单位:亿美元 (100 million USD)

国别(地区)	Country (Region)	1978	1990	2000	2005	2006	2007
总　计	**Total**	**1.33**	**21.10**	**293.56**	**956.23**	**1 139.16**	**1 390.45**
亚　洲	**Asia**	**0.75**	**11.15**	**161.59**	**585.84**	**699.01**	**825.55**
#中国香港	Hong Kong, China	0.02	5.30	16.68	11.33	8.63	14.61
中国台湾	Taiwan, China		0.21	19.44	98.74	117.33	122.73
日　本	Japan	0.69	4.59	70.43	168.87	192.31	224.30
韩　国	Republic of Korea			20.63	81.79	97.40	122.46
新加坡	Singapore	0.02	0.37	9.39	31.84	30.32	30.25
马来西亚	Malaysia	0.01	0.28	6.49	40.13	46.68	52.02
泰　国	Thailand		0.10	4.35	25.02	31.49	40.33
菲律宾	Philippines			1.83	35.15	52.10	80.79
科威特	Kuwait		0.03	0.22	0.44	0.43	1.19
沙特阿拉伯	Saudi Arabia			0.78	4.19	3.99	5.13
阿拉伯联合酋长国	United Arab Emirates			0.40	1.00	1.31	1.15
非　洲	**Africa**		**0.26**	**1.89**	**8.52**	**11.00**	**12.81**
欧　洲	**Europe**	**0.41**	**5.33**	**63.36**	**177.30**	**214.53**	**271.42**
#德　国	Germany	0.13	3.46	26.59	67.27	76.21	101.87
法　国	France	0.02	0.11	7.95	22.67	33.85	37.25
意大利	Italy	0.05	0.30	4.81	15.25	18.99	22.63
荷　兰	Netherlands	0.03	0.09	2.43	6.26	7.02	7.67
比利时	Belgium	0.02	0.21	2.83	7.90	8.74	11.14
英　国	United Kingdoms	0.04	0.48	3.76	11.83	15.45	19.61
瑞　士	Switzerland	0.05	0.22	2.22	9.79	11.21	15.63
瑞　典	Sweden	0.02	0.09	4.53	5.24	6.79	8.27
美　洲	**America**	**0.07**	**3.14**	**58.60**	**160.13**	**187.24**	**244.79**
#美　国	United States	0.01	2.81	40.11	110.04	131.64	146.93
加拿大	Canada	0.02	0.14	7.03	10.43	11.40	17.07
巴　西	Brazil			4.11	13.03	17.08	24.85
大洋洲及太平洋岛屿	**Oceanic and Pacific Island**	**0.10**	**1.22**	**8.07**	**24.33**	**27.26**	**35.74**
#澳大利亚	Australia	0.07	1.08	6.68	20.84	22.56	31.32
新西兰	New Zealand	0.03	0.13	1.25	2.27	2.32	2.66
其　他	**Others**			**0.05**	**0.11**	**0.12**	**0.14**

注：本表数据由上海海关提供。
Note: Data in this table are provided by Shanghai Custom.

表7.9 外贸出口商品总额(2004~2007)
TOTAL VALUE OF FOREIGN TRADE EXPORTS OF MAJOR COMMODITIES

单位:亿美元(100 million USD)

类别	Types	2004	2005	2006	2007
总　计	**Total**	**735.20**	**907.42**	**1 135.73**	**1 439.28**
初级产品	**Primary Products**	**21.38**	**24.79**	**27.53**	**32.09**
食品及活动物	Food and Livestock	4.93	5.60	6.62	8.01
#肉及肉制品	Meat and Meat Products	0.55	0.65	0.70	0.49
蔬菜及水果	Vegetable and Fruits	1.18	1.43	1.93	2.17
饮料及烟类	Beverage and Tobacco	1.04	1.20	1.47	1.98
#烟草及其制品	Tobacco and Tobacco Products	0.90	1.01	1.13	1.16
非食用原料	Non-edible Raw Materials	2.93	4.34	5.21	6.15
矿物燃料、润滑油及其有关原料	Mineral Fuel,Lubricant and Related Raw Materials	12.44	13.62	14.05	15.89
动植物油、脂及蜡	Animal and Plant Oil,Fat and Wax	0.04	0.03	0.18	0.06
工业制成品	**Industrial Products**	**713.82**	**882.63**	**1 108.20**	**1 407.19**
化学成品及有关产品	Chemicals and Related Products	28.52	39.20	52.71	70.05
#医药品	Medical Products	3.56	4.09	4.81	6.05
原料制成品	Raw Material Products	101.94	126.83	177.52	215.29
#橡胶制品	Rubber Products	3.13	3.74	4.75	5.54
纺纱、织物、制成品及有关产品	Spinning,Textile and Related Products	32.00	36.76	41.48	42.11
钢　铁	Steel	16.36	20.90	37.31	51.58
机械及运输设备	Machinery and Transportation Equipments	421.31	526.32	656.61	853.27
#通用工业机械设备及零件	General-purpose Industrial Machinery Equipments and Parts	35.67	46.21	57.64	75.13
电力机械器具及电气零件	Electrical Equipments,Tools and Parts	109.48	124.69	163.80	192.87
杂项制品	Assorted Products	161.38	189.05	220.18	267.35
#服装及衣着附件	Clothing and Dresses	82.40	89.71	99.75	111.62
未分类的商品	Other Commodities	0.67	1.23	1.18	1.23

注：本表数据由上海海关提供。
Note: Data in this table are provided by Shanghai Custom.

表7.10 外贸进口商品总额(2004～2007)
TOTAL VALUE OF FOREIGN TRADE IMPORTS OF MAJOR COMMODITIES

单位:亿美元 (100 million USD)

类别	Types	2004	2005	2006	2007
总　计	**Total**	**865.06**	**956.23**	**1 139.16**	**1 390.45**
初级产品	**Primary Products**	**83.36**	**99.46**	**121.33**	**156.70**
食品及活动物	Food and Livestock	6.26	7.63	9.44	13.26
#肉及肉制品	Meat and Meat Products	0.98	1.59	1.17	1.61
蔬菜及水果	Vegetable and Fruits	0.88	1.28	1.76	2.27
饮料及烟类	Beverage and Tobacco	1.84	3.21	4.32	5.85
#烟草及其制品	Tobacco and Tobacco Products	0.17	0.31	0.20	0.08
非食用原料	Non-edible Raw Materials	51.80	63.19	74.67	97.43
矿物燃料、润滑油及其有关原料	Mineral Fuel, Lubricant and Related Raw Materials	17.97	20.33	27.97	26.89
动植物油、脂及蜡	Animal and Plant Oil, Fat and Wax	5.49	5.10	4.93	13.27
工业制成品	**Industrial Products**	**781.70**	**856.77**	**1 017.83**	**1 233.75**
化学成品及有关产品	Chemicals and Related Products	110.75	121.65	142.58	175.24
#医药品	Medical Products	6.12	7.35	9.76	12.50
原料制成品	Raw Material Products	115.46	120.93	141.31	176.37
#橡胶制品	Rubber Products	3.65	3.71	5.91	6.68
纺纱、织物、制成品及有关产品	Spinning, Textile and Related Products	20.42	19.80	19.53	19.21
钢　铁	Steel	34.61	32.52	28.15	30.72
机械及运输设备	Machinery and Transportation Equipments	461.84	514.51	628.08	761.91
#通用工业机械设备及零件	General-purpose Industrial Machinery Equipments and Parts	50.56	48.79	55.25	79.58
电力机械、器具及电气零件	Electrical Equipments, Tools and Parts	200.39	244.15	321.51	403.05
杂项制品	Assorted Products	93.32	99.10	104.96	119.16
#服装及衣着附件	Clothing and Dresses	2.13	2.94	3.36	5.11
未分类的商品	Other Commodities	0.33	0.58	0.90	1.07

注：本表数据由上海海关提供。
Note: Data in this table are provided by Shanghai Custom.

表 7.11 主要年份进出口商品检验情况
IMPORTS AND EXPORTS INSPECTION IN MAIN YEARS

指标	Indicators	1990	2000	2006	2007
进口商品检验	**Imports Inspection**				
检验批数(批)	Groups of Inspection(group)	7 991	51 940	633 858	792 800
检验金额(亿美元)	Values of Inspection(100 million USD)	32.26	76.16	595.26	788.80
不合格批数(批)	Unqualified Groups (group)	1 327	1 539	8 706	4 783
占检验批数比重(%)	Percentage in Total (%)	16.6	3.0	1.4	0.6
不合格金额(亿美元)	Unqualified Values (100 million USD)	10.75	0.99	14.58	11.33
占检验金额比重(%)	Percentage in Total (%)	33.3	1.3	2.5	1.4
出口商品检验	**Exports Inspection**				
检验批数(批)	Groups of Inspection(group)	101 301	344 138	637 453	712 085
检验金额(亿美元)	Values of Inspection (100 million USD)	95.53	100.86	226.60	258.22
不合格批数(批)	Unqualified Groups (group)	1854	564	327	386
占检验批数比重(%)	Percentage in Total (%)	1.8	0.2	0.1	0.1
不合格金额(亿美元)	Unqualified Values (100 million USD)	1.82	0.11	0.07	0.14
占检验金额比重(%)	Percentage in Total (%)	1.9	0.1	…	0.1

注：本表数据由市出入境检验检疫局提供。
Note: Data in this table are provided by Shanghai Entry-Exit Inspection and Quarantine Bureau.

表 7.12 主要年份直接吸收外资情况
FOREIGN DIRECT INVESTMENT IN MAIN YEARS

指标	Indicators	1990	2000	2006	2007
签订合同项目(个)	**Number of Signed Contracts (item)**	**203**	**1 814**	**4 061**	**4 206**
# 合资经营	Joint Ventures	161	441	540	511
合作经营	Cooperative Ventures	12	226	27	24
独资经营	Sole-foreign Funded Enterprises	30	1 146	3 486	3 668
签订合同金额(亿美元)	**Contracted Foreign Capital (100 million USD)**	**2.14**	**63.9**	**145.74**	**148.69**
# 合资经营	Joint Ventures	1.10	13.86	24.27	21.69
合作经营	Cooperative Ventures	0.38	5.86	2.86	4.31
独资经营	Sole-foreign Funded Enterprises	0.66	44.14	117.37	117.84
实际吸收外资金额(亿美元)	**Foreign Investment Actually Absorbed (100 million USD)**	**1.77**	**31.60**	**71.07**	**79.20**
# 合资经营	Joint Ventures	1.08	12.94	15.84	17.12
合作经营	Cooperative Ventures	0.67	2.99	1.86	1.56
独资经营	Sole-foreign Funded Enterprises	0.02	15.67	53.30	60.43

注：本表部分数据由市外国投资工作委员会提供。
Note: Data in this table are provided by Shanghai Foreign Investment Commission.

表7.13 外商直接投资合同项目和金额（2007）
NUMBER OF CONTRACTS SIGNED AND VALUES OF FOREIGN DIRECT INVESTMENT PROJECTS

类别	Types	签订合同项目(个) Number of Contracts Signed(item) 2007	签订合同项目(个) 至2007年底累计 Total by the End of 2007	签订合同金额(亿美元) Contracted Foreign Capital (100 million USD) 2007	签订合同金额(亿美元) 至2007年底累计 Total by the End of 2007	实际吸收外资金额(亿美元) Foreign Investment Actually Absorbed (100 million USD) 2007	实际吸收外资金额(亿美元) 至2007年底累计 Total by the End of 2007
总计	**Total**	**4 206**	**48 753**	**148.69**	**1 294.04**	**79.20**	**746.83**
#1 000万美元以上项目	Projects of Over 10 Million USD	260	4 011	110.09	942.03		
#工业	Industry	107	2 095	39.42	264.51		
按投资方式分	**Grouped by Investment Mode**						
#合资经营	Joint Ventures	511	15 417	21.69	352.11	17.12	262.26
合作经营	Cooperative Ventures	24	5 047	4.31	128.24	1.56	85.87
独资经营	Sole-foreign Funded Enterprises	3 668	28 216	117.84	777.02	60.43	371.08
按产业分	**Grouped by Industry**						
第一产业	Primary Industry	5	258	0.37	3.92	0.08	1.55
第二产业	Secondary Industry	806	24 456	52.45	702.96	25.97	362.47
#工业	Industry	794	23 618	52.19	687.7	25.79	357.59
第三产业	Tertiary Industry	3 395	24 039	95.87	587.16	53.15	382.81
按主要国别(地区)分	**Grouped by Country and Region**						
#中国香港	Hong Kong, China	1 141	14 010	55.07	328.60	19.74	194.28
中国澳门	Macao, China	9	228	0.07	3.76	0.07	1.37
中国台湾	Taiwan, China	348	5 587	2.98	48.13	1.02	34.2
日本	Japan	468	6 844	11.26	142.05	8.73	103.93
韩国	Republic of Korea	268	1 358	2.66	15.13	1.32	8.99
新加坡	Singapore	219	2 540	8.41	68.36	3.05	31.48
泰国	Thailand	8	374	-0.02	4.16	0.05	2.44
德国	Germany	119	1 052	4.17	54.85	3.60	37.24
英国	United Kingdoms	77	758	1.36	23.20	0.88	17.54
法国	France	60	458	2.79	17.18	1.43	8.11
意大利	Italy	82	453	0.82	5.36	0.7	1.87
美国	United States	470	5 758	7.95	113.63	5.27	76.06
加拿大	Canada	59	849	0.14	7.85	0.27	3.34
澳大利亚	Australia	73	936	0.30	10.66	0.30	5.04

注：本表数据由市外国投资工作委员会提供。
Note: Data in this table are provided by Shanghai Foreign Investment Commission.

表 7.14　主要年份外商投资企业生产经营情况
PRODUCTION AND OPERATION OF OVERSEAS-FUNDED ENTERPRISES IN MAIN YEARS

指　标	Indicators	1990	2000	2006	2007
销售（经营）收入（亿元）	Sales (Operation) Revenues (100 million yuan)	111.02	3 977.90	15 618.76	19 197.58
利润总额（亿元）	Total Pre-tax Profits (100 million yuan)	11.04	217.79	837.19	1 211.94
交纳税金总额（亿元）	Total Tax Payment (100 million yuan)	3.90	158.93	455.36	542.00
外汇总收入（亿美元）	Total Foreign Exchange Inflow (100 million USD)		209.58	907.23	1 087.54
#经常项目外汇收入	Foreign Exchange Inflow of Current Accounts	11.92	126.39	743.68	870.95
外汇总支出(亿美元)	Total Foreign Exchange Outflow(100 million USD)		205.24	876.18	1 074.90
#经常项目外汇支出	Foreign Exchange Outflow of Current Accounts	10.81	140.43	720.50	848.23
年末外汇结存(亿美元)	Foreign Exchange Balance at Year End(100 million USD)	5.46	29.55	48.99	48.99
从业人员薪金总额（亿元）	Total Wages and Salaries for Employees (100 million yuan)		180.37	587.39	732.66

表 7.15　主要年份引进技术设备实际到货金额
ARRIVED CAPITAL THROUGH IMPORTED TECHNOLOGY AND EQUIPMENT IN MAIN YEARS

单位:万美元(10 000 USD)

国　别(地区)	Country(Region)	1990	2000	2006	2007
总　计	**Total**	**15 063**	**104 558**	**2 062 857**	**2 520 296**
#中国香港	Hong Kong, China	1 688	10 746	16 986	13 546
日　本	Japan	2 868	10 069	438 295	503 809
德　国	Germany	2 925	16 314	371 729	546 324
意大利	Italy	1 755	622	73 693	77 294
美　国	United States	2 226	49 431	284 945	309 671
瑞　士	Switzerland	1 060	1 862	37 118	56 855
英　国	United Kingdoms	667	712	46 172	56 907
瑞　典	Sweden	576	639	28 803	34 669
奥地利	Austria	603	1 162	11 751	24 139
法　国	France	70	1 926	82 374	92 089

注：本表数据由上海海关提供。
Note: Data in this table are provided by Shanghai Custom.

表 7.16 主要年份对外经济合作情况
ECONOMIC COOPERATION WITH FOREIGN COUNTRIES OR REGIONS IN MAIN YEARS

指 标	Indicators	1990	2000	2006	2007
签订合同项目（个）	**Number of Contracted Projects（item）**	**78**	**1 076**	**7 346**	**6 185**
#对外承包工程	Overseas Contracted Projects	12	143	2 724	821
对外劳务合作	Overseas Labor Services Cooperation	66	836	4 599	5 315
签订合同金额(万美元)	**Value of Contract（10 000 USD）**	**6 010**	**98 050**	**545 723**	**734 747**
#对外承包工程	Overseas Contracted Projects	3 929	76 058	508 953	669 931
对外劳务合作	Overseas Labor Services Cooperation	2 081	20 837	34 960	50 778
实际营业额(万美元)	**Actual Business Volume(10 000 USD)**	**5 131**	**83 790**	**470 179**	**502 441**
#对外承包工程	Overseas Contracted Projects	4 083	61 906	429 336	449 076
对外劳务合作	Overseas Labor Services Cooperation	1 048	21 049	40 170	51 689
年末在外人员(人)	**Persons Abroad(year-end)(person)**	**2 041**	**30 052**	**27 561**	**30 231**
#对外承包工程	Overseas Contracted Projects	121	1 327	3 531	6 374
对外劳务合作	Overseas Labor Services Cooperation	1 920	28 710	24 002	23 834

注：本表数据由市对外经济贸易委员会提供。
Note：Data in this table are provided by Shanghai Foreign Economic Relation & Trade Commission.

表 7.17 海外企业情况(2006～2007)
ENTERPRISES ABROAD

指 标	Indicators	2006 年新增 Established in 2006	至 2006 年底累计 Total by the end of 2006	2007 年新增 Established in 2007	至 2007 年底累计 Total by the end of 2007
企业数(个)	Number of Enterprises（unit）	75	981	78	1 059
投资额(万美元)	Investment Value（10 000 USD）	52 977	236 875	64 937	301 812

表 7.18 国际会展(2006～2007)
INTERNATIONAL CONFERENCE AND EXHIBITION

指 标	Indicators	2006	2007
举办国际会展次数(次)	International Exhibit(time)	295	309
国际会展展出总面积(万平方米)	Total Square of International Exhibit(10 000 sq · m)	434	475

表 7.19 旅行社接待经营情况（2004～2007）
TOURISTS RECEIVED BY TOUR AGENCIES

指标	Indicators	2004	2005	2006	2007
接待境内外来沪旅游者（万人次）	**Overseas and Domestic Tourists (10 000 person-times)**	**633.47**	**750.89**	**880.24**	**904.73**
境外旅游者	Overseas Tourists	78.40	95.01	107.34	111.50
#外国人	Foreigners	74.92	90.01	101.67	108.51
中国香港	Tourists from Hong Kong, China	1.83	1.48	2.28	1.29
中国澳门	Tourists from Macao, China	0.01	0.01	0.03	0.01
中国台湾	Tourists from Taiwan, China	1.64	3.51	3.36	1.69
境内旅游者	Domestic Tourists	555.07	655.88	772.90	793.23
出境旅游者（万人次）	Tourists Going Abroad (10 000 person-times)	49.86	51.71	58.54	68.91
经营和财务状况	Operation and Financial Status				
营业收入（亿元）	Operational Revenues (100 million yuan)	108.22	132.43	169.49	228.84
利润总额（亿元）	Total Profits (100 million yuan)	1.81	1.61	1.71	1.91

注：本表数据由市旅游事业管理委员会提供。
Note: Data in this table are provided by Shanghai Municipal Tourism Administrative Commission.

表 7.20 住宿业接待经营情况（2004～2007）
OPERATION OF HOTELS

指标	Indicators	2004	2005	2006	2007
年末客房数（万间）	**Year-end Guest Rooms (10 000 rooms)**	**11.49**	**12.57**	**13.71**	**18.06**
年末客房床位数（万张）	Year-end Guest Beds (10 000 beds)	21.72	24.05	25.95	31.79
客房平均出租率（%）	**Average Room Occupancy Rate (%)**	**62.9**	**67.3**	**64.8**	**61.2**
#星级宾馆	Star-rated Hotels	69.0	65.6	63.9	61.5
实际住宿人次数（万人次）	**Actual Number of Guests (10 000 person-times)**	**2 070.13**	**2 378.86**	**2 422.34**	**2 792.83**
#境外来沪	Overseas Visitors	345.04	558.51	570.90	582.07
实际住宿人天数（万人天）	**Actual Number of Guests and Days of Stay (10 000 person-day)**	**3 595.18**	**4 036.98**	**4 110.44**	**4 772.11**
#境外来沪	Overseas Visitors	863.49	1 150.65	1 212.11	1 429.26
营业收入（亿元）	**Operational Revenues (100 million yuan)**	**165.59**	**194.47**	**212.03**	**271.65**
#客房收入	Room Rate Revenues	89.99	110.19	121.95	153.52
餐饮收入	Catering Revenues	49.80	55.36	59.99	76.68
商品收入	Commodity Sales Revenues	3.68	4.04	4.14	4.87
利润总额（亿元）	**Total Profits (100 million yuan)**	**22.67**	**23.97**	**27.93**	**32.11**

注：本表数据由市旅游事业管理委员会提供。
Note: Data in this table are provided by Shanghai Municipal Tourism Administrative Commission.

表 7.21 旅游景点基本情况(2005～2007)
BASIC STATISTICS OF SCENIC SPOTS

指标	Indicators	2005	2006	2007
A 级旅游景点数(家)	Scenic Spots of A Level and above	18	18	20
#5A 级景点	AAAAA-Level			2
4A 级景点	AAAA-Level	17	17	17
红色旅游基地数(个)	Red Travelling Base			22
#全国红色旅游基地	National Red Travelling Base			4

注：本表数据由市旅游事业管理委员会提供。
Note: Data in this table are provided by Shanghai Municipal Tourism Administrative Commission.

表 7.22 旅游星级饭店基本情况(2007)
BASIC STATISTICS OF STAR-RATED TOURISM HOTELS

指标	Indicators	合计 Total	五星级 Five-Star	四星级 Four-Star	三星级 Three-Star	二星级 Two-Star	一星级 One-Star
饭店数(个)	Number of Hotels(unit)	320	32	47	128	105	8
客房数(万间)	Number of Rooms (10 000 rooms)	6.14	1.43	1.63	2.17	0.87	0.04
床位数(万张)	Number of Beds (10 000 beds)	9.85	1.94	2.47	3.82	1.55	0.07
客房平均出租率(%)	Average Occupancy Rate (%)	61.48	68.23	63.47	56.89	57.37	65.93
营业收入(亿元)	Business Revenues (100 million yuan)	159.70	82.19	41.82	28.57	6.93	0.19
平均房价 (元/间天)	Average Room Rates (yuan/room. day)	668.06	1 335.79	648.09	325.52	211.82	153.87

注：本表数据由市旅游事业管理委员会提供。
Note: Data in this table are provided by Shanghai Municipal Tourism Administrative Commission.

表 7.23 国内旅游者来沪人数和人均消费支出 (2003～2007)
NUMBER OF DOMESTIC TOURISTS VISITING SHANGHAI AND PER CAPITA CONSUMPTION EXPENDITURES

指标	Indicators	2003	2004	2005	2006	2007
国内旅游者来沪人数(万人次)	**Number of Domestic Tourists Visiting Shanghai(10 000 person-times)**	**7 603**	**8 505**	**9 012**	**9 684**	**10 210**
外省市来沪旅游人数(万人次)	Number of Tourists from other Provinces Visiting Shanghai (10 000 person-times)	5 630	6 346	6 805	7 327	7 766
本市市民在本地旅游人数(万人次)	Number of Local Tourists (10 000 person-times)	1 973	2 159	2 207	2 357	2 444
国内旅游者人均消费支出 (元)	**Consumption Expenditure Per Person (yuan)**	**1 465**	**1 430**	**1 452**	**1 466**	**1 578**
#长途交通费	Long-distance Traffic Expenditure	170	194	176	174	165
住宿费	Accommodation Expenditure	233	220	219	211	234
餐饮费	Food Expenditure	249	232	220	217	210
购物费	Shopping Expenditure	521	420	553	536	650
门票费	Ticket Expenditure	44	119	96	112	109
娱乐费	Entertainment Expenditure	52	33	30	47	46
市内交通费	Local Traffic Expenditure	79	87	88	94	87
邮电通信费	Post and Telecommunications Expenditure	19	27	37	35	35

注：本表为抽样调查资料。
Note: Data in this table are from the sampling survey.

表 7.24 主要年份国际旅游入境人数
NUMBER OF OVERSEAS TOURISTS IN MAIN YEARS

指　标	Indicators	1978	1990	2000	2006	2007
国际旅游入境人数（万人次）	**Number of Overseas Tourists (10 000 person-times)**	**24.02**	**89.30**	**181.40**	**605.67**	**665.59**
#外国人	Foreigner	17.07	46.06	139.14	485.40	536.76
#日　本	Japanese	5.73	22.60	53.76	136.93	142.68
新加坡	Singaporean	0.34	1.02	5.29	15.23	17.01
德　国	German	0.73	1.60	7.11	21.79	25.45
法　国	French	0.70	1.19	5.39	15.68	18.83
英　国	Briton	0.44	1.11	1.69	16.69	19.25
意大利	Italian	0.39	0.99	1.88	8.52	9.90
加拿大	Canadian	0.34	0.81	2.25	10.13	12.12
美　国	American	3.87	4.67	13.78	54.60	63.59
澳大利亚	Australian	0.42	0.53	3.23	13.08	15.17
港澳同胞	Hong Kong and Macao Chinese	6.29	10.33	17.62	47.74	51.25
台湾同胞	Taiwanese		31.03	19.88	72.53	77.58
平均每天来沪旅游人数（人次/天）	**Average Number of Tourists Visiting Shanghai Everyday (person-time/day)**	**658**	**2 447**	**4 970**	**16 594**	**18 235**
来沪旅游者平均逗留天数（天/人）	**Average Time Tourists Staying in Shanghai (day/person)**	**3.87**	**2.83**	**3.92**	**3.60**	**3.69**
国际旅游（外汇）收入（亿美元）	**Foreign Exchange Earnings from International Tourism (100 million USD)**	**0.56**	**2.31**	**16.13**	**39.61**	**47.37**

注：本表数据由市旅游事业委员会、市出入境边防检查总站等提供。
Note: Data in this table are provided by Shanghai Municipal Tourism Administrative Commission, Shanghai Entry-Exit Inspection and Quarantine Bureau and ect.

表 7.25 上海国际友好城市、与上海建立国际友好交流关系的城市一览 (2007 年末)
FOREIGN CITIES WITH SISTER-CITY RELATIONSHIP OR FRIENDLY EXCHANGE RELATIONSHIP WITH SHANGHAI (BY THE END OF YEAR 2007)

城市	Cities	国家	Countries	缔结日期	Relationship Eastablished Date
上海国际友好城市	**Cities with Sister-city Relationship**				
横滨市	Yokohama	日本	Japan	1973 年 11 月 30 日	Nov. 30, 1973
大阪市	Osaka	日本	Japan	1974 年 4 月 18 日	Apr. 18, 1974
米兰市	Milan	意大利	Italy	1979 年 6 月 25 日	Jun. 25, 1979
鹿特丹市	Rotterdam	荷兰	Netherlands	1979 年 11 月 23 日	Nov. 23, 1979
旧金山市	San Francisco	美国	United States	1980 年 1 月 28 日	Jan. 28, 1980
萨格勒布市	Zagreb	克罗地亚	Croatia	1980 年 6 月 18 日	Jun. 18, 1980
大阪府	Osaka	日本	Japan	1980 年 11 月 21 日	Nov. 21, 1980
咸兴市	Hamhung	朝鲜	D. P. R. Korea	1982 年 6 月 18 日	Jun. 18, 1982
大马尼拉市	Manila	菲律宾	Philippines	1983 年 6 月 15 日	Jun. 15, 1983
卡拉奇市	Karachi	巴基斯坦	Pakistan	1984 年 2 月 15 日	Feb. 15, 1984
安特卫普市	Antwerp	比利时	Belgium	1984 年 5 月 27 日	May. 27, 1984
蒙特利尔市	Montreal	加拿大	Canada	1985 年 5 月 14 日	May. 14, 1985
比雷埃夫斯市	Piraiev	希腊	Greece	1985 年 6 月 24 日	Jun. 24, 1985
滨海省	Binhai City	波兰	Poland	1985 年 7 月 4 日	Jul. 4, 1985
汉堡市	Hamburg	德国	Germany	1985 年 6 月 29 日	Jun. 29, 1985
卡萨布兰卡市	Casablanca	摩洛哥	Morocco	1986 年 9 月 8 日	Sep. 8, 1986
马赛市	Marseilles	法国	France	1987 年 10 月 26 日	Oct. 26, 1987
圣堡罗市	Sao Paul	巴西	Brazil	1988 年 7 月 7 日	Jul. 7, 1988
圣彼得堡市	St Petersburg	俄罗斯	Russia	1988 年 12 月 15 日	Dec. 15, 1988
昆士兰州	Queensland	澳大利亚	Australia	1989 年 5 月 24 日	May. 24, 1989
伊斯坦布尔市	Istanbul	土耳其	Turkey	1989 年 10 月 23 日	Oct. 23, 1989
亚历山大省	Alexandria	埃及	Egypt	1992 年 5 月 12 日	May. 12, 1992
海法市	Haifa	以色列	Israel	1993 年 6 月 22 日	Jun. 22, 1993
釜山市	Pusan	韩国	Republic of Korea	1993 年 8 月 24 日	Aug. 24, 1993
胡志明市	Ho Chi Minh City	越南	Viet Nam	1994 年 5 月 14 日	May. 14, 1994
维拉港	Port-Vila	瓦努阿图	Vanuatu	1994 年 6 月 8 日	Jun. 8, 1994
达尼丁市	Dunedin	新西兰	New Zealand	1994 年 10 月 21 日	Oct. 21, 1994

注：本表数据由市外事办公室提供。
Note: Data in this table are provided by Shanghai Municipal Foreign Affairs Office.

表 7.25 续表 1 continued

城市	Cities	国家	Countries	缔结日期	Relationship Eastablished Date
市级国际友好城市	Shanghai's International Sister Cities				
塔什干市	Tashkent	乌兹别克	Uzbekistan	1994 年 12 月 15 日	Dec. 15,1994
波尔图市	Oporto	葡萄牙	Portugal	1995 年 4 月 15 日	Apr. 15,1995
亚丁省	Aden	也门	Yemen	1995 年 9 月 14 日	Sep. 14,1995
温得和克市	Windhoek	纳米比亚	Namibia	1995 年 11 月 1 日	Nov. 1,1995
圣地亚哥省	Santiago	古巴	Cuba	1996 年 7 月 30 日	Jul. 30,1996
罗萨里奥市	Rosario	阿根廷	Argentina	1997 年 6 月 17 日	Jun. 17,1997
埃斯波市	Espoo	芬兰	Finland	1998 年 9 月 4 日	Sep. 4,1998
哈利斯科州	Jalisco Estado	墨西哥	Mexico	1998 年 11 月 18 日	Nov. 18,1998
利物浦市	Liverpool City	英国	United Kingdom	1999 年 10 月 18 日	Oct. 18,1999
马普托市	Maputo	莫桑比克	Mozambique	1999 年 10 月 25 日	Oct. 25,1999
清迈府	Chiengmai	泰国	Thailand	2000 年 4 月 2 日	Apr. 2,2000
迪拜市	Dubai	阿联酋	United Arab Emirates	2000 年 5 月 30 日	May. 30,2000
夸祖鲁－纳塔尔省	KwaZulu-Natal	南非	South Africa	2001 年 5 月 16 日	May. 16,2001
瓜亚基尔市	Guayaquil	厄瓜多尔	Ecuador	2001 年 7 月 6 日	Jul. 6,2001
瓦尔帕莱索	Valparaiso	智利	Chile	2001 年 7 月 10 日	Jul. 10,2001
巴塞罗那	Barcelona	西班牙	Spain	2001 年 10 月 31 日	Oct. 31,2001
奥斯陆市	Oslo	挪威	Norway	2001 年 11 月 10 日	Nov. 10,2001
康斯坦察县	Constanta	罗马尼亚	Romania	2002 年 4 月 15 日	Apr. 15,2002
科伦坡市	Colombo	斯里兰卡	Srilanka	2003 年 8 月 11 日	Aug. 11,2003
哥德堡市	Gothenburg	瑞典	Sweden	2003 年 10 月 23 日	Oct. 23,2003
布拉迪斯拉发州	Bratislara	斯洛伐克	Slovak	2003 年 11 月 10 日	Nov. 10,2003
奥胡斯州	Arhus	丹麦	Danmark	2003 年 11 月 10 日	Nov. 10,2003
科克	Cork	爱尔兰	Ireland	2005 年 5 月 19 日	May. 19,2005
东爪哇省	East Jawa Province	印尼	Indonesia	2006 年 8 月 30 日	Aug 30,2006
巴赛尔州	Basel-stadt	瑞士	Switzerland	2007 年 11 月 19 日	Nov. 19,2007
芝加哥市	Chicago	美国	United States	1985 年 9 月 5 日	Sep. 5,1985
区镇级国际友好城市	Shanghai Districts International Friendship Cities				
日本枚方市－长宁区	Hirakata-Changning	日本	Japan	1987 年 12 月 16 日	Dec. 16,1987
日本八尾市－嘉定区	Yao-Jiading	日本	Japan	1986 年 9 月 13 日	Sep. 13,1986
日本寝屋川市－卢湾区	Neyagawa-Luwan	日本	Japan	1994 年 5 月 12 日	May. 12,1994
日本泉佐野市－徐汇区	Yizumisano-Xuhui	日本	Japan	1994 年 10 月 21 日	Oct. 21,1994
纳米比亚奥卡汉贾市－马桥镇	Okahandja-Maqiao Town	纳米比亚	Namibia	1998 年 12 月 16 日	Dec. 16,1998
菲律宾大马尼拉署马卡蒂市－黄浦区	City of Makati-Huangpu	菲律宾	Philippines	2002 年 9 月 26 日	Sep. 26,2002
汉堡中心区－虹口区	Hamburg-mitte-Hongkou	德国	Germany	2007 年 6 月 21 日	Jun. 21,2007

表 7.25 续表 2 continued

城 市 Cities		国 家 Countries		缔结日期 Relationship Eastablished Date	
上海与国外建立友好交流关系的城市	**Cities with Friendly Exchange Relations**				
罗纳－阿尔卑斯大区	Rhone-Aples	法 国	France	1986 年 1 月 20 日	Nov. 20,1986
符拉迪沃斯托克市	Vladivostok	俄罗斯	Russia	1993 年 4 月 27 日	Apr. 27,1993
全罗南道	Cholla-Namdo	韩 国	Republic of Korea	1996 年 4 月 19 日	Apr. 19,1996
伦敦城	London City	英 国	United Kingdom	1996 年 9 月 4 日	Sep. 4,1996
长崎县	Nagasaki	日 本	Japan	1996 年 10 月 14 日	Oct. 14,1996
伦巴底大区	Lombardy Region	意大利	Italy	2002 年 11 月 19 日	Nov. 19,2002
全罗北道	Jeollabukdo Trade	韩 国	Korea	2003 年 4 月 16 日	Apr. 16,2003
尼科西亚市	Nicosia	塞浦路斯	Cyprus	2004 年 9 月 4 日	Sep. 4,2004
萨尔茨堡	Salzburg	奥地利	Austria	2004 年 11 月 3 日	Nov. 3,2004

表 7.26 各国驻沪总领事馆一览 (2007 年底)
LIST OF GENERAL CONSULATES OF FOREIGN COUNTRIES IN SHANGHAI (BY THE END OF YEAR 2007)

馆 名 Consulates		领区地域 Consular Region	
俄罗斯	Russia	上海、浙江、江苏、安徽	Shanghai,Zhejiang,Jiangsu and Anhui
波 兰	Poland	上海、浙江、江苏、安徽、福建	Shanghai,Zhejiang,Jiangsu,Anhui and Fujian
印 度	India	上海、浙江、江苏	Shanghai,Zhejiang and Jiangsu
韩 国	Republic of Korea	上海、浙江、江苏、安徽	Shanghai,Zhejiang,Jiangsu and Anhui
日 本	Japan	上海、浙江、江苏、安徽	Shanghai,Zhejiang,Jiangsu and Anhui
澳大利亚	Australia	上海、浙江、江苏、安徽	Shanghai,Zhejiang,Jiangsu and Anhui
古 巴	Cuba	上海、浙江、江苏、安徽	Shanghai,Zhejiang,Jiangsu and Anhui
法 国	France	上海、浙江、江苏	Shanghai,Zhejiang and Jiangsu
以色列	Israel	上海、浙江、江苏	Shanghai,Zhejiang and Jiangsu
美 国	United States	上海、浙江、江苏、安徽	Shanghai,Zhejiang,Jiangsu and Anhui
荷 兰	Netherlands	上海、浙江、江苏、安徽	Shanghai,Zhejiang,Jiangsu and Anhui
英 国	United Kingdom	上海、浙江、江苏	Shanghai,Zhejiang and Jiangsu
捷 克	Czech	上海、浙江、江苏、安徽	Shanghai,Zhejiang,Jiangsu and Anhui
德 国	Germany	上海、浙江、江苏、安徽	Shanghai,Zhejiang,Jiangsu and Anhui

注：本表数据由市外事办公室提供。
Note: Data in this table are provided by Shanghai Municipal Foreign Affairs Office.

表 7.26 续表 1 continued

馆名	Consulates	领区地域	Consular Region
瑞士	Switzerland	上海、浙江、江苏、安徽	Shanghai,Zhejiang,Jiangsu and Anhui
加拿大	Canada	上海、浙江、江苏、安徽	Shanghai,Zhejiang,Jiangsu and Anhui
新西兰	New Zealand	上海、浙江、江苏、安徽	Shanghai,Zhejiang,Jiangsu and Anhui
墨西哥	Mexico	上海、浙江、江苏、福建、湖南、江西	Shanghai,Zhejiang ,Jiangsu,Fujian,Hunan and Jiangxi
丹麦	Denmark	上海、浙江、江苏、安徽	Shanghai,Zhejiang,Jiangsu and Anhui
意大利	Italy	上海、浙江、江苏、安徽	Shanghai,Zhejiang,Jiangsu and Anhui
伊朗	Iran	上海、浙江、江苏、安徽	Shanghai,Zhejiang,Jiangsu and Anhui
新加坡	Singapore	上海、浙江、江苏	Shanghai,Zhejiang and Jiangsu
奥地利	Austria	上海、浙江、江苏、安徽	Shanghai,Zhejiang,Jiangsu and Anhui
芬兰	Finland	上海、浙江、江苏、安徽	Shanghai,Zhejiang,Jiangsu and Anhui
智利	Chile	上海、浙江、江苏、安徽	Shanghai,Zhejiang,Jiangsu and Anhui
瑞典	Sweden	上海、浙江、江苏、安徽	Shanghai,Zhejiang,Jiangsu and Anhui
挪威	Norway	上海、浙江、江苏、安徽	Shanghai,Zhejiang,Jiangsu and Anhui
比利时	Belgium	上海、浙江、江苏、安徽	Shanghai,Zhejiang,Jiangsu and Anhui
泰国	Thailand	上海、浙江、江苏、安徽	Shanghai,Zhejiang,Jiangsu and Anhui
土耳其	Turkey	上海、浙江、江苏、安徽	Shanghai,Zhejiang,Jiangsu and Anhui
埃及	Egypt	上海、浙江、江苏、安徽	Shanghai,Zhejiang,Jiangsu and Anhui
西班牙	Spain	上海、浙江、江苏	Shanghai,Zhejiang and Jiangsu
柬埔寨	Camboclia	上海、浙江、江苏、安徽	Shanghai,Zhejiang,Jiangsu and Anhui
马来西亚	Malaysia	上海、浙江、江苏	Shanghai,Zhejiang and Jiangsu
罗马尼亚	Romania	上海、浙江、江苏	Shanghai,Zhejiang and Jiangsu

表 7.26 续表 2 continued

馆名	Consulates	领区地域	Consular Region
阿根廷	Argentina	上海、浙江、江苏、安徽	Shanghai,Zhejiang,Jiangsu and Anhui
爱尔兰	Ireland	上海、浙江、江苏、安徽、江西	Shanghai,Zhejiang,Jiangsu ,Anhui,and Jiangxi
乌克兰	Ukraine	上海、浙江、江苏、安徽、福建、江西	Shanghai,Zhejiang,Jiangsu ,Anhui,Fujian and Jiangxi
巴西	Brazil	上海、浙江、江苏、安徽	Shanghai,Zhejiang,Jiangsu and Anhui
秘鲁	Peru	上海、浙江、江苏、安徽、福建、江西	Shanghai,Zhejiang,Jiangsu ,Anhui,Fujian and Jiangxi
菲律宾	The Philippines	上海、江苏、安徽、湖北	Shanghai,Jiangsu,Anhui and Hubai
南非	South Africa	上海、浙江、江苏、安徽、山东、福建、广东	Shanghai,Zhejiang,Jiangsu ,Anhui,Shantong, Fujian and Guangdong
乌拉圭	Uruguay	上海、浙江、江苏、安徽	Shanghai,Zhejiang,Jiangsu and Anhui
巴基斯坦	Pakistan	浙江、江苏、安徽	Zhejiang,Jiangsu and Anhui
摩纳哥	Monaco	浙江、江苏、安徽	Zhejiang,Jiangsu and Anhui
尼泊尔	Nepal	上海	Shanghai
斯洛伐克	Slovakia	浙江、江苏、安徽、福建、江西	Zhejiang,Jiangsu and Anhui,Fujian and Jiangxi
希腊	Greece	浙江、江苏、安徽、山东、福建、江西	Zhejiang,Jiangsu and Anhui,Shantong,Fujian and Jiangxi
匈牙利	Hungary	浙江、江苏、安徽	Zhejiang,Jiangsu and Anhui
牙买加	Jamaice	浙江、江苏、安徽	Zhejiang,Jiangsu and Anhui
哈萨克斯坦	Kazakhstan	浙江、江苏、安徽、福建、江西	Zhejiang,Jiangsu and Anhui,Fujian and Jiangxi
保加利亚	Bulgaria	浙江、江苏、安徽、福建、江西	Zhejiang,Jiangsu and Anhui,Fujian and Jiangxi
葡萄牙	Portugal	浙江、江苏、安徽、江西	Zhejiang,Jiangsu ,Anhui and Jiangxi
斯里兰卡	Sri Lanka	浙江、江苏、安徽、湖南、福建	Zhejiang,Jiangsu and Anhui,Hunan and Fujian
塞尔维亚	Serbia	浙江、江苏、安徽	Zhejiang,Jiangsu and Anhui
委内瑞拉	Venezuela	浙江、江苏	Zhejiang and Jiangsu
卢森堡	Luxembourg	浙江、江苏、安徽、福建	Zhejiang,Jiangsu, Anhui and Fujian
乌兹别克	Uzbekistan	浙江、江苏、安徽、福建、江西	Zhejiang,Jiangsu and Anhui,Fujian and Jiangxi
巴布亚新几内亚	Papua New Guinea	上海	Shanghai
马尔代夫	Maldives	上海	Shanghai
瓦努阿图	Vanuatu	上海、浙江、江苏、安徽	Shanghai,Zhejiang,Jiangsu and Anhui
尼日利亚	Nigeria	尚未开馆	Not Opened
越南	Vietnam	上海	Shanghai

①波兰领馆原设天津，1954 年 10 月 22 日迁来上海，当时系领事馆，1955 年 6 月 17 日升格为总领事馆。
②原苏联驻上海总领事馆于 1991 年 12 月更名为俄罗斯驻上海总领事馆。
❶Poland consulate was in Tianjin formerly and moved to Shanghai in Oct. 22,1954. In Jun. 17,1955,it was upgraded as Consulate General.
❷ In Dec. 1991,former U. S. S. R. Consulate General renamed as Russian Consulate General.

上 / 海 / 统 / 计 / 年 / 鉴

主要统计指标解释

口岸进出口总额

指由海关统计的进出口商品总额。统计方法依据联合国的国际贸易统计原则，反映进出上海而引起物质资源储备增加或减少的商品运动。按上述原则应具备条件：实际进出上海(海关关境)，不仅包括经商业交易行为的进出口货品，也包括援助、捐赠等未发生买卖关系的货品价值。出口按离岸价(FOB)统计，进口按到岸价(CIF)统计。

外贸进出口总额

指海关统计中按经营单位即进出口企业在海关注册地的行政区域口径统计的数据，它反映的是上海行政辖区内各类具有进出口经营权企业（外贸企业）的进出口。它不包含外省市外贸企业途经上海口岸由上海海关结关放行及统计的进出口商品，但包含上海外贸企业经由非上海口岸进出口结关放行及统计的商品。

外商直接投资

指外国企业和经济组织或个人(包括华侨、港澳台胞以及我国在境外注册的企业)按我国有关政策、法规，用现汇、实物、技术等在我国境内开办外商独资企业、与我国境内的企业或经济组织共同举办中外合资经营企业、合作经营企业或合作开发资源的投资（包括外商投资收益的再投资）以及企业投资总额内直接投资者对企业的贷款,即外方股东贷款(需在报告期内将相应合同及贷款协议报商务部备案核查)。

引进技术

指通过贸易途径从国外获得发展我国国民经济和提高技术水平所需要的技术装备。引进方式有:许可证贸易(技术贸易)、生产线(包括成套设备)、单机(包括关键设备)、软硬件结合(同时引进技术和设备)和其他。

对外承包工程

对外承包工程包括各对外承包公司以招标议标承包方式承揽的下列业务:(1)承包国外工程建设项目。(2)承包我国对外经济援助项目。(3)承包我国驻外机构的工程建设项目。(4)承包我国境内利用外资进行建设的工程项目。(5)与外国承包公司合营或联合承包工程项目时我国公司分包部分。(6)以服务成果向业主收费的技术服务项目(包括承担地形地貌测绘;地质资源勘探与普查;建设区域规划;提供设计文件、图纸、生产工艺技术资料和工程技术经济咨询;工程项目的可行性考察、研究和评估;进行技术指导和培训人员等)。(7)对外承包兼营的房屋开发业务。对外承包工程的营业额是以货币表现的本期内完成的对外承包工程的工作量，包括以前年度签订的合同和本年度新签订的合同在报告期完成的工作量。

对外劳务合作

指以收取工资的形式向业主或承包商提供技术和劳动服务的活动。上海对外承包公司在境外开办的合营企业,上海公司同时又提供劳务的,其劳务部分也纳入劳务合作统计。劳务合作营业额按报告期内向雇主提交的结算数(包括工资、加班费和奖金等)统计。

国际旅游入境人数

指来上海参观、访问、旅行、探亲、访友、休养、考察、参加会议和从事经济、科技、文化、教育、体育、宗教等活动的外国人、华侨、港澳和台湾同胞的人数。不包括来上海常住1年以上的外国专家、留学生等。上海入境的境外旅游人数包括从上海口岸入境的境外旅游人数和从我国其他口岸入境的境外旅游人数。

国际旅游(外汇)收入

指入境旅游的外国人、华侨、港澳台同胞在上海旅游过程中发生的一切旅游支出。

SHANGHAI STATISTICAL YEARBOOK

EXPLANATORY NOTES TO MAJOR STATISTICAL INDICATORS

□ Total Value of Port Imports and Exports

Total Port Trade Volume refers to the aggregate volume of commodities that are imported or exported through Shanghai's ports. The statistics method follows the international trade statistics principles set by the United Nations. It reflects the fluctuation of Shanghai's material reserves caused by export or import. Requirements involved in the principle is: the commodities refer to those enter or leave Shanghai's ports, including not only the business trading activities but also the commodities value of the aid and donations that haven't been involved in sales . Exports are calculated according to FOB price, and imports are calculated according to CIF.

□ Total Value of Foreign Trade Imports and Exports

The Volume of Foreign Trade is offered by Customs authorities, covering the operation units, or the enterprises involved in import and export, that have registered in the administrative regions where the Customs operate. It reflects the import and export of all the enterprises with import and export rights (foreign trade enterprises) under the administration of Shanghai Municipality. It excludes those commodities of foreign trade enterprises from out of town that underwent customs clearance at Shanghai ports but includes commodities of foreign trade enterprises of Shanghai that underwent customs clearance in non-Shanghai ports.

□ Foreign Direct Investment

Foreign Direct Investment refers to the investments made inside China by foreign enterprises and economic organizations or individuals (including overseas Chinese, compatriots in Hong Kong, Macao and Chinese enterprises registered abroad), in line with the relevant policies and laws of China, for the establishment of wholly foreign-owned enterprises, and joint ventures or development projects launched in China (including re-investment of profits from foreign businesses), and the funds that enterprises borrow from abroad in the total investment of projects which are approved by the relevant departments of the governments and the loans from the direct investors within the total investment of the projects, i.e., foreign shareholders' loans. (The related contracts and loans agreements in the report period should be filed with the Ministry of Commerce)

□ Import of Technology and Equipment

Import of Technology refers to technology and equipments obtained through the trade channel from other countries which are needed for advancing China's national economy and improving its technological level. The import form includes: licensing (technological trade), production lines (including complete plant), single machine (including key equipments), combination of hardware and software (importing technology and equipments simultaneously) and others.

□ Overseas Contracted Projects

Overseas Contracted Projects refer to projects undertaken by Chinese contractors (project contracting companies) through bidding process. They include: (1) overseas civil engineering construction projects financed by foreign investors. (2) overseas projects financed by the Chinese government through its foreign-aid programs. (3) construction projects of Chinese diplomatic missions, trade offices and other institutions stationed abroad. (4) construction projects in China financed by foreign investment. (5) sub-contracted projects to be taken by Chinese contractors through a joint umbrella project with foreign contractor(s). (6) technical assistance projects in the form of service results and chargeable to the owners (such as topographic surveying, geological prospecting, development zone programming, provision of documents, blueprint, materials on production process, technical consultation, project feasibility studies and evaluation, personnel training, etc.). and (7) housing development projects. The business turnover from international contracting is the work of contracted projects completed during the reporting period, expressed in monetary terms, including completed work on project contracts signed in previous years.

□ Overseas Labor Service Cooperation

Overseas Labor Service refers to activities of providing technology and labor services to employers or contractors by collecting salaries and wages. Labor services provided by Shanghai's international contrasting corporations to their overseas joint ventures shall be included into the statistics of over-

EXPLANATORY NOTES TO MAJOR STATISTICAL INDICATORS

seas services. The business turn over of overseas labor services is the settlement price (including salaries, overtime pay and bonuses) submitted to the employers during the reporting period.

□ Quantity of Overseas Tourists

Number of Overseas Tourists refers to the number of foreigners, overseas Chinese, and compatriots from Hong Kong, Macao and Taiwan coming to Shanghai for sightseeing, visits, tours, family reunions, meeting friends, vacations, study tours, attending meetings and other activities of an economic, scientific and technological, cultural, physical culture and religious nature. This does not include foreign experts and students residing in Shanghai for over 1 year. The number of overseas tourists to Shanghai includes those overseas tourists entering China through Shanghai customs and through customs other than Shanghai.

□ Foreign Exchange Earnings from International Tourism

Foreign Exchange Earnings from International Tourism refer to the total expenditures of foreigners, overseas Chinese, Chinese compatriots from Hong Kong, Macao and Taiwan during their stay in Shanghai.

第八篇

CHAPTER 8

价格水平

PRICES

表 8.1 居民消费价格和商品零售价格指数(1978～2007)
OVERALL RESIDENTS CONSUMER PRICE INDEX AND RETAIL PRICE INDEX

年 份 Year	居民消费价格指数 Overall Residents Consumer Price Index		年 份 Year	商品零售价格指数 Retail Price Index	
	以上年价格为 100 preceding year = 100	以 1978 年价格为 100 1978 = 100		以上年价格为 100 preceding year = 100	以 1978 年价格为 100 1978 = 100
1978	100.5	100.0	1978	100.1	100.0
1979	100.9	100.9	1979	101.0	101.0
1980	105.9	106.9	1980	106.5	107.6
1981	101.4	108.3	1981	101.5	109.2
1982	100.3	108.7	1982	100.3	109.5
1983	100.2	108.9	1983	100.1	109.6
1984	102.2	111.3	1984	102.2	112.0
1985	115.2	128.2	1985	116.4	130.4
1986	106.3	136.3	1986	106.7	139.1
1987	108.1	147.3	1987	108.8	151.4
1988	120.1	176.9	1988	121.3	183.6
1989	115.9	205.1	1989	116.7	214.3
1990	106.3	218.0	1990	104.8	224.6
1991	110.5	240.9	1991	109.5	245.9
1992	110.0	265.0	1992	109.7	269.8
1993	120.2	318.5	1993	117.5	317.0
1994	123.9	394.6	1994	117.5	372.4
1995	118.7	468.4	1995	113.0	420.9
1996	109.2	511.5	1996	105.0	441.9
1997	102.8	525.8	1997	98.8	436.6
1998	100.0	525.8	1998	95.1	415.2
1999	101.5	533.7	1999	97.3	404.0
2000	102.5	547.0	2000	96.4	389.5
2001	100.0	547.0	2001	98.6	384.0
2002	100.5	549.8	2002	98.7	379.0
2003	100.1	550.3	2003	99.0	375.4
2004	102.2	562.2	2004	100.9	378.8
2005	101.0	567.6	2005	99.4	376.7
2006	101.2	574.5	2006	100.2	377.4
2007	103.2	592.6	2007	102.4	386.5

注：本表数据由国家统计局上海调查总队提供。
Note: Date on this table are provided by Survey Office of the National Bureau of Statistics in Shanghai.

表8.2 居民消费价格指数(1991～2007, 以1990年价格为100)
OVERALL RESIDENTS CONSUMER PRICE INDEX (1990 = 100)

年 份 Year	居民消费价格指数 Overall Residents Consumer Price Index	食 品 Food	烟酒及用品 Cigarettes, Liquors and Related Items	衣 着 Clothing
1991	110.5	113.5	103.0	105.7
1992	121.6	128.7	113.0	115.7
1993	146.1	157.2	124.5	137.3
1994	181.0	207.1	139.5	158.8
1995	214.9	261.2	149.1	172.8
1996	234.6	288.6	149.1	187.8
1997	241.2	288.6	134.6	189.9
1998	241.2	282.3	129.2	178.5
1999	244.8	274.9	129.8	175.5
2000	250.9	270.0	126.1	167.2
2001	250.9	270.8	124.7	165.4
2002	252.2	278.6	123.4	161.2
2003	252.5	282.3	123.1	157.2
2004	257.8	305.6	121.0	148.1
2005	260.3	319.4	120.6	136.4
2006	263.4	327.5	120.9	145.2
2007	271.7	358.3	121.7	147.1

注：本表数据由国家统计局上海调查总队提供。
Note: Date in this table are provided by Survey Office of the National Bureau of Statistics in Shanghai.

表8.2 续表 continued

年 份 Year	家庭设备用品及维修服务 Home Appliances and Repair Service	医疗保健和个人用品 Medicine, Medical Services and Personal Aricles	交通和通信 Transportation and Communication	娱乐教育文化用品及服务 Recreation, Education and Culture Articles	居 住 Residence
1991	112.5	113.1	108.5	96.9	129.3
1992	115.4	132.7	108.9	93.8	153.9
1993	126.4	151.8	127.5	115.7	206.8
1994	140.2	180.9	149.5	136.1	249.4
1995	145.5	199.0	171.5	158.2	300.0
1996	144.2	210.9	181.9	187.6	329.1
1997	131.8	215.4	210.3	205.6	396.9
1998	121.9	219.5	218.1	218.6	450.9
1999	117.5	223.6	245.1	244.1	477.5
2000	112.5	223.4	271.9	296.6	493.3
2001	109.3	217.6	266.7	302.8	504.6
2002	106.8	212.4	258.4	305.3	504.6
2003	105.1	212.4	248.9	306.2	510.2
2004	102.8	212.2	240.4	306.0	518.5
2005	103.6	212.9	234.3	300.8	533.7
2006	106.4	215.2	227.8	295.5	549.2
2007	109.9	215.7	220.8	287.4	573.9

表8.3 居民消费价格指数(1991～2007，以上年价格为100)
OVERALL RESIDENTS CONSUMER PRICE INDEX (PRECEDING YEAR = 100)

年 份 Year	居民消费价格指数 Overall Residents Consumer Price Index	食 品 Food	烟酒及用品 Cigarettes, Liquors and Related Items	衣 着 Clothing
1991	110.5	113.5	103.0	105.7
1992	110.0	113.4	109.7	109.5
1993	120.2	122.1	110.2	118.6
1994	123.9	131.8	112.0	115.7
1995	118.7	126.1	106.9	108.8
1996	109.2	110.5	100.0	108.7
1997	102.8	100.0	90.3	101.1
1998	100.0	97.8	96.0	94.0
1999	101.5	97.4	100.4	98.3
2000	102.5	98.2	97.2	95.3
2001	100.0	100.3	98.9	98.9
2002	100.5	102.9	98.9	97.5
2003	100.1	101.3	99.8	97.5
2004	102.2	108.3	98.3	94.2
2005	101.0	104.5	99.7	92.1
2006	101.2	102.5	100.2	106.4
2007	103.2	109.4	100.7	101.3

注：本表数据由国家统计局上海调查总队提供。
Note: Date in this table are provided by Survey Office of the National Bureau of Statistics in Shanghai.

表8.3 续表 continued

年 份 Year	家庭设备用品 及维修服务 Home Appliances and Repair Service	医疗保健 和个人用品 Medicine, Medical Services and Personal Aricles	交通和通信 Transportation and Communication	娱乐教育 文化用品及服务 Recreation, Education and Culture Articles	居 住 Residence
1991	112.5	113.1	108.5	96.9	129.3
1992	102.6	117.3	100.4	96.8	119.0
1993	109.5	114.4	117.0	123.4	134.4
1994	110.9	119.2	117.3	117.6	120.6
1995	103.8	110.0	114.7	116.2	120.3
1996	99.1	106.0	106.1	118.6	109.7
1997	91.4	102.1	115.6	109.6	120.6
1998	92.5	101.9	103.7	106.3	113.6
1999	96.4	101.9	112.4	111.7	105.9
2000	95.7	99.9	110.9	121.5	103.3
2001	97.2	97.4	98.1	102.1	102.3
2002	97.7	97.6	96.9	100.8	100.0
2003	98.4	100.0	96.3	100.3	101.1
2004	97.8	100.0	96.5	99.9	101.6
2005	100.8	100.3	97.5	98.3	102.9
2006	102.7	101.1	97.3	98.2	102.9
2007	103.3	100.2	96.9	97.3	104.5

表8.4　主要年份居民消费价格指数(以上年价格为100)
CLASSIFIED RESIDENTS CONSUMER PRICE INDEX IN MAIN YEARS(PRECEDING YEAR = 100)

类　别	Types	2001	2006	2007
居民消费价格指数	**Overall Residents Consumer Price Index**	**100.0**	**101.2**	**103.2**
#服务项目价格	Services Items Price	105.4	101.2	100.9
食　品	**Food**	**100.3**	**102.5**	**109.4**
粮　食	Grain	102.9	101.9	101.6
淀　粉	Starch	103.6	95.6	101.8
干豆类及豆制品	Dry Beans and Bean Products	95.6	99.0	108.7
油　脂	Oil or Fat	84.5	97.6	129.8
肉禽及其制品	Meat Poultry and Their Products	99.3	100.6	123.0
蛋	Eggs	102.4	95.4	121.8
水产品	Aquatic Products	100.1	102.0	101.4
菜	Vegetables	108.9	105.2	113.5
#鲜　菜	Fresh Vegetables	110.2	104.8	114.0
调味品	Flavoring	99.2	104.4	104.6
糖	Sugars	101.4	102.1	99.8
茶及饮料	Tea and Beverages	98.4	100.5	101.8
干鲜瓜果	Dried and Fresh Fruits	104.3	111.5	111.8
#鲜瓜果	Fresh Fruits	105.8	114.8	110.9
糕点饼干	Cakes, Biscuits and Bread	100.5	98.9	101.5
液体乳及乳制品	Milk and Its Products	100.8	102.3	106.2
在外用膳食品	Dining Out	98.0	102.5	107.6
其他食品	Other Food	99.2	102.8	100.9
烟酒及用品	**Cigarettes, Liquors and Related Items**	**98.9**	**100.2**	**100.7**
烟　草	Tobacco	99.2	99.8	100.6
酒	Liquors	98.2	100.2	101.0
吸烟饮酒用品	Cigarettes and Spirits Related Items	100.0	104.8	100.5
衣　着	**Clothing**	**98.9**	**106.4**	**101.3**
服　装	Garments	96.4	106.3	103.1
男式服装	Men' Wear	99.0	101.6	100.6
女式服装	Women's Wear	94.7	109.6	104.6
儿童服装	Children's Wear	95.4	109.3	106.1
衣着材料	Clothing Materials	98.7	97.8	100.7
鞋袜帽	Shoes, Socks and Hats	106.2	107.9	95.4
#鞋	Shoes	106.6	109.1	94.4
衣着加工服务	Garment Processing Service	100.0	100.0	102.0

注：本表数据由国家统计局上海调查总队提供。
Note: Date in this table are provided by Survey Office of the National Bureau of Statistics in Shanghai.

表 8.4 续表 continued

类 别	Types	2001	2006	2007
家庭设备用品及维修服务	**Home Appliances and Repair Service**	**97.2**	**102.7**	**103.3**
耐用消费品	Durable Consumer Goods	94.7	101.2	102.9
室内装饰品	Interior Decorations	101.0	100.0	100.2
床上用品	Bed Articles	100.5	100.6	103.1
家庭日用杂品	Daily Use Household Articles	98.6	102.8	102.1
家庭服务及加工维修服务	Other Daily Use Articles	100.0	112.0	108.5
医疗保健和个人用品	**Medicine, Medical Services and Personal Aricles**	**97.4**	**101.1**	**100.2**
医疗保健	Medicine and Medical Services	96.5	98.1	98.4
#中药材及中成药	Herbs and Ready-made Traditional Chinese Medicine	105.5	100.9	98.2
西 药	Western Medicine	92.0	95.1	95.6
保健器具及用品	Healthcare Equipment	95.4	99.7	101.7
医疗保健服务	Medical and Healthcare Service	100.0	98.8	97.9
个人用品及服务	Personal Aricles and Service	99.8	107.1	103.0
交通和通信	**Transportation and Communication**	**98.1**	**97.3**	**96.9**
交 通	Transport	102.3	98.9	98.8
#交通工具	Transport Tools	97.9	91.3	96.2
通 信	Communications	94.4	94.9	94.3
通信工具	Communications Tools	69.7	70.4	70.7
通信服务	Communications Service	103.1	100.0	98.9
娱乐教育文化用品及服务	**Recreation, Education and Culture Articles**	**102.1**	**98.2**	**97.3**
文娱用耐用消费品及服务	Durable Consumer Goods for Recreational Use	91.2	87.8	83.8
教 育	Education	109.6	100.0	99.8
文化娱乐类	Recreation and Culture Articles	105.2	101.6	99.8
旅 游	Tourism	96.2	103.0	103.4
居 住	**Residence**	**102.3**	**102.9**	**104.5**
建房及装修材料	Construction and Decoration Materials	97.5	107.0	106.9
租 房	Renting	111.0	99.5	108.7
自有住房	Self-owned House	99.8	102.3	105.6
水电燃料	Water, Electricity and Fuels	101.7	100.4	100.3
#水	Water	109.3	100.0	100.0
电	Electricity	100.0	100.6	100.6
液化石油气	LPG	118.4	104.3	101.3
管道煤气	Gas	100.0	100.0	100.0

表8.5 商品零售价格指数（2001～2007，以上年价格为100）
COMMODITY RETAIL PRICE INDEX (PRECEDING YEAR =100)

类别	Types	2001	2002	2003
商品零售价格指数	**Overall Retail Price Index**	**98.6**	**98.7**	**99.0**
食　品	Food	98.4	100.3	101.5
粮　食	Grain	100.1	96.7	100.5
淀　粉	Starch	100.4	101.3	109.2
干豆类及豆制品	Dry Beans and Bean Products	111.3	94.3	102.7
油　脂	Oil or Fat	81.4	97.9	106.8
肉禽及其制品	Meat Poultry and Their Products	100.4	99.0	101.7
蛋	Eggs	110.7	100.5	101.0
水产品	Aquatic Products	90.1	101.1	103.9
菜	Vegetables	107.1	106.4	101.5
调味品	Flavoring	99.5	100.8	98.4
糖	Sugars	104.4	98.5	98.9
干鲜瓜果	Dried and Fresh Fruits	107.3	104.6	97.6
糕点饼干面包	Cakes,Biscuits and Bread	99.8	98.9	101.4
液体乳及乳制品	Milk and Its Products	99.8	99.9	101.4
在外用膳食品	Dinging Out	100.7	98.9	100.7
其他食品	Other Food	99.5	99.9	101.5
饮料、烟酒	Beverages, Tobacco and Liquor	98.4	97.7	99.5
服装、鞋帽	Garments, Shoes and Hats	107.7	95.0	96.7
纺织品	Textiles	98.8	99.4	99.8
家用电器及音像器材	Household Appliances and Audio-video Appliances	95.0	93.5	95.8
文化办公用品	Cultural Office Articles	98.7	92.7	93.7
日用品	Daily Use Articles	99.0	99.8	99.1
体育娱乐用品	Sports and Recreation Goods	99.1	97.9	97.4
交通、通信用品	Transportation and Communication Goods	97.4	96.6	91.2
家　具	Furniture	90.4	100.1	99.5
化妆品	Cosmetics	100.7	97.4	100.4
金银珠宝	Jewelry	87.2	100.0	106.5
中西药品及医疗保健用品	Traditional Chinese and Western Medicines	98.7	99.5	98.3
书报杂志及电子出版物	Newspapers and Magazines and Electronic Publications	99.5	98.9	98.3
燃　料	Fuels	111.4	106.8	108.6
建筑材料及五金电料	Building Materials and Hardwares	101.8	103.8	100.8

注：本表数据由国家统计局上海调查总队提供。
Note: Date in this table are provided by Survey Office of the National Bureau of Statistics in Shanghai.

表 8.5 续表 continued

	类 别 Types	2004	2005	2006	2007
商品零售价格指数	**Overall Retail Price Index**	**100.9**	**99.4**	**100.2**	**102.4**
食 品	Food	108.6	104.7	102.7	109.6
粮 食	Grain	128.8	102.1	102.4	101.4
淀 粉	Starch	107.2	105.2	95.6	101.8
干豆类及豆制品	Dry Beans and Bean Products	124.8	103.6	99.5	108.6
油 脂	Oil or Fat	114.4	91.2	97.6	129.8
肉禽及其制品	Meat Poultry and Their Products	117.6	105.5	100.6	123.0
蛋	Eggs	118.6	105.8	95.4	121.8
水产品	Aquatic Products	107.7	114.4	102.0	101.4
菜	Vegetables	95.5	103.4	105.2	113.5
调味品	Flavoring	103.0	102.1	104.4	104.6
糖	Sugars	103.1	103.8	103.8	99.1
干鲜瓜果	Dried and Fresh Fruits	118.3	99.4	111.5	111.8
糕点饼干面包	Cakes, Biscuits and Bread	100.9	98.4	98.9	101.5
液体乳及乳制品	Milk and Its Products	99.6	100.8	102.3	106.2
在外用膳食品	Dining Out	103.1	104.4	102.5	107.6
其他食品	Other Food	96.9	101.1	102.8	100.9
饮料、烟酒	Beverages, Tobacco and Liquor	98.8	99.6	100.1	100.9
服装、鞋帽	Garments, Shoes and Hats	93.9	92.6	106.6	101.2
纺织品	Textiles	102.2	99.4	100.1	102.6
家用电器及音像器材	Household Appliances and Audio-video Appliances	93.4	93.1	92.6	92.2
文化办公用品	Cultural Office Articles	91.9	91.6	95.2	93.9
日用品	Daily Use Articles	98.4	100.5	102.5	101.8
体育娱乐用品	Sports and Recreation Goods	96.8	94.7	95.6	92.9
交通、通信用品	Transportation and Communication Goods	90.2	88.5	87.5	90.8
家 具	Furniture	98.2	100.1	101.2	101.8
化妆品	Cosmetics	99.0	96.1	98.0	101.2
金银珠宝	Jewelry	107.9	107.3	114.7	106.2
中西药品及医疗保健用品	Traditional Chinese and Western Medicines	95.6	97.7	97.6	98.0
书报杂志及电子出版物	Newspapers and Magazines and Electronic Publications	99.6	98.0	100.8	103.6
燃 料	Fuels	107.0	109.1	110.0	103.0
建筑材料及五金电料	Building Materials and Hardwares	104.7	104.0	106.1	107.6

表8.6 工业品出厂价格指数（2001～2007，以2000年价格为100）
PRODUCER PRICE INDEX OF INDUSTRIAL PRODUCTS (2000 = 100)

	类 别 Types	2001	2002	2003
工业品出厂价格指数	**Producer Price Index of Industrial Products**	**96.7**	**93.2**	**94.5**
按轻重工业分	**Grouped by Light or Heavy Industries**			
轻工业	Light Industry	97.8	94.9	94.1
以农产品为原料	Using Farm Products as Raw Materials	99.8	98.7	99.7
以非农产品为原料	Using Non-farm Products as Raw Materials	95.4	90.5	89.0
重工业	Heavy Industry	96.1	92.4	95.1
采 掘	Mining and Guarrying	100.0	100.4	113.1
原 料	Raw Material	98.7	96.8	104.5
加 工	Manufacturing	94.7	90.0	90.8
按用途分	**Grouped by Use**			
生产资料	Means of Production	96.3	92.3	95.2
生活资料	Consumer Goods	97.3	94.7	92.9
#食 品	Food	102.6	105.3	105.4
衣 着	Clothing	99.6	99.4	99.1
一般日用品	Non-Durable Consumer Goods	97.2	94.4	93.7
耐用消费品	Durable Consumer Goods	95.1	90.1	86.6
按工业部门分	**Grouped by Sector**			
冶金工业	Metallurgy Industry	98.4	95.2	107.1
电力工业	Electric Power Industry	100.2	99.8	99.1
煤碳及炼焦工业	Coal and Coling Industry	103.8	108.7	126.5
石油工业	Petroleum Industry	99.8	97.5	113.4
化学工业	Chemical Industry	96.2	92.6	95.7
机械工业	Machinery Industry	93.6	88.2	85.2
建筑材料工业	Building Material Industry	102.2	98.5	98.7
森林工业	Forest Industry	97.6	94.0	92.3
食品工业	Food Industry	102.8	105.2	107.0
纺织工业	Textile Industry	96.2	91.2	94.1
缝纫工业	Sewing Industry	99.1	98.9	98.7
皮革工业	Leather Industry	100.7	99.5	98.9
造纸工业	Paper Making Industry	97.8	92.6	90.8
文教艺术用品工业	Cultural Educational and Art Goods	96.9	95.9	95.1
其他工业	Others Industry	100.5	105.5	107.1

①采掘业工业品出厂价格指数以2001年价格为100计算。
②本表数据由国家统计局上海调查总队提供。
❶The prices of minging and quarrying industry in 2001 are set at 100.
❷Date in this table are provided by Survey Office of the National Bureau of Statistics in Shanghai.

表 8.6 续表 continued

	类 别 Types	2004	2005	2006	2007
工业品出厂价格指数	**Producer Price Index of Industrial Products**	**97.9**	**99.6**	**100.2**	**101.4**
按轻重工业分	**Grouped by Light or Heavy Industries**				
轻工业	Light Industry	95.0	95.6	94.5	94.5
以农产品为原料	Using Farm Products as Raw Materials	102.9	103.3	103.9	107.1
以非农产品为原料	Using Non-farm Products as Raw Materials	88.8	89.4	87.8	87.0
重工业	Heavy Industry	99.9	102.2	104.7	107.1
采 掘	Mining and Guarrying	134.9	168.0	192.7	195.6
原 料	Raw Material	118.2	129.7	140.3	145.9
加 工	Manufacturing	92.9	92.8	93.1	94.7
按用途分	**Grouped by Use**				
生产资料	Means of Production	101.0	104.2	105.5	107.0
生活资料	Consumer Goods	91.7	90.5	89.5	89.7
#食 品	Food	106.8	107.4	107.9	113.1
衣 着	Clothing	101.6	103.0	103.4	105.2
一般日用品	Non-Durable Consumer Goods	94.9	95.6	96.5	97.5
耐用消费品	Durable Consumer Goods	81.9	78.4	74.8	71.5
按工业部门分	**Grouped by Sector**				
冶金工业	Metallurgy Industry	126.8	138.6	144.3	156.0
电力工业	Electric Power Industry	101.0	102.3	103.1	103.6
煤碳及炼焦工业	Coal and Coking Industry	142.1	143.4	144.8	163.3
石油工业	Petroleum Industry	131.9	159.2	182.3	188.9
化学工业	Chemical Industry	103.5	110.6	112.8	116.2
机械工业	Machinery Industry	82.9	80.5	79.0	77.3
建筑材料工业	Building Material Industry	104.5	99.1	95.5	97.0
森林工业	Forest Industry	90.9	91.9	92.8	95.2
食品工业	Food Industry	111.4	113.1	114.2	120.7
纺织工业	Textile Industry	97.6	97.2	97.8	98.3
缝纫工业	Sewing Industry	101.3	102.8	103.0	105.0
皮革工业	Leather Industry	99.2	99.1	99.9	100.0
造纸工业	Paper Making Industry	90.1	88.7	88.3	88.5
文教艺术用品工业	Cultural Educational and Art Goods	94.1	93.8	92.1	91.3
其他工业	Others Industry	112.6	114.4	120.2	122.8

表8.7　工业品出厂价格指数（2000～2007，以上年价格为100）
PRODUCER PRICE INDEX OF INDUSTRIAL PRODUCTS IN MAIN YEARS (PRECEDING YEAR＝100)

类　别	Types	2000	2001	2002	2003
工业品出厂价格指数	**Producer Price Index of Industrial Products**	**102.5**	**96.7**	**96.4**	**101.4**
按轻重工业分	**Grouped by Light or Heavy Industries**				
轻工业	Light Industry	99.9	97.8	97.0	99.2
以农产品为原料	Using Farm Products as Raw Materials	99.4	99.8	98.9	101.0
以非农产品为原料	Using Non-farm Products as Raw Materials	100.2	95.4	94.9	98.3
重工业	Heavy Industry	104.3	96.1	96.1	102.9
采　掘	Mining and Guarrying		100.0	100.4	112.6
原　料	Raw Material	110.9	98.7	98.1	108.0
加　工	Manufacturing	99.0	94.7	95.0	100.9
按用途分	**Grouped by Use**				
生产资料	Means of Production	105.4	96.3	95.8	103.1
生活资料	Consumer Goods	98.0	97.3	97.3	98.1
#食　品	Food	98.2	102.6	102.6	100.1
衣　着	Clothing	99.9	99.6	99.8	99.7
一般日用品	Non-Durable Consumer Goods	97.4	97.2	97.1	99.3
耐用消费品	Durable Consumer Goods	97.3	95.1	94.7	96.1
按工业部门分	**Grouped by Sector**				
冶金工业	Metallurgy Industry	104.6	98.4	96.7	112.5
电力工业	ElectricPower Industry	98.3	100.2	99.6	99.3
煤碳及炼焦工业	Coal and Coking Industry	102.7	103.8	104.7	116.4
石油工业	Petroleum Industry	135.9	99.8	97.7	116.3
化学工业	Chemical Industry	108.7	96.2	96.3	103.4
机械工业	Machinery Industry	96.9	93.6	94.2	96.6
建筑材料工业	Building Material Industry	108.4	102.2	96.4	100.2
森林工业	Forest Industry	97.4	97.6	96.3	98.2
食品工业	Food Industry	98.2	102.8	102.3	101.7
纺织工业	Textile Industry	105.5	96.2	94.8	103.2
缝纫工业	Sewing Industry	97.4	99.1	99.8	99.8
皮革工业	Leather Industry	97.6	100.7	98.8	99.4
造纸工业	Paper Making Industry	110.0	97.8	94.7	98.1
文教艺术用品工业	Cultural Educational and Art Goods	99.4	96.9	99.0	99.2
其他工业	Other Industry	98.2	100.5	105.0	101.5

注：本表数据由国家统计局上海调查总队提供。
Note: Date in this table are provided by Survey Office of the National Bureau of Statistics in Shanghai.

表8.7 续表 continued

	类 别 Types	2004	2005	2006	2007
工业品出厂价格指数	**Producer Price Index of Industrial Products**	**103.6**	**101.7**	**100.6**	**101.2**
按轻重工业分	**Grouped by Light or Heavy Industries**				
轻工业	Light Industry	101.0	100.6	98.8	100.0
以农产品为原料	Using Farm Products as Raw Materials	103.2	100.4	100.6	103.1
以非农产品为原料	Using Non-farm Products as Raw Materials	99.8	100.7	98.2	99.1
重工业	Heavy Industry	105.0	102.3	102.4	102.3
采 掘	Mining and Guarrying	119.3	124.5	114.7	101.5
原 料	Raw Material	113.1	109.7	108.2	104.0
加 工	Manufacturing	102.3	99.9	100.3	101.7
按用途分	**Grouped by Use**				
生产资料	Means of Production	106.1	103.2	101.2	101.4
生活资料	Consumer Goods	98.7	98.7	98.9	100.2
#食 品	Food	101.3	100.6	100.5	104.8
衣 着	Clothing	102.5	101.4	100.4	101.7
一般日用品	Non-Durable Consumer Goods	101.3	100.7	100.9	101.0
耐用消费品	Durable Consumer Goods	94.6	95.7	95.4	95.6
按工业部门分	**Grouped by Sector**				
冶金工业	Metallurgy Industry	118.4	109.3	104.1	108.1
电力工业	Electric Power Industry	101.9	101.3	100.8	100.5
煤碳及炼焦工业	Coal and Coking Industry	112.3	100.9	101.0	112.8
石油工业	Petroleum Industry	116.3	120.7	114.5	103.6
化学工业	Chemical Industry	108.2	106.9	102.0	103.0
机械工业	Machinery Industry	97.3	97.1	98.1	97.8
建筑材料工业	Building Material Industry	105.9	94.8	96.4	101.6
森林工业	Forest Industry	98.5	101.1	101.0	102.6
食品工业	Food Industry	104.1	101.5	101.0	105.7
纺织工业	Textile Industry	103.7	99.6	100.6	100.5
缝纫工业	Sewing Industry	102.6	101.5	100.2	101.9
皮革工业	Leather Industry	100.3	99.9	100.8	100.1
造纸工业	Paper Making Industry	99.2	98.5	99.6	100.2
文教艺术用品工业	Cultural Educational and Art Goods	99.0	99.7	98.2	99.1
其他工业	Other Industry	105.1	101.6	105.1	102.2

表8.8 原材料、燃料、动力购进价格指数（2001～2007，以2000年价格为100）
PURCHASING PRICE INDEX OF RAW MATERIALS, FUELS AND POWER (2000 = 100)

	类 别 Types	2001	2002	2003	2004
原材料、燃料、动力购进价格指数	**Purchasing Price Index of Raw Materials, Fuels and Power**	**98.7**	**96.4**	**102.6**	**119.4**
燃料、动力类	Fuel and Power	99.9	101.5	109.3	136.4
黑色金属材料类	Ferrous Metals	104.5	104.6	118.9	160.0
#钢　材	Rolled-steel	99.7	96.6	105.2	129.6
有色金属材料和电线类	Nonferrous Metals and Electric Wire	93.2	88.6	90.8	108.9
化工原料类	Chemical Raw Materials	90.4	83.8	89.9	102.8
木材及纸浆类	Wood and Paper Pulps	94.9	92.6	92.0	92.8
建筑材料及非金属矿类	Building Materials and Nonmetal Minerals	101.6	97.8	100.7	115.9
其他工业原材料及半成品类	Other Industrial Raw and Processed Materials	100.9	98.6	97.5	100.4
农副产品类	Farm and Sideline Products	99.3	98.8	107.9	119.1
纺织原料类	Textile Raw Material	96.8	91.5	93.3	97.9

注：本表数据由国家统计局上海调查总队提供。
Note: Date in this table are provided by Survey Office of the National Bureau of Statistics in Shanghai.

表8.8 续表 continued

	类 别 Types	2005	2006	2007
原材料、燃料、动力购进价格指数	**Purchasing Price Index of Raw Materials, Fuels and Power**	**127.5**	**133.6**	**139.1**
燃料、动力类	Fuel and Power	169.3	187.8	195.9
黑色金属材料类	Ferrous Metals	165.1	153.0	163.1
#钢　材	Rolled-steel	142.4	136.6	142.6
有色金属材料和电线类	Nonferrous Metals and Electric Wire	122.2	170.0	182.2
化工原料类	Chemical Raw Materials	114.2	117.9	124.0
木材及纸浆类	Wood and Paper Pulps	94.2	94.5	96.4
建筑材料及非金属矿类	Building Materials and Nonmetal Minerals	103.0	102.8	105.6
其他工业原材料及半成品类	Other Industrial Raw and Processed Materials	99.7	103.0	105.3
农副产品类	Farm and Sideline Products	116.8	122.8	131.0
纺织原料类	Textile Raw Material	99.7	100.2	102.0

表8.9 原材料、燃料、动力购进价格指数（2000～2007，以上年价格为100）
PURCHASING PRICE INDEX OF RAW MATERIALS ,FUELS AND POWER IN MAIN YEARS (PRECEDING YEAR =100)

类别	Types	2000	2001	2002	2003
原材料、燃料、动力购进价格指数	**Purchasing Price Index of Raw Materials Fuels and Power**	**107.1**	**98.7**	**97.7**	**106.4**
燃料、动力类	Fuels and Power	116.7	99.9	101.6	107.7
黑色金属材料类	Ferrous Metals	96.7	104.5	100.1	113.7
#钢　材	Rolled-steel	102.6	99.7	96.9	108.9
有色金属材料和电线类	Nonferrous Metals and Electric Wire	111.4	93.2	95.1	102.5
化工原料类	Chemical Raw Materials	123.5	90.4	92.7	107.3
木材及纸浆类	Wood and Paper Pulps	101.6	94.9	97.6	99.3
建筑材料及非金属矿类	Building Materials and Nonmetal Minerals	99.5	101.6	96.3	103.0
其他工业原材料及半成品类	Other Industrial Raw and Processed Materials	104.6	100.9	97.7	98.9
农副产品类	Farm and Sideline Products	97.2	99.3	99.5	109.2
纺织原料类	Textile Raw Material	96.9	96.8	94.5	102.0

注：本表数据由国家统计局上海调查总队提供。
Note: Date in this table are provided by Survey Office of the National Bureau of Statistics in Shanghai.

表8.9 续表 continued

类别	Types	2004	2005	2006	2007
原材料、燃料、动力购进价格指数	**Purchasing Price Index of Raw Materials, Fuels and Power**	**116.4**	**106.8**	**104.8**	**104.1**
燃料、动力类	Fuels and Power	124.8	124.1	110.9	104.3
黑色金属材料类	Ferrous Metals	134.6	103.2	92.7	106.6
#钢　材	Rolled-steel	123.2	109.9	95.9	104.4
有色金属材料和电线类	Nonferrous Metals and Electric Wire	119.9	112.2	139.1	107.2
化工原料类	Chemical Raw Materials	114.3	111.1	103.2	105.2
木材及纸浆类	Wood and Paper Pulps	100.9	101.5	100.3	102.0
建筑材料及非金属矿类	Building Materials and Nonmetal Minerals	115.1	88.9	99.8	102.7
其他工业原材料及半成品类	Other Industrial Raw and Processed Materials	103.0	99.3	103.3	102.2
农副产品类	Farm and Sideline Products	110.4	98.1	105.1	106.7
纺织原料类	Textile Raw Material	104.9	101.8	100.5	101.8

表8.10　固定资产投资价格指数（1996～2007，以1995年价格为100）
PRICE INDEX OF INVESTMENT IN FIXED ASSETS (1995 ＝100)

年 份 Year	固定资产投资价格指数 Price Index of Fixed Asset Investment	建筑安装、装饰工程 Building Project Price Index	#人工费 Manpower Cost Price Index	#材料费 Material Price Index	#机械使用费 Machinery Used Price Index	设备、工器具购 置 Equipment and Instrument Price Index	其他费用投 资 Other Investment Price Index
1996	107.0	108.9	114.2	97.4	118.5	101.7	107.7
1997	107.5	110.4	124.5	96.1	123.8	99.5	108.6
1998	105.8	109.2	119.5	94.5	123.5	95.6	108.1
1999	103.8	106.8	123.6	90.8	124.1	92.6	107.9
2000	103.8	108.4	124.3	92.4	123.8	89.8	107.8
2001	104.5	111.0	135.5	93.6	123.5	86.7	109.2
2002	104.8	113.1	149.7	93.4	126.9	83.8	109.5
2003	107.4	119.0	156.5	98.5	133.1	81.7	111.1
2004	114.6	131.6	165.4	110.3	144.7	81.3	116.3
2005	115.5	132.8	173.3	109.7	152.8	79.1	120.0
2006	115.6	132.9	181.6	108.1	157.3	77.0	122.4
2007	119.6	139.0	194.9	112.7	161.1	76.5	127.4

表8.11　固定资产投资价格指数（1995～2007，以上年价格为100）
PRICE INDEX OF INVESTMENT IN FIXED ASSETS (PRECEDING YEAR ＝100)

年 份 Year	固定资产投资价格指数 Price Index of Fixed Asset Investment	建筑安装、装饰工程 Building Project Price Index	#人工费 Manpower Cost Price Index	#材料费 Material Price Index	#机械使用费 Machinery Used Price Index	设备、工器具购 置 Equipment and Instrument Price Index	其他费用投 资 Other Investment Price Index
1995	103.1	101.9	108.7	99.5		104.8	107.0
1996	107.0	108.9	114.2	97.4	118.5	101.7	107.7
1997	100.5	101.4	109.0	98.7	104.5	97.8	100.8
1998	98.4	98.9	96.0	98.3	99.7	96.1	99.6
1999	98.1	97.8	103.4	96.1	100.5	96.9	99.8
2000	100.0	101.5	100.6	101.8	99.8	97.0	99.9
2001	100.7	102.4	109.0	101.2	99.7	96.5	101.3
2002	100.3	101.9	110.5	99.8	102.8	96.7	100.3
2003	102.4	105.2	104.5	105.5	104.9	97.5	101.4
2004	106.7	110.6	105.7	112.0	108.7	99.4	104.7
2005	100.8	100.9	104.8	99.4	105.6	97.4	103.2
2006	100.1	100.1	104.8	98.6	102.9	97.3	102.0
2007	103.5	104.6	107.3	104.3	102.4	99.4	104.1

注：本表数据由国家统计局上海调查总队提供。
Note：Date on this page are provided by Survey Office of the National Bureau of Statistics in Shanghai.

表8.12 房地产价格指数（2001～2007，以2000年价格为100）
REAL ESTATE PRICE INDEX (2000 = 100)

	类 别 Types	2001	2002	2003
房屋销售价格指数	**Price Index of Real Estate Sales**	**104.4**	**112.0**	**134.5**
商品房	Commodity Housing	101.8	110.1	132.7
住 宅	Residence	102.1	111.0	134.7
非住宅	Non-residence	98.3	102.0	114.0
公 房	Public Housing	107.4	108.2	108.2
二手房	Second-hand Housing	110.8	117.1	142.4
房屋租赁价格指数	**Price Index of Real Estate Leasing**	**104.9**	**103.9**	**106.0**
住 宅	Residence	107.4	107.4	108.7
#公 房	Public Housing	115.2	115.2	115.2
办公楼	Offices	98.6	97.9	103.0
商业娱乐用房	Commercial and Entertainment Housing	107.2	104.0	102.8
工业仓储用房	Workshops and Warehouses	118.8	121.2	125.5
土地交易价格指数	**Price Index of Land Exchange**	**97.2**	**103.3**	**118.9**
#居住用地	Residential	92.2	102.3	125.1
工业仓储用地	Workshops and Warehouses	91.6	82.7	84.0

注：本表数据由国家统计局上海调查总队提供。
Note: Date in this table are provided by Survey Office of the National Bureau of Statistics in Shanghai.

表8.12 续表 continued

	类 别 Types	2004	2005	2006	2007
房屋销售价格指数	**Price Index of Real Estate Sales**	**155.9**	**171.1**	**168.9**	**174.6**
商品房	Commodity Housing	153.7	167.8	162.8	167.8
住 宅	Residence	156.0	170.4	165.0	170.6
非住宅	Non-residence	132.3	143.6	141.6	144.6
公 房	Public Housing	108.2			
二手房	Second-hand Housing	167.3	185.1	188.4	195.6
房屋租赁价格指数	**Price Index of Real Estate Leasing**	**111.9**	**115.9**	**120.6**	**126.8**
住 宅	Residence	110.1	113.7	116.4	123.9
#公 房	Public Housing	115.2			
办公楼	Offices	110.1	117.2	121.6	127.1
商业娱乐用房	Commercial and Entertainment Housing	110.4	111.4	118.2	125.1
工业仓储用房	Workshops and Warehouses	131.8	133.7	135.1	137.2
土地交易价格指数	**Price Index of Land Exchange**	**143.1**	**153.0**	**154.8**	**166.9**
#居住用地	Residential	161.8	170.6	169.7	177.2
工业仓储用地	Workshops and Warehouses	85.1	88.3	90.8	103.4

注：按照国家统计局新的调查制度规定，取消房屋价格统计中原“私房、公房”调查指标。“私房”指标改为“二手房”指标。2005年以前的二手房数据指私房。
Note: According to the new investigation system regulation of National Bureau of Statistics, the investigate indicator of Private Housing and Public Housing were canceled. Private Housing was changed to Second-hand Housing. Second-hand Housing data of 2005 and the year before refer to Private Housing.

表8.13 房地产价格指数（2000～2007，以上年价格为100）
REAL ESTATE PRICE INDEX (PRECEDING YEAR = 100)

	类 别 Types	2000	2001	2002	2003
房屋销售价格指数	**Price Index of Real Estate Sales**	**98.6**	**104.4**	**107.3**	**120.1**
商品房	Commodity Housing	98.5	101.8	108.2	120.5
住 宅	Residence	98.5	102.1	108.7	121.4
非住宅	Non-residence	98.2	98.3	103.8	111.7
公 房	Public Housing	100.0	107.4	100.7	100.0
二手房	Second-hand Housing	99.1	110.8	105.7	121.6
房屋租赁价格指数	**Price Index of Real Estate Leasing**	**95.8**	**104.9**	**99.0**	**102.1**
住 宅	Residence	104.1	107.4	100.0	101.2
#公 房	Public Housing	104.1	115.2	100.0	100.0
办公楼	Offices	87.6	98.6	99.3	105.2
商业娱乐用房	Commercial and Entertainment Housing	103.6	107.2	97.0	98.9
工业仓储用房	Workshops and Warehouses	92.3	118.8	102.0	103.6
土地交易价格指数	**Price Index of Land Exchange**	**91.9**	**97.2**	**106.3**	**115.1**
#居住用地	Residential	86.3	92.2	111.0	122.2
工业仓储用地	Workshops and Warehouses	93.3	91.6	90.3	101.5

注：本表数据由国家统计局上海调查总队提供。
Note: Date in this table are provided by Survey Office of the National Bureau of Statistics in Shanghai.

表8.13 续表 continued

	类 别 Types	2004	2005	2006	2007
房屋销售价格指数	**Price Index of Real Estate Sales**	**115.9**	**109.7**	**98.7**	**103.4**
商品房	Commodity Housing	115.8	109.2	97.0	103.1
住 宅	Residence	115.8	109.2	96.8	103.4
非住宅	Non-residence	116.1	108.5	98.6	102.1
公 房	Public Housing	100.0			
二手房	Second-hand Housing	117.5	110.6	101.8	103.8
房屋租赁价格指数	**Price Index of Real Estate Leasing**	**105.5**	**103.6**	**104.0**	**105.1**
住 宅	Residence	101.3	103.3	102.3	106.5
#公 房	Public Housing	100.0			
办公楼	Offices	106.9	106.4	103.8	104.5
商业娱乐用房	Commercial and Entertainment Housing	107.3	101.0	106.1	105.8
工业仓储用房	Workshops and Warehouses	105.0	101.4	101.1	101.5
土地交易价格指数	**Price Index of Land Exchange**	**120.3**	**106.9**	**101.2**	**107.8**
#居住用地	Residential	129.4	105.4	99.5	104.4
工业仓储用地	Workshops and Warehouses	101.4	103.7	102.9	113.8

上/海/统/计/年/鉴

主要统计指标解释

■ 居民消费价格指数

是度量一组代表性消费商品及服务项目价格水平随着时间而变动的相对数，反映居民家庭购买的消费品及服务价格水平的变动情况。它是宏观经济分析和决策、价格总水平监测和调控以及国民经济核算的重要指标。其按年度计算的变动率通常被用来作为反映通货膨胀或紧缩程度的指标。

现行的居民消费价格指数按用途分为八个大类，包括食品、烟酒及用品、衣着、家庭设备用品及维修服务、医疗保健和个人用品、交通和通信、娱乐教育文化用品及服务、居住。

■ 商品零售价格指数

是反映一定时期内城乡商品零售价格变动趋势和程度的相对数。商品零售价格的变动直接影响城乡居民的生活支出和国家的财政收入，影响居民购买力和市场供需的平衡，影响消费与积累的比例关系。因此，该指数可以从一个侧面对上述经济活动进行观察和分析。

■ 工业品出厂价格指数

是反映一定时期内全部工业产品出厂价格总水平的变动趋势和程度的相对数，包括工业企业售给本企业以外所有单位的各种工业产品和生活消费产品。该指数可以观察出厂价格变动对工业总产值及增加值的影响。

■ 原材料、燃料、动力购进价格指数

是反映工业企业作为生产投入，从物资交易市场和能源、原材料生产企业购买原材料、燃料和动力产品时，所支付的价格水平变动趋势和程度的统计指标，是扣除工业企业物质消耗成本中的价格变动影响的重要依据。

目前，我国编制的原材料燃料和动力购进价格指数所调查的产品包括燃料动力、黑色金属、有色金属、化工、建材等九大类近1800种产品。

■ 固定资产投资价格指数

是反映一定时期内固定资产投资品及项目的价格变动趋势和程度的相对数。固定资产投资额是由建筑安装工程投资完成额、设备工器具购置投资完成额和其他费用投资完成额三部分组成的。编制固定资产投资价格指数应首先分别编制上述三部分投资的价格指数，然后采用加权算术平均法求出固定资产投资价格总指数。

该指数可以准确地反映固定资产投资中涉及的各类投资品和收费项目价格变动趋势和变动幅度，消除按现价计算的固定资产投资指标中的价格变动因素，真实地反映固定资产投资的规模、速度、结构和效益，为国家科学地制定、检查固定资产投资计划并提高宏观调控水平，为完善国民经济核算体系提供科学的、可靠的依据。

■ 房屋销售价格指数

房屋销售指以买卖方式转移房地产的所有权。它包括商品房销售和二手房交易二部分。房屋销售价格指数是指房屋销售价格总水平变动趋势的相对数。

■ 房屋租赁价格指数

房屋租赁指以支付租金形式取得房屋使用权。它包括住宅租赁、办公楼租赁 、商业娱乐用房租赁和工业仓储用房租赁部分。房屋租赁价格指数是指房屋租赁价格总水平变动趋势和程度的相对数。

■ 土地交易价格指数

指房地产开发商或其他建设单位在进行商品房开发之前，为取得土地使用权而实际支付的价格的变动趋势和程度的相对数。

■ 二手房

二手房是指进入房屋市场进行交易，第二次以上进行产权登记的商品房。

EXPLANATORY NOTES TO MAJOR STATISTICAL INDICATORS

□ Consumer Price Index

The Consumer Price Index is an index that reflects the time–based change of prices of a group of representative consumption commodities and services. It is an important reference factor for macro–economic analysis and strategy, monitoring and adjustment of overall price level and the national economic budgeting. The year–on–year change of the index is often a norm reflecting the inflation or deflation.

The current CPI covers eight categories of goods and services: food; tobacco, liquor and related articles; garments; household facilities, articles and repair services; medical and health care and personal items; traffic and telecommunications; education, culture and recreation articles and services and residence.

□ Retail Price Index

Retail Price Index reflects the trend and degree of change in retail prices of commodities during a given period. The change in retail prices of commodities directly affect the living expenditure of urban and rural residents, government revenue, purchasing power of residents and the equilibrium of market supply and demand, and the ratio of consumption to accumulation. Therefore, the retail price indices are useful to analyze the changes of the above economic activities.

□ Producer Price Index of Industrial Products

Producer Price Indices of Industrial Products reflects the trend and degree of changes in general ex–factory prices of all industrial products during a given period, including sales of industrial products and consumer goods by an industrial enterprise to all units outside the enterprise. It can be used to analyze the impact of ex–factory prices on gross output value and value–added of the industrial sector.

□ Purchasing Price of Index of Raw Materials, Fuels and Power

Purchasing Price of Index of Raw Materials, Fuels and Power reflect changes in the level and degree of prices paid by industrial enterprises when they purchase production input such as raw materials, fuels and power from the market or from other energy or raw materials producing enterprises. These indices provide important basis for measuring the material consumption of industrial enterprises after removing influence of price changes.

At present, close to 1,800 products in 9 categories, including fuels and power, ferrous metals, non–ferrous metals, chemicals, building materials, are covered in China for the survey to produce indices of purchasing prices of raw materials, fuels and power.

□ Price Index of Investment in Fixed Assets

Price Index of Investment in Fixed Assets reflects the trend and degree of changes in prices of investment goods and projects in fixed assets during a given period. The investment in fixed assets consists of three components, namely the investment in construction and installation, the investment in purchases of equipment and instrument, and the investment in other items. Price indices of investment in fixed assets are calculated as the weighted arithmetic mean of the price indices of the three components of investment in fixed assets.

Removing the factor of price change in the aggregates of investment at current prices, this indicator shows the changes in the prices of commodities and fees involved in the investment of fixed assets, and can be used to observe the actual size, growth, structure, and efficiency of investment in fixed assets and provides reliable and scientific data for government planning, management, decision–making, and further improving the current national accounting system.

□ Price Index of Real Estate Sales

Price Index of Real Estate Sales refers to the transference of ownership of real estate through selling and buying. Included are the sales of commodity housings and second–hand housing, public housings and private housings. The Price Index of Real Estate Sales is an indicator of the general trend and variation degrees of the sales price of the real estate.

□ Price Index of Real Estate Leasing

Price Index of Real estate leasing refers to the acquisition of

EXPLANATORY NOTES TO MAJOR STATISTICAL INDICATORS

the real estate ownership by means of paying rent. Included are the leasing of residential houses, offices, commercial and Entertain-ment housing, and workshops and warehouses. The Price Index of Real Estate leasing is an indicator of general trend and variation of the leasing price of real estate.

□ Price Index of Land Exchange

Price Index of Land Exchange is an indicator of the general trend and variation of the paid price in order to obtain the owner-ship of the land by the real estate developer or other construction organizations before the development.

□ Second-hand Housing

Second-hand Housing refers to the houses traded in the housing market, and its property righthed been registered for more than once. Data of 2005 and the year before refers to Private Housing.

第九篇

CHAPTER 9

人民生活

LIVING STANDARDS

表 9.1 从业人员报酬(1978～2007)
COMPENSATION OF EMPLOYEES

年 份 Year	从业人员报酬 (亿元) Compensation of Employees (100 million yuan)	按产业分 Grouped by Industry			按登记注册类型分 Classified According to the Categories of registration		
		第一产业 Primary Industry	第二产业 Secondary Industry	第三产业 Tertiary Industry	国有单位 State-owned Units	集体单位 Collective-owned Units	其他单位 Other Ownership Units
1978	28.18	1.31	17.18	9.69	23.88	4.30	
1979	32.90	1.44	20.43	11.03	27.77	5.13	
1980	38.26	1.66	23.42	13.18	31.71	6.55	
1981	39.76	1.61	24.40	13.75	32.55	7.21	
1982	41.55	1.59	25.15	14.81	33.83	7.72	
1983	43.21	1.48	26.07	15.66	35.07	8.14	
1984	54.13	1.63	33.29	19.21	43.39	10.29	0.45
1985	69.63	2.10	42.86	24.67	55.96	13.18	0.49
1986	84.89	2.45	51.70	30.74	68.32	15.84	0.73
1987	96.36	2.64	58.18	35.54	78.15	17.46	0.75
1988	117.04	3.18	70.35	43.51	94.78	20.91	1.35
1989	134.04	3.60	81.41	49.03	106.57	25.17	2.30
1990	150.48	4.02	89.48	56.98	121.56	25.64	3.28
1991	177.55	4.64	105.25	67.66	142.00	30.24	5.31
1992	223.36	2.47	135.49	85.40	179.43	35.40	8.53
1993	290.42	2.57	157.10	130.75	212.10	39.56	38.76
1994	374.44	3.11	186.81	184.52	268.19	48.59	57.66
1995	465.67	3.53	232.10	230.04	324.72	56.99	83.96
1996	521.63	3.72	250.94	266.97	359.56	60.18	101.89
1997	547.87	3.69	245.59	298.59	366.61	60.11	121.15
1998	554.86	3.47	255.43	276.61	342.88	49.65	162.33
1999	635.84	3.35	277.11	332.39	380.58	48.36	206.90
2000	647.55	3.32	283.20	361.03	369.65	38.88	239.02
2001	716.95	3.25	301.93	411.77	389.26	36.91	290.78
2002	788.55	3.76	333.64	451.15	404.89	34.18	349.48
2003	873.06	2.53	373.19	497.34	434.93	32.43	405.70
2004	925.33	2.69	383.84	538.80	435.30	31.00	459.03
2005	1 245.44	3.21	478.97	763.26	474.39	30.28	740.77
2006	1 598.09	3.92	646.41	937.76	559.02	31.15	1 007.92
2007	1 976.54	4.35	796.03	1 176.16	704.35	35.94	1 236.25

①至 2006 年起，从业人员报酬包括 120 人以上私营企业从业人员报酬 。
②本表"其他单位"包括港澳台及外商企业。
❶Since 2006, Compensation of Employees included those of private enterprises above 120 persons.
❷"Other" in this table includes foreign invested and HongKong, Macao and Taiwan funded enterprises.

表9.2 从业人员报酬(2007)
COMPENSATION OF EMPLOYEES

单位:亿元 (100 million yuan)

行 业	Sectors	合 计 Total	其中 of which: 国有单位 State-owned Units	集体单位 Collective-owned Units	港澳台及外商投资单位 Units with Investment from Hong Kong, Macao, Taiwan and Foreign Countries	其他单位 Other Units
全 市	**Total**	**1 976.54**	**704.35**	**35.94**	**503.08**	**733.17**
一、按产业分	**Grouped by Industry**					
第一产业	Primary Industry	4.35	1.67	0.38	0.05	2.25
第二产业	Secondary Industry	796.03	120.93	6.10	374.90	294.10
第三产业	Tertiary Industry	1 176.16	581.75	29.46	128.13	436.82
二、按行业分	**Grouped by Sector**					
农、林、牧、渔业	Farming, Forestry, Animal Husbandry and Fishery	4.35	1.67	0.38	0.05	2.25
工 业	Industry	717.81	99.86	5.16	371.54	241.25
采矿业	Mining	0.44	0.40		0.01	0.03
制造业	Manufacturing	683.16	75.03	4.88	368.27	234.97
电力、燃气及水的生产和供应业	Power, Gas and Water Production and Supply	34.21	24.43	0.28	3.26	6.25
建筑业	Construction	78.22	21.07	0.94	3.36	52.85
交通运输、仓储和邮政业	Transportation, Warehousing and Post	158.04	68.79	1.31	13.40	74.53
#交通运输	Transportation	141.91	55.94	1.18	12.03	72.75
邮政业	Post	11.74	11.51			0.23
信息传输、计算机服务和软件业	Information Transmission, Computer Servcies and Software Industries	64.45	14.32	0.16	21.32	28.65
#信息传输	Information Transmission	25.98	13.06	0.15	7.78	4.99
批发和零售业	Wholesale and Retail	130.75	17.07	4.45	21.58	87.66
批发业	Wholesale	85.79	10.60	2.43	18.11	54.65
零售业	Retail	44.96	6.46	2.02	3.46	33.01
住宿和餐饮业	Hoteling and Catering	31.94	5.64	0.36	7.93	18.01
#餐饮业	Catering	9.22	1.10	0.26	5.11	2.76
金融业	Financial Industry	171.12	51.94		24.43	94.75
房地产业	Real Estate	46.96	11.55	0.58	10.28	24.56
租赁和商务服务业	Leasing and Business Services	106.12	23.10	8.48	20.28	54.27
科学研究、技术服务和地质勘查业	Scientific Research, Technological Service and Geological Prospecting	95.88	80.05	0.64	5.07	10.12
水利、环境和公共设施管理业	Water Conservancies, Environment and Public Facilities Management	18.09	14.12	0.82	0.51	2.64
居民服务和其他服务业	Resident Service and Other Services	35.19	3.21	0.96	0.78	30.24
教 育	Education	119.90	115.35	0.69	1.24	2.62
卫生、社会保障和社会福利业	Healthcare, Social Security and Social Welfare	83.00	71.21	9.62	0.18	1.99
卫 生	Healthcare	78.10	67.52	9.22	0.18	1.18
社会保障	Social Security	3.20	2.09	0.31		0.80
社会福利业	Social Welfare	1.69	1.59	0.09		0.01
文化、体育和娱乐业	Culture, Sports and Entertainment	27.98	19.59	0.50	1.12	6.78
文 化	Culture	21.34	16.23	0.48	0.40	4.23
体 育	Sports	3.08	3.02	0.02	0.04	
娱乐业	Entertainment	3.56	0.33		0.68	2.55
公共管理和社会组织	Public Administration and Social Organizations	86.73	85.84	0.89		

表9.3 从业人员平均报酬(2007)
AVERAGE ANNUAL COMPENSATION OF EMPLOYEES

单位:元 (yuan)

行业	Sectors	合计 Total	国有单位 State-owned Units	集体单位 Collective-owned Units	港澳台及外商投资单位 Units with Investment from Hong Kong, Macao,Taiwan and Foreign Countries	其他单位 Other Units
全市	**Total**	**35 952**	**50 311**	**27 949**	**41 536**	**26 584**
一、按产业分	**Grouped by Industry**					
第一产业	Primary Industry	21 550	27 425	32 571	19 917	17 735
第二产业	Secondary Industry	31 361	45 839	21 189	36 732	24 007
第三产业	Tertiary Industry	40 016	51 479	29 868	67 332	28 734
二、按行业分	**Grouped by Sector**					
农、林、牧、渔业	Farming, Forestry, Animal Husbandry and Fishery	21 550	27 425	32 571	19 917	17 735
工业	Industry	31 474	46 749	21 306	36 589	23 481
采矿业	Mining	51 745	62 766		21 270	18 075
制造业	Manufacturing	30 700	43 441	20 644	36 381	23 113
电力、燃气及水的生产和供应业	Power, Gas and Water Production and Supply	62 716	60 692	48 104	104 741	58 886
建筑业	Construction	30 361	41 968	20 572	64 404	26 742
交通运输、仓储和邮政业	Transportation, Warehousing and Post	40 763	54 142	17 783	58 577	32 350
#交通运输	Transportation	40 496	56 501	17 203	61 361	32 344
邮政业	Post	46 275	47 386			21 130
信息传输、计算机服务和软件业	Information Transmission, Computer Servcies and Software Industries	73 799	93 789	42 862	77 889	64 646
#信息传输	Information Transmission	87 456	98 034	50 441	80 171	78 156
批发和零售业	Retail and Wholesale	24 001	47 325	23 930	63 837	19 210
批发业	Wholesale	25 537	59 238	28 040	80 159	19 055
零售业	Retail	21 531	35 585	20 354	30 912	19 474
住宿和餐饮业	Hoteling and Catering	24 406	30 094	20 080	24 445	23 121
#餐饮业	Catering	21 065	33 616	19 751	19 521	21 152
金融业	Financial Industry	94 674	120 924	17 125	172 289	76 654
房地产业	Real Estate	34 363	38 722	25 735	35 790	32 364
租赁和商务服务业	Leasing and Business Services	26 794	30 021	27 684	116 988	20 013
科学研究、技术服务和地质勘查业	Scientific Research, Technological Service and Geological Prospecting	61 501	58 209	39 040	141 713	76 863
水利、环境和公共设施管理业	Water Conservancies, Environment and Public Facilities Management	33 721	35 639	20 079	33 926	31 252
居民服务和其他服务业	Resident Service and Other Services	18 287	27 387	20 495	18 649	17 598
教育	Education	45 833	46 399	31 417	123 851	26 733
卫生、社会保障和社会福利业	Healthcare, Social Security and Social Welfare	49 958	53 547	46 200	71 717	16 467
卫生	Healthcare	52 107	54 783	47 038	71 717	17 355
社会保障	Social Security	30 122	45 108	39 954		15 341
社会福利业	Social Welfare	30 166	31 309	19 868		14 918
文化、体育和娱乐业	Culture, Sports and Entertainment	42 592	54 433	34 770	37 031	26 831
文化	Culture	48 501	59 362	34 960	46 170	29 332
体育	Sports	39 229	39 452	44 417	27 289	
娱乐业	Entertainment	25 724	34 128		33 815	23 501
公共管理和社会组织	Public Administration and Social Organizations	48 285	48 537	32 233		

表9.4 职工工资总额和平均工资(1978～2007)
TOTAL WAGES AND AVERAGE ANNUAL WAGES OF STAFF AND WORKERS

年份 Year	职工工资总额(亿元) Total Wages of Staff and Workers (100 million yuan)	其中 of which 国有单位 State-owned Units	集体单位 Collective-owned Units	其他单位 Other Ownership Units	职工平均工资(元) Average Annual Wages of Staff and Workers (yuan)	其中 of which 国有单位 State-owned Units	集体单位 Collective-owned Units	其他单位 Other Units
1978	28.12	23.82	4.30		672	716	500	
1979	32.73	27.63	5.10		784	834	590	
1980	38.10	31.59	6.51		873	918	702	
1981	39.59	32.42	7.17		870	910	727	
1982	41.34	33.71	7.63		883	920	750	
1983	42.91	34.93	7.98		897	935	763	
1984	53.72	43.19	10.08	0.45	1 110	1 160	938	1 149
1985	68.99	55.50	13.00	0.49	1 416	1 467	1 227	1 628
1986	83.35	67.49	15.15	0.71	1 689	1 752	1 443	2 029
1987	94.78	77.19	16.87	0.72	1 893	1 960	1 623	2 510
1988	114.47	93.62	19.55	1.30	2 277	2 354	1 951	2 715
1989	131.10	105.08	23.77	2.25	2 608	2 691	2 259	3 235
1990	146.78	119.26	24.30	3.22	2 917	3 037	2 394	3 611
1991	172.84	139.12	28.51	5.21	3 375	3 487	2 817	4 363
1992	217.21	175.95	32.89	8.37	4 273	4 451	3 363	5 486
1993	279.33	206.12	36.60	36.61	5 650	5 784	4 253	7 043
1994	357.89	259.78	44.73	53.38	7 401	7 529	5 389	9 617
1995	440.75	314.69	51.61	74.45	9 279	9 578	6 309	11 518
1996	492.70	348.96	54.92	88.82	10 663	11 015	7 051	13 186
1997	510.10	353.69	53.69	102.72	11 425	11 733	7 329	14 313
1998	510.35	330.10	44.13	136.12	12 059	12 361	7 138	14 430
1999	583.54	366.21	43.22	174.11	14 147	14 419	7 935	16 736
2000	614.53	371.39	39.35	203.79	15 420	15 737	8 041	17 942
2001	678.29	389.91	35.79	252.59	17 764	17 820	8 525	20 865
2002	733.31	404.44	31.54	297.33	19 473	19 777	8 707	21 886
2003	803.84	430.92	30.52	342.40	22 160	22 541	9 844	24 359
2004	837.39	428.49	29.36	379.54	24 398	24 726	11 539	26 270
2005	1 146.97	463.24	28.44	655.29	26 823	28 803	12 819	26 792
2006	1 475.93	539.88	28.41	907.64	29 569	36 010	15 209	27 459
2007	1 802.17	673.20	32.75	1 096.22	34 707	46 426	19 244	30 687

①至2006年起，职工工资总额和平均工资包括120人以上的私营企业职工工资。
②本表"其他单位"包括港澳台及外商企业。
❶Since 2006, Tatal Wages and Average Wages of Workers induded those of private enterprises above 120 persons.
❷"Other" in this table inoludes foreign invested and HongKong, Macao and Taiwan funded enterprises.

表 9.5 职工工资总额（2007）
TOTAL WAGES OF STAFF AND WORKERS

单位：亿元（100 million yuan）

行　业	Sectors	合　计 Total	国有单位 State-owned Units	集体单位 Collective-owned Units	港澳台及外商投资单位 Units with Investment from Hong Kong, Macao, Taiwan and Foreign Countries	其他单位 Other Units
全　市	**Total**	**1 802.17**	**673.20**	**32.75**	**413.20**	**683.02**
一、按产业分	**Grouped by Industry**					
第一产业	Primary Industry	3.57	1.39	0.35	0.04	1.79
第二产业	Secondary Industry	714.56	119.41	5.16	312.76	277.23
第三产业	Tertiary Industry	1 084.04	552.40	27.24	100.40	404.00
二、按行业分	**Grouped by Sector**					
农、林、牧、渔业	Farming, Forestry, Animal Husbandry and Fishery	3.57	1.39	0.35	0.04	1.79
工　业	Industry	642.89	100.28	4.57	310.37	227.67
采矿业	Mining	0.35	0.31			0.03
制造业	Manufacturing	608.68	75.83	4.26	307.13	221.46
电力、燃气及水的生产和供应业	Power, Gas and Water Production and Supply	33.86	24.13	0.30	3.24	6.18
建筑业	Construction	71.67	19.13	0.59	2.39	49.56
交通运输、仓储和邮政业	Transportation, Warehousing and Post	145.12	62.64	1.17	11.62	69.70
#交通运输	Transportation	133.15	53.50	1.05	10.47	68.13
邮政业	Post	7.84	7.80			0.04
信息传输、计算机服务和软件业	Information Transmission, Computer Servcies and Software Industries	59.89	14.41	0.16	17.92	27.40
#信息传输	Information Transmission	24.11	13.16	0.15	5.98	4.82
批发和零售业	Retail and Wholesale	117.16	17.61	3.96	18.29	77.30
批发业	Wholesale	78.69	10.25	2.07	15.41	50.96
零售业	Retail	38.47	7.36	1.89	2.88	26.34
住宿和餐饮业	Hoteling and Catering	26.53	4.87	0.32	5.11	16.23
#餐饮业	Catering	6.63	1.07	0.22	2.99	2.35
金融业	Financial Industry	158.73	49.71		17.97	91.05
房地产业	Real Estate	38.16	9.56	0.47	6.59	21.54
租赁和商务服务业	Leasing and Business Services	98.29	21.17	8.67	17.10	51.35
科学研究、技术服务和地质勘查业	Scientific Research, Technological Service and Geological Prospecting	89.79	76.95	0.58	3.46	8.80
水利、环境和公共设施管理业	Water Conservancies, Environment and Public Facilities Management	16.68	13.19	0.71	0.48	2.30
居民服务和其他服务业	Resident Service and Other Services	33.16	2.72	0.83	0.68	28.93
教　育	Education	114.07	112.07	0.48	0.30	1.21
卫生、社会保障和社会福利业	Healthcare, Social Security and Social Welfare	76.80	66.17	8.67	0.08	1.89
卫　生	Healthcare	72.19	62.76	8.27	0.08	1.09
社会保障	Social Security	3.14	2.03	0.32		0.80
社会福利业	Social Welfare	1.47	1.38	0.08		0.01
文化、体育和娱乐业	Culture, Sports and Entertainment	24.90	17.35	0.44	0.82	6.29
文　化	Culture	18.87	14.23	0.42	0.34	3.88
体　育	Sports	2.89	2.84	0.01	0.04	
娱乐业	Entertainment	3.14	0.28	0.01	0.44	2.41
公共管理和社会组织	Public Administration and Social Organizations	84.77	84.01	0.77		

表9.6　职工平均工资(2007)
AVERAGE ANNUAL WAGES OF STAFF AND WORKERS

单位:元(yuan)

行业	Sectors	合计 Total	国有单位 State-owned Units	集体单位 Collective-owned Units	港澳台及外商投资单位 Units with Investment from Hong Kong, Macao, Taiwan and Foreign Countries	其他单位 Other Units
全　市	**Total**	**34 707**	**46 426**	**19 244**	**41 006**	**26 633**
一、按产业分	**Grouped by Industry**					
第一产业	Primary Industry	21 352	29 983	36 671	21 076	16 374
第二产业	Secondary Industry	28 916	31 071	10 369	36 209	23 627
第三产业	Tertiary Industry	40 082	52 058	22 802	69 858	29 269
二、按行业分	**Grouped by Sector**					
农、林、牧、渔业	Farming, Forestry, Animal Husbandry and Fishery	21 352	29 983	36 671	21 076	16 374
工　业	Industry	28 792	29 759	9 830	36 076	23 017
采矿业	Mining	59 051	84 113			18 343
制造业	Manufacturing	27 934	25 488	9 333	35 829	22 630
电力、燃气及水的生产和供应业	Power, Gas and Water Production and Supply	63 518	61 746	40 408	104 880	59 551
建筑业	Construction	30 075	40 413	17 956	69 181	26 903
交通运输、仓储和邮政业	Transportation, Warehousing and Post	41 012	53 922	13 052	55 294	33 554
#交通运输	Transportation	40 823	54 826	12 449	57 966	33 712
邮政业	Post	51 552	54 610			3 913
信息传输、计算机服务和软件业	Information Transmission, Computer Servcies and Software Industries	75 119	91 533	41 889	81 984	65 643
#信息传输	Information Transmission	97 064	95 047	46 494	127 418	80 669
批发和零售业	Retail and Wholesale	22 662	28 724	12 958	63 678	19 501
批发业	Wholesale	24 720	49 299	16 774	77 845	19 201
零售业	Retail	19 365	18 165	10 379	32 266	20 109
住宿和餐饮业	Hoteling and Catering	25 080	28 980	13 413	33 224	22 796
#餐饮业	Catering	23 168	26 931	12 263	28 232	19 166
金融业	Financial Industry	98 966	128 654		169 522	81 921
房地产业	Real Estate	37 315	48 386	27 408	34 186	35 018
租赁和商务服务业	Leasing and Business Services	24 740	30 350	20 477	110 434	19 039
科学研究、技术服务和地质勘查业	Scientific Research, Technological Service and Geological Prospecting	61 054	58 390	28 317	104 442	88 803
水利、环境和公共设施管理业	Water Conservancies, Environment and Public Facilities Management	38 790	41 171	22 149	33 891	36 293
居民服务和其他服务业	Resident Service and Other Services	17 510	16 646	17 213	18 975	17 572
教　育	Education	48 367	49 216	23 937	44 036	22 333
卫生、社会保障和社会福利业	Healthcare, Social Security and Social Welfare	52 932	57 083	49 538	36 038	16 497
卫　生	Healthcare	55 511	58 404	51 201	36 038	17 455
社会保障	Social Security	28 743	41 216	39 508		15 318
社会福利业	Social Welfare	35 700	39 040	14 893		21 800
文化、体育和娱乐业	Culture, Sports and Entertainment	42 311	53 992	30 720	37 154	27 254
文　化	Culture	48 049	58 252	37 392	42 798	30 009
体　育	Sports	40 448	40 791	44 848	23 547	
娱乐业	Entertainment	25 248	37 704	1 833	35 156	23 749
公共管理和社会组织	Public Administration and Social Organizations	50 136	50 281	38 099		

表9.7 在岗职工工资总额（2007） TOTAL WAGES OF WORKING STAFF AND WORKERS

单位：亿元(100 million yuan)

行业	Sectors	合计 Total	国有单位 State-owned Units	集体单位 Collective-owned Units	港澳台及外商投资单位 Units with Investment from Hong Kong, Macao, Taiwan and Foreign Countries	其他单位 Other Units
全　市	**Total**	**1 766.52**	**651.93**	**30.32**	**410.95**	**673.32**
一、按产业分	**Grouped by Industry**					
第一产业	Primary Industry	3.40	1.31	0.34	0.04	1.71
第二产业	Secondary Industry	700.04	111.19	4.52	310.88	273.45
第三产业	Tertiary Industry	1 063.08	539.43	25.46	100.03	398.16
二、按行业分	**Grouped by Sector**					
农、林、牧、渔业	Farming, Forestry, Animal Husbandry and Fishery	3.40	1.31	0.34	0.04	1.71
工　业	Industry	629.96	93.01	3.95	308.49	224.51
采矿业	Mining	0.35	0.31			0.03
制造业	Manufacturing	595.90	68.68	3.67	305.25	218.31
电力、燃气及水的生产和供应业	Power, Gas and Water Production and Supply	33.71	24.02	0.28	3.24	6.18
建筑业	Construction	70.07	18.19	0.57	2.39	48.92
交通运输、仓储和邮政业	Transportation, Warehousing and Post	141.08	60.83	1.06	11.46	67.73
#交通运输	Transportation	129.35	51.84	0.95	10.32	66.23
邮政业	Post	7.77	7.73			0.04
信息传输、计算机服务和软件业	Information Transmission, Computer Servcies and Software Industries	59.48	14.22	0.15	17.73	27.37
#信息传输	Information Transmission	23.87	12.97	0.15	5.95	4.80
批发和零售业	Retail and Wholesale	113.96	15.83	3.41	18.28	76.43
批发业	Wholesale	77.93	9.94	1.85	15.40	50.74
零售业	Retail	36.02	5.89	1.56	2.88	25.70
住宿和餐饮业	Hoteling and Catering	25.78	4.51	0.27	5.11	15.89
#餐饮业	Catering	6.24	0.87	0.19	2.99	2.19
金融业	Financial Industry	157.39	48.82		17.95	90.61
房地产业	Real Estate	37.60	9.30	0.46	6.59	21.25
租赁和商务服务业	Leasing and Business Services	93.95	19.04	7.98	17.10	49.84
科学研究、技术服务和地质勘查业	Scientific Research, Technological Service and Geological Prospecting	89.20	76.40	0.57	3.46	8.76
水利、环境和公共设施管理业	Water Conservancies, Environment and Public Facilities Management	15.74	12.37	0.69	0.48	2.20
居民服务和其他服务业	Resident Service and Other Services	32.54	2.43	0.75	0.68	28.69
教　育	Education	112.22	110.24	0.46	0.30	1.21
卫生、社会保障和社会福利业	Healthcare, Social Security and Social Welfare	75.54	65.10	8.48	0.08	1.89
卫　生	Healthcare	71.03	61.77	8.10	0.08	1.08
社会保障	Social Security	3.05	1.95	0.31		0.80
社会福利业	Social Welfare	1.46	1.38	0.07		0.01
文化、体育和娱乐业	Culture, Sports and Entertainment	24.13	16.62	0.42	0.82	6.28
文　化	Culture	18.18	13.56	0.41	0.34	3.87
体　育	Sports	2.83	2.78	0.01	0.04	
娱乐业	Entertainment	3.12	0.28		0.44	2.41
公共管理和社会组织	Public Administration and Social Organizations	84.47	83.73	0.75		

表9.8 在岗职工平均工资(2007)
AVERAGE ANNUAL WAGES OF STAFF AND WORKERS

单位:元 (yuan)

	行 业 Sectors	合 计 Total	国 有 单 位 State-owned Units	集 体 单 位 Collective-owned Units	港澳台及外商投资单位 Units with Investment from Hong Kong, Macao,Taiwan and Foreign Countries	其 他 单 位 Other Units
全 市	**Total**	**37 716**	**55 547**	**30 923**	**41 959**	**27 679**
一、按产业分	**Grouped by Industry**					
第一产业	Primary Industry	23 562	33 859	39 242	21 076	18 002
第二产业	Secondary Industry	31 852	50 189	21 843	37 007	24 514
第三产业	Tertiary Industry	43 013	56 888	33 289	71 877	30 449
二、按行业分	**Grouped by Sector**					
农、林、牧、渔业	Farming, Forestry, Animal Husbandry and Fishery	23 562	33 859	39 242	21 076	18 002
工 业	Industry	31 883	50 533	21 810	36 873	23 960
采矿业	Mining	67 439	96 373			18 343
制造业	Manufacturing	30 988	47 225	20 935	36 620	23 562
电力、燃气及水的生产和供应业	Power, Gas and Water Production and Supply	64 464	62 703	48 104	105 669	59 711
建筑业	Construction	31 575	48 501	22 072	69 697	27 424
交通运输、仓储和邮政业	Transportation, Warehousing and Post	44 499	59 667	18 375	57 054	35 793
#交通运输	Transportation	44 181	61 055	17 635	60 004	35 754
邮政业	Post	56 254	56 461			31 412
信息传输、计算机服务和软件业	Information Transmission, Computer Servcies and Software Industries	76 315	95 542	45 705	83 884	65 832
#信息传输	Information Transmission	100 748	99 723	51 039	131 690	81 654
批发和零售业	Retail and Wholesale	25 217	53 702	27 654	64 473	20 023
批发业	Wholesale	25 777	66 878	33 520	79 136	19 330
零售业	Retail	24 087	40 306	22 884	32 380	21 549
住宿和餐饮业	Hoteling and Catering	27 018	35 120	21 286	33 682	24 028
#餐饮业	Catering	27 587	43 775	20 651	28 784	23 477
金融业	Financial Industry	100 849	134 681		171 585	82 871
房地产业	Real Estate	40 657	57 577	30 191	38 175	36 933
租赁和商务服务业	Leasing and Business Services	27 868	38 425	29 809	110 830	20 309
科学研究、技术服务和地质勘查业	Scientific Research, Technological Service and Geological Prospecting	62 951	59 929	43 027	104 567	91 604
水利、环境和公共设施管理业	Water Conservancies, Environment and Public Facilities Management	41 253	43 826	22 869	34 139	39 975
居民服务和其他服务业	Resident Service and Other Services	18 619	38 945	23 516	19 002	17 731
教 育	Education	49 201	49 956	32 652	50 390	22 483
卫生、社会保障和社会福利业	Healthcare, Social Security and Social Welfare	54 296	58 706	51 194	36 038	16 460
卫 生	Healthcare	56 593	59 631	52 285	36 038	17 388
社会保障	Social Security	31 325	51 434	41 132		15 318
社会福利业	Social Welfare	37 674	39 262	22 249		21 800
文化、体育和娱乐业	Culture, Sports and Entertainment	43 582	57 031	38 430	37 269	27 351
文 化	Culture	49 929	62 449	38 289	42 900	30 141
体 育	Sports	40 989	41 348	47 533	23 547	
娱乐业	Entertainment	25 901	39 567		35 292	23 812
公共管理和社会组织	Public Administration and Social Organizations	50 782	50 900	40 279		

表9.9 主要年份离退休、退职人员养老金
LABOUR INSURANCE AND WELFARE FUNDS FOR RETIRED STAFF IN MAIN YEARS

指标	Indicators	2000	2006	2007
离退休、退职人员养老金(亿元)	**Labour Insurance and Welfare Funds for Nonworking Staff and Workers (100 million yuan)**	**205.14**	**394.20**	**488.46**
离休职工的离休费	Pensions for Retired Veteran Cadres	7.32	13.23	15.50
退休职工的退休费	Pensions for Retired	195.90	375.65	466.42
退职人员的退职生活费	Living Expenses for Resigned	1.92	5.32	6.54

表9.10 离退休、退职人员养老金(2007)
WORKERS CLASSIFIED ACCORDING TO THE CATEGORIES OF REGISTRATION

指标	Indicators	合计 Total	国有单位 State-owned Units	集体单位 Collective-owned Units	其他单位 Other Units
离退休、退职人员养老金(亿元)	**Labour Insurance and Welfare Funds for Nonworking Staff and Workers (100 million yuan)**	**488.46**	**288.85**	**62.35**	**137.26**
离休职工的离休费	Pensions for Retired Veteran Cadres	15.50	11.61	0.27	3.62
退休职工的退休费	Pensions for Retired	466.42	274.37	60.76	131.29
退职人员的退职生活费	Living Expenses for Resigned	6.54	2.87	1.32	2.35

注：本表"其他单位"包括港澳台及外商企业。
Note: "Other" in this table inoludes foreign invested and HongKong, Macao and Taiwan funded enterprises.

表9.11 主要年份职工福利费用
LABOUR INSURANCE AND WELFARE FUNDS FOR STAFF AND WORKERS IN MAIN YEARS

指标	Indicators	2000	2006	2007
职工劳保福利费(亿元)	**Labour Insurance and Welfare Funds for Working Staff and Workers (100 million yuan)**	**96.93**	**135.07**	**109.61**
集体福利事业补贴费和设施费	Subsidies for Collective Welfare Funds	8.54	31.31	15.77
文体宣传费	Expenses for Cultural Activities, Sports and Propaganda	1.34	9.44	2.41
其他	Others	87.05	94.32	91.43

①本页数据由上海市劳动和社会保障局提供。
②本表为在职职工口径。
❶Data on this page are provided by Shanghai Municipal Labour and Social Security Bureau.
❷The scope of data in this table refere to working staff and workers.

表9.12 按登记注册类型分的职工福利费用（2007）
WORKERS CLASSIFIED ACCORDING TO THE CATEGORIES OF REGISTRATION

	指 标 Indicators	劳保福利费用 Labour Insurance and Welfare Funds	国有单位 State-owned Units	集体单位 Collective-owned Units	其他单位 Other Units
在职职工福利费(亿元)	**Welfare Funds for Working Staff and Workers (100 million yuan)**	**109.61**	**54.38**	**2.73**	**52.50**
集体福利事业补贴费和设施费	Subsidies for Collective Welfare Funds	15.77	7.37	0.83	7.57
文体宣传费	Expenses for Cultural Activities, Sports and Propaganda	2.41	0.98	0.07	1.36
其 他	Others	91.43	46.03	1.83	43.57

①本表数据由上海市劳动和社会保障局提供。
②本表为在职职工口径。
❶This table is provided by Shanghai Municipal Labour and Social Security Bureau.
❷The scope of data in this table refer to working staff and workers.

表9.13 居民储蓄存款(1997～2007)
DEPOSITS OF RESIDENTS

年 份 Year	居民储蓄存款（亿元）Deposits of Residents (100 million yuan)	其中 of which: 定期储蓄 Time Account	其中 of which: 活期储蓄 Current Account	人均储蓄存款（元）Average Deposits (yuan)
1997	2 109.18	1 843.25	265.93	13 851
1998	2 372.94	2 017.16	355.78	15 303
1999	2 597.12	2 119.82	477.30	16 447
2000	2 627.07	2 084.21	542.86	16 338
2001	3 109.50	2 301.33	808.17	19 218
2002	4 915.54	3 603.05	1 312.49	30 249
2003	6 054.60	4 260.87	1 793.73	35 390
2004	6 960.99	4 904.93	2 056.06	39 956
2005	8 432.49	6 071.83	2 360.66	47 416
2006	9 480.28	6 701.97	2 778.31	52 230
2007	9 326.45	6 185.85	3 140.60	50 194

注：本表数据由中国人民银行上海总部提供。2000年起居民储蓄存款为中外资本外币存款余额。
Note: Data in this table are provided by Shanghai Headquarters of the People's Bank of China. Since 2000, the deposits of residents refered to all deposits in foreign and domestic currrency of foreign and domestic capital.

表 9.14 城市居民家庭生活基本情况(1980~2007)
BASIC STATISTICS OF URBAN HOUSEHOLDS

年份 Year	调查户数(户) Number of Households Surveyed (household)	平均每户家庭人口(人) Average Number Persons per Household (person)	平均每户就业人口(人) Average Number of Employees per Household (person)	平均每户就业面(%) Percentage of Emplyment per Household (%)	平均每一就业者负担人数(人) Persons Supported by Each Employee (person)	平均每人可支配收入(元) Average per Capita Disposable Income (yuan)
1980	500	4.06	2.41	59.4	1.69	637
1981	500	4.06	2.47	60.8	1.65	637
1982	500	4.03	2.48	61.5	1.62	659
1983	500	4.00	2.52	63.0	1.58	691
1984	500	3.94	2.53	64.2	1.56	834
1985	500	3.72	2.27	61.0	1.64	1 075
1986	500	3.66	2.30	62.8	1.60	1 293
1987	500	3.55	2.20	62.0	1.61	1 437
1988	500	3.38	2.08	61.5	1.62	1 723
1989	500	3.27	2.00	61.2	1.63	1 975
1990	500	3.25	1.98	60.9	1.64	2 182
1991	500	3.18	1.91	60.1	1.67	2 486
1992	500	3.11	1.86	59.8	1.68	3 009
1993	500	3.03	1.77	58.4	1.71	4 277
1994	500	3.07	1.69	55.0	1.82	5 868
1995	500	3.11	1.65	53.1	1.88	7 172
1996	500	3.07	1.58	51.5	1.95	8 159
1997	500	3.08	1.58	51.3	1.94	8 439
1998	500	3.09	1.58	51.1	1.95	8 773
1999	500	3.08	1.74	56.5	1.78	10 932
2000	500	3.04	1.64	53.9	1.85	11 718
2001	500	3.00	1.55	51.7	1.94	12 883
2002	500	2.91	1.52	52.2	1.91	13 250
2003	500	2.99	1.55	51.8	1.93	14 867
2004	1 000	3.04	1.53	50.3	1.99	16 683
2005	1 000	3.01	1.55	51.5	1.94	18 645
2006	1 000	3.02	1.60	53.0	1.89	20 668
2007	1 000	3.01	1.64	54.5	1.84	23 623

注：本表数据为城市居民家庭收支抽样调查资料，由国家统计局上海调查总队提供。
Note: Data in this table are obtained from the sample survey of households and provided by Survey Office of the National Bureau of Statistics in Shanghai.

表9.14 续表 continued

年份 Year	平均每人消费支出(元) Average per Capita Consumption Expenditures (yuan)	其中 of which 服务性消费支出 Service Consumption Expenditures	服务性消费支出占消费支出比重(%) Percentage of Service Consumption Expenditures to the Total Expenditure (%)	平均每人可支配收入指数(以1980年价格为100) Index of per Capita Disposable Income (1980 = 100)	平均每人消费支出指数(以1980年价格为100) Index of per Capita consumption Expenditures (1980 = 100)	恩格尔系数 Engel Coefficient
1980	553	75	13.6	100	100	56.0
1981	585	78	13.4	98.6	104.2	56.8
1982	576	82	14.3	101.8	102.4	58.8
1983	615	87	14.2	106.5	109.2	58.6
1984	726	101	13.9	125.8	126.1	56.5
1985	992	121	12.2	140.7	149.5	52.1
1986	1 170	136	11.7	159.2	166.0	52.7
1987	1 282	161	12.6	163.7	168.2	54.5
1988	1 648	170	10.3	163.4	180.1	52.6
1989	1 812	190	10.5	161.6	170.8	55.8
1990	1 937	233	12.0	167.9	171.7	56.5
1991	2 167	294	13.6	173.1	173.9	56.9
1992	2 509	376	15.0	190.6	183.1	55.9
1993	3 530	583	16.5	225.4	214.2	53.1
1994	4 669	762	16.3	249.5	228.7	53.5
1995	5 868	924	15.7	256.9	242.2	53.4
1996	6 763	1 263	18.7	267.6	255.6	50.7
1997	6 820	1 241	18.2	269.3	250.7	51.7
1998	6 866	1 371	20.0	280.0	252.4	50.6
1999	8 248	1 849	22.4	343.7	298.7	45.2
2000	8 868	2 231	25.2	359.4	313.3	44.5
2001	9 336	2 482	26.6	395.2	329.9	43.4
2002	10 464	3 033	29.0	438.4	365.7	39.4
2003	11 040	3 369	30.5	491.4	385.4	37.2
2004	12 631	4 084	32.3	539.6	431.5	36.4
2005	13 773	4 447	32.3	597.1	465.8	35.9
2006	14 762	4 841	32.8	654.0	493.3	35.6
2007	17 255	5 595	32.4	724.3	558.8	35.5

注：平均每人可支配收入指数和平均每人消费支出指数是扣除价格因素后按同口径计算的。

Note: Index of per Caspita Disposable Income and Index of per Capita Consumption Expenditures are calculated by deducting prices according to the same caliber.

表9.15 城市居民家庭生活基本情况(2007，按收入水平分组)
BASIC STATISTICS OF URBAN HOUSEHOLD INCOME AND EXPENDITURES (2007,GROUPED BY INCOME LEVEL)

指标	Indicators	总平均 Total Average	低收入户 Low Income	中低收入户 Medium-low Income
调查户数（户）	Number of Households Surveyed (household)	1 000	200	200
平均每户家庭人口（人）	Average Number of Persons Per Household (person)	3.01	3.15	2.97
平均每户就业人口（人）	Average Number of Employees Per Household (person)	1.64	1.50	1.49
平均每户就业面（%）	Percentage of Employment Per Household (%)	54.5	47.6	50.2
平均每一就业者负担人数（人）	Persons Supported by Each Employee (person)	1.84	2.10	1.99
可支配收入（元）	Average per Capita Disposable Income (yuan)	23 623	10 297	15 131
工资性收入	Salaries	16 598	6 863	9 155
经营净收入	Net Income from Household Business	1 158	301	779
财产性收入	Property Income	369	38	124
转移性收入	Transferred Income	5 498	3 095	5 073
#养老金或离退休金	Pensions and Retirement Pay	4 696	2 544	4 459
出售财物收入（元）	Income from Selling Properties(yuan)	587	8	…
借贷收入（元）	Average per Capita Borrowing(yuan)	5 714	1 195	3 557
#住房贷款	Housing Loan	647		
提取储蓄存款	Pick up Savings Deposits	4 974	1 178	3 555
消费支出(元)	Average Per Capita Consumption Expenditures (yuan)	17 255	9 217	12 959
#服务性消费支出	Service Consumption Expenditure	5 595	2 866	3 832
购房与建房支出（元）	Buying and Building House Expenditure (yuan)	2 451	9	1 207
转移性支出（元）	Transferred Expenditure (yuan)	1 877	440	1 322
社会保障支出(元)	Social Security Expenditure (yuan)	1 972	784	1 176
借贷支出（元）	Lending Expenditure (yuan)	7 296	1 001	2 021

注：本表数据为城市居民家庭收支抽样调查资料，由国家统计局上海调查总队提供。
Note: Data in this table are obtained from the sample survey of households and provided by Survey office of the National Bureau of Statistics in Shanghai.

表 9.15 续表 continued

	指 标 Indicators	中等收入户 Medium Income	中高收入户 Medium-high Income	高收入户 High Income
调查户数（户）	Number of Households Surveyed (household)	200	200	200
平均每户家庭人口（人）	Average Number of Persons Per Household (person)	3.02	3.01	2.89
平均每户就业人口（人）	Average Number of Employees Per Household (person)	1.67	1.72	1.83
平均每户就业面（%）	Percentage of Employment Per Household (%)	55.3	57.1	63.3
平均每一就业者负担人数（人）	Persons Supported by Each Employee (person)	1.81	1.75	1.58
可支配收入（元）	Average per Capita Disposable Income (yuan)	20 249	27 286	47 149
工资性收入	Salaries	13 239	18 486	36 907
经营净收入	Net Income from Household Business	940	1 600	2 272
财产性收入	Property Income	249	408	1 083
转移性收入	Transferred Income	5 821	6 792	6 887
#养老金或离退休金	Pensions and Retirement Pay	5 153	6 009	5 441
出售财物收入（元）	Income from Selling Properties(yuan)	513	1 446	1 003
借贷收入（元）	Average per Capita Borrowing(yuan)	2 494	7 332	14 773
#住房借贷	Housing Loan		1 156	2 203
提取储蓄存款	Pick up Savings Deposits	2 417	6 021	12 344
消费支出(元)	Average per Capita Consumption Expenditures (yuan)	15 468	18 993	30 820
#服务性消费支出	Service Consumption Expenditure	4 700	6 230	10 781
购房与建房支出（元）	Buying and Building House Expenditure(yuan)	591	3 829	7 017
转移性支出（元）	Transferred Expenditure(yuan)	1 310	2 168	4 367
社会保障支出(元)	Social Security Expenditure(yuan)	1 679	2 204	4 203
借贷支出（元）	Lending Expenditure(yuan)	4 592	9 747	20 163

表 9.16 主要年份城市居民家庭人均可支配收入
PER CAPITA DISPOSABLE INCOME OF URBAN HOUSEHOLDS IN MAIN YEARS

单位：元(yuan)

年 份 Year	人均可支配收入 Average per Capita Disposable Income	工资性收入 Salaries	经营净收入 Net Income from Household Business	财产性收入 Property Income	转移性收入 Transferred Income
1980	637	551			86
1985	1 075	795			280
1990	2 182	1 548	1	21	612
1991	2 486	1 780		29	677
1992	3 009	2 138	3	44	824
1993	4 277	3 099	4	37	1 137
1994	5 868	4 224	28	54	1 562
1995	7 172	5 002	69	92	2 009
1996	8 159	5 889	87	61	2 122
1997	8 439	5 969	150	69	2 251
1998	8 773	6 004	98	57	2 614
1999	10 932	7 326	156	68	3 382
2000	11 718	7 832	120	65	3 701
2001	12 883	7 975	119	39	4 750
2002	13 250	7 915	436	94	4 805
2003	14 867	10 097	377	130	4 263
2004	16 683	11 422	507	215	4 539
2005	18 645	12 409	798	292	5 146
2006	20 668	13 962	959	300	5 447
2007	23 623	16 598	1 158	369	5 498

注：2002 年起，人均可支配收入不包括出售财物收入和个人交纳的社会保障支出。其他年份按原口径计算。
Note: Per Capita Disposable exclude income from selling properties and social security expenditure from 2002.

表 9.17 主要年份城市居民家庭人均可支配收入与消费支出
PER CAPITA ANNUAL DISPOSABLE INCOME AND CONSUMPTION EXPENDITURES OF URBAN HOUSEHOLDS IN MAIN YEARS

单位：元(yuan)

指 标	Indicators	2000	2006	2007
人均可支配收入	**Average per Capita Disposable Income**	**11 718**	**20 668**	**23 623**
低收入户	Low Income	6 840	8 973	10 297
中低收入户	Medium-low Income	8 815	13 045	15 131
中等收入户	Medium Income	10 529	16 774	20 249
中高收入户	Medium-high Income	12 892	22 994	27 286
高收入户	High Income	19 959	42 884	47 149
人均消费支出	**Average per Capita Consumption Expenditures**	**8 868**	**14 762**	**17 255**
低收入户	Low Income	6 272	8 004	9 217
中低收入户	Medium-low Income	7 516	11 233	12 959
中等收入户	Medium Income	8 555	13 142	15 468
中高收入户	Medium-high Income	9 445	15 815	18 993
高收入户	High Income	12 763	26 325	30 820

注：本页数据为城市居民家庭收支抽样调查资料，由国家统计局上海调查总队提供。
Note: Data on this page are obtained from the sample survey of households and provided by Survey Office of the National Bureau of Statistics in Shanghai.

表9.18 主要年份城市居民家庭人均消费支出
PER CAPITA CONSUMPTION EXPENDITURES OF URBAN HOUSEHOLDS IN MAIN YEARS

单位:元(yuan)

年 份 Year	消费支出 Total Consumption Expenditures	食 品 Food	衣 着 Clothing	家庭设备用品及服务 Household Facilities, Articles and Services	医 疗 保 健 Medicines and Medical Services	交通和 通 信 Traffic and Communi-cations	教育文化娱乐服务 Education, Culture and Recreation Services	居 住 Residence	其他商品和服务 Other Commodities and Services
1980	553	310	79	50	7	20	49	26	12
1985	992	517	151	118	5	30	91	43	37
1990	1 937	1 095	208	196	11	58	231	90	48
1995	5 868	3 131	561	637	113	321	508	401	196
1996	6 763	3 429	590	614	148	496	827	416	243
1997	6 820	3 526	552	525	197	397	828	605	190
1998	6 866	3 477	472	453	261	406	893	674	230
1999	8 248	3 731	551	772	347	583	1 094	842	328
2000	8 868	3 947	567	683	501	759	1 287	794	330
2001	9 336	4 056	577	579	558	958	1 422	796	390
2002	10 464	4 120	613	653	734	1 115	1 668	1 189	372
2003	11 040	4 102	751	792	603	1 259	1 834	1 280	419
2004	12 631	4 593	797	780	762	1 703	2 195	1 327	474
2005	13 773	4 940	940	800	797	1 984	2 273	1 412	627
2006	14 762	5 249	1 027	877	763	2 333	2 432	1 436	645
2007	17 255	6 125	1 330	959	857	3 154	2 654	1 412	764

表9.19 主要年份城市居民家庭人均消费支出构成
COMPOSITION OF PER CAPITA CONSUMER EXPENDITURES OF URBAN HOUSEHOLDS IN MAIN YEARS

单位:%

年 份 Year	消费支出 Total Consumption Expenditures	食 品 Food	衣 着 Clothing	家庭设备用品及服务 Household Facilities Articles and Services	医 疗 保 健 Medicine and Medical Services	交通和 通 信 Traffic and Communi-cations	教育文化娱乐服务 Education, Cultural and Recreation Services	居 住 Residence	其他商品和服务 Other Commodities and Services
1980	100	56.0	14.3	9.0	1.3	3.6	8.9	4.8	2.1
1985	100	52.1	15.3	11.9	0.5	3.0	9.2	4.3	3.7
1990	100	56.5	10.8	10.1	0.6	3.0	11.9	4.6	2.5
1995	100	53.4	9.6	10.9	1.9	5.5	8.6	6.8	3.3
1996	100	50.7	8.7	9.1	2.2	7.3	12.2	6.2	3.6
1997	100	51.7	8.1	7.7	2.9	5.8	12.1	8.9	2.8
1998	100	50.6	6.9	6.6	3.8	5.9	13.0	9.8	3.4
1999	100	45.2	6.7	9.3	4.2	7.1	13.3	10.2	4.0
2000	100	44.5	6.4	7.7	5.6	8.6	14.5	9.0	3.7
2001	100	43.4	6.2	6.2	6.0	10.3	15.2	8.5	4.2
2002	100	39.4	5.9	6.2	7.0	10.7	15.9	11.4	3.5
2003	100	37.2	6.8	7.2	5.4	11.4	16.6	11.6	3.8
2004	100	36.4	6.3	6.2	6.0	13.4	17.4	10.5	3.8
2005	100	35.9	6.8	5.8	5.8	14.4	16.5	10.2	4.6
2006	100	35.6	6.9	5.9	5.2	15.8	16.5	9.7	4.4
2007	100	35.5	7.7	5.5	5.0	18.3	15.4	8.2	4.4

注：本页数据为城市居民家庭收支抽样调查资料，由国家统计局上海调查总队提供。
Note: Data on this page are obtained from the sample survey of households and provided by Survey Office of the National Bureau of Statistics in Shanghai.

表9.20 主要年份城市居民家庭人均消费支出
PER CAPITA CONSUMPTION EXPENDITURES OF URBAN HOUSEHOLD IN MAIN YEARS

单位:元(yuan)

类 别	Types	2000	2006	2007
消费支出	**Total Consumption Expenditures**	**8 868**	**14 762**	**17 255**
食　品	Food	3 947	5 249	6 125
#粮　油	Grain and Oil	396	452	561
肉禽蛋水产品	Meat, Poultry, Eggs and Aquatic Products	1 324	1 352	1 666
蔬　菜	Vegetables	305	402	443
干鲜瓜果	Dry and Fresh Fruits	293	378	450
糕点、奶及奶制品	Cake, Milk and Dairy Products	315	410	484
在外饮食	Dining Out	710	1 482	1 722
衣　着	Clothing	567	1 027	1 330
#服　装	Garments	387	753	984
家庭设备用品及服务	Household Facilities, Articles and Services	683	877	959
#耐用消费品	Durable Consumer Goods	340	458	438
医疗保健	Medicines and Medical Services	501	763	857
#药品费	Medicines	244	327	343
医疗费	Medical Prouducts	69	192	230
交通和通信	Traffic and Communications	759	2 333	3 154
交　通	Traffic	375	1 396	2 079
#交通费	Traffic Fees	335	581	675
通　信	Communications	384	937	1 075
#电信费	Telecommunication Fees	272	743	847
教育文化娱乐服务	Education, Culture and Recreation Articles and Services	1 287	2 432	2 654
教　育	Education	585	1 225	1 204
#非义务学杂费	Tuition for Non-compulsory Education		574	501
义务学费费	Tuition for Compulsory Education		24	17
成人教育费	Adult Education Fee	78	197	215
文化娱乐服务	Culture and Recreation Services	147	504	709
文化娱乐用品	Culture and Recreation Articles	555	703	741
#家用电脑	Computers	197	243	300
书报杂志	Books, Newspapers and Magazines	73	67	73
居　住	Residence	794	1 436	1 412
#水　费	Water	72	93	100
电　费	Electricity	258	354	379
燃料费	Fuels	157	169	173
租赁房房租	Rent	142	120	163
物业管理费	Estate Management Fee	20	122	154
其他商品和服务	Miscellanecus Commodities and Services	330	645	764

注：本表数据为城市居民家庭收支抽样调查资料，由国家统计局上海调查总队提供。
Note: Data in this table are obtained from the sample survey of households and provided by Survey office of the National Bureau of Statistics in Shanghai.

表9.21 城市居民家庭人均消费支出（2007，按收入水平分组）
PER CAPITA CONSUMPTION EXPENDITURES OF URBAN HOUSEHOLD (2007,GROUPED BY INCOME LEVEL)

单位:元(yuan)

类别	Types	总平均 Total Average	低收入户 Low Income	中低收入户 Medium-low Income
消费支出	**Total Consumer Expenditures**	**17 255**	**9 217**	**12 959**
食　品	Food	6 125	4 148	5 571
#粮　油	Grain and Oil	561	466	559
肉禽蛋水产品	Meat,Poultry,Eggs and Aquatic Products	1 666	1 305	1 651
蔬　菜	Vegetables	443	361	448
干鲜瓜果	Dry and Fresh Fruit	450	321	413
糕点、奶及奶制品	Cake,Milk and Dairy Products	484	354	446
在外饮食	Dining Out	1 722	757	1 277
衣　着	Clothing	1 330	571	869
#服　装	Garments	984	416	602
家庭设备用品及服务	Household Facilities Articles and Services	959	351	661
#耐用消费品	Durable Consumer Goods	438	119	323
医疗保健	Medicine and Medical Services	857	527	571
#药品费	Medicines	343	224	295
医疗费	Medical Prouducts	230	216	100
交通和通信	Traffic and Communications	3 154	1 029	1 617
交　通	Traffic	2 079	423	678
#交通费	TrafficFees	675	335	479
通　信	Telecommunications	1 075	606	939
#电信费	Communication Fees	847	526	748
教育文化娱乐服务	Education,Culture and Recreation Articles and Services	2 654	1 635	1 908
教　育	Education	1 204	1 096	1 119
#非义务学杂费	Tuition for Non-compulsory Education	501	620	581
义务学费费	Tuition for Compulsory Education	17	22	21
成人教育费	Adult Education Fee	215	99	140
文化娱乐服务	Culture and Recreation Services	709	193	308
文化娱乐用品	Culture and Recreation Articles	741	346	481
#家用电脑	Computers	300	159	212
书报杂志	Books,Newspapers and Magazines	73	31	53
居　住	Residence	1 412	677	1 219
#水　费	Water	100	84	95
电　费	Electricity	379	284	348
燃料费	Fuels	173	144	166
租赁房房租	Rent	163	66	126
物业管理费	Estate Management Fee	154	57	86
其他商品和服务	Miscellanecus Commodities and Services	764	279	543

注：本表数据为城市居民家庭收支抽样调查资料，由国家统计局上海调查总队提供。
Note: Data in this table are obtained from the sample survey of households and provided by Survey office of the National Bureau of Statistics in Shanghai.

表 9.21 续表 continued

单位:元(yuan)

类 别	Types	中等收入户 Medium Income	中高收入户 Medium-high Income	高收入户 High Income
消费支出	**Total Consumer Expenditures**	**15 468**	**18 993**	**30 820**
食 品	Food	6 088	6 551	8 500
#粮 油	Grain and Oil	590	574	623
肉禽蛋水产品	Meat, Poultry, Eggs and Aquatic Products	1 763	1 747	1 893
蔬 菜	Vegetables	459	462	491
干鲜瓜果	Dry and Fresh Fruit	455	515	560
糕点、奶及奶制品	Cake, Milk and Dairy Products	520	515	597
在外饮食	Dining Out	1 440	1 918	3 365
衣 着	Clothing	1 140	1 629	2 547
#服 装	Garments	835	1 211	1 938
家庭设备用品及服务	Household Facilities Articles and Services	912	1 230	1 713
#耐用消费品	Durable Consumer Goods	454	582	741
医疗保健	Medicine and Medical Services	1 007	860	1 363
#药品费	Medicines	414	332	465
医疗费	Medical Prouducts	200	266	377
交通和通信	Traffic and Communications	2 234	3 570	7 691
交 通	Traffic	1 196	2 369	6 046
#交通费	Traffic Fees	622	785	1 197
通 信	Telecommunications	1 038	1 200	1 645
#电信费	Communication Fees	830	930	1 238
教育文化娱乐服务	Education, Culture and Recreation Articles and Services	2 237	2 655	5 026
教 育	Education	1 046	949	1 857
#非义务学杂费	Tuition for Non-compulsory Education	422	375	503
义务学费费	Tuition for Compulsory Education	13	13	19
成人教育费	Adult Education Fee	176	158	527
文化娱乐服务	Culture and Recreation Services	527	878	1 723
文化娱乐用品	Culture and Recreation Articles	664	828	1 446
#家用电脑	Computers	269	375	504
书报杂志	Books, Newspapers and Magazines	63	80	143
居 住	Residence	1 342	1 634	2 272
#水 费	Water	102	102	120
电 费	Electricity	391	395	489
燃料费	Fuels	168	180	209
租赁房房租	Rent	190	275	163
物业管理费	Estate Management Fee	144	166	336
其他商品和服务	Miscellanecus Commodities and Services	508	864	1 708

表9.22 主要年份城市居民家庭平均每人主要消费品消费量
PER CAPITA CONSUMPTION OF MAJOR CONSUMER GOODS OF URBAN HOUSEHOLDS IN MAIN YEARS

商品名称	Name of Commodities	2000	2006	2007
大 米(千克)	Grain(kg)	53.4	43.4	40.3
食用植物油(千克)	Edible Vegetable Oil(kg)	10.9	9.5	10.2
猪 肉(千克)	Pork(kg)	17.3	19.0	17.4
牛羊肉(千克)	Beef and Mutton(kg)	2.2	2.8	2.9
鸡(千克)	Poultry(kg)	7.5	5.5	7.3
鸭(千克)	Duck (kg)	1.3	2.3	2.6
鲜 蛋(千克)	Eggs(kg)	11.3	9.2	9.4
鱼(千克)	Fish (kg)	6.9	15.3	15.7
虾(千克)	Shrimp (kg)	4.9	5.2	5.5
鲜 菜(千克)	Vegetables(kg)	104.7	98.8	99.6
啤 酒(千克)	Beer (kg)	8.9	7.0	7.7
糕点类(千克)	Cake (kg)	4.6	5.3	6.0
鲜瓜果(千克)	Fresh Melon and Fruit (kg)	60.5	67.6	71.5
鲜乳品和酸奶(千克)	Fresh Milk and Yogurt (kg)	29.6	29.7	31.9
服 装(件)	Clothing (unit)	7.3	9.3	10.2
生活用水(立方米)	Household Water Consumption (cubic meters)	53.3	51.7	55.2
生活用电(千瓦时)	Household Power Consumption (kwh)	421.3	593.4	627.4
液化石油气(千克)	Liquified Petroleum Gas (kg)	3.3	0.7	0.7
管道煤气(立方米)	Pipeline Gas (cubic meters)	155.7	139.6	139.5

表9.23 主要年份平均每百户城市居民家庭年末耐用消费品拥有量
PER 100 URBAN HOUSEHOLDS YEAR-END POSSESSION OF DURABLE CONSUMER GOODS IN MAIN YEARS

商品名称	Name of Commodities	2000	2006	2007
彩色电视机(台)	Color TV Set (unit)	147	179	183
照相机(架)	Camera (unit)	71	86	89
摄像机(架)	Video Camera (unit)	3	11	15
家用电脑(台)	Personal Computer (unit)	26	91	104
健身器材(台)	Gymnasfic Equipment (unit)	6	11	10
移动电话(部)	Mobile Phone (unit)	29	200	217
钢 琴(架)	Piano (unit)	3	5	6
组合音响(台)	Music Center (unit)	32	48	52
家用空调器(台)	Household Air Conditioner (unit)	96	175	189
洗衣机(台)	Washing Machine (unit)	93	98	98
电冰箱(台)	Household Refrigerator (unit)	102	104	103
热水淋浴器(台)	Water Heater (unit)	64	93	96
微波炉(台)	Microwave Oven (unit)	78	96	96
消毒碗柜(台)	Dish-sterilization Boxes(unit)		13	14

注：本页数据为城市居民家庭收支抽样调查资料，由国家统计局上海调查总队提供。
Note: Data on this page are obtained from the sample survey of households and provided by Survey Office of the National Bureau of Statistics in Shanghai.

表 9.24 农村居民家庭生活基本情况（1990～2007）
BASIC STATISTICS OF RURAL HOUSEHOLDS

年 份 Year	调查户数 （户） Number of Households Surveyed (household)	平均每户人口 （人） Average Number of Person per Household (person)	平均每户劳动力 （人） Average Number of Labours per Household (person)	平均每一劳动力负担人数 （人） Persons Supported by Each Person (person)	平均每人总收入 （元） Average Gross Income per Capita (yuan)	平均每人可支配收入 （元） Average Disposable Income per Capita (yuan)	平均每人总支出 （元） Average Expenditures per Capita (yuan)
1990	1 000	3.68	2.46	1.49	1 990	1 665	1 592
1991	600	3.49	2.36	1.48	2 376	2 003	1 893
1992	600	3.43	2.36	1.46	2 581	2 226	2 322
1993	600	3.41	2.45	1.39	3 149	2 727	2 660
1994	600	3.41	2.51	1.36	3 940	3 437	3 320
1995	600	3.47	2.54	1.37	4 861	4 246	4 041
1996	600	3.40	2.54	1.34	5 506	4 846	4 581
1997	600	3.35	2.48	1.35	5 933	5 277	4 953
1998	600	3.33	2.50	1.33	5 965	5 407	4 924
1999	600	3.31	2.54	1.30	5 924	5 481	4 431
2000	600	3.31	2.53	1.31	6 400	5 565	5 578
2001	600	3.29	2.48	1.33	6 827	5 850	6 353
2002	600	3.33	2.52	1.32	7 080	6 212	6 988
2003	600	3.34	2.59	1.29	7 260	6 658	6 931
2004	600	3.33	2.54	1.31	7 994	7 337	7 580
2005	600	3.21	2.19	1.47	9 234	8 342	8 663
2006	600	3.20	2.24	1.43	10 225	9 213	9 344
2007	600	3.18	2.17	1.47	11 382	10 222	10 429

注：本表数据为农村居民家庭收支抽样调查资料，由国家统计局上海调查总队提供。
Note: Data in this table are obtained from the sample survey of households and provided by Survey office of the National Bureau of Statistics in Shanghai.

表 9.24 续表 continued

年　份 Year	平均每人生活消费支出（元）per Capita Consumpition Expenditures (yuan)	平均每人可支配收入指数（以 1990 年为 100）Index of per Capita Disposable Income (1990 = 100)	平均每人生活消费支出指数（以 1990 年为 100）Index of Per Capita Consumption Expenditures (1990 = 100)	平均每人年底居住房屋面积（平方米）Average per Capita Living Space Year-end (sq. m)	平均每百户购买商品房面积（平方米）Commodity Housing Floor Space Purchased by Every 100 Households(sq. m)	平均每百户购买商品房金额（万元）Commodity Housing Value Purchased by Every 100 Households (10 000 yuan)
1990	1 262	100.0	100.0	37.08		
1991	1 540	120.3	122.0	39.60		
1992	1 967	133.7	155.7	42.07		
1993	2 200	163.8	174.3	44.22		
1994	2 715	206.4	215.1	44.15		
1995	3 368	255.0	266.9	43.08		
1996	3 868	291.1	306.5	45.47	159.20	8.27
1997	4 228	316.9	335.0	46.44	147.80	12.10
1998	4 207	324.7	333.4	47.24	128.70	12.10
1999	3 867	329.2	306.4	49.00	53.00	6.55
2000	4 138	336.1	327.9	53.58	48.30	5.30
2001	4 753	351.3	376.6	54.70	75.80	6.40
2002	5 311	373.1	420.8	57.08	196.80	20.90
2003	5 670	399.9	449.3	59.03	121.78	20.63
2004	6 329	440.7	502.0	59.84	126.50	23.84
2005	7 265	501.0	575.7	56.56	67.20	10.13
2006	8 006	553.3	634.4	59.99	57.80	17.64
2007	8 845	613.9	700.9	61.22	90.67	25.92

注：2000 年前平均每人可支配收入按纯收入口径计算，平均每人总收入不包括内部亲友赠送。
Note: The per Capita Disposable Income before 2000 refers to the Net Income. The Gross Income excludes the donations from relatives and friends.

表 9.25 农村居民家庭人均可支配收入分组占全部户数比重(1990～2007)
PERCENTAGE OF RURAL HOUSEHOLDS IN TOTAL GROUPED BY DISPOSABLE INCOME

单位:%

年 份 Year	2 000 元以下 Below 2 000 yuan	2 000～3 000 元 2 000～3 000 yuan	3 000～4 000 元 3 000～4 000 yuan	4 000～5 000 元 4 000～5 000 yuan	5 000～6 000 元 5 000～6 000 yuan	6 000～7 000 元 6 000～7 000 yuan	7 000～8 000 元 7 000～8 000 yuan
1990	69.9	24.5	4.1	1.5			
1991	55.3	33.3	8.0	2.2	1.2		
1992	44.0	35.3	14.7	4.0	2.0		
1993	27.0	37.3	22.5	8.5	4.7		
1994	16.0	29.8	23.0	14.8	8.3	4.2	1.3
1995	9.5	19.5	23.2	17.2	13.0	7.5	4.0
1996	6.3	13.7	20.8	20.3	16.8	7.0	5.7
1997	5.0	11.5	18.8	17.5	14.8	12.3	5.5
1998	5.6	9.3	18.0	17.7	13.7	13.7	7.3
1999	6.5	11.3	17.7	17.5	11.2	10.0	8.0
2000	5.2	10.5	15.7	13.7	16.2	11.2	10.3
2001	5.0	11.2	12.5	12.8	13.3	14.3	9.0
2002	4.5	10.2	12.0	14.3	13.2	11.8	8.3
2003	2.8	7.8	11.8	12.5	12.5	13.3	8.8
2004	2.7	5.0	7.8	11.0	11.2	12.2	13.3
2005	3.5	4.3	8.8	9.8	10.7	9.0	11.5
2006	1.0	3.3	4.2	7.5	11.8	9.0	8.8
2007	1.3	1.5	3.5	6.3	7.7	8.2	9.0

表 9.25 续表 continued

单位:%

年 份 Year	8 000～9 000 元 8 000～9 000 yuan	9 000～10 000 元 9000～10 000yuan	10 000～11 000 元 10 000～11 000yuan	11 000～12 000 元 11 000～12 000yuan	12 000～13 000 元 12 000～13 000yuan	13 000～14 000 元 13 000～14 000yuan	14 000 元以上 14 000 yuan Over
1994	1.2	0.7	0.7				
1995	1.8	1.8	2.5				
1996	4.0	2.5	2.9				
1997	6.2	2.0	6.4				
1998	4.7	3.2	6.8				
1999	5.7	4.0	2.7	5.4			
2000	6.2	2.8	2.5	1.3	1.8	0.8	1.8
2001	6.7	4.3	3.0	2.5	1.2	1.0	3.2
2002	6.5	6.5	3.8	2.2	1.5	1.2	4.0
2003	8.9	6.7	3.9	3.0	2.0	1.7	4.3
2004	10.0	5.8	5.5	5.2	2.5	2.0	5.8
2005	6.7	6.2	6.7	4.8	2.8	3.3	11.9
2006	11.2	8.0	6.5	5.0	4.7	4.3	14.7
2007	8.3	10.2	8.0	6.5	6.0	4.2	19.3

注：本页数据为农村居民家庭收支抽样调查资料,由国家统计局上海调查总队提供。
Note: Data on this page are obtained from the sample survey of households and provided by Survey Office of the National Bureau of Statistics in Shanghai.

表 9.26 农村居民家庭人均可支配收入情况（1990～2007）
PER CAPITA DISPOSABLE INCOME OF RURAL HOUSEHOLDS

年 份 Year	人均可支配收入(元) Average Disposable Income per Capita (yuan)	工资性收入 Wages	家庭经营纯收入 Household Business Income	转移性和财产性收入 Property and Transferred Income	比重(以人均可支配收入为100) Proportion (Average Disposable Income Per Capita = 100)		
					工资性收入 Wages	家庭经营纯收入 Household Business Income	转移性和财产性收入 Property and Transferred Income
1990	1 665	1 066	539	60	64.0	32.4	3.6
1991	2 003	1 235	681	87	61.7	34.0	4.3
1992	2 226	1 454	685	87	65.3	30.8	3.9
1993	2 727	1 662	949	116	60.9	34.8	4.3
1994	3 437	2 112	1 084	241	61.5	31.5	7.0
1995	4 246	2 734	1 183	329	64.4	27.9	7.7
1996	4 846	3 240	1 278	328	66.9	26.4	6.7
1997	5 277	3 736	1 226	315	70.8	23.2	6.0
1998	5 407	3 869	1 185	353	71.6	21.9	6.5
1999	5 481	4 192	929	360	76.5	16.9	6.6
2000	5 565	4 310	934	321	77.4	16.8	5.8
2001	5 850	4 491	967	392	76.8	16.5	6.7
2002	6 212	4 920	774	518	79.2	12.5	8.3
2003	6 658	5 284	813	561	79.4	12.2	8.4
2004	7 337	5 757	886	694	78.5	12.1	9.4
2005	8 342	6 364	811	1 167	76.3	9.7	14.0
2006	9 213	6 892	766	1 555	74.8	8.4	16.8
2007	10 222	7 498	754	1 970	73.3	7.4	19.3

注：2000 年前平均每人可支配收入按纯收入口径计算。
Note: The per Capita Annual Disposable Income before 2000 refers to the Net Income.

表 9.27 农村居民家庭人均可支配收入和人均生活消费支出(2000～2007)
PER CAPITA DISPOSABLE INCOME AND LIVING EXPENDITURES FOR CONSUMPTION OF RURAL HOUSEHOLDS

单位:元(yuan)

年 份 Year	总平均 Average	低收入户 Low Income	中低收入户 Medium-low Income	中等收入户 Medium Income	中高收入户 Medium-high Income	高收入户 High Income
人均可支配收入	**Average per Capita Disposable Income**					
2000	5 565	2 330	3 906	5 264	6 725	10 405
2001	5 850	2 351	4 078	5 649	7 122	10 930
2002	6 212	2 429	4 266	5 701	7 513	11 989
2003	6 658	2 761	4 621	6 213	7 972	12 777
2004	7 337	3 122	5 148	7 006	8 775	13 652
2005	8 342	3 347	5 594	7 612	9 755	15 309
2006	9 213	3 830	6 194	8 412	10 714	16 843
2007	10 222	4 321	7 098	9 442	11 807	18 443
人均生活消费支出	**Average per Capita Consumption Expenditures**					
2000	4 138	2 390	3 387	3 887	5 487	5 880
2001	4 753	2 921	3 250	4 334	5 356	8 449
2002	5 311	2 350	4 341	4 834	5 873	9 683
2003	5 670	2 886	3 681	5 363	6 286	10 769
2004	6 329	4 076	4 914	5 309	6 992	10 971
2005	7 265	4 618	5 690	6 317	7 059	12 975
2006	8 006	4 788	6 001	6 951	8 015	15 058
2007	8 845	4 890	6 077	7 305	9 541	17 317

注：本页数据为农村居民家庭收支抽样调查资料，由国家统计局上海调查总队提供。
Note: Data on this page are obtained from the sample survey of households and provided by Survey Office of the National Bureau of Statistics in Shanghai.

表9.28 农村居民家庭人均生活消费支出(1990～2007)
PER CAPITA CONSUMPTION EXPENDITURES OF RURAL HOUSEHOLDS

单位:元(yuan)

年 份 Year	生活消费支出 Total Consumption Expenditures	食 品 Food	衣 着 Clothing	居 住 Residence	家庭设备用品及服务 Household Facilities, Articles and Services	交通和通 信 Traffic and Communi-cations	文教娱乐用品及服务 Education, Culture and Recreation Articles and Services	医 疗 保 健 Medicines and Medical Services	其他商品和服务 Other Commodities and Services
1990	1 262	586	107	272	129	6	59	33	70
1991	1 540	739	134	324	151	15	85	35	57
1992	1 967	853	148	451	232	31	121	45	86
1993	2 200	1 022	157	357	259	65	220	50	70
1994	2 715	1 315	213	454	267	79	222	75	90
1995	3 368	1 491	233	761	284	159	256	73	111
1996	3 868	1 657	256	816	363	200	347	108	121
1997	4 228	1 756	267	921	338	240	414	174	118
1998	4 207	1 775	239	876	369	226	463	170	89
1999	3 867	1 669	202	681	389	197	474	160	95
2000	4 138	1 823	201	724	225	279	559	209	118
2001	4 753	1 915	226	890	294	340	673	265	150
2002	5 311	1 872	226	1 392	281	462	661	280	137
2003	5 670	2 004	250	1 437	297	587	676	333	86
2004	6 329	2 191	280	1 446	344	720	806	425	117
2005	7 265	2 676	367	1 323	458	739	936	562	204
2006	8 006	3 024	418	1 658	481	780	920	549	176
2007	8 845	3 259	476	2 097	452	884	857	571	249

表9.29 农村居民家庭人均生活消费支出构成(1990～2007)
COMPOSITION OF PER CAPITA CONSUMER EXPENDITURES OF RURAL HOUSEHOLDS

单位:%

年 份 Year	生活消费支出 Total Consumption Expenditures	食 品 Food	衣 着 Clothing	居 住 Residence	家庭设备用品及服务 Household Facilities, Articles and Services	交通和通 信 Traffic and Communi-cations	文教娱乐用品及服务 Education, Culture and Recreation Articles and Services	医 疗 保 健 Medicines and Medical Services	其他商品和服务 Other Commodities and Services
1990	100	46.4	8.5	21.6	10.2	0.5	4.7	2.6	5.5
1991	100	48.0	8.7	21.0	9.8	1.0	5.5	2.3	3.7
1992	100	43.4	7.5	22.9	11.8	1.6	6.1	2.3	4.4
1993	100	46.4	7.1	16.2	11.8	3.0	10.0	2.3	3.2
1994	100	48.4	7.9	16.7	9.8	2.9	8.2	2.8	3.3
1995	100	44.3	6.9	22.6	8.4	4.7	7.6	2.2	3.3
1996	100	42.8	6.6	21.1	9.4	5.2	9.0	2.8	3.1
1997	100	41.5	6.3	21.8	8.0	5.7	9.8	4.1	2.8
1998	100	42.2	5.7	20.8	8.8	5.4	11.0	4.0	2.1
1999	100	43.1	5.2	17.6	10.1	5.1	12.3	4.1	2.5
2000	100	44.0	4.9	17.5	5.4	6.7	13.5	5.1	2.9
2001	100	40.3	4.7	18.7	6.2	7.1	14.2	5.6	3.2
2002	100	35.2	4.3	26.2	5.3	8.7	12.4	5.3	2.6
2003	100	35.4	4.4	25.3	5.2	10.4	11.9	5.9	1.5
2004	100	34.6	4.4	22.9	5.4	11.4	12.7	6.7	1.9
2005	100	36.8	5.1	18.2	6.3	10.2	12.9	7.7	2.8
2006	100	37.8	5.2	20.7	6.0	9.7	11.5	6.9	2.2
2007	100	36.8	5.4	23.7	5.1	10.0	9.7	6.5	2.8

注：本页数据为农村居民家庭收支抽样调查资料，由国家统计局上海调查总队提供。
Note: Data on this page are obtained from the sample survey of households and provided by Survey Office of the National Bureau of Statistics in Shanghai.

表 9.30 农村居民家庭人均可支配收入(2007,按收入水平分组)
AVERAGE PER CAPITA DISPOSABLE INCOME OF RURAL HOUSEHOLDS (2007, GROUPED BY INCOME LEVEL)

单位:元(yuan)

指 标	Indicators	总平均 Total Average	低收入户 Low Income	中低收入户 Medium-low Income
平均每人可支配收入	**Average Per Capita Disposable Income**	**10 222**	**4 321**	**7 098**
工资性收入	Wage	7 498	3 156	5 286
家庭经营纯收入	Household Business Income	754	488	562
#农业纯收入	Agricultural Income	472	429	429
财产性收入	Property Income	673	261	371
#利息收入	Interest Income	53	5	31
租金收入	Rental Income	423	149	268
土地征用补偿	Compensation for Land Requisition	52	13	19
转移性收入	Transferred Income	1 297	416	879
#离退休金、养老金	Pension	1 286	404	879

注:本表数据为农村居民家庭收支抽样调查资料,由国家统计局上海调查总队提供。
Note: Data in this table are obtained from the sample survey of households and provided by Survey office of the National Bureau of Statistics in Shanghai.

表 9.30 续表 continued

单位:元(yuan)

指 标	Indicators	中等收入户 Medium Income	中高收入户 Medium-high Income	高收入户 High Income
平均每人可支配收入	**Average Per Capita Disposable Income**	**9 442**	**11 807**	**18 443**
工资性收入	Wage	6 924	8 806	14 043
家庭经营纯收入	Household Business Income	585	779	1 424
#农业纯收入	Agricultural Income	479	566	458
财产性收入	Property Income	642	545	1 351
#利息收入	Interest Income	43	13	186
租金收入	Rental Income	379	425	950
土地征用补偿	Compensation for Land Requisition	32	42	165
转移性收入	Transferred Income	1 291	1 677	1 625
#离退休金、养老金	Pension	1 230	1 639	1 472

表 9.31 农村居民家庭人均生活消费支出（2007，按收入水平分组）
PER CAPITA EXPENDITURES OF RURAL HOUSEHOLDS(2007,GROUPED BY INCOME LEVEL)

单位:元(yuan)

指 标	Indicators	总平均 Total Average	低收入户 Low Income	中低收入户 Medium-low Income
生活消费支出	**Consumption Expenditures**	**8 845**	**4 890**	**6 077**
食 品	Food	3 259	2 119	2 491
衣 着	Clothing	476	219	318
居 住	Residence	2 097	924	1 336
家庭设备用品及服务	Household Faclities, Articles and Services	452	215	295
交通和通信	Traffic and Communications	884	411	614
文教娱乐用品及服务	Education, Culture and Recreation Articles and Services	857	491	607
医疗保健	Medicine and Medical Services	571	438	337
其 他	Others	249	73	79

注：本表数据为农村居民家庭收支抽样调查资料，由国家统计局上海调查总队提供。
Note: Data in this table are obtained from the sample survey of households and provided by Survey office of the National Bureau of Statistics in Shanghai.

表 9.31 续表 continued

单位:元(yuan)

指 标	Indicators	中等收入户 Medium Income	中高收入户 Medium-high Income	高收入户 High Income
生活消费支出	**Consumption Expenditures**	**7 305**	**9 541**	**17 317**
食 品	Food	3 149	3 874	4 858
衣 着	Clothing	398	544	950
居 住	Residence	1 157	1 873	5 537
家庭设备用品及服务	Household Faclities, Articles and Services	419	567	802
交通和通信	Traffic and Communications	710	998	1 783
文教娱乐用品及服务	Education, Culture and Recreation Articles and Services	796	915	1 554
医疗保健	Medicine and Medical Services	456	561	1 122
其 他	Others	220	209	711

表 9.32 主要年份农村居民家庭平均每人主要消费品消费量
PER CAPITA CONSUMPTION OF MAJOR CONSUMER GOODS OF RURAL HOUSEHOLDS IN MAIN YEARS

商品名称	Name of Commodities	2000	2006	2007
粮 食（千克）	Grain (kg)	222.27	160.58	158.00
#稻 谷	Rice	205.25	152.14	151.73
豆类及豆制品(千克)	Beans and Their Products(kg)	5.71	7.19	7.52
油脂类（千克）	Edible Oil (kg)	7.99	8.17	9.00
蔬菜及菜制品(千克)	Vegetables and Their Products(kg)	92.41	66.84	69.64
肉禽及其制品（千克）	Meat, Poultry and Their Products (kg)	29.68	35.92	33.95
蛋类及蛋制品（千克）	Eggs and Their Products (kg)	10.71	7.68	7.93
奶及奶制品（千克）	Milk and Dairy Products(kg)	2.07	9.68	9.89
水产品（千克）	Aquatic Products (kg)	14.51	20.64	19.40
#鱼 类	Fish	10.11	12.90	12.19
虾、贝、蟹类	Shrimp, Testacean, Crab	2.61	5.39	5.04
水果及水果制品(千克)	Fruits and Their Products(kg)	36.94	33.21	31.96
食 糖（千克）	Suger (kg)	2.47	1.86	1.75
卷 烟（盒）	Cigarette (case)	44.49	50.66	48.65
酒（千克）	Licuor (kg)	16.58	18.31	18.63

表 9.33 主要年份平均每百户农村居民家庭年末耐用消费品拥有量
PER 100 RURAL HOUSEHOLD YEAR-END POSSESSION OF DURABLE CONSUMER GOODS IN MAIN YEARS

商品名称	Name of Commodities	2000	2006	2007
黑白电视机（台）	Black/ White TV Set (unit)	61	19	17
彩色电视机（台）	Color TV Set (unit)	97	167	179
电冰箱（台）	Household Refrigerator (unit)	74	94	96
洗衣机（台）	Washing Machine (unit)	69	89	91
影碟机（台）	VCD Player (unit)	27	31	28
轻骑、摩托车（辆）	Moped and Motorcycle (vehicle)	73	74	60
家用空调器（台）	Household Air Conditioner (unit)	14	99	120
抽油烟机（台）	Cooking Soat Inducer (unit)	35	65	69
微波炉（台）	Microwave Oven (unit)	14	71	76
吸尘器（台）	Vacuum Cleaner (unit)	9	24	26
热水淋浴器（台）	Water Heater (unit)	44	83	89
移动电话（部）	Mobile Phone (unit)	19	148	147
家用电脑（台）	Personal Computer (unit)	5	38	43

注：本页数据为农村居民家庭收支抽样调查资料，由国家统计局上海调查总队提供。
Note: Data on this page are obtained from the sample survey of households and provided by Survey Office of the National Bureau of Statistics in Shanghai.

上 / 海 / 统 / 计 / 年 / 鉴

主要统计指标解释

从业人员报酬

指各单位在一定时期内直接支付给本单位全部从业人员的劳动报酬总额。包括在岗职工工资总额和本单位其他从业人员劳动报酬两部分。

职工工资总额

指在报告期内直接支付给本单位职工的劳动报酬或生活费。职工工资总额包括在岗职工工资和离岗职工生活费两部分。

在岗职工工资是指单位在报告期内直接支付给本单位在岗职工的劳动报酬。包括计时工资、计件工资、计件标准工资、奖金和计件超额工资、津贴和补贴、加班加点工资和其他工资。

(1)计时工资是指按计时工资标准和工作时间支付给个人的劳动报酬。

(2)计件工资是指对已做工作按计件单价支付的劳动报酬。

(3)计件标准工资是指实行计件工资制的单位,按照批准的计件单价和规定的劳动定额或工作量支付给计件工人的劳动报酬。

(4)奖金和计件超额工资．奖金是指支付给在岗职工的超额劳动报酬和增收节支的劳动报酬。计件超额工资是计件工资的一部分，按计件工人超额完成定额任务后所得的工资。

(5)津贴和补贴:是指为了补偿职工特殊或额外的劳动消耗和因其他特殊原因支付给职工的津贴，以及为了保证职工工资水平不受物价影响支付给职工的物价补贴。津贴包括补偿职工特殊或额外劳动消耗的津贴及岗位性津贴、保健性津贴、技术性津贴、年功性津贴,地区津贴、其他津贴。补贴包括:为保证职工工资水平不受物价上涨或变动影响而支付的各种补贴，如副食品价格补贴(含肉类等价格补贴)、粮、油、蔬菜等价格补贴、煤价补贴、房贴、水电贴、房改补贴以及提高煤炭价格后,部分地区实行的民用燃料和照明电价格补贴等。

(6)加班加点工资是指对法定节假日和公休假日工作的职工，以及在正常工作日以外延长工作时间的职工按规定支付的加班工资和加点工资。

(7)其他工资是指其他根据国家规定支付的工资。如附加工资、保留工资以及调整工资补发的上年工资等。

离岗职工生活费是离岗职工已不在本单位从事其他工作但仍保留劳动关系期间从本单位领取的生活费

职工平均工资

指企业、事业、机关单位的职工在一定时期内平均每人所得的货币工资额。它表明一定时期职工工资收入的高低程度,是反映职工工资水平的主要指标。计算公式为:

职工平均工资＝报告期实际支付的全部职工工资总额／报告期全部职工平均人数

城市居民可支配收入

指居民可用于最终消费支出和其他非义务性支出以及储蓄的总和,即居民家庭可以用来自由支配的收入。它是家庭总收入扣除交纳的所得税、个人交纳的社会保障费以及调查户的记账补贴后的收入。不包括出售财物和借贷收入。

城市居民家庭消费支出

指城市居民家庭用于日常生活的全部支出。包括食品、衣着、家庭设备用品及服务、医疗保健、交通和通信、教育文化娱乐服务、居住、杂项商品和服务等八大类。

城市居民家庭人均服务性消费支出

指调查户用于本家庭支付社会提供的各种文化和生活方面的非商品性服务费用。服务性消费的特点在于其劳动过程和消费过程在时间与空间上的统一。在居民家庭八大类消费中,服务性消费支出包括:1、食品类中加工服务费和部分在外饮食费用;2、衣着类中衣着加工服务费;3、家庭设备用品及服务类中家庭服务(如家政服务费用);4、医疗保健类中医疗费(如诊疗费、上门出诊费、护工费用);5、交通和通信类中交通工具服务费(如汽车使用、维修费用)、交通费中使用飞机、轮船、火车等交通工具费用、通信服务费(如电信费、邮费);6、教育文化娱乐服务类中文化娱乐服务费(如参观、游览费用、健身活动费、团体旅游、其他文娱活动费)、文娱用品修理服务费、教育费(如义务、非义务教育支出)、成人教育支出、家教费、培训班费用、择校费;7、居住类中租赁费用、部分房屋装潢费用(人工费用)、居住服务费(如物业管理、维修费

主要统计指标解释

用);8、杂项商品和服务(如美容、洗澡、理发费用,旅馆住宿等费用)。

城乡居民储蓄存款余额

指某一时点城乡居民存入银行及农村信用社的储蓄金额,包括城镇居民储蓄存款和农民个人储蓄存款,不包括居民的手存现金和工矿企业、部队、机关、团体等单位存款。

农村居民可支配收入

指农村居民获得的经过初次分配与再分配后的收入。可支配收入可用于住户的最终消费、非义务性支出以及储蓄。

农村居民可支配收入＝总收入－家庭经营费用支出－税费支出－生产性固定资产折旧－财产性支出－转移性支出。

工资性收入

指农村住户成员受雇于单位或个人，靠出卖劳动而获得的收入。

财产性收入

指金融资产或有形非生产性资产的所有者向其他机构单位提供资金或将有形非生产性资产供其支配，作为回报而从中获得的收入。

转移性收入

指农村住户和住户成员无须付出任何对应物而获得的货物、服务、资金或资产所有权等,不包括无偿提供的用于固定资本形成的资金。一般情况下,是指农村住户在二次分配中的所有收入。

农村居民家庭生活消费支出

指农村住户用于物质生活和精神生活方面的支出。包括食品,衣着,居住,家庭设备用品及服务,医疗保健,交通和通信,文化教育娱乐用品及服务,其他商品和服务等消费支出。

SHANGHAI STATISTICAL YEARBOOK

EXPLANATORY NOTES TO MAJOR STATISTICAL INDICATORS

□ Labor Compensation

Labor Compensation refers to total payment by various units to their employees during a certain period of time, including wages to permanent staff and workers and payment to other employees.

□ Total Wages of Staff and Workers

Total Wages of Staff and Workers refers to the compensation for services or living cost a unit pays to its employees on the payroll, including the living cost paid to those not on duty.

Wages of working staff and workers refers to the compensation for services paid to its employees who are on duty, including time wages, piece rate wage, standard piece-rate wage, bonuses and extra piece-rate wages, allowances and subsidies, overtime payment and other remunerations.

(1)Time wages refer to the payment for services rated on the hourly system.

(2)Piece rate wages refer to payment for work rated on the piece system.

(3)Standard piece-rate wages refer to payment a unit pays to a worker according to a rate approved by an authority.

(4)Bonus and extra piece-rate wages. Bonus refers to the payment to an on-duty employee for his or her work above their quota and for their work in increasing production and savings for the unit. Extra piece-rate wages are part of the piece-rate wages and paid for the work an employee finishes above his or her quota.

(5)Allowances and subsidies refer to the compensation paid for special or extra services, the loss the price factors cost an employee, or for other reasons. Allowances refer to payment for special or extra services or special fund for post, healthcare, professional skills, yearly achievement, regional economic gap and other reasons. Subsidies are paid to secure an employee's salary against the fluctuating prices, including price compensation for non-staple food (such as meat products), grain, oil, vegetable, coal, housing, tap water, housing reforms, as well as price compensation paid during a coal price hike for consumption of fuel and power in some regions.

(6)Overtime payment is paid to employees for work he or she does during state holidays amd other holidays or outside the working hours.

(7)Other remunerations refer to the payment stipulated by the state, such as extra salary, reserve salary and money paid for the previous year arising from a salary raise.

Living cost for off-duty employees refer to the payment for living cost to an employee who keeps his or her labor relationship with a unit though they are not working for it.

□ Average Wages of Staff and Workers

Average Wages of Staff and Workers refers to the average wage in money terms per person during a certain period of time for staff and workers in enterprises, institutions, and government agencies, which reflects the general level of wage income during a certain period of time and is calculated as follows:

Average Wages of Staff and Workers = Total Wages of Staff and Workers at Reference Time /Average Number of Staff and Workers at Reference Time.

□ Disposable Income of Urban Households

Disposable Income of Urban Households refers to the actual income at the disposal of members of the households which can be used for final consumption, other non-compulsory expenditure and savings, which is part of the urban households' income that can be disposed by the urban households themselves. It is the income after deducting personal income tax, social insurance paid by individuals and investigation allowance from the total income of the households. The income from selling properties and borrowing are not included.

□ Consumption Expenditures of Urban Households

Consumption Expenditures of Urban Households refer to all the expenditures paid by urban households for consumption in daily life, including 8 categories as follows: food; clothing; household facilities, articles and services; medical care; traffic and telecommunication; education, culture and recreation services; housing; miscellaneous commodities and services.

□ Urbanities' Per-capita Spending on Srvices

Urbanities' per-capita spending on services refers to urbanites pay for services rather than commodities. Services are offered and consumed at the same time and place. The service spending

EXPLANATORY NOTES TO MAJOR STATISTICAL INDICATORS

for an urban family falls into the following eight types: 1. Money paid for food processing and money spent while eating out; 2. Money paid for clothing processing; 3. Domestic services and services for home amenities; 4. Medical cost (including medical diagnosis and treatment, in-home medical services and nursing cost); 5. Transport tool service fees (such as for the use of a car and maintenance fee thereby arising), transport tools (plane, ship, train) fees, post and telecommunications fees; 6. Fees for culture and entertainment services (such as tour and fitness building), fees for repair of sports and entertainment items, education cost (spending on obligatory and non-obligatory education), adult education cost, tutor fees, training courses fees and extra money paid as sponsorship fee to a school a student outside his or her education community; 7. Housing rents, some interior decoration cost (for labor), residence service fees (such as for property management and repairs); 8. Fees for other services (such as at a beauty salon, bathhouse, hairdresser's and hotels).

□ The Saving Deposits of Urban and Rural Residents

The Saving Deposits of Urban and Rural Residents refer to the total value of saving deposits of urban and rural households in banks and rural credit cooperatives at a given point of time, including the saving deposit of urban households and the savings deposit of rural households. The cash in hand by households and the deposits of organizations such as enterprises, military units, government agencies, institutions, etc. are not included.

□ Disposable Income of Rural Households

Disposable Income of Rural Households refers to the actual income at the disposal of rural households after initial distribution and reallocation. Disposal Income can be used for final consumption, non-compulsory expenditure and savings.

Disposal Income of Rural Households=total household income−expenditure for household operations−taxes and fees− depreciation of productive fixed assets−expenses on properties−expenses on transfers.

□ Income from Wages and Salaries

Income from Wages and Salaries refers to income from labour earned by the members of rural households employed by other units of individuals.

□ Income from Properties

Income from Properties refers to the income received as returns by owners of financial assets or tangible non-productive assets by providing capitals or tangible non-productive assets to other institutional units.

□ Income from Transfers

Income from Transfers refers to the receipt by rural households and their members of goods, services, capitals or rights of assets without giving or repaying accordingly, excluding capitals provided to them for the formation of fixed assets. In general, it refers to all income received by rural households through redistribution.

□ Living Expenditures for Consumption of Rural Households

Living Expenditures for Consumption of Rural Households refer to expenditures of material and culture life of rural household, including expenses on food, clothing, housing, household appliances and service, medical and health care, traffic and communication items, cultural, education and recreation items and service and other commodities and service.

第十篇

CHAPTER 10

城市建设

URBAN CONSTRUCTION

表 10.1 主要年份城市基础设施投资额
URBAN INFRASTRUCTURE INVESTMENT IN MAIN YEARS

单位：亿元（100 million yuan）

年 份 Year	合 计 Total	其中 of which 电力建设 Power Generation	运输邮电 Transportation, Postal and Telecommunications	其中 of which 交通运输 Transportation	邮电通信 Postal and Telecommunications	公用设施 Facilities for Public Use	其中 of which 公用事业 Public Utilities	市政建设 Civil Construction
1950～1978	60.08	19.71	23.25	19.41	3.84	17.12	6.85	10.27
1980	9.55	5.31	2.91	2.31	0.60	1.33	0.64	0.69
1985	23.49	3.97	6.75	5.52	1.23	12.77	7.88	4.89
1986	24.78	5.68	8.40	6.56	1.84	10.70	5.67	5.03
1987	32.64	9.31	12.39	10.02	2.37	10.94	5.36	5.58
1988	37.08	14.18	12.35	8.80	3.55	10.55	4.01	6.54
1989	36.09	11.69	9.96	6.16	3.80	14.44	6.84	7.60
1990	47.22	17.53	10.06	7.17	2.90	19.63	10.83	8.80
1991	61.38	19.79	19.07	14.49	4.58	22.52	9.15	13.37
1992	84.35	19.70	21.44	15.01	6.43	43.21	12.58	30.63
1993	167.94	25.77	46.44	31.75	14.69	95.73	37.91	57.82
1994	238.16	41.57	72.68	36.83	35.85	123.91	26.77	97.14
1995	273.78	57.33	79.36	25.94	53.42	137.09	35.03	102.06
1996	378.78	77.61	147.21	69.66	77.55	153.96	48.31	105.65
1997	412.85	80.24	146.10	85.06	61.04	186.51	52.24	134.27
1998	531.38	89.58	181.46	108.79	72.67	260.34	58.37	201.97
1999	501.39	83.05	166.16	102.24	63.92	252.18	64.20	187.98
2000	449.90	64.61	117.52	48.83	68.69	267.77	104.43	163.34
2001	510.78	72.22	168.42	60.72	107.70	270.14	92.25	177.89
2002	583.49	62.14	171.24	63.01	108.23	350.11	148.42	201.69
2003	604.62	66.00	350.35	273.77	76.58	188.28	36.91	151.36
2004	672.58	89.52	371.35	316.96	54.39	211.71	26.92	184.80
2005	885.74	124.22	443.90	385.58	58.32	317.62	41.33	276.28
2006	1 125.54	116.23	703.24	589.52	113.72	306.07	56.23	249.84
2007	1 466.33	163.30	942.03	840.46	101.57	361.01	60.90	300.11

注：本表各项投资额均不包括住宅建设投资。从 2003 年起，交通运输投资包括公用设施中市内公共交通投资。

Note: All items in this table exclude investment in Residential Rousing. Since 2003, Public Traffic Investment, which is belong to facilities for Public Use has been included in Transportation Investment.

表 10.2 用于公用事业和市政建设的投资额(1985~2007)
INVESTMENT IN PUBLIC UTILITIES AND CIVIL CONSTRUCTION

单位:亿元(100 million yuan)

年份 Year	公用事业 Public Utilities	其中 of which 自来水 Tap Water	其中 of which 煤气 Gas	市政建设 Civil Construction	其中 of which 园林绿化 Parks and Green Areas	其中 of which 环境卫生 Environmental Sanitation	其中 of which 市政工程管理 Administration of Civil Utilities	其中 of which 其他 Others
1985	7.88			4.89				
1986	5.67	2.74	1.78	5.03	0.43	0.71	3.84	0.05
1987	5.36	2.53	1.79	5.58	0.30	0.34	4.94	…
1988	4.01	0.72	1.25	6.54	0.24	0.58	5.72	…
1989	6.84	0.90	1.03	7.60	0.01	0.52	7.02	0.05
1990	10.83	1.06	1.81	8.80	0.11	0.37	8.31	0.01
1991	9.15	2.35	4.46	13.37	0.15	0.45	12.77	…
1992	12.58	3.24	6.14	30.63	0.32	0.79	28.45	1.07
1993	37.91	6.90	16.72	57.82	0.52	1.06	56.24	…
1994	26.77	11.49	7.80	97.14	2.42	1.01	93.47	0.24
1995	35.03	13.12	12.97	102.06	4.27	1.26	96.21	0.32
1996	48.31	22.12	14.61	105.65	2.66	1.14	101.80	0.05
1997	52.24	27.08	10.03	134.27	5.11	1.62	127.41	0.13
1998	58.37	14.59	13.15	201.97	9.10	3.35	189.41	0.11
1999	64.20	6.41	9.89	187.98	28.62	2.97	155.73	0.66
2000	104.43	5.35	6.88	163.34	38.76	19.34	102.36	2.88
2001	92.25	5.97	5.83	177.89	32.92	2.97	140.63	1.37
2002	148.42	8.62	6.83	201.69	38.83	1.47	160.64	0.75
2003	36.91	22.89	14.02	151.36	33.85	9.25	107.73	0.53
2004	26.92	16.66	10.26	184.80	16.69	7.01	160.22	0.88
2005	41.33	29.66	11.67	276.28	13.88	15.36	246.58	0.46
2006	56.23	43.79	12.44	249.84	26.41	10.17	213.26	…
2007	60.90	50.12	10.78	300.11	34.66	11.26	254.19	…

表 10.3 主要年份各类房屋构成情况
COMPOSITION OF BUILDINGS IN MAIN YEARS

单位：万平方米(10 000 sq. m)

指 标	Indicators	1978	1990	2000	2006	2007
总 计	**Total**	**8 653**	**17 256**	**34 206**	**70 282**	**74 873**
居住房屋	**Residential Buildings**	**4 117**	**8 901**	**20 865**	**40 857**	**43 283**
花园住宅	Villas	128	158	250	1 464	1 639
公 寓	Apartments	90	118	206	528	531
职工住宅	Staff Dwellings	1 140	4 884	17 939	36 504	38 836
新式里弄	Improved Residential Blocks	433	474	428	534	531
旧式里弄	Old Residential Blocks	1 777	3 067	1 896	1 689	1 366
简 屋	Simple Housings	464	123	84	37	35
其 他	Others	85	77	62	101	345
非居住房屋	**Non-Residential Buildings**	**4 536**	**8 355**	**13 341**	**29 425**	**31 590**
工 厂	Plants	2 543	4 822	5 739	13 276	14 526
学 校	Schools	504	927	1 417	2 456	2 562
仓库堆栈	Warehouses	354	472	650	1 305	1 342
办公建筑	Offices	228	599	2 416	4 674	4 972
商场店铺	Stores	228	403	1 191	3 788	4 029
医 院	Hospitals	123	203	367	591	602
旅 馆	Hotels	55	237	376	651	679
影剧院	Theatres and Cinemas	20	34	47	72	72
其 他	Others	481	658	1 138	2 612	2 806

表 10.4 主要年份八层以上房屋情况
BUILDINGS OVER EIGHT STOREYS IN MAIN YEARS

类 别	Types	单 位 Unit	1980	1990	2000	2006	2007
总 计	**Total**	**幢（building）**	**121**	**748**	**3 529**	**11 989**	**13 114**
		万平方米（10 000 sq. m）	**127**	**914**	**6 180**	**14 821**	**15 766**
8～10 层	8～10 Storeys	幢（building）	78	207	536	1 556	1 658
		万平方米（10 000 sq. m）	68	170	451	969	1 049
11～15 层	11～15 Storeys	幢（building）	33	244	684	4 897	5 515
		万平方米（10 000 sq. m）	42	242	875	3 597	3 990
16～19 层	16～19 Storeys	幢（building）	7	145	831	2 486	2 739
		万平方米（10 000 sq. m）	12	182	1 100	2 966	3 191
20～29 层	20～29 Storeys	幢（building）	3	137	1 266	2 316	2 425
		万平方米（10 000 sq. m）	4	229	2 695	4 695	4 850
30 层以上	Over 30 Storeys	幢（building）		15	212	734	777
		万平方米（10 000 sq. m）		92	1 059	2 594	2 686

①本页数据由市房屋土地资源管理局提供。
②本页数据按建筑面积计算。
❶Data on this page are provided by Shanghai Municipal Building and Land Administration Bureau.
❷Data on this page are calculated according to floor space of builings.

表 10.5 各区、县房屋建筑分布情况(2007)
DISTRIBUTION OF BUILDINGS IN DIFFERENT DISTRICTS AND COUNTIES

单位：万平方米(10 000 sq. m)

地区 District		建筑面积合计 Total	其中 of which #年内新增 Newly Constructed	居住房屋 Residential	其中 of which #年内新增 Newly Constructed	非居住房屋 Non-Residential	其中 of which #年内新增 Newly Constructed
总计	**Total**	**74 873**	**4 591**	**43 283**	**2 426**	**31 590**	**2 164**
浦东新区	Pudong New Area	11 504	347	7 148	258	4 356	89
黄浦区	Huangpu	1 922	14	839	9	1 083	5
卢湾区	Luwan	1 278	3	745	1	533	2
徐汇区	Xuhui	4 459	187	3 025	65	1 434	123
长宁区	Changning	3 046	81	1 940	47	1 106	34
静安区	Jing'an	1 538	25	822	2	716	23
普陀区	Putuo	4 711	140	3 128	59	1 584	82
闸北区	Zhabei	2 684	66	1 526	51	1 159	16
虹口区	Hongkou	2 992	46	1 854	28	1 137	16
杨浦区	Yangpu	4 454	165	2 807	114	1 648	51
宝山区	Baoshan	6 075	681	3 759	341	2 316	340
闵行区	Minhang	7 676	448	5 174	342	2 502	106
嘉定区	Jiading	5 097	615	216	105	3 081	509
金山区	Jinshan	1 882	253	141	119	841	135
松江区	Songjiang	7 200	741	2 842	366	4 358	376
青浦区	Qingpu	3 413	252	1 408	114	2 005	138
南汇区	Nanhui	2 534	406	1 804	332	729	73
奉贤区	Fengxian	1 642	72	931	25	710	46
崇明县	Chongming	766	49	474	48	292	

注：本表数据由市房屋土地资源管理局提供。
Note: Data in this table are provided by Shanghai Municipal Building and Land Administration Bureau.

表 10.6 各区、县各类房屋分布情况(2007)
DISTRIBUTION OF BUILDINGS IN DIFFERENT DISTRICTS AND COUNTIES

单位：万平方米(10 000 sq. m)

地区	District	居住房屋 Residential Buildings	其中 of which				
			花园住宅 Villas	公寓 Apartments	一类职工住宅 Staff Dwellings of 1st Class	二类职工住宅 Staff Dwellings of 2nd Class	三类职工住宅 Staff Dwellings of 3rd Class
总计	**Total**	**43 283**	**1 639**	**531**	**12 634**	**24 904**	**1 298**
浦东新区	Pudong New Area	7 148	334	20	2 730	3 963	55
黄浦区	Huangpu	839	1	3	505	127	7
卢湾区	Luwan	745	16	272	156	140	7
徐汇区	Xuhui	3 025	78	114	1 057	1 572	27
长宁区	Changning	1 940	55	17	801	997	8
静安区	Jing'an	822	21	36	491	135	3
普陀区	Putuo	3 128	30	17	1 330	1 638	24
闸北区	Zhabei	1 526	1		643	706	27
虹口区	Hongkou	1 854	10	16	800	531	274
杨浦区	Yangpu	2 807	4	1	972	1 607	14
宝山区	Baoshan	3 759	5		555	3 158	2
闵行区	Minhang	5 174	245	3	1 267	3 101	465
嘉定区	Jiading	2 016	40		31	1 707	202
金山区	Jinshan	1 041	0		177	772	59
松江区	Songjiang	2 842	551		603	1 562	
青浦区	Qingpu	1 407	202	31	157	875	91
南汇区	Nanhui	1 806	14	1	250	1 106	25
奉贤区	Fengxian	931	32		91	792	2
崇明县	Chongming	474			18	415	6

注：本表数据由市房屋土地资源管理局提供。
Note: Data in this table are provided by Shanghai Municipal Building and Land Administration Bureau.

表 10.6 续表 1 continued

单位：万平方米(10 000 sq. m)

地区 District		其中 of Which				
		新式里弄 Improved Residential Blocks	旧式里弄 Old Residential Blocks 一等 1st Class	旧式里弄 Old Residential Blocks 二等 2 nd Class	简屋 Simple Housings	其他 Others
总 计	**Total**	**531**	**470**	**896**	**35**	**345**
浦东新区	Pudong New Area	2	23	14	7	
黄 浦 区	Huangpu	29	108	23		36
卢 湾 区	Luwan	72	64	17		2
徐 汇 区	Xuhui	75	15	47	3	36
长 宁 区	Changning	22	1	36	1	2
静 安 区	Jing'an	93	24	14		5
普 陀 区	Putuo	5	11	63	3	6
闸 北 区	Zhabei	1	65	79	2	1
虹 口 区	Hongkou	64	97	52	4	7
杨 浦 区	Yangpu	5	27	167	10	1
宝 山 区	Baoshan		17	22		
闵 行 区	Minhang			90	2	
嘉 定 区	Jiading	1	1	34		
金 山 区	Jinshan		2	31		
松 江 区	Songjiang			34		91
青 浦 区	Qingpu	1	6	43	1	
南 汇 区	Nanhui	160	5	86	1	158
奉 贤 区	Fengxian	1	1	12		
崇 明 县	Chongming		3	32		

表 10.6 续表 2 continued

单位：万平方米(10 000 sq. m)

地 区 District		非居住房屋 Non-Residential Buildings	其中 of Which			
			工厂 Plants	学校 Schools	仓库堆栈 Warehouses	办公楼 Offices
总 计	**Total**	**31 590**	**14 526**	**2 562**	**1 342**	**4 972**
浦东新区	Pudong New Area	4 356	724	279	93	1 518
黄 浦 区	Huangpu	1 083	80	50	26	556
卢 湾 区	Luwan	533	80	41	7	212
徐 汇 区	Xuhui	1 434	274	197	44	367
长 宁 区	Changning	1 106	260	141	29	326
静 安 区	Jing'an	716	127	43	5	299
普 陀 区	Putuo	1 584	466	148	225	274
闸 北 区	Zhabei	1 159	460	111	68	140
虹 口 区	Hongkou	1 137	362	147	75	167
杨 浦 区	Yangpu	1 648	907	218	78	130
宝 山 区	Baoshan	2 316	1 050	151	237	242
闵 行 区	Minhang	2 502	1 528	135	98	130
嘉 定 区	Jiading	3 081	2 288	183	31	123
金 山 区	Jinshan	841	523	54	25	57
松 江 区	Songjiang	4 358	3 230	305	158	130
青 浦 区	Qingpu	2 005	1 406	135	73	133
南 汇 区	Nanhui	729	296	133	31	52
奉 贤 区	Fengxian	710	348	48	18	75
崇 明 县	Chongming	292	117	43	21	41

表 10.6 续表 3 continued

单位：万平方米(10 000 sq. m)

地区 District		其中 of Which 商场店铺 Stores	医院 Hospitals	旅馆 Hotels	影剧院 Theatres and Cinemas	其他 Others
总计	**Total**	**4 029**	**602**	**679**	**72**	**2 806**
浦东新区	Pudong New Area	1 213	73	141	13	303
黄浦区	Huangpu	189	33	63	10	77
卢湾区	Luwan	100	20	37	2	34
徐汇区	Xuhui	135	45	55	2	314
长宁区	Changning	109	35	80	2	125
静安区	Jing'an	97	31	68	3	44
普陀区	Putuo	230	27	25	2	186
闸北区	Zhabei	232	39	19	1	89
虹口区	Hongkou	164	37	38	2	144
杨浦区	Yangpu	132	56	17	3	106
宝山区	Baoshan	208	23	30	5	370
闵行区	Minhang	153	13	16	5	424
嘉定区	Jiading	252	22	9	1	171
金山区	Jinshan	101	19	10	3	49
松江区	Songjiang	283	27	38	7	180
青浦区	Qingpu	138	21	13	3	84
南汇区	Nanhui	131	18	5	6	58
奉贤区	Fengxian	137	45	9	1	28
崇明县	Chongming	25	18	6	1	20

表 10.7 各区、县八层以上房屋分布(2007)
DISTRIBUTION OF BUILDINGS OVER EIGHT STOREYS BY DISTRICTS AND COUNTIES

单位：万平方米(10 000 sq. m)

地 区 District		合 计 Total		8～10 层 8～10 Storeys		11～15 层 11～15 Storeys	
		幢 Building	面 积 Floor Space	幢 Building	面 积 Floor Space	幢 Building	面 积 Floor Space
总 计	**Total**	**13 114**	**15 766**	**1 658**	**1 049**	**5 515**	**3 990**
浦东新区	Pudong New Area	2 281	2 891	244	151	1 011	754
黄 浦 区	Huangpu	454	1 007	88	97	59	78
卢 湾 区	Luwan	324	672	30	20	52	62
徐 汇 区	Xuhui	1 077	1 467	123	76	276	209
长 宁 区	Changning	760	1 407	123	78	180	212
静 安 区	Jing'an	445	945	43	40	40	40
普 陀 区	Putuo	1 397	1 618	125	71	432	305
闸 北 区	Zhabei	511	765	53	35	211	180
虹 口 区	Hongkou	679	1 097	87	74	158	152
杨 浦 区	Yangpu	1 588	1 132	204	61	783	340
宝 山 区	Baoshan	493	423	55	34	324	264
闵 行 区	Minhang	1 801	1 205	342	220	1 112	677
嘉 定 区	Jiading	64	79	7	3	43	52
金 山 区	Jinshan	216	149	32	24	110	72
松 江 区	Songjiang	520	456	36	28	387	304
青 浦 区	Qingpu	112	144	14	8	84	106
南 汇 区	Nanhui	262	187	30	17	172	111
奉 贤 区	Fengxian	95	101	4	4	65	64
崇 明 县	Chongming	35	20	18	8	16	10

注：本表数据由市房屋土地资源管理局提供。
Note: Data in this table are provided by Shanghai Municipal Building and Land Administration Bureau.

表 10.7 续表 continued

单位：万平方米(10 000 sq. m)

地 区 District		16～19 层 16～19 Storeys		20～29 层 20～29 Storeys		30 层以上 Over 30 Storeys	
		幢 Building	面 积 Floor Space	幢 Building	面 积 Floor Space	幢 Building	面 积 Floor Space
总 计	**Total**	**2 739**	**3 191**	**2 425**	**4 850**	**777**	**2 686**
浦东新区	Pudong New Area	495	578	419	844	112	564
黄浦区	Huangpu	79	144	145	361	83	328
卢湾区	Luwan	54	84	121	278	67	228
徐汇区	Xuhui	288	324	282	567	108	291
长宁区	Changning	156	220	228	563	73	334
静安区	Jing'an	69	98	212	461	81	305
普陀区	Putuo	338	334	364	617	138	292
闸北区	Zhabei	109	291	118	211	20	49
虹口区	Hongkou	198	277	180	376	56	218
杨浦区	Yangpu	377	323	194	344	30	64
宝山区	Baoshan	80	82	34	43		
闵行区	Minhang	263	209	76	90	8	9
嘉定区	Jiading	9	11	4	9	1	4
金山区	Jinshan	66	37	8	16		
松江区	Songjiang	64	74	33	51		
青浦区	Qingpu	10	18	4	12		
南汇区	Nanhui	60	59				
奉贤区	Fengxian	24	29	2	5		
崇明县	Chongming			1	3		

表 10.8 主要年份市政工程设施情况
CIVIL FACILITIES IN MAIN YEARS

	指　标 Indicators	1990	2000	2006	2007
道路长度(公里)	Length of Roads(km)	1 631	6 641	14 619	15 458
道路面积(万平方米)	Area of Roads (10 000 sq. m)	1 787	8 147	21 490	22 579
城市桥梁(座)	Bridges (bridge)	553	4 432	10 199	10 747
防洪堤长度(公里)	Length of Floodwalls (km)		335	1 069.73	985.93
城市排水管道长度(公里)	Length of Sewage Pipelines (km)	1 892	3 920	7 430	8 120
污水处理厂污水处理能力(万吨/日)	Capacity of Sewage Treatment(10 000 tons/day)	41	463	488	556.55
防汛泵站(座)	Pumping Stations of Flood Prevention (bridge)	134	160	166	183

①本表数据由市水务局、市政工程管理局提供。
②2005、2006 年,防洪堤包括海塘。
③2006 年起,道路中包括公路中的村道。
❶Data in this table are provided by Shanghai Water Authority and Shanghai Municipal Administration Bureau.
❷The floodwall includes seawall in 2005 and 2006.
❸Data of village road has been included in that of roads since 2006.

表 10.9 主要年份自来水情况
TAP WATER SUPPLY IN MAIN YEARS

	指　标 Indicators	1990	2000	2006	2007
水厂个数(个)	Number of Water Works (unit)	8	218	146	123
自来水供水能力(万立方米/日)	Production Capacity (10 000 cu. m/day)	462	1 048	1 138	1 080
供水管道长度(公里)	Length of Water Supply Pipelines (km)	3 483	15 943	26 619	27 659
供水总量(亿立方米)	Volume of Water Supply (100 million cu. m)	13.32	24.00	29.19	30.34
售水总量(亿立方米)	Sales Volume of Tap Water (100 million cu. m)	12.25	19.75	23.30	23.90
#工业用水	Industrial Use	5.90	5.49	6.43	6.78
生活用水	Living Use	6.36	14.26	16.88	17.12
#居民生活用水	Living Use for Residents	3.29	6.82	8.52	8.98
日用水量(万立方米)	Daily Average Water Consumed (10 000 cu. m)	335.64	541.20	638.50	654.66

注：本表数据由市水务局提供。
Note: Data in this table are provided by Shanghai Water Authority.

表 10.10 主要年份用电量
ELECTRICITY POWER CONSUMPTION IN MAIN YEARS

	指　标 Indicators	1990	2000	2006	2007
用电量(亿千瓦.时)	Power Consumption (100 million kwh)	264.74	559.42	990.15	1 072.38
#工业用电	Industrial Consumption	220.97	393.13	656.10	705.90
农业用电	Agricultural Consumption	7.22	8.92	5.34	5.27
城市居民生活用电	Urban Residential Consumption	14.44	53.20	122.37	131.12

注：本表数据由市电力公司提供。
Note: Data in this table are provided by Shanghai Electric Power Corporation.

表 10.11 主要年份煤气、液化石油气、天然气情况
GAS,LIQUEFIED PETROLEUM GAS AND NATURAL GAS IN MAIN YEARS

指标	Indicators	1990	2000	2006	2007
煤　气	Gas				
煤气生产能力(万立方米/日)	Production Capacity (10 000 cu. m/day)	488	984	1 013	1 013
煤气管线长度(公里)	Length of Gas Pipelines (km)	2 700	6 606	8 778	8 097
煤气销售总量(亿立方米)	Total Sales Volume (100 million cu. m)	12.15	18.40	19.22	18.50
#家庭用量	Household Consumption		11.5	10.9	10.3
家庭煤气用户数(万户)	Households Users (10 000 households)	113.19	255.89	230.22	213.40
液化石油气	Liquefied Petroleum Gas				
液化石油气销售总量(万吨)	Sales of LPG (10 000 tons)	5.97	45.94	45.86	50.65
#家庭用量	Household Consumption	4.27	20.47	26.70	28.75
#家庭液化石油气用户数	Household Users	29.64	239.30	260.10	277.30
天然气	Natural Gas				
天然气销售总量(亿立方米)	Sales of Natural Gas (100 million cu. m)		2.16	22.58	26.60
#家庭用量	Household Consumption		0.45	3.7	4.6
天然气管线长度(公里)	Length of Natural Gas Pipelines (km)		1 742	8 349	10 867
家庭天然气用户数(万户)	Household Users of Natural Gas (10 000 households)		38.10	216.93	257.90

注：本表数据由市市政工程管理局提供。
Note: Data in this table are provided by Shanghai Municipal Administration Bureau.

表 10.12 主要年份公共交通和轮渡情况
PUBLIC TRANSPORTATION AND FERRY IN MAIN YEARS

指标	Indicators	1990	2000	2006	2007
公共汽电车	Buses and Trolley Buses				
公交线路长度(公里)	Length of Public Bus Lines (km)	18 593	23 260	21 776	22 375
公交线路条数(条)	Number of Public Bus Lines (line)	390	978	944	991
运营公交车辆数(辆)	Operating Public Transportation Vehicles (vehicle)	6 264	17 939	17 284	16 944
#公共汽车	Buses	5 341	17 358	16 899	16 672
客运总量(亿人次)	Passenger Volume (100 million person-times)	54.37	26.49	27.40	26.50
出租汽车	Taxi				
运营车辆(辆)	Operating Vehicles (vehicle)	11 298	42 943	48 022	48 614
#小客车	Small Passenger Car	8 095	40 806	45 959	46 758
载客车次(万次)	Number of Carryings(10 000 times)	2 129	37 599	58 920	57 764
运营里程(亿公里)	Operation Length (100 million km)	3.76	46.48	61.05	60.66
#营业里程	Operation Lengths	2.97	24.35	36.72	36.68
运营收入(亿元)	Operation Revenues(100 million yuan)	5.76	76.68	124.97	127.52
运营单位(个)	Operation Unit (unit)	1 666	1 178	3 646	3 375
轮　渡	Ferry				
年末轮渡船数(艘)	Year-end Number of Ferry Boats (ship)	111	95	53	50
乘客人数(亿人次)	Passenger Volume (100 million person-times)	3.74	1.85	1.19	1.13

注：本表数据由市城市交通管理局、市航务管理处提供。
Note: Data in this table are provided by Shanghai Urban Traffic Management Bureau and Shanghai Municipal Navigation Management Department.

表 10.13 轨道交通、高架道路、黄浦江大桥和隧道基本情况（2005～2007）
BASIC FACTS OF URBAN RAILWAY COMMUNICATION, ELEVATED ROADS, BRIDGES ACROSS HUANGPU RIVER AND TUNNELS

指　标	Indicators	2005	2006	2007
轨道交通	**Urban Metro**			
运营车辆（节）	Operating Vehicles(car)	695	829	1 117
轨道交通线路条数（条）	Number of Operation Lines(line)	6	6	9
运营线路长度（公里）	Length of Operation Lines(km)	147.80	169.40	262.83
行驶里程（万列.公里）	Mileage(10 000 vehicle-km)	1 205	1 457	1 697
客运总量（万人次）	Volume of Passenger Traffic (10 000 person-times)	59 406	65 569	81 395
利润总额（万元）	Total Pre-tax Profits (10 000 yuan)	2 300	1 692	1 601
年末从业人数（人）	Year-end Number of Staff and Workers (person)	7 411	8 458	12 581
高架、大桥和隧道	**Elevated Roads, Bridges and Tunnels**			
高架道路长度（公里）	Length of Elevated Roads (km)	77	77	77
越江大桥数（座）	Number of Bridges Across Huangpu River (bridge)	6	6	7
越江隧道数（条）	Tunnels Across Huangpu River (tunnel)	6	6	6

注：本表数据由市市政工程管理局、城市交通管理局提供。
Note: Data in this table are provided by Shanghai Municipal Administration Bureau and Shanghai Municipal Traffic Management Bureau.

表 10.14 主要年份城市设施水平
LEVEL OF URBAN FACILITIES IN MAIN YEARS

指　标	Indicators	1990	2000	2006	2007
人均日综合生活用水量（升）	Per Capita Daily Consumption of Tap Water for Daily Life	223	241	256	253
人均日居民生活用水量（升）	Per Capita Daily Consumption of Tap Water for Residential Use(liter)	116	114	129	133
自来水普及率（%）	Percentage of Population with Access to Tap Water (%)	100.00	99.97	99.99	99.99
拥有道路长度（公里/万人）	Per Capita Length of Roads (km/10 000 persons)	2.08	5.84	10.69	11.21
人均拥有道路面积（平方米）	Per Capita Area of Roads (sq. m)	2.28	7.17	15.70	16.38
每万人拥有城市排水管道长度（公里）	Length of Sewage Pipelines Per 10 000 Persons (km)	1.47	2.86	5.43	5.89
每万人拥有公共车辆（辆）	Number of Public Transportation Vehicles Per 10 000 Persons (vehicle)	7.43	14.30	12.63	12.29
每万人拥有出租汽车（辆）	Number of Taxi Per 10 000 Persons (vehicle)	8.80	32.49	35.10	35.26
人均拥有公共绿地面积（平方米）	Per Capita Public Green Areas (sq. m)	1.02	4.60	11.50	12.01
每万人拥有公共厕所（座）	Number of Public Lavatories Per 10 000 Persons (unit)	0.79	1.67	2.74	3.93

①本表数据由市水务局、市政工程管理局、市绿化局等单位提供。
②1990 年平均每人生活用水、自来水普及率为中心城区数据。
❶Data in this table are provided by Shanghai Water Authority, Shanghai Municipal Administration Bureau, Shanghai Municipal Virescence Bureau, and etc.
❷Per Captita Water Consumption for Residential Use and Percentage of Population with Access to Tap Water only cover the downtown areas for 1990.

表 10.15 主要年份城市园林绿化情况
PARKS,GARDENS AND GREEN AREAS IN MAIN YEARS

单位：公顷(hectare)

年 份 Year	城市园林绿地面积 Total Area of Urban Parks, Gardens and Green Areas	#公共绿地 Public Green Area	其中 of which：公园面积 Area of Parks	其中 of which：街道绿地 Roadside Green Area	#专用绿地 Special-Purpose Green Area	#园林苗圃 Gardens and Nurseries
1978	761	383	309	75		308
1980	1 738	390	319	71	970	303
1985	2 339	522	412	110	1 551	143
1990	3 570	983	712	271	2 255	294
1995	6 561	1 793	920	873	4 429	309
1996	7 231	2 008	933	1 076	4 889	305
1997	7 849	2 484	961	1 523	5 083	253
1998	8 855	3 117	976	2 141	5 456	253
1999	11 117	3 856	993	2 863	6 888	318
2000	12 601	4 812	1 153	3 658	7 346	388
2001	14 771	5 820	1 291	4 529	8 624	248
2002	18 758	7 810	1 411	6 399	9 591	267
2003	24 426	9 450	1 473	7 977	10 218	335
2004	26 689	10 979	1 481	9 498	10 921	335
2005	28 865	12 038	1 521	10 516	11 591	335
2006	30 609	13 307	1 529	11 782	12 202	331
2007	31 795	13 899	1 675	12 224	13 590	204

表 10.15 续表 continued

年 份 Year	公园数(个) Parks (unit)	游园人数(万人次) Visitors to Parks and Zooes (10 000 person-times)	植树数(万株) Trees Planted (10 000 trees)	行道树实有数(万株) Roadside Trees (10 000 trees)	新辟绿地面积(公顷) Greenlands Newly Created (hectare)	绿化覆盖率(%) Coverage Rate of Urban Green Areas(%)
1978	42	3 876	35	13		8.2
1980	45	6 404	60	13	44	8.2
1985	52	8 372	208	15	226	9.7
1990	83	8 474	130	23	186	12.4
1995	100	9 064	279	33	516	16.0
1996	105	9 797	355	41	587	17.0
1997	108	9 757	383	43	728	17.8
1998	111	9 285	773	48	1 077	19.1
1999	115	9 601	845	54	1 315	20.3
2000	122	8 184	827	57	1 458	22.2
2001	125	8 561	1 384	65	1 374	23.8
2002	133	8 796	2 729	68	2 600	30.0
2003	136	9 629	2 540	74	4 904	35.2
2004	136	13 381	2 037	80	2 434	36.0
2005	144	13 656	2 117	83	2 116	37.0
2006	144	16 652	2 187	86	1 691	37.3
2007	146	18 342	1 693	69	1 629	37.6

注：本页数据由市绿化管理局提供。
Note: Data on this page are provided by Shanghai Landscape Bureau.

表 10.16 各区、县绿化面积(2007)
URBAN GREEN AREA IN DIFFERENT DISTRICTS

地　区 District		园林绿地面积 (公顷) Total Area of Parks, Gardens and Green Areas (hectare)	其　中　of which #公共绿地面积 Public Green Areas	公园数 (个) Number of Parks (unit)	公园游园人数 (万人次) Visitors to Parks and Zoos (10 000 person-times)
总　计	**Total**	**31 795.37**	**13 898.83**	**146**	**18 342.30**
浦东新区	Pudong New Area	8 300.37	4 369.94	18	1 406.95
黄 浦 区	Huangpu	122.04	85.94	7	2 297.41
卢 湾 区	Luwan	100.90	49.78	5	569.95
徐 汇 区	Xuhui	1 139.97	432.40	11	1 713.79
长 宁 区	Changning	1 068.09	403.08	13	1 501.61
静 安 区	Jing'an	87.01	34.85	2	479.89
普 陀 区	Putuo	1 048.21	462.51	16	1 670.41
闸 北 区	Zhabei	572.74	212.83	7	1 277.52
虹 口 区	Hongkou	385.24	147.85	9	2 306.16
杨 浦 区	Yangpu	993.68	423.15	14	1 858.07
宝 山 区	Baoshan	3 955.73	1 531.02	11	1 642.00
闵 行 区	Minhang	3 337.14	1 894.04	9	847.33
嘉 定 区	Jiading	2 042.76	1 041.15	5	132.66
金 山 区	Jinshan	1 210.11	483.43	7	148.07
松 江 区	Songjiang	1 417.83	442.23	4	219.63
青 浦 区	Qingpu	2 211.12	850.53	3	32.93
南 汇 区	Nanhui	1 621.30	534.49	2	67.22
奉 贤 区	Fengxian	2 012.09	429.43	1	161.14
崇 明 县	Chongming	169.06	70.17	2	9.56

注：本表数据由市绿化管理局提供。
Note: Data in this table are provided by Shanghai Landscape Bureau.

上 / 海 / 统 / 计 / 年 / 鉴

主要统计指标解释

城市基础设施

城市基础设施包括电力建设、交通运输、邮电通信、公用事业和市政建设等。

道路长度

指道路长度和与道路相通的桥梁、隧道的长度，按车行道中心线计算。

城市园林绿地面积

指报告期末用作园林和绿化的各种绿地面积。包括公共绿地、居住区绿地、单位附属绿地、防护绿地、生产绿地、道路绿地和风景林地面积。

不包括：

（1）屋顶绿化、垂直绿化、阳台绿化和室内绿化。

（2）以物质生产为主的林地、耕地、牧草地、果园和竹园等。

（3）城市总体规划中不列入绿地的水域。

公共绿地

指向公众开放的市级、区级、居住区级各类公园、街旁游园，包括其范围内的水域。其中居住区级公园应不小于 1 万平方米，街旁游园的宽度不小于 8 米，面积不小于 400 平方米。

供水管道长度

指从送水泵至用户水表之间所有管道的长度。不包括新安装尚未使用的管道。

供水总量

指报告期供水企业（单位）供出的全部水量。包括有效供水量和漏损水量。

生活用水

生活用水包括公共服务用水和居民家庭用水。公共服务用水指为城市社会公共生活服务的用水。包括行政事业单位、部队营区和公共设施服务、社会服务业、批发零售贸易业、旅馆饮食业以及其他公共服务业等单位的用水。居民家庭用水指城市范围内所有居民家庭的日常生活用水。包括城市居民、农民家庭、公共供水站用水。

煤气生产能力

指报告期末煤气生产厂制气、净化、输送等环节的综合生产能力，不包括备用设备能力。一般按设计能力计算，如果实际生产能力大于设计能力时，应按实际测定的生产能力计算。测定时应以制气、净化、输送三个环节中最薄弱的环节为主。

供气总量

指全年燃气企业（单位）向用户供应的燃气数量。包括销售量和损失量。

排水管道长度

指所有排水总管、干管、支管、检查井及连接井进出口等长度之和。

运营公交车辆数

指年末公交企业（单位）用于运营业务的全部车辆数。以企业(单位)固定资产台帐中已投入运营的车辆数为准。

污水日处理能力

指污水处理厂（或处理装置）每昼夜处理污水量的设计能力。

SHANGHAI STATISTICAL YEARBOOK

EXPLANATORY NOTES TO MAJOR STATISTICAL INDICATORS

□ Urban Infrastructure Facilities

Urban Infrastructure Facilities include facilities for power generating, transportation, post and telecommunication, public utilities, development of municipal engineering.

□ Length of Roads

The length of roads refers to the length of roads and of the bridges and tunnels connected to the roads, calculated by the center line of the roads

□ Area of Urban Gardens and Green Areas

Area of Urban Gardens and Green Areas refers to the total area occupied for green projects at the end of the reference period, including public green land, green land in residential quarters, green land attached to institutions, protection green land, production green land, roadside green land and forest in scenic spots. It does not include the following:

(1) Greenery and plants on roofs, balconies, indoors and vertical green areas;

(2) Forest, cultivated land grassland, orchards and bamboo grooves that are for production purpose and etc.;

(3) Water areas that are not included in urban master plan as green land.

□ Public Green Area

Public Green Area refers to green areas open to the public such as municipal, community and neighborhood parks and roadside parks, including waters within parks. Neighborhood parks should occupy an area larger than 10,000 square meters, and the width of roadside parks should occupy an area larger than 400 square meters, with a width of more that 8 meters.

□ Length of Water Supply Pipelines

Length of Water Supply Pipelines refers to the total length of all the pipelines between the water pumps and the user's water meters, excluding pipelines newly installed but not used yet.

□ Volume of Water Supply

Volume of Water Supply refers to the total volume of water supplied by water-works (units) during the reference period, including both the effective water supply and loss during the water supply.

□ Consumption of Water for Residential Use

Consumption of Water for Living Use refers to the water consumption of households for daily life and the water consumption of public service facilities. The latter refers to water consumption for urban public services, including the consumption of government agencies and public institutions, military barracks, public facilities, wholesale and retail outlets, restaurants, hotels, and other units providing public services. Household water consumption refers to consumption of water for daily life of all households in the boundary of cities, including households of urban residents and farmers, and public water supply stations.

□ Production Capacity of Gaswork Gas

Production Capacity of Gaswork Gas refers to the comprehensive production capacity of the urban gasworks in gas generation, purification and delivery at the end of the reference period, excluding capacity of the reserved facilities. In general, it is determined by the designed capacity, and when actual production capacity is larger than the designed capacity, the capacity is determined by the actual measurement on the weakest link in the production, purification and delivery.

□ Volume of Gas Supply

Volume of Gas Supply refers to the total volume of gas provided to users by gas-producing enterprises (units) in a year, including the volume sold and the volume lost.

□ Length of Sewage Pipes

Length of Sewage Pipes refers to the total length of general drainage, trunks, branch and inspection wells, connection wells, inlets and outlets, etc.

□ Number of Vehicles under Operation

Number of Operating Public Transportation Vehicles refers to the total number of vehicles under operation by public transport

EXPLANATORY NOTES TO MAJOR STATISTICAL INDICATORS

enterprises (units) at the end of the year, based on the records of operational vehicles by the enterprises (units).

□ Daily Disposal Capacity of Urban Sewage

Daily Capacity of Sewage Treatment refers to the designed 24 hour capacity of sewage disposal by the sewage treatment works or facilities.

第十一篇

CHAPTER 11

农　业

AGRICULTURE

表 11.1 农业总产值(1978～2007)
GROSS OUTPUT VALUE OF AGRICULTURE

单位:亿元(100 million yuan)

年 份 Year	农业总产值 Gross Output Value of Agriculture	其 中 of which				
		种植业 Planting	林 业 Forestry	畜牧业 Animal Husbandry	渔 业 Fishery	农林牧渔服务业 Service Industry for Agriculture
1978	18.26	13.49	0.06	3.67	0.86	
1979	20.41	15.10	0.04	4.22	0.90	
1980	18.90	11.40	0.06	6.27	0.97	
1981	20.33	11.91	0.21	6.38	1.23	
1982	23.97	13.80	0.23	7.81	1.56	
1983	22.68	12.59	0.20	7.80	1.29	
1984	26.59	16.41	0.21	8.06	1.40	
1985	31.38	15.63	0.21	12.25	2.82	
1986	33.76	16.83	0.24	12.75	3.45	
1987	38.84	17.69	0.34	15.48	4.79	
1988	53.07	22.47	0.45	22.18	7.43	
1989	60.63	25.53	0.39	26.41	7.88	
1990	68.16	29.09	0.37	30.25	8.04	
1991	73.65	30.51	0.39	33.38	8.97	
1992	80.01	32.80	0.43	37.19	9.18	
1993	96.20	40.52	0.41	42.95	12.31	
1994	140.24	60.19	0.49	62.04	17.52	
1995	182.47	77.71	0.45	81.48	22.83	
1996	200.95	87.64	0.67	85.46	27.18	
1997	204.41	85.20	0.47	88.37	30.37	
1998	206.75	89.10	0.84	87.27	29.54	
1999	206.90	87.86	0.98	86.35	31.71	
2000	216.50	89.81	1.41	87.35	37.92	
2001	227.61	95.53	3.52	88.43	40.13	
2002	233.57	97.21	7.75	83.48	45.13	
2003	247.29	98.17	13.05	81.13	49.21	5.73
2004	248.89	109.32	13.14	70.77	49.9	5.76
2005	233.39	111.25	11.11	54.34	51.64	5.05
2006	237.01	119.99	10.43	46.29	55.25	5.05
2007	255.98	126.74	10.05	58.00	54.19	7.00

注：从 2003 年起，农业总产值包括农林牧渔服务业。
Note: The Gross Qutput Value of Agriculture did not include the output value of service industry for planting, forestry, animal husbandary and fishery before 2003.

表11.2　农业总产值指数（以1978年为100，1978～2007）
GROSS OUTPUT VALUE INDEXS OF AGRICULTURE (1978 = 100)

年　份 Year	农业总产值指数 Indexs of Gross Output Value of Agriculture	其　中　of which				
		种植业 Planting	林　业 Forestry	畜牧业 Animal Husbandry	渔　业 Fishery	农林牧渔服务业 Service Industry for Agriculture
1978	100.0	100.0	100.0	100.0	100.0	
1979	101.4	92.9	121.9	128.1	101.6	
1980	92.1	78.6	152.9	115.8	104.1	
1981	100.0	83.9	144.0	140.2	97.3	
1982	117.4	97.4	161.1	170.1	107.3	
1983	109.9	86.0	116.1	167.3	123.6	
1984	124.5	109.0	98.4	167.5	114.7	
1985	113.0	88.2	107.2	181.4	127.6	
1986	119.7	89.5	134.5	201.2	149.5	
1987	122.5	90.6	138.9	206.7	158.1	
1988	130.3	95.3	166.0	227.0	160.0	
1989	132.0	92.3	134.9	245.6	171.8	
1990	139.5	96.3	139.7	271.2	164.3	
1991	146.2	95.6	153.7	299.0	172.7	
1992	154.7	101.3	144.0	322.9	168.8	
1993	147.9	94.1	129.4	313.8	166.8	
1994	159.4	96.0	130.5	336.7	215.0	
1995	177.0	104.0	125.2	363.0	252.4	
1996	191.6	114.5	168.6	389.1	269.6	
1997	202.5	123.1	133.0	404.3	288.4	
1998	207.3	129.4	185.2	412.1	278.6	
1999	212.6	133.2	258.3	418.0	289.2	
2000	220.9	141.2	414.9	414.6	321.9	
2001	236.5	145.2	629.7	433.7	392.0	
2002	243.6	145.7	1 546.0	416.4	442.6	100.0
2003	246.3	135.3	2 062.4	395.5	544.4	102.6
2004	229.6	144.0	2 070.6	306.5	526.4	103.2
2005	205.5	136.7	1 613.0	221.6	555.4	91.4
2006	206.9	141.1	1 514.6	205.0	587.6	90.3
2007	210.0	142.9	1 458.6	214.2	573.5	121.6

注：根据国家统计局方法制度规定，从2006年起，农业总产值指数按可比价计算，2006年以前按不变价计算。

Note: According to the regulation of National Bureau of Statistics, since 2006, index of gross output value of agriculture has been calculated by comparable price. and before 2006, it was calculated by constant price.

表 11.3 耕地面积(1978～2007)
AREAS UNDER CULTIVATION

年 份 Year	耕地面积 (万公顷) Cultivated Area (10 000 hectares)	其 中 of which 水 田 Paddy Fields	旱 田 Dry Fields	平均每个农村人口占有耕地(平方米) Cultivated Area Per Rural Person (sq · m)	平均每个农村从业人员占有耕地(平方米) Cultivated Area Per Rural Employee (sq · m)
1978	36.01	31.88	4.14	800	1 240
1979	35.58	31.49	4.08	793	1 220
1980	35.41	31.26	4.15	787	1 193
1981	35.27	31.02	4.25	773	1 173
1982	35.17	30.96	4.21	767	1 173
1983	34.99	31.00	4.00	760	1 193
1984	34.58	30.89	3.69	760	1 207
1985	33.96	30.45	3.51	753	1 200
1986	33.30	29.75	3.56	740	1 200
1987	33.09	29.67	3.42	740	1 207
1988	32.72	29.28	3.44	740	1 213
1989	32.40	28.95	3.45	733	1 227
1990	32.32	28.54	3.78	773	1 293
1991	32.10	28.38	3.72	731	1 236
1992	31.78	28.03	3.75	718	1 303
1993	30.20	26.42	3.78	712	1 215
1994	29.38	25.81	3.58	735	1 262
1995	29.00	25.39	3.61	740	1 189
1996	30.06	27.16	2.89	753	1 051
1997	29.80	26.93	2.87	762	1 052
1998	29.38	26.67	2.71	758	1 087
1999	29.09	26.15	2.94	732	1 058
2000	28.59	25.74	2.85	731	1 048
2001	28.06	26.02	2.04	722	1 029
2002	27.04	25.06	1.98	693	986
2003	25.73	24.19	1.54	668	951
2004	24.57	22.88	1.69	654	918
2005	23.73	22.34	1.39	647	899
2006	20.80	18.83	1.97	583	901
2007	20.60	18.65	1.95	580	942

表 11.4 主要年份农村户数、人口和从业人员
RURAL HOUSEHOLDS, POPULATION AND EMPLOYEES IN MAIN YEARS

指 标	Indicators	2000	2006	2007
户 数 (万户)	**Households (10 000 households)**	**115.17**	**121.11**	**101.60**
人 口 (万人)	Population (10 000 persons)	360.71	356.47	355.23
从业人员 (万人)	Employees (10 000 persons)	253.45	230.76	218.76
#农 业	Agriculture	81.45	46.08	51.78
工 业	Industry	108.75	113.37	108.56
建筑业	Construction	11.14	12.21	9.80
交通运输、仓储及邮政业	Transportation, Storage and Post	7.07	9.48	7.97
批发和零售业	Wholesale and Retail	13.49	10.18	6.65

表 11.5 主要年份农作物总播种面积
TOTAL SOWN AREA OF PLANTING IN MAIN YEARS

年 份 Year	总播种面积 (万公顷) Total Sown Area (10 000 hectare)	粮食作物 Grain Crops		经济作物 Cash Crops		其他作物 Others	
		播种面积 Sown Area	占总播种面积(%) Percentage of the Total(%)	播种面积 Sown Area	占总播种面积(%) Percentage of the Total(%)	播种面积 Sown Area	占总播种面积(%) Percentage of the Total(%)
1990	63.11	41.71	66.1	11.16	17.7	10.24	16.2
1995	54.22	34.40	63.5	8.88	16.4	10.94	20.1
1996	57.01	35.38	62.1	8.33	14.6	13.30	23.3
1997	55.23	36.58	66.2	6.91	12.5	11.74	21.3
1998	55.64	35.25	63.4	7.42	13.3	12.97	23.3
1999	55.17	33.50	60.7	7.97	14.5	13.70	24.8
2000	52.15	25.88	49.6	8.84	17.0	17.43	33.4
2001	49.09	21.12	43.0	8.08	16.5	19.89	40.5
2002	47.67	18.77	39.4	8.07	16.9	20.83	43.7
2003	41.92	14.83	35.4	6.07	14.5	21.02	50.1
2004	40.44	15.47	38.3	4.90	12.1	20.07	49.6
2005	40.36	16.61	41.1	4.75	11.8	19.00	47.1
2006	40.14	16.55	41.2	3.73	9.3	19.86	49.5
2007	39.07	16.96	43.4	2.77	7.1	19.34	49.5

表 11.6 主要年份农副产品产量
OUTPUT OF MAJOR FARM AND SIDELINE PRODUCTS IN MAIN YEARS

指标	Indicators	1990	2000	2006	2007
农副产品	**Farm and Sideline Products**				
粮　食(万吨)(包括大豆)	Grain (10 000 tons) (Including Soybean)	244.36	174.00	111.30	109.20
棉　花(万吨)	Cotton (10 000 tons)	1.22	0.12	0.20	0.25
油　料(万吨)	Oil Plants (10 000 tons)	18.20	16.37	5.31	3.62
#油菜籽	Rapeseed	18.17	15.71	4.91	3.28
蔬　菜(万吨)	Vegetables (10 000 tons)	186.79	377.00	418.76	413.49
西甜瓜(万吨)	Watermelons and Muskmelons (10 000 tons)	30.77	49.88	66.99	66.30
蚕　茧(吨)	Pod (ton)	311	79	3	2
水　果(万吨)	Fruits (10 000 tons)	9.42	22.54	38.93	43.93
#生　梨	Pear	1.15	1.74	3.16	3.19
柑　桔	Citrus Fruits	2.58	10.18	19.66	24.04
畜禽产品	**Livestock and Poultry**				
生猪出栏量(万头)	Quantity of Sold Hogs(10 000 heads)	411.80	471.46	206.12	205.09
生猪年末圈存量(万头)	Hogs in Pens By Year-end (10 000 heads)	237.53	241.60	108.31	122.93
奶牛年末头数(万头)	Cows in Pens By Year-end (10 000 heads)	7.09	5.83	5.46	5.82
羊年末头数(万头)	Sheep in Pens By Year-end (10 000 heads)	37.19	55.44	11.46	10.96
兔年末圈存量(万头)	Rabbits in Pens By Year-end (10 000 heads)	130.62	88.90	29.08	27.38
猪　肉(万吨)	Pork (10 000 tons)	23.32	25.96	15.20	15.15
牛羊肉(万吨)	Beef and Mutton (10 000 tons)	0.30	0.79	0.26	0.26
家禽出栏量(万羽)	Quantity of Poultry Sold Birds (10 000 fowls)	7 357	17 213	4 743	4 459
牛　奶(万吨)	Milk (10 000 tons)	22.68	25.95	22.09	22.04
鲜　蛋(万吨)	Fresh Egg(10 000 tons)	15.07	16.64	5.55	5.54
水产品	**Aquatic Products**				
海水产品(万吨)	Seawater Aquatic Products (10 000 tons)	17.04	12.23	19.44	18.00
淡水产品(万吨)	Freshwater Aquatic Products (10 000 tons)	10.32	16.64	19.31	19.02

表 11.7 农牧业特色种养产品产量(2006～2007)
OUTPUT OF SPECIAL PRODUCTS IN FARMING AND ANIMAL HUSBANDRY

指标	Indicators	2006	2007	指标	Indicators	2006	2007
桃　子(万吨)	Peach (10 000 tons)	11.32	10.89	鸵　鸟(只)	Ostrich(fowl)	804	325
葡　萄(万吨)	Graper (10 000 tons)	3.39	4.57	肉　鸽(万只)	Meat Dove (10 000 fowls)	496	612.21
草　莓(万吨)	Strawberry (10 000 tons)	2.33	2.15	甲　鱼(吨)	Soft-shelled Turtle (ton)	1 038	470
无花果(吨)	Fig (ton)	36	119	牛　蛙(吨)	Bullforg (ton)	16	10
弥猴桃(吨)	Kiwi (ton)	312	240	河　蟹(万吨)	Hairy Crab (10 000 tons)	1.61	1.52

表 11.8　主要年份农业商品产值和商品率
OUTPUT VALUE OF AGRICULTURAL COMMODITY AND COMMODITY RATE IN MAIN YEARS

指　标	Indicators	2000	2006	2007
农业商品产值(亿元)	**Output Value of Agricultural Commodity (100 million yuan)**	**179.79**	**188.90**	**208.78**
#种植业	Planting	61.84	89.46	99.55
#粮食作物	Grain Crops	10.15	9.53	9.98
牧　业	Animal Husbandry	80.75	42.85	54.32
#猪	Hogs	29.82	21.05	31.44
禽	Poultry	33.41	9.20	9.80
蛋	Eggs	7.94	3.89	4.30
渔　业	Fishery	36.53	53.98	52.02
#淡水产品	Freshwater Aquatic Products	25.14	38.33	35.10
农业商品率(%)	**Agricultural Commodity Rate (%)**	**83.0**	**79.7**	**81.6**
#种植业	Planting	68.8	74.6	78.5
#粮食作物	Grain Crops	45.4	46.6	47.5
牧　业	Animal Husbandry	92.4	92.6	93.7
#猪	Hogs	95.8	97.3	98.4
禽	Poultry	91.9	89.2	86.9
蛋	Eggs	82.3	88.1	88.5
渔　业	Fishery	96.3	97.7	96.0
#淡水产品	Freshwater Aquatic Products	95.9	97.0	94.6

表 11.9　主要年份农产品出口情况
EXPORTS OF AGRICULTURAL PRODUCTS IN MAIN YEARS

单位:亿元(100 million yuan)

指　标	Indicators	2000	2006	2007
农产品出口总额	**Output Value of Exports of Agricultural Products**	**7.88**	**17.63**	**17.52**
#农业产品	Farm Products	0.63	2.93	3.63
牧业产品	Animal Husbardry Products	1.71	0.25	0.15
渔业产品	Fishery Products	5.55	14.45	13.75
农产品直接出口总额	**Output Value of Direct Exports of Agricultural Products**	**6.82**	**13.34**	**13.15**
#农业产品	Farm Products	0.47	2.35	1.92
牧业产品	Animal Husbardry Products	0.99	0.19	0.10
渔业产品	Fishery Products	5.37	10.80	11.14
主要出口产品	**Main Products of Exports**			
蔬　菜	Vegetables	0.19	1.75	1.54
活　猪	Hogs	0.63	0.22	0.15
水产品	Aquatic Products	5.55	14.45	13.75
海水产品	Seawater Aquatic Products	5.29	11.83	10.72
淡水产品	Freshwater Aquatic Products	0.26	2.62	3.03

表 11.10 主要年份农田水利工程投资
INVESTMENT IN FARM WATER CONSERVANCY PROJECTS IN MAIN YEARS

单位:万元(10 000 yuan)

年 份 Year	合 计 Total	国家投资 State Investment	其 中 of which 海 塘 Seadike	农田水利 Farm Water Conservancy	基本建设 Capital Construction	乡、镇自筹 Funds Raised by Township and Town	企事业和区县自筹 Funds Raised by Enterprises and Public Affairs Departments
1978	17 431	13 542	719	8 512	4 134	3 889	
1980	13 172	8 080	623	4 519	2 765	5 092	
1990	26 143	15 959	907	10 877	1 506	10 184	
1995	62 474	44 651	6 103	10 583	21 800	17 823	
1996	76 467	56 421	6 470	16 159	20 693	20 046	
1997	83 097	60 497	14 467	27 153	22 447	22 600	
1998	108 565	83 596	9 660	25 712	37 780	24 969	
1999	150 324	119 193	18 580	32 882	53 660	31 131	
2000	184 102	151 539	22 063	31 282	53 532	32 563	
2001	244 337	188 477	10 598	42 406	120 575	32 178	23 682
2002	382 935	264 370	23 548	59 869	140 875	28 140	90 425
2003	516 075	375 688	13 083	78 515	199 341	27 568	112 819
2004	576 050	219 506	7 317	71 920	97 328	57 676	298 868
2005	543 780	176 215	7 010	34 973	55 290	66 421	301 145
2006	467 449	202 815	2 603	85 161	30 423	37 330	227 304
2007	577 116	379 071	4 138	131 779	193 886	56 843	141 202

表 11.11 主要年份农村用电量
RURAL ELECTRICITY POWER CONSUMPTION IN MAIN YEARS

年 份 Year	农村用电量(亿千瓦·时) Rural Electricity Power Consumption (100 million kwh)	其 中 of which 机电排灌 Motorized Drainage and Irrigation	农、副业加工 Farming and Sideline Products Processing	乡村办工业 Rural Enterprises
1978	8.93	1.51	2.78	3.36
1980	12.23	1.24	3.10	6.28
1985	21.87	1.44	3.01	14.73
1990	32.16	1.75	4.00	22.85
1995	58.19	2.00	7.26	41.24
1996	62.07	2.01	7.79	44.16
1997	64.98	1.94	6.92	47.55
1998	67.91	2.09	6.79	49.55
1999	70.89	2.09	6.34	52.67
2000	73.19	2.34	6.12	49.71
2001	79.66	1.51	3.57	62.51
2002	81.79	1.24	3.62	57.56
2003	89.70	1.12	3.24	61.53
2004	114.35	1.17	2.41	79.01
2005	124.53	0.99	2.70	99.72
2006	143.54	1.03	2.84	97.98
2007	171.68	0.85	2.44	108.11

表 11.12　主要年份农业机械拥有量
POSSESSION OF AGRICULTURAL MACHINERY IN MAIN YEARS

机械名称	Name of Machinery	2000	2006	2007
农业机械总动力（万千瓦）	**Total Power of Agricultural Machinery (10 000 kw)**	**142.50**	**97.23**	**97.68**
耕作机械动力合计（万千瓦）	Total Power of Farming Machinery (10 000 kw)	37.60	23.46	24.45
#大、中型拖拉机（台）	Large and Medium Tractors (set)	7 844	4 262	4 584
（万千瓦）	(10 000 kw)	29.30	16.28	18.09
小型拖拉机（台）	Small Tractors (set)	9 253	7 904	6 926
（万千瓦）	(10 000 kw)	8.30	7.18	6.36
排灌机械动力合计（万千瓦）	**Total Power of Drainage and Irrigation Machinery (10 000 kw)**	**25.92**	**21.32**	**21.45**
收获机械动力合计（万千瓦）	Total Power of Harvest Machinery (10 000 kw)	33.30	13.58	12.82
#联合收割机（台）	Combined Harvesters (set)	4 991	2 030	1 934
（万千瓦）	(10 000 kw)	2.70	3.40	3.75
机动收割机（台）	Swathers (set)	87	10	14
机动脱粒机（万台）	Motorized Threshers (10 000 sets)	11.34	3.91	3.08
（万千瓦）	(10 000 kw)	30.05	9.94	7.81
植物保护机械动力合计（万千瓦）	Total Power of Plant Protecting Machine (10 000 kw)	3.07	2.36	3.84
#机动喷雾器（万台）	Motorized Nebulizers (10 000 sets)	2.07	1.39	1.84
（万千瓦）	(10 000 kw)	3.07	2.35	3.66
渔业机械动力合计（万千瓦）	Total Power of Fishery Machinery (10 000 kw)	23.40	24.16	22.90
#机动渔船（艘）	Motorized Fishing Boats (ship)	2905	1420	1396
（万千瓦）	(10 000 kw)	20.50	18.15	17.99
运输机械动力合计（万千瓦）	Total Power of Transport Machinery (10 000 kw)	8.11	4.08	3.30
#农用载重汽车（万千瓦）	Agricultural Camions (10 000 kw)	5.89	2.93	2.27
（辆）	(automobile)	953	519	424
机动运输船（万千瓦）	Motorized Transport Vessels (10 000 kw)	2.22	1.15	1.02
（艘）	(ship)	1 545	403	283
其他农业机械动力合计（万千瓦）	Total Power of Other Agricultural Machine (10 000 kw)	11.13	8.27	8.92
#推土机（万千瓦）	Bulldozers (10 000 kw)	0.25	0.29	0.27
（辆）	(automobile)	45	47	44

表 11.13 主要年份农业技术应用和综合开发情况
TECHNOLOGY APPLICATIONS AND INTEGRATIVE EXPLOITATION IN AGRICULTURE IN MAIN YEARS

指 标	Indicators	2000	2006	2007
机耕面积（万公顷）	Areas of Motorized Cultivation (10 000 hectares)	23.46	17.18	16.51
机电排灌总控制面积（万公顷）	Total Area with Motorized Drainage and Irrigation Facilities (10 000 hectares)	28.59	19.30	17.85
机种面积（万公顷）	Areas of Motorized Planting (10 000 hectares)	6.08	4.14	4.15
占粮食播种面积（%）	Percentage in Total Planting Area of Grain (%)	23.5	25.0	24.5
机收面积（万公顷）	Areas of Motorized Harvesting (10 000 hectares)	16.42	14.74	15.00
占粮食收获面积（%）	Percentage in Total Harvesting Area of Grain (%)	63.4	89.0	88.4
喷、滴管灌面积（万公顷）	Areas of Irrigating by Insufflantion and Dripping Pipeline (10 000 hectares)	0.43	0.22	0.16
机械植保面积（万公顷）	Areas of Mechancial Protecting (10 000 hectares)	41.10	27.01	31.3
化肥施用面积（万公顷）	Areas of Chemical Fertilizing (10 000 hectares)	32.10	23.72	23.41
化肥施用量（实物量）（万吨）	Chemical Fertilizer Consumption (real) (10 000 tons)	82.54	59.19	56.84
化肥施用量（折纯量）（万吨）	Chemical Fertilizer Consumption (convert to pure amount) (10 000 tons)	19.33	14.53	14.08
农药施用面积（万公顷）	Areas of Farm Pesticides (10 000 hectares)	31.02	25.81	25.14
农药施用量(万吨)	Farm Pesticides Consumption (10 000 tons)	1.10	0.83	0.81
农用塑料薄膜使用量（万吨）	Agricultural Plastic Film Consumption (10 000 tons)	2.13	2.21	2.13
地膜覆盖面积（万公顷）	Areas Covered by Plastic Film (10 000 hectares)	2.05	3.12	3.22
蔬菜大棚面积（万公顷）	Areas of Trellis of Vegetables (10 000 hectares)	0.15	0.59	0.76
温室面积（公顷）	Areas of Greenhouse (hectares)	88.15	362.80	283.3
科技攻关重点项目数（个）	Number of Key Science and Technology Projects (unit)	103	20	48
科技攻关重点项目投资额（亿元）	Investment of Key Science and Techndogy Projects (100 million yuan)	1.00	0.30	0.54
常年菜田面积（万公顷）	Areas of Perennial Vegetable Farmland (10 000 hectares)	1.25	3.23	3.15
#设施菜田	Established Vegetable Farmland	0.27	0.66	1.00
精养渔塘面积（万公顷）	Areas of Find-breed Ponds (10 000 hectares)	1.05	0.65	0.62
粮食良种使用面积（万公顷）	Areas of Well-bred Provision Farmland (10 000 hectares)	23.56	15.32	15.8

上/海/统/计/年/鉴

主要统计指标解释

农村从业人员

指乡村人口中16岁以上实际参加生产经营活动并取得实物或货币收入的人员，既包括劳动年龄内实际参加劳动人员，也包括超过劳动年龄但实际参加劳动的人员，但不包括户口在家的在外学生、现役军人和丧失劳动能力的人，也不包括待业人员和家务劳动者。劳动者年龄为16岁以上。

农业总产值

农业总产值是以货币表现的农、林、牧、渔业全部产品的总量和对农林牧渔生产活动进行的各种支持性服务活动的价值。它反映一定时期内农业生产的总规模和总成果。

农、林、牧、渔业的统计范围是：

(1)农业 包括农作物种植业和其他农业。

农作物种植业包括谷物、豆类、薯类、棉、油料、糖料、麻类、烟叶、蔬菜、药材、瓜类和其他农作物的种植，以及茶园、桑园、果园的生产经营。

(2)林业 包括林木的栽培(不包括茶园、桑园和果园的栽培、管理和收获等活动)、林产品的采集和村及村以下合作经济组织和农户的竹木采伐。

(3)牧业 包括除渔业养殖以外的一切动物饲养和放牧，以及野生动物的捕猎和饲养。

(4)渔业 包括水生动物和海藻类植物的养殖和捕捞。

(5)农林牧渔服务业 包括农林牧渔业生产活动进行的各种支持性服务活动。但不包括各种科学技术和专业技术服务活动。

从所有制看，包括国有经济的各种专业农(农、林、牧、渔)场以及国家各级机关团体学校、科研机构、部队经营的农业；集体所有制的乡镇村各级办农场；农村各种经济组织经营的农、林、牧、渔业以及工矿企业家属集体经营的农业；农民家庭自营的农林牧渔业及兼营商品性工业等。

农业总产值的计算方法通常是按农林牧渔业产品及其副产品的产量分别乘以各自单位产品价格求得，少数生产周期较长、当年没有产品或产品产量不易统计的，则采用间接方法匡算其产值，然后将四业产品产值和服务业产值相加即为农业总产值。

1957年以前的农业总产值中包括了厩肥和农民自给性手工业(如农民自制衣服、鞋、袜，自己从事粮食初步加工等)。1958年及以后的农业总产值，林业中增加了村及村以下竹木采伐产值；牧业中取消了厩肥产值；副业中取消了农民自给性手工业产值，增加了村及村以下办的工业产值；渔业中增加了海洋捕捞水产品产值。1980年及以后的农业总产值，在副业中增加了农民家庭兼营工业商品部分的产值。从1984年起村及村以下办工业产值划归工业。从1993年起，取消副业。将野生动物的捕猎划入牧业，野生植物采集和农民家庭兼营商品性工业划归农业。从2003年起，农业总产值中包括了农林牧渔服务业产值。

农业机械总动力

指用于农、林、牧、渔业生产的各种动力机械的动力总和。动力机械包括耕作、排灌、种植、植物保护、收获、农产品加工、运输、畜牧、渔业、农田水利等各种机械。不包括专门用于乡办工业、基本建设、非农业运输、科学试验和教学等非农业生产方面用的动力机械与作业机械的数量。

农作物播种面积

指报告期内收获农产品的作物的实际播种或移植有农作物的面积。凡是实际种植农作物的面积，不论种植在耕地上还是种植在非耕地上，均包括在农作物播种面积中。在播种季节基本结束后，因遭灾而重新改种和补种的农作物面积，也包括在内。

粮食产量

指全社会的产量。包括国有经济经营的、集体统一经营的和农民家庭经营的粮食产量，还包括工矿企业办的农场和其他生产单位的产量。粮食除包括稻谷、小麦、玉米、高粱、谷子及其他杂粮外，还包括薯类和豆类。其产量计算方法，豆类按去豆荚后的干豆计算；薯类(包括甘薯和马铃薯，不包括芋头和木薯)1963年以前按每4公斤鲜薯折1公斤粮食计算，从1964年开始改为按5公斤鲜薯折1公斤粮食计算。城市郊区作为蔬菜的薯类(如马铃薯等)按鲜品计算，并且不作粮食统计。其他粮食一律按脱粒后的原粮计算。1989年以前粮食产量数据主要靠全面

上 / 海 / 统 / 计 / 年 / 鉴

报表取得，1989年开始使用抽样调查数据。

■ 棉花产量

指全社会的产量。包括春播棉和夏播棉。产量按皮棉计算。3公斤籽棉折1公斤皮棉，不包括木棉。

■ 油料产量

指全部油料作物的生产量。包括花生、油菜籽、芝麻、向日葵籽、胡麻籽（亚麻籽）和其他油料。不包括大豆、木本油料和野生油料。花生以带壳干花生计算。

■ 水产品产量

指人工养殖的水产品和天然生长的水产品的捕捞量。包括海水的鱼类、虾蟹类、贝类和藻类以及内陆水域的鱼类、虾蟹类和贝类，不包括淡水生植物。水产品产量是通过各级水产和统计部门逐级上报取得数据。1995年及以前，贝类中牡蛎按鲜肉计算；蚶、蛤、蛏按 5 斤鲜品折 1 斤计算。1996年以后则统一按鲜品计算。

■ 猪、牛、羊肉产量

指当年出栏并已屠宰、除去头蹄下水后带骨肉(即胴体重)的重量。包括全社会范围内的产量。1996年前为各级逐级上报数据。1996年第一次农业普查以后，由于畜牧业产品年报数据与普查数据之间存在一定的差距，国家统计局农调总队对畜牧业年报数据与普查数据进行衔接。1999年以后，国家统计局开展了猪、牛、羊、禽等主要畜禽品种的抽样调查，并用抽样数据作为国家定案数据使用。未开展抽样调查的品种，仍使用各级统计部门逐级上报数据。

SHANGHAI STATISTICAL YEARBOOK

EXPLANATORY NOTES TO MAJOR STATISTICAL INDICATORS

□ Rural Employees

Rural Employees refers to people in rural areas who are older than 16 years and engaged in production and business activities that generate incomes in cash or in practicality. It includes all working laborers, no matter whether they are within the working age or not, whereas students studying outside but with their registered residence at home, active serviceman, people who lost their ability to work, unemployed people, and those engaged in housework are not included. The working age is defined as older than 16 years.

□ Gross Output Value of Agriculture

Gross Output Value of Agriculture refers to the total volume of products of farming, forestry, animal husbandry and fishery expressed in the monetary terms and output value of all kinds of service activities that support farming, forestry, animal husbandry and fishery production. It reflects the overall scale and achievements of agricultural production during a given period of time.

The scope of statistics on farming, forestry, animal husbandry, and fishery are as follows:

(1)Farming includes cultivation of farm crops and other agricultural activities.

Cultivation of farm crops include cultivation of grain crops, legume crops, tuber-crops, cotton, oil-bearing crops, sugar crops, bastfiber plants, tobacco, vegetables, medicinal herbs, melon crops, and cultivation and management of tea plantations, mulberry fields and orchards.

Other agricultural activities include harvesting wild fruits, fiber, tree gum, resin, oil-bearing plants, firewood, wild medicinal herbs, fungus, and rural-household commodity industries.

(2)Forestry refers to planting trees of various kinds (excluding tea plantations, mulberry fields and orchards), collection of forestry products and cutting and felling of bamboo and trees by villages and other cooperative organizations under village level.

(3)Animal husbandry refers to raising and grazing of all kinds of farm animals except fishing and aquatic cultivating, and hunting and rising of wild animals.

(4)Fishery refers to cultivation and catching of fish and other aquatic products and cultivation and collection of seaweed and other aquatic plants.

(5)Service Industry for Farming, Forestry, Animal Husbandry and Fishery refers to all kinds of service activities that support farming, forestry, animal husbandry and fishery production, whereas activities of science, technology and professional service are not included.

In terms of ownership, China's agriculture includes specialized state farms (for farming, forestry, animal husbandry, fishery), farms managed by various government agencies, organizations, schools, research institutions, and army; farms managed by rural collective organizations at levels of the township, town, and village; farming, forestry, animal husbandry, fishery run by various rural collective organizations and farming run by collective family members' organizations of mining and industrial enterprises; farming, forestry, animal husbandry and fishery and some commodity industries run by individual farmers.

Gross output value of agriculture is obtained by first multiplying the output of products or by-products by their unit price. For a small number of products, annual output of which is not available or difficult to get due to the long production/growing process involved, the output value will be estimated through an indirect approach. The sum of output value of all products of farming, forestry, animal husbandry and fishery and output value of service activities will then and together to form gross output value of agriculture.

Before 1957, China's gross agricultural output value included the value of barnyard manure and handicraft products for self-consumption (clothes, shoes, stockings, and initial grain processing under-taken by peasants). After 1958, the output value of cutting and felling of bamboo and trees by villages and other cooperative organizations under villages have been included in forestry; value of barnyard manure has been excluded from animal husbandry; the value of self-consumed handicrafts has been excluded from sideline occupations, while output value of industries run by villages and cooperative organizations under village level has been included in sideline occupations and output value of fish catches by motor fishing boats has been added to fishery. Since 1980, the output value of handicraft products made for sale by farmer households has been added to sideline occupations, From 1984, industries run by villages and cooperative organizations under village level have been included in the sector of industry. Af-

EXPLANATORY NOTES TO MAJOR STATISTICAL INDICATORS

ter 1993, the category of sideline occupations has been canceled and hunting of wild animals has been classified into husbandry, and harvesting of wild vegetation and commodity industry run by rural households have been grouped into the category of agriculture. Since 2003, the output value of service industry for farming, forestry, animal husbandry and fishery is included in the gross output value of agriculture.

□ Total Power of Agricultural Machinery

Total Power of Agricultural Machinery refers to the total mechanical power of machinery used in farming, forestry animal husbandry and fishery, including machines used for ploughing, irrigation and drainage, crop growing, plant protection, harvesting, farm product processing, transport, stock breeding, fishery and water conservancy. Machinery employed for non-agricultural purposes such as township industry, capital construction, non-agricultural transport, scientific experiments and for teaching is excluded.

□ Sown Area of Planting

Sown Area of Planting refers to area of land sown or transplanted with crops that have been harvested during report period, regardless of being in cultivated area or non-cultivated area. Area of land re-sown due to natural disasters is also included.

□ Grain Output

Grain Output refers to the total output in the whole country including grains produced by state farms, collective units, rural households, as well as by farms affiliated to industrial and mining enterprises and other production units. Grain includes rice, wheat, corn, sorghum, millet and other miscellaneous grains as well as tubers and bean. Output of beans refers to dry beans without pods. The output of tubers (sweet potatoes and potatoes, not including taros and cassava) was converted into that of grain at the ratio 4:1, i.e. 4 kilograms of fresh tubers was equivalent to 1 kilogram of grain up to 1963. Since 1964 the ratio for conversion has been 5:1. Tubers supplied as vegetables (such as potatoes) in cities and suburbs are calculated as fresh vegetables and their output is not included in the output of grain. Output of all other grains refers to husked grain. Data on grain production before 1989 were obtained through Comprehensive Statistical Reporting System. Since 1989, data from sample surveys are used.

□ Cotton Output

Cotton Output refers to the cotton production in the whole country including cotton sown in spring and in autumn. Output is measured as the weight of ginned cotton. Three kilograms of seed-cotton are equivalent to 1 kilogram of ginned cotton, excluding ceiba.

□ Output of Oil Plants

Output of Oil Plants refers to the total production of oil-bearing crops of various kinds, including peanuts, (dry, in shell) rapeseeds, sesame, sunflower seeds, flax seeds, and other oil-bearing crops. Soybeans, oil-bearing woody plants, and wild oil-bearing crops are not included.

□ Output of Aquatic Products

Output of Aquatic Products refers to catches of both artificially cultured and naturally grown aquatic products, including fish, shrimps, crabs and shellfish in sea and inland water as well as seaweed. Freshwater plants are not included. Data on output of aquatic products are reported by aquatic product and statistical agencies level by level. Before 1995, among the shellfish, the oyster was counted as fresh meat; 5 kilograms of ark shell, clams and frogs are equivalent to 1 kilogram of fresh aquatic products; they are all counted as fresh aquatic products since 1996.

□ Output of Pork, Beef, and Mutton

Output of Pork, Beef, and Mutton refers to the meat of slaughtered hogs, cattle, sheep and goats with head, feet, and offal taken away. Data refers to the production of the whole country. The first agriculture census of China in 1996 revealed some discrepancy between the production of animal products from the annual reports and that from the census. Efforts were made by the Rural Socio-economic Survey Organization of NBS to adjust the output value of animal husbandry to make the figures from the annual reports consistent with the census data. Since 1999, NBS conducted sample survey for the major animal husbandry products, such as hogs, cattle, sheep and goats and fowls, and the data from sample surveys are used as national finalized data. Those products, which are not covered by the sample survey, are still reported by statistical agencies level by level.

第十二篇

CHAPTER 12

工 业

INDUSTRY

表 12.1 工业总产值及指数(1978～2007)
GROSS OUTPUT VALUE AND INDEX OF INDUSTRY

年 份 Year	工业总产值(亿元) Gross Output Value of Industry(100 million yuan)			工业总产值指数(以 1978 年为 100) Indices of Gross Output Value of Industry(1978 = 100)		
	合 计 Total	轻工业 Light Industry	重工业 Heavy Industry	总指数 Index	轻工业 Light Industry	重工业 Heavy Industry
1978	514.01	266.02	247.99	100.0	100.0	100.0
1979	556.30	290.78	265.52	108.6	109.7	107.6
1980	598.75	331.13	267.62	115.7	123.4	108.3
1981	620.12	360.12	260.00	120.0	135.9	104.6
1982	634.65	359.62	275.03	125.6	139.9	111.9
1983	663.53	363.92	299.61	134.4	147.6	121.8
1984	728.12	395.60	332.52	147.7	163.3	132.7
1985	862.73	456.59	406.14	167.7	184.3	151.9
1986	952.21	493.09	459.12	177.0	192.2	162.6
1987	1 073.84	556.96	516.88	188.9	206.3	172.4
1988	1 304.66	679.17	625.49	208.8	227.2	191.4
1989	1 524.67	789.57	735.10	215.0	233.6	197.3
1990	1 642.75	846.63	796.12	223.6	241.8	206.7
1991	1 947.18	976.34	970.84	255.2	269.2	241.9
1992	2 429.96	1 132.75	1 297.21	306.7	306.4	306.6
1993	3 327.04	1 401.33	1 925.71	368.2	352.7	380.1
1994	4 255.19	1 890.12	2 365.06	435.3	429.9	437.6
1995	5 349.53	2 432.67	2 916.86	510.9	504.2	513.9
(1995)	(4 547.47)	(2 092.89)	(2 454.57)			
1996	5 126.22	2 334.29	2 791.73	590.1	568.7	606.4
1997	5 649.93	2 528.19	3 121.74	675.7	640.4	704.1
1998	5 763.67	2 527.56	3 236.11	728.5	657.7	788.7
1999	6 213.24	2 679.71	3 533.53	805.1	709.1	887.5
2000	7 022.98	2 903.40	4 119.59	913.7	782.2	1 027.7
2001	7 806.18	2 986.59	4 819.59	1 063.8	865.2	1 234.8
2002	8 730.00	3 169.30	5 560.70	1 219.1	934.7	1 463.2
2003	11 708.49	3 550.80	8 157.68	1 601.9	1 064.0	2 061.3
2004	14 595.29	3 871.33	10 723.97	1 927.1	1 268.2	2 492.2
2005	16 876.78	4 299.31	12 577.48	2 195.0	1 395.0	2 873.5
2006	19 631.23	4 747.28	14 883.94	2 500.1	1 494.0	3 341.9
2007	23 108.63	5 318.85	17 789.78	2 892.6	1 641.9	3 926.7

注：从 1996 年开始，工业总产值按新规定计算，括号内数为 1995 年新规定数。

Note: Since 1996, new regulations have been adopted in calculating Gross Output Value of Industry. The figures of 1995 in brackets are calculated in line with the new regulations.

表12.2 各区、县工业企业主要指标(2007)
MAJOR INDICATIORS OF INDUSTRIAL ENTERPRISES IN DISTRICTS AND COUNTIES

地 区 District		单位数(个) Number of Enterprises (unit)	从业人员(万人) Employees (10 000 persons)	工业总产值(亿元) Gross Output Value of Industry (100 million yuan)	年末资产总计(亿元) Total Assets (year-end) (100 million yuan)	主营业务收入(亿元) Prime Operating Revenue (100 million yuan)	利润总额(亿元) Total Pre-tax Profits (100 million yuan)
总 计	**Total**	**15 099**	**287.45**	**22 259.94**	**20 656.75**	**23 112.35**	**1 329.21**
浦东新区	Pudong New Area	2 306	46.49	4 689.38	4 984.86	5 157.49	346.14
黄浦区	Huangpu	56	1.89	116.36	167.33	163.35	4.79
卢湾区	Luwan	40	1.45	103.23	201.29	100.90	4.91
徐汇区	Xuhui	362	7.95	525.71	461.74	561.86	31.36
长宁区	Changning	114	1.79	82.27	123.08	92.05	5.86
静安区	Jing'an	38	0.48	29.02	58.67	32.27	9.36
普陀区	Putuo	323	4.87	232.47	221.10	226.97	18.68
闸北区	Zhabei	167	3.33	148.16	167.94	146.32	4.64
虹口区	Hongkou	93	1.82	61.51	73.84	74.09	4.10
杨浦区	Yangpu	222	4.89	575.77	886.46	598.63	92.59
宝山区	Baoshan	2 015	40.87	3 020.68	2 487.73	2 307.48	191.91
闵行区	Minhang	895	15.29	2 075.31	2 289.19	2 307.48	191.91
嘉定区	Jiading	1 967	35.59	2 132.15	1 559.52	2 193.15	120.56
金山区	Jinshan	822	13.98	1 122.30	736.36	1 064.34	38.96
松江区	Songjiang	1 073	17.41	978.9	775.32	969.48	53.90
青浦区	Qingpu	1 334	16.40	791.64	720.81	775.81	36.60
南汇区	Nanhui	1 656	40.17	3 440.96	1 823.62	3 439.27	94.20
奉贤区	Fengxian	1 299	24.62	967.02	848.78	953.36	49.53
崇明县	Chongming	280	5.21	164.83	141.03	158.40	6.20
其 他	Others	37	2.92	1 002.29	1 928.09	1 030.05	53.41

注：本表数据为主营业务收入在500万元以上企业。
Note: Data in this table are collected from enterprises with revenue of prime Operating Revenue more than 5 million yuan.

表 12.3 规模以上工业企业主要指标(2007)
MAJOR INDICATORS OF THE CITY'S INDUSTRIAL ENTERPRISES ABOVE THE SET SCALE

类别	Types	单位数(个) Number of Enterprises (unit)	从业人员(万人) Employees (10 000 persons)
总计	**Total**	**15 099**	**287.45**
按隶属关系分	**Grouped by Subordination**		
#中央工业	Central Government	181	14.9
市(局)属工业	Municipality	1 046	44.47
区属工业	District	737	11.89
县属工业	County	21	0.52
街道属工业	Subdistrict	113	1.65
镇属工业	Town	2 236	39.5
乡属工业	Township	129	3.07
村属工业	Village	1 214	14.37
按登记注册类型分	**Grouped by Registration Categories**		
内资	Domestic	9 217	122.7
国有	State-owned	343	12.85
集体	Collective-owned	837	9.18
股份合作	Share-holding Cooperation	450	4.71
联营	Joint Owned	170	2.52
有限责任公司	Companies with Limited Liabilities	1 057	24.39
股份有限公司	Share-holding Companies with Limited Liabilities	113	7.41
私营	Private	6 214	61.33
其他	Others	33	0.31
港澳台商投资	Hong Kong, Macao and Taiwan Funded	1 796	41.23
外商投资	Foreign Funded	4 086	123.53
按轻、重工业分	**Grouped by Light and Heavy Industry**		
轻工业	Light Industry	6 208	114.62
重工业	Heavy Industry	8 891	172.84
按企业规模分	**Grouped by Size of Enterprises**		
大型企业	Large	106	48.52
中型企业	Medium	1 564	104.77
小型企业	Small	13 429	134.16
按工业行业分	**Grouped by Sectors**		
采矿业	Mining Industry	1	0.02
制造业	Manufacture Industry	15 023	283.4
农副食品加工业	Farm and Sideline Products Processing	170	2.62
食品制造业	Food Manufacturing	259	5.63

注：本表数据为主营业务收入在500万元以上企业。
Note: Data in this table are collected from enterprises with revenue of prime Operating Revenue more than 5 million yuan.

工业总产值（亿元）Gross Output Value of Industry (100 million yuan)	年末资产总计（亿元）Total Assets (year-end) (100 million yuan)	固定资产净值年平均余额（亿元）Average Net Value of Fixed Assets (100 million yuan)	流动资产年平均余额（亿元）Average Current Assets (100 million yuan)
22 259.94	**20 656.75**	**6 399.9**	**10 316.11**
4 480.66	5 861.05	2 388.88	2 106.64
4 612.79	5 232.61	1 433.36	2 530.71
653.45	705.18	224.4	365.24
11.66	9.76	2.97	5.82
84.00	73.37	13.82	45.79
1 585.74	1 288.86	330.46	759.43
179.89	103.49	21.8	68.95
538.26	400.55	80.8	279.86
7 611.13	9 497.03	3 034.63	4 156.61
1 328.65	2 515.11	1 211.53	773.25
316.11	233.83	42.3	165.58
178.56	129.29	26.89	83.38
93.58	77.84	22.37	45.65
1 782.29	2 252.37	561.54	1 289.11
1 578.95	2 503.16	754.74	732.8
2 278.00	1 749.66	407.08	1 048.06
54.98	35.77	8.18	18.78
2 637.21	2 560.38	746.69	1 249.29
12 011.60	8 599.34	2 618.58	4 910.21
4 914.51	4 666.62	1 201.5	2 617.93
17 345.43	15 990.14	5 198.4	7 698.18
9 109.71	8 273.27	2 734.41	3 500.57
6 774.4	6 585.10	1 997.42	3 472.05
6 375.83	5 798.39	1 668.08	3 343.48
18.32	41.19	15.33	22.28
21 425.13	18 834.03	5 087.24	10 130.64
208.44	145.91	29.12	89.42
288.56	300.51	75.6	150.27

表 12.3 续表 1 continued

类 别	Types	单位数（个）Number of Enterprises (unit)	从业人员（万人）Employees (10 000 persons)
饮料制造业	Beverage Manufacturing	60	1.23
烟草制品业	Tabacco Manufacturing	2	0.39
纺织业	Textile	910	14.47
纺织服装、鞋、帽制造业	Garments, Shoes and Accessories Manufacturing	1 039	22.25
皮革、毛皮、羽毛(绒)及其制品业	Leather, Fur, and Wool Products Manufacturing	227	5.57
木材加工及木、竹、藤、棕、草制品业	Timber Processing and Timber, Bamboo, Rattan, Coir and Straw Products Manufacturing	164	2.3
家具制造业	Furniture Manufacturing	261	5.65
造纸及纸制品业	Paper-making and Paper Products Manufacturing	335	3.76
印刷业和记录媒介的复制	Printing and Record Duplicating	378	4.7
文教体育用品制造业	Stationary, Education and Sports Goods Manufacturing	278	6.61
石油加工、炼焦及核燃料加工业	Oil Processing, Coking and Nuclear Fuel Processing	51	2.36
化学原料及化学制品制造业	Raw Chemical Materials and Chemical Products Manufacturing	1 069	11.65
医药制造业	Medicine Manufacturing	223	5.71
化学纤维制造业	Chemical Fiber Manufacturing	51	0.85
橡胶制品业	Rubber Products Manufacturing	233	4.50
塑料制品业	Plastic Products Manufacturing	971	12.67
非金属矿物制品业	Nonmetal Mineral Products	612	8.36
黑色金属冶炼及压延加工业	Smelting and Pressing of Ferrous Metals	163	4.55
有色金属冶炼及压延加工业	Smelting and Pressing of Nonferrous Metals	252	4.32
金属制品业	Metal Products Manufacturing	1 350	17.33
通用设备制造业	General Equipment Manufacturing	1 759	26.89
专用设备制造业	Special Purpose Equipment Manufacturing	915	13.19
交通运输设备制造业	Transportation Equipment Manufacturing	797	22.51
电气机械及器材制造业	Electric Machinery Equipments and Manufacturing	1 247	25.63
通信设备、计算机及其他电子设备制造业	Communications Equipment, Computer and Other Electronic Equipment Manufacturing	700	38.34
仪器仪表及文化、办公用机械制造业	Instruments, Meters, Culture and Office Equipments Manufacturing	338	6.53
工艺品及其他制造业	Artworks and Other Manufacturing	167	2.56
废弃资源和废旧材料回收加工业	Waste Resources and Materials Recycling and Processing	42	0.25
电力、燃气及水的生产和供应业	**Production and Supply of Power, Gas and Water**	**75**	**4.04**
电力、热力的生产和供应业	Production and Supply of Electricity and Thermal Power	30	2.09
燃气生产和供应业	Production and Supply of Gas	12	0.90
水的生产和供应业	Production and Supply of Water	33	1.04

工业总产值（亿元）Gross Output Value of Industry (100 million yuan)	年末资产总计（亿元）Total Assets (year-end) (100 million yuan)	固定资产净值年平均余额（亿元）Average Net Value of Fixed Assets (100 million yuan)	流动资产年平均余额（亿元）Average Current Assets (100 million yuan)
134.42	132.78	49.18	69.17
282.34	532.92	29.88	346.41
364.74	349.7	93.54	193.7
434.31	298.38	65.08	192.65
131.33	101.94	21.54	72.65
85.12	77.47	18.58	50.23
198.71	132.68	29.91	82.28
187.62	188.94	73.38	92.78
164.97	205.21	74.37	93.72
164.93	129.36	28.57	80.21
973.74	515.1	205.29	148.83
1 623.23	1 620.7	610.32	703.29
272.23	346.71	105.18	178.98
108.94	93.53	40.03	46.39
166.54	175.87	56.9	98.54
463.52	440.07	137.39	231.56
418.99	534.72	143.39	301.72
1 609.98	1 966.47	827.82	628.03
430.45	231.55	59.79	135.14
831.7	658.72	151.12	418.96
1 890.42	1 941.63	332.59	1 240.66
600.57	664.96	153.03	403.87
2 358.92	2 688.07	543.83	1 389.38
1 573.37	1 161.86	241.18	764.82
4 976.89	2 803.49	812.64	1 661.46
322.54	278.69	44.63	202.63
115.08	92.66	24.98	49.81
42.54	23.45	8.39	13.07
816.49	**1 781.53**	**1 297.33**	**163.19**
724.32	1 453.8	1 109.33	93.02
60.64	111.83	51.87	42.96
31.53	215.9	136.12	27.21

表 12.3 续表 2 continued

	类　别 Types	年末负债合计 Total Liabilities (year-end)	年末所有者权益 Owners' Equity (year-end)
总　计	**Total**	**10 815.5**	**9 841.25**
按隶属关系分	**Grouped by Subordination**		
#中央工业	Central Government	2 448.71	3 412.34
市(局)属工业	Municipality	2 718.08	2 514.53
区属工业	District	371.15	334.03
县属工业	County	5.39	4.36
街道属工业	Subdistrict	37.59	35.78
镇属工业	Town	715.07	573.79
乡属工业	Township	65.19	38.31
村属工业	Village	209.21	191.34
按登记注册类型分	**Grouped by Registration Categories**		
内　资	Domestic	4 492.64	5 004.39
国　有	State-owned	816.94	1 698.17
集　体	Collective-owned	126.13	107.7
股份合作	Share-holding Cooperation	67.92	61.36
联　营	Joint Owned	47.18	30.66
有限责任公司	Companies with Limited Liabilities	1 320.05	932.32
股份有限公司	Share-holding Companies with Limited Liabilities	1 004.8	1 498.36
私　营	Private	1 086.24	663.43
其　他	Others	23.38	12.39
港澳台商投资	Hong Kong, Macao and Taiwan Funded	1 316.11	1 244.27
外商投资	Foreign Funded	5 006.75	3 592.59
按轻、重工业分	**Grouped by Light and Heavy Industry**		
轻工业	Light Industry	2 265.69	2 400.93
重工业	Heavy Industry	8 549.81	7 440.33
按企业规模分	**Grouped by Size of Enterprises**		
大型企业	Large	3 966.18	4 307.09
中型企业	Medium	3 588.06	2 997.04
小型企业	Small	3 261.26	2 537.13
按工业行业分	**Grouped by Sectors**		
采矿业	Mining Industry	10.42	30.77
制造业	Manufacture Industry	10 295.93	8 538.11
农副食品加工业	Farm and Sideline Products Processing	81.53	64.38
食品制造业	Food Manufacturing	176.28	124.23

单位:亿元(100 million yuan)

主营业务收入 Prime Operating Revenue	利润总额 Total After-tax Profits	税金总额 Total Tax and Duties	成本费用总额 Total Cost and Expenses
23 112.35	**1 329.21**	**840.91**	**21 741.14**
4 733.21	410.68	364.64	4 207.05
5 099.97	324.45	222.47	4 831.56
699.15	45.21	20.96	662.75
11.19	0.58	0.5	10.44
87.06	5.37	2.85	82.37
1 532.6	74.48	36.39	1 461.5
178.55	6.26	3.47	176.66
534.35	34.04	15.28	502.86
7 941.49	589.08	464.83	7 331.66
1 342.75	121.13	219.15	1 119.18
310.35	17.07	11.67	299.12
177.54	10.54	6.15	171.29
94.44	3.57	3.23	89.63
1 951.35	135.20	62.54	1 838.05
1 794.41	197.85	99.00	1 644.5
2 221.05	102.90	61.87	2 121.31
49.61	0.83	1.23	48.57
2 690.42	139.63	63.57	2 566.49
12 480.44	600.51	312.5	11 842.99
5 001.4	327.52	309.87	4 577.99
18 110.95	1 001.69	531.04	17 163.16
9 807.7	557.17	478.36	9 117.26
6 916.3	423.16	173.86	6 541.76
6 388.35	348.88	188.68	6 082.12
18.54	8.48	1.98	9.29
22 244.97	1 267.84	784.61	20 920.51
226.23	13.10	3.47	216.07
312.15	16.86	16.78	297.97

表 12.3 续表 3 continued

	类 别 Types	年末负债合计 Total Liabilities (Year-end)	年末所有者权益 Owners Equity (Year-end)
饮料制造业	Beverage Manufacturing	70.93	61.86
烟草制品业	Tabacco Manufacturing	28.73	504.19
纺织业	Textile	182.31	167.38
纺织服装、鞋、帽制造业	Garments, Shoes and Accessories Manufacturing	169.12	129.26
皮革、毛皮、羽毛(绒)及其制品业	Leather, Fur, and Wool Products Manufacturing	60.79	41.14
木材加工及木、竹、藤、棕、草制品业	Timber Processing and Timber, Bamboo, Rattan, Coir and Straw Products Manufacturing	45.81	31.66
家具制造业	Furniture Manufacturing	85.24	47.45
造纸及纸制品业	Paper-making and Paper Products Manufacturing	106.52	82.43
印刷业和记录媒介的复制	Printing and Record Duplicating	93.58	111.63
文教体育用品制造业	Stationary, Education and Sports Goods Manufacturing	73.13	56.23
石油加工、炼焦及核燃料加工业	Oil Processing, Coking and Nuclear Fuel Processing	193.91	321.19
化学原料及化学制品制造业	Raw Chemical Materials and Chemical Products Manufacturing	916.62	704.08
医药制造业	Medicine Manufacturing	177.71	169.00
化学纤维制造业	Chemical Fiber Manufacturing	47.78	45.74
橡胶制品业	Rubber Products Manufacturing	102.91	72.96
塑料制品业	Plastic Products Manufacturing	230.64	209.44
非金属矿物制品业	Nonmetal Mineral Products	301.62	233.10
黑色金属冶炼及压延加工业	Smelting and Pressing of Ferrous Metals	948.55	1 017.92
有色金属冶炼及压延加工业	Smelting and Pressing of Nonferrous Metals	142.89	88.66
金属制品业	Metal Products Manufacturing	370.81	287.92
通用设备制造业	General Equipment Manufacturing	1 146.52	795.11
专用设备制造业	Special Purpose Equipment Manufacturing	385.48	279.48
交通运输设备制造业	Transportation Equipment Manufacturing	1 471.71	1 216.35
电气机械及器材制造业	Electric Machinery Equipments and Manufacturing	671.21	490.65
通信设备、计算机及其他电子设备制造业	Communications Equipment, Computer and Other Electronic Equipment Manufacturing	1 815.68	987.81
仪器仪表及文化、办公用机械制造业	Instruments, Meters, Culture and Office Equipments Manufacturing	137.61	141.08
工艺品及其他制造业	Artworks and Other Manufacturing	44.98	47.67
废弃资源和废旧材料回收加工业	Waste Resources and Materials Recycling and Processing	15.33	8.12
电力、燃气及水的生产和供应业	**Production and Supply of Power, Gas and Water**	**509.15**	**1 272.38**
电力、热力的生产和供应业	Production and Supply of Electricity and Thermal Power	340.71	1 113.09
燃气生产和供应业	Production and Supply of Gas	61.78	50.04
水的生产和供应业	Production and Supply of Water	106.65	109.25

单位:亿元(100 million yuan)

主营业务收入 Prime Operating Revenue	利润总额 Total After-tax Profits	税金总额 Total Tax and Duties	成本费用总额 Total Cost and Expenses
128.66	7.00	7.78	121.06
281.92	83.00	169.60	69.80
367.24	11.53	9.97	358.85
424.14	22.29	13.14	402.92
128.87	9.40	2.72	119.41
85.42	3.58	2.98	81.25
198.35	11.77	3.93	188.23
186.14	5.54	5.71	181.56
168.12	14.40	7.61	156.45
168.35	2.81	1.86	166.72
997.59	12.85	44.87	980.20
1 646.84	104.02	53.53	1 555.85
281.67	23.89	16.11	263.07
98.38	4.61	1.51	94.87
188.25	8.00	6.03	181.71
460.10	19.18	12.16	443.12
428.65	14.72	15.06	415.39
1 788.30	156.82	89.35	1 627.09
464.72	10.90	6.15	455.83
845.77	46.37	18.43	807.88
1 876.88	148.03	55.69	1 731.77
593.74	42.32	17.01	556.67
2 667.83	238.17	137.47	2 448.29
1 575.35	103.76	32.18	1 480.67
5 133.06	90.82	19.35	5 034.82
325.08	32.09	9.19	295.61
146.09	8.33	3.89	137.82
51.08	1.69	1.08	49.55
848.84	**52.9**	**54.32**	**811.35**
718.67	54.61	51.42	670.75
98.47	-1.05	1.41	102.26
31.71	-0.67	1.49	38.34

表 12.4 工业企业销售产值和新产品产值(2007)
SALES VALUE AND NEW PRODUCTS VALUE OF INDUSTRIAL ENTERPRISES

单位:亿元(100 million yuan)

类 别	Types	工业销售产值 Sales Value of Industry	其中 of which: #出口交货值 Delivery Value of Industry Export	新产品产值 New Products Value
总 计	**Total**	**21 949.97**	**7 312.68**	**3 349.28**
按隶属关系分	**Grouped by Subordination**			
#中央工业	Central Government	4 467.5	686.81	882.37
市(局)属工业	Municipality	4 541.39	800.96	2 006.51
区属工业	District	642.57	115.50	72.97
县属工业	County	11.10	2.90	0.43
街道属工业	Subdistrict	84.88	13.54	0.78
镇属工业	Town	1 549.25	397.43	32.84
乡属工业	Township	176.58	72.78	19.93
村属工业	Village	531.01	100.42	2.28
按登记注册类型分	**Grouped by Registration Categories**			
内 资	Domestic	7 511.95	812.05	941.18
国 有	State-owned	1 326.67	65.07	101.48
集 体	Collective-owned	314.22	10.62	4.99
股份合作	Share-holding Cooperation	175.84	8.95	1.72
联 营	Joint Owned	93.05	6.04	5.04
有限责任公司	Companies with Limited Liabilities	1 763.99	296.33	529.79
股份有限公司	Share-holding Companies with Limited Liabilities	1 554.88	212.52	244.24
私 营	Private	2 231.93	201.21	49.77
其 他	Others	51.39	11.30	4.15
港澳台商投资	Hong Kong, Macao and Taiwan Funded	2 603.43	858.41	324.66
外商投资	Foreign Funded	11 834.59	5 642.23	2 083.44
按轻、重工业分	**Grouped by Light and Heavy Industry**			
轻工业	Light Industry	4 849.47	1 443.41	444.77
重工业	Heavy Industry	17 100.50	5 869.27	2 904.50
按企业规模分	**Grouped by Size of Enterprises**			
大型企业	Large	9 019.38	4 049.57	2 071.80
中型企业	Medium	6 650.23	2 158.54	1 029.91
小型企业	Small	6 280.36	1 104.57	247.57
按工业行业分	**Grouped by Sectors**			
采矿业	Mining Industry	18.51		
制造业	Manufacture Industry	21 117.15	7 312.66	3 311.56
农副食品加工业	Farm and Sideline Products Processing	207.36	11.60	1.31
食品制造业	Food Manufacturing	277.71	19.99	1.30

注：本表数据为主营业务收入在500万元以上企业。
Note: Data in this table are collected from enterprises with revenue of prime Operating Revenue more than 5 million yuan.

表 12.4 续表 continued

单位:亿元(100 million yuan)

类　别	Types	工业销售产值 Sales Value of Industry	其中 of which #出口交货值 Delivery Value of Industry Export	新产品产值 New Products Value
饮料制造业	Beverage Manufacturing	136.75	4.52	1.71
烟草制品业	Tabacco Manufacturing	283.88	6.55	
纺织业	Textile	359.73	112.89	16.90
纺织服装、鞋、帽制造业	Garments, Shoes and Accessories Manufacturing	426.62	180.65	12.82
皮革、毛皮、羽毛(绒)及其制品业	Leather, Fur, and Wool Products Manufacturing	129.34	67.71	2.29
木材加工及木、竹、藤、棕、草制品业	Timber Processing and Timber, Bamboo, Rattan, Coir and Straw Products Manufacturing	85.20	31.36	0.36
家具制造业	Furniture Manufacturing	198.87	85.91	18.42
造纸及纸制品业	Paper-making and Paper Products Manufacturing	186.23	19.45	0.21
印刷业和记录媒介的复制	Printing and Record Duplicating	163.06	14.61	1.72
文教体育用品制造业	Stationary, Education and Sports Goods Manufacturing	164.63	105.38	7.96
石油加工、炼焦及核燃料加工业	Oil Processing, Coking and Nuclear Fuel Processing	977.01	4.98	49.01
化学原料及化学制品制造业	Raw Chemical Materials and Chemical Products Manufacturing	1 604.61	176.73	105.65
医药制造业	Medicine Manufacturing	257.2	36.29	56.51
化学纤维制造业	Chemical Fiber Manufacturing	97.02	24.19	0.56
橡胶制品业	Rubber Products Manufacturing	165.95	50.24	19.76
塑料制品业	Plastic Products Manufacturing	458.26	96.65	10.97
非金属矿物制品业	Nonmetal Mineral Products	405.9	66.69	8.29
黑色金属冶炼及压延加工业	Smelting and Pressing of Ferrous Metals	1 595.58	215.63	158.69
有色金属冶炼及压延加工业	Smelting and Pressing of Nonferrous Metals	422.28	43.26	14.56
金属制品业	Metal Products Manufacturing	819.55	260.11	60.67
通用设备制造业	General Equipment Manufacturing	1 860.22	459.98	557.73
专用设备制造业	Special Purpose Equipment Manufacturing	585.51	140.72	75.32
交通运输设备制造业	Transportation Equipment Manufacturing	2 316.74	430.90	1 250.31
电气机械及器材制造业	Electric Machinery Equipments and Manufacturing	1 567.26	498.05	173.98
通信设备、计算机及其他电子设备制造业	Communcations Equipment, Computer and Other Electronic Equipment Manufacturing	4 896.58	4 003.19	630.96
仪器仪表及文化、办公用机械制造业	Instruments, Meters, Culture and Office Equipments Manufacturing	313.58	130.53	72.58
工艺品及其他制造业	Artworks and Other Manufacturing	112.70	13.66	0.89
废弃资源和废旧材料回收加工业	Waste Resources and Materials Recycling and Processing	41.81	0.25	0.10
电力、燃气及水的生产和供应业	**Production and Supply of Power, Gas and Water**	**814.3**	**0.03**	**37.71**
电力、热力的生产和供应业	Production and Supply of Electricity and Thermal Power	724.27		37.71
燃气生产和供应业	Production and Supply of Gas	60.26	0.03	
水的生产和供应业	Production and Supply of Water	29.76		

表 12.5 工业企业经济效益指标(2007)
ECONOMIC EFFICIENCY INDICATORS OF INDUSTRIAL ENTERPRISES

类 别	Types	工业经济效益综合指数 Industrial Economic Benefit Synthetic Index	总资产贡献率(%) Total Assets Contribution Ratio (%)	资产保值增值率(%) Ratio of Capital Hold and Rise (%)	资 产 负债率(%) Asset-debt Ratio (%)
总 计	**Total**	**219.4**	**11.9**	**108.2**	**52.4**
#国有及国有控股企业	Enterprises Owned by the State or with the State Holding Major Shares	358.9	13.5	109.7	45.6
#大中型企业	Large and Medium Enterprises	393.5	13.9	110.1	44.9
按隶属关系分	**Grouped by Subordination**				
中央工业	Central Government	628.5	14.7	111.0	41.8
地方工业	Municipality	191.9	10.8	106.7	56.5
按轻、重工业分	**Grouped by Light and Heavy Industry**				
轻工业	Light Industry	192.6	15.1	107.9	48.6
重工业	Heavy Industry	240.0	11.0	108.3	53.5
按企业规模分	**Grouped by Size of Enterprise**				
大型企业	Large	353.1	13.9	108.2	47.9
中型企业	Medium	201.1	10.5	111.9	54.5
小型企业	Small	179.8	10.7	104.1	56.2

注：本表数据为主营业务收入在500万元以上企业。
Note: Data in this table are collected from enterprises with revenue of prime Operating Revenue more than 5 million yuan.

表 12.5 续表 continued

类 别	Types	工业全员劳动生产率(元/人) Overall Industrial Labor Productivity (yuan/person)	流动资产周转次数(次) Turnover of Current Assets (time)	成本费用利润率(%) Ratio of pre-tax Profits to Cost and Expenses(%)	工业产品销售率(%) Sales Rate of Industrial Products(%)
总 计	**Total**	**185 008**	**2.2**	**6.1**	**98.6**
#国有及国有控股企业	Enterprises Owned by the State or with the State Holding Major Shares	398 247	2.1	8.3	99.3
#大中型企业	Large and Medium Enterprises	451 503	2.2	8.6	99.3
按隶属关系分	**Grouped by Subordination**				
中央工业	Central Government	827 923	2.2	9.8	99.7
地方工业	Municipality	148 956	2.2	5.2	98.3
按轻、重工业分	**Grouped by Light and Heavy Industry**				
轻工业	Light Industry	129 935	1.9	7.2	98.7
重工业	Heavy Industry	221 881	2.4	5.8	98.6
按企业规模分	**Grouped by Size of Enterprise**				
大型企业	Large	390 389	2.8	6.1	99.0
中型企业	Medium	160 366	2.0	6.5	98.2
小型企业	Small	131 971	1.9	5.7	98.5

表 12.6　国有及国有控股企业主要指标占全市比重(2007)
PROPORTION OF THE MAJOR INDICATORS OF ENTERPRISES OWNED BY THE STATE OR WITH THE STATE HOLDING MAJOR SHARES

指　标	Indicators	合　计 Total	国有及国有控股企业 Enterprises Owned by the State or with the State Holding Major Shares	占全市比重(%) Proportion(%)
企业单位数(个)	Number of Enterprises(unit)	15 099	1 164	7.7
从业人员(万人)	Year-end Employees(10 000 persons)	287.45	51.39	17.9
工业总产值(亿元)	Gross Output Value of Industry(100 million yuan)	22 259.94	7 912.98	35.5
年末资产总计(亿元)	Total Assets(year-end)(100 million yuan)	20 656.75	10 030.39	48.6
流动资产年平均余额(亿元)	Average Current Assets(100 million yuan)	10 316.11	4 076.84	39.5
固定资产净值年平均余额(亿元)	Average Net Value of Fixed Assets (100 million yuan)	6 399.9	3 468.79	54.2
年末负债合计(亿元)	Total Liabilities(year-end)(100 million yuan)	10 815.5	4 575.75	42.3
年末所有者权益(亿元)	Owners Equity(year-end)(100 million yuan)	9 841.25	5 454.64	55.4
主营业务收入(亿元)	Prime Operating Revenue(100 million yuan)	23 112.35	8 673.60	37.5
主营业务税金及附加(亿元)	Product Sales Tax and Addition(100 million yuan)	238.6	224.72	94.2
利润总额(亿元)	Total Pre-Tax Profits(100 million yuan)	1 329.21	658.87	50.0
税金总额(亿元)	Total Tax and Duty(100 million yuan)	840.91	559.82	66.6
亏损企业数(个)	Number of Loss-making Enterprises(unit)	2 895	245	8.5
亏损企业亏损额(亿元)	Total Losses Made by Enterprises-in-red (100 million yuan)	176.84	49.92	28.2

注：本表数据为主营业务收入在500万元以上企业。
Note: Data in this table are collected from enterprises with revenue of prime Operating Revenue more than 5 million yuan.

表 12.7 六个重点发展工业行业主要指标(2007)
MAJOR INDICATORS OF SIX KEY INDUSTRIES ABOVE THE SET SCALE

行 业	Sectors	单位数(个) Number of Enterprises (unit)	从业人员(万人) Year-end Employees (10 000 persons)	工业总产值(亿元) Gross Output Value of Industry (100 million yuan)
总 计	**Total**	**5 227**	**126.78**	**14 502.94**
电子信息产品制造业	Electronic Information Product Manufacturing	1 554	54.95	5 744.25
汽车制造业	Automobile Manufacturing	469	14.43	1 807.52
石油化工及精细化工制造业	Petrochemical and Fine Chemical Products Manufacturing	920	12.49	2 511.46
精品钢材制造业	Fine Steel Manufacturing	162	4.55	1 609.88
成套设备制造业	Equipment Complex Manufacturing	1 712	31.53	2 440.87
生物医药制造业	Bio-medicine Manufacturing	410	8.83	388.96
六个重点发展工业行业占全市比重(%)	**Percentage of the Six Key Industries in Shanghai(%)**	**34.6**	**44.1**	**65.2**

注：本表数据为主营业务收入在500万元以上企业。
Note: Data in this table are collected from enterprises with revenue of prime Operating Revenue more than 5 million yuan.

表 12.7 续表 1 continued

行 业	Sectors	工业增加值(亿元) Value Added of Industry (100 million yuan)	工业销售产值(亿元) Sales Value of Industry (100 million yuan)	年末资产总计(亿元) Total Property (year-end) (100 million yuan)
总 计	**Total**	**2 968.24**	**14 293.27**	**12 532.83**
电子信息产品制造业	Electronic Information Product Manufacturing	878.42	5 661.59	3 409.92
汽车制造业	Automobile Manufacturing	436.79	1 775.57	1 816.64
石油化工及精细化工制造业	Petrochemical and Fine Chemical Products Manufacturing	444.80	2 487.14	2 003.13
精品钢材制造业	Fine Steel Manufacturing	432.14	1 595.49	1 966.32
成套设备制造业	Equipment Complex Manufacturing	642.24	2 402.3	2 868.75
生物医药制造业	Bio-medicine Manufacturing	133.86	371.18	468.07
六个重点发展工业行业占全市比重(%)	**Percentage of the Six Key Industries in Shanghai(%)**	**59.9**	**65.1**	**60.7**

表 12.7 续表 2 continued

行 业	Sectors	主营业务收入(亿元) Prime Operating Revenue (100 million yuan)	利润总额(亿元) Total Pre-tax Profits (100 million yuan)	税金总额(亿元) Total Tax and Duties (100 million yuan)
总 计	**Total**	**15 179.73**	**833.78**	**421.67**
电子信息产品制造业	Electronic Information Product Manufacturing	5 902.96	143.53	30.87
汽车制造业	Automobile Manufacturing	2 114.45	185.61	130.47
石油化工及精细化工制造业	Petrochemical and Fine Chemical Products Manufacturing	2 548.18	110.72	93.08
精品钢材制造业	Fine Steel Manufacturing	1 788.19	156.83	89.21
成套设备制造业	Equipment Complex Manufacturing	2 427.18	202.81	58.68
生物医药制造业	Bio-medicine Manufacturing	398.77	34.29	19.36
六个重点发展工业行业占全市比重(%)	**Percentage of the Six Key Industries in Shanghai(%)**	**65.7**	**62.2**	**50.1**

表 12.8 信息产品制造业主要指标(2007)
MAJOR INDICATORS OF INFORMATION PRODUCTS MANUFACTURING INDUSTRY

单位:亿元(100 million yuan)

指 标	Indicators	工业总产值 Gross Output Value of Industry	工业销售产值 Sales Value of Industry	年末资产总计 Total Assets (year-end)
总 计	**Total**	**5 744.25**	**5 661.59**	**3 409.92**
通信设备制造	Communications Equipment	520.68	512.96	437.22
雷达及配套产品制造	Radar ane Supported Product	0.94	0.90	0.87
广播电视设备制造	Broadcast and Television Equipment	11.89	11.96	8.04
电子计算机制造	Computer	3 114.93	3 077.86	922.40
家用视听设备制造	Household Seeing and Hearing Equipment	234.44	231.59	120.92
电子测量仪器制造	Geodesic Equipment of Electron	119.25	115.43	105.52
电子专用设备制造	Special Equipment of Electron	157.55	153.10	145.06
电子元件制造	Electronic Component	444.28	435.60	432.41
电子器件制造	Electronic Equipment	677.97	656.05	912.54
#集成电路制造	Integrated Circuit	410.90	390.08	625.55
电子机电产品制造	Machinery and Electronic Products of Electron	451.03	455.08	314.66
电子专用材料制造	Special Materials of Electron	11.31	11.05	10.29

表 12.8 续表 continued

单位:亿元(100 million yuan)

指 标	Indicators	主营业务收入 Prime Operating Revenue	利润总额 Total Pre-tax Profits	税金总额 Total Tax and Duty
总 计	**Total**	**5 902.96**	**143.53**	**30.87**
通信设备制造	Communications Equipment	527.11	17.35	3.25
雷达及配套产品制造	Radar ane Supported Product	1.00	0.14	0.12
广播电视设备制造	Broadcast and Television Equipment	12.01	0.11	0.23
电子计算机制造	Computer	3 261.18	27.66	3.85
家用视听设备制造	Household Seeing and Hearing Equipment	234.38	2.99	0.92
电子测量仪器制造	Geodesic Equipment of Electron	118.43	16.88	2.98
电子专用设备制造	Special Equipment of Electron	158.28	11.20	3.67
电子元件制造	Electronic Component	448.8	32.54	6.28
电子器件制造	Electronic Equipment	673.42	12.69	3.01
#集成电路制造	Integrated Circuit	399.64	17.98	1.27
电子机电产品制造	Machinery and Electronic Products of Electron	458.84	20.98	6.32
电子专用材料制造	Special Materials of Electron	9.51	1.00	0.24

表 12.9 高技术产业主要指标(2006～2007)
MAIN FACT ABOUT HIGH TECHNOLOGY INDUSTRY

类 别	Types	工业总产值(亿元) Cross Output Value of Industry (100 million yuan)	
		2006	2007
总 计	**Total**	**4 460.97**	**5 606.63**
占全市比重(%)	**Proportion(%)**	**24.4**	**25.6**
按登记注册类型分	**Grouped by Registration Categories**		
#国 有	State-owned	38.39	54.52
集 体	Collective-owned	5.65	6.26
股份制企业	Share Holding	265.90	277.43
外商投资企业	Foreign Funded	4 122.71	5 231.62
按技术领域分	**Grouped by Technology Areas**		
信息化学品制造	Information Chemical Product	9.23	10.11
医药制造业	Medical and Pharmaceutical Product	234.03	269.20
航空航天器制造	Aviation and Aircraft Manufaturing	22.01	29.34
电子及通信设备制造业	Electron and Communicate Equipments	1 534.92	1 810.70
电子计算机及办公设备制造业	Electronic Computers and Office Equipments	2 429.43	3 214.89
医疗设备及仪器仪表制造业	Medical Treatment Instrument and Meter	231.35	272.39

表 12.9 续表 1 continued

类 别	Types	工业销售产值(亿元) Sales Value of Industry (100 million yuan)		年末资产总计(亿元) Total Property(year-end) (100 million yuan)	
		2006	2007	2006	2007
总 计	**Total**	**4 410.8**	**5 530.86**	**3 014.34**	**3 471.34**
占全市比重(%)	**Proportion(%)**	**24.3**	**25.47**	**17.1**	**16.95**
按登记注册类型分	**Grouped by Registration Categories**				
#国 有	State-owned	38.27	54.93	65.25	106.30
集 体	Collective-owned	5.23	5.81	5.12	6.44
股份制企业	Share Holding	261.47	273.15	369.83	382.37
外商投资企业	Foreign Funded	4 078.57	5 163.19	2 547.93	2 949.95
按技术领域分	**Grouped by Technology Areas**				
信息化学品制造	Information Chemical Product	8.93	9.83	9.01	12.68
医药制造业	Medical and Pharmaceutical Product	226.04	254.86	309.50	344.58
航空航天器制造	Aviation and Aircraft Manufaturing	21.35	23.50	31.89	56.82
电子及通信设备制造业	Electron and Communicate Equipments	1 506.41	1 789.49	1 708.57	1 833.48
电子计算机及办公设备制造业	Electronic Computers and Office Equipments	2 422.91	3 130.0	753.25	976.69
医疗设备及仪器仪表制造业	Medical Treatment Instrument and Meter	225.16	268.18	202.12	247.09

表 12.9 续表 2 continued

类别	Types	主营业务收入(亿元) Prime Operating Revenue (100 million yuan) 2006	2007	利润总额(亿元) Total Pre-tax Profits (100 million yuan) 2006	2007
总 计	**Total**	**4 601.42**	**5 811.97**	**119.26**	**159.25**
占全市比重(%)	**Proportion(%)**	**24.2**	**25.33**	**11.0**	**12.0**
按登记注册类型分	**Grouped by Registration Categories**				
#国 有	State-owned	37.83	53.98	2.78	3.35
集 体	Collective-owned	4.93	5.92	0.30	0.23
股份制企业	Share Holding	293.34	309.48	16.49	21.71
外商投资企业	Foreign Funded	4 235.78	5 408.68	98.04	132.70
按技术领域分	Grouped by Technology Areas				
信息化学品制造	Information Chemical Product	9.92	14.52	1.09	1.18
医药制造业	Medical and Pharmaceutical Product	244.22	283.14	18.51	23.85
航空航天器制造	Aviation and Aircraft Manufaturing	19.86	26.72	1.23	2.22
电子及通信设备制造业	Electron and Communicate Equipments	1 530.06	1 844.65	55.88	65.54
电子计算机及办公设备制造业	Electronic Computers and Office Equipments	2 562.99	3 364.82	15.35	32.93
医疗设备及仪器仪表制造业	Medical Treatment Instrument and Meter	234.37	278.13	27.20	33.52

表 12.9 续表 3 continued

类别	Types	税金总额(亿元) Total Tax and Duties (100 million yuan) 2006	2007	产品销售率(%) Sales Rate of Industrial Products(%) 2006	2007
总 计	**Total**	**42.14**	**46.70**	**98.9**	**98.7**
占全市比重(%)	**Proportion(%)**	**6.2**	**5.6**		
按登记注册类型分	**Grouped by Registration Categories**				
#国 有	State-owned	1.73	2.26	99.7	100.74
集 体	Collective-owned	0.25	0.21	92.6	92.8
股份制企业	Share Holding	10.85	12.05	98.3	98.5
外商投资企业	Foreign Funded	30.72	30.72	98.9	98.7
按技术领域分	**Grouped by Technology Areas**				
信息化学品制造	Information Chemical Product	0.23	0.2	96.7	97.3
医药制造业	Medical and Pharmaceutical Product	14.61	16.28	96.6	94.7
航空航天器制造	Aviation and Aircraft Manufaturing	0.18	0.72	97.0	97.1
电子及通信设备制造业	Electron and Communicate Equipments	13.93	14.16	98.1	98.8
电子计算机及办公设备制造业	Electronic Computers and Office Equipments	5.03	5.82	99.7	98.9
医疗设备及仪器仪表制造业	Medical Treatment Instrument and Meter	8.17	9.53	97.3	98.5

表 12.10 都市型工业主要指标(2006~2007)
MAIN STATISTICS OF URBAN INDUSTRIES

类别	Types	单位数(个) Number of Enterprises (unit)		从业人员(万人) Employees (10 000 persons)		工业总产值(亿元) Gross Output Value of Industry(100 million yuan)	
		2006	2007	2006	2007	2006	2007
总计	**Total**	**3 643**	**3 745**	**71.19**	**74.11**	**2 271.47**	**2 606.09**
按企业规模分	**Grouped by Size of Enterprises**						
大型	Large	16	19	4.92	6.00	202.01	269.09
中型	Medium	380	416	25.16	28.29	1 043.75	1 218.95
小型	Small	3 247	3 310	41.10	39.82	1 025.71	1 118.05
按登记注册类型分	**Grouped by Registration Categories**						
内资	Domestic Investment	2 051	2 075	28.39	27.7	700.97	822.21
国有	State-owned	76	62	0.93	1.10	30.19	43.53
集体	Collective-owned	163	144	2.00	1.81	38.67	39.19
股份合作	Share-holding Cooperative	81	79	1.07	1.00	22.20	23.97
联营	Joint Owned	37	32	0.69	0.62	16.23	19.91
有限责任公司	Companies with Limited Liabilities	244	220	4.77	3.92	181.16	201.79
股份有限公司	Share-holding Companies with Limited Liabilities	18	27	0.95	1.19	39.25	75.49
私营	Private	1 422	1 500	17.79	17.94	370.44	415.66
其他	Others	10	11	0.18	0.14	2.83	2.66
港澳台商投资	Hong Kong, Macao and Taiwan Funded	538	541	13.76	13.95	378.25	391.89
外商投资	Foreign Funded	1 054	1 129	29.04	32.46	1 192.25	1 391.99
按行业分	**Grouped by Sectors**						
服装服饰业	Garment and Trappings	1 282	1 299	27.46	27.92	517.67	559.5
食品加工制造业	Food Processing	449	446	8.78	8.99	489.61	606.35
包装、印刷业	Packaging and Printing	490	513	5.66	6.03	198.75	231.83
室内装饰用品制造业	Indoor Decoration Materials and Equipments Manufacturing	615	640	10.95	11.50	369.17	415.65
化妆品及清洁洗涤用品制造业	Cosmetics and Cleaning Manufacturing	171	179	2.25	2.34	165.55	203.60
工艺美术品、旅游用品制造业	Art Crafts and Tourism Equipments Manufacturing	435	445	9.49	9.68	275.10	299.12
小型电子信息产品制造业	Small Electronic Information Products Manufacturing	201	223	6.61	7.67	255.61	290.05

表 12.10 续表 1 continued

单位:亿元(100 million yuan)

类 别	Types	工业销售产值 Sales Value of Industry 2006	2007	年末资产总计 Total Assets (year-end) 2006	2007	主营业务收入 Prime Operating Revenue 2006	2007
总 计	**Total**	**2 248.61**	**2 585.37**	**1 961.93**	**2 230.61**	**2 351.20**	**2 696.47**
按企业规模分	**Grouped by Size of Enterprises**						
大 型	Large	201.44	272.6	168.85	219.34	223.77	292.51
中 型	Medium	1 025.94	1 194.08	889.19	1 035.96	1 070.22	1 254.99
小 型	Small	1 021.23	1 118.69	903.89	975.31	1 057.21	1 148.97
按登记注册类型分	**Grouped by Registration Categories**						
内 资	Domestic Investment	694.7	809.59	658.21	729.25	738.52	875.35
国 有	State-owned	29.88	42.32	43.78	59.71	32.66	47.71
集 体	Collective-owned	37.50	38.20	37.58	41.90	37.67	38.05
股份合作	Share-holding Coorperative	22.12	23.81	21.30	23.39	22.11	24.39
联 营	Joint Owned	16.02	20.26	10.05	18.12	16.27	19.96
有限责任公司	Companies with Limited Liabilities	182.21	201.07	173.89	166.58	209.06	244.28
股份有限公司	Share-holding Companies with Limited Liabilities	39.22	72.13	92.77	116.47	55.51	92.38
私 营	Private	364.93	409.20	276.75	300.72	362.44	406.21
其 他	Others	2.83	2.61	2.10	2.38	2.80	2.37
港澳台商投资	Hong Kong, Macao and Taiwan Funded	379.24	394.14	358.88	356.54	411.95	419.52
外商投资	Foreign Funded	1 174.67	1 381.64	944.84	1 144.81	1 200.74	1 401.61
按行业分	**Grouped by Sectors**						
服装服饰业	Garment and Trappings	496.89	550.36	347.74	388.00	497.07	547.41
食品加工制造业	Food Processing	489.40	595.74	454.59	553.08	540.77	640.77
包装、印刷业	Packaging and Printing	197.54	230.61	243.28	275.73	201.89	235.84
室内装饰用品制造业	Indoor Decoration Materials and Equipments Manufacturing	369.25	415.62	279.67	301.47	374.57	417.03
化妆品及清洁洗涤用品制造业	Cosmetics and Cleaning Manufacturing	166.79	212.75	166.03	194.73	172.85	229.44
工艺美术品、旅游用品制造业	Art Crafts and Tourism Equipments Manufacturing	275.05	295.88	217.97	246.47	306.62	334.22
小型电子信息产品制造业	Small Electronic Information Products Manufacturing	253.69	284.40	252.64	271.14	257.42	291.76

表 12.10 续表 2 continued

单位:亿元(100 million yuan)

类　别	Types	利润总额 Total Pre-tax Profits		税金总额 Total Tax and Duties	
		2006	2007	2006	2007
总　计	**Total**	**133.04**	**150.80**	**77.01**	**85.28**
按企业规模分	**Grouped by Size of Enterprises**				
大　型	Large	13.13	20.66	5.43	7.61
中　型	Medium	71.62	78.64	41.80	43.94
小　型	Small	48.29	51.50	29.78	33.73
按登记注册类型分	**Grouped by Registration Categories**				
内　资	Domestic Investment	35.86	44.99	25.41	28.39
国　有	State-owned	1.97	3.89	1.86	2.23
集　体	Collective-owned	2.06	1.96	1.36	1.29
股份合作	Share-holding Coorperative	1.72	1.33	1.05	1.06
联　营	Joint Owned	0.72	1.24	0.58	0.68
有限责任公司	Companies with Limited Liabilities	9.01	13.79	7.63	7.58
股份有限公司	Share-holding Companies with Limited Liabilities	3.89	8.79	1.87	3.45
私　营	Private	16.22	13.79	10.90	11.97
其　他	Others	0.26	0.20	0.16	0.13
港澳台商投资	Hong Kong, Macao and Taiwan Funded	18.35	20.38	11.76	12.26
外商投资	Foreign Funded	78.84	85.43	39.84	44.63
按行业分	**Grouped by Sectors**				
服装服饰业	Garment and Trappings	23.08	27.10	11.58	15.38
食品加工制造业	Food Processing	23.07	35.92	28.14	27.18
包装、印刷业	Packaging and Printing	15.20	16.80	8.98	9.69
室内装饰用品制造业	Indoor Decoration Materials and Equipments Manufacturing	22.25	21.51	7.96	7.94
化妆品及清洁洗涤用品制造业	Cosmetics and Cleaning Manufacturing	11.85	13.99	10.74	13.68
工艺美术品、旅游用品制造业	Art Crafts and Tourism Equipments Manufacturing	16.87	13.88	6.10	6.54
小型电子信息产品制造业	Small Electronic Information Products Manufacturing	20.72	21.61	3.51	4.86

表12.11　主要年份工业产品产量
OUTPUT OF INDUSTRIAL PRODUCTS IN MAIN YEARS

年　份 Year	化学纤维 （万吨） Chemical Fibers （10 000 tons）	食用植物油 （万吨） Vegetatble Oil （10 000 tons）	啤　酒 （亿升） Beer （100 million litres）	照相机 （万台） Cameras （10 000 units）	彩色电视机 （万部） Color TV Set （10 000 units）
1978	11.59	7.32	0.50	10.57	0.24
1980	15.15	6.77	0.66	20.69	0.55
1985	22.49	11.13	0.83	53.51	71.75
1990	25.74	13.42	1.66	20.62	81.48
1995	37.83	39.94	2.16	153.23	111.77
1996	38.61	17.38	2.00	198.99	42.59
1997	39.26	12.35	2.61	373.95	70.42
1998	40.93	19.46	2.69	428.58	107.80
1999	37.38	8.03	2.65	517.75	152.05
2000	47.15	11.55	3.04	1 116.94	147.97
2001	45.46	10.32	3.33	630.13	108.30
2002	51.67	9.65	3.62	723.81	137.02
2003	54.17	8.64	3.99	1 212.88	158.15
2004	48.45	3.51	5.92	1 514.39	135.08
2005	49.78	45.11	7.05	1 164.73	145.46
2006	50.60	72.86	7.17	760.73	251.67
2007	51.48	85.24	7.30	106.09	158.37

表12.11 续表1　continued

年　份 Year	家用洗衣机 （万台） Household Washing Machines （10 000 units）	家用电冰箱 （万台） Household Refrigerators （10 000 units）	房间空调器 （万台） Household Airconditioners （10 000 units）	燃气热水器 （万台） Water Heaters （10 000 units）	传真机 （万部） Facsimile Printers （10 000 units）
1980	0.81	0.42	0.10		
1985	113.85	20.49	0.74		
1990	101.29	53.36	1.83		
1995	144.80	128.72	62.46		
1996	141.52	93.12	86.75	37.90	3.03
1997	124.81	30.72	88.20	36.25	11.89
1998	72.55	38.61	113.98	36.52	10.67
1999	57.03	43.03	180.70	35.07	23.89
2000	62.11	43.12	186.08	32.27	23.60
2001	70.79	43.44	223.57	27.86	22.45
2002	95.92	35.97	217.57	36.32	28.17
2003	134.27	34.46	239.72	37.24	22.97
2004	165.67	33.14	399.16	51.86	22.68
2005	183.26	42.68	358.57	65.64	22.40
2006	288.74	101.08	410.60	69.89	27.22
2007	289.68	100.66	395.21	80.46	27.37

表 12.11 续表 2 continued

年 份 Year	机制纸及纸板(万吨) Machine-Made Paper and Paperboards (10 000 tons)	钢(万吨) Steel (10 000 tons)	成品钢材(万吨) Rolled-Steel Products (10 000 tons)	生 铁(万吨) Pig Iron (10 000 tons)	塑 料(万吨) Plastic (10 000 tons)	轮胎外胎(万条) Tires (10 000 tires)
1978	27.34	476.52	360.08	149.86	12.86	149.59
1980	29.57	521.61	412.63	171.12	14.57	174.85
1985	41.29	570.16	451.18	215.37	17.46	219.00
1990	46.49	914.62	609.59	526.90	25.35	318.78
1995	47.08	1 006.92	738.08	664.04	33.91	375.31
1996	38.85	1 441.92	1 175.74	964.03	65.46	942.69
1997	40.00	1 532.42	1 296.48	1 054.56	64.56	829.57
1998	45.46	1 603.75	1 417.58	1 208.57	77.42	957.75
1999	45.42	1 668.62	1 486.08	1 337.75	89.67	804.43
2000	43.54	1 778.70	1 544.46	1 473.00	95.47	830.66
2001	41.35	1 874.71	1 641.11	1 468.91	104.19	545.97
2002	42.61	1 719.42	1 626.98	1 276.12	129.57	704.80
2003	44.40	1 726.65	1 710.80	1 300.24	158.26	846.92
2004	35.96	1 823.65	1 818.41	1 356.47	163.44	927.17
2005	35.73	1 927.96	1 964.16	1 582.89	61.93	932.27
2006	85.87	1 902.82	2 129.78	1 639.13	66.21	1 055.47
2007	83.76	2 081.58	2 144.16	1 790.00	72.46	932.54

表 12.11 续表 3 continued

年 份 Year	水 泥(万吨) Cement (10 000 tons)	平板玻璃(万重量箱) Plate Glass (10 000wt. cases)	发电设备(万千瓦) Power Generating Equipments (10 000 kw)	金属切削机床(台) Metal-cutting Machines (unit)	发电量(亿千瓦·时) Electric Power Generation (100 million kwh)	硫 酸(万吨) Sulfuric (10 000 tons)
1978	139.47	111.87	109.80	17 384	199.32	34.49
1980	161.28	132.79	58.20	16 949	206.41	38.76
1985	219.31	160.08	133.00	19 408	256.25	35.22
1990	230.30	503.05	210.20	13 796	284.10	40.04
1995	433.22	634.63	496.50	15 833	403.42	31.03
1996	443.77	687.63	494.30	15 379	428.64	36.24
1997	338.47	691.08	541.60	18 700	458.48	36.79
1998	330.95	701.45	403.85	11 916	482.16	32.59
1999	251.14	641.81	314.55	17 822	498.01	38.38
2000	311.69	751.88	179.00	22 346	553.09	34.22
2001	334.75	755.80	336.20	21 839	572.86	36.15
2002	351.58	718.42	461.90	27 252	608.92	30.41
2003	568.24	789.21	1 013.70	33 497	684.99	31.41
2004	665.01	845.81	1 520.3	13 975	766.15	33.67
2005	719.97	830.61	2 138.05	13 158	728.74	33.32
2006	818.28	762.75	2 944.71	13 372	710.96	30.37
2007	786.24	742.79	2 845.59	14 266	737.80	30.46

表 12.11 续表 4 continued

年 份 Year	程控交换机(万线) Program Controlled Exchanges (10 000 lines)	微型电子计算机(万部) Personal Computers (10 000 units)	彩色显像管(万只) Color Tubes (10 000 units)	移动通信基站设备(万信道) Mobile Communication Facilities (10 000 channels)
1990	95.23	0.77	74.83	
1995	476.60	4.07	244.31	
1996	580.93	6.20	255.22	
1997	631.62	40.39	298.69	
1998	794.96	21.16	422.16	
1999	915.46	40.09	457.17	
2000	1 091.64	42.04	515.08	1.60
2001	1 752.90	47. 13	519.23	39.49
2002	1 227.25	75.25	631.55	24.82
2003	1 883.47	734.68	713.53	28.20
2004	2 054.28	996.09	745.73	57.67
2005	796.59	2 176.17	533.18	115.03
2006	553.53	2 670.09	507.57	174.16
2007	447.54	4 478.78	170.27	307.46

表 12.11 续表 5 continued

年 份 Year	集成电路(万块) Semi-conduct IC (10 000 units)	汽车(万辆) Motor Vehicles (10 000 vehicles)	其中 of which #轿车 Cars	民用钢质船舶(万总吨) Civil Steel Ships (10 000 syn-tons)
1978		1.04	0.26	25.18
1980		1.47	0.53	17.26
1985		1.22	0.86	40.13
1990	1 167	2.81	2.46	39.07
1995	15 290	16.27	16.07	83.33
1996	11 624	20.17	20.02	77.54
1997	88 098	23.30	23.15	85.29
1998	92 908	23.64	23.50	79.93
1999	170 001	25.58	25.42	62.47
2000	239 330	25.29	25.15	118.81
2001	225 315	29.00	28.88	177.59
2002	339 494	39.19	39.05	87.08
2003	397 313	59.58	58.84	109.77
2004	548 727	55.96	54.99	296.17
2005	677 003	48.45	48.09	235.59
2006	640 483	65.28	64.47	295.48
2007	891 138	82.12	81.15	303.24

注：2000 年开始移动通信设备不包括手机。
Note: The figure of mobile communication facilities has excluded mobile phones since 2000.

表 12.12 主要工业产品生产、销售总量(2007)
OUTPUT AND SALES OF MAIN INDUSTRIAL PRODUCTS

产品名称	Product	单位 Unit	生产量 Output	销售量 Sales
发电量	Electric Power Generation	亿千瓦·时(100 million kwh)	737.80	585.41
啤酒	Beer	亿升(100 million liters)	7.30	7.27
无酒精饮料(软饮料)	Non-alcoholic Beverage	万吨(10 000 tons)	247.69	244.94
卷烟	Cigarettes	亿支(100 million pieces)	855.47	857.99
化学纤维	Chemical Fibers	万吨(10 000 tons)	51.48	44.56
纱	Yarn	万吨(10 000 tons)	8.04	7.36
布	Cloth	亿米(100 million m)	0.77	0.78
丝织品	Silk Products	万米(10 000 m)	297.58	285.38
呢绒	Wool Fabric	万米(10 000 m)	1 954.59	2 091.41
毛线	Knitting Wool	吨(ton)	6 481	6 044
服装	Garments	亿件(100 million cases)	6.60	6.56
皮鞋	Leather Shoes	万双(10 000 pairs)	2 113.71	2 068.14
机制纸及纸版	Paperboard	万吨(10 000 tons)	83.76	82.57
汽油	Gasoline	万吨(10 000 tons)	211.10	189.05
柴油	Diesel Oil	万吨(10 000 tons)	603.47	600.35
焦炭	Coke	万吨(10 000 tons)	749.89	178.98
硫酸	Sulphuric Acid	万吨(10 000 tons)	30.46	27.95
烧碱	Caustic Soda	万吨(10 000 tons)	63.90	61.72
合成氨	Synthetic Ammonia	万吨(10 000 tons)	6.15	3.42
农用化肥	Ag-fertilizer	万吨(10 000 tons)	2.91	2.86
#氮肥	Nitrogen	万吨(10 000 tons)	2.09	2.06
磷肥	Phophate	万吨(10 000 tons)	0.82	0.80
化学农药	Chemical Pesticides	万吨(10 000 tons)	2.95	2.87
乙烯	Ethylene	万吨(10 000 tons)	187.24	36.17
合成橡胶	Synthetic Rubber	万吨(10 000 tons)	26.52	26.41
合成洗涤剂	Synthetic Detergents	万吨(10 000 tons)	22.95	23.21
中成药	Chinese Patent Medicines	万吨(10 000 tons)	1.32	1.19
轮胎外胎	Tires	万条(10 000 tires)	932.54	934.06
水泥	Cement	万吨(10 000 tons)	786.24	782.99
平板玻璃	Plate Glass	万重量箱(10 000 wt. cases)	742.79	721.43
生铁	Pig Iron	万吨(10 000 tons)	1 790.36	4.19
钢	Steel	万吨(10 000 tons)	2 081.58	63.11
金属切削机床	Metal-cutting Machines	台(unit)	14 440	14 728
#数控机床	Digital Machine Tools	台(unit)	1 537	1 618

表 12.12 续表 continued

	产品名称 Product	单 位 Unit	生产量 Output	销售量 Sales
成品钢材	Rolled-steel Products	万吨(10 000 tons)	2 144.16	2 162.60
内燃机	Internal Combustion Engines	万千瓦(10 000 kw)	8 357.01	4 295.77
缝纫机	Sewing Machines	万架(10 000 units)	82.79	82.47
大中型拖拉机	Large and Medium Size Tractors	万台(10 000 units)	0.93	1.00
汽 车	Motor Vehicles	万辆(10 000 vehicles)	82.12	81.92
#轿 车	Cars	万辆(10 000 vehicles)	81.15	81.04
摩托车	Motorcycles	万辆(10 000 vehicles)	67.94	68.11
自行车	Bicycles	万辆(10 000 vehicles)	640.19	635.87
民用钢质船舶	Civil Steel Ships	万总吨(10 000 syn-tons)	303.24	303.24
发电设备	Power Generating Equipments	万千瓦(10 000 kw)	2 845.59	2 748.93
电力电缆	Electric Cable	万公里(10 000 km)	11.85	11.83
家用洗衣机	Household Washing Machines	万台(10 000 units)	289.68	290.58
家用电冰箱	Household Refrigerators	万台(10 000 units)	100.66	98.43
电风扇	Electric Fans	万台(10 000 units)	160.44	166.12
房间空调器	Household Air-conditioners	万台(10 000 units)	395.21	392.08
排油烟机	Range Hoods	万台(10 000 units)	4.28	4.10
微波炉	Microware Oven	万台(10 000 units)	435.16	423.57
电饭锅	Electric Rice Cookers	万个(10 000 units)	112.26	111.71
吸尘器	Vacuum Cleaners	万台(10 000 units)	18.06	18.66
燃气热水器	Water Heaters	万台(10 000 units)	80.46	77.36
程控交换机	Program-controlled Exchanges	万线(10 000 lines)	447.54	448.82
传真机	Facsimile Printers	万部(10 000 units)	27.37	27.41
微型电子计算机	Personal Computers	万部(10 000 units)	4 478.78	4 424.44
彩色显像管	Color Tubes	万只(10 000 units)	170.27	201.51
电视机	Television Sets	万部(10 000 units)	158.37	161.39
#彩色电视机	Color TV Sets	万部(10 000 units)	158.37	161.39
组合音响	Stereo System	万部(10 000 units)	0.52	0.53
照相机	Cameras	万台(10 000 units)	106.09	106.09
表	Watches	万只(10 000 units)	163.77	163.28
移动通信基站设备	Mobile Communication Base Station Facilities	万信道(10 000 channels)	307.46	307.40
光学仪器	Optical Instruments	万台(10 000 units)	13.97	13.81

表 12.13 国有工业企业主要指标(2007)
MAJOR INDICATORS OF STATE-OWNED INDUSTRIAL ENTERPRISES

类别	Types	单位数(个) Number of Enterprises (unit)	从业人员(万人) Employees (10 000 persons)
总　计	**Total**	**343**	**12.85**
按隶属关系分	**Grouped by Subordination**		
#中央工业	Central Government	66	5.46
市(局)属工业	Municipality	195	6.03
区属工业	District	60	0.93
县属工业	County	2	0.19
按轻、重工业分	**Grouped by Light and Heavy Industry**		
轻工业	Light Industry	118	4.01
重工业	Heavy Industry	225	8.84
按企业规模分	**Grouped by Size of Enterprises**		
大型企业	Large	8	3.35
中型企业	Medium	86	6.10
小型企业	Small	249	3.40
按工业行业分	**Grouped by Sectors**		
#制造业	**Manufacture Industry**	**317**	**10.44**
农副食品加工业	Farm and Sideline Products Processing	4	0.03
食品制造业	Food Manufacturing	6	0.08
烟草制品业	Tabacco Manufacture	1	0.36
纺织业	Textile	11	0.60
纺织服装、鞋、帽制造业	Garments, Shoes and Accessories Manufacturing	6	0.01
皮革、毛皮、羽毛(绒)及其制品业	Leather, Fur, and Wool Products Manufacturing	3	0.07
木材加工及木、竹、藤、棕、草制品业	Timber Processing and Timber, Bamboo, Rattan, Coir and Straw Products Manufacturing	1	

工业总产值（亿元）Gross Output Value of Industry (100 million yuan)	年末资产总计（亿元）Total Assets (year-end) (100 million yuan)	固定资产净值年平均余额（亿元）Average Net Value of Fixed Assets (100 million yuan)	流动资产年平均余额（亿元）Average Current Assets (100 million yuan)
1 328.65	**2 515.11**	**1 211.53**	**773.25**
1 044.19	2 045.76	1 047.82	576.94
252.14	412.69	138.89	173.04
24.45	45.84	20.40	18.01
1.52	1.97	1.17	0.96
391.77	783.61	139.93	426.71
936.88	1 731.50	1 071.60	346.54
911.53	1 904.40	993.19	519.43
248.07	359.49	114.20	164.61
169.05	251.21	104.15	89.21
785.72	**1 341.58**	**282.86**	**703.26**
0.94	1.44	0.59	0.45
10.02	5.94	1.76	3.76
280.63	528.80	28.01	344.41
9.27	21.98	4.98	11.57
1.22	0.93	0.18	0.68
1.10	1.32	0.79	0.92
0.09	0.05	0.01	0.04

表 12.13 续表 1 continued

类别	Types	单位数（个）Number of Enterprises (unit)	从业人员（万人）Employees (10 000 persons)
家具制造业	Furniture Manufacturing	4	0.04
造纸及纸制品业	Paper-making and Paper Products Manufacturing	2	0.03
印刷业和记录媒介的复制	Printing and Record Duplicating	20	0.54
文教体育用品制造业	Stationary, Education and Sports Goods Manufacturing	6	0.15
化学原料及化学制品制造业	Raw Chemical Materials and Chemical Products Manufacturing	31	0.63
医药制造业	Medicine Manufacturing	13	0.87
化学纤维制造业	Chemical Fiber Manufacturing	1	0.03
橡胶制品业	Rubber Products Manufacturing	5	0.18
塑料制品业	Plastic Products Manufacturing	16	0.29
非金属矿物制品业	Nonmetal Mineral Products	18	0.55
黑色金属冶炼及压延加工业	Smelting and Pressing of Ferrous Metals	7	0.36
有色金属冶炼及压延加工业	Smelting and Pressing of Nonferrous Metals	3	0.02
金属制品业	Metal Products Manufacturing	12	0.32
通用设备制造业	General Equipment Manufacturing	45	1.60
专用设备制造业	Special Purpose Equipment Manufacturing	25	0.73
交通运输设备制造业	Transportation Equipment Manufacturing	35	2.24
电气机械及器材制造业	Electric Machinery Equipments and Manufacturing	16	0.20
通信设备、计算机及其他电子设备制造业	Communcations Equipment, Computer and Other Electronic Equipment Manufacturing	11	0.22
仪器仪表及文化、办公用机械制造业	Instruments, Meters, Culture and Office Equipments Manufacturing	12	0.25
工艺品及其他制造业	Artworks and Other Manufacturing	2	0.03
废弃资源和废旧材料回收加工业	Recycling and Disposal of Waste	1	0.01
电力、燃气及水的生产和供应业	**Production and Supply of Power, Gas and Water**	**26**	**2.42**
电力、热力的生产和供应业	Production and Supply of Electricity and Thermal Power	8	1.38
燃气生产和供应业	Production and Supply of Gas	5	0.45
水的生产和供应业	Production and Supply of Water	13	0.58

工业总产值 (亿元) Gross Output Value of Industry (100 million yuan)	年末资产总计 (亿元) Total Assets (year-end) (100 million yuan)	固定资产净值年平均余额 (亿元) Average Net Value of Fixed Assets (100 million yuan)	流动资产年平均余额 (亿元) Average Current Assets (100 million yuan)
0.70	0.85	0.19	0.64
1.21	1.93	1.01	0.85
24.24	39.79	18.45	12.23
1.63	2.81	0.75	2.03
69.18	72.25	35.14	19.63
23.93	46.91	15.84	21.25
0.57	1.34	0.62	0.62
2.24	4.99	1.13	2.68
8.89	7.82	3.26	3.15
23.59	30.00	6.19	16.80
53.80	167.24	93.22	25.90
1.55	0.44	0.08	0.23
22.05	23.46	9.66	10.38
60.00	63.81	8.75	38.45
25.81	37.83	6.38	20.85
120.41	250.98	41.92	146.67
6.16	6.11	1.31	3.99
8.35	8.17	1.31	4.67
7.23	5.83	0.86	3.76
0.16	2.69	0.17	1.69
20.74	5.87	0.30	4.95
542.93	**1 173.53**	**928.67**	**69.99**
506.82	1 011.90	842.97	33.27
20.61	48.87	23.23	20.85
15.49	112.76	62.47	15.86

表 12.13 续表 2 continued

类别	Types	年末负债合计 Total Liabilities (year-end)	年末所有者权益 Owner's Equity (year-end)
总 计	**Total**	**816.94**	**1 698.17**
按隶属关系分	**Grouped by Subordination**		
#中央工业	Central Government	554.28	1 491.48
市(局)属工业	Municipality	234.43	178.26
区属工业	District	22.08	23.77
县属工业	County	1.36	0.61
按轻、重工业分	**Grouped by Light and Heavy Industry**		
轻工业	Light Industry	155.46	628.15
重工业	Heavy Industry	661.48	1 070.02
按企业规模分	**Grouped by Size of Enterprises**		
大型企业	Large	485.18	1 419.22
中型企业	Medium	191.59	167.9
小型企业	Small	140.17	111.04
按工业行业分	**Grouped by Sectors**		
#制造业	**Manufacture Industry**	**573.8**	**767.77**
农副食品加工业	Farm and Sideline Products Processing	1.15	0.29
食品制造业	Food Manufacturing	4.23	1.71
烟草制品业	Tabacco Manufacture	28.23	500.57
纺织业	Textile	15.16	6.82
纺织服装、鞋、帽制造业	Garments, Shoes and Accessories Manufacturing	0.40	0.53
皮革、毛皮、羽毛(绒)及其制品业	Leather, Fur, and Wool Products Manufacturing	1.91	-0.59
木材加工及木、竹、藤、棕、草制品业	Timber Processing and Timber, Bamboo, Rattan, Coir and Straw Products Manufacturing	0.04	0.01

单位:亿元(100 million yuan)

主营业务收入 Prime Operating Revenue	利润总额 Total Pre-tax Profits	税金总额 Total Tax and Duties	成本费用总额 Total Cost and Expenses
1 342.75	**121.13**	**219.15**	**1 119.18**
1 024.62	118.08	207.55	792.38
285.16	3.16	10.43	293.03
24.39	0.13	0.68	25.01
1.67	-0.14	0.11	1.84
400.19	88.20	175.10	187.59
942.56	32.92	44.05	931.59
904.47	108.77	203.61	676.44
265.81	10.50	9.93	266.44
172.47	1.86	5.62	176.30
787.04	**101.79**	**186.86**	**578.16**
0.90	-0.18	0.01	1.00
8.98	0.59	0.18	8.57
280.18	82.68	169.35	68.37
13.03	-0.87	0.62	13.69
1.18	0.01	0.14	1.19
1.06	-0.10	0.03	1.23
0.09			0.09

表 12.13 续表 3 continued

类别	Types	年末负债合计 Total Liabilities (year-end)	年末所有者权益 Owners' Equity (year-end)
家具制造业	Furniture Manufacturing	0.39	0.46
造纸及纸制品业	Paper-making and Paper Products Manufacturing	1.26	0.67
印刷业和记录媒介的复制	Printing and Record Duplicating	12.24	27.55
文教体育用品制造业	Stationary, Education and Sports Goods Manufacturing	2.42	0.40
化学原料及化学制品制造业	Raw Chemical Materials and Chemical Products Manufacturing	42.04	30.21
医药制造业	Medicine Manufacturing	20.54	26.37
化学纤维制造业	Chemical Fiber Manufacturing	0.98	0.36
橡胶制品业	Rubber Products Manufacturing	3.67	1.33
塑料制品业	Plastic Products Manufacturing	4.44	3.37
非金属矿物制品业	Nonmetal Mineral Products	18.89	11.11
黑色金属冶炼及压延加工业	Smelting and Pressing of Ferrous Metals	128.07	39.17
有色金属冶炼及压延加工业	Smelting and Pressing of Nonferrous Metals	0.25	0.19
金属制品业	Metal Products Manufacturing	10.46	13.00
通用设备制造业	General Equipment Manufacturing	42.42	21.40
专用设备制造业	Special Purpose Equipment Manufacturing	21.59	16.24
交通运输设备制造业	Transportation Equipment Manufacturing	193.73	57.25
电气机械及器材制造业	Electric Machinery Equipments and Manufacturing	4.63	1.49
通信设备、计算机及其他电子设备制造业	Communcations Equipment, Computer and Other Electronic Equipment Manufacturing	4.24	3.94
仪器仪表及文化、办公用机械制造业	Instruments, Meters, Culture and Office Equipments Manufacturing	3.87	1.96
工艺品及其他制造业	Artworks and Other Manufacturing	1.54	1.16
废弃资源和废旧材料回收加工业	Recycling and Disposal of Waste	5.04	0.82
电力、燃气及水的生产和供应业	**Production and Supply of Power, Gas and Water**	**243.14**	**930.40**
电力、热力的生产和供应业	Production and Supply of Electricity and Thermal Power	167.25	844.65
燃气生产和供应业	Production and Supply of Gas	21.06	27.82
水的生产和供应业	Production and Supply of Water	54.83	57.93

单位:亿元(100 million yuan)

主营业务收入 Prime Operating Revenue	利润总额 Total Pre-tax Profits	税金总额 Total Tax and Duties	成本费用总额 Total Cost and Expenses
1.01	0.01	0.03	1.03
1.12	-0.08	0.15	1.27
27.39	3.71	1.64	25.22
1.74	-0.32	0.14	2.02
68.62	6.61	1.53	67.82
23.42	1.50	1.35	22.20
0.57	-0.05	0.02	0.63
2.35	0.03	0.11	2.73
8.67	0.34	0.33	8.51
21.48	-0.08	0.98	21.48
58.09	-1.18	2.76	64.86
1.41	0.01	0.01	1.42
23.50	1.58	1.00	22.20
59.19	1.44	1.93	58.76
27.62	1.37	1.22	27.33
105.31	3.76	2.21	106.99
6.07	0.05	0.28	6.10
8.34	0.39	0.14	8.26
4.18	0.12	0.21	4.35
1.79	0.07	0.01	1.79
29.74	0.38	0.48	29.06
555.71	**19.34**	**32.29**	**541.02**
500.43	20.96	31.23	481.04
38.36	-1.51	0.42	40.44
16.91	-0.12	0.65	19.54

表 12.14 股份制、港澳台商和外商投资企业主要指标(2007)
MAJOR INDICATORS OF SHARE-HOLDING ENTERPRISES AND ENTERPRISES WITH INVESTMENT FROM OTHER COUNTRIES OR FROM HONG KONG, MACAO AND TAIWAN

指标	Indicators	股份有限公司 Stock-holding Companies with Limited Liabilities	港澳台商投资企业 Enterprises with Investment from Hong kong, Macao and Taiwan
单位数(个)	Number of Enterprises(unit)	113	1 796
从业人员(万人)	Employees(10 000 persons)	7.41	41.23
工业总产值(亿元)	Gross Output Value of Industry(100 million yuan)	1 578.95	2 637.21
出口交货值(亿元)	Delivery Value of Exports(100 million yuan)	212.52	858.41
实收资本(股本)(亿元)	Paid-up Capital(Stock Capital)(100 million yuan)	376.19	820.75
#国家资本(国家股)	State Capital(State Stock)	174.44	58.79
年末资产总计(亿元)	Total Assets(year-end)(100 million yuan)	2 503.16	2 560.38
流动资产合计(亿元)	Total Current Assets(100 million yuan)	825.40	1 312.41
流动资产年平均余额(亿元)	Average Current Assets(100 million yuan)	732.80	1 249.29
固定资产合计(亿元)	Total Fixed Assets(100 million yuan)	797.75	818.66
固定资产原价(亿元)	Original Value of Fixed Assets(100 million yuan)	1 830.76	1 483.06
固定资产净值(亿元)	Net Value of Fixed Assets(100 million yuan)	790.09	764.87
固定资产净值年平均余额(亿元)	Average Net Value of Fixed Assets(100 million yuan)	754.74	746.69
年末负债合计(亿元)	Total Liabilities(year-end)(100 million yuan)	1 004.80	1 316.11
流动负债合计(亿元)	Total Current Liabilities(100 million yuan)	722.83	1 128.64
长期负债合计(亿元)	Long-Term Liabilities(100 million yuan)	279.52	178.40
年末所有者权益(亿元)	Owners' Equity(year-end)(100 million yuan)	1 498.36	1 244.27
主营业务收入(亿元)	Prime Operating Revenue(100 million yuan)	1 794.41	2 690.42
利润总额(亿元)	Total Pre-tax Profits(100 million yuan)	197.85	139.63
税金总额(亿元)	Total Tax and Duties(100 million yuan)	99.00	63.57

其中 of which			外商投资企业 Foreign-invested Enterprises	其中 of which		
# 与港澳台商合资合作经营 Joint and Cooperation Enterprises with Investment from Hong Kong, Macao and Taiwan	# 港澳台商独资 Ventures Solely Invested by Business from Hong kong, Macao and Taiwan	# 港澳台商投资股份有限公司 Stock-holding Companies with Limited Liabilities with Investment from Hong Kong, Macao and Taiwan		# 中外合资合作企业 Sino-foreign Joint and Cooperation Enterprises	# 外商独资 Solely Foreign-invested Ventures	# 外商投资股份有限公司 Stock-holding Companies with Limited Liabilities with Foreign Investment
754	1 018	24	4 086	1 578	2 454	54
16.23	22.28	2.71	123.53	45.26	74.26	4.01
865.62	970.45	801.13	12 011.60	4 695.05	6 563.00	753.56
236.68	417.38	204.35	5 642.23	1 015.17	4 541.54	85.52
222.62	391.69	206.44	2 980.89	1 362.80	1 382.54	235.54
12.66	0.00	46.12	99.68	50.51	0.00	49.17
697.62	939.59	923.17	8 599.34	3 872.63	4 096.74	629.97
441.08	530.33	341.00	5 231.32	2 255.96	2 612.30	363.06
417.62	513.94	317.73	4 910.21	2 176.98	2 405.49	327.73
202.60	347.76	268.30	2 853.92	1 344.18	1 328.39	181.36
318.11	590.14	574.81	4 478.35	2 175.82	1 955.74	346.79
183.55	320.86	260.46	2 605.06	1 265.22	1 177.50	162.34
180.85	320.09	245.75	2 618.58	1 274.70	1 182.51	161.37
404.79	506.57	404.74	5 006.75	2 095.84	2 593.08	317.82
373.48	412.31	342.85	4 350.96	1 734.37	2 306.16	310.43
27.49	91.45	59.47	609.34	333.46	268.88	7.00
292.83	433.02	518.43	3 592.59	1 776.79	1 503.66	312.15
886.18	973.79	830.45	12 480.44	5 003.85	6 704.16	772.43
43.00	53.43	43.21	600.51	362.70	226.95	10.86
18.57	18.42	26.58	312.50	207.91	75.00	29.60

表 12.15 大中型工业企业主要指标(2007)
MAJOR INDICATORS OF LARGE AND MEDIUM SIZED INDUSTRIAL ENTERPRISES

类 别	Types	单位数（个）Number of Enterprises (unit)	从业人员（万人）Employees (10 000 persons)	工业总产值（亿元）Gross Output Value of Industry (100 million yuan)
总 计	**Total**	**1 670**	**153.29**	**15 884.11**
按轻、重工业分	**Grouped by Light and Heavy Industry**			
大型企业	Large Enterprises	106	48.52	9 109.71
轻工业	Light Industry	29	9.38	758.98
重工业	Heavy Industry	77	39.14	8 350.73
中型企业	Medium Enterprises	1 564	104.77	6 774.40
轻工业	Light Industry	661	42.98	2 155.47
重工业	Heavy Industry	903	61.79	4 618.92
按隶属关系分	**Grouped by Subordination**			
大型企业	Large Enterprises	106	48.52	9 109.71
中央工业	Central Government	16	9.53	3 428.38
地方工业	Local Government	90	38.99	5 681.33
中型企业	Medium Enterprises	1 564	104.77	6 774.40
中央工业	Central Government	53	4.03	901.49
地方工业	Local Government	1 511	100.74	5 872.91
按从业人员分	**Grouped by Number of Employees**			
1 万人及以上	10 000 persons and above	9	13.01	4 694.89
5 000 ~ 9 999 人	5 000 ~ 9 999 persons	17	11.38	1 248.55
3 000 ~ 4 999 人	3 000 ~ 4 999 persons	38	14.40	2 122.25
1 000 ~ 2 999 人	1 000 ~ 2 999 persons	288	46.33	3 475.82
1 000 人以下	Below 1 000 persons	1 318	68.16	4 342.61
按工业总产值分	**Grouped by Gross Output Value of Industry**			
10 亿元及以上	1 000 million yuan and above	209	53.78	12 109.6
5 ~ 9.99 亿元	500 ~ 999 million yuan	207	22.10	1 474.28
1 ~ 4.99 亿元	100 ~ 499 million yuan	862	58.61	2 033.11
5 000 ~ 9 999 万元	50 ~ 99.99 million yuan	310	15.18	233.88
1 000 ~ 4 999 万元	10 ~ 49.99 million yuan	82	3.63	33.16
按固定资产原价分	**Grouped by Original Value of Fixed Assets**			
10 亿元及以上	1 000 million yuan and above	96	33.64	8 974.87
1 ~ 9.99 亿元	100 ~ 999 million yuan	636	65.47	4 875.71
5 000 ~ 9 999 万元	50 ~ 99.99 million yuan	372	23.35	1 034.41
1 000 ~ 4 999 万元	10 ~ 49.99 million yuan	499	27.48	899.28
1 000 万元以下	Below 10 million yuan	67	3.36	99.84

工业销售产值（亿元） Sales Value of Industry Products(100 million yuan)	实收资本（股本）（亿元） Paid-in Capital (fixed capital stock)(100 million yuan)	年末资产总计（亿元） Total Assets (year-end) (100 million yuan)	年末负债合计（亿元） Total Liabilities (year-end) (100 million yuan)	主营业务收　入（亿元） Prime Operation Revenue (100 million yuan)	利润总额（亿元） Total Pre-tax Profits (100 million yuan)	税金总额（亿元） Total Tax and Duties (100 million yuan)	成本费用总额（亿元） Total Costs and Expenses (100 million yuan)
15 669.61	**3 665.63**	**14 858.37**	**7 554.24**	**16 724.00**	**980.33**	**652.22**	**15 659.02**
9 019.38	1 460.52	8 273.27	3 966.18	9 807.70	557.17	478.36	9 117.26
768.49	115.09	923.11	244.97	800.76	118.23	182.88	559.82
8 250.88	1 345.43	7 350.16	3 721.21	9 006.94	438.94	295.48	8 557.44
6 650.23	2 205.10	6 585.10	3 588.06	6 916.30	423.16	173.86	6 541.76
2 099.32	639.90	1 912.45	1 016.83	2 179.92	120.54	67.87	2 072.96
4 550.91	1 565.21	4 672.65	2 571.23	4 736.38	302.62	105.99	4 468.80
9 019.38	1 460.52	8 273.27	3 966.18	9 807.70	557.17	478.36	9 117.26
3 417.87	586.23	4 634.45	1 846.03	3 647.88	304.05	330.23	3 221.08
5 601.50	874.30	3 638.81	2 120.15	6 159.82	253.12	148.13	5 896.19
6 650.23	2 205.10	6 585.10	3 588.06	6 916.30	423.16	173.86	6 541.76
898.89	282.84	1 044.08	501.09	920.20	97.96	27.69	828.19
5 751.35	1 922.27	5 541.02	3 086.97	5 996.10	325.21	146.16	5 713.57
4 644.81	455.29	3 629.64	1 480.55	4 899.29	227.03	174.57	4 638.13
1 209.37	423.02	1 569.34	782.29	1 485.31	112.76	66.31	1 413.48
2 126.97	289.31	1 685.33	860.89	2 301.09	119.33	205.56	2 023.79
3 421.26	1 147.00	3 930.60	2 248.89	3 589.18	255.93	89.10	3 370.46
4 267.20	1 351.01	4 043.46	2 181.62	4 449.13	265.27	116.68	4 213.16
11 971.41	2 292.20	10 795.80	5 368.75	12 828.80	760.53	546.87	11 938.61
1 443.30	438.55	1 429.14	825.97	1 536.10	84.11	39.14	1 469.99
1 989.13	755.04	2 181.52	1 129.09	2 073.06	123.06	57.03	1 967.76
230.90	139.99	352.06	180.00	243.82	11.13	7.64	238.40
34.87	39.85	99.85	50.43	42.21	1.51	1.54	44.26
8 887.39	2 072.98	9 106.32	4 241.29	9 549.35	581.67	491.01	8 872.00
4 783.30	1 243.82	4 218.72	2 414.05	5 080.94	267.15	116.52	4 808.56
1 019.12	197.39	793.99	448.43	1 078.61	69.83	23.40	1 022.77
882.77	142.76	673.96	404.08	917.82	56.49	19.46	863.40
97.03	8.68	65.37	46.39	97.28	5.19	1.84	92.30

表 12.15 续表 continued

	类 别 Types	单位数（个）Number of Enterprises (unit)	从业人员（万人）Employees (10 000 persons)	工业总产值（亿元）Gross Output Value of Industry (100 million yuan)
按工业行业分	**Grouped by Sectors**			
制造业	**Manufacture Industry**	**1 648**	**150.04**	**15 184.15**
农副食品加工业	Farm and Sideline Products Processing	19	1.36	114.40
食品制造业	Food Manufacturing	39	3.26	182.67
饮料制造业	Beverage Manufacturing	15	0.82	110.11
烟草制品业	Tabacco Manufacturing	2	0.39	282.34
纺织业	Textile	76	5.12	137.74
纺织服装、鞋、帽制造业	Garments, Shoes and Accessories Manufacturing	95	6.85	190.36
皮革、毛皮、羽毛(绒)及其制品业	Leather, Fur, and Wool Products Manufacturing	23	2.50	69.57
木材加工及木、竹、藤、棕、草制品业	Timber Processing and Timber, Bamboo, Rattan, Coir and Straw Products Manufacturing	14	0.95	33.54
家具制造业	Furniture Manufacturing	32	3.13	126.20
造纸及纸制品业	Paper-making and Paper Products Manufacturing	28	1.33	78.63
印刷业和记录媒介的复制	Printing and Record Duplicating	31	1.60	66.25
文教体育用品制造业	Stationary, Education and Sports Goods Manufacturing	47	3.48	97.36
石油加工、炼焦及核燃料加工业	Oil Processing, Coking and Nuclear Fuel Processing	4	2.16	942.50
化学原料及化学制品制造业	Raw Chemical Materials and Chemical Products Manufacturing	64	4.34	743.00
医药制造业	Medicine Manufacturing	46	3.57	171.25
化学纤维制造业	Chemical Fiber Manufacturing	5	0.33	63.95
橡胶制品业	Rubber Products Manufacturing	31	2.32	98.18
塑料制品业	Plastic Products Manufacturing	89	5.20	148.06
非金属矿物制品业	Nonmetal Mineral Products	48	3.32	161.36
黑色金属冶炼及压延加工业	Smelting and Pressing of Ferrous Metals	15	3.38	1 462.22
有色金属冶炼及压延加工业	Smelting and Pressing of Nonferrous Metals	27	2.67	209.35
金属制品业	Metal Products Manufacturing	97	6.56	350.20
通用设备制造业	General Equipment Manufacturing	139	11.52	1 132.30
专用设备制造业	Special Purpose Equipment Manufacturing	96	5.74	273.46
交通运输设备制造业	Transportation Equipment Manufacturing	139	14.92	1 981.55
电气机械及器材制造业	Electric Machinery Equipments and Manufacturing	160	15.45	1 005.92
通信设备、计算机及其他电子设备制造业	Communications Equipment, Computer and Other Electronic Equipment Manufacturing	206	32.68	4 686.73
仪器仪表及文化、办公用机械制造业	Instruments, Meters, Culture and Office Equipments Manufacturing	46	4.01	202.04
工艺品及其他制造业	Artworks and Other Manufacturing	15	1.11	62.91
废弃资源和废旧材料回收加工业	Reclaim and Processing of Abandoned Resources and Materials			
电力、燃气及水的生产和供应业	**Production and Supply of Power, Gas and Water**	**22**	**3.25**	**699.96**
电力、热力的生产和供应业	Production and Supply of Electricity and Thermal Power	9	1.91	638.66
燃气生产和供应业	Production and Supply of Gas	8	0.85	47.75
水的生产和供应业	Production and Supply of Water	5	0.49	13.56

工业销售产值（亿元）Sales Value of Industry Products(100 million yuan)	实收资本（股本）（亿元）Paid-in Capital (fixed capital stock) (100 million yuan)	年末资产总计（亿元）Total Assets (year-end) (100 million yuan)	年末负债合计（亿元）Total Liabilities (year-end) (100 million yuan)	主营业务收入（亿元）Prime Operation Revenue (100 million yuan)	利润总额（亿元）Total Pre-tax Profits (100 million yuan)	税金总额（亿元）Total Tax and Duties (100 million yuan)	成本费用总额（亿元）Total Costs and Expenses (100 million yuan)
14 971.08	**3 408.62**	**13 392.44**	**7 201.70**	**16 000.03**	**923.89**	**607.34**	**14 957.76**
113.62	16.95	67.81	42.31	128.23	6.96	1.74	121.49
172.89	61.27	183.31	91.20	196.84	14.90	13.06	184.87
111.99	35.60	93.86	49.53	106.36	6.34	5.99	99.80
283.88	20.30	532.92	28.73	281.92	83.00	169.60	69.80
135.04	56.69	170.81	81.54	138.10	6.49	3.74	134.91
184.43	43.18	142.78	78.89	186.33	14.65	6.78	172.35
68.24	9.06	64.53	33.19	68.68	8.52	1.33	60.17
32.15	7.64	33.66	18.87	33.31	2.07	1.33	30.97
126.72	16.25	77.67	50.35	127.45	9.42	2.36	119.53
77.08	30.81	85.71	54.44	77.40	2.31	2.32	75.57
65.21	31.51	83.90	35.33	68.17	6.93	3.65	62.99
97.50	18.56	67.11	41.48	100.15	0.57	0.40	100.35
945.72	176.81	499.78	186.82	966.29	10.62	43.86	951.13
735.38	293.90	813.57	418.54	763.37	58.52	28.70	712.61
161.97	72.51	220.32	118.99	184.07	16.62	10.98	171.89
58.53	21.09	52.50	33.48	61.49	-0.35	0.08	62.21
97.54	35.81	113.42	70.27	117.54	1.41	3.11	116.96
147.33	60.11	179.76	89.84	148.79	7.61	4.59	142.19
154.47	68.57	218.70	124.50	169.01	6.19	5.41	162.62
1 447.93	295.64	1 865.07	890.07	1 645.60	151.79	86.58	1 487.99
207.84	44.24	130.17	77.34	252.88	6.78	3.28	247.36
345.47	66.00	283.61	155.70	346.71	22.82	5.41	328.12
1 111.06	235.92	1 283.57	778.32	1 128.37	89.98	31.58	1 037.47
263.62	99.47	333.06	191.32	270.43	20.00	7.96	253.80
1 950.17	518.93	2 346.28	1 275.74	2 302.12	220.92	126.63	2 096.69
1 001.15	175.18	700.05	411.57	1 006.58	65.10	16.74	943.46
4 613.39	837.87	2 529.31	1 666.94	4 838.75	79.47	11.98	4 749.14
197.81	45.76	170.41	84.64	209.01	18.36	5.42	191.75
62.97	12.96	48.80	21.79	76.08	6.12	2.72	69.58
698.53	**257.01**	**1 465.93**	**352.54**	**723.97**	**36.21**	**44.88**	**701.26**
638.65	163.01	1 266.08	240.59	632.02	39.40	42.92	600.12
47.38	55.90	101.25	58.80	79.90	-1.51	1.12	84.04
12.50	38.11	98.60	53.15	12.05	-1.67	0.83	17.10

表 12.16 国有大中型工业企业主要指标(2007)

MAJOR INDICATORS OF STATE-OWNED LARGE AND MEDIUM-SIZED INDUSTRIAL ENTERPRISES

类 别	Types	单位数(个) Number of Enterprises (unit)	从业人员(万人) Employees (10 000 persons)	工业总产值(亿元) Gross Output Value of Industry (100 million yuan)
总 计	**Total**	**94**	**9.45**	**1 159.60**
按轻、重工业分	**Grouped by Light and Heavy Industry**			
大型企业	Large Enterprises	8	3.35	911.53
轻工业	Light Industry	3	0.85	298.33
重工业	Heavy Industry	5	2.51	613.19
中型企业	Medium Enterprises	86	6.10	248.07
轻工业	Light Industry	22	1.75	45.29
重工业	Heavy Industry	64	4.35	202.78
按隶属关系分	**Grouped by Subordination**			
大型企业	Large Enterprises	8	3.35	911.53
中央工业	Central Government	7	3.07	906.57
地方工业	Local Government	1	0.28	4.96
中型企业	Medium Enterprises	86	6.10	248.07
中央工业	Central Government	22	1.89	105.35
地方工业	Local Government	64	4.20	142.72
按从业人员分	**Grouped by Number of Employees**			
1 万人及以上	10 000 persons and above	1	1.19	492.28
5 000 ~ 9 999 人	5 000 ~ 9 999 persons			
3 000 ~ 4 999 人	3 000 ~ 4 999 persons	3	1.19	361.58
1 000 ~ 2 999 人	1 000 ~ 2 999 persons	20	3.42	160.42
1 000 人以下	Below 1 000 persons	70	3.65	145.32
按工业总产值分	**Grouped by Gross Output Value of Industry**			
10 亿元及以上	1 000 million yuan and above	8	3.13	946.27
5 ~ 9.99 亿元	500 ~ 999 million yuan	12	1.30	79.56
1 ~ 4.99 亿元	100 ~ 499 million yuan	49	4.05	117.22
5 000 ~ 9 999 万元	50 ~ 99.99 million yuan	19	0.75	13.97
1 000 ~ 4 999 万元	10 ~ 49.99 million yuan	6	0.24	2.58
按固定资产原价分	**Grouped by Original Value of Fixed Assets**			
10 亿元及以上	1 000 million yuan and above	10	3.34	957.81
1 ~ 9.99 亿元	100 ~ 999 million yuan	36	3.69	117.63
5 000 ~ 9 999 万元	50 ~ 99.99 million yuan	27	1.41	53.49
1 000 ~ 4 999 万元	10 ~ 49.99 million yuan	18	0.89	25.43
1 000 万元以下	Below 10 million yuan	3	0.12	5.24

工业销售产值（亿元）Sales Value of Industry Products(100 million yuan)	实收资本（股本）（亿元）Paid-in Capital (fixed capital stock)(100 million yuan)	年末资产总计（亿元）Total Assets (year-end)(100 million yuan)	年末负债合计（亿元）Total Liabilities (year-end)(100 million yuan)	主营业务收入（亿元）Prime Operation Revenue (100 million yuan)	利润总额（亿元）Total Pre-tax Profits (100 million yuan)	税金总额（亿元）Total Tax and Duties (100 million yuan)	成本费用总额（亿元）Total Costs and Expenses (100 million yuan)
1 161.50	**282.87**	**2 263.90**	**676.77**	**1 170.27**	**119.27**	**213.53**	**942.88**
918.21	152.06	1 904.40	485.18	904.47	108.77	203.61	676.44
301.77	26.87	560.06	43.28	301.39	85.49	170.72	87.90
616.44	125.19	1 344.35	441.90	603.07	23.28	32.89	588.53
243.30	130.80	359.49	191.59	265.81	10.50	9.93	266.44
44.51	25.87	92.58	46.86	47.63	2.64	2.46	45.73
198.78	104.94	266.91	144.73	218.18	7.85	7.47	220.71
918.21	152.06	1 904.40	485.18	904.47	108.77	203.61	676.44
911.35	149.46	1 889.90	475.91	896.00	108.41	203.23	667.99
6.86	2.60	14.50	9.27	8.46	0.36	0.38	8.45
243.30	130.80	359.49	191.59	265.81	10.50	9.93	266.44
101.82	40.12	131.68	65.26	104.33	9.29	3.55	100.19
141.47	90.68	227.82	126.33	161.48	1.21	6.37	166.25
492.28	62.32	999.57	162.83	487.51	20.55	29.61	466.63
364.05	47.25	705.44	172.20	349.00	85.09	170.28	138.05
161.93	96.33	357.34	227.79	183.71	9.96	8.25	188.31
143.25	76.97	201.54	113.95	150.06	3.66	5.40	149.89
950.86	166.73	1 914.42	474.46	937.59	114.87	204.53	707.17
79.14	42.94	119.19	67.85	95.93	2.69	4.08	96.25
115.32	60.13	183.68	103.60	117.16	1.72	4.05	118.16
13.53	8.98	35.94	26.48	14.78	-0.22	0.68	15.94
2.66	4.09	10.67	4.38	4.82	0.20	0.19	5.36
962.40	190.31	1 951.59	489.93	966.27	114.84	204.76	736.28
117.64	66.98	218.37	128.89	117.33	1.85	6.04	119.88
51.45	19.90	65.39	35.80	56.15	1.98	1.63	56.06
24.96	5.26	25.27	19.34	25.66	0.58	1.00	25.79
5.05	0.42	3.28	2.82	4.87	0.02	0.10	4.87

表 12.16 续表 continued

类别	Types	单位数（个）Number of Enterprises (unit)	从业人员（万人）Employees (10 000 persons)	工业总产值（亿元）Gross Output Value of Industry (100 million yuan)
按工业行业分	**Grouped by Sectors**			
制造业	**Manufacture Industry**	**86**	**7.56**	**636.03**
烟草制品业	Tabacco Manufacturing	1	0.36	280.63
纺织业	Textile	3	0.52	7.48
印刷业和记录媒介的复制	Printing and Record Duplicating	4	0.35	20.08
文教体育用品制造业	Stationary, Education and Sports Goods Manufacturing	2	0.10	0.93
化学原料及化学制品制造业	Raw Chemical Materials and Chemical Products Manufacturing	5	0.35	41.51
医药制造业	Medicine Manufacturing	6	0.78	21.78
化学纤维制造业	Chemical Fiber Manufacturing	1	0.03	0.57
橡胶制品业	Rubber Products Manufacturing	2	0.11	1.69
非金属矿物制品业	Nonmetal Mineral Products	1	0.03	0.73
黑色金属冶炼及压延加工业	Smelting and Pressing of Ferrous Metals	6	0.42	16.15
有色金属冶炼及压延加工业	Smelting and Pressing of Nonferrous Metals	2	0.31	40.62
金属制品业	Metal Products Manufacturing	3	0.21	12.80
通用设备制造业	General Equipment Manufacturing	22	1.28	51.13
专用设备制造业	Special Purpose Equipment Manufacturing	9	0.46	19.45
交通运输设备制造业	Transportation Equipment Manufacturing	13	1.95	112.85
电气机械及器材制造业	Electric Machinery Equipments and Manufacturing	1	0.06	1.09
通信设备、计算机及其他电子设备制造业	Communications Equipment, Computer and Other Electronic Equipment Manufacturing	2	0.14	4.93
仪器仪表及文化、办公用机械制造业	Instruments, Meters, Culture and Office Equipments Manufacturing	3	0.12	1.63
电力、燃气及水的生产和供应业	**Production and Supply of Power, Gas and Water**	**8**	**1.89**	**523.57**
电力、热力的生产和供应业	Production and Supply of Electricity and Thermal Power	2	1.33	501.14
燃气生产和供应业	Production and Supply of Gas	4	0.44	20.25
水的生产和供应业	Production and Supply of Water	2	0.12	2.19

工业销售产值（亿元） Sales Value of Industry Products(100 million yuan)	实收资本（股本）（亿元） Paid-in Capital (fixed capital stock)(100 million yuan)	年末资产总计（亿元） Total Assets (year-end) (100 million yuan)	年末负债合计（亿元） Total Liabilities (year-end) (100 million yuan)	主营业务收入（亿元） Prime Operation Revenue (100 million yuan)	利润总额（亿元） Total Pre-tax Profits (100 million yuan)	税金总额（亿元） Total Tax and Duties (100 million yuan)	成本费用总额（亿元） Total Costs and Expenses (100 million yuan)
637.91	**182.69**	**1 192.28**	**477.37**	**636.21**	**100.66**	**182.25**	**425.55**
282.16	17.40	528.80	28.23	280.18	82.68	169.35	68.37
9.43	3.56	16.83	10.98	11.22	0.14	0.55	11.42
19.94	12.21	30.5	9.95	23.04	3.52	1.45	20.81
0.91	0.84	2.00	1.78	1.05	-0.24	0.08	1.24
41.48	16.99	39.48	18.43	41.99	5.72	0.66	40.55
21.43	10.71	43.42	18.69	21.29	1.58	1.22	19.99
0.58	1.11	1.34	0.98	0.57	-0.05	0.02	0.63
1.74	0.08	3.20	2.30	1.74	0.04	0.08	1.74
0.73	0.01	0.68	0.26	0.73	0.04	0.03	0.71
15.84	2.98	19.74	13.23	15.37	0.31	0.69	15.18
43.67	40.13	160.46	122.98	49.67	-1.20	2.61	56.18
12.61	5.47	15.46	5.97	13.63	1.49	0.86	12.38
48.81	13.93	51.04	34.40	49.86	1.53	1.52	49.17
18.92	11.05	29.34	15.57	20.55	1.29	0.99	20.17
112.19	43.88	241.77	188	97.55	3.47	1.88	99.2
1.05	0.40	1.01	0.63	1.03		0.05	1.05
4.76	1.15	3.55	2.22	4.76	0.23	0.10	4.73
1.65	0.79	3.68	2.77	1.97	0.10	0.12	2.04
523.59	**100.18**	**1 071.62**	**199.40**	**534.06**	**18.61**	**31.28**	**517.32**
501.14	63.65	1 005.71	165.02	494.44	20.55	30.73	475.2
20.63	32.97	46.69	20.97	37.99	-1.51	0.40	40.03
1.82	3.55	19.23	13.41	1.63	-0.44	0.15	2.09

表 12.17 闵行经济技术开发区主要指标(2007)
MAJOR INDICATORS OF MINHANG ECONOMIC AND TECHNICAL DEVELOPMENT ZONE

类　别	Types	单位数(个) Number of Enterprises (unit)	工业总产值(亿元) Gross Output Value of Industry (100 million yuan)
总　计	**Total**	**82**	**405.37**
按登记注册类型分	**Grouped by Registration Categories**		
其他有限责任公司	Other Limited Liability Company	4	0.98
私营有限责任公司	Private Limited Liability Company	1	0.72
合资经营(港或澳、台资)	Joint Ventures with Investment from Hong Kong, Macao and Taiwan	10	9.48
港澳台商独资	Hong Kong, Macao and Taiwan Enterprises	2	2.09
中外合资经营	Joint Ventures	25	194.49
中外合作经营	Cooperation Ventures	1	1.80
外商独资企业	Solily Foreign-funded Enterprese	35	167.37
外商投资股份有限公司	Foreign-funded share-holding companies with Limited Liabilities	4	28.43
按轻重工业分	**Grouped by Light and Heavy Industry**		
轻工业	Light Industry	44	197.00
重工业	Heavy Industry	38	208.37
按企业规模分	**Grouped by Size of Enterprises**		
大型企业	Large	2	81.24
中型企业	Medium	37	272.61
小型企业	Small	43	51.52
按行业分	**Grouped by Sectors**		
食品制造业	Food Manufacturing	6	18.49
饮料制造业	Beverage Manufacturing	4	54.00
纺织业	Textile	7	3.60
纺织服装、鞋、帽制造业	Garments, Shoes and Accessories Manufacturing	7	3.60
家具制造业	Furniture Manufacturing	1	1.08
印刷业和记录媒介的复制	Printing and Record Duplicating	2	0.63
化学原料及化学制品制造业	Raw Chemical Materials and Chemical Products Manufacturing	6	36.89
医药制造业	Medicine Manufacturing	6	31.06
化学纤维制造业	Chemical Fibre Manufacturing	1	0.48
橡胶制品业	Robber Products Manufacturing	1	10.67
塑料制品业	Plastic Products Manufacturing	6	8.59
非金属矿物制品业	Nonmetal Mineral Products	4	15.58
有色金属冶炼及压延加工业	Smelting and Pressing of Nonferrous Metals	1	7.27
金属制品业	Metal Products Manufacturing	2	0.74
通用设备制造业	General Equipment Manufacturing	8	97.17
专用设备制造业	Special Prupose Equipment Manufacturing	3	3.05
交通运输设备制造业	Transportation Equipment Manufacturing	2	13.53
电气机械及器材制造业	Electric Machinery Equipments and Manufacturing	7	47.90
通信设备、计算机及其他电子设备制造	Communications Equipment, Computer and Other Electronic Equipment Manufacturing	2	3.69
仪器仪表及文化、办公用机械制造业	Instruments, Meters, Culture and Office Equipments Manufacturing	4	31.34
工艺品及其他制造业	Artworks and Other Manufacturing	2	16.02

工业销售产值（亿元）Sales Value of Industrial Products (100 million yuan)	实收资本（股本）（亿元）Paid-in Capital (fixed capital stock) (100 million yuan)	年末资产总计（亿元）Total Assets (year-end) (100 million yuan)	年末负债合计（亿元）Total Liabilities (year-end) (100 million yuan)	主营业务收入（亿元）Prime Operating Revenue (100 million yuan)	利润总额（亿元）Total Pre-tax Profits (100 million yuan)	税金总额（亿元）Total Tax and Duties (100 million yuan)
404.20	**98.81**	**356.69**	**196.80**	**412.22**	**38.90**	**20.49**
1.06	0.58	1.08	0.55	1.11	-0.21	0.06
0.72	0.05	0.59	0.54	0.78	0.00	0.01
10.37	3.47	8.77	2.81	11.41	1.50	0.57
2.55	2.18	3.42	0.99	2.56	0.11	0.04
191.36	32.34	158.71	81.79	190.45	20.78	9.44
2.18	1.30	7.90	8.98	1.93	-0.21	0.13
166.57	43.03	134.35	79.57	172.35	13.84	8.44
29.39	15.86	41.88	21.58	31.63	3.08	1.82
198.98	42.63	150.19	76.06	200.40	16.57	10.67
205.22	56.18	206.49	120.74	211.82	22.33	9.83
81.22	17.99	82.60	35.29	79.32	11.68	5.19
273.90	61.91	219.78	128.30	281.41	21.49	12.23
49.08	18.91	54.31	33.21	51.48	5.73	3.07
18.86	3.61	10.36	6.01	22.63	1.65	1.38
58.22	6.28	49.03	31.20	54.56	3.22	1.42
4.15	2.57	4.87	1.07	4.17	0.17	0.11
3.54	0.81	2.28	0.97	3.42	0.09	0.02
1.06	0.06	0.56	0.35	1.04	0.13	0.10
0.65	0.87	1.72	0.65	0.65	0.08	0.08
37.01	10.93	25.34	11.79	37.30	1.66	3.39
28.36	7.21	21.30	10.25	27.85	4.45	3.01
0.44	0.61	0.55	0.42	0.45		
10.69	9.63	18.75	16.73	12.96	-0.76	0.30
8.66	1.97	5.73	2.46	8.58	0.32	0.10
15.65	11.26	23.66	22.83	16.59	-5.64	0.49
7.17	2.10	4.29	1.76	7.17	-0.09	0.58
0.76	0.10	0.55	0.24	0.77		0.03
95.28	17.69	94.01	45.55	97.63	20.95	5.78
2.31	2.94	4.14	1.85	2.92	0.24	0.12
13.49	2.03	10.66	6.92	14.06	1.89	0.14
47.94	7.61	40.20	22.52	48.22	5.38	1.91
3.68	1.46	2.56	0.78	3.65	0.15	0.04
30.24	3.06	15.01	7.90	31.59	1.33	0.26
16.02	6.03	21.12	4.56	16.02	3.67	1.24

表 12.18 漕河泾新兴技术开发区主要指标(2007)
MAJOR INDEXES OF CAOHEJING NEW TECHNICAL DEVELOPMENT ZONE

类 别	Types	单位数(个) Number of Enterprises (unit)	工业总产值(亿元) Gross Output Value of Industry (100 million yuan)	工业销售产值(亿元) Sales Value of Industrial Products (100 million yuan)
总 计	**Total**	**171**	**295.26**	**290.90**
按登记注册类型分	**Grouped by Registration Categories**			
国 有	State-owned	8	5.66	5.50
集 体	Collective-owned	6	1.48	1.5
股份合作	Share-holding Cooperation	2	1.12	1.12
集体联营	Collective Joint Owned	1	0.07	0.07
国有独资公司	Solely State Fund Company	1	0.06	0.06
其他有限责任公司	Other Companies with Limited Liabilities	22	13.59	13.84
股份有限公司	Share-holding Companies with Limited Liabilities	3	1.20	1.19
私营有限责任公司	Private Companies with Limited Liabilities	30	9.18	8.91
合资经营(港或澳、台资)	Joint Venture(Hong Kong, Macao and Taiwan Funded)	5	1.85	1.66
港澳台商独资	Solely Hong Kong, Macao and Taiwan Funded	17	41.41	41.26
港澳台商投资股份有限公司	Funded share-holding Companies with Limited Liabites from HongKong, Macao and Taiwan	2	11.91	11.84
中外合资经营	Sino-foreign Joint Ventures	11	49.31	49.21
中外合作经营	Sino-foreign Cooperation	1	6.12	5.71
外商独资企业	Solely Foreign Funded	57	133.94	130.24
外商投资股份有限公司	Foreign Funded Share-holding Companies with Limited Liabilities	5	18.36	18.79
按轻、重工业分	**Grouped by Light and Heavy Industry**			
轻工业	Light Industry	43	26.94	26.49
重工业	Heavy Industry	128	268.32	264.41
按企业规模分	**Grouped by Size of Enterprises**			
大型企业	Large	4	108.83	108.95
中型企业	Medium	24	114.18	112.70
小型企业	Small	143	72.26	69.25
按工业行业分	**Grouped by Sectors**			
食品制造业	Food Manufacturing	4	6.45	6.48
纺织业	Textile	1	0.15	0.15
纺织服装、鞋、帽制造业	Garments, Shoes and Accessories Manufacturing	3	0.40	0.29
木材加工及木、竹、藤、棕、草制品业	Timber Processing and Timber, Bamboo, Rattan, Coir and Straw Products Manufacturing	1	0.11	0.10
印刷业和记录媒介的复制	Printing and Record Duplicating	6	4.41	4.69
化学原料及化学制品制造业	Raw Chemical Materials and Chemical Products	8	28.27	28.04
医药制造业	Medicine Manufacturing	7	3.50	3.02
塑料制品业	Plastic Products Manufacturing	1	0.09	0.09
有色金属冶炼及压延加工业	Smelting and Pressing of Nonferrous Metals	1	0.16	0.16
金属制品业	Metal Products Manufacturing	6	1.46	1.50
通用设备制造业	General Equipment Manufacturing	15	16.70	14.04
专用设备制造业	Special Purpose Equipment Manufacturing	13	4.57	4.48
交通运输设备制造业	Transportation Equipment Manufacturing	2	33.12	32.97
电气机械及器材制造业	Electric Machinery Equipments Manufacturing	21	16.85	17.08
通信设备、计算机及其他电子设备制造业	Communications Equipment, Computer and Other Electric Machinery Equipments and Manufacturing	57	150.52	149.65
仪器仪表及文化、办公用机械制造业	Instruments, Meters, Culture and Office Equipments Manufacturing	23	28.33	28.00
工艺品及其他制造业	Artworks and Other Manufacturing	2	0.16	0.16

实收资本（股本）（亿元） Paid-in Capital (fixed capital stock) (100 million yuan)	年末资产总计（亿元） Total Assets (year-end) (100 million yuan)	年末负债合计（亿元） Total Liabilities (year-end) (100 million yuan)	主营业务收入（亿元） Prime Operating Revenue (100 million yuan)	利润总额（亿元） Total Pre-tax Profits (100 million yuan)	税金总额（亿元） Total Tax and Duties (100 million yuan)
99.01	**295.86**	**152.93**	**307.25**	**18.57**	**7.29**
2.32	8.38	3.55	6.16	0.34	0.15
0.12	0.89	0.37	1.50	0.08	0.04
0.05	0.44	0.22	1.12	0.09	0.04
0.07	0.13	0.07	0.07	-0.01	0.00
0.03	0.04	0.01	0.06	0.00	0.00
7.34	23.52	15.62	15.51	0.58	0.76
1.01	1.86	0.67	1.60	0.13	0.03
1.14	7.26	5.03	8.88	0.57	0.29
1.66	2.23	0.78	1.70	0.13	0.08
10.99	23.62	13.83	41.53	1.00	0.32
15.36	22.92	6.36	11.94	-1.50	0.00
12.86	44.85	22.65	50.28	5.86	1.30
0.49	6.00	3.91	8.54	0.78	0.26
32.31	108.30	62.04	135.28	10.16	3.48
13.28	45.43	17.83	23.09	0.37	0.55
15.30	40.25	23.14	26.64	1.87	0.90
83.71	255.61	129.79	280.60	16.70	6.39
16.08	67.91	45.70	110.77	7.14	1.52
51.08	146.24	64.83	121.67	6.63	3.02
31.84	81.71	42.40	74.81	4.80	2.76
2.55	7.66	3.92	6.62	0.64	0.37
0.02	0.08	0.05	0.14	0.01	
0.36	0.44	0.12	0.26	0.02	0.02
0.02	0.25	0.23	0.10		
1.85	6.87	1.83	4.94	0.63	0.22
8.03	29.00	15.98	27.86	2.54	1.69
3.33	4.42	1.81	2.18	0.10	0.11
0.01	0.05	0.03	0.09		0.01
0.05	0.29	0.12	0.15	0.01	0.01
0.34	0.82	0.70	1.38	-0.07	0.03
3.15	11.16	4.19	14.22	2.84	0.84
1.59	4.41	2.64	4.60	0.30	0.11
6.74	29.29	14.14	34.26	6.11	1.03
5.18	14.70	7.41	18.89	0.77	0.23
54.77	157.52	81.67	159.38	2.67	1.20
10.83	28.15	17.54	32.00	1.96	1.41
0.17	0.75	0.54	0.16	0.04	0.02

表 12.19 国家级、市级工业园区主要经济指标(2007)
MAJOR ECONOMIC INDICATORS OF MUNICIPAL AND NATIONAL INDUSTRIAL ZONE

指标	Indicators	国家级开发区 National Level Develop Zone	其中 of which	
			外高桥保税区 Waigaoqiao Free Trade Zone	金桥出口加工区 Jinqiao Export Processing Zone
单位数(个)	Number of Enterprises(unit)	878	213	256
从业人员(万人)	Employees(10 000 persons)	41.87	5.44	11.16
工业总产值(亿元)	Gross Output Value of Industry(100 million yuan)	6 009.43	488.32	1 650.61
出口交货值(亿元)	Delivery Value of Industry Exports(100 million yuan)	3 781.75	241.78	390.24
实收资本(股本)(亿元)	Paid-in Capital(Fixed capital stock)(100 million yuan)	1 190.95	96.60	479.18
年末资产总计(亿元)	Total Assets(year-end)(100 million yuan)	4 087.38	390.58	1 362.99
流动资产合计(亿元)	Total Current Assets(100 million yuan)	2 504.20	265.26	905.22
流动资产年平均余额(亿元)	Average Current Assets (100 million yuan)	2 295.80	246.57	842.30
固定资产合计(亿元)	Total Fixed Assets(100 million yuan)	1 002.27	105.86	316.91
固定资产原价(亿元)	Original Value of Fixed Assets(100 million yuan)	1 815.77	190.73	625.26
固定资产净值年平均余额(亿元)	Average Net Value of Fixed Assets (100 million yuan)	918.77	102.89	285.29
年末负债合计(亿元)	Total Liabilities(year-end)(100 million yuan)	2 364.96	233.42	784.86
年末流动负债合计(亿元)	Total Current Liabilities(year-end)(100 million yuan)	2 111.29	216.22	730.29
长期负债合计(亿元)	Total Long-term Liabilities(100 million yuan)	243.06	17.02	49.03
年末所有者权益(亿元)	Owners' Equity(year-end)(100 million yuan)	1 722.42	157.17	578.13
主营业务收入(亿元)	Prime Operating Revenue(100 million yuan)	6 445.26	501.58	2 041.41
利润总额(亿元)	Total Pre-tax Profits(100 million yuan)	294.96	38.73	118.66
税金总额(亿元)	Total Tax and Duties(100 million yuan)	131.49	7.22	83.61
亏损总额(亿元)	Total Loss(100 million yuan)	32.55	2.27	5.88

张江高科技园区 Zhangjiang Hi-Tec Park	漕河泾新兴技术开发区 Caohejing Hi-tec Park	漕河泾出口加工区 Caohejing Export Processing Zone	闵行经济技术开发区 Minhang Hi-tec Park	上海松江出口加工区 Songjiang Export Processing Zone	市级开发区 Municipal Level Development Zone	其中 of which 上海宝山工业园区 Baoshan Industrial Park	上海月杨工业园区 Yueyang Industrial Park
97	171	4	82	55	3 773	151	108
4.75	4.72	2.69	3.65	9.45	80.73	2.73	1.84
399.36	295.26	641.86	405.37	2 128.66	5 383.50	147.29	128.01
204.71	127.08	642.08	77.71	2 098.15	1 545.22	39.64	21.78
340.43	99.01	11.19	98.81	65.73	1 641.73	36.37	30.31
955.34	295.86	136.05	356.69	589.87	4 788.19	126.76	97.41
322.62	171.63	104.57	253.35	481.54	2 633.52	77.42	61.01
265.58	175.81	87.44	236.08	442.02	2 463.18	70.74	58.89
274.57	84.60	29.18	86.91	104.24	1 804.43	38.80	27.55
513.51	158.03	40.68	156.36	131.20	2 433.04	48.63	34.50
244.41	77.04	27.56	81.97	99.61	1 642.72	34.45	22.89
366.56	152.93	121.89	196.80	508.49	2 696.74	73.74	54.91
218.22	140.98	121.89	192.24	491.45	2 161.93	66.25	51.69
147.85	11.55		0.59	17.01	508.19	7.03	2.60
588.78	142.92	14.16	159.88	81.38	2 091.45	53.03	42.50
390.26	307.25	641.88	412.22	2 150.66	5 427.8	144.33	146.20
52.41	18.57	3.07	38.90	24.61	317.31	7.87	7.61
12.71	7.29	0.01	20.49	0.14	149.62	2.93	3.31
10.88	4.90		7.50	1.11	59.17	0.82	0.86

表 12.19 续表 1 continued

指 标	Indicators	上海富盛经济开发区 Fusheng Economic Development Zone	上海浦东空港工业园区 Pudong Konggang Industrial Park	上海市嘉定区工业园区 Jiading Industrial Park
单位数(个)	Number of Enterprises(unit)	2	144	549
从业人员(万人)	Employees(10 000 persons)	0.03	2.08	11.80
工业总产值(亿元)	Gross Output Value of Industry(100 million yuan)	0.44	87.9	698.35
出口交货值(亿元)	Delivery Value of Industry Exports(100 million yuan)	0.19	15.33	274.93
实收资本(股本)(亿元)	Paid-in Capital(Fixed capital stock)(100 million yuan)	0.06	17.88	169.87
年末资产总计(亿元)	Total Assets(year-end)(100 million yuan)	0.46	78.22	498.47
流动资产合计(亿元)	Total Current Assets(100 million yuan)	0.29	51.29	310.29
流动资产年平均余额(亿元)	Average Current Assets (100 million yuan)	0.29	45.74	293.24
固定资产合计(亿元)	Total Fixed Assets(100 million yuan)	0.15	21.47	154.43
固定资产原价(亿元)	Original Value of Fixed Assets(100 million yuan)	0.20	26.84	230.82
固定资产净值年平均余额(亿元)	Average Net Value of Fixed Assets (100 million yuan)	0.15	19.00	145.7
年末负债合计(亿元)	Total Liabilities(year-end)(100 million yuan)	0.37	42.64	277.43
年末流动负债合计(亿元)	Total Current Liabilities(year-end)(100 million yuan)	0.37	39.45	250.83
长期负债合计(亿元)	Total Long-term Liabilities(100 million yuan)		2.90	24.36
年末所有者权益(亿元)	Owners' Equity(year-end)(100 million yuan)	0.09	35.59	221.04
主营业务收入(亿元)	Prime Operating Revenue(100 million yuan)	0.40	85.09	705.38
利润总额(亿元)	Total Pre-tax Profits(100 million yuan)	0.01	8.35	31.32
税金总额(亿元)	Total Tax and Duties(100 million yuan)	0.01	1.75	11.64
亏损总额(亿元)	Total Loss(100 million yuan)		0.55	5.48

上海市嘉定区汽车产业园区 Jiading Automobile Industrial Park	上海莘庄工业区 Xinzhuang Industrial Park	上海青浦工业园区 Qingpu Industrial Park	上海西郊经济开发区 Xijiao Economic Development Zone	上海松江工业园区 Songjiang Industrial Park	上海松江经济开发区 Songjiang Economic Development Zone	上海奉贤经济开发区 Fengxian Economic Development Zone	上海金山工业园区 Jinshan Industrial Park
316	342	379	220	627	114	107	110
7.15	7.30	8.18	4.88	16.50	2.00	2.07	1.89
787.91	508.95	385.74	157.9	772.42	107.74	152.06	91.6
70.21	199.89	122.34	57.33	248.53	32.16	92.12	13.52
178.56	202.96	144.04	61.62	291.43	25.1	46.41	23.96
533.10	544.32	366.11	161.95	754.8	83.21	135.64	72.27
304.58	283.30	221.09	91.25	441.77	57.82	89.14	34.54
303	270.07	198.51	84.71	402.42	54.88	73.91	34.81
186.95	202.87	125.02	60.47	266.03	22.13	36.21	30.56
334.33	271.83	176.39	82.18	392.51	34.86	41.86	33.09
168.21	183.92	115.64	55.71	248.72	21.58	29.08	25.67
225.65	299.77	197.26	83.62	419.97	46.62	79.65	42.17
202.10	243.63	177.16	76.95	366.74	44.24	74.43	34.4
10.78	54.91	18.60	6.13	50.62	1.89	3.71	7.72
307.46	244.55	168.85	78.34	334.83	36.58	55.99	30.10
845.71	518.68	373.02	158.02	768.45	100.52	149.8	85.50
58.61	29.31	22.85	7.84	44.12	6.54	8.01	1.68
46.93	12.96	10.5	4.69	16.74	2.23	1.98	1.97
1.17	8.06	7.27	1.76	7.67	0.36	3.10	0.90

表 12.19 续表 2 continued

指 标	Indicators	上海枫泾工业园区 Fengjing Industrial Park	上海市北工业园区 Shibei Industrial Park	上海崇明工业园区 Congming Industrial Park
单位数(个)	Number of Enterprises(unit)	105	35	20
从业人员(万人)	Employees(10000 persons)	1.63	0.65	0.43
工业总产值(亿元)	Gross Output Value of Industry(100 million yuan)	101.43	29.56	11.19
出口交货值(亿元)	Delivery Value of Industry Exports(100 million yuan)	13.62	8.14	4.35
实收资本(股本)(亿元)	Paid-in Capital(Fixed capital stock)(100 million yuan)	24	10.32	2.04
年末资产总计(亿元)	Total Assets(year-end)(100 million yuan)	71.83	26.58	10.87
流动资产合计(亿元)	Total Current Assets(100 million yuan)	37.94	17.67	6.19
流动资产年平均余额(亿元)	Average Current Assets (100 million yuan)	35.06	16.19	6.58
固定资产合计(亿元)	Total Fixed Assets(100 million yuan)	20.64	6.46	3.60
固定资产原价(亿元)	Original Value of Fixed Assets(100 million yuan)	24.87	14.88	4.66
固定资产净值年平均余额(亿元)	Average Net Value of Fixed Assets (100 million yuan)	17.75	6.63	2.89
年末负债合计(亿元)	Total Liabilities(year-end)(100 million yuan)	36.75	12.28	5.99
年末流动负债合计(亿元)	Total Current Liabilities(year-end)(100 million yuan)	31.56	11.01	5.39
长期负债合计(亿元)	Total Long-term Liabilities(100 million yuan)	4.74	0.46	0.31
年末所有者权益(亿元)	Owners' Equity(year-end)(100 million yuan)	35.08	14.3	4.88
主营业务收入(亿元)	Prime Operating Revenue(100 million yuan)	95.81	28.64	10.74
利润总额(亿元)	Total Pre-tax Profits(100 million yuan)	2.41	1.55	0.43
税金总额(亿元)	Total Tax and Duties(100 million yuan)	2.21	0.66	0.39
亏损总额(亿元)	Total Loss(100 million yuan)	1.22	0.12	0.11

上海星火工业园区 Xinghuo Industrial Park	上海紫竹高新技术产业园区 Zizhu High and new Technical Industrial Park	上海浦东康桥工业园区 Pudong Kangqiao Industial Park	上海化学工业园区 Chemical Industrial Park	上海新杨工业园区 Xinyang Industrial Psrk	上海浦东合庆工业园区 Pudong Heqing Industrial Park	上海南汇工业园区 Nanhui Industrial Park	上海奉贤工业园区 Fengxian Industrial Park	上海未来岛物流科技园区 Future Island Logistic Technology Zone
26	2	179	18	16	70	75	48	6
0.79	0.05	4.86	0.37	0.29	1.11	1.11	0.74	0.18
105.64	2.05	494	437.67	17.22	64.98	47.06	18.56	22.89
10.85	0.97	253.42	31.91	0.64	9.38	16.8		5.72
28.42	0.14	100.75	204.61	1.81	16.92	17.71	3.50	2.77
93.64	2.85	384.6	580.39	12.71	62.74	58.96	12.66	15.96
44.84	1.46	249.44	148.84	7.57	43.22	30.49	7.79	13.23
43.30	0.95	230.62	142.68	6.69	42.66	26.96	7.52	11.71
46.63	1.23	113.18	394.13	3.62	14.59	21.06	3.96	2.12
64.09	1.59	155.45	400.21	4.66	21.65	22.3	5.63	4.21
44.52	1.07	108.58	349.88	2.99	13.21	18.02	3.95	1.91
68.96	1.79	250.20	391.63	7.10	30.04	28.41	7.35	11.13
49.64	1.70	228.41	125.65	6.87	28.87	24.98	7.30	11.01
19.32	0.08	21.17	265.98	0.23	1.07	3.43	0.02	0.12
24.69	1.06	134.4	188.75	5.6	32.7	30.55	5.30	4.83
104.43	1.34	493.2	437.95	17.59	64.00	47.45	17.82	23.45
0.12	0.35	32.08	30.68	1.83	5.67	4.68	0.54	2.85
1.66	0.22	8.95	13.69	0.55	1.37	1.17	0.32	0.73
2.46		2.08	14.00	0.03	0.41	0.61		0.09

上/海/统/计/年/鉴

主要统计指标解释

工　业

指从事自然资源的开采，对采掘品和农产品进行加工和再加工的物质生产部门。具体包括：(1)对自然资源的开采，如采矿、晒盐等(但不包括禽兽捕猎和水产捕捞)；(2)对农副产品的加工、再加工，如粮油加工、食品加工、缫丝、纺织、制革等；(3)对采掘品的加工、再加工，如炼铁、炼钢、化工生产、石油加工、机器制造、木材加工等，以及电力、自来水、煤气的生产和供应等；(4)对工业品的修理、翻新，如机器设备的修理、交通运输工具(包括小卧车)的修理等。

1984年以前农村的村及村以下办工业归属农业，1984年以后划归工业。

工业统计调查单位为独立核算法人工业企业。

法人工业企业指从事工业生产经营活动的单位。独立核算法人工业企业应同时具备以下条件：①依法成立，有自己的名称、组织机构和场所，能够承担民事责任；②独立拥有和使用资产，承担负债，有权与其他单位签订合同；③独立核算盈亏，并能够编制资产负债表。

轻工业

指主要提供生活消费品和制作手工工具的工业。按其所使用的原料不同，可分为两大类：(1)以农产品为原料的轻工业，是指直接或间接以农产品为基本原料的轻工业。主要包括食品制造、饮料制造、烟草加工、纺织、缝纫、皮革和毛皮制作、造纸以及印刷等工业；(2)以非农产品为原料的轻工业，是指以工业品为原料的轻工业。主要包括文教体育用品、化学药品制造、合成纤维制造、日用化学制品、日用玻璃制品、日用金属制品、手工工具制造、医疗器械制造、文化和办公用机械制造等工业。

重工业

指为国民经济各部门提供物质技术基础的主要生产资料的工业。按其生产性质和产品用途，可以分为下列三类：(1)采掘工业，是指对自然资源的开采，包括石油开采、煤炭开采、金属矿开采、非金属矿开采等工业；(2)原材料工业，指向国民经济各部门提供基本材料、动力和燃料的工业。包括金属冶炼及加工、炼焦及焦炭、化学、化工原料、水泥、人造板以及电力、石油和煤炭加工等工业；(3)加工工业，是指对工业原材料进行再加工制造的工业。包括装备国民经济各部门的机械设备制造工业、金属结构、水泥制品等工业，以及为农业提供的生产资料如化肥、农药等工业。

根据上述划分原则，修理业中以重工业产品为修理作业对象的划为重工业，反之划为轻工业。

工业总产值

(1)定义：工业总产值是以货币形式表现的，工业企业在一定时期内生产的工业最终产品或提供工业性劳务活动的总价值量。它反映一定时间内工业生产的总规模和总水平。

(2)计算原则：

工业生产的原则，即凡是企业在报告期生产的经检验合格的产品，不管是否在报告期销售，均包括在内。

最终产品的原则，即凡是计入工业总产值的产品，必须是本企业生产的经检验合格的，不需要再进行任何加工的最终产品。如果企业有中间产品(半成品)对外销售，则对外销售的中间产品应视为企业的最终产品。

工厂法原则，即工业总产值是以工业企业作为基本计算(核算)单位，即按企业的最终产品计算工业总产值。按这种方法计算的工业总产值，不允许同一产品价值在企业内部重复计算，不能把企业内部各个车间(分厂)生产的成果相加，但允许企业间的重复计算。

(3)内容及计算方法：1995年全国工业普查对工业总产值(原规定)的内容及计算原则和方法做了某些修订，修订后的工业总产值(新规定)包括三项内容：即本期生产成品价值、对外加工费收入、在制品半成品期末期初差额价值三部分。

本期生产成品价值：指企业本期生产，并在报告期内不再进行加工，经检验、包装入库的全部工业成品(半产品)价值合计，包括企业生产的自制设备及提供给本企业在建工程、其他非工业部门和福利部门等单位使用的成品价值。本期生产成品价值按成品实物量乘以本期不含销项税额的产品实际销售平均单价计算；自制设备和自产自用的成品，按会计核算成本价格计算价值。生产成品价值中不包括用定货者来料加工的成品(半产品)价值。

对外加工费收入：指企业在报告期内完成的对外承接的工业品加工(包括用定货者来料加工产品)的加工费收入和对外工业修理作业所取得的加工费收入。对外加

主要统计指标解释

工费收入按不含增值税(销项税额)的价格计算,可根据会计"产品销售收入"科目的有关资料取得。

对于本企业对内非工业部门提供的加工修理、设备安装的劳务收入,如果企业会计核算基础较好,能取得这部分资料,而且这部分价值所占比重较大,应包括在对外加工费收入中。

自制半成品在制品期末期初差额价值:指企业报告期在制品期末减期初的差额价值,本指标一般可以从会计核算资料中取得。如果会计产品成本核算中不计算半成品、在制品的成本,则总产值中也不包括这部分价值,反之则包括。

(4)工业总产值统计范围变化和计算方法修订情况:

1984 年以前工业总产值不包括村办工业,村办工业总产值划归农业。1984 年以后工业总产值包括村办工业。

1995 年工业普查对工业总产值计算方法做了修订,即从 1995 年始按新修订(新规定)方法计算工业总产值。新规定与原规定的区别如下:

全价与加工费的计算原则不同:新规定为凡自备原材料,不论其生产繁简程度如何,一律按全价计算工业总产值;凡来料加工,允许按加工费计算工业总产值。原规定则视生产加工的繁简程度不同,规定哪些行业按全价,哪些行业按加工费计算工业总产值。

自制半成品、在产品期末期初差额价值的计算原则不同:新规定要求,凡会计产品成本核算时计算了成本的差额价值,总产值中就应包括,否则可不包括;原规定则按生产周期六个月的界限区分,凡生产周期六个月以上的企业,总产值计算中应包括这部分差额价值,否则可不包括。

计算价格不同:新规定按不含增值税(销项税额)的价格计算;原规定则按含增值税(销项税额)的价格计算。

大、中、小型企业

大中小型企业划分标准:自 2003 年年报起,大中小型企业划分标准执行"统计上大中小型企业划分办法(暂行)"(国统字[2003]17 号)。即大型企业必须同时达到从业人员数 ≥2000 人、销售收入≥ 30000 万元、资产总额 ≥ 40000 万元;中型企业必须同时达到 2000 人 ≥从业人员数 ≥300 人、30000 万元 ≥销售收入≥ 3000 万元、40000 万元≥ 资产总额 ≥4000 万元;其余的均为小型企业。

资产总计

资产是指企业拥有或者控制的能以货币计量的经济资源,包括各种财产、债权和其他权利。资产按其流动性(即资产的变现能力和支付能力)划分为:流动资产、长期投资、固定资产、无形资产、递延资产和其他资产。该指标根据企业会计"资产负债表"中"资产总计"项目的期末数增列。

流动资产合计

指可以在一年或者超过一年的一个营业周期内变现或者耗用的资产,包括现金及各种存款、短期投资、应收及预付货款、存款等。

流动资产平均余额

指企业在报告期内全部流动资产的平均余额。

固定资产净值年平均余额

指固定资产净值在报告期内余额的平均数。计算公式为:

固定资产净值年平均余额 =1 至 12 月各月月初、月末固定资产净值之和 /24

该指标根据"资产负债表"中"固定资产原价"、"累计折旧"指标的期初、期末数计算填列。

固定资产净值指固定资产原价减去历年已提折旧额后的净额。计算公式为:

固定资产净值 = 固定资产原价 - 累计折旧

负债合计

指企业所承担的能以货币计量,将以资产或劳务偿付的债务总计。负债一般按偿还期长短分为流动负债和长期负债。流动负债合计是指企业在一年内或超过一年的一个营业周期内偿还的债务;长期负债合计是指偿还期在一年以上或者超过一年的一个营业周期内偿还债务。

所有者权益

指企业投资人对企业净资产的所有权。企业净资产等于企业全部资产减去全部负债后的余额,包括企业投资人对企业的最初投入的实际到位的资产及资本公积金、盈余公积金和未分配利润。所有者权益合计数小于零,表示企业资不抵债。

利润总额

指企业生产经营活动的最终成果,是企业在一定时期内实现的盈亏相抵后的利润总额(亏损以"-"号表示),它等于营业利润加上补贴收入加上投资收益加上营业外

主要统计指标解释

净收入再加上以前年度损益调整。

总资产贡献率

反映企业全部资产的获利能力，是企业经营业绩和管理水平的集中体现，是评价和考核企业盈利能力的核心指标。计算公式为：

总资产贡献率(%)= 利润总额 + 税金总额 + 利息支出 / 平均资金总额 × 100%

公式中：税金总额为产品销售税金及附加与应缴增值税之和；平均资产总额为期初期末资产之和的算术平均值。

资产负债率

该指标既反映企业经营风险的大小，也反映企业利用债权人提供的资金从事经营活动的能力。计算公式为：

资产负债率(%)= 负债总额 / 资产总额 × 100%

资产与负债均为报告期期末数。

流动资产周转次数

指一定时期内流动资产完成的周转次数，反映投入工业企业流动资金的周转速度。计算公式为：

流动资产周转资转 = 产品销售收入 / 全部流动资产平均余额

公式中：全部流动资产平均余额为期初和期末的流动资产之和的算术平均值。

成本费用利润率

反映企业投入的生产成本及费用的经济效益，同时也反映企业降低成本所取得的经济效益。计算公式为：

成本费用利润(%)= 利润总额 / 成本费用总额 × 100%

公式中：成本费用总额为产品销售成本、销售费用、管理费用、财务费用之和。

产品销售率

该指标反映工业产品已实现销售的程度，是分析工业产销衔接情况、研究工业产品满足社会需求的指标。计算公式为：

产品销售率 (%)= 工业销售产值 / 工业总产值（现价）× 100%

资产保值增值率

该指标反映企业净资产的变动状况，是企业发展能力的集中体现。计算公式为：

资产保值增值率＝报告期期末所有者权益 / 上年同期期末所有者权益

所有者权益等于资产总计减负债总计。

全员劳动生产率

该指标反映企业的生产效率和劳动投入的经济效益。计算公式为：

$$\text{全员劳动生产率(元/人)}=\frac{\text{工业增加值}}{\text{全部从业人员平均人数}}$$

SHANGHAI STATISTICAL YEARBOOK

EXPLANATORY NOTES TO MAJOR STATISTICAL INDICATORS

□ Industry

Industry refers to the material production sector which is engaged in extraction of natural resources and processing and reprocessing of minerals and agricultural products, including (1) extraction of natural resources, such as mining, salt production (but not including hunting and fishing); (2) processing and reprocessing of farm and sideline produces, such as rice husking, flour milling, wine making, oil pressing, silk reeling, spinning and weaving, and leather making; (3) manufacture of industrial products, such as steel making, iron smelting, chemicals manufacturing, petroleum processing, machine building, timber processing; water and gas production and electricity generation and supply; (4)repairing of industrial products such as the repairing of machinery and means of transport (including cars).

Prior to 1984, the rural industry run by villages and cooperative organizations under village was classified into agriculture. Since 1984, it has been grouped into industry.

Units of industrial statistics survey corporate industrial enterprises with independent accounting system.

Corporate industrial enterprises with independent accounting system refer to enterprises engaging in industrial production activities, which meet the following requirements: ①They are established legally, having their own names, organizations, location, able to take civil liability; ②They possess and use their assets independently, assume liabilities, and are entitled to sign contracts with other units; ③They are financially independent and compile their own balance sheets.

□ Light Industry

Light Industry refers to the industry that produces consumer goods and hand tools. It consists of two categories, depending on the materials used:

(1) Industries using farm products as raw materials. These are branches of light industry which directly or indirectly use farm products as basic raw materials, including the manufacture of food and beverages, tobacco processing, textile, clothing, fur and leather manufacturing, paper making, printing, etc.

(2) Industries using non farm products as raw materials. These are branches of light industry which use manufactured goods as raw materials, including the manufacture of cultural, educational articles and sports goods, chemicals, synthetic fiber, chemical products for daily use, glass products for daily use, metal products for daily use, hand tools, medical apparatus and instruments, and the manufacture of cultural and clerical machinery.

□ Heavy Industry

Heavy Industry refers to the industry which produces capital goods, and provides various sectors of the national economy with necessary material and technical basis. It consists of the following three branches according to the purpose of production or the use of products:

(1) Mining, quarrying and logging industry refers to the industry that extracts natural resources, including extraction of petroleum, coal, metal and non-metal ores.

(2) Raw materials industry refers to the industry that provides various sectors of the national economy with raw materials, fuels and power. It includes smelting and processing of metals, coking and coke chemistry, chemical materials and building materials such as cement, plywood, and power, petroleum refining and coal dressing.

(3) Manufacturing industry refers to the industry that processes raw materials. It includes machine building industry which equips sectors of the national economy, industries of metal structure and cement products, industries producing means of agricultural production, such as chemical fertilizers and pesticides. According to the above principle of classification, the repairing trades which are engaged primarily in repairing products of heavy industry are classified into heavy industry while these engaged in repairing products of light industry are classified into light industry.

□ Gross Output Value of Industry

(1) Definition: Gross industrial output value is the total volume of final industrial products produced and industrial services provided during a given period. It reflects the total achievements and overall scale of industrial production during a given period.

(2) Principles for calculation:

Statistics on industrial production follow the principle that all products produced by the enterprises and accepted during the

EXPLANATORY NOTES TO MAJOR STATISTICAL INDICATORS

reference period are to be included no matter whether they are sold or not during the reference period.

Determination of final products follow the principle that all products that are included in the calculation of grow industrial output value are the final products of the enterprise which have been accepted through quality check and require no further processing. If an enterprise has intermediate (semi-finished) products to sell, these intermediate products are considered as the final products of the enterprise.

Gross industrial output value is calculated following the principle of factory approach, i.e. industrial enterprise is used as the basic accounting unit in calculating the gross industrial output value. By this approach, value of the same product is not to be double counted, and the output value of different workshops (branch factories) should not be added. However, this approach does not exclude the possibility of double counting between enterprises.

(3)Content and calculation method: The old definition of gross industrial output value was modified during the national industrial census in 1995. The revised (new) definition of gross industrial output value consists of 3 components: value of the finished products during the reference period, income from external processing, and value of change in semi-finished products at the end and at the beginning of the reference period.

Value of the finished products during the reference period: refers to the value of all finished (semi-finished) industrial products that are produced during the reference period without the need for further processing, checked for acceptance, packed and put into the warehouse of the enterprise, including the value of own-produced equipment and the value of products provided to the projects under construction of the enterprise, and to other non-industrial or welfare units. Value of finished products during the reference period is calculated by the quantity of products produced using own materials multiplied by the average unit prices at which products are sold (excluding value-added tax). Own-produced equipment and products produced for own use are value at cost prices as in the case of enterprise accounting. Value of finished products does not include the value of finished products (semi-finished products) that are produced using the materials from the clients who make the orders.

Income from external processing: refers to income from contracted external processing of industrial products (including processing of industrial products using materials from the clients), and the income from industrial repairing work provided to other units. Income from external processing is calculated using information from the item "products sales income" in the enterprise accounting at the prices excluding value-added tax.

For income from services such as processing, repairing and installation of equipment provided to non-industrial units within the enterprise, if the accounting work of the enterprise is good enough to separate it from other records, and the share of such services is significant, it should also be included in the income from external processing.

Value of change in semi-finished products at the end and at the beginning of the reference period: refers to the value of change in semi-finished products at the end and at the beginning of the reference period, which generally can be obtained from accounting records of enterprises. If the enterprise accounting excludes the cost of semi-finished products, then it should not be included in the gross industrial output value, and vice versa.

(4) Changes in the coverage and method of calculation of gross industrial output value

Prior to 1984, the value of rural industry run by villages was classified into agriculture instead of industry. Since 1984, it has been included in the gross industrial output value.

Method of calculation for the gross industrial output value was modified in the industrial census in 1995. The difference in the new method as compared with the old one is outlined below:

Principle in using full value vs. processing fee: The new method stipulates that all products produced using own materials are to be calculated with full value in reporting the gross industrial output value irrespective of sophistication of production, and for external processing, it allows calculation using processing fee. In the old method, however, the use of full value or processing fee was determined by the degree of sophistication of production in different branches of industries.

Principle in determining the value of change in semi-finished products: The new method requires that value of the change in semi-finished products should be included in the gross industrial output value if it is included in the accounting record of the enterprise, otherwise it should not be included. By the old method, it is determined by the type of enterprises in terms of production cycle. If the production cycle is over 6 months, the value of change in semi-finished products is included in the gross industrial output value, otherwise it is excluded.

Difference in prices: The new method uses prices excluding value-added tax in the calculation of gross industrial output value, while the old method used prices including value-added tax.

EXPLANATORY NOTES TO MAJOR STATISTICAL INDICATORS

□ Large, Medium and Small Enterprises

Since 2003 annual report enforcement, the criteria for classifying large, medium and small enterprises has been based on The Method for Classifying Large, Medium and Small Enterprises (Provisional) (State Statistics Bureau[2003] No.17). That is, an enterprise could be entitled Large Enterprise only when it has more than 2000 employees, its sales revenue exceeds 300 million yuan and total property exceeds 400 million yuan , simultaneously. An enterprise could be entitled Medium Enterprise when its employee number ranges from 300 to 2000, its sales revenue ranges from 30 million to 300 million yuan and its total property ranges from 40 million to 400 million yuan, simultaneously. All other enterprises should be entitled Small Enterprises.

□ Aggregate Assets

Total Assets refer to all economic resources, in monetary terms, that is owned or controlled by enterprises, including properties, creditors equity and other economic rights of all forms. Classified by the degree of equitability, total assets include circulating assets, long-term investment, fixed assets, intangible assets and deferred assets, and other assets. Data on this indicator can be obtained by the year-end figures of total assets in the Assets and Liability Table of accounting records of enterprises.

□ Total of Working Capitals

Total of Working Capitals refer to capitals which can be cashed in or spent or consumed in an operating cycle of one year or over one year, including cash, all kinds of deposits, short term investment, receivable and payable payment for goods or deposits.

□ Average Value of Working Capitals

Average Value of Working Capitals refers to the average value of all working capitals of the enterprise during the reference period.

□ Annual Average of Net Value of Fixed Assets

Annual Average of Net Value of Fixed Assets refer to average of the net value of fixed assets during the reference period, calculated with the following formula:

Annual Average of Net Value of Fixed Assets = sum of net value of fixed assets at the beginning and at the end of each month from January to December / 24.

Information on this indicator can be obtained from the beginning and ending figures of the original value of fixed assets and cumulative depreciation from the Assets and Liability Table of enterprises.

Net value of fixed assets refers to the original value of fixed assets minus depreciation over the years, i.e.:

Net value of fixed assets = original value of fixed assets – cumulative depreciation

□ Aggregate Liabilities

Aggregate liabilities refer to the total debts of an enterprise which can be calculated in monetary term and will be repaid in the forms of assets or service. Usually, the debts are divided into liquid liability and long-term debt according to the length of the payback period. The liquid liability is the debt that an enterprise will pay back during an operation cycle which is either shorter or longer than a year. The long-term debt refers to a debt whose payback period is longer than a year or which will be repaid during an operation cycle that is longer than a year.

□ Creditors' Equity

Creditors' Equity refers to investors ownership of net assets of the enterprise, which is equal to the total assets of the enterprise minus its total liabilities, including the primary input actually received at the enterprise from investors, capital accumulation fund, surplus accumulation fund and undistributed profit. When the total of creditors' equity is less than zero, that indicates the liability of the enterprise is larger that its assets.

□ Total Profits

Total Profits refer to the final achievements of production and operation of the enterprises, represented by the total profits after deducting losses (loss is expressed by the negative figure). It is the sum of profits from operation, income from subsidies, investment earnings, net income from activities other than operation, and adjustment of profits and losses of previous years.

□ Ratio of Profits, Taxes and Interests to Average Assets

Ratio of Profits, Taxes and Interests to Average Assets reflects the profit-making capability of all assets of the enterprise and is a key indicator manifesting the performance and management and evaluating the profit-making potential of the enterprise. It is calculated as follows:

Ratio of Profits, Taxes and Interests to Average Assets (%) = [(total profits + total taxes + interest payment) / average assets] ×

EXPLANATORY NOTES TO MAJOR STATISTICAL INDICATORS

100%

In the above formula, total taxes is the sum of tax and extra charges on the sales of products and value-added tax payable; and average assets is the arithmetic mean of the sum of beginning assets and ending assets.

□ Ratio of Debts to Assets

Ratio of Debts to Assets reflect both the operation risk and the capability of the enterprise in making use of the capital from the creditors. It is calculated as follows:

Ratio of Debts to Assets (%) =(total debts / total assets) × 100%

Both assets and debts are figures at the end of the reference period.

□ Turnover of Working Capital

Turnover of Working Capital refers to the number of times of turnover of working capital in a given period of time, which reflects the speed of the turnover of working capital of industrial enterprises, and is calculated as follows:

Turnover of Current Assets= (sales revenue of products) / (average balance of total working capital)

In the above formula, average balance of total working capital refers to the arithmetic mean of the sum of working capital at the beginning and at the end of the reference period.

□ Ratio of Profits to Total Industrial Costs

Ratio of Profits to Total Industrial Costs refers to the ratio of profits realized in a given period to the total costs in the same period, which reflects the economic efficiency of input cost and is calculated as follows:

Ratio of Pre-tax Profits to Cost and Expenses (%)=(total profits/ total costs) × 100%

Total costs in the above formula is the sum of cost of products sold, marketing cost, management cost and financial cost.

□ Ratio of Sales to Gross Output Value

Ratio of Sales to Gross Output Value reflects the degree at which industrial products are sold. It helps to analyze the linkage between production and sales and the extent of the needs of the society that has been met by the supply of industrial products. It is calculated as follows:

Ratio of Sales to Gross Output Value= (Industrial sales / Gross industrial output value at current prices) × 100%

□ Capital Maintenance and Appreciation Rate

Capital Maintenance and Appreciation Rate reflects the changes of an enterprise's net assets. It epitomizes the growth capability of an enterprise. Its calculating formula is:

Capital maintenance and appreciation rate = Ownership equity at the end of the reporting period/Ownership equity at the same period of the previous year.

Ownership equity is the result of total assets minus total liabilities.

□ Overall Labour Productivity

Overall Labour Productivity is an indicator reflecting the production efficiency of an enterprise and the economic efficiency of its labour input, calculated by the formula:

Overall Labour Productivity (yuan/person)=industrial value-added/average of all persons engaged.

第十三篇

CHAPTER 13

建筑业

CONSTRUCTION

表 13.1 建筑业主要指标(1978~2007)
MAJOR INDICATORS OF CONSTRUCTION ENTERPRISES

年份 Year	年末从业人员（万人）Year-end Employees (10 000 persons)	总产值（亿元）Output Value (100 million yuan)	房屋竣工面积（万平方米）Floor Space of Building Completed (10 000 sq. m)	平均每个职工房屋竣工面积（平方米/人）Area of Completed Building for Every Staff and Worker (sq. m/person)	全员劳动生产率（按总产值计算）（元/人）Overall Labor Productivity (In Term of Output Value) (yuan/person)
1978	10.07	5.55	234.03	26.32	6 005
1979	23.35	13.98	564.62	26.10	6 226
1980	27.27	17.07	607.91	24.13	6 513
1981	30.21	18.03	649.93	22.28	5 941
1982	30.73	21.56	684.61	22.90	6 928
1983	33.35	24.64	736.34	22.46	7 189
1984	32.94	30.62	799.40	23.10	8 402
1985	33.35	36.73	819.24	23.78	10 070
1986	35.53	49.91	867.08	22.87	12 147
1987	35.83	59.45	872.25	22.66	14 455
1988	36.70	68.83	836.73	21.26	16 251
1989	34.43	74.75	758.34	19.70	18 053
1990	34.01	75.62	747.88	20.01	18 569
1991	34.62	84.30	775.63	20.14	21 022
1992	36.33	117.68	860.49	19.92	26 221
1993	36.90	193.00	1 144.16	26.10	44 020
1994	39.95	309.68	1 557.87	29.33	58 305
1995	41.10	391.42	1 485.87	25.44	67 023
1996	36.19	450.41	1 514.58	26.95	80 161
1997	37.40	564.37	1 777.41	29.60	93 995
1998	40.88	593.11	1 913.55	33.08	102 531
1999	39.01	573.06	1 950.76	33.86	99 473
2000	35.91	631.64	1 909.11	33.02	109 244
2001	35.52	730.33	2 434.73	39.55	118 641
2002	41.97	822.27	2 596.95	42.23	133 698
2003	50.52	1 195.80	3 609.20	71.44	153 910
2004	74.26	1 724.40	4 672.53	62.92	168 719
2005	72.23	1 889.25	5 648.85	78.21	182 299
2006	73.44	2 285.38	6 506.41	88.59	208 368
2007	69.33	2 524.18	6 090.22	87.84	228 710

注：本表从业人员是指本行业的全部从业人员。
Note: Employees in this table refer to all the employees in the sector.

表 13.2 建筑业主要指标（2007）
MAJOR INDICATORS OF CONSTRUCTION ENTERPRISES

类 别	Types	企业数（个）Number of Enterprises (unit)	年末从业人员（万人）Year-end Employees (10 000 persons)	竣工产值（亿元）Output Value of Construction Completed (100 million yuan)
总 计	**Total**	**2 784**	**69.33**	**1 570.97**
按登记注册类型分	**Grouped By Registration Categories**			
内 资	Domestic Investment	2 641	67.28	1 479.08
#国 有	State-owned	132	4.55	146.91
集 体	Collective Owned	128	2.85	51.14
股份合作	Stock-holding Cooperation	22	0.20	2.58
联 营	Joint Owned	23	0.27	6.16
有限责任公司	Companies with Limited Liabilition	585	23.73	643.53
股份有限公司	Stock-holding Companies Liabilities	44	3.45	170.78
私 营	Private	1 703	32.20	457.78
港澳台商投资	Hong Kong, Macao and Taiwan Funded	79	1.08	28.87
外商投资	Foreign Funded	64	0.98	63.01
按行业分	**By Sectors**			
房屋和土木工程建筑业	Housing Construction and Civil Engineering Industry	1 239	53.89	1 192.04
建筑安装业	Construction and Installation Industry	690	8.16	218.05
建筑装饰业	Construction and Decoration Industry	642	5.42	122.48
其他建筑业	Other Construction Industries	213	1.85	38.40
按资质标准分	**By Qualification Standard**			
#施工总承包	Chief Construction Contract	1 311	56.59	1 277.12
专业承包	Professional Contract	1 473	12.75	293.85

表 13.2 续表 1 continued

类 别	Types	总产值（亿元）Output Value (100 million yuan)	其中 of which #建筑工程 Construction	#安装工程 Installation
总 计	**Total**	**2 524.18**	**2 036.98**	**385.59**
按登记注册类型分	**Grouped By Registration Categories**			
内 资	Domestic Investment	2 374.62	1 930.89	365.60
#国 有	State-owned	231.07	184.65	39.63
集 体	Collective Owned	70.04	49.43	17.23
股份合作	Stock-holding Cooperation	3.83	2.01	1.75
联 营	Joint Owned	5.77	4.63	0.43
有限责任公司	Companies with Limited Liabilition	1 070.80	868.69	176.54
股份有限公司	Stock-holding Companies Liabilities	242.90	212.69	23.27
私 营	Private	750.01	608.60	106.74
港澳台商投资	Hong Kong, Macao and Taiwan Funded	52.77	47.31	4.36
外商投资	Foreign Funded	96.79	58.79	15.63
按行业分	**By Sectors**			
房屋和土木工程建筑业	Housing Construction and Civil Engineering Industry	1 959.75	1 763.25	143.77
建筑安装业	Construction and Installation Industry	300.47	59.56	227.55
建筑装饰业	Construction and Decoration Industry	203.72	194.17	7.56
其他建筑业	Other Construction Industries	60.23	20.00	6.72
按资质标准分	**By Qualification Standard**			
#施工总承包	Chief Construction Contract	2 081.96	1 752.29	271.75
专业承包	Professional Contract	442.22	284.69	113.85

表 13.2 续表 2 continued

类 别	Types	房屋建筑面积(万平方米) Floor Space of Buildings (10 000 sq. m) 施工面积 Under Construction	竣工面积 Completed	年末自有机械设备 Machines Owned (year-end) 总台数(万台) Number (10 000 units)	总功率(万千瓦) Capacity (10 000 kw)
总 计	**Total**	**16 040.51**	**6 090.22**	**15.63**	**309.96**
按登记注册类型分	**Grouped By Registration Categories**				
内 资	Domestic Investment	15 591.44	5 856.60	15.09	304.38
#国 有	State-owned	1 449.93	641.11	1.17	26.14
集 体	Collective Owned	645.12	328.48	0.73	6.64
股份合作	Stock-holding Cooperation	6.70	5.70	0.04	0.20
联 营	Joint Owned	33.70	15.85	0.07	1.61
有限责任公司	Companies with Limited Liabilition	5 224.69	1 724.78	5.25	148.23
股份有限公司	Stock-holding Companies Liabilities	2 487.12	721.15	0.57	36.55
私 营	Private	5 744.18	2 419.55	7.27	84.92
港澳台商投资	Hong Kong, Macao and Taiwan Funded	78.42	13.75	0.29	2.56
外商投资	Foreign Funded	370.66	219.88	0.26	3.02
按行业分	**By Sectors**				
房屋和土木工程建筑业	Housing Construction and Civil Engineering Industry	15 882.43	6 043.54	10.85	250.86
建筑安装业	Construction and Installation Industry	123.77	30.98	2.27	36.97
建筑装饰业	Construction and Decoration Industry	12.76	11.81	1.90	10.03
其他建筑业	Other Construction Industries	21.55	3.89	0.61	12.10
按资质标准分	**By Qualification Standard**				
#施工总承包	Chief Construction Contract	15 611.87	5 828.17	11.43	266.19
专业承包	Professional Contract	428.64	262.05	4.21	43.77

表 13.3 建筑业主要财务指标(2007)
MAJOR ACCOUNTING INDICATORS OF CONSTRUCTION ENTERPRISES

指　标	Indicators	合　计 Total	内　资 Domestic Investment
施工企业单位数（个）	Number of Construction Enterprises (unit)	2 784	2 641
固定资产原价（亿元）	Fixed Assets (Original Value) (100 million yuan)	385.25	371.26
固定资产净值（亿元）	Fixed Assets (Net Value) (100 million yuan)	214.76	207.08
自有机械设备台数（万台）	Machinery and Equipment (10 000 units)	15.63	15.09
自有机械设备净值（亿元）	Machinery and Equipment (Net Value) (100 million yuan)	97.22	95.85
自有机械设备总功率（万千瓦）	Capacity of Machinery and Equipment (10 000 kw)	309.96	304.38
总产值（亿元）	Output Value(100 million yuan)	2 524.18	2 374.62
资产合计（亿元）	Assets at Year-end (100 million yuan)	2 955.30	2 792.43
#流动资产	Total Current Assets	2 440.81	2 290.32
固定资产	Total Fixed Assets	249.52	240.56
无形及递延资产	Intangible and Defered Assets	31.08	30.58
负债合计（亿元）	Total Liabilities at Year-end (100 million yuan)	2 180.96	2 059.48
流动负债	Current Liabilities	2 127.03	2 007.52
长期负债	Long-term Liabilities	53.92	51.96
所有者权益（亿元）	Total Owners,Equity (100 million yuan)	774.34	732.95
企业总收入（亿元）	Total Revenue of Enterprises (100 million yuan)	2 948.07	2 775.46
工程结算收入	Revenue of Engineering Settlement Accounts	2 883.71	2 712.55
其他业务收入	Other Revenue	64.36	62.92
施工面积（万平方米）	Floor Space of Building Under Construction (10 000 sq m)	16 040.51	15 591.44
竣工面积（万平方米）	Floor Space of Building Completed (10 000 sq. m)	6 090.22	5 856.60
利润总额（亿元）	Total Profits (100 million yuan)	82.38	75.18
全员劳动生产率（元/人）（按总产值计算）	Overall Labor Productivity (yuan/person) (In Term of Output Value)	228 710	224 607
技术装备率（元/人）	Per Capita Machinery Value (yuan/person)	14 022	14 246
动力装备率（千瓦/人）	Per Capita Machinery Capacity (kw/person)	4.5	4.5
房屋建筑面积竣工率（%）	Rate of Buiding Completed (%)	38.0	37.6
产值利润率（%）	Ratio of Profit/Gross Output Value (%)	3.3	3.2
产值利税率（%）	Ratio of Profit and Taxes/Gross Output Value (%)	6.7	6.7

其中 of which					
国有 State-owned	集体 Collective-Owned	股份合作 Stock-holding Cooperation	联营 Joint Owned	有限责任公司 Companies With Limited Liabilition	股份有限公司 Stock-holding Companies Liabilities
132	128	22	23	585	44
30.53	6.28	0.48	0.88	179.41	55.45
17.66	3.78	0.30	0.48	92.97	27.10
1.17	0.73	0.04	0.07	5.25	0.57
7.69	0.96	0.02	0.17	43.65	20.62
26.14	6.64	0.20	1.61	148.23	36.55
231.07	70.04	3.83	5.77	1 070.80	242.90
292.04	85.77	4.10	6.87	1 306.29	272.46
225.03	75.63	3.65	5.78	1 065.39	206.87
20.31	6.76	0.42	0.50	106.47	31.92
4.59	0.24	0.00	0.09	19.79	1.92
225.24	65.78	2.83	4.58	1 028.89	196.67
216.76	62.12	2.83	4.57	1 002.92	191.13
8.49	3.66	0.00	0.02	25.97	5.54
66.80	19.99	1.27	2.29	277.40	75.79
306.35	77.16	4.19	6.39	1 269.51	355.77
297.54	76.17	4.16	6.33	1 227.70	352.93
8.81	0.99	0.03	0.06	41.80	2.84
1 449.93	645.12	6.70	33.70	5 224.69	2 487.12
641.11	328.48	5.70	15.85	1 724.78	721.15
5.21	1.02	0.07	0.16	40.93	7.06
201 311	174 163	146 454	138 065	290 218	243 777
16 876	3 357	784	6 220	18 398	59 760
5.7	2.3	1.0	5.8	6.2	10.6
44.2	50.9	85.1	47.0	33.0	29.0
2.3	1.5	1.7	2.7	3.8	2.9
6.0	5.3	4.6	5.6	7.4	7.2

表 13.3 续表 Continued

指标	Indicators	其中 of which 私营 Private	港澳台商投资 Hong Kong, Macao and Taiwan Funded	外商投资 Foreign Funded
施工企业单位数（个）	Number of Construction Enterprises (unit)	1 703	79	64
固定资产原价（亿元）	Fixed Assets (Original Value) (100 million yuan)	98.13	4.62	9.37
固定资产净值（亿元）	Fixed Assets (Net Value) (100 million yuan)	64.77	2.12	5.56
自有机械设备台数（万台）	Machinery and Equipment (10 000 units)	7.27	0.29	0.26
自有机械设备净值（亿元）	Machinery and Equipment (Net Value) (100 million yuan)	22.73	0.54	0.84
自有机械设备总功率（万千瓦）	Capacity of Machinery and Equipment (10 000 kw)	84.92	2.56	3.02
总产值（亿元）	Output Value(100 million yuan)	750.01	52.77	96.79
资产合计（亿元）	Assets at Year-end (100 million yuan)	824.22	42.93	119.94
#流动资产	Total Current Assets	707.34	37.41	113.09
固定资产	Total Fixed Assets	74.16	3.07	5.88
无形及递延资产	Intangible and Defered Assets	3.93	0.08	0.42
负债合计（亿元）	Total Liabilities at Year-end (100 million yuan)	535.21	27.60	93.88
流动负债	Current Liabilities	526.92	27.53	91.98
长期负债	Long-term Liabilities	8.28	0.07	1.90
所有者权益（亿元）	Total Owners, Equity (100 million yuan)	289.02	15.33	26.06
企业总收入（亿元）	Total Revenue of Enterprises (100 million yuan)	755.51	46.75	125.86
工程结算收入	Revenue of Engineering Settlement Accounts	747.14	46.59	124.58
其他业务收入	Other Revenue	8.38	0.16	1.28
施工面积（万平方米）	Floor Space of Building Under Construction (10 000 sq. m)	5 744.18	78.42	370.66
竣工面积（万平方米）	Floor Space of Building Completed (10 000 sq. m)	2 419.55	13.75	219.88
利润总额（亿元）	Total Profits (100 million yuan)	20.73	1.38	5.82
全员劳动生产率（元/人）（按总产值计算）	Overall Labor Productivity (yuan/person) (In Term of Output Value)	175 845	249 513	382 903
技术装备率（元/人）	Per Capita Machinery Value (yuan/person)	7 060	5 041	8 515
动力装备率（千瓦/人）	Per Capita Machinery Capacity (kw/person)	2.6	2.4	3.1
房屋建筑面积竣工率（%）	Rate of Buiding Completed (%)	42.1	17.5	59.3
产值利润率（%）	Ratio of Profit/Gross Output Value (%)	2.8	2.6	6.0
产值利税率（%）	Ratio of Profit and Taxes/Gross Output Value (%)	5.8	4.8	8.4

表 13.4 各区、县建筑业主要指标(2007)
MAIN CONSTRUCTION INDUSTRY STATISTICS OF DISTRICTS AND COUNTIES

地 区	District	企业数 (个) Number of Enterprises (unit)	年末从业人员 (万人) Year-end Employees (10 000 persons)	总产值 (亿元) Output Value (100 million yuan)
总 计	**Total**	**2 784**	**69.33**	**2 524.18**
浦东新区	Pudong New Area	389	13.41	473.02
黄 浦 区	Huangpu	129	1.97	122.02
卢 湾 区	Luwan	77	0.60	19.91
徐 汇 区	Xuhui	182	4.11	233.65
长 宁 区	Changning	139	2.09	95.09
静 安 区	Jing'an	103	1.01	54.26
普 陀 区	Putuo	175	3.66	138.35
闸 北 区	Zhabei	89	3.67	184.34
虹 口 区	Hongkou	174	5.76	203.05
杨 浦 区	Yangpu	189	3.75	121.72
宝 山 区	Baoshan	177	6.84	318.83
闵 行 区	Minhang	147	4.00	99.75
嘉 定 区	Jiading	121	2.49	52.15
金 山 区	Jinshan	114	2.92	60.75
松 江 区	Songjiang	144	3.99	81.98
青 浦 区	Qingpu	82	2.08	54.74
南 汇 区	Nanhui	134	2.40	99.25
奉 贤 区	Fengxian	184	3.13	73.25
崇 明 县	Chongming	35	1.45	38.06

表 13.4 续表 Continued

地 区	District	房屋建筑施工面积(万平方米) Floor Space of Buildings Under Construction (10 000 sq. m)	房屋建筑竣工面积(万平方米) Floor Space of Buildings Completed (10 000 sq. m)	其中 of which #住宅 Residence
总 计	**Total**	**16 040.51**	**6 090.22**	**2 558.70**
浦东新区	Pudong New Area	3 399.91	962.73	417.25
黄 浦 区	Huangpu	387.87	136.05	77.55
卢 湾 区	Luwan	111.67	39.36	7.90
徐 汇 区	Xuhui	477.87	140.06	78.07
长 宁 区	Changning	1 063.08	353.06	80.64
静 安 区	Jing'an	495.32	145.73	91.07
普 陀 区	Putuo	1 018.20	245.34	158.01
闸 北 区	Zhabei	481.33	156.50	74.01
虹 口 区	Hongkou	1 426.98	370.71	175.35
杨 浦 区	Yangpu	464.64	155.07	68.48
宝 山 区	Baoshan	1 553.45	855.97	226.17
闵 行 区	Minhang	941.13	391.53	213.50
嘉 定 区	Jiading	626.94	274.31	108.37
金 山 区	Jinshan	360.84	190.41	61.91
松 江 区	Songjiang	1 082.95	546.29	160.61
青 浦 区	Qingpu	499.12	303.12	106.99
南 汇 区	Nanhui	774.08	433.52	206.95
奉 贤 区	Fengxian	521.56	234.15	114.82
崇 明 县	Chongming	353.57	156.32	131.06

上 / 海 / 统 / 计 / 年 / 鉴

主要统计指标解释

建筑业总产值

建筑业总产值是以货币形式表现的建筑(安装)业企业在一定时期内生产的建筑业产品和提供的服务的总和。建筑业总产值包括:

(1)建筑工程产值: 指列入建筑工程预算内的各种工程价值。

(2)(设备)安装工程产值: 指设备安装工程价值,不包括被安装设备本身价值。

(3)其他产值:建筑业总产值中除建筑工程、安装工程以外的产值。包括房屋构筑物修理产值、非标准设备制造产值、总包企业向分包企业收取的管理费以及不能明确划分的施工活动所完成的产值。

a. 房屋构筑物修理产值: 指房屋和构筑物修理所完成的产值,但不包括被修理房屋、构筑物本身价值和生产设备的修理产值。

b. 非标准设备制造产值: 指加工制造没有定型的非标准生产设备的加工费和原材料价值(如化工厂、炼油厂用的各种罐、槽,矿井生产统一使用的各种漏斗、三角槽、阀门等) 以及附属加工厂为本企业承建工程制作的非标准设备的价值。

房屋建筑施工面积

指在报告期内施过工的全部房屋建筑面积, 包括本期新开工的房屋面积、上期施工跨入本期继续施工的房屋面积、上期停缓建在本期恢复施工的房屋面积、本期竣工的房屋面积及本期施工后又停缓建的房屋面积。

房屋建筑竣工面积

指在报告期内房屋建筑按照设计要求全部完工,达到了(住人和)使用条件,经验收鉴定合格,正式移交使用单位的房屋建筑面积。

年末自有机械设备总台数

指归本企业所有, 属于本企业固定资产的生产性机械设备年末总台数。包括施工机械、生产设备、运输设备以及其他设备。

年末自有机械设备总功率

指本企业自有施工机械、生产设备、运输设备以及其他设备等列为在册固定资产的生产性机械设备年末总功率,按设定能力或查定能力计算。包括机械本身的动力和为该机械服务的单独动力设备,如电动机等。计算单位用千瓦,动力换算可按 1 马力=0.735 千瓦折合成千瓦数。电焊机、变压器、锅炉不计算动力。

企业总收入

指与企业生产经营直接有关的各项收入, 包括工程结算收入和其他业务收入。计算公式为:

企业总收入 = 工程结算收入 + 其他业务收入

房屋建筑面积

指房屋建筑物勒脚以上外墙外围的水平截面面积,包括房屋建筑物的有效面积和结构面积。该指标是从实物形态上反映建设规模和建设成果的重要指标之一,也是检查工程形象进度、计算工程造价、分析投资效果、研究施工任务和建筑材料之间平衡情况的重要依据。

SHANGHAI STATISTICAL YEARBOOK

EXPLANATORY NOTES TO MAJOR STATISTICAL INDICATORS

□ Gross Output Value of Construction

Gross Output Value of Construction refers to total of construction products and services, expressed in money terms, produced or rendered by (completed by) construction and installation enterprises during a given period of time. It includes:

(1) Output value of construction projects, that is the value of projects covered by the project budgets;

(2) Output value of installation projects, that is the value of the installation of equipment, (excluding the value of the equipment to be installed);

(3) Output value of other projects refers to other output value of gross output value of construction industry besides construction and installation projects. It includes the output value of building repairing, nonstandard equipment manufacturing, the management fees going from subcontractor to original contractor and other construction output value which can not be measure off definitely.

a.Output value of repair of buildings and structures:the value created through the repairs of buildings or structures.It does not include the value of buildings or structures being repaired and the value of the repair of production equipment;

b.Output value of manufactured non-standard equipment:the value of non-standard production equipment,including raw materials and manufacturing cost,made for the construction project(i.e., chemical plant;kettles of tanks used by refineries;various fillers, triangle tanks,valves used by mines).It also includes the output value of equipment manufactured by subsidiary workshops.

□ Floor Space of Buildings Under Construction

Floor Space of Buildings Under Construction refers to floor space of buildings under construction during the reference period, including newly started buildings, buildings started earlier and continued during the reference period, and buildings suspended earlier but restarted during the reference period, buildings completed during the reference period, and buildings under construction and then suspended during the reference period.

□ Floor Space of Buildings Completed

Floor Space of Buildings Completed refers to the floor space of buildings that are completed in the reference period in accordance with the requirements of the design, up to the standard for putting them into use, and have been checked and accepted by concerned departments as qualified ones.

□ Total Number of Machinery and Equipment Owned by the End of Year

Total Number of Machinery and Equipment Owned by the End of Year refers to the number of machines and equipment owned by the enterprises, and listed as the fixed assets of the enterprises by the end of the year, including machinery and equipment for construction, production and transportation.

□ Total Capacity of Machinery and Equipment Owned by the End of Year

Total Capacity of Machinery and Equipment Owned by the End of Year refers to the total power of machinery and equipment owned by the enterprises, and listed as the fixed assets of the enterprises by the end of the year, including machinery and equipment for construction, production and transportation. The power of the machinery is calculated on basis of the designed or verified capacity, covering the power of the machinery/equipment and the separate power equipment serving the machinery/equipment (such as electric motors), but excluding welders, transformers and boilers. The unit used for the calculation of power is kilowatt, with horsepower converted to kilowatt by 1 horsepower=0.735 kilowatt.

□ Total Revenue of Enterprises

Total Revenue of Enterprises refers to the sum of income from production and operation of enterprises, including income from settlement of projects and other operational income, namely:

Total Revenue of Enterprises=Income from Settlement of Projects + Other Operational Income

□ Floor Space of Buildings

Floor Space of Buildings refers to total floor space of the horizontal section of outer walls above the plinth of the building, including the effective area and the area occupied by the structure. This indicator is one of the important indicators in physical terms to reflect the scale and accomplishment of the construction industry, and important basis for monitoring the progress, calculating the cost, analyzing the efficiency and studying the supply of building materials in relation with the construction projects.

第十四篇

CHAPTER 14

交通运输、邮政和信息传输

TRANSPORTATION, POSTS AND INFORMATION TRANSMISSION

表 14.1 主要年份运输线路长度
LENGTHS OF TRAFFIC LINES IN MAIN YEARS

指 标	Indicators	1990	2000	2006	2007
铁路运输	**Railway**				
运营里程(公里)	Operation Mileage (km)	259	257	269	281
正线延展里程(公里)	Mainline Railway Length Extended (km)	356	397	412	415
公路运输	**Highway**				
通车里程(公里)	Operation Mileage(km)	3 050	6 078	10 392	15 458
#高速公路	High Speed Highways	36	98	581	635
内河航道	Navigable Inland Waterways				
航道里程(公里)	Length of Navigable Inland Waterways (km)	2 100	2 100	2 110	2 110

表 14.2 主要年份交通运输主要指标
MAJOR INDICATORS OF TRANSPORTATION IN MAIN YEARS

指 标	Indicators	1990	2000	2006	2007
公路运输	**Highway Transportation**				
货运汽车每车吨年产量(万吨·公里)	Annual Tonnage of Each Ton-wagon (10 000 tons · km)	1.72	1.50	0.85	0.79
汽油车耗油 (升/百吨·公里)	Oil Consumption of Gasoline Trucks (litre/100 tons · km)	6.50	6.87	8.50	8.30
柴油车耗油 (升/百吨·公里)	Oil Consumption of Diesel Trucks (litre/100 tons · km)	4.00	4.77	6.60	7.53
港 口	**Harbor**				
船舶平均在港停泊时间 (天)	Average Days of Vessel Berthed at Harbor (day)	1.5	0.9	0.4	0.4
民用航空	**Civil Aviation**				
起降航班数(架次)	Aircraft Movements(sortie)			40.95	44.08
进出港旅客人次(万人次)	Passenger Turnover(10 000 person-times)			4 601.54	5 156.64
#国内航线	Domestic Flight			2 996.76	3 370.13
国际及地区航线	International and Regional Flight			1 604.78	1 786.51

注：本页数据由上海铁路局、市城市交通管理局、市港口管理局、上海机场集团、市航务管理处等单位提供。

Note: Data on this page are provided by Shanghai Railway Bureau, Shanghai Municipal Traffic Administrative Bureau, Shanghai Port Administrative Bureau, Shanghai Airport Group and Shanghai Navigation Administrative Department.

表 14.3 主要年份旅客发送量
PASSENGER DEPARTING IN MAIN YEARS

单位:万人次(10 000 person-times)

年份 Year	旅客发送量 Passenger Departures	其中 of which			
		铁路 Railway	公路 Highway	港口 Harbor	民用航空 Civil Aviation
1980	2 369	1 692	200	446	31
1985	3 434	2 320	410	622	82
1990	3 835	2 476	605	555	199
1995	5 265	2 929	1 257	512	567
1996	5 822	2 804	1 974	422	622
1997	6 057	2 779	2 277	328	673
1998	6 139	2 760	2 006	678	695
1999	6 406	2 906	2 178	581	741
2000	6 893	2 980	2 482	539	892
2001	6 324	3 231	1 508	543	1 042
2002	7 326	3 518	2 046	526	1 236
2003	7 212	3 391	2 052	528	1 241
2004	8 968	4 076	2 465	621	1 806
2005	9 487	4 313	2 468	626	2 080
2006	9 619	4 458	2 784	68	2 309
2007	10 371	4 795	2 872	95	2 609

①2000 年前旅客发送量是专业运输部门的数字，2001 年开始改为跨省市旅客运输的行业统计数字。
②港口旅客发送量从 2006 年起口径不包含海港到内河部分。
❶The passenger departures volume before 2000 is based on the figures for special traffic departments and the volume since 2001 is based on the figures for the inter-provincial passenger transport industries.
❷Starting from 2006, the volume of Passenger Departures excludes those from seaports to freshwater.

表 14.4 主要年份旅客周转量
TURNOVER VOLUME OF PASSENGER TRAFFIC IN MAIN YEARS

单位:亿人·公里 (100 million persons·km)

年份 Year	旅客周转量 Turnover Volume of Passenger Traffic	其中 of which			
		铁路 Railway	公路 Highway	水运 Waterway	民用航空 Civil Aviation
1980	49.31	15.67	1.24	32.39	
1985	87.20	24.30	4.32	44.63	13.95
1990	113.94	26.85	8.42	40.84	37.84
1995	170.98	34.18	8.23	31.71	96.86
1996	171.81	31.49	8.83	24.13	107.36
1997	181.99	31.44	12.61	16.52	121.42
1998	199.15	30.68	12.07	9.97	146.43
1999	217.95	34.18	15.81	7.94	160.02
2000	234.72	35.40	16.44	6.77	176.11
2001	286.93	37.81	42.31	5.48	201.30
2002	332.12	39.48	50.43	4.41	237.80
2003	353.62	38.10	58.00	4.65	252.88
2004	599.62	46.35	72.09	4.49	476.70
2005	663.93	48.86	75.06	4.52	535.48
2006	742.87	51.23	86.85	4.52	600.28
2007	883.25	51.34	94.02	6.10	731.79

注：本页数据由上海铁路局、市城市交通管理局、市港口管理局、上海机场集团、市航务管理处等单位提供。
Note: Data on this page are provided by Shanghai Railway Bureau, Shanghai Municipal Traffic Administrative Bureau, Shanghai Port Administrative Bureau, Shanghai Airport Group and Shanghai Navigation Administrative Department.

表 14.5　主要年份货物运输量
FREIGHT TRAFFIC VOLUME IN MAIN YEARS

单位:万吨(10 000 tons)

年份 Year	货物运输量 Freight Traffic Volume	其中 of which 铁路 Railway	公路 Highway	水运 Waterway	其中 of which #远洋运输 Ocean Shipping	民用航空 Civil Aviation
1980	20 037	4 484	7 284	8 267	1 098	2
1985	24 243	5 059	9 216	9 965	1 402	3
1990	22 848	1 257	8 714	12 864	2 246	13
1995	22 531	1 376	6 273	14 845	2 778	37
1996	40 928	1 320	25 023	14 544	3 594	41
1997	41 373	1 252	25 991	14 082	4 201	48
1998	42 090	1 152	26 352	14 529	4 844	57
1999	44 485	997	27 171	16 241	5 783	76
2000	47 954	1 055	28 369	18 442	7 022	88
2001	49 545	1 080	28 869	19 496	7 129	100
2002	54 196	1 131	29 759	23 174	7 210	132
2003	58 669	1 208	30 678	26 621	7 832	162
2004	63 180	1 284	31 554	30 148	8 603	194
2005	68 741	1 278	32 684	34 557	10 091	222
2006	72 616	1 223	33 799	37 342	11 766	253
2007	78 108	1 143	35 634	41 041	12 575	290

注：2005 年起民航货物吞吐量不包括旅客行李。
Note: The Freight transportation volume of civil aviation in 2005 doesnt include the freight transportation volume.

表 14.6　主要年份货物周转量
TURNOVER VOLUME OF FREIGHT TRAFFIC IN MAIN YEARS

单位:亿吨·公里(100 million tons·km)

年份 Year	货物周转量 Turnover Volume of Freight Traffic	其中 of which 铁路 Railway	公路 Highway	水运 Waterway	其中 of which #远洋运输 Ocean Shipping	民用航空 Civil Aviation
1980	1 487	87	8	1 392	778	
1985	2 015	102	11	1 902	1 072	
1990	3 359	111	11	3 236	1 957	1
1995	4 187	143	9	4 030	2 259	5
1996	3 814	133	49	3 627	2 721	5
1997	4 016	123	47	3 840	3 049	6
1998	4 838	117	49	4 665	3 794	7
1999	5 606	113	51	5 432	4 020	10
2000	6 620	122	56	6 430	5 285	12
2001	6 992	113	60	6 808	5 511	11
2002	7 472	100	65	7 295	5 674	12
2003	8 587	118	69	8 385	6 376	15
2004	10 036	42	71	9 899	7 486	24
2005	12 132	47	73	11 986	9 285	27
2006	13 837	55	80	13 683	10 817	19
2007	15 949	35	85	15 789	12 039	40

①2004 年起，上海铁路分局改为上海铁路局，货物周转量数据有所调整。
②2006 年民航货物周转量未包括中国货运航空公司的数据。
③本页数据由上海铁路局、市城市交通管理局、市港口管理局、上海机场集团、市航务管理处等单位提供。
❶Since 2004, Shanghai Railway Branch Bureau has been change into Shanghai Reailway Bureau, the turnover volume of freigh has been adjusted accordingly.
❷In 2006, the data of China Cargo Airlines wasn't included in the turnover volume of fright of aviotion.
❸Data on this page are provided by Shanghai Railway Bureau, Shanghai Municipal Traffic Administrative Bureau, Shanghai Port Administrative Bureau, Shanghai Airport Group and Shanghai Navigation Administrative Department.

表 14.7 主要年份港口码头情况 PORTS IN MAIN YEARS

年份 Year	码头长度（万米）Length of Harbor (10 000 m)	泊位（个）Berths (unit)	其中 of which #万吨级 10 000 Tonnage	其中 of which #集装箱泊位 Container Berths	港口货物吞吐量(万吨) Cargo at Ports Throughput (10 000 tons)	其中 of which 进港 Input	出港 Output
1980	1.28	92	46	2	8 483	5 800	2 683
1985	1.39	98	46	4	11 291	7 972	3 319
1990	1.77	122	64	7	13 959	9 461	4 498
1995	1.90	140	68	12	16 567	12 097	4 470
1996	1.90	138	69	12	16 402	11 947	4 455
1997	1.96	142	71	12	16 397	11 851	4 546
1998	7.58	1 108	109	13	16 388	11 839	4 549
1999	7.69	1 110	113	18	18 641	12 936	5 705
2000	7.64	1 098	111	18	20 440	13 791	6 649
2001	7.67	1 087	112	18	22 099	14 922	7 177
2002	7.92	1 096	115	20	26 384	17 444	8 940
2003	8.76	1 202	125	24	31 621	20 607	11 014
2004	8.90	1 198	123	24	37 896	24 113	13 783
2005	8.95	1 181	124	28	44 317	27 539	16 778
2006	9.16	1 140	131	32	53 748	34 598	19 151
2007	10.15	1 155	133	37	56 145	35 477	20 668

注：1997 年以前，码头长度、泊位为原港务局数据，从 1998 年后，为全港数据。

Note: Before 1997, the figures of length of harbor and berths were from the ports belonged Port Administration Bureau, and after 1998, they have been collected from all types of ports.

表 14.8 主要年份国际集装箱和外贸货物吞吐量 INTERNATIONAL CONTAINERS AND CARGO THROUGHPUT OF FOREIGN TRADE IN MAIN YEARS

年份 Year	国际标准集装箱吞吐量重量(万吨) Weight of International Containers (10 000 tons)	国际标准集装箱吞吐量(万 TEU) International Containers (10 000 TEU)	其中 of which 进港 Input	出港 Output	外贸货物吞吐量(万吨) Cargo Throughput of Foreign Trade (10 000 tons)	其中 of which 进港 Input	出港 Output
1980	23	3	1.6	1.4	1 791	1 360	431
1985	184	20	11	10	2 871	2 411	460
1990	446	46	22	23	2 593	1 869	724
1995	1 389	153	69	83	4 086	2 605	1 481
1996	1 785	197	92	105	4 136	2 681	1 454
1997	2 304	253	115	138	4 713	2 931	1 782
1998	2 766	307	141	166	4 904	3 024	1 879
1999	3 949	422	197	225	6 285	3 899	2 386
2000	5 170	561	266	295	7 633	4 549	3 084
2001	5 911	634	305	329	8 653	5 216	3 437
2002	7 822	861	414	447	10 609	6 349	4 260
2003	10 225	1 128	544	584	12 968	7 607	5 361
2004	13 294	1 455	700	756	15 836	9 091	6 745
2005	16 250	1 808	887	921	18 492	10 098	8 394
2006	19 595	2 172	1 064	1 108	21 268	10 987	10 281
2007	23 850	2 615	1 276	1 339	25 570	12 860	12 709

①TEU 是“折合 20 英尺标准箱”英文缩写语。

②本页数据市港口管理局提供。

❶TEU is the abbreviation, which refers to 20-foot equivalent unit.

❷Data on this page are proviaed by Shanghai port Admintraive Bureau.

表 14.9 车辆拥有量(2005～2007)
MOTOR VEHICLES

单位:万辆(10 000 vehicles)

指 标	Indicators	2005	2006	2007
总 计	**Total**	**221.74**	**238.13**	**253.6**
# 汽 车	Civil Automobile	95.15	107.04	119.7
载客汽车	Passenger Vehicles	76.00	87.06	98.92
# 轿 车	Cars	53.59	62.81	72.81
载货汽车	Freight Trucks	19.16	19.98	20.78
摩托车	Motorcycle	120.42	124.15	125.97
农用运输车	Farm Vehicles	0.17	0.18	0.19
拖拉机	Tractors	1.24	1.22	1.15

注：本表不包括军用车辆和码头、机场等专用特种车辆。
Note: This table doestn't include the quantity of military vehicles and special vehicles for port and airport.

表 14.10 个人车辆拥有量 (2005～2007)
INDIVIDUAL MOTOR VEHICLES

单位:万辆(10 000 vehicles)

指 标	Indicators	2005	2006	2007
总 计	**Total**	**157.65**	**171.23**	**183.66**
# 汽 车	Civil Automobile	41.00	50.94	61.29
载客汽车	Passenger Vehicles	41.00	50.91	61.25
# 轿 车	Cars	32.21	40.95	50.15
载货汽车	Freight Trucks	0.04	0.03	0.04
摩托车	Motorcycle	116.52	120.13	122.2
农用运输车	Farm Vehicles	0.14	0.16	0.17

①本页数据由上海市公安局车管所提供，拖拉机数据由市农机办提供。
②2006 年、2007 年个人车辆拥有量不包括拖拉机。
❶Data on this page are provided by Shanghai Land-carriage Administration and the data of tractors are provided by Crivil Agricultural Engineering Office.
❷The data of individual civil motor vehicles doesn't include tractors in 2006 and 2007.

表 14.11　主要年份邮政电信情况
POST AND TELECOMMUNICATION IN MAIN YEARS

	指　标 Indicators	1990	2000	2006	2007
邮电局、所(个)	Post Office (unit)	535	580	649	638
报刊图书销售点(个)	Publications Sales Outlet (unit)	346	3 212	2 330	2 195
邮政信筒信箱(个)	Mail Boxe (unit)	3 914	4 224	3 842	3 778
集邮品销售点(个)	Stamps Sales Outlet (unit)	203	296	351	356
邮政储蓄网点(个)	Postal Savings Office (unit)	271	422	440	444
邮路条数(条)	Number of Mail Route (route)	427	638	768	883
邮路总长度(万公里)	Total Length of Mail Routes (10 000 km)	16.10	21.17	18.97	25.25
农村投递路线总长度(万公里)	Length of Rural Delivery Routes (10 000 km)	2.30	2.73	3.00	3.04
长途电话业务电路(2M)	Long Distance Call Line (2M)			94 818	178 337
长途光缆线路长度(公里)	Long-distance Cable (km)		1 770	3 042	2 973

注：本表数据由市邮政局、市通信管理局提供。
Note: Data in this table are provided by Shanghai Municipal Post Bureau and Shanghai Communications Administration.

表 14.12　主要年份邮政业务主要指标
MAJOR INDICATORS OF POSTAL BUSINESS IN MAIN YEARS

	指　标 Indicators	1990	2000	2006	2007
邮政业务总量(亿元)	Volume of Postal Business (100 million yuan)		22.40	43.59	47.48
函　件(亿件)	Mails (100 million units)	2.96	4.61	10.36	11.17
国内特快专递(万件)	Domestic Express Mails (10 000 pieces)	33.00	709.90	1 930.10	2 444.00
国际特快专递(万件)	International Express Mails (10 000 pieces)	15.00	52.10	182.30	222.00
邮政储蓄期末余额(亿元)	Postal Saving Deposit Balance (100 million yuan)	10.98	153.50	522.90	540.00
报纸、杂志累计订销数(亿份)	Total Copies of Newspapers and Magazines Subscribed and Sold (100 million pieces)	8.71	11.30	12.45	11.98
集邮业务(万枚)	Stamp Collection Business (10 000 stamps)	5 132	9 467	3 560	3 655

注：本表数据由市邮政局提供。
Note: Data in this table are provided by Shanghai Municipal Post Bureau.

表 14.13 电信业务主要指标（2004～2007）
MAJOR INDICATORS OF TELECOM BUSINESS

指 标	Indicators	2004	2005	2006	2007
电信业务总量(亿元)	Volume of Telecom Business (100 million yuan)	311.20	375.77	511.41	668.00
年末固定电话用户（万户）	Year-end Installed Telephones (10 000 households)	868	997	1 112	1 022
#住宅电话	Household Phones Installed	542	685	738	669
移动电话用户（万户）	Mobile Phone Subscribers Users (10 000 households)	1 311	1 444	1 610	1 777
全年长途通话时长（亿分钟）	Long-distance Call Lasting Time (100 million minutes)	100.7	110.0	151	189.8
#固定电话长途通话时长	Installed Telephone Domestic Long-distance Call Lasting Time	32.8	31.2	32.6	36.4
#固定电话国内长途电话通话量	Domestic Trunk Calls	31.5	30.0	31.2	34.8
固定电话国际及港澳台电话通话量	Overseas Calls	1.3	1.3	1.4	1.6
移动电话长途通话时长	Mobile Telephone Long-distance Call Lasting Time	20.4	19.6	27.2	40.1
IP 电话通话时长	IP Telephone Long-distance Call Lasting Time	47.5	59.2	91.6	113.3
移动电话通话时长（亿分钟）	Mobile Calls (100 million minutes)	223.20	290.1	453.4	661.6
#本地通话时长	Local Calls	202.80	270.5	426.2	621.5
数字数据用户（万户）	Digital and Data Users (10 000 households)	2.5	2.4	1.8	1.7
局用交换机容量（含接入网设备容量）（万门）	Capacity of Office Telephone Exchanges (Including Access Network Capacity) (10 000 units)	912	1 357	1 391	1 455

注：本表数据由市信息化委员会、市通信管理局提供。
Note: Data in this table are provided by Shanghai Municipal Information Commission and Shanghai Communications Administration.

表 14.14　邮电通信水平(2004 ~ 2007)
POSTAL AND TELECOM LEVEL

	指　标 Indicators	2004	2005	2006	2007
固定电话普及率（%）*	Popularity Rate of Telephone Line（%）	49.8	56.1	61.3	55.0
住宅电话普及率（%）	Popularity Rate of Household Telephone（%）	110.5	137.9	147.7	133.0
平均每一邮政局所服务面积（平方公里）	Average Area Served by One Post Office (sq. km)	10.3	10.0	9.8	9.9
平均每一邮政局所服务人口（万人）	Average Population Served by Every Post Office (10 000 persons)	2.20	2.10	2.11	2.16
人均每年发函件数(件)	Average Number of Letters Mailed (piece)	44	52	57	60
人均每年购报刊数(份)	Average Number of Newspaper and Magazine Purchased (piece)	98	91	91	87
移动电话普及率(%)	Popularity Rate of Mobile Telephone(%)	75.3	81.0	88.7	95.6

注：本表数据由市通信管理局提供。
Note: Data in this table are provided by Shanghai Communications Administration.

表 14.15　信息化基础设施情况(2004 ~ 2007)
INFRASTRUCTURE OF INFORMATIZATION

	指　标 Indicators	2004	2005	2006	2007
长途光缆线路长度(公里)	Long-distance Cable (km)	4 603	5 141	3 042	2 973
信息通信管线长度(沟公里)	Length of Information Communication Pielines (channel km)	1 255	1 621	2 451	3 131
卫星站点(个)	Satellite Station (unit)	917	925	831	805
互联网国际出口宽带(千兆比特每秒)	Wide Band of Internet (Gbps)	18.5	30	40	72
本地信息交互流量(万亿字节)	Local Information Exchange Flow (TB)	1 330	1 300	2 113	2 188
有线电视双向改造用户数(万户)	Users of CATV Bil-rebuilding (10 000 households)	172.89	185.66	200.3	210.81
国际互联网用户(万人)	Users of Internet (10 000 persons)	633	803	957	1 080
互联网用户普及率(%)	Users of Internet per Thousand People (%)	37.0	45.2	52.7	58.1
家庭宽带接入用户(万户)	Users of Wide Band for Public (10 000 household)	142.94	222.66	301.60	327.60
家庭宽带接入用户普及率(%)	Users of Wide Band for Public per Hundred Household (%)	23.4	33.8	44.9	47.6

注：本表数据由市信息化委员会提供。
Note: Data in this table is provided by Shanghai Municipal Information Commissiom.

表 14.16 信息服务业经营情况(2005~2007)
OPERATION OF INFORMATION SERVICE INDUSTRY

指　标	Indicators	2005	2006	2007
信息服务业经营收入(亿元)	Operating Revenue of Information Service Industry (100 million yuan)	905.06	1 036.21	1 294.44
#计算机服务及软件业	Computer Service & Software Industry	390.09	478.75	655.19
信息服务业从业人员(万人)	Employees of Information Service Industry (10 000 persons)	18.81	21.03	24.45
#计算机服务及软件业	Computer Service & Software Industry	12.7	14.69	17.34

注：本表数据由市信息化委员会提供。
Note: Data in this table is provided by Shanghai Municipal Information Commissiom.

表 14.17 信息技术应用(2006~2007)
APPLICATION OF INFORMATION TECHNOLOGY

指　标	Indicators	2006	2007
社会公共服务领域信息化	**Informatization of Public Service**		
"市民信箱"累计注册用户(万人)	Accumulative Registered Users of Citizen Mail Box (10 000 persons)	124.26	332.93
"付费通"业务平台交易量(万笔)	All-year Exchange Volum of FFT (10 000 units)	1 976.48	2 907
"付费通"业务平台交易额(亿元)	All-year Exchange Value of FFT (100 million yuan)	16.23	24.69
社保卡累计发放量(万张)	Accumulative Volum of Social Insurance Card (10 000 pieces)	1 004.32	1 112.23
交通卡累计销售量(万张)	Accumulative Volum of Traffic Card (10 000 pieces)	2 568.06	3 240.64
交通卡销售额(亿元)	All-year Sales Value of Traffic Card (100 million yuan)	10.06	11.66
银行卡累计发卡量(万张)	Accumulative Volum of Bank Card (10 000 pieces)	5 610.89	6 781.64
银行卡交易额(亿元)	All-year Exchange Value of Bank Card (100 million yuan)	3 666.19	5 996.81
#持卡消费金额	Consumption Value with Bank Card	1 793.7	2 852.56
社会信用体系	**Social Credit System**		
个人信用信息入库量(万条)	Newly Recorded Individual Credit Information (10 000 pieces)	770	929
个人信用报告累计出具数量(万份)	Accumulative Provided Volum of Individual Credit Information Report (10 000 pieces)	643	780
企业信用信息入库量(万家)	Newly Recorded Enterprise Credit Information (10 000 untis)	60	98

注：本表数据由市信息化委员会提供。
Note: Data in this table is provided by Shanghai Municipal Information Commissiom.

表 14.18 电子商务(2006~2007)
ELECTRONIC COMMERCE

指　标	Indicators	2006	2007
电子商务交易额(亿元)	Trade Value of E-commerce (100 million yuan)	2 087.4	2 426.2
累计发放数字证书(万张)	Accumulative Granted Digital Certificate (10 000 pieces)	71.8	106.5

上 / 海 / 统 / 计 / 年 / 鉴

主要统计指标解释

铁路运营里程

铁路运营里程又称营业长度（包括正式营业和临时营业里程），指办理客货运输业务的铁路正线总长度。凡是全线或部分建成双线及以上的线路，以第一线的实际长度计算；复线、站线、段管线、岔线和特殊用途线以及不计算运费的联络线都不计算营业里程。铁路营业里程是反映铁路运输业基础设施发展水平的重要指标，也是计算客货周转量、运输密度和机车车辆运用效率等指标的基础资料。

内河航道里程

内河航道里程也称内河通航里程，指在一定时期内，能通航运输船舶及排筏的天然河流、湖泊水库、运河及通航渠道的长度。包括全年季节性通航累计三个月以上的航道，不包括仅供零散流放竹、木排的河道。该指标可以反映内河水运网的规模、水平和发展情况。

货物（旅客）周转量

指在一定时期内，由各种运输工具运送的货物（旅客）数量与其相应运输距离的乘积之总和，是反映运输业生产总成果的重要指标，也是编制和检查运输生产计划，计算运输效益、劳动生产率以及核算运输单位成本的主要基础资料。通常以吨公里和人公里为计算单位。计算货物周转量通常按发出站与到达站之间的最短距离，也就是计费距离计算。

货（客）运量

指在一定时期内，各种运输工具实际运送的货物（旅客）数量。它是反映运输业为国民经济和人民生活服务的数量指标，也是制定和检查运输生产计划、研究运输发展规模和速度的重要指标。货运按吨计算，客运按人计算。货物不论运输距离长短、货物类别，均按实际重量统计。旅客不论行程远近或票价多少，均按一人一次客运量统计；半价票、小孩票也按一人统计。

港口货物吞吐量

指经水运进出港区范围，并经过装卸的货物数量，包括邮件及办理托运手续的行李、包裹以及补给运输船舶的燃、物料和淡水。货物吞吐量按货物流向分为进口、出口吞吐量，按货物交流性质分为外贸货物吞吐量和国内贸易货物吞吐量。货物吞吐量的货类构成及其流向，是衡量港口生产能力大小的重要指标。

国际标准集装箱吞吐量

凡经过水运进、出港区范围，并经过装卸的集装箱箱数和重量（含集装箱自重），通常是按进港和出港分别统计。

TEU是“折合20英尺标准箱”的英文缩写。它是指各种尺寸的国际标准集装箱的自然箱数，按各自的换算比例，折算为20英尺标准箱的换算箱数。其换算比例为：40英尺箱1∶2；35英尺箱1∶1.75；20英尺箱1∶1；10英尺箱1∶0.5。

车辆拥有量

指报告期末，在公安交通管理部门按照《机动车注册登记工作规范》，已注册登记领有民用车辆牌照的全部汽车数量。汽车拥有量统计的主要分类：根据汽车结构分为载客汽车、载货汽车及其他汽车；根据汽车所有者不同分为个人（私人）汽车、单位汽车；根据汽车的使用性质分为营运汽车、非营运汽车和特种汽车；根据汽车大小规格不同载客汽车分为大型、中型、小型和微型，载货汽车分为重型、中型、轻型和微型。

邮政业务总量

指以货币表现的邮政部门用于邮政服务的总数量。它综合反映了一定时期邮政工作的总成果，是研究邮政业务量构成和发展趋势的重要指标。它用各种邮政分类业务量，如函件件数、电报份数、订销报刊累计份数等，分别乘以相应的平均单位（不变价），加总后再加上其他业务收入求得。

住宅电话用户

指安装在居民住宅或农民家里并按照住宅电话用户登记注册和收费的电话用户。包括私人付费、单位付费和按规定免费安装的住宅电话用户。

移动电话用户

指通过移动电话交换机进入移动电话网、占用移动

主要统计指标解释

电话号码的电话用户。用户数量以报告期末在移动电话营业部门实际办理登记手续进入移动电话网的户数进行计算，一部移动电话统计为一户。

数字数据用户 (DDN)

指在 DDN 数据通信网上接通的，在邮电部门办理登记手续的数据传输用户。

局用交换机容量

指安装在电信企业用于接续本地固定电话的电话交换机容量。

SHANGHAI STATISTICAL YEARBOOK

EXPLANATORY NOTES TO MAJOR STATISTICAL INDICATORS

□ Operation Mileage of Railways

Operation Mileage of Railways refers to the total length of the trunk line under passenger and freight transportation (including both full operation and temporary operation). The calculation is based on the actual length of the first line even if this line has a full or partial double track or more tracks, excluding double tracks, station sidings, tracks under the charge of stations, branch lines, special-purpose lines and the non-payable connecting lines. The length of railways in operation is an important indicator to show the development of the infrastructure for the railway transport, and also the essential data to calculate volume of passenger freight transport, traffic density and utilization efficiency of the locomotives and carriages.

□ Length of Navigable Inland Waterways

Length of Navigable Inland Waterways it is an indicator reflecting the size and development of inland water network, it refers to the length of the natural rivers, lakes, reservoirs, canals, and ditches open to navigation during a given period, which enables the transport by ships and rafts. It includes the channels open to navigation for over an accumulative 3 months in a year, yet this does not include the river courses, which are only used to float odd logs and bamboo rafts. This indicator can reflect the scale, level and development situation of the inland waterway network.

□ Freight (Passenger) Turnover Volume

Freight (Passenger) Turnover Volume refers to the total of the product of the physical volume of transported cargo (passengers) by the transport distance, usually using ton/kilometer and person/kilometer as calculating units. Normally, the shortest distance between the departure point and the destination is the basis to calculate the freight turnover volume, that is to say, the payable distance. This is an important indicator to show the total results of the transport industry, to prepare and examine the transport plan and to measure the efficiency, the labor productivity and the unit cost of transport.

□ Freight (Passenger) Traffic

Freight (Passenger) Traffic refers to the volume of freight (passenger) transported with various means. The freight (passenger) traffic provides a quantitative measure to show how the transport industry serves the national economy and people, and is also an important indicator for planning the transport industry and for studying the development scale and speed of the transport industry. Freight transport is calculated in tons and passenger traffic is calculated in the number of persons. Despite the type of freight and travelling distance, the freight transport is calculated in the actual weight of the goods: and despite the travelling distance and ticket price, the passenger traffic is calculated by the principle that one person can be counted only once in one travel. The passenger who travels with a half price ticket or a child ticket is also calculated as one person.

□ Volume of Freight Handled in Ports

Volume of Freight Handled in Ports refers to the volume of cargo passing in and out the harbor area of the ports and having been loaded and unloaded. The volume includes that of the postal matters, registered luggage and fuels, materials and fresh water as supplies of the ships. The volume of freight handled may be classified by direction of flow as freight for import and freight for export, or by nature of cargo as freight for domestic trade and freight for foreign trade. As an important indicator, the volume of freight handled by type of cargo and by main flow direction reflects the production capacity of ports.

□ InternationalContainerThroughputCapacity

International Container Throughput Capacity refers to number and weight of containers which are loaded or unloaded within port area via water carriage. It is often calculated by entering and leaving port, respectively. TEU was the abbreviation of twenty foot equivalent unit, which refers to converted number of all kinds of containers. The conversion method is based on respective conversion ratio and the number of all kinds of container is converted to the standard number of twenty foot equivalent unit. The conversion ratio is: 40 feet container 1 ∶ 2, 35 feet container 1 ∶ 1.75, 20 feet container 1 ∶ 1, 10 feet container 1 ∶ 0.5.

□ Motor Vehicles

Motor Vehicles refers to the total numbers of vehicles that are registered and received vehicles' license tags according to the

EXPLANATORY NOTES TO MAJOR STATISTICAL INDICATORS

Work Standard for Motor Vehicles Registration formulated by transport management office under department of public security at the end of reference period. They are divided into following categories according to the structure of motor vehicles: passenger vehicles, trucks and others; and private vehicles and vehicles for units use according to ownerships; working vehicles, non–working vehicles and special motor vehicles according to kind of usage; large passenger vehicles, medium passenger vehicles and small passenger vehicles, heavy trucks, light –heavy trucks and light trucks according to sizes of vehicles.

□ Volume of Post Business

Volume of Post Business refers to the total amount of post services provided by the post department, which reflects the total achievements by the post departments during a given period of time in a comprehensive way, and is an important indicator to study the composition and development of the post business. It is arrived by first multiplying the business volume of different types, such as number of letters, telegrams and accumulated number of newspaper and journals subscribed and sold, etc. by their respective average unit price (fixed price) and then adding these products together, plus the income from other business revenues.

□ Household Telephone Subscribers

Household Telephone Subscribers refer to telephone sets installed in the dwelling units of urban or rural residents, and registered as residence subscribers for payment, including 3 types of payment for the service: private payment, public payment and free service.

□ Mobile Phone Subscribers

Mobile Phone Subscribers refer to the persons who own mobile telephone numbers and are connected with the mobile telephone communication network through the mobile telephone switchboards. The number of subscribers is calculated by the subscribers who have completed registration at mobile communication business centers and entered into the mobile telephone network. One mobile telephone is taken as a user.

□ Digital and Data Users

Digital and Data Users refer to the data transmission users who log to the DDN data telecommunications network and have registered with the post and telecommunications authority.

□ Capacity of Office Telephone Exchanges

Capacity of Office Telephone Exchanges refers to the capacity of telephone exchanges installed in the office of telecommunication service providers for communication between fixed telephones.

第十五篇

CHAPTER 15

批发和零售

WHOLESALEAND RETAIL

表 15.1 批发零售贸易业、餐饮业从业人员(1978~2007)
EMPLOYEES OF WHOLESALES, RETAILERS AND CATERING

年 份 Year	从业人员 (万人) Employees (10 000 persons)	其中 of which 批发零售贸易业 Wholesale and Retail	其中 of which 批发业 Wholesale	零售业 Retail	餐饮业 Catering
1978	39.62	30.70	5.46	25.24	5.57
1979	44.70	32.94	7.87	25.07	5.82
1980	45.78	33.94	7.91	26.03	5.66
1981	48.47	35.31	8.41	26.90	6.25
1982	50.24	36.70	9.05	27.65	6.51
1983	51.30	37.64	8.86	28.78	6.51
1984	55.24	40.57	8.81	31.76	6.86
1985	62.64	45.41	8.99	36.42	7.66
1986	63.76	44.98	8.96	36.02	7.97
1987	66.13	45.98	8.85	37.13	8.18
1988	72.80	50.89	9.42	41.47	8.67
1989	77.31	52.20	9.67	42.53	9.35
1990	74.75	50.48	8.19	42.29	9.33
1991	75.41	52.47	8.53	43.94	10.71
1992	87.27	63.71	13.74	49.97	10.98
1993	109.98	98.44	29.68	68.76	11.54
1994	88.51	77.49	27.58	49.91	11.02
1995	111.24	94.78	34.31	60.47	16.46
1996	145.67	122.21	50.79	71.42	23.46
1997	149.97	125.64	53.68	71.96	24.33
1998	150.96	126.56	53.67	72.89	24.40
1999	153.90	128.18	53.93	74.25	25.72
2000	154.32	128.41	53.79	74.62	25.91
2001	165.68	138.73	56.33	82.40	26.95
2002	179.34	152.19	65.40	86.79	27.15
2003	174.93	147.91	59.31	88.60	27.02
2004	181.25	156.21	74.77	81.44	25.04
2005	195.92	169.60	84.71	84.89	26.32
2006	203.51	174.49	86.32	88.17	29.02
2007	204.46	175.50	86.23	89.27	28.96

注：本表从业人员是指本行业的全部从业人员。
Note: Employees in this table refer to all the employees in the sector.

表 15.2 限额以上批发贸易业产业活动单位和从业人员(2007)
NUMBER OF BUSINESS UNITS AND EMPLOYEES OF WHOLESALE TRADE ABOVE THE SET SCALE

类别	Types	法人企业(个) Number of Corporations (unit)	产业活动单位数(个) Number of Business Units (unit)	从业人员(人) Number of Employees (person)
总计	**Total**	**2 365**	**4 485**	**180 383**
按登记注册类型分	**Grouped by Registration Categories**			
内资企业	Domestic Enterprises	1 889	3 885	119 248
国有	State-owned	194	406	16 376
集体	Collective-owned	69	190	3 514
私营	Private	1 172	1 760	43 753
股份制公司	Share Holding	34	367	15 226
其他内资	Others	420	1 162	40 379
外商投资	Foreign Funded	352	458	45 920
港澳台商投资	Hong Kong, Macao and Taiwan Funded	124	142	15 215
按行业分	**Grouped By Sectors**			
农畜产品批发	Primary and Livestock Products	25	59	1 540
食品、饮料及烟草制品批发	Food, Beverage and Tabacco	189	995	24 826
#米、面制品及食用油批发	Rice, Flour and Cooking Oil	32	102	3 351
烟草制品批发	Tabacco	26	596	8 170
纺织、服装及日用品批发	Textile Products, Gaments and Commodity	301	367	29 916
#服装批发	Garments	101	133	10 868
文化、体育用品及器材批发	Culture & Sports Articles and Equipments	59	283	7 290
医药及医疗器材批发	Medicines and Special Appliances of Medicines	120	339	22 128
矿产品、建材及化工产品批发	Mineral Products, Materials of Construction and Chemical Products	773	1 268	32 284
#煤炭及制品批发	Coal	42	49	2 214
石油及制品批发	Petroleum	80	274	7 716
金属及金属矿批发	Metal Products and Metal Minerals	340	428	10 163
建材批发	Building Materials	63	94	4 411
机械设备、五金交电及电子产品批发	Mechinery Equipments, Hardwares, Electric Appliances and Eletronic Products	549	721	39 545
#汽车、摩托车及零配件批发	Spare and Component Parts for Automobiles and Motorcycles	67	96	4 892
家用电器批发	Household Electrical Equipment	40	48	3 682
计算机、软件及辅助设备批发	Computers, Softwares and Accessorial Equipments	76	117	5 632
贸易经济与代理	Economic Trade and Agency	42	46	1 429
其他批发	Others	307	407	21 425

表 15.3 限额以上零售贸易业产业活动单位和从业人员（2007）
NUMBER OF BUSINESS UNITS AND EMPLOYEES OF RETAIL TRADE ABOVE THE SET SCALE

类别	Types	法人企业（个）Number of Corporations (unit)	产业活动单位数（个）Number of Business Units (unit)	从业人员（人）Number of Employees (person)
总　计	**Total**	**1 180**	**12 483**	**287 533**
按登记注册类型分	**Grouped by Registration Categories**			
内资企业	Domestic Investment Enterprises	1 102	11 702	241 161
国　有	State-owned	118	696	9 745
集　体	Collective-owned	94	535	6 778
私　营	Private	509	1 121	33 898
股份制公司	Share Holding	36	1 258	70 251
其他内资	Others	345	8 092	120 489
外商投资	Foreign Funded	46	531	36 594
港澳台商投资	Hong Kong, Macao and Taiwan Funded	32	250	9 778
按行业分	**Grouped By Sectors**			
综合零售业	Comprehensive Retail Sale	240	6 594	199 417
#百货零售	Articles For Daily Use	90	224	19 991
超级市场零售	Retail Sale of Supermarket	103	1 856	145 132
食品、饮料及烟草制品专门零售	Food, Beverage and Tabacco	93	513	6 639
纺织、服装及日用品专门零售	Textile, Garments and Articles for Daily Use	87	499	14 704
#服装零售	Garments	34	137	764
文化、体育用品及器材专门零售	Culture & Sports Articles and Equipments	66	1 910	8 222
#体育用品零售	Sports Articles	4	43	1 353
图书零售	Books	12	44	1 490
医药及医疗器材专门零售	Medicines and Special Appliances of Medicines	65	1 246	8 504
#药品零售	Medicine	59	1 235	8 273
汽车、摩托车、燃料及零配件专门零售	Automobiles, Motocycles, Fuels and Their Parts	374	877	23 748
#汽车零售	Automobiles	191	220	13 140
机动车燃料零售	Fuels of Power-Vehicles	154	612	9 210
家用电器及电子产品专门零售	Household Electrical Appliances and Electronic Products	97	397	14 827
#家用电器零售	Household Electrical Appliances and Electronic Products	31	197	9 631
计算机、软件及辅助设备零售	Computers, Softwares and Accessorial Equipments	42	134	3 159
通信设备零售	Telecommunication Appliances	14	53	1 754
五金、家具及室内装修材料专门零售	Hardwares, Furnitures and Materials of Decoration	81	249	7 323
无店铺及其他零售	No-Shop and Others	77	198	4 149
#邮购及电子销售	Mail Orders and Electronic Sales	3	3	675

表 15.4 社会消费品零售总额(1978～2007)
TOTAL RETAIL SALES OF CONSUMER GOODS

单位:亿元 (100 million yuan)

年 份 Year	社会消费品零售总额 Total Retail Sales of Consumer Goods	按商品用途分 by use 食品类 Foods	衣着类 Clothing	用品类 Articles	燃料类 Fuels
1978	54.10	26.51	11.60	15.16	0.83
1979	68.28	30.05	16.07	21.28	0.88
1980	80.43	34.30	19.75	25.44	0.94
1981	88.73	38.78	21.27	27.73	0.95
1982	89.80	40.72	19.57	28.52	0.99
1983	100.68	44.20	22.31	33.18	0.99
1984	123.72	50.18	27.71	44.81	1.02
1985	173.39	64.08	35.51	72.70	1.10
1986	196.84	76.99	39.38	79.31	1.16
1987	225.25	91.01	42.52	90.41	1.31
1988	295.83	119.36	53.66	121.17	1.64
1989	331.38	140.03	51.95	137.70	1.70
1990	333.86	142.15	52.33	137.23	2.15
1991	382.06	162.82	52.91	163.30	3.03
1992	464.82	190.70	67.04	202.83	4.25
1993	675.92	259.93	101.30	309.26	5.43
1994	834.76	325.44	123.89	378.86	6.57
1995	1 050.96	407.44	153.74	481.96	7.82
1996	1 258.00	490.97	178.80	579.12	9.11
1997	1 435.38	564.62	200.62	659.61	10.53
1998	1 593.27	640.84	212.85	728.22	11.36
1999	1 722.33	694.03	228.18	787.62	12.50
2000	1 865.28	743.31	248.94	858.33	14.70
2001	2 016.37	802.53	266.31	931.02	16.51
2002	2 203.89	874.76	289.43	1 021.84	17.85
2003	2 404.45	939.29	309.70	1 135.27	20.19
2004	2 656.91	1 043.26	341.28	1 247.39	24.98
2005	2 972.97	1 172.05	381.31	1 388.32	31.29
2006	3 360.41	1 328.30	425.70	1 566.55	39.86
2007	3 847.79	1 524.23	476.65	1 796.05	50.86

表 15.4 续表 1 continued

单位:亿元(100 million yuan)

年 份 Year	按经济类型分 by Type of Ownership				
	国有经济 State-owned	集体经济 Collective-owned	私营经济 Private-owned	个 体 Individual	其 他 Others
1978	39.50	14.41		0.19	
1979	46.47	21.32		0.20	0.29
1980	54.01	25.31		0.24	0.87
1981	56.57	30.28	0.04	0.29	1.55
1982	56.48	31.39	0.03	0.32	1.58
1983	63.17	34.55	0.02	0.70	2.24
1984	75.63	43.80	0.02	1.68	2.59
1985	102.59	59.49	0.18	6.42	4.71
1986	111.73	69.06	0.67	8.47	6.91
1987	123.05	80.38	0.88	11.46	9.48
1988	161.65	103.84	1.72	14.56	14.06
1989	176.07	119.97	1.76	16.16	17.42
1990	179.37	115.59	2.05	16.17	20.68
1991	200.25	135.30	2.72	18.70	25.09
1992	247.68	157.56	5.75	22.88	30.95
1993	250.97	202.05	0.51	41.45	180.94
1994	249.27	198.56	0.64	65.00	321.29
1995	247.10	193.03	0.86	76.44	533.54
1996	238.54	183.50	30.10	92.64	713.22
1997	225.35	173.85	21.83	114.88	899.47
1998	210.92	161.70	59.48	126.94	1 034.23
1999	180.33	141.83	62.77	141.16	1 196.24
2000	150.09	118.26	496.86	153.57	946.50
2001	135.69	105.90	596.21	172.66	1 005.91
2002	131.91	102.19	699.75	190.66	1 079.38
2003	133.36	102.68	803.74	208.45	1 156.22
2004	134.44	102.78	935.44	233.01	1 251.24
2005	135.44	103.00	1 117.73	257.74	1 359.06
2006	138.43	104.62	1 342.60	284.46	1 490.30
2007	148.85	110.10	1 560.09	317.12	1 711.63

注：1997 年以前私营经济为合营。
Note: The figures private basiness before 1997 refer to those joint-owned.

表 15.4 续表 2 continued

单位:亿元(100 million yuan)

年 份 Year	社会消费品零售总额 Total Retail Sales of Consumer Goods	按行业分 by Sectors			
		批发零售贸易业 Wholesale and Retail Trade	餐饮业 Catering Trade	制造业 Manufacturing	其他行业 Others
1978	54.10	47.55	2.39	1.65	2.51
1979	68.28	59.02	2.82	2.54	3.9
1980	80.43	70.28	3.41	4.24	2.5
1981	88.73	77.53	3.68	4.61	2.91
1982	89.80	77.31	3.76	5.44	3.29
1983	100.68	84.93	4.26	7.72	3.77
1984	123.72	103.27	4.9	10.6	4.95
1985	173.39	150.03	7.58	8.41	7.37
1986	196.84	170.12	9.54	8.79	8.39
1987	225.25	193.50	11.09	10.47	10.19
1988	295.83	254.99	14.48	11.90	14.46
1989	331.38	265.87	15.06	16.84	33.01
1990	333.86	265.67	17.08	15.15	35.96
1991	382.06	300.26	20.91	17.7	43.19
1992	464.82	362.03	25.92	20.25	56.62
1993	675.92	559.56	35.47	29.24	51.65
1994	834.76	684.81	42.74	32.75	74.46
1995	1 050.96	864.01	52.61	38.05	96.29
1996	1 258.00	1 032.78	78.50	39.84	106.88
1997	1 435.38	1 173.94	93.49	44.38	123.57
1998	1 593.27	1 298.40	96.58	45.41	152.88
1999	1 722.33	1 391.08	114.93	47.22	169.10
2000	1 865.28	1 493.13	134.12	49.16	188.87
2001	2 016.37	1 619.13	148.88	50.78	197.58
2002	2 203.89	1 756.77	193.68	52.66	200.78
2003	2 404.45	1 920.20	225.83	53.87	204.55
2004	2 656.91	2 108.59	279.44	56.29	212.59
2005	2 972.97	2 340.57	350.32	59.84	222.24
2006	3 360.41	2 695.62	452.16		212.63
2007	3 847.79	3 058.25	556.48		233.06

表 15.4 续表 3 continued

单位：亿元（100 million yuan）

年 份 Year	按销售地区分 by Regions		按类别分 by Sectors		
	区 Districts	县 Counties	#家居类 Home Appliances	#通讯类 Communications	#轿车类 Cars
1978	41.42	12.68			
1979	51.60	16.68			
1980	61.08	19.35			
1981	66.66	22.07			
1982	67.49	22.31			
1983	75.62	25.06			
1984	93.71	30.01			
1985	133.59	39.80			
1990	265.83	68.03			
1991	302.54	79.52			
1992	361.64	103.18			
1993	530.97	144.95			
1994	666.00	174.76			
1995	832.92	218.04			
1996	1 006.15	251.84			
1997	1 156.08	279.30			
1998	1 289.03	304.24			
1999	1 398.60	323.73			
2000	1 521.68	343.60			
2001	1 665.46	350.91			
2002	1 884.77	319.12			
2003	2 063.71	340.74			
2004	2 292.63	364.28	278.44	62.20	196.85
2005	2 588.86	384.11	341.13	78.02	200.03
2006	2 938.73	421.68	393.20	92.00	209.31
2007	3 379.84	467.95	467.96	112.73	230.01

注：县的零售额包括崇明县全部及宝山区、嘉定区、闵行区、浦东新区、松江区、金山区、青浦区、奉贤区和南汇区镇以下地区零售额。

Note: The retail sales of consumer goods include Chongming County and those at town level and below from Baoshan, Jiading, Pudong New Area, Songjiang, Jinshan, Qingpu, Fengxian and Nanhui Districts.

表 15.5 主要消费品零售量(1990 ~ 2007)
RETAIL SALES OF MAIN CONSUMER GOODS

年 份 Year	皮 鞋 (万双) Leather Shoes (10 000 pairs)	化妆品 (亿元) Cosmetics (100 million yuan)	照相机 (万架) Cameras (10 000 units)	彩色电视机 (万台) Color TV Sets (10 000 units)
1990	1 813		13.43	23.04
1991	1 784		11.19	26.67
1992	1 629	2.16	12.73	26.25
1993	1 678	4.16	16.36	35.58
1994	1 977	5.29	16.55	34.33
1995	1 852	11.67	23.35	37.60
1996	1 501	10.32	21.42	36.12
1997	1 606	10.91	21.52	49.03
1998	1 415	12.46	19.49	60.87
1999	1 842	15.42	20.98	71.65
2000	1 623	21.70	25.12	80.69
2001	1 897	28.53	28.52	88.43
2002	2 097	32.87	30.14	99.78
2003	2 257	36.07	32.21	111.96
2004	2 438	40.74	34.64	117.79
2005	2 733	47.71	37.33	127.49
2006	3 086	54.54	40.75	136.49
2007	3 448	67.70	45.52	146.12

表 15.5 续表 1 continued

年 份 Types	洗衣机 (万台) Washing Machines (10 000 units)	家用空调器 (万台) Air-conditioners (10 000 units)	摄像机 (万架) Video Cameras (10 000 units)	电冰箱 (万台) Refrigerators (10 000 units)
1990	13.73	1.12		16.18
1991	15.57	2.34		18.57
1992	15.60	4.59		19.16
1993	19.44	9.68	0.58	22.39
1994	20.73	19.48	0.78	24.06
1995	27.92	33.93	0.95	27.32
1996	24.66	39.11	0.99	26.45
1997	28.81	39.70	1.17	27.48
1998	35.21	40.87	1.63	32.41
1999	34.17	37.27	1.48	30.00
2000	33.75	42.10	1.73	33.75
2001	38.05	43.78	2.36	35.46
2002	44.61	54.97	3.02	41.14
2003	51.17	80.76	4.08	47.48
2004	56.12	108.37	5.11	52.54
2005	64.58	120.00	5.99	58.42
2006	70.84	118.51	6.55	65.16
2007	76.21	143.23	7.08	72.26

表 15.5 续表 2 continued

年 份 Types	汽 车 (万辆) Automobiles (10 000 vehicles)	金饰品 (亿元) Gold Ornaments (100 million yuan)	微波炉 (万台) Microwave Ovens (10 000 units)	热水淋浴器 (万台) Water Heaters (10 000 units)
1992		13.60		14.04
1993		21.38	6.47	24.42
1994	3.45	16.17	16.50	24.66
1995	4.62	24.51	23.19	28.38
1996	3.84	23.95	29.63	26.18
1997	5.11	26.45	35.76	26.78
1998	5.11	27.16	34.94	21.72
1999	4.96	22.51	30.50	20.52
2000	4.81	23.09	31.71	21.55
2001	5.10	26.00	33.53	21.81
2002	6.40	28.93	45.93	24.28
2003	7.84	30.52	55.98	31.38
2004	8.91	33.17	60.21	35.21
2005	9.08	39.95	66.25	40.54
2006	9.55	48.23	68.77	45.14
2007	11.04	58.53	73.86	50.71

表 15.5 续表 3 continued

年 份 Types	电 脑 (台) Computers (set)	脱排油烟机 (万台) Range Hoods (10 000 units)	钢 琴 (台) Pianoes (set)	移动电话机 (万台) Mobile Telephone (10 000 units)
1992		8.63		
1993		11.96		
1994		11.59		
1995		17.36		
1996	3 903	15.59	1 904	
1997	12 564	15.97	2 207	
1998	37 279	16.85	3 660	
1999	76 529	15.41	3 863	13.67
2000	127 854	17.35	3 999	27.41
2001	158 134	17.76	4 190	40.73
2002	170 344	20.59	4 357	61.66
2003	184 665	23.43	4 539	130.43
2004	199 267	27.62	3 766	165.96
2005	220 551	34.83	5 338	186.47
2006	242 472	39.18	6 203	230.29
2007	266 758	43.25	7 311	251.10

表 15.6 主要年份批发零售贸易业购、销、存总额
PURCHASE, SALES AND INVENTORY OF WHOLESALE AND RETAIL TRADE IN MAIN YEARS

单位:亿元(100 million yuan)

指 标	Indicators	1978	1990	2000	2006	2007
商品购进总额	**Purchase of Commodities**	**259.35**	**1 129.49**	**6 615.75**	**13 044.42**	**16 527.98**
#从生产者购进	Purchase from Producers	190.27	597.66	3 498.32	6 142.47	7 537.14
从批发零售贸易业购进	Purchase from Wholesale and Retail	69.08	113.79	3 067.15	5 646.35	7 199.50
商品销售总额	**Sales of Commodities**	**303.43**	**1 305.41**	**7 474.81**	**15 504.05**	**20 400.79**
零 售	Retail	47.55	265.67	1 723.31	2 896.29	3 278.25
批 发	Wholesale	255.88	1 039.74	5 751.50	12 607.76	17 122.54
#售给批发零售贸易	Sales to Retail and Wholesale	110.61	168.14	3 548.54	7 232.73	9 413.45
年末库存总额	**Year-end Inventory**	**47.27**	**230.97**	**262.50**	**419.76**	**473.49**

注：本表为国内批发零售贸易业、物资供销业、对外贸易业统计口径。
Note: The figures in this table are based on wholesale, retail trade, purchase and sales of commodities and foreign trade.

表 15.7 批发零售贸易业商品购、销、存总额(2007)
PURCHASE, SALES AND INVENTORY OF WHOLESALE AND RETAIL TRADE

单位:亿元 (100 million yuan)

类 别	Types	商品购进总额 Purchase of Commodities	商品销售总额 Sales of Commodities	商品库存总额 Year-end Inventory
总 计	**Total**	**16 527.98**	**20 400.79**	**473.49**
限额以上单位	Above the Set Scale	13 869.50	16 110.31	357.43
#国有及国有控股	State-owned and State-controlled	4 820.82	5 519.97	231.82
限额以下单位	Below the Set Scale	2 658.48	4 290.48	116.06

表 15.8 批发零售贸易业商品销售总额(2004 ~ 2007)
SALES OF COMMODITIES OF WHOLESALE AND RETAIL

单位:亿元(100 million yuan)

类别	Types	2004	2005	2006	2007
商品销售总额	**Sales of Commodities**	**11 254.81**	**12 943.25**	**15 504.05**	**20 400.79**
#食 品	Food	706.17	814.22	960.78	1 198.52
饮 料	Beverage	103.60	115.20	140.38	169.07
烟 酒	Tabacco and Liquor	462.80	574.33	711.21	889.13
服装、鞋帽	Garments, Shoes and Hats	559.71	659.90	678.30	734.74
针、纺织品	Textile Products	317.25	352.46	405.48	452.14
化妆品	Cosmetics	100.18	120.11	150.14	165.23
金银珠宝	Jewelry	68.56	75.90	94.61	104.94
日用品	Articles for Daily Use	271.30	301.14	435.17	538.29
五金、电料	Hardware and Electrical Appliances	110.93	118.25	121.79	134.59
体育、娱乐用品	Recreation and Sports Articles	52.74	60.34	73.05	80.43
书报、杂志	Books and Newspapers	88.45	97.83	106.21	117.42
电子出版物及音像制品	Electronic Publications and Audio-video Products	29.31	34.56	41.47	50.19
家用电器和音响器材	Household Appliances and Audio-video Equipments	293.95	375.67	459.59	502.10
中西药品	Medicines	308.19	340.55	361.87	410.33
文化、办公用品	Culture and Office Articles	290.97	371.86	481.93	646.27
家 具	Furnitures	80.28	95.78	147.02	160.24
通信器材	Telecommunication Appliances	201.35	265.38	345.00	400.18
建筑及装潢材料	Materials for Construction and Decoration	240.80	280.05	313.92	368.95
机电产品及设备	Mechanical and Electrical Equipments	1 905.04	2 044.11	2 217.86	2 831.48

表 15.9 批发零售贸易业主要工业品购进量(2004 ~ 2007)
PURCHASE OF MAJOR INDUSTRIAL PRODUCTS OF WHOLESALE AND RETAIL TRADE

商品名称	Name of Commodities	2004	2005	2006	2007
卷　烟 (万箱)	Cigarettes (10 000 cases)	290.11	323.79	352.75	389.08
酒 (万吨)	Liquor (10 000 tons)	58.29	61.94	65.07	71.12
棉　布 (万米)	Cotton Cloth (10 000 m)	1 801	1 861	2 005	2 177
呢　绒 (万米)	Wool Fabric (10 000 m)	1 355	1 331	1 345	1 401
绸　缎 (万米)	Silk and Statins (10 000 m)	601	647	698	722
各种服装 (万件)	Garments (10 000 pieces)	12 556	12 988	13 450	14 304
皮　鞋 (万双)	Leather Shoes (10 000 pairs)	1 451	2 211	2 338	2 519
自行车 (万辆)	Bicycles (10 000 vehicles)	80.22	94.41	100.03	118.22
电风扇 (万台)	Electrical Fans (10 000 units)	92.11	96.19	98.23	115.15
电视机 (万台)	TV Sets (10 000 units)	101.59	126.04	132.99	144.43
#彩色电视机	Color TV Sets	100.05	125.90	130.87	143.22
录音机 (万台)	Recorders (10 000 units)	56.13	71.57	81.48	93.12
照相机 (万架)	Cameras (10 000 units)	34.52	44.45	62.29	80.10
电冰箱 (万台)	Refrigerators (10 000 units)	58.12	66.17	70.39	77.57
洗衣机 (万台)	Washing Machines (10 000 units)	49.37	59.86	72.76	88.01
家用空调器 (万台)	Household Air-conditioners (10 000 units)	95.22	142.44	159.72	179.13
影碟机 (万台)	Video Player (10 000 units)	60.10	86.35	87.41	90.48
脱排油烟机 (万架)	Range Hoods (10 000 units)	28.12	30.61	35.56	41.22
热水淋浴器 (万架)	Water Heaters (10 000 units)	29.18	38.71	46.35	55.18
微波炉 (万台)	Microware Ovens (10 000 units)	61.34	61.10	69.36	78.50
电话机 (万只)	Telephones (10 000 units)	133.58	121.45	130.74	172.58
电　脑 (万台)	Computers (10 000 units)	12.22	17.20	23.69	32.01
煤　油 (万吨)	Kerosene (10 000 tons)	398.19	488.95	508.58	530.41
柴　油 (万吨)	Diesel Oil (10 000 tons)	2 627.25	2 889.97	3 095.38	3 516.13

表 15.10 批发零售贸易业主要工业品销售量(2004～2007)
SALES OF MAJOR INDUSTRIAL PRODUCTS OF WHOLESALE AND RETAIL

商品名称	Name of Commodities	2004	2005	2006	2007
卷　烟（万箱）	Cigarettes (10 000 cases)	295.06	311.77	332.15	353.90
酒（万吨）	Liquor (10 000 tons)	59.19	62.13	68.31	75.41
棉　布（万米）	Cotton Cloth (10 000 m)	1 899	1 957	2 218	2 573
呢　绒（万米）	Wool Fabric (10 000 m)	1 301	1 334	1 434	1 515
绸　缎（万米）	Silk and Satins (10 000 m)	597	521	701	993
服　装（万件）	Garments (10 000 pieces)	12 848	14 183	16 764	19 835
皮　鞋（万双）	Leather Shoes (10 000 pairs)	1 501	1 722	2 464	3 648
自行车（万辆）	Bicycles (10 000 vehicles)	82.31	85.83	110.23	130.38
电风扇（万台）	Electrical Fans (10 000 units)	93.21	85.14	100.63	120.31
电视机（万台）	TV Sets (10 000 units)	125.47	130.14	137.03	151.07
#彩色电视机	Color TV Sets	128.39	130.00	135.03	150.12
录音机（万台）	Recorders (10 000 units)	60.50	70.87	84.51	103.71
照相机（万架）	Cameras (10 000 units)	38.35	42.10	63.61	85.15
电冰箱（万台）	Refrigerators (10 000 units)	60.77	64.96	77.88	88.26
洗衣机（万台）	Washing Machines (10 000 units)	59.44	61.73	76.87	93.21
家用空调器（万台）	Household Air-conditioners (10 000 units)	115.29	135.87	162.66	189.96
影碟机（万台）	Video Players (10 000 units)	65.25	80.28	90.61	105.20
脱排油烟机（万架）	Range Hoods (10 000 units)	32.89	35.08	40.34	49.34
热水淋浴器（万架）	Water Heaters (10 000 units)	35.51	47.91	51.66	59.71
微波炉（万台）	Microware Ovens (10 000 units)	65.12	68.01	78.88	89.33
电话机（万只）	Telephones (10 000 units)	118.84	130.37	139.05	150.87
煤　油（万吨）	Kerosene (10 000 tons)	474.01	487.35	492.13	565.10
柴　油（万吨）	Diesel Oil (10 000 tons)	3 440.17	3 501.08	3 611.12	4 346.30

表 15.11 批发零售贸易业主要农副产品纯购进量(2004～2007)
NET PURCHASE OF MAJOR FARM AND SIDELINE PRODUCTS OF WHOLESALE AND RETAIL TRADE

单位:万吨 (10 000 tons)

商品名称	Name of Commodities	从生产者购进 Purchase from Producers			
		2004	2005	2006	2007
粮　食(贸易粮)	Grain (for Trading)	92.10	95.25	97.80	100.52
食用植物油	Edible Vegetable Oil	6.25	8.01	10.27	12.57
猪和猪肉	Hogs and Porks	9.23	10.54	11.48	12.66
牛和牛肉	Oxes and Beef	0.78	0.75	0.87	1.09
家　禽	Poultries	0.95	0.91	0.90	1.11
鲜　蛋	Fresh Eggs	1.70	1.65	2.25	2.83
水产品	Aquatic Products	9.55	11.46	14.19	15.75
鲜　菜	Fresh Vegetable	79.14	89.75	95.05	100.36
棉　花	Cotton	0.62	0.50	0.84	0.89

表 15.11 续表 continued

单位:万吨 (10 000 tons)

商品名称	Name of Commodities	从市外批发零售贸易购进 Purchase from Wholesale and Retail of Outside City			
		2004	2005	2006	2007
粮　食(贸易粮)	Grain (for Trading)	160.11	170.47	185.93	190.78
食用植物油	Edible Vegetable Oil	53.19	56.14	60.16	66.67
猪和猪肉	Hogs and Pork	14.58	18.33	20.27	24.92
牛和牛肉	Oxes and Beef	1.28	1.35	1.01	1.35
家　禽	Poultries	1.59	0.98	0.73	0.83
鲜　蛋	Fresh Eggs	4.15	4.05	3.98	4.83
水产品	Aquatic Products	0.71	0.86	0.99	1.11
鲜　菜	Fresh Vegetable	75.33	83.45	100.07	136.73
棉　花	Cotton	6.01	6.85	7.67	8.00

表 15.12 限额以上批发贸易业商品购、销、存总额(2007)
PURCHASE, SALES AND INVENTORY OF WHOLESALE TRADE ABOVE THE SET SCALE

单位:亿元(100 million yuan)

类 别	Types	商品购进总额 Purchase of Commodities	商品销售总额 Sales of Commodities	商品库存总额 Year-end Inventory
总 计	**Total**	**11 270.21**	**13 385.32**	**169.01**
按登记注册类型分	**Grouped by Type of Registration**			
内资企业	Domestic Fund Enterprises	7 997.60	9 716.22	113.87
国有企业	State-Owned Enterprises	2 973.05	3 576.71	14.13
集体企业	Collective-Owned Enterprises	128.14	134.11	10.95
股份合作企业	Share Holding Cooperative Enterprises	54.94	51.30	2.91
联营企业	Joint-Owned Enterprises	104.27	109.49	16.11
有限责任公司	Companies with Limited Liabilities	2 051.81	2 574.96	23.35
股份有限公司	Share Holding Companies with Limited Liabilities	661.38	700.12	28.16
私营企业	Private Enterprises	2 008.90	2 558.43	18.03
其他企业	Others	10.11	11.10	0.23
港澳台商投资企业	Hong Kong, Macao and Taiwan Funded Enterprises	624.98	677.17	21.04
外商投资企业	Foreign Funded Enterprises	2 647.63	2 991.93	34.10
按行业分	**Grouped by Sector**			
农畜产品批发	Primary and Livestock Products	33.46	37.18	3.85
食品、饮料及烟草制品批发	Food, Beverage and Tabacco	706.88	981.78	28.27
#米、面制品及食用油批发	Rice, Flour and Cooking Oil	57.90	57.64	7.06
烟草制品批发	Tabacco	343.28	403.74	7.03

表 15.12 续表 continued

单位:亿元(100 million yuan)

类 别	Types	商品购进总额 Purchase of Commodities	商品销售总额 Sales of Commodities	商品库存总额 Year-end Inventory
纺织、服装及日用品批发	Textile Products, Garments and Commodity	880.14	1 170.45	20.19
#服装批发	Garments	311.97	421.30	10.30
文化、体育用品及器材批发	Culture & Sports Articles and Equipments	130.08	148.24	21.45
医药及医疗器材批发	Medicines and Special Appliances of Medicines	493.30	535.44	12.60
矿产品、建材及化工产品批发	Mineral Products, Materials of Construction and Chemical Products	6 406.61	7 291.31	40.67
#煤炭及制品批发	Coal	280.61	283.92	2.74
石油及制品批发	Petroleum	2 165.96	2 234.29	13.14
金属及金属矿批发	Metal Products and Metal Minerals	2 973.52	3 005.09	3.40
建材批发	Building Materials	158.40	162.27	10.69
化肥批发	Chemical Fertilizer	39.18	41.36	5.46
机械设备、五金交电及电子产品批发	Mechinery Equipments, Hardwares, Electric Appliances and Eletronic Products	2 370.12	2 929.78	35.42
#汽车、摩托车及零配件批发	Spare and Component Parts for Automobiles and Motorcycles	700.27	823.07	20.37
家用电器批发	Household Electrical Equipment	70.39	86.75	8.16
计算机、软件及辅助设备批发	Computers, Softwares and Accessorial Equipments	421.28	531.20	2.98
贸易经纪与代理	Economic Trade and Agency	129.57	142.33	3.38
其他批发	Others	120.05	148.81	3.18

表 15.13 限额以上零售贸易业商品购、销、存总额(2007)
PURCHASE, SALES AND INVENTORY OF RETAIL TRADE ABOVE THE SET SCALE

单位:亿元(100 million yuan)

类别	Types	商品购进总额 Purchase of Commodities	商品销售总额 Sales of Commodities	商品库存总额 Year-end Inventory
总计	**Total**	**2 599.29**	**2 724.99**	**188.42**
按登记注册类型分	**Grouped by Type of Registration**			
内资企业	Domestic Enterprises	2 150.56	2 218.59	146.27
国有企业	State-Owned Enterprises	73.81	83.58	7.95
集体企业	Collective-Owned Enterprises	34.65	40.88	5.78
股份合作企业	Share Holding Cooperative Enterprises	10.92	12.90	0.42
联营企业	Joint-Owned Enterprises	22.26	22.63	0.77
有限责任公司	Companies with Limited Liabilities	793.18	774.25	42.62
股份有限公司	Share Holding Companies with Limited Liabilities	728.06	777.87	42.98
私营企业	Private Enterprises	420.07	443.26	39.34
其他企业	Others	67.61	63.22	6.41
港澳台商投资企业	Hong Kong, Macao and Taiwan Funded	135.80	145.78	8.76
外商投资企业	Foreign Funded Enterprises	312.93	360.62	33.39
按行业分	**Grouped by Sector**			
#综合零售业	Comprehensive Retail Sale	1 270.13	1 339.82	87.99
食品、饮料及烟草制品专门零售	Food, Beverage and Tabacco	53.75	47.82	3.41
纺织、服装及日用品专门零售	Textile Products, Garments and Commodity	82.04	98.26	18.73
文化、体育用品及器材专门零售	Culture & Sports Articles and Equipments	109.33	111.58	15.69
医药及医疗器材专门零售	Medicines and Special Appliances of Medicines	37.71	39.52	6.23
汽车、摩托车、燃料及零配件专门零售	Automobiles, Motocycles, Fuels and Their Parts	752.33	735.81	25.64
家用电器及电子产品专门零售	Household Electrical Appliances and Electronic Products	185.39	227.00	20.06
五金、家具及室内装修材料专门零售	Hardwares, Furnitures and Materials of Decoration	72.45	78.30	6.52

表 15.14 限额以上批发零售贸易业主要生产资料销售量(2004~2007)
SALES OF MAJOR PRODUCT MATERIAL OF WHOLESALE AND RETAIL SALES TRADE ABOVE THE SET SCALE

单位:万吨 (10 000 tons)

生产资料名称	Names of Product Material	2004	2005	2006	2007
钢材	Steels	1 168.86	1 807.99	2 656.65	3 590.85
铜	Cuprum	44.61	57.38	60.06	46.34
铝	Aluminium	15.02	21.34	33.76	42.54
煤炭	Coal	1 453.86	3 016.67	3 315.22	4 818.79
汽油	Gasoline	1 390.34	1 213.18	1 186.33	2 046.81
煤油	Coal Oil	474.01	502.88	309.40	365.10
柴油	Diesel Oil	3 440.17	2 961.25	3 085.83	4 346.30
水泥	Concrete	93.52	118.73	169.20	251.79

表 15.15 限额以上批发零售贸易业主要商品销售额(2007)
TOTAL SALES OF ENTERPRISES ABOVE THE SET SCALE IN WHOLESALE AND RETAIL TRADE OF MAIN COMMODITIES

单位:亿元(100 million yuan)

类 别	Types	合 计 Total	批 发 Wholesale Trade	零 售 Retail Trade
食品、饮料、烟酒	Food, Beverages, Tobacco and Liquor	2 558.07	1 743.46	814.61
#肉禽蛋	Meat, Poultry and Eggs	138.36	67.30	71.06
饮 料	Beverages	117.08	56.98	60.10
烟 酒	Tobacco and Liquor	668.77	512.73	156.04
服装鞋帽、针、纺织品	Clothing, Shoes, Hats and Textiles	1 026.56	696.47	330.09
#服 装	Clothing	657.05	402.17	254.88
针、纺织品	Knitwear and Textiles	281.05	230.11	50.94
化妆品	Cosmetics	139.04	84.03	55.01
金银珠宝	Gold, Silver and Jewelry	96.62	46.14	50.48
日用品	Articles for Daily Use	500.61	311.74	188.87
#洗涤用品	Washing Articles	52.93	29.26	23.67
五金、电料	Hardware and Electrical Materials	118.80	70.49	48.31
体育、娱乐用品	Sports and Recreation Articles	65.22	28.94	36.28
书报杂志	Newspapers and Magazines	93.86	41.31	52.55
电子出版物及音像制品	E-journal and Video Products	9.39	5.86	3.53
家用电器和音像器材	Household Appliances and Video Appliances	425.04	200.69	224.35
中西药品	Traditional Chinese and Western Medicines	357.71	204.13	153.58
#西 药	Western Medicines	182.92	92.22	90.70
中草药及中成药	Traditional Chinese Medicines	101.57	38.69	62.88
文化办公用品	Cultural and Official Goods	513.80	443.78	70.02
家 具	Furniture	101.15	53.29	47.86
通讯器材	Communication Appliances	252.61	180.43	72.18
汽 车	Automobile	1 259.69	1 023.14	236.55
建筑及装潢材料	Building and Decoration Materials	256.15	165.46	90.69
机电产品及设备	Mechanical and Electrical Products	887.54	867.23	20.31
其 他	Others	7 448.45	7 209.30	239.15

表 15.16 限额以上批发零售贸易业商品销售量(2007)

TOTAL SALES NUMBER OF ENTERPRISES ABOVE THE SET SCALE IN WHOLESALE AND RETAIL TRADE BY COMMODITIES

名 称	Name of Commodities	销售合计 Total	批 发 Wholesale Trade	零 售 Retail Trade
粮 食(万吨)	Grain(10 000 tons)	313.74	263.95	49.79
食用植物油(万吨)	Edible Vegetable Oil(10 000 tons)	60.27	39.74	20.53
卷 烟(万箱)	Tobacco(10 000 boxes)	213.81	186.17	27.64
酒(万吨)	Alcohol(10 000 tons)	59.17	38.33	20.84
#白 酒	Distilled spirit	22.57	16.44	6.13
啤 酒	Beer	21.03	13.48	7.55
布(万米)	Colth(10 000 meters)	795.34	784.81	10.53
服 装(万件)	Dress(10 000 units)	544.27	351.97	192.30
鞋(万双)	Shoes(10 000 pairs)	150.00	95.60	54.40
彩色电视机(万台)	Colour TV Sets(10 000 units)	179.38	33.26	146.12
电 脑(微型计算机)(万台)	Personal Computers(10 000 units)	39.72	31.37	8.35
组合音响(万台)	Hi-Fi Stereo Component System(10 000 unit)	37.28	20.67	16.61
电冰箱(万台)	Refrigerators(10 000 units)	114.88	42.62	72.26
洗衣机(万台)	Washing Machines(10 000 units)	108.68	32.47	76.21
摄像机(万台)	Pickup Cameras(10 000 units)	7.76	0.69	7.07
影碟机(万台)	Video Disc Players(10 000 units)	109.85	27.83	82.02
家用空调器(万台)	Household Air Conditioners(10 000 units)	193.52	60.86	132.66
微波炉(万台)	Micro-ovens(10 000 units)	98.36	24.50	73.86
普通电话机(万台)	Telephones(10 000 units)	178.28	90.49	87.79
移动电话(万台)	Hand Telephones(10 000 units)	963.19	712.09	251.10
照相机(万台)	Cameras(10 000 units)	52.51	20.13	32.38
#数码照相机	Numeral Cameras	20.28	8.79	11.49
煤 油(万吨)	Kerosene(10 000 tons)	365.10	363.97	1.13
煤 炭(万吨)	Coal(10 000 tons)	4 818.79	4 812.30	6.49
柴 油(万吨)	Diesel Oil(10 000 tons)	4 346.30	4 329.44	16.86
汽 车(万辆)	Automobiles(10 000 vehicles)	64.57	53.53	11.04
#轿 车	Car	60.18	49.98	10.20
汽 油(万吨)	Gasoline(10 000 tons)	2 046.81	2 032.40	14.41
钢 材(万吨)	Steel Products(10 000 tons)	3 590.85	3 588.29	2.56
水 泥(万吨)	Cement(10 000 tons)	251.79	245.63	6.16
木 材(万立方米)	Wood(10 000 cu. m)	54.40	53.92	0.48

表 15.17 限额以上批发零售贸易业主要财务指标（2005～2007）
MAIN FINANCIAL INDICATORS OF WHOLESALE AND RETAIL SALES ABOVE THE SET SCALE

单位：亿元(100 million yuan)

指 标	Indicators	2005	2006	2007
流动资产	Current Assets	2 929.27	3 229.85	3 770.34
#存 货	Inventory	722.78	811.94	863.09
固定资产原价	Fixed Assets Original Value	546.78	632.69	610.48
累计折旧	Accumulative Depreciation	169.94	201.05	212.11
#本年折旧	Depreciation	31.20	38.47	37.25
资产总计	Total Assets	3 926.22	4 317.05	5 013.88
负债合计	Total Liabilities	2 727.25	2 961.32	3 530.89
所有者权益合计	Total Owner's Equities	1 198.97	1 355.73	1 482.99
实收资本	Paid-up Capital	862.49	858.18	826.15
#国家资本	State Capital	132.19	123.22	140.25
港澳台资本	Hongkong, Macao and Taiwan Capital	38.17	40.74	22.48
外商资本	Foreign Capital	242.71	222.50	280.22
主营业务收入	Prime Operating Revenues	11 236.19	13 065.98	14 721.69
主营业务成本	Operating Costs	9 874.12	12 065.15	13 297.33
营业费用	Operating Expenses	501.98	553.29	694.63
主营业务税金及附加	Sales Taxes and Extra Charges	10.10	14.81	16.79
主营业务利润	Profits of Major Management	737.71	952.92	1 168.26
管理费用	Management Expenses	243.12	256.52	302.45
财务费用	Financial Expenses	24.09	23.52	25.38
营业利润	Operating Profits	248.71	283.07	391.16
利润总额	Total Profits	223.35	325.83	457.80
主营业务应付工资总额	Total Payable Salaries Involved in Major Business	130.25	137.49	127.37
主营业务应付福利费总额	Total Payable Welfare Involved in Major Business	21.89	20.44	25.85

表 15.18 限额以上批发零售贸易业主要财务指标(2007)
MAIN FINANCIAL INDICATORS OF WHOLESALE AND RETAIL ENTERPRISES ABOVE THE SET SCALE

类别	Types	流动资产 Current Assets	固定资产原价 Fixed Assets Original Value	资产总计 Total Assets
总计	**Total**	**3 770.34**	**610.48**	**5 013.88**
一、按登记注册类型分	**Grouped by Type of Registration**			
批发贸易业	Wholesale Trade	3 050.35	246.21	3 725.24
内资企业	Domestic Enterprises	1 905.14	189.16	2 461.45
国有企业	State-Owned Enterprises	451.59	32.19	543.38
集体企业	Collective-Owned Enterprises	31.96	4.52	37.46
股份合作企业	Share Holding Cooperative Enterprises	9.99	0.69	11.83
联营企业	Joint-Owned Enterprises	30.7	2.74	34.85
有限责任公司	Companies with Limited Liabilities	569.87	77.5	754.35
股份有限公司	Share Holding Companies with Limited Liabilities	80.46	21.48	231.91
私营企业	Private Enterprises	724.75	48.77	835.87
其他企业	Others	5.82	1.27	11.8
港澳台商投资企业	Hong Kong, Macao and Taiwan Funded	211.22	7.91	224.26
外商投资企业	Foreign Funded Enterprises	933.99	49.14	1 039.53
零售贸易业	Retail Trade	719.99	364.27	1 288.64
内资企业	Domestic Enterprises	544.46	254.55	1 018.75
国有企业	State-Owned Enterprises	31.32	12.09	63.54
集体企业	Collective-Owned Enterprises	11.37	8.89	19.68
股份合作企业	Share Holding Cooperative Enterprises	2.83	0.57	6.94
联营企业	Joint-Owned Enterprises	3.58	1.84	4.75
有限责任公司	Responsibility Co. Ltd.	198.26	74.42	295.72
股份有限公司	Share Holding Co. Ltd.	147.64	128.71	433.35
私营企业	Private Enterprises	125.6	25.36	168.72
其他企业	Others	23.86	2.67	26.05
港澳台商投资企业	Hong Kong, Macao and Taiwan Funded	40.47	39.37	69.81
外商投资企业	Foreign Funded Enterprises	135.06	70.35	200.08

单位:亿元(100 million yuan)

负债合计 Total Liabilities	所有者权益合计 Total Owner's Equity	实收资本 Paid-up Capital	主营业务收入 Prime Operating Revenues	主营业务成本 Operating Costs	主营业务利润 Profits from Major Business	利润总额 Total Profits
3 530.89	**1 482.99**	**826.15**	**14 721.69**	**13 297.33**	**1 168.26**	**457.80**
2 617.89	1 107.34	553.88	12 183.67	11 080.99	872.16	377.09
1 699.92	761.53	383.04	8 683.99	8 120.84	419.18	229.25
392.45	150.92	64.23	3 216.47	3 005.57	130.25	109.45
27.99	9.47	3.06	123.78	118	4.95	1.93
8.95	2.89	1.09	52.15	50.66	1.45	0.98
25.27	9.59	4.51	104.49	96.8	5.24	2.04
498.97	255.38	124.04	2 121.32	1 973.48	135.38	72.52
126.04	105.87	41.56	628.83	583.37	29.96	8.98
613.3	222.57	140.95	2 426.9	2 283.39	111.53	33.26
6.95	4.84	3.6	10.05	9.57	0.42	0.09
174.4	49.86	25.89	616.99	529.21	59.41	17.15
743.57	295.95	144.95	2 882.19	2 430.94	393.57	130.69
913	375.65	272.27	2 538.02	2 216.34	296.1	80.71
679.86	338.9	171.29	2 058.7	1 820.64	217.80	61.33
33.19	30.35	12.23	76.22	62.94	12.49	2.74
10.46	9.22	4.47	43.73	38.51	4.17	1.91
6.06	0.89	0.63	11.69	10.68	0.89	0.25
3.5	1.25	0.99	20.69	19.11	1.21	0.43
212.97	82.75	40.81	759.01	669.49	82.62	22.79
257.23	176.11	80.76	676.24	593.77	79.30	30.26
134.32	34.4	30.09	411.53	372.70	33.19	2.57
22.13	3.93	1.31	59.59	53.44	3.93	0.38
47.71	22.1	22.97	131.58	99.90	30.34	11.13
185.43	14.65	78.01	347.74	295.80	47.96	8.25

表 15.18 续表 continued

	类　别 Types	流动资产 Current Assets	固定资产原价 Fixed Assets Original Value	资产总计 Total Assets
二、按行业分	**Grouped by Sector**			
批发贸易业	**Wholesale Trade**	**3 050.35**	**246.21**	**3 725.24**
农畜产品批发	Primary and Livestock Products	13.03	3.78	16.93
食品、饮料及烟草制品批发	Food, Beverage and Tabacco	188.93	43.23	272.61
纺织、服装及日用品批发	Textile Products, Gaments and Commodity	368.96	30.82	456.44
文化、体育用品及器材批发	Culture & Sports Articles and Equipments	61.68	9.52	82.61
医药及医疗器材批发	Medicines and Special Appliances of Medicines	143.5	21.44	251.11
矿产品、建材及化工产品批发	Mineral Products, Materials of Construction and Chemical Products	1 070.18	68.64	1 258.56
机械设备、五金交电及电子产品批发	Mechinery Equipments, Hardwares, Electric Appliances and Eletronic Products	692.06	36.78	826.24
贸易经济与代理	Economy on Trade and Agency	42.96	2.28	46.74
其他批发	Others	469.05	29.72	514
零售贸易业	**Retail Trade**	**719.99**	**364.27**	**1 288.64**
综合零售业	Comprehensive Retail Sale	394.76	257.41	718.77
食品、饮料及烟草制品专门零售	Food, Beverage and Tabacco	18.32	5	46.42
纺织、服装及日用品专门零售	Textile Products, Gaments and Commodity	34.97	11.2	46.32
文化、体育用品及器材专门零售	Culture & Sports Articles and Equipments	39.4	4.25	46.75
医药及医疗器材专门零售	Medicines and Special Appliances of Medicines	11.7	3.4	23.89
汽车、摩托车、燃料及零配件专门零售	Automobiles, Motocycles, Fuels and Their Parts	115.59	58.47	188.94
家用电器及电子产品专门零售	Household Electrical Appliances and Electronic Products	38.13	4.84	110.38
五金、家具及室内装修材料专门零售	Hardwares, Furnitures and Materials of Decoration	30.4	8.39	48.92
无店铺及其他零售	No-Shop and Others	36.72	11.31	58.25

单位:亿元(100 million yuan)

负债合计 Total Liabilities	所有者权益合计 Total Owner's Equity	实收资本 Paid-up Capital	主营业务收入 Prime Operating Revenues	主营业务成本 Operating Costs	主营业务利润 Profits from Major Business	利润总额 Total Profits
2 617.89	**1 107.34**	**553.88**	**12 183.67**	**11 080.99**	**872.16**	**377.09**
12.37	4.56	2.79	36.86	36.06	0.71	0.04
144.79	127.82	53.04	698.79	582.26	101.89	66.19
308.56	147.88	87.16	1 128.11	902.65	167.77	42.82
56	26.61	14.22	140.53	125.83	12.85	3.94
184.8	66.31	26.62	521.12	461.15	53.31	9.31
905.26	353.30	192.61	5 831.92	5 522.91	211.77	132.11
590.99	235.25	124.95	2 556.80	2 344.43	192.27	63.36
37.09	9.65	5.51	139.55	133.03	6.01	2.53
378.03	135.96	46.98	1 129.99	972.67	125.58	56.79
913	**375.65**	**272.27**	**2 538.02**	**2 216.34**	**296.10**	**80.71**
537.00	181.78	145.55	1 215.85	1 025.95	177.47	49.84
14.34	32.08	7.85	53.68	46.02	6.82	3.20
34	12.32	8.49	92.32	64.46	27.03	5.14
34.5	12.25	10.14	101.23	86.27	12.90	4.27
10.73	13.16	9.13	38.43	30.18	7.43	1.09
109.43	79.51	62.09	703.05	663.46	37.07	10.45
93.64	16.74	5.65	205.31	190.63	11.83	1.54
35.34	13.58	14.43	79.17	67.13	9.15	2.41
44.02	14.23	8.94	48.98	42.24	6.40	2.77

表 15.19　限额以上餐饮业主要财务指标(2005～2007)
MAIN FINANCIAL INDICATORS OF CATERING SECTOR ABOVE THE SET SCALE

单位:亿元(100 million yuan)

指　标	Indicators	2005	2006	2007
流动资产	Current Assets	43.60	64.37	71.87
#存　货	Inventory	5.10	6.32	5.17
固定资产原价	Fixed Assets Original Value	44.76	56.92	57.43
累计折旧	Accumulative Depreciation	15.65	20.56	24.12
#本年折旧	Depreciation	3.83	4.54	4.74
资产总计	Total Assets	94.49	124.56	130.99
负债合计	Total Liabilities	64.13	87.84	93.98
所有者权益合计	Total Owner's Equities	30.36	36.73	37.01
实收资本	Paid-up Capital	31.05	39.57	39.44
#国家资本	State Capital	0.78	1.42	1.63
港澳台资本	Hongkong, Macao and Taiwan Capital	6.95	8.33	6.18
外商资本	Foreign Capital	6.66	9.67	10.98
主营业务收入	Prime Operating Revenues	157.66	195.49	220.43
主营业务成本	Operating Costs	72.03	88.55	95.21
营业费用	Operating Expenses	53.86	67.17	73.37
主营业务税金及附加	Sales Taxes and Extra Charges	8.14	9.87	11.04
主营业务利润	Profits of Major Management	65.75	84.83	96.44
管理费用	Management Expenses	19.42	23.06	24.69
财务费用	Financial Expenses	1.15	1.90	2.57
营业利润	Operating Profits	5.49	6.41	6.12
利润总额	Total Profits	5.49	6.16	7.40
主营业务应付工资总额	Total Payable Salaries Involved in Major Business	17.54	21.44	25.30
主营业务应付福利费总额	Total Payable Welfare Involved in Major Business	2.26	2.24	3.25

表 15.20　限额以上连锁零售业、住宿和餐饮业经营情况(2005～2007)
THE BASIC STATISTICS OF CHAIN RETAIL, ACCOMMODATION AND CATERING ABOVE SET SCALE

指　标	Indicators	2005	2006	2007
门店总数(个)	Quantity of Stores(unit)	15 775	16 547	17 202
营业面积(万平方米)	Operational Area(10 000 sq. m)	809.16	865.81	898.68
从业人数(万人)	Quantity of Persons Employed(10 000 person)	24.47	26.01	28.30
商品购进总额(亿元)	Purchase of Commodities(100 million yuan)	1 222.94	1 460.66	1 762.11
商品销售总额 (亿元)	Sales of Commodities (100 million yuan)	1 815.32	2 048.13	2 333.94
#零售额	Retail Sales	1 201.03	1 321.55	1 779.47
餐饮业营业收入(亿元)	Total Operating Revenue(100 million yuan)	35.69	40.89	48.32

表 15.24 成交额前 30 位的商品交易市场一览(2007)
BASIC STATISTICS OF 30 COMMODITY EXCHANGE MARKETS WITH TRANSACTION VOLUME BEFORE NO.30

名 称	Name	摊位数量（个）Number of Stalls (unit)	成交额（亿元）Transaction Volume (100 million yuan)
上海市物贸中心有色金属交易市场	Shanghai Commodity Center Non-ferreous Metal Exchange Market	300	910.78
上海逸仙钢材市场经营管理有限公司	Shanghai Yixian Steel on Hand Exchange Market	850	450.00
宝山钢材交易市场地址管理有限公司	Baoshan Steel Material Exchange Market	600	249.48
上海新沪办钢材交易市场经营管理有限公司	Shanghai New Huban Steel Exchange Market	142	230.00
上海中油石油交易中心有限公司	Shanghai Zhongyou Oil Exchange Center	280	200.00
上海石化物资交易中心有限公司	Shanghai Petrochemical Commodity Exchange Center	200	197.00
上海长江有色金属现货市场	Changjiang Non-ferreous Metal on Hand Market	1	98.25
中昊化工网上交易中心	Shanghai Zhonghao Network Exchange Center	300	89.00
上海柏树钢铁交易市场管理有限公司	Shanghai Baishu Steel Exchange Market	131	75.26
上海华东钢材市场	Shanghai East China Steel Market	200	72.01
上海铁闵钢材市场经营管理有限公司	Shanghai Tiemin Steel Exchange Market	236	60.06
上海诚通香山金属交易有限公司	Xiangshan Steel Material Exchange Market	274	53.75
上海农产品中心批发市场	Shanghai Agriculture Center Distribution Market	728	46.83
铜川水产市场	Tongchuan Aquatic Product Market	950	45.83
沪西水产市场	Shanghai Huxi Aquatic Product Market	548	44.13
上海砖贸综合市场经营管理有限公司	Shanghai Zhuanmao Integrative Market	3 067	42.56
上海曹安路市场	Shanghai Caoan Road Market	2 006	38.51
上海江杨农产品批发市场经营管理有限公司	Shanghai Jiangyang Agriculture Products Distribution Market	766	37.23
上海中山化工市场	Shanghai Zhongshan Chemical Products Market	500	36.00
上海高境金属交易市场管理有限公司	Shanghai Gaojing Steel Material Exchange Market	63	33.56
上海市旧机动车交易市场	Shanghai Secondhand Automobile Exchange Market	68	33.20
上海东方国际水产中心市场经营管理有限公司	Oriental International Fisheries Market	910	30.00
上海毛家塘南北货批发市场经营管理有限公司	Maojiatang Local Products Wholesale Market	445	28.24
上海市江桥批发市场经营管理有限公司	Shanghai Jiangqiao Wholesale Market	252	24.02
上海金山市场有限公司	Shanghai Jinshan Market	3 271	23.81
上海东方汽配城	Shanghai Orient Automobile Parts Market	620	22.77
上海国泰路综合市场经营管理有限公司	Shanghai Guotai Road Intergrative Market	247	21.57
上海新七浦服装批发市场	Shanghai Xinqipu Fashion Market	1 000	20.00
恒大陶瓷建材市场	Shanghai Hengda Ceramic Building Materials Trade Market	800	20.00
上海二手车交易市场有限公司	Shanghai Secondhand Aotumobile Exchange Market	23	18.22

上/海/统/计/年/鉴

主要统计指标解释

社会消费品零售总额

指批发和零售业、餐饮业、新闻出版业、邮政业和其他服务业等,售予城乡居民用于生活消费的商品和社会集团用于公共消费的商品之总量。社会消费品零售总额包括:

一、批发和零售业企业(单位):

1. 售予城乡居民的各种生活消费品;

2. 售予入境旅游的外国人、华侨、港澳台同胞的各类商品;

3. 售予行政事业单位、社会团体、军队和武警等机构的商品,以及以零售方式售予各类企业的商品。具体包括:用于非生产和社会交往的办公用品,如通讯设备、计算器具和设备、电讯网络设备、文印设备、音像视听器材和设备、纸张、本册、文具及装订文印材料、家具、日用电器、针纺织品、清洁卫生用品、文体用品、奖品、纪念品、礼品等;供内部人员乘坐的交通工具和燃料;用于办公设施修缮的各类配件、材料、工具等;用于取暖和防暑降温的设备、燃料、材料及食品等;专用于教学的用品和设备;非营利医疗机构的中、西药品、中药材和医疗设备器材;非专用的劳动保护用品;不对外营业的内部食堂用的餐具、炊具、设备、清洁卫生工具和食品、燃料等;军队、武警用于其人员生活的衣着品和个人用品;其他各类非生产性设备和用品。

二、餐饮业出售的主食、菜肴、烟酒饮料和其他商品。

三、新闻出版业、邮政业售予城乡居民、企事业单位、军队和武警等机构的书报杂志、音像制品、邮品等。

四、其他服务业出售的食品、烟酒饮料、服装鞋帽、日常生活用品、医药保健用品、艺术品、工艺美术品、玩具、殡葬用品以及其他消费品。

商品购进总额

指从本企业(单位)以外的单位和个人购进(包括从境外直接进口)作为转卖或加工后转卖的商品总额。它反映批发零售贸易业从国内、国外市场上购进商品的总量。商品购进总额包括:(1)从工农业生产者购进的商品;(2)从出版社、报社的出版发行部门购进的图书、杂志和报纸;(3)从各种登记注册类型的批发零售贸易企业(单位)购进的商品;(4)从其他单位购进的商品,如从机关、团体、企业等单位购进的剩余物资,从餐饮业、服务业购进的商品,从海关、市场管理部门购进的缉私和没收的商品,从居民手中收购的废旧商品等;(5)从国(境)外直接进口的商品。不包括企业(单位)为自身经营用和未通过买卖行为而收入的商品以及销售退回、商品升溢等。

商品销售总额

指对本企业以外的单位和个人出售(包括对国(境)外直接出口)的商品。这个指标反映批发零售贸易业在上海市场以及上海以外市场上销售商品的总量。商品销售总额包括:(1)售给城乡居民和社会集团消费用的商品;(2)售给工业、农业、建筑业、运输邮电业、批发零售贸易业、餐饮业、服务业等作为生产、经营使用的商品;(3)售给批发零售贸易业作为转卖或加工后转卖的商品;(4)对国(境)外直接出口的商品。不包括:出售本企业自用的废旧包装用品,未通过买卖行为付出的商品,经本单位介绍,由买卖双方直接结算,本单位只收取手续费的业务,购货退出的商品以及商品损耗和损失等。

主营业务收入

指企业在销售商品、提供劳务等日常活动中所产生的收入总额。

主营业务成本

指企业已销商品应负担的进货原价和商品进价成本。

营业费用

指批发零售贸易企业在购、销、存过程中发生的各项经营费用。包括运输费、装卸费、包装费、保险费、展览费、差旅费、广告费、商品损耗、进出口商品累计佣金、经营人员的工资及福利费等。

SHANGHAI STATISTICAL YEARBOOK

EXPLANATORY NOTES TO MAJOR STATISTICAL INDICATORS

□ Total Retail Sales of Consumer Goods

Total Retail Sales of Consumer Goods refer to the sum of retail sales of commodities sold by wholesale, retail, catering, publishing, post and telecommunications and other service industries to urban and rural households for private consumption and to social institutions for public consumption. Retail sales of consumer goods include:

Sales by wholesale and retail units:

of consumer goods sold to urban and rural households

of commodities sold to foreigners, overseas Chinese and Chinese compatriots from Hong Kong, Macao and Taiwan visiting in China

of commodities sold to government agencies, institutions, social organizations, military and armed police units, and commodities sold to enterprises in the form of retail sales. More specifically, they include: office facilities and articles for non-production purposes such as communications equipment, computing equipment and instruments, TV and network equipment, printing and copying equipment, audio-visual equipment and instruments, paper, notebooks, stationeries, furniture, electric appliances, knitwear, sanitation and cleaning articles, cultural and sport articles, articles for prizes, souvenirs, etc.; transport vehicles and fuels for employees; materials, spare parts and tools for the maintenance of office facilities; equipment, fuels, materials and food for winter heating or summer cooling purposes; articles and equipment for teaching purpose; Chinese and western medicines and medical equipment and facilities purchased by non profit-making medical institutes; non-specialized work safety articles; cooking utensils, tableware, equipment, cleaning articles, food and fuels purchased by internal cafeterias; clothes and personal articles purchased by military or armed police units for their officials and soldiers; and other equipment and articles for non-production purposes.

Sales of stable food, cooked dishes, beverages, tobaccos and other articles by catering units.

Sales of books, newspapers, magazines, audio-visual products and post products by publishing, post and telecommunications departments to urban and rural households and to enterprises, institutions, military and armed police units.

Sales of food, beverages, tobaccos, clothing, hats, footwear, articles for daily use, medicines, medical and health articles, work of art, handicrafts, toys, funeral articles and other articles by other service industries.

□ Total Purchase of Commodities

Total Purchases of Commodities refer to the total value of purchases of commodities by enterprises (establishments) from other establishments or individuals (including direct import from abroad) for the purpose of re-selling, either with or without further processing of the commodities purchased. This indicator is used to show the total value of purchases of commodities by wholesale and retail establishments from domestic and overseas markets. The total purchases include: (1) agricultural and industrial products purchased from producers; (2) books, magazines and newspapers purchased from distribution departments of the publishers; (3) commodities purchased from wholesale and retail establishments of different status of registration; (4) commodities purchased from other units, such as surplus materials purchased from government agencies, enterprises or institutions, commodities purchased from catering and service establishments, confiscated goods purchased from customs authorities or market management agencies, second-hand goods and wastes purchased from residents; and (5) commodities directly imported from abroad. Excluded are commodities purchased by enterprises (establishments) for use in their own business operation, commodities obtained without buying or selling procedures, rejected commodities, etc.

□ Total Sales of Commodities

Total Sales of Commodities refer to the selling of commodities to other establishments and individuals (including direct export). Reflecting the total value of sales of commodities at Shanghai markets and out-of-Shanghai markets, this indicator includes: (1)commodities sold to urban and rural households and institutions for their consumption; (2)commodities sold to establishments in industry, agriculture, construction, transportation, post and telecommunications, wholesale and retail trade, catering and service trade and public utility for their production and operation; (3)commodities sold to wholesale and retail establishments for re-selling, with or without further processing; and (4) commodities for direct export to other countries. Excluded are selling of

EXPLANATORY NOTES TO MAJOR STATISTICAL INDICATORS

waste packaging materials used by enterprises themselves commodities transferred without buying or selling procedures, commission income from brokerage in transactions whose settlement is directly handled by buyers and sellers, rejected commodities in the purchase, loss in commodities, etc.

□ Prime Operating Revenue

Prime Operating Revenue refers to the earnings a corporation receives in daily activity such as selling goods and offering labor service.

□ Operating Cost

Operating Cost refers to the cost a corporation paid to buy and deliver the commodities.

□ Operating Expenses

Operating Expenses refer to the spendings that a wholesaler or retailer pays in buying, selling or stocking goods. It includes fees incurred in transport, loading and unloading, packaging, insurance, exhibition, business trip, advertisement, commodity wastage, commissions in import and export, salaries and bonus paid to workers involved.

第十六篇

CHAPTER 16

金融业

FINANCE

表 16.1 金融机构(2006~2007)
FINANCIAL INSTITUTIONS

单位:家(Unit)

指 标	Indicators	2006	2007
金融机构	Financial Institutions	504	604
#银行业机构	Banking Institutions	82	109
保险业机构	Insurance Institutions	222	261
证券业机构	Security Institutions	90	94
#外资金融机构	Year-end Foreign Financial Institutions Operating	110	140
#外资银行及财务公司	Year-end Foreign Bank and Finance Company Operating	63	84
#获准经营人民币业务	Permission of Operating RMB Business Gained	43	45

表 16.2 主要年份保险及保险中介机构
INSURERS AND INSURANCE AGENTS IN MAIN YEARS

单位:家(Unit)

指 标	Indicators	2000	2006	2007
保险机构	**Insurers**	**21**	**76**	**96**
#中 资	Domestic-funded	9	52	68
外 资	Foreign-funded	12	24	28
#财产险公司	Property Insurance Company	11	31	41
人寿险公司	Life Insurance Company	10	36	41
再保险公司	Reinsurance Company		3	4
保险中介机构	**Insurance Agents**	**1**	**146**	**165**

注：本表数据由中国保监委上海保监局提供。
Note：Data in this table are provided by Shanghai Insurance Regulatory Bureau.

表 16.3 外资金融机构实到资本金(2006~2007)
REAL CAPITAL OF FOREIGN FINANCIAL INSTITUTIONS

单位:亿元(100 million yuan)

指 标	Indicators	2006	2007
外资金融机构	Year-end Foreign Financial Institutions Operating in Shanghai	35.69	51.67
外资银行及财务公司	Year-end Foreign Bank and Finance Company Operating	26.56	30.67
保险机构	Insurance Institutions	5.70	6.43
证券机构	Security Institutions	3.43	14.57

表 16.4 主要年份金融机构存贷款余额
SAVING DEPOSIT AND LOAN BALANCE OF FINANCIAL INSTITUTIONS IN MAIN YEARS

单位:亿元(100 million yuan)

指 标	Indicators	2000	2006	2007
金融机构存款余额	**Saving Deposit Balance of Financial Institutions**	**9 349.83**	**26 454.88**	**30 315.53**
中资金融机构	Chinese Financial Institutions	9 088.66	24 924.65	28 168.50
人民币	RMB	7 771.50	23 535.24	27 044.75
外汇(折人民币)	Foreign Currencies(Converting into RMB)	1 317.16	1 389.41	1 123.75
外资金融机构	Foreign-funded Financial Institutions	261.17	1 530.23	2 147.03
外汇(折人民币)	Foreign Currencies (Converting into RMB)	196.41	636.86	702.75
人民币	RMB	64.76	893.37	1 444.28
金融机构贷款余额	**Loan Balance of Financial Institutions**	**7 254.26**	**18 603.92**	**21 709.95**
中资金融机构	Chinese Financial Institutions	6 427.84	15 968.94	18 019.40
人民币	RMB	5 959.51	14 826.93	16 607.77
外汇(折人民币)	Foreign Currencies (Converting into RMB)	468.33	1 142.01	1 411.63
外资金融机构	Foreign-funded Financial Institutions	826.42	2 634.99	3 690.55
外汇(折人民币)	Foreign Currencies (Converting into RMB)	635.50	1 479.64	1 702.52
人民币	RMB	190.92	1 155.35	1 988.03

表 16.5 主要年份中资金融机构人民币存款余额
RMB SAVING DEPOSIT OF CHINESE FINANCIAL INSTITUTIONS IN MAIN YEARS

单位:亿元(100 million yuan)

指 标	Indicators	2000	2006	2007
各项存款余额	**All Deposits**	**7 771.50**	**23 535.24**	**27 044.75**
企业存款	Enterprise Deposits	4 424.97	11 565.63	13 586.77
活期存款	Current Deposits	3 433.00	8 349.92	9 516.28
定期存款	Time Deposits	991.97	3 215.71	4 070.49
财政存款	Fiscal Deposits	179.68	396.74	740.98
机关团体存款	Deposits of Institutions and Organizations	91.12	956.05	1 653.58
储蓄存款	Savings Deposits	2 524.05	8 726.99	8 695.41
活期储蓄	Savings on Current Account	536.96	2 566.39	2 946.48
定期储蓄	Savings on Time Account	1 987.09	6 160.60	5 748.93
农业存款	Agricultural Deposits	171.29	502.58	617.88
委托存款	Entrusted Deposits	133.55	244.77	361.56
其他存款	Other Deposits	186.71	1142.48	1 388.57

注：本页数据由中国人民银行上海总部提供。
Note: Data on this page are provided by Shanghai Branch of People's Bank of China.

表 16.6 主要年份中资金融机构人民币贷款余额
RMB LOAN BALANCE OF CHINESE FINANCIAL INSTITUTIONS IN MAIN YEARS

单位：亿元（100 million yuan）

指 标	Indicators	2000	2006	2007
各项贷款余额	**All Loans**	**5 959.51**	**14 826.93**	**16 607.77**
#短期贷款	Short-term Loans	4 343.10	4 674.67	5 691.66
工业贷款	Industrial Loans	1 159.99	1 460.69	1 719.68
商业贷款	Commercial Loans	685.41	692.85	740.97
建筑业贷款	Construction Industry Loans	179.52	376.42	418.63
农业贷款	Agricultural Loans	31.59	9.98	15.59
乡镇企业贷款	Township Enterprise Loans	291.11	92.82	127.02
三资企业贷款	Overseas-funder Enterprise	439.39	138.90	152.42
私营企业及个体贷款	Private Business Loans	21.39	112.19	135.33
其他短期贷款	Other Short-term Loans	1 534.71	1 790.82	2 382.02
#个人短期消费贷款	Personal Short-term Consumption Loans		42.97	94.23
中长期贷款	Mid and Long-term Loans	1 071.39	8 963.10	10 156.13
基本建设贷款	Capital Construction Loans	523.79	3 271.30	3 584.76
技术改造贷款	Loans For Technical Updates and Transformation	404.71	155.83	122.87
其他中长期贷款	Other Mid and Long-term Loans	142.89	5 535.97	6 448.50
#个人中长期消费贷款	Mid and Long-term Loans For Personal Consumption		2 610.19	2 976.97
融资租赁	Financing Leasing	2.79	6.98	1.39
委托贷款	Trusted Loans	124.01	203.35	238.45
票据融资	Bill Financing		964.02	506.63
各项垫款	All Advanced Money		14.81	13.51

表 16.7 个人贷款总额(2005～2007)
TOTAL AMOUNT OF PERSONAL LOANS

单位：亿元（100 million yuan）

指 标	Indicators	2005	2006	2007
个人贷款总额	**Total Amount of Personal Loans**	**3 149.01**	**3 069.15**	**3 653.20**
个人消费贷款	Personal Consumption Loan	2 814.16	2 653.16	3 071.20
#个人住房贷款	Housing Mortgage Loan	2 644.94	2 483.73	2 859.92
汽车消费贷款	Car Consumption Loan	47.85	28.04	27.07
公积金贷款	Accumulation Fund Loan	334.85	415.99	582.00
个人住房贷款占个人消费贷款额比重(%)	**Percentage of Housing Mortgage Loan in Personal Consumption Loan**	**94.0**	**93.6**	**93.1**

注：本页数据由中国人民银行上海总部提供。
Note: Data on this page are provided by Shanghai Branch of People's Bank of China.

表 16.8 银行现金收入和支出(1990～2007)
CASH INCOME AND PAYOUT OF BANKS

单位:亿元(100 million yuan)

年 份 Year	现金收入 Cash Income	其中 of which #商品销售收入 Commodity Sales Income	#储蓄存款收入 Savings Income	#服务事业收入 Service Income	现金支出 Cash Payout	其中 of which #工资及对个人支出 Wage and Personal Payout	#储蓄存款支出 Savings Payout	#行政管理支出 Administrative Payout
1990	554.62	267.02	166.78	45.30	523.97	213.50	126.17	52.04
1991	697.34	312.02	220.87	59.38	667.14	256.55	178.78	64.94
1992	1 107.00	407.75	369.79	85.01	1 089.77	344.11	342.68	103.08
1993	1 766.29	594.21	647.16	126.20	1 776.11	495.36	585.66	208.33
1994	2 218.79	690.47	893.00	181.97	2 300.72	680.32	703.91	285.53
1995	3 017.36	828.25	1 398.83	208.13	3 102.50	913.91	1 201.86	342.88
1996	3 469.05	938.91	1 596.81	241.53	3 650.54	932.22	1 734.95	518.44
1997	4 026.57	998.75	1 877.66	279.41	4 219.72	779.27	2 404.84	606.30
1998	5 681.56	1 384.74	2 866.31	439.09	5 856.38	1 023.70	3 117.37	744.89
1999	6 430.00	1 506.02	3 370.06	493.27	6 612.87	949.15	3 749.12	856.16
2000	7 946.79	1 827.34	4 042.11	552.84	8 041.05	897.47	4 738.28	1 085.23
2001	10 102.34	2 085.64	5 937.10	574.42	10 305.35	977.28	6 268.39	1 426.58
2002	11 698.86	2 428.06	7 155.32	616.39	11 947.35	1 079.77	7 196.26	1 789.68
2003	15 378.63	2 918.36	10 064.82	693.09	15 730.94	1 407.72	9 836.08	2 274.99
2004	19 969.87	3 195.19	13 704.06	775.16	20 358.79	1 734.34	13 487.46	2 478.33
2005	21 195.88	3 152.31	14 838.14	745.68	21 701.53	1 919.32	14 417.49	2 615.49
2006	24 114.40	3 232.63	16 842.89	974.62	24 708.35	2 135.47	16 533.01	2 808.89
2007	30 070.03	3 637.62	22 071.51	1 271.51	30 721.55	2 488.74	21 724.99	3 162.89

注：本表数据由中国人民银行上海总部提供。
Note: Data in this table are provided by Shanghai Branch of People's Bank of China.

表 16.9 主要年份主要要素市场交易情况和资金拆借情况
TRANSACTIONS OF MAIN MATERIAL MARKETS AND INTERBANK FUNDING IN MAIN YEARS

指标	Indicators	2000	2006	2007
银行间市场成交总额(亿元)	**Interbank Funding (100 million yuan)**	**23 191.99**	**390 643.62**	**712 948.82**
拆借市场成交额	Total Funding	6 728.07	21 503.11	106 465.68
债券市场成交额	Total Bond Turnover	16 463.92	369 140.51	606 483.14
回购交易	Bonds Repurchase.	15 781.24	265 912.71	447 924.95
现券交易	Currency Transaction	682.68	102 563.93	156 043.39
远期交易	Forward Transaction		663.87	2 514.80
年末资金拆借余额	Year-end Total Funding Balance	289.00	500.35	1 258.98
黄金交易所成交金额(亿元)	**Total Gold Turnover (100 million yuan)**		**2 245.50**	**3 324.65**
钻石交易所成交金额(亿美元)	**Total Diamond Tumover (100 million USD)**		**5.73**	**10.02**
产权交易市场	**Property Right Market**			
交易项目(项)	Trade Volume (item)		2 866	2 610
交易金额(亿元)	Trade Turnover (100 million yuan)		844.12	956.93

注：本表数据由中国银行间同业拆借中心、上海黄金交易所、上海钻石交易所、上海产权交易所等提供。
Note: Data in this table are provided by China Foreign Exchange Trade System, Nation Intertank Funding. Center, Shanghai stock Exchange, Shanghai.

表 16.10　金融机构人民币存款基准利率(1990～2007)
BENCHMARK INTEREST RATE OF RMB DEPOSIT FOR FINANCIAL INSTITUTIONS

单位:年利率%(annual interest rate)

调整时间 Adjust Time	活　期 Checking Deposit	定　期 fixed deposit					
		3 个月 3 Months	6 个月 6 Months	1 年 1 Year	2 年 2 Year	3 年 3 Year	5 年 5 Year
1990.04.15	2.88	6.30	7.74	10.08	10.98	11.88	13.68
1990.08.21	2.16	4.32	6.48	8.64	9.36	10.08	11.52
1991.04.21	1.80	3.24	5.40	7.56	7.92	8.28	9.00
1993.05.15	2.16	4.86	7.20	9.18	9.90	10.80	12.06
1993.07.11	3.15	6.66	9.00	10.98	11.70	12.24	13.86
1996.05.01	2.97	4.86	7.20	9.18	9.90	10.80	12.06
1996.08.23	1.98	3.33	5.40	7.47	7.92	8.28	9.00
1997.10.23	1.71	2.88	4.14	5.67	5.94	6.21	6.66
1998.03.25	1.71	2.88	4.14	5.22	5.58	6.21	6.66
1998.07.01	1.44	2.79	3.96	4.77	4.86	4.95	5.22
1998.12.07	1.44	2.79	3.33	3.78	3.96	4.14	4.50
1999.06.10	0.99	1.98	2.16	2.25	2.43	2.70	2.88
2002.02.21	0.72	1.71	1.89	1.98	2.25	2.52	2.79
2004.10.29	0.72	1.71	2.07	2.25	2.70	3.24	3.60
2006.08.19	0.72	1.80	2.25	2.52	3.06	3.69	4.14
2007.03.18	0.72	1.98	2.43	2.79	3.33	3.96	4.41
2007.05.19	0.72	2.07	2.61	3.06	3.69	4.41	4.95
2007.07.21	0.81	2.34	2.88	3.33	3.96	4.68	5.22
2007.08.22	0.81	2.61	3.15	3.60	4.23	4.95	5.49
2007.09.15	0.81	2.88	3.42	3.87	4.50	5.22	5.76
2007.12.21	0.72	3.33	3.78	4.14	4.68	5.40	5.85

注：本表数据由中国人民银行提供。
Note: Data in this table are provided by People's Bank of China.

表 16.11 金融机构人民币贷款基准利率
BENCHMARK INTEREST RATE OF RMB LOAN FOR FINANCIAL INSTITUTIONS

单位:年利率%(annual interest rate)

调整时间 Adjust Time	6 个月 6 Month	1 年 1 Year	1~3 年(含) 1~3 Years	3~5 年(含) 3~5 Years	5 年以上 Above 5 Years
1991.04.21	8.10	8.64	9.00	9.54	9.72
1993.05.15	8.82	9.36	10.80	12.06	12.24
1993.07.11	9.00	10.98	12.24	13.86	14.04
1995.01.01	9.00	10.98	12.96	14.58	14.76
1995.07.01	10.08	12.06	13.50	15.12	15.30
1996.05.01	9.72	10.98	13.14	14.94	15.12
1996.08.23	9.18	10.08	10.98	11.70	12.42
1997.10.23	7.65	8.64	9.36	9.90	10.53
1998.03.25	7.02	7.92	9.00	9.72	10.35
1998.07.01	6.57	6.93	7.11	7.65	8.01
1998.12.07	6.12	6.39	6.66	7.20	7.56
1999.06.10	5.58	5.85	5.94	6.03	6.21
2002.02.21	5.04	5.31	5.49	5.58	5.76
2004.10.29	5.22	5.58	5.76	5.85	6.12
2006.04.28	5.40	5.85	6.03	6.12	6.39
2006.08.19	5.58	6.12	6.30	6.48	6.84
2007.03.18	5.67	6.39	6.57	6.75	7.11
2007.05.19	5.85	6.57	6.75	6.93	7.20
2007.07.21	6.03	6.84	7.02	7.20	7.38
2007.07.21	6.03	6.84	7.02	7.20	7.38
2007.07.21	6.03	6.84	7.02	7.20	7.38
2007.08.22	6.21	7.02	7.20	7.38	7.56
2007.09.15	6.48	7.29	7.47	7.65	7.83
2007.12.21	6.57	7.47	7.56	7.74	7.83

注：本表数据由中国人民银行提供。
Note: Data in this table are provided by People's Bank of China.

表 16.12 主要年份上海证券交易所上市公司股本结构
CAPITAL STOCK STRUCTURES OF PUBLIC COMPANIES IN SHANGHAI STOCK EXCHANGE IN MAIN YEARS

单位：亿元（100 million yuan）

指 标	Indicators	1995	2000	2006	2007
总 计	**Total**	**557.76**	**2 127.93**	**12 366.62**	**19 394.22**
非流通股份	Non-circulation Shares	365.48	1 383.43	8 025.07	10 773.80
国家股	State Shares	245.38	926.68	4 466.65	7 340.08
境内法人股	Domestic Sponsoring Corporate Shares	74.31	278.17	523.98	638.83
外资法人股	Foreign Corporate Shares	5.59	21.76	60.12	85.50
募集法人股	Raised Corporate	34.87	119.22	62.21	14.29
内部职工股	Employees Shares	1.29	13.11	2.09	
机构配售及其他	Transferred, Left and Others	4.04	24.49	2 910.02	2 695.10
可流通股份	Circulation Shares	192.28	744.50	4 341.55	8 620.42
A 股	A Shares	95.21	563.92	2 144.31	3 283.92
B 股	B Shares	34.65	85.07	110.17	115.38
H 股	H Shares	62.42	95.51	2 087.07	5 221.12

表 16.13 上海证券交易所有价证券成交总额（1991～2007）
TOTAL VOLUME OF PRICED SECURITIES TRADING IN SHANGHAI STOCK EXCHANGE

单位：亿元（100 million yuan）

年 份 Year	合 计 Total	股 票 Shocks	其 中 of which A 股 A Shares	B 股 B Shares	基 金 Funds	债 券 Bonds	其 中 of which 国债现货 State Treasury Bond	国债回购 Repo	其 他 Others
1991	46	8	8			38	32		6
1992	324	247	233	14		77	70		7
1993	2 455	2 341	2 262	79	12	62	61		40
1994	6 427	5 735	5 627	108	117	520	457	63	55
1995	5 460	3 103	3 042	61	306	1 937	764	1 172	114
1996	27 661	9 115	9 020	95	497	17 403	4 962	12 439	646
1997	29 843	13 763	13 550	213	220	15 396	3 468	11 912	464
1998	34 336	12 386	12 304	82	605	21 267	6 047	15 188	78
1999	35 992	16 966	16 826	140	1 366	17 447	5 277	12 124	213
2000	49 901	31 374	31 030	344	1 334	16 896	3 657	13 147	297
2001	44 144	22 709	19 877	2 833	1 349	19 794	4 383	15 343	292
2002	48 528	16 959	16 442	517	557	30 877	6 381	24 419	135
2003	82 912	20 824	20 541	283	362	61 596	5 500	52 982	130
2004	76 927	26 470	26 229	241	249	49 998	2 962	44 086	210
2005	49 718	19 240	19 061	179	156	28 138	2 773	23 621	2 184
2006	91 912	57 817	57 245	572	777	18 130	1 537	15 487	15 188
2007	380 026	305 434	301 960	3 474	3 101	20 400	1 262	18 345	51 091

注：本页数据由上海证券交易所提供。
Note: Data on this page are provided by Shanghai Stock Exchange.

表 16.14 上证综合指数(1990～2007)
SHANGHAI COMPOSITE INDEX

年份 Year	开盘 Open	最高 High	日期 Date		最低 Low	日期 Date		收盘 Close
1990	96.05	127.61	12月31日	31,Dec	95.79	12月19日	19,Dec	127.61
1991	127.61	292.75	12月31日	31,Dec	104.96	5月17日	17,May	292.75
1992	293.74	1 429.01	5月26日	26,May	292.76	1月2日	2,Jan	780.39
1993	773.89	1 558.98	2月16日	16,Feb	750.46	12月20日	20,Dec	833.80
1994	837.70	1 052.94	9月13日	13,Sep	325.89	7月29日	29,July	647.87
1995	637.72	926.41	5月22日	22,May	524.43	2月7日	7,Feb	555.29
1996	550.26	1 258.69	12月11日	11,Dec	512.83	1月19日	19,Jan	917.02
1997	914.06	1 510.18	5月12日	12,May	870.80	2月20日	20,Feb	1 194.10
1998	1 200.95	1 422.95	6月4日	4,June	1 043.02	8月18日	18,Aug	1 146.70
1999	1 144.89	1 756.18	6月30日	30,June	1 047.83	5月17日	17,May	1 366.58
2000	1 368.69	2 125.72	11月23日	23,Nov	1 361.21	1月4日	4,Jan	2 073.48
2001	2 077.08	2 245.44	6月14日	14,June	1 514.86	10月22日	22,Oct	1 645.97
2002	1 643.49	1 748.89	6月25日	25,June	1 339.20	1月29日	29,Jan	1 357.65
2003	1 347.43	1 649.60	4月16日	16,Apr	1 307.40	11月13日	13,Nov	1 497.04
2004	1 492.72	1 777.52	4月6日	6,Apr	1 260.32	9月13日	13,Sep	1 266.50
2005	1 260.78	1 318.27	3月8日	8, Mar	1 011.50	7月11日	11, July	1 161.06
2006	1 163.88	2 698.90	12月29日	29,Dec	1 161.91	1月4日	4,Jan	2 675.47
2007	2 728.19	6 124.04	10月16日	16,Oct	2 541.53	2月6日	6,Feb	5 261.56

表 16.15 新上证综指、上证 180 指数等指数(2006～2007)
SSE NEW COMPOSITE, SSE 180, SSE 50 AND SSE DIVIDEND

年份 Year	开盘 Open	最高 High	日期 Date		最低 Low	日期 Date		收盘 Close
新上证综指 SSE New Composite								
2006	997.05	2 317.86	12月29日	29, Dec	992.91	1月4日	4, Jan	2 297.03
2007	2 343.56	5 210.71	10月16日	16, Otc	2 166.51	2月6日	6, Feb	4 470.90
上证 180 指数 SSE 180								
2006	2 174.72	4 810.86	12月29日	29, Dec	2 172.26	1月4日	4, Jan	4 780.23
2007	4 864.31	13 325.04	10月16日	16, Otc	4 750.22	1月5日	5, Jan	12 024.60
上证 50 指数 SSE 50								
2006	801.41	1 819.04	12月29日	29, Dec	800.21	1月4日	4, Jan	1 805.31
2007	1 842.63	4 772.93	10月16日	16, Otc	1 791.64	1月5日	5, Jan	4 226.72
上证红利指数 SSE Dividend								
2006	888.19	1 803.50	12月29日	29, Dec	886.01	1月4日	4, Jan	1 788.75
2007	1 817.02	5 272.32	10月16日	16, Otc	1 817.02	1月4日	4, Jan	4 661.24

注：本页数据由上海证券交易所提供。
Note: Data on this page are provided by Shanghai Stock Exchange.

表 16.16 上证基金指数(2000～2007)
SHANGHAI FUND INDEX

年 份 Year	开 盘 Open	最 高 High	日 期 Date		最 低 Low	日 期 Date		收 盘 Close
2000	996.69	1 121.71	12 月 29 日	29,Dec	968.70	5 月 16 日	16,May	1 121.71
2001	1 133.17	1 367.37	7 月 3 日	3,July	1 077.73	2 月 16 日	16,Feb	1 183.13
2002	1 168.82	1 237.98	6 月 24 日	24,June	934.54	11 月 27 日	27,Nov	942.33
2003	933.96	1 057.46	4 月 14 日	14,Apr	889.81	10 月 21 日	21,Otc	1 016.96
2004	1 012.37	1 101.88	4 月 7 日	7,Apr	836.81	11 月 8 日	8,Nov	872.01
2005	866.93	866.93	1 月 4 日	4,Jan	706.53	6 月 6 日	6,June	840.19
2006	837.92	2 091.30	12 月 29 日	29,Dec	837.82	1 月 4 日	4,Jan	2 090.52
2007	2 132.24	5 112.83	12 月 24 日	24,Dec	2 041.89	2 月 5 日	5,Feb	5 070.79

表 16.17 主要年份上海证券交易所市场概况
SHANGHAI STOCK EXCHANGE MARKET IN MAIN YEARS

指 标	Indicators	2000	2006	2007
上市公司数(个)	Quantity of Public Company (unit)	572	842	860
上市股票数(个)	Quantity of Listed Stock(unit)	614	886	904
上市证券数(个)	Quantity of Negotiable Securities(unit)	657	1 126	1 125
股票发行股数(亿股)	Shares of Stocks Issued (100 million shares)	2 032.42	10 279.54	14 173.1
A 股	A Shares	1 947.35	10 169.37	14 057.73
B 股	B Shares	85.07	110.17	115.38
股票市价总值(亿元)	Aggregate Value of Stocks in Market Price (100 million yuan)	26 930.86	71 612.38	269 838.87
A 股	A Shares	26 596.32	71 117.95	268 497.27
B 股	B Shares	334.54	494.43	1 341.60
流通股数(亿股)	Shares in Circulation (100 million shares)	648.99	2 254.48	3 399.30
A 股	A Shares	563.92	2 144.31	3 283.92
B 股	B Shares	85.07	110.17	115.38
流通市值(亿元)	Value in circulation (100 million yuan)	8 481.33	16 428.33	64 532.17
A 股	A Shares	8 146.79	15 933.90	63 190.57
B 股	B Shares	334.54	494.43	1 341.60
市场筹资额(亿元)	Funds Raised from Market (100 million yuan)	919.95	1 743.18	6 668.95
首次发行 A 股	IPO of A Shares	591.18	1 180.23	4 379.92
再次发行 A 股	Additional A Shares Issued	325.13	534.18	2 236.43
首次发行 B 股	IPO of B Shares	3.64		
可转换债券	Convertible Loan Stock		28.77	52.60

①本页数据由上海证券交易所提供。
②2006、2007 年未发行 B 股。
❶Data on this page are provided by Shanghai Stock Exchange.
❷There were no IPO of B shares in 2006 and 2007.

表 16.18 主要年份上海证券交易所投资者开户情况
ACCOUNT-OPENING BY INVESTORS IN SHANGHAI STOCK EXCHANGE IN MAIN YEARS

单位：万户（10 000 households）

	指 标 Indicators	1995	2000	2006	2007
年末开户总数	**Total Accounts Year-end**				
总 数	Total	685.20	2 957.84	3 901.53	5 817.01
个 人	Private	682.32	2 944.89	3 878.76	5 788.22
机 构	Institution	2.88	12.95	22.77	28.79
A 股开户数	**A Shares Accounts**				
总 数	Total	682.50	2 943.32	3 799.94	5 673.18
个 人	Private	680.00	2 931.20	3 778.51	5 645.87
机 构	Institution	2.50	12.12	21.43	27.31
B 股开户数	**B Shares Accounts**				
总 数	Total	2.70	14.52	101.59	143.83
个 人	Private	2.32	13.69	100.25	142.35
机 构	Institution	0.38	0.83	1.34	1.48
当年新开户总数	**Newly Opened Accounts During the Year**				
总 数	Total	110.31	676.72	153.62	1 915.47
个 人	Private	109.75	672.09	152.13	1 909.45
机 构	Institution	0.56	4.64	1.49	6.02
A 股新开户数	**Newly Opened Accounts of A Shares**				
总 数	Total	109.50	671.08	151.88	1 873.24
个 人	Private	109.00	666.52	150.51	1 867.36
机 构	Institution	0.50	4.56	1.37	5.88
B 股新开户数	**Newly Opened Accounts of B Shares**				
总 数	Total	0.81	5.64	1.74	42.23
个 人	Private	0.75	5.56	1.62	42.09
机 构	Institution	0.06	0.08	0.12	0.14

①本页数据由上海证券交易所提供。
②本表数据不含基金帐户。
❶Data on this page are provided by Shanghai Stock Exchange.
❷The data in this table don't include fund account.

表 16.19 上海股份制企业首次发行 A 股一览
LIST OF IPO OF A SHARES OF SHANGHAI ENTERPRISES

名　称	Name	股票面值 Par Value of Stocks (元) (yuan)	发行价 Issued Price (元) (yuan)	总股本 Aggregate of Capital Stock (万股) (10 000 shares)	发行量 Issued Volume (万股) (10 000 shares)	筹资额 Capital Raised (万元) (10 000 yuan)
1984 年	**Year of 1984**			**50**	**50**	**50**
飞乐音响	Feile Accoustics	1.00	1.00	50	50	50
1985 年	**Year of 1985**			**530**	**530**	**530**
延中实业	YanZhong	1.00	1.00	500	500	500
爱使股份	AiShi	1.00	1.00	30	30	30
1987 年	**Year of 1987**			**17 895**	**2 410**	**2 410**
真空电子	Vacuum Electron	1.00	1.00	15 694	1 450	1 450
申华实业	Shenhua	1.00	1.00	100	100	100
飞乐股份	Feile	1.00	1.00	2 101	860	860
1988 年	**Year of 1988**			**650**	**485**	**485**
豫园商城	Yuyuan Bazar	1.00	1.00	650	485	485
1991 年	**Year of 1991**			**3 400**	**2 703**	**12 961**
兴业房产	Xingye Real Estate	1.00	3.50	2 000	1 303	4 561
浦东大众	Pudong Dazhong	1.00	6.00	1 400	1 400	8 400
1992 年	**Year of 1992**			**1 036 691**	**184 676**	**823 737**
二纺机	ErfangJi	1.00	3.80	17 954	3 820	14 516
轻工机械	Light Ind Mach	1.00	2.40	16 516	1 000	2 400
嘉丰股份	Jiafeng	1.00	3.50	7 063	1 150	4 025
联合实业	United Holding	1.00	4.30	9 293	1 100	4 730
异型钢管	Special Steel Tube	1.00	2.80	3 610	1 275	3 570
中纺机	China Textile Mach	1.00	3.80	13 810	2 800	10 640
大众出租	DaZhong Taxi	1.00	4.90	6 090	1 000	4 900
第一铅笔	First Pencil	1.00	4.00	3 900	1 008	4 032
永生制笔	Wing Sung	1.00	7.20	5 604	1 200	8 640
胶带股份	Rubber Belt	1.00	3.50	4 395	1 000	3 500
丰华圆珠	Fenghua Ballpen	1.00	5.50	5 672	1 800	9 900
第一食品	1st Provision Store	1.00	5.80	2 839	1 300	7 540
联华合纤	Lian Hua Fibre	1.00	5.58	7 289	2 000	11 160
氯碱化工	Chlor Alkali	1.00	5.40	59 181	8 643	46 672
冰箱压缩	Refrige Compressor	1.00	4.80	11 991	4 000	19 200
联农股份	United Agriculture	1.00	5.00	2 500	1 700	8 500
金陵股份	Jinling	1.00	4.20	5 099	1 817	7 631
嘉宝实业	Jiabao	1.00	5.00	10 626	2 500	12 500
轮胎橡胶	Tyre and Rubber	1.00	6.80	45 201	2 000	13 600
复华实业	Forward	1.00	5.20	4 339	1 500	7 800
水仙电器	Narcissus Electric	1.00	4.60	8 578	2 500	11 500

① 本表数据由上海证券交易所提供。
② 每股面值为 1 元人民币，对历史曾出现的大于 1 元面额的股票，均被换算到当前 1 元面额。
③ “＊”表示在深圳交易所中小板上市。
④未列入的年份是因为该年未发行 A 股。
❶Data in this table are provided by Shanghai Stock Exchange.
❷Par value of each share is one yuan. The par value of the stocks used to be above one yuan have all been converted to one yuan.
❸The mark ＊ refers to the stocks came into market in Shenzhen Stock Exchange.
❹There are some years unlisted because there were no IPO of A shares in those years.

表 16.19 续表 1 continued

名称	Name	股票面值 Par Value of Stocks (元) (yuan)	发行价 Issued Price (元) (yuan)	总股本 Aggregate of Capital Stock (万股) (10 000 shares)	发行量 Issued Volume (万股) (10 000 shares)	筹资额 Capital Raised (万元) (10 000 yuan)
申达实业	Shenda	1.00	3.00	13 655	3 500	10 500
电器股份	Electric	1.00	4.40	40 651	4 500	19 800
新世界	New World	1.00	8.80	1 500	641	5 641
棱光实业	Lengguang	1.00	2.20	3 380	1 500	3 300
龙头股份	Dragon Head	1.00	3.80	17 447	4 500	17 100
中百一店	No. 1 Store	1.00	8.90	12 108	5 300	47 170
华联商厦	Shanghai Hualian	1.00	9.28	8 153	4 500	41 760
双鹿电器	Shuanglu Elec	1.00	5.66	9 217	3 500	19 810
海鸟电子	Albatronics	1.00	4.00	1 529	600	2 400
三爱富	3F New Material	1.00	3.40	5 000	2 000	6 800
广电股份	Radio and Audio	1.00	4.80	45 922	6 538	31 382
黄浦房产	Huangpu Real Estate	1.00	6.08	8 024	2 893	17 589
浦东金桥	Jin Qiao	1.00	2.50	30 000	3 000	7 500
国脉实业	Guo Mai	1.00	5.18	7 000	2 879	14 913
众城实业	Zhongcheng	1.00	1.20	6 180	1 000	1 200
申能股份	Shenergy	1.00	2.80	240 274	27 988	78 366
爱建股份	Aijian	1.00	7.00	15 000	4 500	31 500
望春花	Wang Chun Hua	1.00	5.00	3 022	1 200	6 000
国嘉实业	Citic-Jiading	1.00	3.60	2 998	1 000	3 600
新亚快餐	New Asia Fast Food	1.00	3.28	1 700	700	2 296
外高桥	Outer Gaoqiao	1.00	2.80	28 000	1 000	2 800
原水股份	Raw Water	1.00	3.80	66 242	17 249	65 546
新锦江	Jinjiang Tower	1.00	5.20	16 630	8 000	41 600
豫园商城	Yuyuan Bazar	1.00	8.00	11 290	5 350	42 800
南洋实业	Nanyang Int'l	1.00	5.58	6 600	2 574	14 363
浦东强生	Qiang Sheng Taxi	1.00	2.85	1 800	720	2 052
陆家嘴	Lujiazui	1.00	2.80	71 500	1 500	4 200
沪昌特钢	Huchang Sp Steel	1.00	2.80	40 000	8 931	25 007
良华实业	Liang Hua	1.00	2.45	6 269	2 300	5 636
东方明珠	Oriential Pearl	1.00	5.10	41 000	4 000	20 400
商业网点	Commercial Re	1.00	4.10	4 850	2 000	8 200
凌桥股份	Lingqiao Tapwater	1.00	1.50	18 200	3 700	5 550
1993 年	**Year of 1993**			**802 423**	**117 441**	**470 986**
中华企业	China Enterprise	1.00	6.50	7 863	2 000	13 001
钢运股份	Steel Trans	1.00	4.00	5 084	1 500	6 000
上海凤凰	Phoenix Bicycle	1.00	6.00	25 176	3 000	18 000
邮通设备	Posts and Telecoms	1.00	5.00	6 661	1 900	9 500
上海石化	Shanghai Petrochem	1.00	3.00	455 000	55 000	165 000
上海三毛	Sanmao Textile	1.00	4.00	6 659	1 750	7 000
亚通股份	Ya Tong	1.00	2.80	5 016	1 800	5 040
大江股份	Dajiang (Group)	1.00	4.00	45 935	2 500	10 000

表 16.19 续表 2 continued

名 称	Name	股票面值 Par Value of Stocks (元) (yuan)	发行价 Issued Price (元) (yuan)	总股本 Aggregate of Capital Stock (万股) (10 000 shares)	发行量 Issued Volume (万股) (10 000 shares)	筹资额 Capital Raised (万元) (10 000 yuan)
上海永久	Forever Bicycle	1.00	5.50	17 101	2 300	12 650
耀皮玻璃	Yaohua Pilkington	1.00	6.30	28 999	2 952	18 598
隧道股份	Tunnel Engineering	1.00	3.40	8 433	2 900	9 860
物贸中心	Goods and Materials	1.00	3.70	13 987	1 900	7 030
万象集团	Wan Xiang	1.00	5.00	5 000	2 000	10 000
益民集团	Yimin	1.00	6.60	5 033	1 270	8 382
时装股份	Fashion Clothing	1.00	5.40	5 000	2 000	10 800
兰生股份	Lansheng	1.00	5.50	14 163	3 550	19 525
友谊华侨	Friendship	1.00	5.20	4 500	1 500	7 800
上菱电器	Shangling Electric	1.00	5.50	20 365	2 700	14 850
界龙实业	Jielong	1.00	4.00	5 000	1 859	7 436
农垦商社	Saic Trading	1.00	5.00	5 019	1 260	6 300
第九百货	No. 9 Store	1.00	5.00	5 000	2 000	10 000
上股份柴	Diesel Engine	1.00	5.20	22 942	2 800	14 560
中西药业	Zhongxi Pharm	1.00	5.00	5 000	1 920	9 600
工业缝纫	Industrial Sewing	1.00	5.80	11 920	2 200	12 760
英雄股份	Hero	1.00	5.80	7 501	1 680	9 744
钢管股份	Steel Tube	1.00	4.00	15 840	2 200	8 800
同济科技	Tongji Science	1.00	6.00	5 009	1 300	7 800
自仪股份	Auto Instrument	1.00	3.50	19 086	3 200	11 200
四药股份	No. 4 Pharm	1.00	4.50	5 797	1 500	6 750
华东电脑	East-china Computer	1.00	3.00	5 000	2 000	6 000
海欣股份	Haixin	1.00	7.00	9 334	1 000	7 000
1996 年	**Year of 1996**			**122 255**	**23 810**	**128 078**
东海股份	Shanghai Donghai	1.00	5.80	12 392	2 710	15 718
民丰实业	Minfeng	1.00	4.90	8 689	1 950	9 555
上海港机	Shanghai Port Ma	1.00	5.18	11 960	4 000	20 720
浦东不锈	Pudong Stainless	1.00	5.40	24 000	6 000	32 400
新亚股份	New Asia	1.00	4.90	35 464	1 900	9 310
巴士股份	Shanghai Bus	1.00	5.80	5 200	2 200	12 760
张江高科	Zhangjiang Hi-te	1.00	6.15	10 000	2 500	15 375
中国高科	China High Tech	1.00	4.80	14 550	2 550	12 240
1997 年	**Year of 1997**			**679 249**	**88 250**	**431 558**
江南重工	Jiangnan Heavy Industry	1.00	5.37	13 201	6 000	32 220
中纺投资	China Textile Investment	1.00	6.20	11 000	3 000	18 600
上海梅林	Shanghai Meilin	1.00	4.00	27 000	10 000	40 000
华源股份	China Energy	1.00	7.04	23 853	4 000	28 160
东方航空	Eastern Airline	1.00	2.45	486 695	30 000	73 500
上海汽车	Shanghai Auto	1.00	7.02	100 000	30 000	210 600
东风电仪	Dongfeng Elec Instruments	1.00	7.55	5 000	1 250	9 438
长江投资	Changjiang Investment	1.00	4.76	12 500	4 000	19 040

表 16.19 续表3 continued

	名 称 Name	股票面值 Par Value of Stocks (元) (yuan)	发行价 Issued Price (元) (yuan)	总股本 Aggregate of Capital Stock (万股) (10 000 shares)	发行量 Issued Volume (万股) (10 000 shares)	筹资额 Capital Raised (万元) (10 000 yuan)
1998 年	**Year of 1998**			**241 343**	**75 800**	**472 438**
沪东重机	Hudong Heavy Machine	1.00	3.83	21 954	7 000	26 810
航天机电	Hangtian Elec	1.00	5.76	27 200	6 800	39 168
上海贝岭	Shanghai Belling	1.00	6.53	33 419	12 000	78 360
上海建工	Shanghai Construction	1.00	6.67	53 700	15 000	100 050
虹桥机场	Hongqiao Airport	1.00	6.41	90 000	30 000	192 300
复星实业	Shanghai Fuxing	1.00	7.15	15 070	5 000	35 750
1999 年	**Year of 1999**			**273 340**	**48 500**	**466 640**
浦发银行	Pudong Development Bank	1.00	10.00	241 000	40 000	400 000
紫江实业	Zijiang	1.00	7.84	32 340	8 500	66 640
2000 年	**Year of 2000**			**1 373 420**	**216 700**	**1 086 166**
上港集箱	Shanggang Containers	1.00	11.98	90 220	21 000	251 580
宝钢股份	Baosteel	1.00	4.18	1 251 200	187 700	784 586
东方创业	Dongfang	1.00	6.25	32 000	8 000	50 000
2001 年	**Year of 2001**			**87 151**	**24 000**	**241 290**
上海家化	Shanghai Jahwa	1.00	9.18	27 000	8 000	73 440
上海能源	Shanghai Energy	1.00	9.00	40 151	11 000	99 000
交大昂立	Jiao Tong University	1.00	13.77	20 000	5 000	68 850
2002 年	**Year of 2002**			**340 218**	**70 000**	**286 700**
中海发展	Zhonghai Development	1.00	2.36	203 000	35 000	82 600
上海航空	Shanghai Airlines	1.00	5.33	72 100	20 000	106 600
光明乳业	Brightness Milk	1.00	6.50	65 118	15 000	97 500
2003 年	**Year of 2003**			**171 934**	**29 500**	**175 950**
上海电力	Shanghai Power	1.00	5.80	156 351	24 000	139 200
中科合臣	Synica	1.00	7.00	7 600	3 000	21 000
置信电气	Zhixin Electric	1.00	6.30	7 983	2 500	15 750
2004 年	**Year of 2004**			**43 494**	**14 440**	**107 523**
浦东建设	Pudong Construction	1.00	4.85	22 600	8 000	38 800
现代制药	Modern Oharmacy	1.00	8.08	8 719	3 300	26 664
科华生物 *	Kehua Bio-engineering	1.00	11.12	6 875	1 800	20 016
思源电器 *	Sieyuan Electric	1.00	16.45	5 300	1 340	22 043
2006 年	**Year of 2006**			**349 577**	**121 800**	**456 144**
招商轮船	CMES	1.00	3.71	343 340	120 000	445 200
威尔泰 *	Welltech	1.00	6.08	6 237	1 800	10 944
2007 年	**Year of 2007**			**6 926 944**	**675 148**	**7 237 050**
交通银行	Bank of Communications	1.00	7.90	4 899 438	319 035	2 520 377
中国太保	CPIC	1.00	30.00	770 000	100 000	3 000 000
中海集运	CSCL	1.00	6.62	1 168 313	233 663	1 546 846
中国海诚 *	China Haicheng Engineering	1.00	6.88	11 400	2 900	19 952
汉钟精机 *	Hanbell Precise Machinery	1.00	9.08	15 050	3 800	34 504
斯米克 *	Cimic	1.00	5.08	38 000	9 500	48 260
延华智能 *	Yanhua Smartech	1.00	7.89	8 000	2 000	15 780
海得控制 *	Hi-tech Control System	1.00	12.90	11 000	2 800	36 120
海隆软件 *	Hyron Software	1.00	10.49	5 740	1 450	15 211

表 16.20 上海股份制企业首次发行 B 股一览
LIST OF IPO OF B SHARES OF SHANGHAI ENTERPRISES

名称	Name	股票面值(元) Face Value (yuan)	发行价 Issued Price 美元 USD	发行价 Issued Price 折人民币(元) Converting into RMB (yuan)	发行量(万股) Issual Volume (10 000 shares)	筹资额 Capital Raised 万美元 10 000 USD	筹资额 Capital Raised 折人民币(万元) Converting into RMB (10 000 yuan)
1992 年	**Year of 1992**				**85 500**	**65 558**	**426 891**
真空	Vacuum	1.00	0.712	4.20	10 000	7 120	42 000
二纺	Erfang Ji	1.00	0.610	3.88	12 500	7 625	48 500
大众	Dazhong	1.00	0.650	4.30	2 500	1 625	10 750
永生	Wing Sung	1.00	0.836	5.30	2 500	2 090	13 250
中铅	First Pencil	1.00	0.520	3.47	2 500	1 300	8 675
中纺	China Textile	1.00	0.610	4.00	7 000	4 270	28 000
胶带	Bubber Belt	1.00	0.531	3.50	2 500	1 328	8 750
氯碱	Chlor Alkali	1.00	0.800	5.25	24 000	19 200	126 000
轮胎	Tyre and Rubber	1.00	1.100	7.30	17 000	18 700	124 066
冰箱	Refrigerator	1.00	0.460	3.38	5 000	2 300	16 900
1993 年	**Year of 1993**				**85 300**	**38 464**	**339 100**
金桥	Jinqiao	1.00	0.344	2.80	11 000	3 784	30 800
外高桥	Outer Gaoqiao	1.00	0.380	4.07	8 500	3 230	34 595
联华	Lian Hua	1.00	0.380	3.34	3 000	1 140	10 020
新锦江	Jinjiang Tower	1.00	0.379	3.30	9 000	3 411	29 700
永久	Forever Bicycle	1.00	0.355	3.09	6 000	2 130	18 540
凤凰	Phoenix Bicycle	1.00	0.405	3.52	10 000	4 050	35 200
海欣	HaiXin	1.00	0.700	6.09	3 500	2 450	21 315
耀皮	Yaohua Pilkinton	1.00	0.720	6.27	10 000	7 200	62 664
大江	Dajiang (Group)	1.00	0.402	3.50	3 500	1 407	12 250
上柴	Diesel Engine	1.00	0.523	4.55	10 000	5 230	45 500
英雄	Hero	1.00	0.439	3.82	3 500	1 537	13 370
三毛	Sanmao	1.00	0.344	2.98	3 300	1 135	9 834
友谊	Friendship	1.00	0.440	3.83	4 000	1 760	15 312

①本表数据由上海证券交易所提供。
②每股面值为 1 元人民币，对历史曾出现的大于 1 元面额的股票，均被换算到当前 1 元面额。
③未列出的年份是因为该年未发行 B 股。
❶Data in this table are provided by Shanghai Stock Exchange.
❷Par value of each share is one yuan. The par value of the stocks used to be above one yuan have all been converted to one yuan.
❸There are some years unlisted because there were no IPO of B shares in those years.

表 16.20 续表 1　continued

名　称 Name		股票面值(元) Face Value (yuan)	发行价 Issued Price 美　元 USD	折人民币(元) Converting into RMB (yuan)	发行量(万股) Issued Volume (10 000 shares)	筹资额 Capital Raised 万美元 10 000 USD	折人民币(万元) Converting into RMB (10 000 yuan)
1994 年	**Year of 1994**				**86 500**	**39 400**	**349 970**
工　缝	Industrial Sewing	1.00	0.420	3.65	7 500	3 150	27 405
上　菱	Shangling	1.00	0.750	6.52	7 000	5 250	45 654
钢　管	Steel Tube	1.00	0.398	4.00	8 000	3 184	32 000
物　贸	Goods and Materials	1.00	0.258	3.70	5 000	1 290	18 500
自　仪	Auto Instrument	1.00	0.248	2.16	7 000	1 736	15 103
国　旅	Int'L Travel	1.00	0.360	3.08	6 000	2 160	18 461
邮　通	Posts and Telecoms	1.00	0.520	4.44	6 000	3 120	26 614
水　仙	Narcissus	1.00	0.265	2.26	10 000	2 650	22 602
陆家嘴	Lujiazui	1.00	0.668	5.69	20 000	13 360	113 850
新　亚	New Asia	1.00	0.350	2.98	10 000	3 500	29 781
1995 年	**Year of 1995**				**8 000**	**2 216**	**18 400**
金　泰	Jintai	1.00	0.277	2.30	8 000	2 216	18 400
1996 年	**Year of 1996**				**26 000**	**6 344**	**52 577**
汇　丽	Huili	1.00	0.187	1.54	8 000	1 496	12 320
华源股份	Huayuan Stocks	1.00	0.280	2.33	10 000	2 800	23 300
开　开	Kai Kai	1.00	0.256	2.12	8 000	2 048	16 957
1997 年	**Year of 1997**				**10 000**	**4 330**	**35 900**
振　华	Zhenghua	1.00	0.433	3.59	10 000	4 330	35 900
1998 年	**Year of 1998**				**35 000**	**9 704**	**80 408**
凯　马	Kaima B	1.00	0.276	2.29	24 000	6 624	54 888
茉织华	Mozhihua	1.00	0.280	2.32	11 000	3 080	25 520
2000 年	**Year of 2000**				**18 400**	**4 379**	**36 248**
凌　云	Lingyun	1.00	0.238	1.97	18 400	4 379	36 248

表 16.21 上海股份制企业在境外首次发行股票一览
LIST OF OVERSEAS IPO OF SHANGHAI ENTERPRISES

	股票名称 Stock Title	上市日期 Date of IPO	上市地点 Place of IPO		发行价(元) 港币/美元 Issued Price(yuan) HKD/USD	发行量 (万股) Circulation (10 000 shares)	筹资额(万元) 港币/美元 Capital Raised (10 000 yuan) HKD/USD
1993 年	**Year of 1993**						
上海石化	SPC	1993.11.08	香　港	Hong Kong	1.58	168 000	265 440
1994 年	**Year of 1994**						
海兴轮船	Haixing Shipping	1994.11.11	香　港	Hong Kong	1.46	108 000	157 680
1997 年	**Year of 1997**						
东方航空	China Eastern	1997.02.05	香　港	Hong Kong	1.38	156 695	216 239
2000 年	Year of 2000						
复旦微电子	Fudan Microelectronics	2000.08.04	香　港	Hong Kong	0.80	12 500	10 000
2002 年	**Year of 2002**						
交大慧谷	Jiaoda Withub Information	2002.07.31	香　港	Hong Kong	0.66	13 200	8 712
复旦张江	Fudan-Zhangjiang	2002.08.13	香　港	Hong Kong	0.80	19 800	15 840
2003 年	**Year of 2003**						
联华超市	Lianhua Super Market	2003.06.27	香　港	Hong Kong	3.88	15 000	58 125
携程网	Ctrip	2003.12.09	美　国	USA	18.00	420	7 560
2004 年	**Year of 2004**						
复地集团	Forte Land	2004.02.06	香　港	Hong Kong	2.35	73 300	172 258
灵通网	Linktone	2004.03.04	美　国	USA	14.00	614	8 596
中芯国际	SMIC	2004.03.17	美　国	USA	17.50	9 788	171 290
中芯国际	SMIC	2004.03.18	香　港	Hong Kong	2.69	25 758	69 289
盛大网	Shanda	2004.05.13	美　国	USA	11.00	1 380	15 180
中海集装箱	CSCL	2004.06.16	香　港	Hong Kong	3.18	242 000	768 350
青浦消防	Qingpu Fire	2004.06.24	香　港	Hong Kong	0.54	5 556	3 000
前程无忧	51job	2004.09.28	美　国	USA	14.00	525	7 350
第九城市	The9 Limited	2004.12.15	美　国	USA	17.00	607	10 319
2005 年	**Year of 2005**						
上海电气	Shanghai Electric	2005.04.28	香　港	Hong Kong	1.70	297 291	505 395
交通银行	Communication Bank	2005.06.23	香　港	Hong Kong	2.50	585 600	1 464 000
上海栋华	Shanghai Donghua	2005.07.13	香　港	Hong Kong	0.53	10 300	5 459
分众传媒	Focus Media	2005.07.13	美　国	USA	17.00	1 010	17 170
新宇亨得利	Xinyu Hendry	2005.09.27	香　港	Hong Kong	1.32	28 750	37 950
2006 年	**Year of 2006**						
先进半导体	ASMC	2006.04.07	香　港	Hong Kong	1.60	40 666	65 066
上海集优	PMC	2006.04.27	香　港	Hong Kong	2.10	60 056	126 118
盛高置地	SPGLand	2006.10.10	香　港	Hong Kong	4.78	28 750	137 425
锦江酒店	Jin Jiang Hotel	2006.12.15	香　港	Hong Kong	2.20	110 000	242 000
2007 年	**Year of 2007**						
橡果国际	Acorn International	2007.05.03	美　国	USA	15.50	770	11 935
展讯通信	Spreadtrum	2007.06.27	美　国	USA	14.00	890	12 460
复星国际	Fosun International	2007.07.16	香　港	Hong Kong	9.23	125 000	1 153 750
易居中国	Ehouse China	2007.08.08	美　国	USA	13.80	1 460	20 148
药明康德	Wuxi Pharma Tech	2007.08.09	美　国	USA	14.00	1 320	18 480
巨人网络	Ztgame	2007.11.01	美　国	USA	15.50	5 720	88 660

①本表数据由上海证券交易所提供。
②香港上市的货币币种为港元，美国上市的货币币种为美元。
❶ Data in this table are provided by Shanghai Stock Exchange.
❷ The Currency of stock issued in Hong Kong refers to HK Dollar, while the counterpart refers to US dollar.

表 16.22 保险公司主要业务指标(2007) MAJOR BUSINESS INDICES OF INSURANCE COMPANIES

单位:亿元(100 million yuan)

指 标	Indicators	保 费 Premium	赔款及给付 Compensation and Claims
总 计	**Total**	**482.64**	**139.82**
财产保险	**Property Insurance**	**119.43**	**53.03**
#企业财产险	Enterprise Property Insurance	15.84	4.58
家庭财产险	Household Property Insurance	1.82	0.30
机动车辆险	Motor Vehicles Insurance	65.41	36.17
责任险	Liability Insurance	8.11	2.25
人寿保险	**Liability Insurance**	**363.22**	**86.79**
寿 险	Life Insurance	317.12	75.70
健康险	Health Insurance	35.59	9.00
人身意外伤害险	Accidents Insurance	10.51	2.09

注：本表数据由中国保监委上海保监局提供。
Note: Data in this table are provided by Shanghai Insurance Regulatory Bureau.

表 16.23 保险费收入和赔款及给付(1990～2007) PREMIUM INCOME, COMPENSATION AND PAYMENT

年 份 Year	保险费收入(亿元) Premium Income (100 million yuan)	其中 of which #人寿保险 Liability Insurance	#财产保险 Property Insurance	赔款及给付支出(亿元) Compensation and Payment (100 millon yuan)	其中 of which #人寿保险 Liability Insurance	#财产保险 Property Insurance	赔付率(%) Compensation Ratio (%)
1990	8.99			2.22			24.7
1991	11.16			4.47			40.1
1992	18.20	5.70	12.50	4.23			23.2
1993	25.91	12.21	13.70	5.89			22.7
1994	39.48	16.61	22.87	11.91			30.2
1995	44.04	17.08	26.96	12.75			29.0
1996	58.10	28.64	29.46	15.00			25.8
1997	87.72	58.13	29.59	19.10			21.8
1998	102.92	70.50	32.42	28.67			27.9
1999	115.28	81.53	33.75	39.46			34.2
2000	127.23	92.14	35.09	36.44	20.56	15.88	28.6
2001	180.25	140.30	39.95	38.82	19.61	19.21	21.5
2002	237.61	193.30	44.31	49.97	28.38	21.59	21.0
2003	289.93	232.50	57.43	61.97	34.87	27.10	21.4
2004	307.11	231.30	75.81	70.86	36.79	34.07	23.1
2005	333.62	245.76	87.86	87.46	40.20	47.26	26.2
2006	407.04	305.72	101.33	91.31	46.14	45.17	22.4
2007	482.64	363.22	119.43	139.82	86.79	53.03	29.0

注：本表数据由中国保监委上海保监局提供。
Note: Data in this table are provided by Shanghai Insurance Regulatory Bureau.

上/海/统/计/年/鉴

主要统计指标解释

存　款

是企业、机关、团体或居民等根据资金必须收回的原则，把货币资金存入银行或其他信用机构保管并取得一定利息的一种信用活动形式。根据存款对象的不同可划分为企业存款、财政存款、机关团体存款、储蓄存款等科目。它是银行信贷资金的主要来源。

贷　款

是银行或其他信用机构根据资金必须归还的原则，按一定利率，为企业、个人等提供资金的一种信用活动形式。我国银行贷款分为短期贷款、中期流动资金贷款、中长期贷款、信托贷款以及工业贷款、商业贷款等科目。

综合指数

以全部上市公司作为样本计算的股票价格指数。

股票筹资额

上市公司发行股票所筹集的资金数量，等于股票发行量乘以发行价。

保险公司

在中国境内的、经过保险监督管理部门批准设立，并依法登记注册的各类商业保险公司。

保险金额

指保险人承担赔偿或者给付保险金责任的最高限额。

保险费

是指投保人根据保险合同的有关规定，为保险受益人取得因保险事故发生所造成的经济损失予以补偿（或给付）权利，付给保险人的代价。包括财产险和人身险储金类支出。

保险赔款及给付

指保险事故发生后，经查证确属保险责任范围以内的保险标的损失，保险人根据保险合同的规定履行赔偿义务，给予被保险人（或投保人指定的受益人）的款项。

SHANGHAI STATISTICAL YEARBOOK

EXPLANATORY NOTES TO MAJOR STATISTICAL INDICATORS

□ Deposits

Deposits are a form of credit by which enterprises, institutions, organizations or residents put money into banks and other credit institutions for safekeeping and earn interests under the principle of free withdrawal. According to different depositors, deposits are divided into enterprise deposits, treasury deposits, deposits of institutions and organizations, urban savings deposits and other deposits. Deposits constitute a major source of bank credit funds.

□ Loans

Loans are a form of credit by which banks and other credit institutions provide funds with a specified interest to enterprises and individuals under the principle of free repayment. Loans from Chinese banks include short term loans, medium term circulating capital loans, long term loans, trust loans, industrial loans and commercial loans.

□ Composite Index

Composite Index refers to stock price index taking all the listed companies as samples.

□ Raised Capital

Raised Capital refers to money raised by listed companies, i.e., volume of issued shares times the issue prices.

□ Insurance Companies

Insurance Companies refer to commercial insurance companies of various forms registered by law and established in China with the approval of insurance regulatory agencies.

□ Amount Insured

Amount Insured refers to the maximum that the insurant will get for the claim of the case insured.

□ Premium

Premium is the fee paid by the insurant to the insurer to obtain the obligation of compensation from the insurance within the agreed terms. It includes saving payment for property and life insurance.

□ Insurance Indemnity

Insurance Indemnity is the compensation paid by the insurer to the insurant or the beneficiary, when an accident has happened to the insured property or life and the loss has been investigated and verified to be within the insurance obligation.

第十七篇

CHAPTER 17

房地产业

REAL ESTATE

表 17.1 全社会房屋施工面积、竣工面积(1985~2007)
TOTAL FLOOR SPACE OF CONSTRUCTION AND COMPLETED BUILDINGS

年 份 Year	施 工 面 积 (万平方米) Floor Area of Construction (10 000 sq. m.)	其中 of which #住 宅 Residential Housing	竣 工 面 积 (万平方米) Floor Area Completed (10 000 sq. m.)	其中 of which #住 宅 Residential Housing	房屋建筑面积竣工率 (%) Construction Completion Rate (%)	其中 of which #住 宅 Residential Housing
1985	4 162.15	2 651.52	2 909.58	2 112.04	69.9	79.7
1986	4 874.44	2 469.27	2 493.93	1 790.01	51.2	72.5
1987	4 382.40	2 658.05	2 700.96	1 874.90	61.6	70.5
1988	4 369.20	2 667.00	2 457.34	1 758.29	56.2	65.9
1989	3 683.77	2 048.20	1 941.80	1 246.58	52.7	60.9
1990	3 801.46	2 269.06	2 138.44	1 339.02	56.3	59.0
1991	3 611.53	2 157.46	1 923.92	1 160.61	53.3	53.8
1992	4 709.52	2 463.79	2 608.20	1 379.18	55.4	56.0
1993	4 724.30	2 142.39	2 031.76	1 017.54	43.0	47.5
1994	6 720.70	3 520.27	2 519.09	1 349.24	37.5	38.3
1995	10 566.42	6 195.12	3 093.93	1 746.82	29.3	28.2
1996	10 730.85	5 874.26	3 254.57	1 872.65	30.3	31.9
1997	9 955.21	5 450.13	3 614.19	2 179.68	36.3	40.0
1998	9 364.36	5 113.52	3 364.43	1 963.51	35.9	38.4
1999	8 364.48	4 608.49	3 257.57	1 731.55	38.9	37.6
2000	8 636.31	4 804.12	3 266.52	1 724.02	37.8	35.9
2001	8 588.49	5 236.93	3 215.12	1 743.90	37.4	33.3
2002	9 425.42	5 994.70	3 102.54	1 880.50	32.9	31.4
2003	11 023.24	6 974.27	3 582.34	2 280.79	32.5	32.7
2004	12 291.81	7 873.44	4 932.57	3 270.43	40.1	41.5
2005	14 477.85	8 267.24	4 873.82	2 819.35	33.7	34.1
2006	14 596.49	8 085.28	4 901.46	2 746.80	33.6	34.0
2007	14 979.37	7 789.91	5 068.46	2 843.62	33.8	36.5

表 17.2 住宅投资和竣工建筑面积(1978～2007)
INVESTMENT IN RESIDENTIAL HOUSING AND FLOOR SPACE OF BUILDINGS COMPLETED

年 份 Year	住宅投资额 (亿元) Investment in Residential Housing (100 million yuan)	占全社会固定资产投资总额比重(%) As Percentage of Total Investment in Fixed Asset	住宅竣工建筑面积 (万平方米) Floor Area of Floor Area of Residence Building Completed (10 000 sq. m.)	市区人均居住面积 (平方米) Dwelling Area per Capita(sq. m.)
1978	1.79	7.4	199.61	4.5
1979	2.23	6.9	215.99	4.3
1980	4.24	10.4	304.32	4.4
1981	9.87	18.1	1 380.70	4.5
1982	10.95	15.3	1 363.63	4.7
1983	11.16	14.7	1 347.79	4.9
1984	15.72	17.0	1 788.44	5.0
1985	25.18	21.2	2 112.04	5.4
1986	28.03	19.1	1 790.01	6.0
1987	35.79	19.2	1 874.90	6.2
1988	44.73	18.2	1 758.29	6.3
1989	34.67	16.1	1 246.58	6.4
1990	42.94	18.9	1 339.02	6.6
1991	48.92	18.9	1 160.61	6.7
1992	61.23	17.1	1 379.18	6.9
1993	77.14	11.8	1 017.54	7.3
1994	300.65	26.8	1 349.24	7.5
1995	433.76	27.1	1 746.82	8.0
1996	466.99	23.9	1 872.65	8.7
1997	458.22	23.2	2 179.68	9.3
1998	404.96	20.6	1 963.51	9.7
1999	378.82	20.4	1 731.55	10.9
2000	443.90	23.7	1 724.02	11.8
2001	466.71	23.4	1 743.90	12.5
2002	584.51	26.7	1 880.50	13.1
2003	694.30	28.3	2 280.79	13.8
2004	922.61	29.9	3 270.43	14.8
2005	936.36	26.4	2 819.35	15.5
2006	854.15	21.8	2 746.80	16.0
2007	853.13	19.1	2 843.62	16.5

注：1981 年以前住宅投资额和住宅竣工建筑面积数据不包括城乡私人建房和农村投资，从 1981 年开始为全社会口径。
Note: Before 1981, investments and floor area of residential housing completed in this table don't cover private-built houses in urban and rural areas and rural investment, the whole society is covered since 1981.

表 17.3 主要年份房地产开发投资和经营情况
INVESTMENT AND OPERATION IN REAL ESTATE DEVELOPMENT IN MAIN YEARS

单位:亿元(100 million yuan)

指标	Indicators	1995	2000	2006	2007
投资总额	**Total Investment**	**466.20**	**566.17**	**1 275.59**	**1 307.53**
#商品房屋建设投资	Investment in Commodity Housing	286.45	476.32	1 153.71	1 187.63
土地开发投资	Investment in Land Development	53.19	25.91	63.36	55.62
在投资总额中	**Of Total Investment**				
住　宅	Residence	280.38	408.82	835.63	837.53
#别墅、高档公寓	Villas and Apartment	31.75	40.72	203.24	228.79
办公楼	Office Building	81.74	57.47	124.29	157.51
商业营业用房	Commercial Building	32.39	51.51	155.07	158.94
其　他	Others	71.69	48.38	160.60	153.55
新增固定资产	**Newly Increased Fixed Assets**	**151.06**	**477.39**	**1 058.94**	**1 048.47**
资金来源合计	**Total Capital Source**	**670.83**	**778.16**	**2 775.76**	**3 153.31**
上年末结余资金	Balance at End of Previous Year	112.00	113.48	598.87	600.12
本年资金来源小计	Sub-total Capital Source of this Year	558.83	664.68	2 176.89	2 553.19
国内贷款	Domestic Loans	122.63	155.37	575.10	558.43
利用外资	Foreign Capital Utilized	51.81	28.11	55.96	74.05
#外商直接投资	Foreign Direct Investment	34.87	16.24	51.30	65.41
自筹资金	Self-Financed Capital	214.53	211.86	577.98	583.75
其他资金	Other Capital	169.86	269.34	967.85	1 336.96

表 17.4　主要年份房地产开发企业房屋建筑面积和造价
CONSTRUCTION AREA AND COST OF PROPERTY DEVELOPED BY REAL ESTATE COMPANIES IN MAIN YEARS

指　标	Indicators	1995	2000	2006	2007
房屋施工面积(万平方米)	**Floor Area of Construction(10 000 sq. m)**	**5 074.80**	**5 523.23**	**10 938.75**	**10 766.72**
住　宅	Residence	3 843.22	4 263.50	7 988.73	7 642.79
#别墅、高档公寓	Villas and Apartment	246.47	254.11	1 381.8	1 492.75
办公楼	Office Building	634.46	515.10	723.78	935.23
商业营业用房	Commercial Building	274.68	438.47	1 074.06	1 131.86
其　他	Others	322.44	306.16	1 152.18	1 056.84
房屋竣工面积(万平方米)	**Floor Area Completed(10 000 sq. m)**	**700.39**	**1 643.62**	**3 274.27**	**3 380.12**
住　宅	Residence	529.77	1 388.01	2 699.11	2 752.45
#别墅、高档公寓	Villas and Apartment	75.50	66.38	343.99	406.39
办公楼	Office Building	30.82	95.93	108.53	138.89
商业营业用房	Commercial Building	50.74	100.16	239.39	256.46
其　他	Others	89.06	59.52	227.24	232.32
房屋竣工价值(亿元)	**Value of Building Completed(100 million yuan)**	**102.55**	**355.79**	**1 011.31**	**1 046.58**
住　宅	Residence	72.21	270.29	799.75	829.59
#别墅、高档公寓	Villas and Apartment	18.41	20.66	178.81	211.22
办公楼	Office Building	9.48	45.41	71.55	62.97
商业营业用房	Commercial Building	7.88	24.29	82.16	87.49
其　他	Others	12.99	15.80	57.85	66.53
竣工房屋平均造价(元/平方米)	**Average Construction Cost(yuan/sq. m)**	**1 464**	**2 164**	**3 089**	**3 096**
住　宅	Residence	1 363	1 947	2 963	3 014
#别墅、高档公寓	Villas and Apartment	2 438	3 112	5 198	5 197
办公楼	Office Building	3 075	4 733	6 593	4 534
商业营业用房	Commercial Building	1 552	2 425	3 432	3 411
其　他	Others	1 458	2 654	2 546	2 864

表 17.5 商品房建筑面积(2007)
FLOOR AREA OF COMMODITY HOUSING

指标	Indicators	合计 Total	其中 of which 内环线以内 Inside Inner-Ring	内、外环线间 Between Inner-Ring and Out-Ring	外环线以外 Outside Out-Ring
房屋施工面积(万平方米)	**Floor Area Under Construction(10 000 sq. m)**	**10 766.72**	**1 826.31**	**3 417.83**	**5 522.59**
住宅	Residence	7 642.79	828.6	2 297.62	4 516.57
别墅、高档公寓	Villas and Apartment	1 492.75	274.08	364.29	854.37
其他住宅	Other Residence	6 150.04	554.52	1 933.33	3 662.20
办公楼	Office Building	935.23	480.90	331.54	122.80
商业营业用房	Commercial Building	1 131.86	274.57	372.05	485.25
其他	Others	1 056.83	242.24	416.62	397.97
新开工面积(万平方米)	**Floor Area Started(10 000 sq. m)**	**2 251.75**	**210.78**	**679.7**	**1 361.27**
住宅	Residence	1 633.94	90.38	433.64	1 109.92
别墅、高档公寓	Villas and Apartment	282.79	22.01	42.16	218.61
其他住宅	Other Residence	1 351.15	68.36	391.48	891.31
办公楼	Office Building	201.06	60.28	90.58	50.20
商业营业用房	Commercial Building	202.89	21.59	73.52	107.78
其他	Others	213.87	38.53	81.96	93.38
房屋竣工面积(万平方米)	**Floor Area Completed(10 000 sq. m)**	**3 380.12**	**427.31**	**1 052.12**	**1 900.69**
住宅	Residence	2 752.45	265.24	786.87	1 700.34
别墅、高档公寓	Villas and Apartment	406.39	67.88	96.65	241.86
其他住宅	Other Residence	2 346.06	197.36	690.22	1 458.48
办公楼	Office Building	138.89	66.91	63.89	8.09
商业营业用房	Commercial Building	256.46	35.45	98.40	122.61
其他	Others	232.32	59.71	102.96	69.65
房屋竣工价值(亿元)	**Value of Building Completed(100 million yuan)**	**1 046.58**	**226.40**	**326.88**	**493.31**
住宅	Residence	829.59	154.39	231.56	443.64
别墅、高档公寓	Villas and Apartment	211.22	67.14	52.92	91.17
其他住宅	Other Residence	618.36	87.25	178.64	352.47

表 17.5 续表 continued

指　标	Indicators	合　计 Total	其中 of which: 内环线以内 Inside Inner-Ring	内、外环线间 Between Inner-Ring and Out-Ring	外环线以外 Outside Out-Ring
办公楼	Office Building	62.97	35.09	26.09	1.80
商业营业用房	Commercial Building	87.49	18.77	39.52	29.20
其　他	Others	66.53	18.15	29.71	18.67
商品房销售面积（万平方米）	**Sold Area of Commodity Housing (10 000 sq. m)**	**3 694.96**	**363.75**	**1 016.76**	**2 314.45**
住　宅	Residence	3 279.17	268.38	877.27	2 133.52
别墅、高档公寓	Villas and Apartment	503.14	58.73	134.31	310.10
其他住宅	Other Residence	2 776.03	209.65	742.96	1 823.42
办公楼	Office Building	150.93	56.72	72.96	21.25
商业营业用房	Commercial Building	198.38	25.97	49.47	122.94
其　他	Others	66.47	12.68	17.06	36.73
商品房销售额（亿元）	**Sales Volume of Commodity Housing (100 million yuan)**	**3 089.35**	**672.91**	**1 000.63**	**1 415.81**
住　宅	Residence	2 706.30	519.42	858.71	1 328.17
别墅、高档公寓	Villas and Apartment	654.04	130.16	188.70	335.18
其他住宅	Other Residence	2 052.26	389.26	670.01	992.99
办公楼	Office Building	214.67	107.55	87.01	20.11
商业营业用房	Commercial Building	131.19	34.32	38.99	57.88
其　他	Others	37.19	11.62	15.92	9.65
房屋出租面积（万平方米）	**Leasing Area of Buildings (10 000 sq. m)**	**1 128.69**	**474.77**	**551.98**	**101.94**
住　宅	Residence	110.38	60.95	33.69	15.74
别墅、高档公寓	Villas and Apartment	86.85	50.42	25.87	10.57
其他住宅	Other Residence	23.53	10.53	7.83	5.17
办公楼	Office Building	343.60	241.29	96.29	6.03
商业营业用房	Commercial Building	270.42	146.66	92.74	31.02
其　他	Others	404.28	25.87	329.26	49.15

表 17.6 主要年份商品房销售和出租情况
COMMODITY HOUSING SOLD AND LEASED IN MAIN YEARS

指 标	Indicators	2000	2006	2007
商品房销售面积（万平方米）	**Sold Area of Commodity Housing (10 000 sq. m.)**	**1 557.87**	**3 025.40**	**3 694.96**
住 宅	Residence	1 445.87	2 615.49	3 279.17
#别墅、高档公寓	Villas and Apartment	53.44	498.56	503.14
办公楼	Office Building	47.76	139.05	150.93
商业营业用房	Commercial Building	54.54	188.51	198.38
其 他	Others	9.70	82.35	66.47
商品房销售额(亿元)	**Sales Volume of Commodity Housing(100 million yuan)**	**555.45**	**2 177.08**	**3 089.35**
住 宅	Residence	480.97	1 841.04	2 706.30
#别墅、高档公寓	Villas and Apartment	32.65	540.19	654.04
办公楼	Office Building	44.05	167.95	214.67
商业营业用房	Commercial Building	27.87	122.13	131.19
其 他	Others	2.56	45.96	37.19
商品房出租面积（万平方米）	**Commodity Housing Leased (10 000 Sq. m)**	**358.38**	**977.77**	**1 128.69**
住 宅	Residence	59.29	78.63	110.38
#别墅、高档公寓	Villas and Apartment	37.43	68.88	86.85
办公楼	Office Building	156.15	332.91	343.60
商业营业用房	Commercial Building	62.04	234.85	270.42
其 他	Others	80.91	331.38	404.28

表 17.7 每百户城市居民家庭房屋产权构成(2005～2007)
PROPERTY RIGHT STRUCTURE OF TOWNSMAN TENEMENT PER HUNDRED HOUSEHOLDS

单位:%

类 别	Types	2005	2006	2007
每百户城市居民家庭房屋产权构成	Property Right Structure of Townsman Tenement per hundred households	100	100	100
租赁公房	Leasehold Public Tenement	25.5	23.8	20.4
租赁私房	Leasehold Private Tenement	1.1	1.3	1.6
原有私房	Inhere Private Tenement	2.4	1.3	0.9
房改私房	Reformed Private Tenement	40.4	40.4	37.3
商品房	Commercial Tenement	30.5	32.4	39.4
其 他	Others	0.1	0.8	0.4

表 17.8 房屋拆迁情况(1995 ~ 2007)
BUILDINGS RESETTLEMENT

年 份 Year	拆迁户数(户) Quantity of Resettlements (unit)	其 中 of which #居民住宅 Residence	拆迁面积 (万平方米) Floor Area Resettled (10 000 sq. m.)	其 中 of which #居民住宅 Residence
1995	75 777	73 695	322.77	253.90
1996	89 132	86 481	342.95	258.86
1997	79 857	77 388	479.67	363.16
1998	78 205	75 157	452.22	343.94
1999	75 185	73 709	342.50	248.17
2000	70 606	68 293	365.77	288.35
2001	73 728	71 909	515.65	386.66
2002	101 097	98 714	644.53	485.00
2003	80 858	79 077	584.93	475.47
2004	42 415	41 552	308.40	232.52
2005	75 857	74 483	1 222.53	851.85
2006	81 126	76 874	1 516.85	848.35
2007	51 354	49 092	825.00	690.00

注：此表的统计范围为下表 10 个中心城区。
Note: The scope of statistics in this table is 10 central urban districts, same as the fllowing table, in which the names of districts are listed.

表 17.9 各区房屋拆迁情况(2007)
BUILDINGS RESETTLEMENT IN DIFFERENT DISTRICTS

地 区	District	拆迁户数(户) Quantity of Resettlements (unit)	其 中 of which #居民住宅 Residence	拆迁面积 (万平方米) Floor Area Resettled (10 000 sq. m.)	其 中 of which #居民住宅 Residence
总 计	**Total**	**51 354**	**49 092**	**825.00**	**690.00**
#浦东新区	Pudong New Area	10 328	10 179	289.66	268.00
黄 浦 区	Huangpu	5 749	5 506	42.82	17.18
卢 湾 区	Luwan	2 107	2 008	17.70	8.21
徐 汇 区	Xuhui	1 667	1 628	14.05	9.74
长 宁 区	Changning	1 943	1 798	43.99	13.73
静 安 区	Jing'an	1 816	1 695	10.41	6.12
普 陀 区	Putuo	1 736	1 655	28.21	6.24
闸 北 区	Zhabei	4 311	4 213	17.03	15.98
虹 口 区	Hongkou	4 300	4 049	23.74	11.89
杨 浦 区	Yangpu	1 017	978	7.36	2.76

注：本页数据由市房屋土地资源管理局提供。
Note: Data on this page are provided by Shanghai Municipal Building and Land Administration Bureau.

表 17.10 主要年份土地使用权出让情况
LEASE OF LAND PLOT TENURE IN MAIN YEARS

指 标	Indicators	1995	2000	2006	2007
出让地块(幅)	**Leased Plot(piece)**	**499**	**1 325**	**2 611**	**696**
出让面积(万平方米)	**Leased Area(10 000 sq. m)**	**1 245.42**	**2 183.22**	**7 680.13**	**2 740.22**
区	District	875.11	1 259.94	7 424.17	2 115.57
#浦东新区	Pudong New Area	646.76	534.29	546.25	220.06
县	County	370.31	923.28	255.96	624.65
可建面积(万平方米)	**Area Suitable for Construction(10 000 sq. m)**	**1 343.99**	**3 502.73**	**8 398.51**	**3 346.23**
住 宅	Residence	887.60	1 912.31	1 987.06	915.42
商业服务	Commercial Service	1.27	92.96	295.07	507.73
工矿仓储	Storege of Industry	424.46	1 417.67	5 940.81	1 870.32
其 他	Others	30.66	79.79	175.57	52.75

注：1995 年为外销地块，2000 年起包括内销和外销地块。
Note: The figures before 1995 are of the plots leased to foreigners, and since 2000, the plots leased to domestic leases have been included.

表 17.11 存量房交易情况(1994～2007)
EXCHANGE OF SECOND-HAND HOUSES

年 份 Year	成交套数 (套) Houses Traded (set)	成交面积 (万平方米) Areas Traded (10 000 sq. m.)	其 中 of which		
			住 宅 Residence	办公楼 Office	商业营业用房 Commerce
1994	2 821	31.76	10.59		
1995	4 176	60.87	19.70		
1996	4 689	82.29	25.09		
1997	9 180	162.40	87.68	23.95	14.95
1998	24 501	315.23	197.56	21.49	18.28
1999	44 234	510.84	336.69	37.63	14.61
2000	96 348	778.52	648.23	39.48	21.65
2001	164 598	1 422.43	1 031.48	56.99	57.24
2002	204 239	1 790.50	1 341.60	65.70	91.80
2003	263 297	2 306.28	1 807.57	105.14	114.28
2004	303 291	2 726.70	2 222.24	117.12	121.39
2005	189 896	1 971.50	1 608.20	88.10	78.00
2006	184 194	1 706.81	1 375.22	67.35	46.53
2007	213 733	1 992.59	1 715.05	49.73	36.34

注：本页数据由市房屋土地资源管理局提供。
Note: Data on this page are provided by Shanghai Municipal Building and Land Administration Bureau.

表 17.12　各区、县房地产开发建设和经营情况(2007)
INVESTMENT AND OPERATION IN REAL ESTATE DEVELOPMENT BY DISTRICT AND COUNTY

单位:万平方米(10 000 sq. m.)

地　区	District	施　工 面　积 Floor Area of Construction	竣　工 面　积 Floor Area Completed	其　中 of which #住　宅 Residential Housing
全　市	**Total**	**10 766.72**	**3 380.12**	**2 752.45**
浦东新区	Pudong New Area	1 983.86	516.59	419.29
黄 浦 区	Huangpu	191.71	20.26	9.62
卢 湾 区	Luwan	87.63	7.96	6.06
徐 汇 区	Xuhui	323.04	121.57	84.86
长 宁 区	Changning	350.75	80.61	61.89
静 安 区	Jing'an	190.68	15.46	0.69
普 陀 区	Putuo	561.99	119.23	94.06
闸 北 区	Zhabei	249.59	59.64	29.22
虹 口 区	Hongkou	306.48	93.67	50.70
杨 浦 区	Yangpu	638.38	199.55	114.87
宝 山 区	Baoshan	1 260.95	342.41	311.61
闵 行 区	Minhang	893.61	164.00	141.96
嘉 定 区	Jiading	663.26	295.66	255.77
金 山 区	Jinshan	139.64	87.90	77.95
松 江 区	Songjiang	1 013.16	444.07	389.94
青 浦 区	Qingpu	355.97	87.72	65.90
南 汇 区	Nanhui	1 178.80	583.92	504.02
奉 贤 区	Fengxian	280.34	81.63	78.45
崇 明 县	Chongming	96.88	58.27	55.59

表 17.12 续表 continued

单位:万平方米(10 000 sq. m.)

地 区	District	实际销售面积 Areas Sold	其中 of which #住宅 Residential Housing	实际销售额(亿元) Sales Volume (100 million yuan)	其中 of which #住宅 Residential Housing
全 市	**Total**	**3 694.96**	**3 279.17**	**3 089.35**	**2 706.30**
浦东新区	Pudong New Area	560.78	437.91	522.31	406.70
黄 浦 区	Huangpu	47.02	43.50	56.16	50.47
卢 湾 区	Luwan	22.78	20.82	29.70	28.04
徐 汇 区	Xuhui	93.67	86.35	86.46	78.82
长 宁 区	Changning	54.23	33.00	59.88	41.75
静 安 区	Jing'an	37.25	24.74	40.53	24.26
普 陀 区	Putuo	193.06	156.56	178.04	140.84
闸 北 区	Zhabei	124.62	112.89	118.29	106.14
虹 口 区	Hongkou	64.37	46.06	79.51	52.25
杨 浦 区	Yangpu	178.56	139.54	147.22	109.14
宝 山 区	Baoshan	351.29	310.91	330.44	300.22
闵 行 区	Minhang	448.04	436.79	303.89	295.65
嘉 定 区	Jiading	222.38	204.06	172.68	155.90
金 山 区	Jinshan	59.07	53.98	41.26	37.46
松 江 区	Songjiang	533.38	505.67	415.45	396.38
青 浦 区	Qingpu	119.56	112.67	98.18	92.54
南 汇 区	Nanhui	398.62	370.88	282.52	265.05
奉 贤 区	Fengxian	141.49	138.98	101.38	99.82
崇 明 县	Chongming	44.79	43.86	25.45	24.87

上 / 海 / 统 / 计 / 年 / 鉴

主要统计指标解释

房地产开发投资

指各种登记注册类型的房地产开发公司、商品房建设公司及其他房地产开发法人单位和附属于其他法人单位实际从事房地产开发或经营活动的单位统一开发的包括统代建、拆迁还建的住宅、厂房、仓库、饭店、宾馆、度假村、写字楼、办公楼等房屋建筑物和配套的服务设施，土地开发工程(如道路、给水、排水、供电、供热、通讯、平整场地等基础设施工程)的投资；不包括单纯的土地交易活动。

施工面积

指报告期内施工的全部房屋建筑面积。包括本期新开工的面积和上期开工跨入本期继续施工的房屋面积，以及上期已停建在本期恢复施工的房屋面积。本期竣工和本期施工后又停缓建的房屋，其建筑面积仍计入本期房屋施工面积中。

竣工面积

指在报告期内房屋建筑按照设计要求已经全部完工，达到住人和使用条件，经验收鉴定合格(或达到竣工验收标准)，正式移交使用单位的各栋房屋建筑面积的总和。

房屋建筑面积竣工率

指一定时期内房屋竣工面积占同期房屋施工面积的比率。该指标从房屋建筑施工速度的角度反映投资效果的指标。

别墅、高档公寓

指建筑造价和销售价格明显高于一般商品住宅的商品住宅。别墅一般指地处郊区，独立成栋的商品住宅；高档公寓一般指地处市内高尚社区，高层或多层的商品住宅。别墅、高档公寓的确定标准：一是经有房地产投资计划审批权的主管部门审批建设的别墅、高档公寓开发项目；二是销售价格高于当地同等地段商品住宅平均销售价格一倍以上的别墅、公寓开发项目。该指标可以分析房地产投资结构，反映高收入家庭商品住宅的供求平衡情况。

SHANGHAI STATISTICAL YEARBOOK

EXPLANATORY NOTES TO MAJOR STATISTICAL INDICATORS

□ Investment in Real Estate Development

It includes the investment by the real estate development companies, commercial buildings construction companies and other real estate development units of various types of ownership in the construction of house buildings, such as residential buildings, factory buildings, warehouses, hotels, guesthouses, holiday villages, office buildings, and the complementary service facilities and land development projects, such as roads, water supply, water drainage, power supply, heating, telecommunications, land leveling and other projects of infrastructure. It excludes the activities in simple land transactions.

□ Floor Area of under Construction

Floor Area of Construction refers to total floor space of all buildings under construction during the reference period, including floor space of newly started buildings during the reference period, floor space of construction extended from the previous period to the current period, and floor space of construction suspended during the previous period and resumed in the current period. Floor space of construction completed in the current period, and floor space of construction started and then suspended in the current period are also included in the floor space under construction of the current year.

□ Floor Area of Buildings Completed

Floor Area Completed refers to the floor space of all buildings completed in the reference period, which have been appraised and accepted(or come up to the designed standards) and have been transferred to the owners for use.

□ Completion Rate of Floor Space of Buildings

Completion Rate of Floor Space of Buildings refers to the ratio of the floor space of buildings completed in certain period of time to the floor space of buildings under construction in the same period. This indicator reflects the investment result from the perspective of the speed of construction.

□ Villask, High-Grade Apartments

Villas, High-Grade Apartments refers to commercial houses whose construction costs and marketing prices are significantly higher than ordinary housing. Villas are independent structures generally located in the suburbs; high-grade apartments are multi-story buildings located in elegant urban neighborhoods. Criteria for villas and high-grade apartments include: 1) projects for the construction of villas or high-grade apartments have to be approved by competent departments in charge of real estate development and investment plans, and 2) prices for projects on villas or high-grade apartments are higher by over 100% compared with the average prices of ordinary commercial housing projects in similar location. This indicator helps to analyze the investment structure of the real estate industry and the demand and supply of housing for high-income households.

第十八篇

CHAPTER 18

科学技术

SCIENCE AND TECHNOLOGY

表 18.1 主要年份科技活动主要指标
MAIN INDICATORS OF SCIENTIFIC AND TECHNOLOGICAL ACTIVITIES IN MAIN YEARS

年　份 Year	科技活动机构数（个） Number of Scientific & Technological Research Institutions (unit)	科技活动人员（万人） Personnel Engaged in Scientific and Technological Activities (10 000 persons)	科技活动经费筹集总额（亿元） Funds Financed for Scientific and Technological Research (100 million yuan)	科技活动经费支出总额（亿元） Expenditures of Scientific and Technological Research (100 million yuan)
1980	551			
1985	816	15.12	19.91	13.37
1990	1 053	19.34	32.47	28.25
1995	1 266	18.25	122.49	114.22
1996	1 018	19.11	127.41	134.37
1997	1 133	17.99	153.77	165.61
1998	1 022	18.72	140.24	177.62
1999	915	16.25	153.05	198.00
2000	894	16.31	201.45	221.38
2001	826	15.19	218.18	247.22
2002	848	15.18	243.99	272.93
2003	839	15.07	274.25	304.48
2004	1 050	18.28	362.50	364.94
2005	1 114	19.67	453.94	419.34
2006	1 162	20.07	485.13	436.44
2007	1 108	22.79	561.27	528.72

注：本表从 2003 年起包括高校的人文社科类数据。
Note: Since 2003, this table has included data of humanities and social science of higher education.

表 18.2 主要年份研究与试验发展（R&D）经费与科技经费支出
EXPENDITURES ON R&D AND EXPENDITURES OF SCIENTIFIC AND TECHNOLOGICAL RESEARCH IN MAIN YEARS

年　份 Years	研究与试验发展经费支出（亿元） Expenditures on R&D (100 million yuan)	研究与试验发展经费支出相当于上海市生产总值比例（%） R&D as Percentage of Gross Domestic Product (%)	地方财政科技经费支出（亿元） Local Fiscal Expenditures on Scientific and Technological Research (100 million yuan)	科技经费支出占地方财政支出比重（%） Percentage of Expenditures on Scientific and Technological Research in Local Fiscal (%)
1978	1.32	0.48		
1980	2.04	0.65	1.38	7.2
1985	4.62	0.99	2.49	5.4
1990	10.13	1.30	2.44	3.2
1995	32.60	1.30	5.12	2.0
1996	40.96	1.38	5.63	1.7
1997	49.76	1.45	7.65	1.8
1998	55.69	1.47	8.28	1.7
1999	63.75	1.52	10.82	2.0
2000	76.73	1.61	10.08	1.6
2001	88.08	1.69	12.39	1.7
2002	102.36	1.78	15.25	1.7
2003	128.92	1.93	19.84	1.8
2004	170.28	2.11	39.32	2.8
2005	213.77	2.33	79.34	4.8
2006	258.84	2.50	94.89	5.2
2007	307.50	2.52	112.42	5.1

①本表数据由上海市财政局等部门提供。
②2004 年起地方财政科技经费支出口径范围扩大至其他系统（包括区县）财政安排的事业费中对科技的支出。
❶Data in this table are mainly provided by Shanghai Municipal Finance Bureau.
❷Since 2004, the scope of Local Fiscal Expenditures on Scientific and Technological Research has extended to other expenditures on science and technology arranged by finance department of other economy (including districts and counties).

表 18.3 主要年份科技活动基本情况
BASIC STATISTICS OF SCIENTIFIC AND TECHNOLOGICAL ACTIVITIES IN MAIN YEARS

指 标	Indicators	2000	2005	2006	2007
科技机构数（个）	**Number of Scientific and Technological Research Institutions (unit)**	**1 232**	**1 114**	**1 162**	**1 108**
#科研机构	Research Institutions	304	266	262	259
高等院校	Institutions of Higher Education	326	225	237	238
大中型工业企业	Large and Medium Industrial Enterprises	264	326	355	315
科技活动人员数（万人）	**Personnel Engaged in Scientific and Technological Activities (10 000 persons)**	**20.17**	**19.67**	**20.07**	**22.79**
#科学家、工程师	Scientists and Engineers	13.36	14.55	15.04	16.95
科技活动经费筹集总额（亿元）	**Funds for Scientific and Technological Research (100 million yuan)**	**247.14**	**453.94**	**485.13**	**561.27**
政府资金	Government Allocation	46.90	99.60	100.63	134.94
事业资金	Undertaking Funds	17.65	9.90	7.35	12.40
企业资金	Self-raised Funds	146.68	324.22	323.50	385.92
银行贷款	Bank Loans	22.42	6.73	34.30	6.70
其他收入	Others	13.49	13.49	19.35	21.31
科技活动经费支出总额（亿元）	**Expenditures of Scientific and Technological Research Funds (100 million yuan)**	**221.38**	**419.34**	**436.44**	**528.72**
#劳务费	Service Fees	52.02	86.80	97.20	126.99
固定资产购建费	Purchasing Fixed Assets	38.68	106.14	107.98	138.07
#研究与发展经费支出	**Expenditures on R&D**	**76.73**	**213.77**	**256.78**	**307.50**
基础研究	Basic Research	4.79	10.64	14.00	16.75
应用研究	Applied Research	17.53	32.33	40.98	36.11
试验发展	Experimental Development	54.41	170.80	201.80	254.64
科技成果登记数(项)	**Number of Achievements Registered in Scientific and Technological Activities(item)**	**1 102**	**1 701**	**1 953**	**2 396**
科技成果获奖数(项)	**Number of Achievements Awarded(item)**	**287**	**362**	**351**	**373**
#国家科技成果奖(项人)	National Award for Achievements in Science and Technology	21	44	42	54
上海科技进步奖	Shanghai Scientific and Technological Progress Prize	266	318	309	319
专利申请受理量(件)	**Patent Applications(piece)**	**11 318**	**32 741**	**36 042**	**47 205**
专利申请授权量(件)	**Patent Certified(piece)**	**4 048**	**12 603**	**16 602**	**24 481**

①本表为全社会口径。
②科研机构统计范围包括区县级及以上的科技机构数，高等院校包括理工农医类和人文社科类科技机构数。
③本表部分数据由市科学技术委员会以及市知识产权局提供。
❶All the indicators of this table cover the total society.
❷The statistical scale of Research Institutions include those of districts and counties and above. Institutions of Higher education include the institutions of Science, Engineering, Agriculture, Medicine Science, Humanities and Social Science.
❸Part of the data in this table are provided by Shanghai Municipal Science and Technology Commission and Shanghai Municipal Intellectual Property Rights Bureau.

表 18.4 主要年份国有企事业单位各类专业人员
PROFESSIONAL AND TECHNICAL PERSONNEL IN STATE-OWNED ENTERPRISES AND INSTITUTIONS IN MAIN YEARS

单位：万人(10 000 persons)

类 别	Types	1990	2000	2006	2007
总 计	**Total**	**86.16**	**71.03**	**72.72**	**77.68**
工程技术人员	Engineering	26.30	17.07	19.65	19.85
农业技术人员	Agriculture	0.37	0.31	0.22	0.24
科学研究人员	Scientific Research	2.55	1.76	1.82	2.09
卫生技术人员	Medical Professionals	9.07	9.00	9.11	9.40
教学人员	Teaching	20.12	16.55	16.41	16.43
经济人员	Economic	14.07	10.17	12.92	17.20
财会人员	Financial Accounting	7.46	7.63	6.57	6.63
统计人员	Statistical	1.76	0.78	0.62	0.60
翻译人员	Translator	0.41	0.21	0.16	0.16
新闻出版、播音人员	Media and Publishing	0.55	0.59	0.77	0.84
艺术人员	Art Personnel	0.55	0.40	0.44	0.43
其他专业人员	Others	2.95	6.56	4.03	3.81
在总计中:高级专业人员	**Of Total:Senior and Intermediate**	**4.72**	**6.43**	**7.55**	**7.66**
工程技术人员	Engineering	2.05	2.17	2.17	2.09
农业技术人员	Agriculture	0.01	0.02	0.03	0.04
科学研究人员	Scientific Research	0.51	0.55	0.63	0.65
卫生技术人员	Medical Professionals	0.38	0.64	0.89	0.95
教学人员	Teaching	0.90	1.96	2.60	2.70
经济人员	Economic	0.10	0.32	0.45	0.46
财会人员	Financial Accounting	0.04	0.08	0.12	0.12
统计人员	Statistical	…	0.01	0.01	0.01
新闻出版、播音人员	Media and Publishing	0.07	0.12	0.14	0.13
翻译人员	Translator	0.02	0.02	0.01	0.01
艺术人员	Art Personnel	0.12	0.12	0.12	0.12
其他专业人员	Others	0.52	0.33	0.38	0.38
平均每万职工拥有专业技术人员(人)	**Professional and Technical Personnel Per 10 000 Employees(person)**	**2 169**	**3 099**	**4 968**	**5 474**

注：本表数据由市委组织部提供。
Note: Data in this table are provided by the Organization Department of Shanghai Committee of Chinese Communist Party.

表 18.5 国有企事业单位各类专业人员(2007)
PROFESSIONAL AND TECHNICAL PERSONNEL IN STATE-OWNED ENTERPRISES AND INSTITUTIONS

单位:万人(10 000 persons)

类别 Types		合计 Total	其中 of which #女性 Female	按专业技术职务分 By Profession 高级 Senior	中级 Medium	初级 Junior	未聘 Not Appointed
总计	**Total**	**77.68**	**36.57**	**7.66**	**26.10**	**28.16**	**15.75**
工程技术人员	Engineering	19.85	4.24	2.09	6.30	7.35	4.11
农业技术人员	Agriculture	0.24	0.06	0.04	0.07	0.12	0.01
科学研究人员	Scientific Research	2.09	0.73	0.65	0.70	0.48	0.26
卫生技术人员	Medical Professionals	9.40	6.78	0.95	2.59	5.40	0.46
教学人员	Teaching	16.43	10.72	2.70	8.66	4.53	0.54
经济人员	Economic	17.20	7.36	0.46	3.77	4.58	8.39
财会人员	Financial Accounting	6.63	4.25	0.12	1.85	3.64	1.02
统计人员	Statistical	0.60	0.35	0.01	0.14	0.25	0.20
翻译人员	Translator	0.16	0.08	0.01	0.07	0.06	0.02
新闻出版、播音人员	Media, Publishing & Announcer	0.84	0.38	0.13	0.29	0.27	0.15
艺术人员	Culture & Art	0.43	0.15	0.12	0.16	0.13	0.02
其他专业人员	Others	3.81	1.47	0.38	1.50	1.35	0.57

注：本表数据由市委组织部提供。
Note: Data in this table are provided by the Organization Department of Shanghai Committee of Chinese Communist Party.

表 18.5 续表 continued

单位:万人(10 000 persons)

类别 Types		按学历分 By Education Background 大学本专科及以上 College and university above	中等专业 Specialized Secondary School	高中及以下 Senior Middle School and below	按年龄分 By Age 45 岁及以下 45 and below	46～54 岁 46～54	55 岁及以上 55 and above
总计	**Total**	**62.34**	**10.12**	**5.22**	**57.83**	**15.07**	**4.78**
工程技术人员	Engineering	16.05	2.08	1.72	15.07	3.56	1.22
农业技术人员	Agriculture	0.18	0.05	0.02	0.19	0.04	0.02
科学研究人员	Scientific Research	1.99	0.06	0.05	1.61	0.33	0.15
卫生技术人员	Medical Professionals	5.82	3.39	0.18	6.83	2.27	0.30
教学人员	Teaching	15.50	0.79	0.13	12.88	2.42	1.12
经济人员	Economic	13.40	1.85	1.95	13.13	3.04	1.02
财会人员	Financial Accounting	4.89	1.19	0.55	5.03	1.39	0.22
统计人员	Statistical	0.38	0.13	0.08	0.40	0.17	0.03
翻译人员	Translator	0.16	…	…	0.10	0.05	0.01
新闻出版、播音人员	Media, Publishing & Announcer	0.76	0.04	0.03	0.60	0.16	0.07
艺术人员	Culture & Art	0.24	0.12	0.09	0.24	0.14	0.06
其他专业人员	Others	2.97	0.42	0.42	1.75	1.50	0.56

表 18.6 集体经济单位各类专业人员（2007）
PROFESSIONAL AND TECHNICAL PERSONNEL IN OTHER ECONOMIC ORGANS

单位：人(person)

类别 Types		合计 Total	其中 of which #女性 Female	按专业技术职务分 By Professional Titles 高级 Senior	中级 Medium	初级 Junior	未聘 Not Appointed
总计	**Total**	**26 008**	**13 474**	**561**	**7 072**	**17 117**	**1 258**
工程技术人员	Engineering	2 644	480	109	962	1 488	85
农业技术人员	Agriculture	1 391	211	18	476	836	61
科学研究人员	Scientific Research	10	4	1	1	8	
卫生技术人员	Medical Professionals	13 089	9 118	243	3 345	9 256	245
教学人员	Teaching	352	221	8	84	260	
其他专业人员	Others	8 522	3 440	182	2 204	5 269	867

注：本表数据由市委组织部提供。
Note: Data in this table are provided by the Organization Department of Shanghai Committee of Chinese Communist Party.

表 18.6 续表 continued

单位：人(person)

类别 Types		按学历分 By Education Background 高等院校 Higher Education	中等专业 Specialized Secondary School	高中及以下 Senior Middle School and below	按年龄分 By Age 45岁及以下 45 and below	46～55岁 46～55	55岁及以上 55 and above
总计	**Total**	**12 408**	**9 175**	**4 425**	**14 064**	**9 397**	**2 547**
工程技术人员	Engineering	1 330	542	772	1 398	836	410
农业技术人员	Agriculture	365	494	532	444	639	308
科学研究人员	Scientific Research	3	3	4	5	2	3
卫生技术人员	Medical Professionals	6 558	5 652	879	7 986	4 483	620
教学人员	Teaching	191	127	34	197	120	35
其他专业人员	Others	3 961	2 357	2 204	4 034	3 317	1 171

注：本表包括集体事业和企业单位人数。
Note: The figures include employees at collective and public service organizations and enterprises.

表 18.7 各类技术合同项目（1991～2007）
VARIOUS TECHNOLOGICAL CONTRACTS

单位：项(item)

年份 Year	项目 Item	其中 of which 技术开发 Technological Development	技术转让 Technological Transfer	技术咨询 Technological Consulting	技术服务 Technological Service
1991	25 023	3 038	1 992	3 203	16 790
1992	32 731	3 501	2 159	4 200	22 871
1993	25 507	2 517	1 389	3 671	17 930
1994	25 099	2 368	941	4 215	17 575
1995	21 213	1 915	775	3 672	14 851
1996	20 074	1 841	823	3 821	13 589
1997	18 863	1 643	1 037	3 569	12 614
1998	18 364	1 206	919	3 235	13 004
1999	19 721	1 158	937	3 993	13 633
2000	20 974	1 561	888	3 905	14 620
2001	23 816	2 385	1 294	5 012	15 125
2002	26 010	2 984	1 156	4 983	16 887
2003	27 292	3 512	2 112	5 306	16 362
2004	27 327	4 398	2 453	4 814	15 662
2005	30 290	5 256	2 444	4 753	17 837
2006	28 191	6 165	2 172	3 592	16 262
2007	27 742	6 425	2 133	3 086	16 098

表 18.8 各类技术合同成交金额（1991～2007）
TOTAL CONTRACTED VALUE IN VARIOUS TECHNOLOGICAL CONTRACTS

单位：亿元(100 million yuan)

年份 Year	成交金额 Contracted Value	其中 of which 技术开发 Technological Development	技术转让 Technological Transfer	技术咨询 Technological Consulting	技术服务 Technological Service
1991	9.33	2.15	1.90	0.55	4.72
1992	15.25	3.56	1.33	0.99	9.37
1993	20.32	3.03	2.00	2.16	13.13
1994	22.09	3.31	1.08	2.08	15.62
1995	23.04	4.14	1.57	2.12	15.21
1996	25.65	4.38	1.50	2.81	16.97
1997	28.76	5.72	2.14	3.28	17.61
1998	31.41	4.55	2.58	2.44	21.85
1999	36.63	3.68	3.50	3.24	26.21
2000	73.90	9.96	36.44	3.51	23.99
2001	106.16	28.24	50.71	4.63	22.58
2002	120.22	45.40	46.18	4.63	24.01
2003	142.78	50.96	50.79	6.11	34.92
2004	171.70	61.31	42.32	6.00	62.07
2005	231.73	87.47	110.08	6.42	27.76
2006	344.43	142.79	165.18	7.60	28.86
2007	432.64	181.50	212.49	5.50	33.15

注：本页数据由市技术市场管理办公室提供。
Note: Data on this page are provided by Shanghai Technology Market Administrative Office.

表 18.9 科技成果（1994～2007）
ACHIEVEMENTS IN SCIENTIFIC AND TECHNICAL RESEARCH

单位：项(item)

年 份 Year	科技成果 Achievements in Science and Technology	按成果水平分 By Level of Achievements				
		国际领先 Being First Created in the World	国际先进 Attaining Advanced World Levels	国内领先 Being First Created in China	国内先进 Attaining Advanced Domestic Levels	其 他 Others
1994	1 715	9	386	677	643	
1995	1 350	6	326	525	470	23
1996	1 094	10	348	477	234	25
1997	1 193	8	434	538	181	32
1998	1 305	30	494	539	210	32
1999	1 252	41	457	536	193	25
2000	1 102	45	462	452	117	26
2001	1 338	78	542	444	116	158
2002	1 418	65	603	463	106	181
2003	1 508	71	532	481	155	269
2004	1 629	147	669	480	155	178
2005	1 701	123	629	588	189	172
2006	1 953	250	675	655	191	182
2007	2 396	180	761	938	254	263

表 18.9 续表 continued

单位：项(item)

年 份 Year	按成果分 By Type of Achievements			按推广应用分 By Populization	
	基础理论成果 Fundamental Theory Research Results	应用技术成果 Application of Technological Achievements	软科学成果 Soft Scientific Achievements	已推广应用 Been Populized	未应用 Not Been Populized
1997	118	978	97	796	182
1998	156	1 036	113	883	153
1999	80	1 054	118	835	219
2000	79	953	70	809	144
2001	81	1 196	61	940	256
2002	110	1 250	58	961	289
2003	97	1 281	130	1 045	236
2004	70	1 488	71	1 204	284
2005	61	1 555	85	1 261	294
2006	52	1 799	102	1 506	293
2007	139	2 162	95	1 724	438

表 18.10 主要年份获得科技成果奖励情况
ACHIEVEMENTS AWARDED IN SCIENTIFIC AND TECHNOLOGICAL RESEARCH IN MAIN YEARS

单位：项(item)

指 标	Indicators	1995	2000	2006	2007
一、科技成果获奖总数	**Number of Achievements Awarded**	**335**	**287**	**353**	**373**
1. 获国家科技成果奖	National Award	59	21	44	54
#国家科学技术进步奖	Science and Technology Progress Award	45	17	33	39
国家技术发明奖	Technological Invention Award	7	1	5	4
国家自然科学奖	Natural Science Award	7	3	4	9
中华人民共和国国际科学技术奖(人)	International Science and Technology Award			2	2
2. 获上海市科学技术奖	Shanghai Award for Science and Technology	276	266	309	319

注：本页数据由市科学技术委员会提供。
Note: Data on this page are provided by Shanghai Municipal Science and Technology Commission.

表 18.11 主要年份专利申请量 PATENT APPLICATIONS IN MAIN YEARS

单位：件(item)

指 标	Indicators	1990	2000	2006	2007
总 计	**Total**	**1 526**	**11 337**	**36 042**	**47 205**
按种类分	**By Type of Patents**				
发 明	Inventions	297	4 713	12 050	15 212
实用新型	Utility Models	1 049	2 760	9 881	12 112
外观设计	Designs	180	3 864	14 111	19 881
按对象分	**By Applicant**				
非职务发明创造	Non-position Patents	846	2 137	5 384	6 056
职务发明创造	Position Patents	680	9 200	30 658	41 149
大专院校	Universities and Colleges	87	618	3 066	5 604
科研单位	Research Institutions	153	613	1 428	1 601
工矿企业	Industrial and Mining Enterprises	354	7 936	24 835	30 643
机关团体	Government Agencies and Organizations	86	33	1 329	3 301

表 18.12 主要年份专利授权量 PATENTS CERTIFIED IN MAIN YEARS

单位：件(item)

指 标	Indicators	1990	2000	2006	2007
总 计	**Total**	**924**	**4 050**	**16 602**	**24 481**
按种类分	**By Type of Patents**				
发 明	Inventions	99	304	2 644	3 259
实用新型	Utility Models	769	2 083	6 739	9 718
外观设计	Designs	56	1 663	7 219	11 504
按对象分	**By Applicant**				
非职务发明创造	Non-position Patents	502	1 516	2 360	3 097
职务发明创造	Position Patents	422	2 534	14 242	21 384
大专院校	Universities and Colleges	81	183	1 586	2 616
科研单位	Research Institutions	145	215	864	1 001
工矿企业	Industrial and Mining Enterprises	156	2 101	11 503	15 383
机关团体	Government Agencies and Organizations	40	35	289	2 384

注：本页数据由市知识产权局提供。
Note: Data on this page are provided by Shanghai Municipal Intellectual Property Rights Bureau.

表 18.13 主要年份研究与试验发展(R&D)经费按执行部门分类
EXPENDITURES ON R&D GROUPED BY EXECUTIVE DEPARTMENT IN MAIN YEARS

单位:亿元(100 million yuan)

指 标	Indicators	2000	2006	2007
总 计	**Total**	**76.73**	**256.78**	**307.50**
科研机构	Research Institutions	25.58	52.07	58.01
高等院校	Institutions of Higher Education	7.43	26.51	26.26
企 业	Enterprises	41.44	177.07	222.15
#工业企业	Industrial Enterprises	34.78	161.43	193.58
#大中型工业企业	Large and Medium Industrial Enterprises	30.98	133.80	162.73
其 他	Others	2.28	1.13	1.08

注：本表数据由上海市财政局提供。
Note: Data in this table are provided by Shanghai Municipal Finance Bureau.

表 18.14 主要年份自然科学研究与技术开发机构课题情况
PROJECTS OF NATURAL SCIENCE RESEARCH AND TECHNOLOGICAL DEVELOPMENT INSTITUTIONS IN MAIN YEARS

年 份 Year	机构数 (个) Number of Institutions (unit)	课题数 (项) Number of Projects (item)	投入经费 (万元) Funds Invested (10 000 yuan)	投入人力 (人年) Manpower Input (person-year)	其中 of which #科学家和工程师 Scientists and Engineers
1985	220	6 398	21 235	22 349	
1990	229	8 339	33 061	23 279	16 292
1991	231	8 504	37 736	23 970	17 402
1992	232	8 909	53 501	23 924	17 487
1993	230	6 926	54 480	20 489	14 951
1994	229	6 268	66 158	17 023	13 275
1995	230	6 544	80 957	17 531	13 811
1996	233	5 538	90 504	17 434	14 465
1997	232	5 481	117 199	17 507	14 453
1998	230	5 554	122 513	16 713	13 466
1999	225	5 135	125 620	16 396	13 360
2000	229	4 879	148 846	17 104	13 569
2001	221	4 468	210 910	16 972	13 821
2002	218	4 393	251 837	15 523	11 710
2003	216	4 473	282 865	17 058	11 849
2004	212	4 540	330 063	17 299	12 045
2005	206	4 416	425 266	18 924	12 542
2006	202	4 585	494 657	19 008	12 905
2007	199	5 534	542 601	20 443	14 902

注：本表数据由市科学技术委员会提供。
Note: Data in this table are provided by Shanghai Municipal Science and Technology Commission.

表 18.15 自然科学研究与技术开发机构课题情况(2007)
STATISTICS OF PROJECTS OF NATURAL SCIENCE RESEARCH AND DEVELOPMENT INSTITUTIONS

类 别	Types	机构数（个）Number of Institutions (unit)	课题数（项）Number of Projects (item)	投入经费（万元）Funds Invested (10 000 yuan)	投入人力（人年）Manpower Input (person-year)
总 计	**Total**	**199**	**5 534**	**542 601**	**20 443**
按学科分	**Grouped by Subject**				
自然科学	Natural Science	17	1 985	96 999	2 327
农业科学	Agriculture Science	18	530	9 514	720
医学科学	Medical Science	17	704	24 026	1 256
工程科学与技术	Engineering Science and Technology	143	2 285	411 432	16 081
社会与人文科学	Social Science and Humanities	4	30	630	59
按行业分	**By Sector**				
制造业	Manufacturing	110	1 412	335 340	12 329
建筑业	Construction	4	99	1 339	260
交通运输、仓储和邮政业	Transportation, Warehousing and Post	4	22	369	106
科学研究、技术服务和地质勘查业	Scientific Research, Technical Service and Geological Prospecting	38	2 922	177 167	5 523
水利、环境和公共设施管理业	Water Conservancy, Environment and Public Facility Management	8	193	2 401	301
卫生、社会保障和社会福利业	Health, Social Security and Welfare	14	301	10 569	701
文化、体育和娱乐业	Culture, Sports and Entertainment	2	33	3 263	357

表 18.16 自然科学研究与技术开发机构论文与著作情况（2007）
PAPERS AND WORKS OF NATURAL SCIENCE RESEARCH AND TECHNOLOGICAL DEVELOPMENT INSTITUTIONS

类 别	Types	论 文（篇）Papers (piece)	其中 of which #国外发表 Published Abroad	科技著作（种）Scientific and Technological Works (sort)
总 计	**Total**	**95**	**6 777**	**2 514**
按学科领域分	**Grouped by the Domain of Subject**			
自然科学	Natural Science	20	2 490	1 450
农业科学	Agriculture Science	12	497	22
医学科学	Medical Science	17	1 225	413
工程科学与技术	Engineering Science and Technology	44	2 561	629
社会与人文科学	Social and Humanities Science	2	4	
按行业分	**By Sector**			
#农、林、牧、渔业	Farming, Forestry, Animal Husbandry and Fishery	10	466	35
制造业	Manufacturing	36	1 347	269
水利、环境和公共设施管理业	Water Conservancy, Environment and Public Facility Management	9	206	5
建筑业	Construction		189	5
科学研究、技术服务和地质勘查业	Scientific Research, Technical Service and Geological Prospecting	24	3 700	2 061
卫生、社会保障和社会福利业	Health, Social Security and Welfare	16	778	137

注：本页数据由市科学技术委员会提供。
Note: Data on this page are provided by Shanghai Municipal Science and Technology Commission.

表 18.17 主要年份区县级以上国有单位独立研究与开发机构从事科技活动的科学家和工程师
SCIENTISTS AND ENGINEERS ENGAGED IN SCIENTIFIC AND TECHNOLOGICAL ACTIVITIES OF STATE-OWNED INDEPENDENT RESEARCH AND DEVELOPMENT INSTITUTIONS ABOVE DISTRICT AND COUNTY LEVEL IN MAIN YEARS

单位:人(person)

类别	Types	1990	2000	2006	2007
总计	**Total**	**40 962**	**25 699**	**23 299**	**27 441**
按隶属关系分	**Grouped by Subordination**				
中国科学院	The Chinese Academy of Science	6 091	3 810	2 907	3 967
国务院部门	Departments of the State Council	19 261	13 129	13 043	15 432
地方	Local	15 610	8 760	7 349	8 042
按领域分	**By Subjects**				
自然科学	Natural Science	39 130	24 160	21 584	25 667
科技信息文献	Scientific & Technological Information & Documents	754	732	875	918
社会与人文科学	Social Sciences and Humanities	1 078	807	840	856

表 18.18 区县级以上国有单位独立研究与开发机构人员(2007)
PERSONNEL OF STATE-OWNED INDEPENDENT RESEARCH AND DEVELOPMENT INSTITUTIONS ABOVE DISTRICT AND COUNTY LEVEL

单位:人(person)

类别	Types	从事科技活动人员 Personnel Engaged in Scientific and Technological Activities	其中 of which			
			#科学家和工程师 Scientists and Engineers	#研究生 Post-graduates	#大学 University and College	#大专 Specialized Institutions of Higher Education
总计	**Total**	**38 254**	**27 441**	**8 064**	**15 039**	**6 974**
按隶属关系分	**Grouped by Subordination**					
中国科学院	The Chinese Academy of Science	4 414	3 967	2 007	1 329	526
国务院部门	Departments of the State Council	23 042	15 432	3 646	9 565	3 978
地方	Local	10 798	8 042	2 411	4 145	2 470
按领域分	**By Subject**					
自然科学	Natural Science	36 074	25 667	7 369	14 268	6 484
科技情报文献	Scientific & Technological Information & Documents	1 039	918	552	278	147
社会与人文科学	Social Sciences and Humanities	1 141	856	143	493	343

注：本页数据由市科学技术委员会提供。
Note: Data on this page are provieded by Shanghai Municipal Science and Technology Commission.

表 18.19 主要年份区县级属研究与开发机构状况
RESEARCH AND DEVELOPMENT INSTITUTIONS AT DISTRICT AND COUNTY LEVEL IN MAIN YEARS

指 标	Indicators	1990	2000	2006	2007
机构数（个）	Number of Institutions (unit)	28	35	21	21
从业人员（人）	Number of Employees (person)	1 175	1 261	1 020	1 004
#科学家和工程师	Scientists and Engineers	339	504	332	362
技术员	Technicians	378	198	363	344
经费支出（万元）	Expenditures (10 000 yuan)	770	7 343	10 564	12 198

表 18.20 主要年份民营科技企业状况
SCIENTIFIC AND TECHNOLOGICAL RESEARCH INSTITUTIONS RUN BY LOCAL PEOPLE IN MAIN YEARS

指 标	Indicators	2000	2006	2007
机构数（个）	**Number of Institutions (unit)**	**12 316**	**15 131**	**15 695**
#集体单位	Collective-owned Units	1 401	369	307
从业人员（万人）	**Employment (10 000 persons)**	**26.33**	**62.18**	**72.26**
#从事科技活动人员	Scientific & Technological Personnel	12.95	21.93	24.15
#科学家和工程师	Scientists & Engineers	8.90	12.04	12.73
技术员	Technicians	4.05	9.89	11.42
总产值(亿元)	Gross Output Value(100 million yuan)	311.22	3 516.89	5 239.56
利润总额(亿元)	Total Pre-tax Profits(100 million yuan)	47.58	239.82	421.21
税金总额(亿元)	Total Tax and Duties(100 million yuan)	28.64	215.22	286.88
创汇(亿美元)	Foreign Exchange Income(100 million USD)	2.83	133.22	239.74
资产总额(亿元)	Total Assets(100 million yuan)	1 064	5 074	7 033
科技投入(亿元)	Input Value of Science and Technology (100 million yuan)	33.5	114.46	168.35
总收入（亿元）	Revenue(100 million yuan)	811.35	5 023.79	7 249.40
总支出（亿元）	Expenditures (100 million yuan)	712.97	4 638.57	5 766.60
专利申请量(件)	Patent Applications(piece)	452	9 048	12 453
专利授权量(件)	Patent Certified(piece)	1 169	4 111	7 112

注：本表统计范围是指经上海市科学技术委员会确认的独立核算国有、集体、个体、私营以及国有与集体联营等科技经营机构。
Note: Figures of Scientific and Technological Institutions in this table are the enterprises with independent accounting systems such as state-owned, collective-owned, individual, private and state-collective joint units certified by Shanghai Science and Technology Commission.

表 18.21 高等学校科技活动人员（2007）
SCIENTIFIC AND TECHNOLOGICAL PERSONNEL OF INSTITUTIONS OF HIGHER EDUCATION

单位：人（person）

指 标	Indicators	合 计 Total	其 中 of which 自然科学 Natural Science	工程与技术 Engineering and Technology	医学科学 Medical Science	农业科学 Agriculture Science	其 他 Others
总 计	**Total**	**29 068**	**3 545**	**9 030**	**12 601**	**258**	**3 634**
按职称分	**By Professional Title**						
高 级	Senior	9 987	1 780	3 779	3 561	123	744
中 级	Medium	10 980	1 314	3 715	4 347	86	1 518
初 级	Junior	6 922	331	1 220	4 407	45	919
按技术等级分	**By Technical Level**						
#科学家和工程师	Scientists and Engineers	27 889	3 425	8 714	12 315	253	3 182

表 18.22 主要年份高等学校研究与开发状况
R&D BY INSTITUTIONS OF HIGHER EDUCATION IN MAIN YEARS

指 标	Indicators	1990	2000	2006	2007
科技活动机构数（个）	**R&D Institutions (unit)**	**370**	**326**	**178**	**179**
科技活动人员数（人）	**Technological Personnel (person)**	**53 013**	**49 402**	**26 701**	**29 068**
#自然科学	Natural Science	7 901	5 012	3 288	3 545
工程与技术	Engineering and Technology	17 976	15 854	8 729	9 030
医学科学	Medical Science	12 116	15 817	11 394	12 601
农业科学	Agriculture Science	415	441	230	258
R&D 人员数（人年）	**R&D Personnel (person-Year)**	**18 658**	**13 526**	**13 517**	**12 772**
#科学家和工程师	Scientists & Engineers	15 278	13 055	13 071	12 349
#高级职务	Personnel with Senior Titles	5 363	6 212	6 501	6 143
课题数（个）	**Number of Projects (unit)**	**8 801**	**12 827**	**19 541**	**19 214**
课题投入人数（万人年）	**Personnel Engaged in Projects (10 000 person-year)**	**1.21**	**1.71**	**1.60**	**1.74**
课题投入经费（亿元）	**Funds Financed (100 million yuan)**	**1.36**	**13.56**	**39.41**	**45.49**
课题经费支出（亿元）	**Expenditures (100 million yuan)**	**1.11**	**10.64**	**34.65**	**35.64**

①本页数据由市教育委员会提供。
②本表统计范围是指高等学校中理工农医类口径。
❶Data on this page are provided by Shanghai Education Commission.
❷Figures of scientific and technological personnel in this table refer to those of science, engineering, agriculture and medicine of higher education.

表 18.23 高等学校 R&D 人员、机构及课题情况（2007）
PERSONNEL, INSTITUTIONS AND PROJECTS OF R&D IN INSTITUTIONS OF HIGHER EDUCATION

指标	Indicators	合计 Total	其中 of which #自然科学 Natural Science	#工程与技术 Engineering and Technology	#医学科学 Medical Science	#农业科学 Agriculture Science
R&D 机构数（个）	R&D Institutions (unit)	179	31	67	78	3
R&D 机构人员（人）	R&D Institutions Personnel (person)	6 085	1 003	2 435	2 610	37
课题数（个）	Number of Projects (unit)	19 214	2 993	11 197	4 323	554
课题投入人数（人年）	Personnel Engaged in Projects (person-year)	17 441	2 012	9 580	5 432	278
课题投入经费（万元）	Funds Financed(10 000 yuan)	454 943	64 292	338 299	46 531	5 821
课题经费支出（万元）	Expenditures (10 000 yuan)	356 371	38 950	287 596	25 503	4 322

①本表数据由市教育委员会提供。
②本表统计范围是指高等学校中理工农医类口径。
❶Data in this table is provided by Shanghai Education Commission.
❷Figures of scientific and technological personnel in this table refer to those of science, engineering, agriculture and medicine of higher education.

表 18.24 各级科协机构和人员（2007）
INSTITUTIONS AND PERSONNEL OF SCIENCE AND TECHNOLOGY ASSOCIATIONS AT VARIOUS LEVELS

指标	Indicators	市级科协 Municipal Level Associations	区级科协 District Level Associations	县级科协 County Level Associations
机构数（个）	Number of Institutions (unit)	1	18	1
人员（人）	Personnel (person)	66	303	6
各级学会在册个数（个）	Number of Societies Registered (unit)	180	406	30

注：本表数据由市科学技术协会提供。
Note: Data in this table are provided by Shanghai Municipal Science and Technology Associations.

表 18.24 续表 continued

指标	Indicators	机构数（个） Number of Institutions (unit)	个人会员（万人） Individual Members (10 000 persons)	团体会员数（个） Organization Members (unit)	所属分科学会（个） Attached Associations (unit)
市级学会	Prefectural Societies	180	18.6	13 359	934

表 18.25 科协系统科普活动和科技培训情况（2007）
PROMOTING SCIENCE ACTIVITIES AND TRAINING PROGRAM ORGANIZED BY SCIENCE AND TECHNOLOGY ASSOCIATIONS

指 标	Indicators	合 计 Total	市科协 Municipal Level Associations	#区县科协 District and County Level Associations	学 会 Academies
科普活动	**Promoting Science Activities**				
科普讲座次数（次）	Lectures(time)	7 616	4 550	4 413	3 066
科普讲座参加人次（万人次）	Participants of Lectures(10 000 person-times)	104	59	56	45
科普展览次数(次)	Exhibitions(time)	1 205	1 057	1 039	148
科普展览参加人次（万人次）	Participants of Exhibitions(10 000 person-times)	189.7	122.1	87.6	67.6
科普宣传活动次数(次)	Popular Science Promotion Activities(time)	2 780	1 972	1 937	808
科技夏（冬）令营次数(次)	Technical Summer (Winter) Camps(time)	219	141	140	78
青少年科技竞赛次数(次)	Youth Technical Competitions(time)	685	636	628	49
培训班	**Training Classes**				
36学时以上班数（个）	Classes of More Than 36 Learning Hours (unit)	1 430	678	621	752
培训人次（万人次）	Trainees (10 000 person-times)	17.9	11.4	11.2	6.5

表 18.26 科协系统出版物和科技服务情况（2007）
PUBLICATIONS AND CONSULTATIVE ACTIVITIES OF SCIENCE AND TECHNOLOGY ASSOCIATIONS

指 标	Indicators	合 计 Total	市科协 Municipal Level Associations	#区县科协 District and County Level Associations	学 会 Academies
出版物	Publications				
主办科技期刊种数（种）	Academic Journals (sort)	79	1		78
年发行总数（万册）	Annual Issues (10 000 copies)	446.3	12.6		433.7
年发表论文(篇)	Number of Paper Published over the Year (piece)	15 337	1 279		14 058
编辑论文集种数（种）	Thesis Collections Edited (sort)	135	35		100
年发行总数（册）	Annual Issues (copy)	46 061	2 500		43 561
主办科技报纸种数（种）	Science and Technology Newspaper (sort)	6	2		4
年发行份数（万份）	Annual Circulation (10 000 pieces)	735.3	730.5		4.8
编著科技图书种数（种）	Science and Technology Books (sort)	111	52	8	59
年发行册数（万册）	Annual Issues (10 000 copies)	236.5	207.6	11.6	28.9
咨 询	**Consultation**				
完成技术咨询合同数（项）	Technical Contracts Completed (item)	1 559	778	622	781
无偿咨询项目数（项）	Free Consultation (item)	5 402	121	121	5 281
咨询合同实现金额（万元）	Technical Constracts Revenue (10 000 yuan)	33 374	31 457	27 390	1 913

注：本页数据由市科学技术协会提供。
Note: Data on this page are provided by Shanghai Municipal Science and Technology Associations.

表 18.27 科协系统学术交流情况（2007）
ACADEMIC EXCHANGES OF SCIENCE AND TECHNOLOGY ASSOCIATIONS

指 标	Indicators	合 计 Total	市科协 Municipal Level Associations	学 会 Academies
国内学术会议	**Domestic Academic Conferences**			
举办次数（次）	Times(time)	2 004	683	1 321
参加人次（人次）	Participants (person-times)	220 550	89 049	131 501
交流论文（篇）	Papers Exchanged (piece)	19 135	989	18 146
国际学术会议	**International Academic Conferences**			
举办次数（次）	Times(time)	97	2	95
中方参加人次（人次）	Chinese Participants (person-time)	14 352	300	14 052
中方交流论文（篇）	Chinese Papers Exchanged (piece)	4 287	14	4 273
外方参加人次（人次）	Overseas Participants (person-time)	2 512	15	2 497
外方交流论文（篇）	Overseas Papers Exchanged (piece)	1 537	5	1 532
接待科技来访团组	**Receiving Visiting Science and Technology Delegations**			
接待海外科技团组数（个）	Foreign Science and Technology Groups (unit)	328	30	298
接待海外来访人次（人次）	Foreign Visitors (person-time)	2 727	676	2 051
接待港澳台科技团组(个)	Science and Technology Groups from Hong Kong, Macao and Taiwan (unit)	52	32	20
接待港澳台来访人次(人次)	Visitors from Hong Kong, Macao and Taiwan (person-time)	447	170	277
双边学术会议	**Bilateral Academic Conferences**			
举办次数(次数)	Number of Meetings(time)	25	1	24
参加人数(人次)	Number of Participants(person-times)	1 538	47	1 491
交流论文(篇)	Number of Papers Exchanged(piece)	150	24	126
港澳台地区学术会议	**Number of Academic Meetings Related with Hongkong, Macao and Taiwan**			
举办次数(次)	Number of Meetings(time)	6	6	
参加人次(人次)	Number of Participants(person-times)	294	294	
交流论文(篇)	Number of Papers Exchanged(piece)	126	126	
海峡两岸地区学术会议	**Number of Academic Meetings Related with Mainland and Taiwan**			
举办次数(次)	Number of Meetings(time)	8	1	7
参加人次(人次)	Number of Participants(person-times)	553	189	364
交流论文(篇)	Number of Papers Exchanged(piece)	144	7	137
外派科技团组	**Dispatching Science and Technology Delegations Abroad**			
外派团组数（个）	Number of Delegations Sent Abroad (unit)	96	19	77
外派总人次（人次）	Number of People Sent Abroad (person-time)	511	71	440
#参加国际会议	Attending International Conferences	203	1	202
参加展览、技贸活动	Attending Exhibition and Technical Trade	23	23	
派往港澳台地区科技团组	**Number of Delegations Sent to Hongkong, Macao and Taiwan**			
派出团组数(个)	Number of Delegations Sent Abroad (unit)	61	13	48
派出总人次(人次)	Number of People Sent Abroad (person-time)	556	125	431

注：本表数据由市科学技术协会提供。
Note: Data in this table is provided by Shanghai Municipal Science and Technology Associations.

表 18.28 规模以上工业企业技术开发机构和人员（2007）
TECHNICAL DEVELOPMENT ORGANIZATIONS AND PERSONNEL OF INDUSTRIAL ENTERPRISES ABOVE THE SET SCALE

类 别	Types	技术开发机构数(个) Technological Development Institutions (unit)	从事技术开发人员(万人) Tech. Development Personnel (10 000 persons)	其中 of which #科学家和工程师 Scientists & Engineers
总 计	**Total**	**513**	**10.54**	**7.07**
一、按隶属关系分	**Grouped by Subordination**			
中央单位	Central Units	47	3.00	2.16
地方单位	Local Units	466	7.54	4.91
二、按登记注册类型分	**By Registration Categories**			
#国有企业	State-owned	41	1.37	0.97
股份制及其他有限公司	Share-holding and Other Companies with Limited Liabilities	123	3.01	1.94
外资企业	Foreign Funded	230	4.98	3.37
#国有及国有控股企业	Enterprises Owned by the State or with the State Holding Major Shares	242	6.54	4.51
三、按企业规模分	**By Size of Enterprises**			
大型企业	Large	71	4.51	3.13
中型企业	Medium	244	3.86	2.50
小型企业	Small	198	2.17	1.44
四、按行业分	**By Sectors**			
#高技术产业	High Technology Industry	170	3.09	2.25
医药制造业	Medicine Manufacturing	55	0.44	0.30
航空航天器制造	Aviation and Aircraft Manufacturing	13	0.12	0.09
电子及通信设备制造业	Electronic and Communicantion Equipment Manufacturing	65	1.63	1.22
电子计算机及办公设备制造业	Electronic Computer and Office Equipment Manufacturing	11	0.45	0.34
医疗设备及仪器仪表制造业	Medical Machinery amd Measuring Instrument Manufacturing	26	0.44	0.30
#六个重点发展工业行业	Six Key Industries	371	8.32	5.70
电子信息产品制造业	Electronic Information Product Manufacturing	115	2.72	1.89
汽车制造业	Automobile Manufacturing	38	0.85	0.66
石油化工及精细化工制造业	Petrochemical and Fine Chemical Products Manufacturing	48	0.64	0.43
精品钢材制造业	Fine Steel Manufacturing	5	1.18	0.74
成套设备制造业	Equipment Complex Manufacturing	101	2.34	1.61
生物医药制造业	Bio-medicine Manufacturing	64	0.57	0.37

表 18.28 续表 continued

类别	Types	技术开发机构数(个) Technical Development Organizations	从事技术开发人员(人) Tech. Development Personnel (persons)	其中 of which #科学家和工程师 Scientists & Engineers
总　计	**Total**	**513**	**105 419**	**70 669**
按工业行业分	**By Sectors**			
制造业	**Manufacture Industry**	**506**	**102 190**	**67 904**
#石油和天然气开采业	Petroleum and Natural Gas Exploiting		64	55
农副食品加工业	Farm and Sideline Products Processing	2	213	90
食品制造业	Food Manufacturing	7	633	371
饮料制造业	Beverage Manufacturing	2	145	83
烟草制品业	Tabacco Manufacturing	1	675	370
纺织业	Textile	7	1 005	389
纺织服装、鞋、帽制造业	Garments, Shoes and Accessories Manufacturing	1	28	19
木材加工及木、竹、藤、棕、草制品业	Timber Processing and Timber, Bamboo, Rattan, Coir and Straw Products Manufacturing		6	5
家具制造业	Furniture Manufacturing	1	548	215
造纸及纸制品业	Paper-making and Paper Products Manufacturing	1	200	122
印刷业和记录媒介的复制	Printing and Record Duplicating	11	1 108	643
文教体育用品制造业	Stationary, Education and Sports Goods Manufacturing	8	537	221
石油加工、炼焦及核燃料加工业	Oil Processing, Coking and Nuclear	6	917	664
化学原料及化学制品制造业	Raw Chemical Materials and Chemical	55	6 319	4 170
医药制造业	Medicine Manufacturing	55	4 432	2 973
化学纤维制造业	Chemical Fiber Manufacturing	1	42	15
橡胶制品业	Rubber Products Manufacturing	6	831	403
塑料制品业	Plastic Products Manufacturing	11	821	585
非金属矿物制品业	Nonmetal Mineral Products	10	2 191	1 176
黑色金属冶炼及压延加工业	Smelting and Pressing of Ferrous Metals	5	11 828	7 439
有色金属冶炼及压延加工业	Smelting and Pressing of Nonferrous Metals	2	580	233
金属制品业	Metal Products Manufacturing	11	1 440	883
通用设备制造业	General Equipment Manufacturing	46	13 332	8 853
专用设备制造业	Special Purpose Equipment Manufacturing	30	5 855	3 760
交通运输设备制造业	Transportation Equipment Manufacturing	58	12 946	9 635
电气机械及器材制造业	Electric Machinery Equipments and Manufacturing	67	10 563	6 174
通信设备、计算机及其他电子设备制造业	Communications Equipments, Computer and Other Electronic Equipment Manufacturing	74	20 442	15 326
仪器仪表及文化、办公用机械制造业	Instruments, Meters, Culture and Office Equipments Manufacturing	26	4 343	2 924
工艺品及其他制造业	Artworks and Other Manufacturing		137	99
电力、燃气及水的生产和供应业	**Production and Supply of Power, Gas and Water**	**7**	**3 229**	**2 765**
电力、热力的生产和供应业	Production and Supply of Electricity and Thermal Power	5	2 756	2 441
燃气生产和供应业	Production and Supply of Gas	1	255	169
水的生产和供应业	Production and Supply of Water	1	218	155

表 18.29 规模以上工业企业技术开发经费来源（2007）
TECHNICAL DEVELOPMENT FUNDS OF INDUSTRIAL ENTERPRISES ABOVE THE SET SCALE

单位：亿元(100 million yuan)

类　别	Types	当年筹集额 Funds of 2007	其中 of which #政府资金 Government Capital	#银行贷款 Bank Loans	#企业自筹 Self-raised Funds
总　计	**Total**	**315.27**	**11.13**	**4.72**	**291.36**
一、按隶属关系分	**Grouped by Subordination**				
中央单位	Central Units	85.64	5.92	0.35	77.76
地方单位	Local Units	229.63	5.21	4.37	213.60
二、按登记注册类型分	**By Registration Categories**				
#国有企业	State-owned	27.36	2.62	0.27	23.64
股份制及其他有限公司	Share-holding and Other Companies with Limited Liabilities	91.80	2.29	1.32	87.30
外资企业	Foreign Funded	176.77	2.95	2.19	165.67
#国有及国有控股企业	Enterprises Owned by the State or with the State Holding Major Shares	216.32	8.15	2.95	202.64
三、按企业规模分	**By Size of Enterprises**				
大型企业	Large	167.26	7.00	0.02	155.09
中型企业	Medium	109.92	2.72	2.64	102.95
小型企业	Small	38.09	1.41	2.06	33.32
四、按行业分	**By Sectors**				
#高技术产业	**High Technology Industry**	**81.55**	**4.81**	**0.80**	**70.89**
信息化学品制造	Information Chemical Product Manufacturing	0.02			0.02
医药制造业	Medicine Manufacturing	11.96	0.32	0.11	11.43
航空航天器制造	Aviation and Aircraft Manufacturing	2.65	1.32		1.30
电子及通信设备制造业	Electronic and Communicantion Equipment Manufacturing	47.73	2.80	0.50	44.30
电子计算机及办公设备制造业	Electronic Computer and Office Equipment Manufacturing	10.10	0.07	0.09	5.44
医疗设备及仪器仪表制造业	Medical Machinery and Measuring Instrument Manufacturing	9.10	0.30	0.11	8.40
#六个重点发展工业行业	**Six Key Industries**	**261.11**	**10.45**	**3.19**	**240.23**
电子信息产品制造业	Electronic Information Product Manufacturing	65.76	3.17	0.81	56.87
汽车制造业	Automobile Manufacturing	59.69	0.14	0.15	59.27
石油化工及精细化工制造业	Petrochemical and Fine Chemical Products Manufacturing	15.14	0.37	0.08	14.52
精品钢材制造业	Fine Steel Manufacturing	31.80	0.50	…	31.26
成套设备制造业	Equipment Complex Manufacturing	75.15	5.94	2.04	65.27
生物医药制造业	Bio-medicine Manufacturing	13.57	0.33	0.11	13.04

表 18.29 续表 continued

单位:万元(10 000 yuan)

类别	Types	当年筹集额 Funds of 2007	其中 of which #政府资金 Government Allocation	#银行贷款 Bank Loans	#企业自筹 Self-raised Funds
总 计	**Total**	**3 152 733**	**111 310**	**47 178**	**2 913 564**
制造业	**Manufacture Industry**	**3 067 576**	**110 544**	**47 178**	**2 835 084**
#石油和天然气开采业	Petroleum and Natural Gas Exploiting	9 398			9 398
农副食品加工业	Farm and Sideline Products Processing	2 067	405		1 662
食品制造业	Food Manufacturing	6 739	185	290	6 264
饮料制造业	Beverage Manufacturing	4 385	50		4 335
烟草制品业	Tabacco Manufacturing	31 730	236		31 494
纺织业	Textile	10 185	174		10 005
纺织服装、鞋、帽制造业	Garments, Shoes and Accessories Manufacturing	428			428
木材加工及木、竹、藤、棕、草制品业	Timber Processing and Timber, Bamboo, Rattan, Coir and Straw Products Manufacturing	59			59
家具制造业	Furniture Manufacturing	19 534	10		19 524
造纸及纸制品业	Paper-making and Paper Products Manufacturing	3 219	100	100	3 019
印刷业和记录媒介的复制	Printing and Record Duplicating	16 961	20	182	16 746
文教体育用品制造业	Stationary, Education and Sports Goods Manufacturing	4 530	15		4 515
石油加工、炼焦及核燃料加工业	Oil Processing, Coking and Nuclear	19 694	929		18 765
化学原料及化学制品制造业	Raw Chemical Materials and Chemical	149 036	3 773	4 135	139 412
医药制造业	Medicine Manufacturing	119 586	3 184	1 100	114 327
化学纤维制造业	Chemical Fiber Manufacturing	1 922	102	190	1 631
橡胶制品业	Rubber Products Manufacturing	23 223		300	22 923
塑料制品业	Plastic Products Manufacturing	14 856	498	500	13 758
非金属矿物制品业	Nonmetal Mineral Products	36 400	569	3 094	32 707
黑色金属冶炼及压延加工业	Smelting and Pressing of Ferrous Metals	317 981	4 966	30	312 640
有色金属冶炼及压延加工业	Smelting and Pressing of Nonferrous Metals	10 682	93	4 000	6 589
金属制品业	Metal Products Manufacturing	29 562	283	406	28 818
通用设备制造业	General Equipment Manufacturing	470 305	9 278	17 598	441 030
专用设备制造业	Special Purpose Equipment Manufacturing	100 407	3 165	750	94 742
交通运输设备制造业	Transportation Equipment Manufacturing	740 540	47 071	1 708	681 660
电气机械及器材制造业	Electric Machinery Equipments and Manufacturing	257 715	3 454	3 699	244 085
通信设备、计算机及其他电子设备制造业	Communications Equipments, Computer and Other Electronic Equipment Manufacturing	567 008	28 612	5 887	486 185
仪器仪表及文化、办公用机械制造业	Instruments, Meters, Culture and Office Equipments Manufacturing	92 598	3 191	1 110	83 896
工艺品及其他制造业	Artworks and Other Manufacturing	6 569		2 100	4 469
电力、燃气及水的生产和供应业	**Production and Supply of Power, Gas and Water**	**85 157**	**766**		**78 481**
电力、热力的生产和供应业	Production and Supply of Electricity and Thermal Power	83 582	759		76 913
燃气生产和供应业	Production and Supply of Gas	571			571
水的生产和供应业	Production and Supply of Water	1 004	7		997

表 18.30 规模以上工业企业技术开发项目与技术开发经费支出情况（2007）
TECHNICAL DEVELOPMENT PROJECTS AND EXPENDITURES OF INDUSTRIAL ENTERPRISES ABOVE THE SET SCALE

类 别	Types	项目数（项）Number of Projects (item)	技术开发经费支出（亿元）Expenditures of Technological Development (100 million yuan)	其中 of which: #新产品开发经费支出 on New Products Development	#研究与试验发展经费支出 Expenditures on R&D
总 计	**Total**	**15 972**	**356.58**	**177.07**	**178.12**
一、按隶属关系分	**Grouped by Subordination**				
中央单位	Central Units	2 939	92.59	38.56	51.08
地方单位	Local Units	13 033	263.99	138.51	127.04
二、按登记注册类型分	**By Registration Categories**				
#国有企业	State-owned	1 540	31.53	9.16	11.15
股份制及其他有限公司	Share-holding and Other Companies with Limited Liabilities	4 010	99.51	36.95	42.42
外资企业	Foreign Funded	7 300	204.58	118.19	116.48
#国有及国有控股企业	Enterprises Owned by the State or with the State Holding Major Shares	8 364	240.27	109.71	123.66
三、按企业规模分	**By Size of Enterprises**				
大型企业	Large	4 783	193.59	88.15	103.16
中型企业	Medium	7 403	123.55	65.28	59.57
小型企业	Small	3 786	39.45	23.64	15.39
四、按行业分	**By Sectors**				
#高技术产业	**High Technology Industry**	**4 783**	**109.91**	**60.04**	**51.44**
信息化学品制造	Information Chemical Product Manufacturing	1	0.01	0.01	
医药制造业	Medicine Manufacturing	888	12.38	6.83	6.95
航空航天器制造	Aviation and Aircraft Manufacturing	45	6.83	2.67	2.65
电子及通信设备制造业	Electronic and Communicantion Equipment Manufacturing	2 862	65.77	37.85	33.10
电子计算机及办公设备制造业	Electronic Computer and Office Equipment Manufacturing	311	15.70	7.08	5.30
医疗设备及仪器仪表制造业	Medical Machinery amd Measuring Instrument Manufacturing	676	9.22	5.60	3.44
#六个重点发展工业行业	**Six Key Industries**	**11 913**	**300.89**	**150.82**	**156.18**
电子信息产品制造业	Electronic Information Product Manufacturing	3 639	90.69	49.07	42.09
汽车制造业	Automobile Manufacturing	1 296	65.10	29.62	37.77
石油化工及精细化工制造业	Petrochemical and Fine Chemical Products Manufacturing	2 113	17.10	7.74	7.50
精品钢材制造业	Fine Steel Manufacturing	1 358	33.03	8.30	16.95
成套设备制造业	Equipment Complex Manufacturing	2455	80.87	47.86	43.51
生物医药制造业	Bio-medicine Manufacturing	1 052	14.10	8.23	8.35

注：技术开发经费支出和研究与发展经费支出包括科研基建费支出。
Note: The Expenditure of Technology Development and R&D comprises the payout of infrastructure for scientific research.

表 18.30 续表 continued

类 别	Types	项目数（项）Number of Projects (item)	技术开发经费支出（万元）Expenditures of Technical Development (100 million yuan)	其中 of which #新产品开发经费支出 New Products Development	#研究与试验发展经费支出 Expenditures on R&D
总　计	**Total**	**15 972**	**3 565 797**	**1 770 732**	**1 781 206**
制造业	**Manufacture Industry**	**15 654**	**3 484 007**	**1 767 091**	**1 770 066**
#石油和天然气开采业	Petroleum and Natural Gas Exploiting	9	9 398		135
农副食品加工业	Farm and Sideline Products Processing	42	1 880	256	221
食品制造业	Food Manufacturing	129	7 067	3 066	1 004
饮料制造业	Beverage Manufacturing	25	4 364	1 869	2 398
烟草制品业	Tabacco Manufacturing	103	31 730	1 260	16 167
纺织业	Textile	565	10 117	8 476	6 346
纺织服装、鞋、帽制造业	Garments, Shoes and Accessories Manufacturing	6	549	224	338
木材加工及木、竹、藤、棕、草制品业	Timber Processing and Timber, Bamboo, Rattan, Coir and Straw Products Manufacturing	1	59	59	1
家具制造业	Furniture Manufacturing	136	23 701	19 324	19 649
造纸及纸制品业	Paper-making and Paper Products Manufacturing	9	3 109	2 549	538
印刷业和记录媒介的复制	Printing and Record Duplicating	118	18 701	10 119	6 177
文教体育用品制造业	Stationary, Education and Sports Goods Manufacturing	220	4 687	2 893	1 288
石油加工、炼焦及核燃料加工业	Oil Processing, Coking and Nuclear	140	19 005	8 565	6 912
化学原料及化学制品制造业	Raw Chemical Materials and Chemical	2 091	171 349	79 841	74 415
医药制造业	Medicine Manufacturing	888	123 781	68 342	69 474
化学纤维制造业	Chemical Fiber Manufacturing	4	1 922	1 922	1 922
橡胶制品业	Rubber Products Manufacturing	124	23 079	13 783	12 694
塑料制品业	Plastic Products Manufacturing	115	16 153	11 378	4 500
非金属矿物制品业	Nonmetal Mineral Products	270	38 740	21 974	13 071
黑色金属冶炼及压延加工业	Smelting and Pressing of Ferrous Metals	1 358	330 333	82 964	169 521
有色金属冶炼及压延加工业	Smelting and Pressing of Nonferrous Metals	44	10 785	7 680	5 986
金属制品业	Metal Products Manufacturing	182	35 433	13 876	7 393
通用设备制造业	General Equipment Manufacturing	1 583	474 476	302 742	283 073
专用设备制造业	Special Purpose Equipment Manufacturing	793	101 548	76 484	55 535
交通运输设备制造业	Transportation Equipment Manufacturing	1 672	845 909	379 925	462 872
电气机械及器材制造业	Electric Machinery Equipments and Manufacturing	1 193	271 283	147 837	136 093
通信设备、计算机及其他电子设备制造业	Communications Equipments, Computer and Other Electronic Equipment Manufacturing	3 123	805 866	444 495	377 139
仪器仪表及文化、办公用机械制造业	Instruments, Meters, Culture and Office Equipments Manufacturing	654	91 715	51 138	32 727
工艺品及其他制造业	Artworks and Other Manufacturing	55	6 929	4 032	2 315
电力、燃气及水的生产和供应业	**Production and Supply of Power, Gas and Water**	**318**	**81 790**	**3 641**	**11 140**
电力、热力的生产和供应业	Production and Supply of Electricity and Thermal Power	259	79 918	3 269	10 548
燃气生产和供应业	Production and Supply of Gas	29	426	86	94
水的生产和供应业	Production and Supply of Water	30	1 446	286	498

表 18.31 规模以上工业企业其他技术活动费用支出情况（2007）
SPECIAL TECHNICAL PROJECT FUNDS OF INDUSTRIAL ENTERPRISES ABOVE THE SET SCALE

单位:亿元（100 million yuan）

	类 别 Types	技术改造经费支出 Expenditures of Technical Transformation	技术引进经费支出 Expenditures of Technical Introduction	购买国内技术支出 Expenditures of Buying Domestic Technology
总 计	**Total**	**159.20**	**62.96**	**22.91**
一、按隶属关系分	**Grouped by Subordination**			
中央单位	Central Units	114.16	23.06	20.80
地方单位	Local Units	45.04	39.90	2.11
二、按登记注册类型分	**By Registration Categories**			
#国有企业	State-owned	42.93	5.10	4.71
股份制及其他有限公司	Share-holding and Other Companies with Limited Liabilities	59.40	17.69	16.29
外资企业	Foreign Funded	47.28	38.95	0.79
#国有及国有控股企业	Enterprises Owned by the State or with the State Holding Major Shares	147.44	35.41	22.67
三、按企业规模分	**By Size of Enterprises**			
大型企业	Large	114.17	46.01	21.80
中型企业	Medium	39.60	15.17	0.67
小型企业	Small	5.43	1.78	0.44
四、按行业分	**By Sectors**			
#高技术产业	**High Technology Industry**	**10.91**	**24.65**	**0.63**
信息化学品制造	Information Chemical Product Manufacturing		0.01	
医药制造业	Medicine Manufacturing	0.88	0.20	0.36
航空航天器制造	Aviation and Aircraft Manufacturing	5.12		
电子及通信设备制造业	Electronic and Communicantion Equipment Manufacturing	3.54	9.17	0.02
电子计算机及办公设备制造业	Electronic Computer and Office Equipment Manufacturing	0.51	14.97	
医疗设备及仪器仪表制造业	Medical Machinery amd Measuring Instrument Manufacturing	0.86	0.31	0.25
#六个重点发展工业行业	**Six Key Industries**	**136.21**	**58.58**	**22.37**
电子信息产品制造业	Electronic Information Product Manufacturing	5.40	24.52	0.05
汽车制造业	Automobile Manufacturing	8.63	6.80	0.36
石油化工及精细化工制造业	Petrochemical and Fine Chemical Products Manufacturing	46.59	0.36	0.07
精品钢材制造业	Fine Steel Manufacturing	48.90	18.11	18.99
成套设备制造业	Equipment Complex Manufacturing	25.67	8.54	2.54
生物医药制造业	Bio-medicine Manufacturing	1.02	0.25	0.36

表 18.31 续表 continued

单位:万元（10 000 yuan）

类　别	Types	技术改造经费支出 Expenditures of Technical Transformation	技术引进经费支出 Expenditures of Technical Introduction	购买国内技术支出 Expenditures of Buying Domestic Techniology
总　计	**Total**	**1 591 963**	**629 600**	**229 176**
制造业	**Manufacture Industry**	**1 540 694**	**629 600**	**229 176**
#农副食品加工业	Farm and Sideline Products Processing	605		
食品制造业	Food Manufacturing	333		5
饮料制造业	Beverage Manufacturing	1 895		130
烟草制品业	Tabacco Manufacturing	50 829		
纺织业	Textile	762	1 037	
纺织服装、鞋、帽制造业	Garments, Shoes and Accessories Manufacturing	82		
印刷业和记录媒介的复制	Printing and Record Duplicating	19 663	2 991	1 953
文教体育用品制造业	Stationary, Education and Sports Goods Manufacturing	887		227
石油加工、炼焦及核燃料加工业	Oil Processing, Coking and Nuclear	251 134		370
化学原料及化学制品制造业	Raw Chemical Materials and Chemical	218 907	4 229	334
医药制造业	Medicine Manufacturing	8 782	1 961	3 625
化学纤维制造业	Chemical Fiber Manufacturing	157		
橡胶制品业	Rubber Products Manufacturing	9 819	153	250
塑料制品业	Plastic Products Manufacturing	1 507	588	1
非金属矿物制品业	Nonmetal Mineral Products	7 792	2 819	60
黑色金属冶炼及压延加工业	Smelting and Pressing of Ferrous Metals	488 964	181 090	189 883
有色金属冶炼及压延加工业	Smelting and Pressing of Nonferrous Metals	6 119	480	
金属制品业	Metal Products Manufacturing	23 625	1 815	45
通用设备制造业	General Equipment Manufacturing	106 598	70 652	7 264
专用设备制造业	Special Purpose Equipment Manufacturing	56 083	3 770	2 126
交通运输设备制造业	Transportation Equipment Manufacturing	185 531	81 308	16 967
电气机械及器材制造业	Electric Machinery Equipments and Manufacturing	50 500	32 751	3 263
通信设备、计算机及其他电子设备制造业	Communications Equipments, Computer and Other Electronic Equipment Manufacturing	40 443	239 780	196
仪器仪表及文化、办公用机械制造业	Instruments, Meters, Culture and Office Equipments Manufacturing	7 416	4 177	2 479
电力、燃气及水的生产和供应业	**Production and Supply of Power, Gas and Water**	**51 269**		
电力、热力的生产和供应业	Production and Supply of Electricity and Thermal Power	37 566		
燃气生产和供应业	Production and Supply of Gas	3 661		
水的生产和供应业	Production and Supply of Water	10 042		

表 18.32 规模以上工业企业新产品开发情况（2007）
NEW PRODUCTS DEVELOPMENT OF INDUSTRIAL ENTERPRISES ABOVE THE SET SCALE

单位：亿元（100 million yuan）

类别	Types	新产品产值 Output Value of New Products	新产品主营业务收入 Prime Operating Revenue	其中 of which: #新产品出口 Exports of New Products
总　计	**Total**	**4 614.38**	**4 727.61**	**788.25**
一、按隶属关系分	**Grouped by Subordination**			
中央单位	Central Units	1 138.29	1 115.63	346.31
地方单位	Local Units	3 476.10	3 611.97	441.94
二、按登记注册类型分	**By Registration Categories**			
#国有企业	State-owned	209.08	202.76	36.48
股份制及其他有限公司	Share-holding and Other Companies with Limited Liabilities	856.75	820.28	168.56
外资企业	Foreign Funded	3 330.48	3 488.04	567.67
#国有及国有控股企业	Enterprises Owned by the State or with the State Holding Major Shares	3 012.38	3 143.78	466.38
三、按企业规模分	**By Size of Enterprises**			
大型企业	Large	3 231.23	3 380.24	423.75
中型企业	Medium	1 181.78	1 148.84	338.12
小型企业	Small	201.37	198.52	26.39
四、按行业分	**By Sectors**			
#高技术产业	**High Technology Industry**	**1 502.03**	**1 458.51**	**298.39**
信息化学品制造	Information Chemical Product Manufacturing	0.07	0.07	
医药制造业	Medicine Manufacturing	71.79	64.67	2.52
航空航天器制造	Aviation and Aircraft Manufacturing	4.50	4.24	
电子及通信设备制造业	Electronic and Communicantion Equipment Manufacturing	519.42	496.37	257.78
电子计算机及办公设备制造业	Electronic Computer and Office Equipment Manufacturing	860.66	853.96	25.99
医疗设备及仪器仪表制造业	Medical Machinery amd Measuring Instrument Manufacturing	45.59	39.20	12.10
#六个重点发展工业行业	**Six Key Industries**	**4 055.08**	**4 189.71**	**631.22**
电子信息产品制造业	Electronic Information Product Manufacturing	1 408.42	1 377.49	280.17
汽车制造业	Automobile Manufacturing	1 095.97	1 290.94	16.28
石油化工及精细化工制造业	Petrochemical and Fine Chemical Products Manufacturing	265.70	235.74	9.68
精品钢材制造业	Fine Steel Manufacturing	357.04	356.39	15.66
成套设备制造业	Equipment Complex Manufacturing	845.85	855.53	305.73
生物医药制造业	Bio-medicine Manufacturing	82.08	73.62	3.72

表 18.32 续表 continued

单位:万元(10 000 yuan)

类 别	Types	新产品产值 Output Value of New Products	新产品主营业务收入 Prime Operating Revenue	其中 of which #新产品出口 Exports of New Products
总 计	**Total**	**46 143 830**	**47 276 059**	**7 882 507**
制造业	**Manufacture Industry**	**46 143 830**	**47 276 059**	**7 882 507**
#农副食品加工业	Farm and Sideline Products Processing	8 768	10 712	559
食品制造业	Food Manufacturing	92 573	93 110	4 686
饮料制造业	Beverage Manufacturing	11 288	11 191	
烟草制品业	Tabacco Manufacturing	337 082	352 545	10 796
纺织业	Textile	168 885	157 340	9 190
纺织服装、鞋、帽制造业	Garments,Shoes and Accessories Manufacturing	18 165	18 374	3 672
家具制造业	Furniture Manufacturing	551 717	525 525	101 746
造纸及纸制品业	Paper-making and Paper Products Manufacturing	16 235	16 178	
印刷业和记录媒介的复制	Printing and Record Duplicating	208 215	225 830	2 221
文教体育用品制造业	Stationary,Education and Sports Goods Manufacturing	40 058	44 307	4 163
石油加工、炼焦及核燃料加工业	Oil Processing,Coking and Nuclear	946 624	878 592	
化学原料及化学制品制造业	Raw Chemical Materials and Chemical	1 864 635	1 665 306	129 467
医药制造业	Medicine Manufacturing	717 877	646 749	25 184
化学纤维制造业	Chemical Fiber Manufacturing	5 558	5 946	2 038
橡胶制品业	Rubber Products Manufacturing	291 828	290 545	98 188
塑料制品业	Plastic Products Manufacturing	92 735	110 602	21 223
非金属矿物制品业	Nonmetal Mineral Products	203 510	177 661	29 519
黑色金属冶炼及压延加工业	Smelting and Pressing of Ferrous Metals	3 570 432	3 563 914	156 559
有色金属冶炼及压延加工业	Smelting and Pressing of Nonferrous Metals	169 096	43 252	4 198
金属制品业	Metal Products Manufacturing	338 470	333 297	209 978
通用设备制造业	General Equipment Manufacturing	5 279 987	5 404 175	1 448 156
专用设备制造业	Special Purpose Equipment Manufacturing	881 990	854 670	136 107
交通运输设备制造业	Transportation Equipment Manufacturing	13 571 970	15 496 969	1 697 684
电气机械及器材制造业	Electric Machinery Equipments and Manufacturing	2 473 665	2 409 981	736 404
通信设备、计算机及其他电子设备制造业	Communications Equipments,Computer and Other Electronic Equipment Manufacturing	13 577 701	13 286 752	2 652 052
仪器仪表及文化、办公用机械制造业	Instruments,Meters,Culture and Office Equipments Manufacturing	693 855	641 181	395 260
工艺品及其他制造业	Artworks and Other Manufacturing	10 913	11 355	3 460

表 18.33 主要年份大中型工业企业技术开发情况
TECHNOLOGICAL DEVELOPMENT PROJECTS OF LARGE AND MEDIUM INDUSTRIAL ENTERPRISES IN MAIN YEARS

指标	Indicators	1990	2000	2006	2007
技术开发机构数（个）	Technological Development Institutions（unit）	383	264	355	315
从事技术开发人员数（万人）	Technological Development Personnel（10 000 persons）	6.45	7.48	6.70	8.37
#科学家和工程师	Scientists and Engineers	2.50	4.33	4.78	5.63
研究与发展人员	Research and Development Personnel		2.63	3.47	3.98
经费筹集额(亿元)	Funds（100 million yuan）	12.50	122.64	254.82	277.18
技术开发经费支出(亿元)	Expenditures of Technical Development（100 million yuan）	10.72	100.78	256.25	317.14
各项技术专款(亿元)	Special Technology Funds（100 million yuan）	30.89	117.47	174.40	245.10
技术改造经费支出	Expenditures on Technological Transformation	18.61	75.31	113.87	153.77
技术引进经费支出	Expenditures on Technological Introduction	11.28	39.00	37.05	61.18
用于消化吸收的经费	Expenditures on Technological Digesting and Absorbing	0.31	2.41	13.46	7.67
购买国内技术支出	Expenditures on Buying Domestic Technology	0.70	0.75	10.02	22.47
技术开发项目数（项）*	Number of Projects（item）	3 107	5 140	19 237	12 186
项目组人员（人）*	Personnel of Project Groups（person）		45 254	47 310	57 207
项目经费支出（内部）(亿元)*	Expenditure on Projects（Internal)(100 million yuan）	5.43	63.72	159.31	208.34
新产品主营业务收入(亿元)	Prime Operating Revenue(100 million yuan）	127.63	1 351.69	4 112.78	4 529.09
#新产品出口	New Products Exported		197.41	1 156.53	761.87
新产品产值(亿元)	Output Value of New Products(100 million yuan）	130.34	1 355.19	3 945.62	4 413.01

注：*有关项目指标调整为企业内部当年所有开发的项目
Note: Some related indicators have benn adjusted to all the projects of the year inside the enterprises.

表 18.34 大中型工业企业技术开发情况(2007)
TECHNOLOGICAL DEVELOPMENT PROJECTS OF LARGE AND MEDIUM INDUSTRIAL ENTERPRISES

类别	Types	从事技术开发的人员数(万人) Technological Development Personnel (10 000 persons)	技术开发经费支出(亿元) Expenditures of Technical Development (100 million yuan)	其中 of which #新产品开发经费支出 Expenditures on New Products Development	研究与试验发展经费支出 Expenditures on R&D
总计	**Total**	**8.37**	**317.14**	**153.43**	**162.73**
一、按隶属关系分	**Grouped by Subordination**				
中央单位	Central Units	2.90	91.02	37.38	50.81
地方单位	Local Units	5.47	226.12	116.05	111.92
二、按登记注册类型分	**By Registration Categories**				
#国有企业	State-owned	1.13	29.06	7.59	10.31
股份制及其他有限公司	Share-holding and Other Companies with Limited Liabilities	2.45	88.90	30.18	38.20
外资企业	Foreign Funded	4.22	186.71	108.23	109.44
#国有及国有控股企业	Enterprises Owned by the State or with the State Holding Major Shares	5.62	225.46	100.24	118.07
三、按行业分	**By Sectors**				
制造业	Manufacture Industry	8.05	309.10	153.08	161.62
食品制造业	Food Manufacturing	0.02	0.45	0.18	…
饮料制造业	Beverage Manufacturing	0.01	0.43	0.18	0.23
烟草制品业	Tabacco Manufacturing	0.07	3.17	0.13	1.62
纺织业	Textile	0.07	0.72	0.62	0.43
印刷业和记录媒介的复制	Printing and Record Duplicating	0.09	1.71	0.87	0.57
文教体育用品制造业	Stationary, Education and Sports Goods Manufacturing	0.05	0.40	0.22	0.13
石油加工、炼焦及核燃料加工业	Oil Processing, Coking and Nuclear	0.09	1.87	0.84	0.67
化学原料及化学制品制造业	Raw Chemical Materials and Chemical	0.36	10.44	4.37	3.81
医药制造业	Medicine Manufacturing	0.30	9.89	5.19	5.88
橡胶制品业	Rubber Products Manufacturing	0.06	2.21	1.31	1.24
塑料制品业	Plastic Products Manufacturing	0.03	0.52	0.36	0.21
非金属矿物制品业	Nonmetal Mineral Products	0.13	2.18	1.65	0.93
黑色金属冶炼及压延加工业	Smelting and Pressing of Ferrous Metals	1.16	32.77	8.17	16.78
有色金属冶炼及压延加工业	Smelting and Pressing of Nonferrous Metals	0.04	0.44	0.38	0.07
金属制品业	Metal Products Manufacturing	0.10	2.65	1.00	0.63
通用设备制造业	General Equipment Manufacturing	1.09	43.78	27.71	26.24
专用设备制造业	Special Purpose Equipment Manufacturing	0.38	7.79	5.79	4.85
交通运输设备制造业	Transportation Equipment Manufacturing	1.16	81.57	35.59	45.45
电气机械及器材制造业	Electric Machinery Equipments and Manufacturing	0.78	21.57	12.27	11.61
通信设备、计算机及其他电子设备制造业	Communications Equipments, Computer and Other Electronic Equipment Manufacturing	1.71	75.36	40.93	35.48
仪器仪表及文化、办公用机械制造业	Instruments, Meters, Culture and Office Equipments Manufacturing	0.27	6.20	3.13	2.65
电力、燃气及水的生产和供应业	Production and Supply of Power, Gas and Water	0.32	8.04	0.35	1.11
电力、热力的生产和供应业	Production and Supply of Electricity and Thermal Power	0.27	7.85	0.31	1.05
燃气生产和供应业	Production and Supply of Gas	0.03	0.04	0.01	0.01
水的生产和供应业	Production and Supply of Water	0.02	0.14	0.03	0.05

表 18.35 质量技术监督机构情况(2005 ~ 2007)
THE INSTITUTIONS OF QUALITY AND TECHNICAL SUPERVISION

类别	Types	2005	2006	2007
机构数(个)	**Number of Institutions (unit)**	**62**	**61**	**62**
按地区分	By Districts			
市级	Municipal Level	10	9	10
区县级	Districts Level	52	52	52
按性质分	By Charactors			
行政管理机构	Administrations	21	21	21
事业单位	Public Service Organization	41	40	41
从业人员(人)	**Personnel(Person)**	**3 177**	**3 171**	**3 398**
公务员	Official	771	793	817
管理人员	Management People	286	281	395
专业技术人员	Professional	1 544	1 557	1 655
其他人员	Other People	576	540	531
计量检定、测试与执法	**Metrological Check, Testing and Enforcement**			
计量标准(项)	Metrology Criterion (item)	657	986	755
建立在国家法定计量检定机构的社会公用计量标准	Public Measurement Standards Set by the State Metrological Authority	443	672	462
授权建立的社会公用计量标准	Authorized Public Measurement Standard	1	2	
建立在部门、企事业单位的最高计量标准	Measurment Standard Set by Government Department and Corporations	213	312	87
授权法定计量技术机构(个)	Authorized Metroloical Institutions(unit)	41	36	34
计量检定员(人)	Measurement Inspectors(Person)	1 064	1 360	798
全年完成计量检定、测试(万台、万件)	Number of Products that Underwent measurement Inspection in the year(10 000 unit)	426.39	428.00	473.83
产品质量监督检查	**Supervision and Inspection of Products Quality**			
抽查产品品种(种)	Product types of Spot Test (type)	3 626	3 193	10 835
抽查工业企业(个)	Industrial Enterprises of Spot test (unit)	2 742	2 875	7 239

注：本表数据由上海市质量技术监督局提供。
Note: Data in this table are provided by Shanghai Municipal Bureau of Quality and Technical Supervision.

上 / 海 / 统 / 计 / 年 / 鉴

主要统计指标解释

专业技术人员

指事业、企业单位中已被聘任专业技术职务的从事专业技术工作和专业技术管理的人员，以及虽未被聘任专业技术职务，但现在专业技术岗位上工作的人员。

R&D

是“科学研究与试验发展”(Research and Development)的英文缩写。其含义是指在科学技术领域，为增加知识总量，以及运用这些知识去创造新的应用进行的系统的创造性的活动。R&D 包括基础研究、应用研究、试验发展三类活动。

基础研究

指为了获得关于现象和可观察事实的基本原理的新知识(揭示客观事物的本质、运动规律，获得新发现、新学说)而进行的实验性或理论性研究，它不以任何专门或特定的应用或使用为目的。其成果以科学论文和科学著作为主要形式。用来反映知识的原始创新能力。

应用研究

指为获得新知识而进行的创造性研究，主要针对某一特定的目的或目标。应用研究是为了确定基础研究成果可能的用途，或是为达到预定的目标探索应采取的新方法(原理性)或新途径。其成果形式以科学论文、专著、原理性模型或发明专利为主。用来反映对基础研究成果应用途径的探索。

试验发展

指利用从基础研究、应用研究和实际经验所获得的现有知识，为产生新的产品、材料和装置，建立新的工艺、系统和服务，以及对已产生和建立的上述各项作实质性的改进而进行的系统性工作。其成果形式主要是专利、专有技术、具有新产品基本特征的产品原型或具有新装置基本特征的原始样机等。在社会科学领域，试验发展是指把通过基础研究、应用研究获得的知识转变成可以实施的计划(包括为进行检验和评估实施示范项目)的过程。人文科学领域没有对应的试验发展活动。主要反映将科研成果转化为技术和产品的能力，是科技推动经济社会发展的物化成果。

发　明

指对产品、方法或者其改进所提出的新的技术方案。是国际通行的反映拥有自主知识产权技术的核心指标。

实用新型

指对产品的形状、构造或者其结合所提出的适于实用的新的技术方案。反映具有一定技术含量的技术成果情况。

外观设计

指对产品的形状、图案、色彩或者其结合所作出的富有美感并适于工业上应用的新设计。反映拥有自主知识产权的外观设计成果情况。

独立研究与开发机构

指有明确的任务和研究方向，有一定学术水平的业务骨干和一定数量的研究人员，具有研究、开发、开展学术工作的基本条件，主要进行科学研究与技术开发活动，并且在行政上有独立的组织形式，财务上独立核算盈亏，有权与其他单位签订合同，在银行有单独户头的单位。

科学家和工程师

指科技活动人员中具有高、中级技术职称(职务)的人员和不具有高、中级技术职称(职务)的大学本科及以上学历人员。

科技活动

指在自然科学、农业科学、医药科学、工程与技术科学、人文与社会科学领域(简称科学技术领域)中，与科技知识的产生、发展、传播和应用密切相关的有组织的活动。可分为研究与试验发展(R&D)、研究与试验发展成果应用及相关的科技服务三类活动。该定义是联合国教科文组织考虑成员国特别是发展中国家开展科技统计工作的需要，而对科技活动所作的统计界定。

科技活动人员

指直接从事科技活动、以及专门从事科技活动管理和为科技活动提供直接服务，累计从事科技活动的时间占全年制度工作时间 10%及以上的人员。(1)直接从事科

主要统计指标解释

技活动的人员，包括：在独立核算的科学研究与技术开发机构、高等学校、各类企业及其他事业单位内设的研究室、实验室、技术开发中心及中试车间（基地）等机构中从事科技活动的研究人员、工程技术人员、技术工人及其它人员；虽不在上述机构工作，但编入科技活动项目（课题）组的人员；科技信息与文献机构中的专业技术人员；从事论文设计的研究生等。(2)专门从事科技活动管理和为科技活动提供直接服务的人员包括：独立核算的科学研究与技术开发机构、科技信息与文献机构、高等学校、各类企业及其他事业单位主管科技工作的负责人，专门从事科技活动的计划、行政、人事、财务、物资供应、设备维护、图书资料管理等工作的各类人员，但不包括保卫、医疗保健人员、司机、食堂人员、茶炉工、水暖工、清洁工等为科技活动提供间接服务的人员。该指标用来反映投入科技活动人力的规模。

■ 新产品

指采用新技术原理、新设计构思研制、生产的全新产品，或在结构、材质、工艺等某一方面比原有产品有明显改进，从而显著提高了产品性能或扩大了使用功能的产品。既包括政府有关部门认定并在有效期内的新产品，也包括企业自行研制开发、在统计规定的新产品跟踪期限内的产品。跟踪期限规定如下：装备类跟踪五年，消费品类跟踪二年，其他类跟踪三年。用来反映科技产出及对经济增长的直接贡献。

■ 专　利

是专利权的简称，是对发明人的发明创造经审查合格后，由专利局依据专利法授予发明人和设计人对该项发明创造享有的专有权。包括发明、实用新型和外观设计。反映拥有自主知识产权的科技和设计成果情况。

■ 科技活动经费筹集

指从各种渠道筹集到的计划用于科技活动的经费，包括政府资金、事业资金、企业资金、银行贷款和其他收入等。反映各社会经济主体对促进科技进步所作的努力。

■ 政府资金

指从各级政府部门获得的计划用于科技活动的经费，包括科学事业费、科技三项费、科研基建费、科学基金、教育等部门事业费中计划用于科技活动的经费以及政府部门预算外资金中计划用于科技活动的经费等。

SHANGHAI STATISTICAL YEARBOOK

EXPLANATORY NOTES TO MAJOR STATISTICAL INDICATORS

□ Professional and Technical Personnel

Professional and Technical Personnel refer to professional, technical and managerial staff members in institutions or enterprises who not only have professional and technical titles but also hold professional and technical posts. They also include those who work on professional and technical posts but do not have professional and technical titles.

□ R&D

R&D is an abbreviation which stands for 'Science Research and Experimental Development', which means systematic and creative endeavors aimed at expanding the overall volume of knowledge and applying the knowledge in systematic creation. R&D includes basic studies, application research and experimental development.

□ Basic Research

Basic Research refers to empirical or theoretical research aiming at obtaining new knowledge on the fundamental principles of phenomena of observable facts to reveal the nature and law of movement of objects and to acquire new discoveries or new theories. Basic research takes no specific or designated application as the aim of the research. Results of basic research are mainly released or disseminated in the form of scientific papers or monographs. This indicator reflects the original innovation capacity of knowledge.

□ Applied Research

Applied Research refers to creative research aiming at obtaining new knowledge on a specific objective or target. Purpose of the applied research is to identify the possible use of results from basic research, or to explore new (fundamental) methods or new approaches. Results of applied research are expressed in the form of scientific papers, monographs, fundamental models or invention patents. This indicator reflects the exploration of ways to apply the results of basic research.

□ Experiments and Development

Experiments and Development refer to systematic activities aiming at using the knowledge from basic and applied researches or from practical experience to develop new products, materials and equipment, to establish new production process, systems and services, or to make substantial improvement on the existing products, process or services. Results of experiment and development activities are embodied in patents, exclusive technology, and monotype of new products or equipment. In social sciences, experiment and development activities refer to the process of converting the knowledge from basic or applied researches into feasible programmes (including conduct of demonstration projects for assessment and evaluation). There are no experiment and development activities in the science of humanities. This indicator reflects the capability of transferring the results of S&T into technique and products, which is the materialized measurement of S&T pushing forward the economic and social development.

□ Invention

Inventions refer to the new technical proposals to the products or methods or their modifications. This is universal core indicator reflecting the technologies with independent intellectual property.

□ Utility Models

Utility Models refer to the practical and new technical proposals on the shape and structure of the product or the combination of both. This indicator reflects the condition of technological results with certain technical content.

□ Exterior Design

Designs refer to the aesthetics and industrially applicable new designs for the shape, pattern and color of the product, or their combinations. This indicator reflects the appearance design achievements with independent intellectual property.

□ Independent Research and Development Institutions

Independent Research and Development Institutions refer to the state-owned institutions which have direct mission and research purpose, a certain research level and quantities of personnel, favorable conditions for R&D and engaging in scientific research and technological development. The institutions also

EXPLANATORY NOTES TO MAJOR STATISTICAL INDICATORS

have their own independent organization, accounting system authority to sign contract with other units, and their own accounts in banks.

□ Scientists and Engineers

Scientists and Engineers refer to persons engaged in S&T activities who have obtained titles of senior and middle level professional positions, and those without such position but have completed university or higher education.

□ Scientific and Technological Activities (S&T Activities)

Scientific and Technological Activities (S&T Activities) refer to organized activities which are closely related with the creation, development, dissemination and application of the scientific and technical knowledge in the fields of natural sciences, agricultural sciences, medical sciences, engineering and technological sciences, humanities and social sciences (referred to as scientific and technological fields). S&T activities can be classified into 3 categories: research and development (R&D) activities, application of R&D results, and related S&T services. This statistical definition is made by UNICHIEF for scientific and technological activities to meet the need of carrying out statistical work in this field for its member countries in particular those developing countries.

□ Personnel Engaged in S&T Activities

Personnel Engaged in S&T Activities refer to personnel directly engaged in S&T activities, in the management of S&T activities, and in providing direct service to S&T activities, who spend over 10% of the total working hours in a year in S&T activities. (1) Personnel directly engaged in S&T activities include researchers, engineers, technicians and other related personnel engaged in S&T activities in independent-accounting R&D institutions, institutions of higher learning, and in research institutes, laboratories, technology development centers and central experiment workshops under enterprises and institutions. Also included are people working in S&T information archiving institutes, and graduate students working on the design of their thesis. (2) Personnel engaged in the management of S&T activities and in providing direct service to S&T activities include senior management people responsible for S&T activities in independent-accounting R&D institutions, S&T information archiving institutes, institutions of higher learning, and in enterprises and institutions where S&T activities are undertaken. Also included are people responsible for the planning, administration, personnel management, financial management, logistics supply, equipment maintenance, information and library management that are related with S&T activities. People providing indirect services are excluded, such as security, medical service, drivers, plumbers, cleaners and those providing catering and related service. This indicator reflects the size of personnel engaged in S&T activities.

□ New Products

New Products refer to new products produced with new technology and new design, or products that represent noticeable improvement in terms of structure, material, or production process so as to improve significantly the character or function of the older versions. They include new products certified by relevant government agencies within the period of certification, as well as new products designed and produced by enterprises within the new product track time limit prescribed by the statistical regulations. The new product track time limit is prescribed as following: equipment products 5 years, consumption products 2 years, other products 3 years. This indictor reflects the direct contribution of S&T output to economic growth.

□ Patent

Patent is an abbreviation for the patent right and refers to the exclusive right of ownership by the inventors or designers for the creation or inventions, given from the patent offices after due process of assessment and approval in accordance with the Patent Law. Patents are granted for inventions, utility models and designs. This indicator reflects the achievements of S&T and design with independent intellectual property.

□ Funding for S&T Activities

Funding for S&T Activities refers to funds obtained from various sources for S&T activities, including government funds, self-raised funds by institutions, self-raised funds by enterprises, loans from banks and other funds. This indicator reflects the efforts made by various social economic entities in promoting the development of S&T.

□ Government Funds

Government Funds refer to funds obtained from govern-

EXPLANATORY NOTES TO MAJOR STATISTICAL INDICATORS

ment agencies at all levels to be used for S&T activities, including fund for scientific undertakings, 3 kinds of fund for S&T activities, fund for capital construction for scientific researches, science fund, funds from education expenditures by education departments for S&T activities, and extra-budget fund from government agencies for S&T activities.

第十九篇

CHAPTER 19

环境保护治理

ENVIRONMENT PROTECTION AND TREATMENT

表 19.1 环保投入和"三废"综合利用(1990~2007)
INVESTMENT ON ENVIRONMENT PROTECTION AND WASTE GAS,WASTE WATER AND SOLID WASTES UTILIZED

单位:亿元(100 million yuan)

年 份 Year	环境保护投资 Investment on Environment Protection	其 中 of which #城市环境基础设施建设投资 Urban Environment Infrastructure Investment	环境保护投资相当于GDP(%) Investment on Environment Protection as Percentage of Gross Domestic Product(%)	"三废"综合利用产品产值 Output Value of Products Made from Utilization of Waste Gas, Waste Water and Solid Wastes	自然保护区覆盖率(%) Coverage Rate of Natural Preservation Areas(%)
1990				2.06	
1991	7.60		0.90	2.67	
1992	15.20		1.40	3.94	
1993	32.13		2.10	5.36	
1994	39.09		2.00	5.95	
1995	46.49		1.90	6.63	
1996	68.83		2.40	7.55	
1997	82.35		2.50	12.15	
1998	102.13		2.80	8.01	
1999	111.57		2.80	8.69	
2000	141.91		3.10	9.16	7.8
2001	152.93		3.10	5.00	10.5
2002	162.39	126.99	3.00	7.25	11.8
2003	191.53	144.05	3.10	7.13	11.8
2004	225.37	166.90	3.03	13.04	11.8
2005	281.18	201.01	3.07	9.11	11.8
2006	310.85	177.81	3.00	9.72	11.8
2007	366.12	233.22	3.00	15.33	12.1

表 19.2 主要年份工业固体废弃物防治
PREVENTION AND CURE OF INDUSTRIAL SOLID WASTES IN MAIN YEARS

指 标	Indicators	2000	2006	2007
工业固体废弃物产生量(万吨)	Volume of Industrial Solid Wastes Produced (10 000 tons)	1 354.74	2 063.19	2 165.40
#危险废物	Dangerous Wastes	28.32	40.79	45.43
工业废弃物综合利用量(万吨)	Volume of Industrial Wastes Treated and Utilized (10 000 tons)	1 515.90	1 953.11	2 040.08
#危险废物	Dangerous Wastes	27.05	29.13	30.94
工业废弃物综合利用率(%)	Ratio of Industrial Wastes Treated and Utilized (%)	93.26	94.66	94.21
工业固体废物处置量(万吨)	Volume of Industrial Solid Wastes Disposed (10 000 tons)	90.96	103.22	106.39
#危险废物	Dangerous Wastes	1.08	14.10	14.68

注:本页数据由上海市环境保护局提供。
Note: Data on this page are provided by Shanghai Environmental Protection Bureau.

表 19.3 水环境保护(1991～2007)
WATER ENVIRONMENT PROTECTION

年 份 Year	废 水 排放总量 (亿吨) Total Waste Water Discharged (100 million tons)	其 中 of which 工 业 Industrial Waste Water	生活及其他 Residential Waste Water	废水化学需氧量排放总量(万吨) Total Emission of Oxygen of Waste Water Needed by Chemistry (10 000 tons)	其 中 of which 工 业 Industrial Waste Water	生活及其他 Residential Waste Water
1991	19.58	13.25	6.33		24.75	
1992	20.28	13.70	6.58		19.60	
1993	20.32	12.81	7.51		16.76	
1994	20.37	11.81	8.56		16.37	
1995	22.45	11.61	10.84		12.29	
1996	22.85	11.41	11.44	27.46	12.16	15.30
1997	21.10	9.99	11.11	38.55	11.70	26.85
1998	20.81	9.00	11.81	36.55	9.63	26.92
1999	20.28	8.52	11.76	34.98	8.92	26.06
2000	19.37	7.25	12.12	31.87	6.93	24.94
2001	19.50	6.80	12.70	30.48	5.27	25.21
2002	19.21	6.49	12.72	32.96	4.78	28.18
2003	18.22	6.11	12.11	28.38	4.38	24.00
2004	19.34	5.64	13.70	29.38	3.76	25.62
2005	19.97	5.11	14.86	30.44	3.66	26.78
2006	22.37	4.83	17.54	30.20	3.53	26.67
2007	22.66	4.76	17.90	29.44	3.38	26.06

表 19.3 续表 continued

年 份 Year	工业废水排放达标量(万吨) Volume of Meeting Standard for Industrial Sewage Discharge (10 000 tons)	工业废水排放达标率(%) Up-to-Standard Rate of Industrial Waste Water Discharge(%)	工业重复用水量(万吨) Volume of Interative Used Water by Industry (10 000 tons)	污水处理厂数(个) Number of Sewage Disposal Plants (unit)	污水处理厂污水处理量(万吨) Volume of Sewage Disposed by Sewage Disposal Plants (10 000 tons)
1991	86 594	65.3		17	11 984
1992	90 559	66.1	384 830	13	13 246
1993	90 721	70.8	390 629	16	14 133
1994	83 683	70.8	427 236	17	12 644
1995	89 365	77.0	445 391	17	14 665
1996	99 721	87.4	486 278	20	12 876
1997	86 568	86.6	495 622	22	14 790
1998	79 356	88.2	475 656	22	15 605
1999	76 664	89.9	605 772	22	17 479
2000	67 553	93.2	592 055	27	23 028
2001	64 876	95.4	709 913	26	29 487
2002	61 521	94.9	654 133	27	30 658
2003	58 020	94.9	690 068	30	39 891
2004	54 255	96.3	750 803	37	95 301
2005	49 590	97.1	886 503	42	117 833
2006	47 146	97.5	843 970	43	155 726
2007	46 492	97.7	899 098	45	152 886

注：本页数据由上海市环境保护局提供。
Note: Data on this page are provided by Shanghai Environmental Protection Bureau.

表 19.4 大气环境保护(1991～2007)
ATMOSPHERE ENVIRONMENT PROTECTION

年 份 Year	废气排放总量(亿标立方米) Total Waste Gas Emission (100 million cu. m)	其中 of which 工业 Industrial Sector	生活及其他 Residential Sector and Others	烟尘排放总量(万吨) Total Emission of Smoke and Dust (10 000 tons)	其中 of which 工业 Industrial Sector	生活及其他 Residential Sector and Others
1991	4 617	4 000	617	21.54	14.68	6.86
1992	5 110	4 418	692	22.50	14.81	7.69
1993	4 231	3 859	371	18.93	14.80	4.13
1994	4 577	4 184	393	18.45	14.08	4.37
1995	5 095	4 625	471	20.78	13.33	7.45
1996	5 132	4 757	375	15.78	14.77	1.01
1997	5 249	4 755	494	17.08	13.38	3.70
1998	5 493	4 912	580	15.63	10.74	4.89
1999	5 480	4 947	533	13.57	9.00	4.57
2000	6 398	5 755	643	14.12	8.32	5.80
2001	7 620	6 964	656	13.52	6.23	7.29
2002	7 902	7 440	462	10.74	5.60	5.14
2003	8 391	7 799	592	11.54	4.97	6.57
2004	9 466	8 834	632	12.27	5.25	7.02
2005	9 103	8 482	621	11.52	4.95	6.57
2006	10 045	9 428	617	11.29	4.73	6.56
2007	10 231	9 591	640	10.60	4.04	6.56

表 19.4 续表 continued

年 份 Year	废气二氧化硫排放总量(万吨) Total Emission of SO_2 (10 000 tons)	其中 of which 工业 Industrial Sector	生活及其他 Residential Sector and Others	工业废气二氧化硫去除量(万吨) SO_2 Dispeled from Industrial Waste Gas (10 000 tons)	工业烟尘去除量(万吨) Industrial Smoke and Dust Dispeled (10 000 tons)	工业粉尘去除量(万吨) Industrial Powder and Dust Dispeled (10 000 tons)
1991	47.92	33.87	14.05	4.13	255.60	89.05
1992	51.36	35.62	15.74	3.90	258.49	117.86
1993	44.12	35.67	8.45	3.70	279.15	123.44
1994	45.19	36.24	8.95	3.47	306.39	123.61
1995	53.41	38.15	15.26	3.34	325.16	117.72
1996	54.00	43.30	7.70	5.58	403.95	89.11
1997	50.85	43.62	7.23	4.16	359.85	141.80
1998	48.89	39.09	9.80	3.11	273.54	151.77
1999	40.31	31.09	9.22	3.36	261.04	184.61
2000	46.49	32.68	13.81	3.77	308.35	218.08
2001	47.26	30.00	17.26	2.14	326.35	263.89
2002	44.66	32.49	12.17	5.58	366.44	301.92
2003	43.54	30.07	13.47	4.86	402.89	348.02
2004	47.31	34.95	12.36	5.53	655.27	208.07
2005	51.28	37.52	13.76	7.49	574.24	150.53
2006	50.80	37.43	13.37	9.45	520.54	146.80
2007	49.78	36.44	13.34	9.03	450.86	145.85

注：本页数据由上海市环境保护局提供。
Note: Data on this page are provided by Shanghai Environmental Protection Bureau.

表 19.5 主要年份环境空气状况
AMBIENT AIR CONDITION IN MAIN YEARS

指 标	Indicators	2000	2006	2007
中心城区二氧化硫年日平均值（毫克/立方米）	Annual Daily Mean Concentration of SO_2 in Urban Area（mg/m^3）	0.045	0.055	0.055
中心城区二氧化氮年日平均值（毫克/立方米）	Annual Daily Mean Concentration of NO_2 in Urban Area（mg/m^3）	0.090	0.051	0.054
中心城区可吸入颗粒平均浓度（毫克/立方米）	Mean Concentration of Inhalable Particulate in Urban Area（mg/m^3）		0.086	0.088
降水 PH 平均值	Rain PH Value	5.19	4.73	4.55
酸雨频率(%)	Frequency of Acid Rain（%）	26.0	56.4	75.6
环境空气质量优良天数(天)	Number of Days with Good Ambient Air Quality（day）	295	324	328
环境空气质量优良率(%)	Rate of Good Ambient Air Quality（%）	80.8	88.8	89.9

表 19.6 主要年份声环境及治理
NOISE ENVIRONMENT AND TREATMENT IN MAIN YEARS

指 标	Indicators	2000	2006	2007
区域环境噪声平均等效声级	**Average Equivalent Sound Level of Area Ambient Noise**			
昼间时段(LeqdB(A))	Daytime（LeqdB(A)）	56.6	56.6	56.8
夜间时段(LeqdB(A))	Nighttime（LeqdB(A)）	49.2	49.7	49.4
交通环境噪声平均等效声级	**Average Equivalent Sound Level of Traffic Noise**			
昼间时段(LeqdB(A))	Daytime（LeqdB(A)）	70.5	72.0	71.9
夜间时段(LeqdB(A))	Nighttime（LeqdB(A)）	64.1	64.9	65.9

注：本页数据由上海市环境保护局提供。
Note：Data on this page are provided by Shanghai Environmental Protection Bureau.

表 19.7 城市环境卫生情况(1978～2007)
URBAN ENVIRONMENTAL SANITATION

年 份 Year	垃圾产生量 (万吨) Garbage Produced (10 000 tons)	其 中 of which 生活垃圾 Residential Garbage	建筑垃圾 Construction Garbage	清运粪便 (万吨) Night Soil Disposal Cleared (10 000 tons)
1978	214	108	106	418
1979	250	125	126	374
1980	272	131	141	331
1981	272	146	126	329
1982	296	169	127	325
1983	280	166	113	311
1984	308	185	123	272
1985	305	196	109	252
1986	328	226	102	263
1987	325	229	97	262
1988	329	240	89	249
1989	344	250	94	246
1990	382	279	103	243
1991	393	296	97	229
1992	428	301	127	242
1993	488	335	152	234
1994	558	358	200	240
1995	668	372	296	216
1996	736	419	317	217
1997	755	454	301	227
1998	824	470	353	218
1999	767	500	267	172
2000	858	641	217	256
2001	901	644	257	219
2002	760	467	293	238
2003	800	585	215	251
2004	802	610	192	258
2005	777	622	155	254
2006	805	658	146	247
2007	852	702	150	232

注：本页数据由上海市环境保护局提供。
Note: Data on this page are provided by Shanghai Environmental Protection Bureau.

表 19.8 环境卫生设施(1978 ~ 2007)
URBAN ENVIRONMENTAL SANITATION

年 份 Year	公共厕所 (座) Public Lavatories (unit)	生活垃圾收集点(处) Collection Points of Residential Garbage(unit)	废物箱 (只) Trash Cans (unit)	倒粪站 (座) Excrements Stations (unit)	化粪池 (只) Septic Tanks (unit)
1978	706	13 840	2 333	3 303	25 540
1979	696	12 695	3 151	3 382	25 915
1980	713	15 707	3 402	3 445	26 754
1981	740	17 905	2 546	3 464	27 407
1982	760	18 824	2 821	3 484	28 652
1983	778	17 859	2 733	3 467	29 977
1984	798	20 384	3 890	3 481	30 943
1985	952	22 870	5 700	3 470	33 477
1986	950	31 142	5 983	3 537	39 175
1987	978	37 751	6 341	3 587	40 042
1988	992	42 802	5 117	3 342	41 171
1989	1 057	46 149	5 276	3 107	41 349
1990	1 016	46 368	4 921	2 973	43 655
1991	1 033	40 309	4 980	3 006	43 089
1992	1 048	44 752	4 961	2 655	43 694
1993	1 104	46 741	5 756	2 732	43 323
1994	1 100	50 292	6 993	2 739	43 125
1995	1 100	48 563	9 019	2 532	43 151
1996	1 112	51 456	9 522	2 412	38 657
1997	1 120	53 643	12 735	2 207	44 440
1998	1 203	59 498	15 968	2 127	41 760
1999	1 311	66 067	17 326	2 192	44 694
2000	2 215	22 470	23 189	2 045	46 921
2001	2 406	17 694	24 672	1 890	47 500
2002	3 776	26 787	29 517	1 846	49 220
2003	3 468	27 814	31 272	1 709	48 831
2004	3 640	28 649	34 571	1 611	47 579
2005	3 640	28 388	39 539	1 689	47 424
2006	3 746	29 812	44 888	2 253	46 217
2007	5 415	29 538	47 739	2 158	45 841

注：本页数据由上海市环境保护局提供。
Note: Data on this page are provided by Shanghai Environmental Protection Bureau.

上/海/统/计/年/鉴

主要统计指标解释

"三废"综合利用产品产值

指报告期内利用"三废"作为主要原料生产的产品价值(现行价);已经销售或准备销售的应计算产品价值,留作生产自用的不应计算产品价值。

自然保护区

指对有代表性的自然生态系统、珍稀濒危野生动植物物种的天然分布区、水源涵养区、有特殊意义的自然历史遗迹等保护对象所在的陆地、陆地水体或海域,依法划出一定面积进行特殊保护和管理的区域。以县及县以上各级人民政府正式批准建立的自然保护区为准(包括"六五"以前由部门或"革委会"批准且现仍存在的自然保护区)。风景名胜区、文物保护区不计在内。自然保护区分国家级、省级、地市级和县级。按主管部门分属:环保、林业、农业、地矿、海洋、水利和其他部门。

工业固体废弃物产生量

指报告期内企业在生产过程中产生的固体状、半固体状和高浓度液体状废弃物的总量,包括危险废物、冶炼废渣、粉煤灰、炉渣、煤矸石、尾矿、放射性废物和其他废物等;不包括矿山开采的剥离废石和掘进废石(煤矸石和呈酸性或碱性的废石除外)。酸性或碱性废石指采掘的废石其流经水、雨淋水的 pH 值小于 4 或 pH 值大于 10.5 者。

危险废物

指列入国家危险废物名录或根据国家规定的危险废物鉴别标准和鉴别方法认定的,具有爆炸性、易燃性、易氧化性、毒性、腐蚀性、易传染疾病等危险特性之一的废物。

工业废弃物综合利用量

指报告期内企业通过回收、加工、循环、交换等方式,从废弃物中提取或者使其转化为可以利用的资源、能源和其他原材料的废弃物量(包括当年利用往年的工业废弃物贮存量),如用作农业肥料、生产建筑材料、筑路等。综合利用量由原产生废弃物的单位统计。

工业废弃物综合利用率

指工业废弃物综合利用量占工业废弃物产生量(包括综合利用往年贮存量)的百分率。计算公式为:

$$\text{工业废弃物综合利用率}=\frac{\text{工业废弃物综合利用量}}{\text{工业废弃物产生量}+\text{综合利用往年贮存量}}\times 100\%$$

工业固体废物处置量

指报告期内企业将固体废物焚烧或者最终置于符合环境保护规定要求的场所,并不再回取的工业固体废物量(包括当年处置往年的工业固体废物贮存量)。处置方式有填埋(其中危险废物应安全填埋)、焚烧、专业贮存场(库)封场处理、深层灌注、回填矿井及海洋处置(经海洋管理部门同意投海处置)等。

工业废水排放量

指经过企业厂区所有排放口排到企业外部的工业废水量。包括生产废水、外排的直接冷却水、超标排放的矿井地下水和与工业废水混排的厂区生活污水,不包括外排的间接冷却水(清污不分流的间接冷却水应计算在内)。

工业废水排放达标量

指报告期内废水中各项污染物指标都达到国家或地方排放标准的外排工业废水量,包括未经处理外排达标的,经废水处理设施处理后达标排放的,以及经污水处理厂处理后达标排放的。

工业废水排放达标率

指工业废水排放达标量占工业废水排放量的百分率,计算公式为:

$$\text{工业废水排放达标率}=\frac{\text{工业废水排放达标量}}{\text{工业废水排放量}}\times 100\%$$

工业废气排放量

指企业厂区内燃料燃烧和生产工艺过程中产生的各种排入空气的含有污染物的气体总量,按标准状态〔273K,101 325Pa〕计算。测算公式为:

$$\text{工业废气排放量}=\text{燃料燃烧过程中废气排放量}+\text{生产工艺过程中废气排放量}$$

工业二氧化硫排放总量

指报告期内企业在燃料燃烧和生产工艺过程中排入

主要统计指标解释

大气的 SO_2 总量,计算公式为:

工业二氧化硫排放量 = 燃料燃烧过程中二氧化硫排放量 + 生产工艺过程中二氧化硫排放量

■ 工业烟尘排放量

指企业厂区内燃料燃烧过程中产生的烟气中夹带的颗粒物排放量。

■ 酸雨频率

指酸雨出现的次数占降水出现次数的比例,通常称PH值小于5.6的降水为酸雨。

■ 生活垃圾清运量

指报告期内收集和运送到垃圾处理厂(场)的生活垃圾数量。生活垃圾指城市日常生活或为城市日常生活提供服务的活动中产生的固体废物以及法律行政规定的视为城市生活垃圾的固体废物。包括:居民生活垃圾、商业垃圾、集市贸易市场垃圾、街道清扫垃圾、公共场所垃圾和机关、学校、厂矿等单位的生活垃圾。

SHANGHAI STATISTICAL YEARBOOK

EXPLANATORY NOTES TO MAJOR STATISTICAL INDICATORS

□ Output Value of Products Made from Waste Gas, Waste Water and Solid Wastes

Output Value of Products Made from Waste Gas, Waste Water and Solid Wastes refers current value of products with waste gas, waste water and solid wastes as main materials of production. Products sold and ready to sell shall be included while those produced for own use shall not be included.

□ Natural Preservation

Natural Reserves refer to all the land, water areas on land and sea areas are under special protection or management due to the possess ion of representative natural ecological system, natural distribution of rare and dying out animal zones, water–resource conservation areas, and natural historical relics. Also included are natural reserves formally approved by people ' s governments at various levels at and above county level (including those approved before the Sixth–five–year Program and still active natural reserves).Scenic spots and historical sites and zones for preservation of cultural relics are not included. Natural reserves are classified as national level, provincial level, prefecture level and county level ones. They are under the jurisdiction of different departments, such as: environment protection, forestry, agriculture, geological and mining, oceanic and water conservancy and so on.

□ Industrial Solid Wastes Produced

Industrial Solid Wastes Produced refers to total volume of solid, semi–solid and high concentration liquid residues produced by industrial enterprises from production process in a given period of time, including hazardous wastes, slag, coal ash, gangue, tailings, radioactive residues and other wastes, but excluding stones stripped or dug out in mining (gangue and acid or alkaline stones not included). A stone is acid or alkaline depending on the pH value of the water below 4 or above 10.5 when the stone is in, or soaked by, the water.

□ Hazardous Wastes

Hazardous Wastes refers to those included in the national hazardous wastes catalogue or specified as any one of the following properties in the national hazardous wastes identification standards: explosive, ignitable, oxidizable, toxic, corrosive or liable to cause infectious diseases or lead to other dangers.

□ Industrial Wastes Utilized

Industrial Wastes Utilized refers to volume of wastes from which useful materials can be extracted or which can be converted into usable resources, energy or other materials by means of reclamation, processing, recycling and exchange (including utilizing in the year the stocks of industrial wastes of the previous year). Examples of such utilizations include fertilizers, building materials and road materials. The information shall be collected by the producing units of the wastes.

□ Ratio of Industrial Wastes Utilized

Ratio of Industrial Wastes Utilized refers to the percentage of industrial wastes utilized over industrial wastes produced (including stocks of the previous years). It is calculated as:

$$\text{Ratio of industrial wastes utilized} = \frac{\text{volume of industrial wastes utilized}}{\text{(industrial wastes produced + stock of previous years)}} \times 100\%$$

□ Industrial Solid Wastes Disposed

Industrial Solid Wastes Disposed refers to quantity of industrial solid wastes which are burnt or placed ultimately in the sites meeting the requirements for environmental protection and not salvaged or recycled (including disposition in the year of those wastes of previous years). The disposition includes landfill (Safe landfills should be conducted for hazardous wastes), incineration, containment spaces, deep underground disposal, backfill in mining pits and disposal at sea.

□ Volume of Industrial Waste Water Discharged

Volume of Industrial Waste Water Discharged refers to the volume of industrial waste water discharged, through all outlets, to the outside of industrial enterprises, including waste water produced, direct–cooling water, underground water from mines that does not meet the standard of discharge, and the domestic sewage mixed up with industrial waste water when discharged, but excluding discharged indirect–cooling water.

EXPLANATORY NOTES TO MAJOR STATISTICAL INDICATORS

□ Industrial Waste Water Meeting Discharge Standards

Industrial Waste Water Meeting Discharge Standards refers to volume of industrial waste water discharge which, with or without treatment, reaches national or local standards with regard to all pollutants.

□ Ratio of Standard Waste Water Discharged to the Total Discharge

Ratio of Standard Waste Water Discharged to the Total Discharge refers to the share of the volume of waste water up to the standard for discharge of the total volume. The formula is as follows:

$$\text{Ratio of Standard Waste Water Discharged to the Total Discharge} = \frac{\text{Volume of Waste Water up to the Standard for Discharge}}{\text{Volume of Industrial Waste Water Discharged}} \times 100\%$$

□ Volume of Waste Industrial Gas Emission

Industrial Waste Air Emission refers to discharge into atmosphere of waste air containing pollutants generated from fuel burning and production process in enterprises within a given period of time. It is calculated at standard status (273K, 101325Pa) as:

Industrial waste air emission=emission through fuel burning +emission through production process

□ SO_2 Emission through Industrial Activities

SO_2 Emission through Industrial Activities refers to volume of sulphur dioxide emission from fuel burning and production process by enterprises during a given period of time. It is calculated as:

SO_2 emission through industrial activities = SO_2 emission from fuel burning + SO_2 emission from production process

□ Industrial Soot Emission

Industrial Soot Emission refers to volume of soot in smoke emitted in process of fuel burning in premises of enterprises.

□ Acid Rain Frequency

Acid Rain Frequency refers to the proportion of frequencies of acid rainfall to the total rainfall times. Rainfall is defined as acid rain when the PH value of its rainwater is small than 5.6.

□ Consumption Wastes Transported

Consumption Wastes Transported refers to volume of consumption wastes collected and transported to disposal factories or sites. Consumption wastes are solid wastes produced from urban households or from service activities for urban households, and solid wastes regarded by laws and regulations as urban consumption wastes, including those from households, commercial activities, markets, cleaning of streets, public sites, offices, schools, factories, mining units and other sources.

第二十篇

CHAPTER 20

教　育

EDUCATION

表 20.1 主要年份教育事业基本情况
BASIC STATISTICS OF EDUCATION IN MAIN YEARS

指 标	Indicators	2000	2006	2007
学校数（所）	**Quantity of Schools（unit）**	**2 225**	**1 672**	**1 640**
普通高等学校	Regular Institutions of Higher Education	37	60	60
普通中等学校	Secondary Schools	1 133	958	937
中等专业学校	Specialized Secondary Schools	84	81	76
职业中学	Vocational Secondary Schools	60	37	32
技工学校	Technical Worker Schools	115	33	30
普通中学	Regular Secondary Schools	861	794	786
工读学校	Reformatory	13	13	13
普通小学	Primary Schools	1 021	626	615
特殊教育学校	Special Education Schools	34	28	28
教职工数（万人）	**Quantity of Teachers and Staff（10 000 persons）**	**22.73**	**21.35**	**21.03**
普通高等学校	Regular Institutions of Higher Education	6.01	7.17	7.18
普通中等学校	Secondary Schools	10.43	9.16	8.85
中等专业学校	Specialized Secondary Schools	1.27	1.06	1.00
职业中学	Vocational Secondary Schools	0.66	0.50	0.48
技工学校	Technical Worker Schools	0.77	0.21	0.20
普通中学	Regular Secondary Schools	7.66	7.33	7.11
工读学校	Reformatory	0.07	0.06	0.06
普通小学	Primary Schools	6.13	4.86	4.84
特殊教育学校	Special Education Schools	0.16	0.16	0.16
专任教师（万人）	**Quantity of Full-time Teachers（10 000 persons）**	**12.83**	**13.36**	**13.59**
普通高等学校	Regular Institutions of Higher Education	2.05	3.39	3.55
普通中等学校	Secondary Schools	6.26	6.12	6.08
中等专业学校	Specialized Secondary Schools	0.53	0.52	0.51
职业中学	Vocational Secondary Schools	0.39	0.30	0.29
技工学校	Technical Worker Schools	0.30	0.12	0.11
普通中学	Regular Secondary Schools	5.01	5.14	5.13
高 中	Senior Secondary Schools	1.42	1.80	1.79
初 中	Junior Secondary Schools	3.59	3.34	3.34
工读学校	Reformatory	0.03	0.04	0.04
普通小学	Primary Schools	4.43	3.75	3.85
特殊教育学校	Special Education Schools	0.09	0.10	0.11

①本表数据由上海市人民政府教育委员会提供。
②普通中学学校数中，完全中学 174 所，高级中学 143 所，初级中学 338 所，一贯制学校 139 所。
❶Data in this table are provided by Shanghai Municipal Education Commission.
❷In regular secondary schools, there are 174 whole secondary schools , 143 senior high schools, 338 junior high schools and 139 system schools

表 20.1 续表 continued

指　标	Indicators	2000	2006	2007
毕业生数(万人)	**Graduates (10 000 persons)**	**55.67**	**50.71**	**49.97**
普通高等学校	Regular Institutions of Higher Education	4.09	11.05	11.85
普通中等学校	Secondary Schools	32.76	28.72	27.48
中等专业学校	Specialized Secondary Schools	3.86	3.52	3.86
职业中学	Vocational Secondary Schools	3.99	2.00	1.52
技工学校	Technical Worker Schools	1.86	0.84	0.79
普通中学	Regular Secondary Schools	22.92	22.24	21.23
高　中	Senior Secondary Schools	7.18	10.21	10.24
初　中	Junior Secondary Schools	15.74	12.03	10.99
工读学校	Reformatory	0.13	0.12	0.08
普通小学	Primary Schools	18.73	10.85	10.55
特殊教育学校	Special Education Schools	0.09	0.09	0.09
招生数(万人)	**New Student Enrollment (10 000 persons)**	**52.23**	**48.65**	**47.59**
普通高等学校	Regular Institutions of Higher Education	8.13	14.04	14.46
普通中等学校	Secondary Schools	33.71	23.67	22.06
中等专业学校	Specialized Secondary Schools	3.00	3.47	3.23
职业中学	Vocational Secondary Schools	2.44	1.76	1.53
技工学校	Technical Worker Schools	1.68	0.44	0.46
普通中学	Regular Secondary Schools	26.46	17.84	16.72
高　中	Senior Secondary Schools	7.84	7.00	6.15
初　中	Junior Secondary Schools	18.62	10.84	10.57
工读学校	Reformatory	0.13	0.16	0.12
普通小学	Primary Schools	10.28	10.87	11.00
特殊教育学校	Special Education Schools	0.11	0.07	0.07
在校学生(万人)	**Student Enrollment (10 000 persons)**	**207.61**	**193.04**	**187.79**
普通高等学校	Regular Institutions of Higher Education	22.68	46.63	48.49
普通中等学校	Secondary Schools	105.53	92.54	85.47
中等专业学校	Specialized Secondary Schools	11.89	13.70	12.81
职业中学	Vocational Secondary Schools	8.48	5.33	5.20
技工学校	Technical Worker Schools	5.37	2.05	1.56
普通中学	Regular Secondary Schools	79.54	71.17	65.60
高　中	Senior Secondary Schools	23.94	27.17	22.90
初　中	Junior Secondary Schools	55.60	44.00	42.70
工读学校	Reformatory	0.25	0.29	0.30
普通小学	Primary Schools	78.86	53.37	53.33
特殊教育学校	Special Education Schools	0.54	0.50	0.50

表20.2 每万人口在校学生数、每个教师负担学生数(1978～2007)
STUDENTS ENROLLMENT PER 10 000 PERSONS AND STUDENTS TAUGHT

单位:人(person)

年 份 Year	平均每万人口在校学生数 Students Enrollment Per 10 000 Persons				平均每个教师负担学生数 Students Taught by Each Teacher		
	大学生 College and University	中专生 Speciallized Secondary School	中学生 Secondary School	小学生 Primary School	普通高等学校 Institution of Higher Education	普通中等学校 Regular Secondary School	普通小学 Primary School
1978	46	14	913	793	3	17	18
1979	60	21	722	777	4	16	19
1980	67	24	547	746	4	13	18
1981	78	25	429	716	5	11	17
1982	71	28	453	668	4	12	16
1983	66	30	436	669	4	10	16
1984	75	37	408	693	4	11	17
1985	89	49	396	692	4	12	17
1986	95	56	392	702	5	11	17
1987	98	56	386	715	5	11	17
1988	102	52	362	779	5	11	18
1989	99	50	361	831	5	11	19
1990	94	48	376	859	5	11	19
1991	91	47	398	865	5	12	19
1992	93	50	425	879	5	13	22
1993	101	58	445	901	6	14	21
1994	108	71	504	877	6	15	21
1995	110	83	556	843	7	16	20
1996	113	76	584	816	7	16	20
1997	118	85	570	785	8	16	20
1998	126	95	565	736	8	17	19
1999	142	99	584	664	9	17	19
2000	172	90	602	597	11	17	18
2001	211	91	605	545	13	16	17
2002	249	95	592	504	14	17	17
2003	282	102	562	483	16	16	17
2004	307	104	612	397	15	17	14
2005	325	101	566	393	14	16	14
2006	341	100	520	390	14	15	14
2007	352	93	476	387	14	14	14

注：本表数据由市教育委员会提供。
Note：Data in this table are provided by Shanghai Municipal Education Commission.

表20.3　各级各类学校在校学生数(1978～2007)
STUDENTS ENROLLMENT BY VARIOUS SCHOOLS

单位:万人(10 000 persons)

年　份 Year	普通高等学校 Institutions of Higher Education	普通中等学校 Secondary School	其中 of which: 中等专业学校 Specialized Secondary School	普通中学 Regular Secondary School	职业学校 Secondary Vocational School	技工学校 Technical Worker School	普通小学 Primary School	特殊教育学校 Special Education School
1978	5.06	101.81	1.55	100.26			87.06	0.18
1979	6.74	90.80	2.42	81.72		6.66	88.00	0.18
1980	7.67	71.68	2.81	62.71	0.29	5.87	85.47	0.18
1981	9.11	58.82	2.94	49.93	0.45	5.50	83.22	0.16
1982	8.39	61.69	3.30	53.53	0.85	4.01	78.88	0.16
1983	7.87	60.53	3.61	52.04	1.71	3.17	79.82	0.23
1984	8.99	61.01	4.48	49.18	3.07	4.28	83.47	0.21
1985	10.79	63.50	5.92	48.23	4.69	4.66	84.18	0.23
1986	11.77	64.82	6.86	48.31	4.71	4.94	86.56	0.25
1987	12.25	64.50	7.03	48.21	4.08	5.18	89.35	0.28
1988	12.82	61.20	6.52	45.68	3.69	5.31	98.39	0.30
1989	12.61	61.01	6.45	46.10	3.54	4.92	106.02	0.32
1990	12.13	62.59	6.17	48.31	3.66	4.45	110.19	0.33
1991	11.69	65.92	6.01	51.24	3.97	4.70	111.38	0.35
1992	11.95	70.84	6.41	54.77	4.90	4.76	113.37	0.38
1993	13.10	76.54	7.58	57.69	6.39	4.88	116.70	0.44
1994	14.04	87.23	9.23	65.56	7.54	4.90	113.98	0.52
1995	14.41	96.38	10.85	72.40	8.64	4.49	109.78	0.57
1996	14.79	99.97	9.95	76.23	9.12	4.67	106.46	0.62
1997	15.38	100.81	11.10	74.43	10.29	4.99	102.44	0.63
1998	16.51	102.53	12.38	73.85	10.72	5.58	96.14	0.52
1999	18.63	105.66	13.06	76.69	10.21	5.70	87.16	0.53
2000	22.68	105.28	11.89	79.54	8.48	5.37	78.86	0.54
2001	28.00	104.37	12.12	80.23	7.48	4.54	72.28	0.48
2002	33.16	103.59	12.66	78.97	7.56	4.40	67.24	0.55
2003	37.85	100.71	13.69	75.47	7.04	4.51	64.83	0.55
2004	41.57	106.94	14.05	82.78	6.43	3.68	53.74	0.54
2005	44.26	99.24	13.67	77.02	5.76	2.79	53.50	0.52
2006	46.63	92.25	13.70	71.17	5.33	2.05	53.37	0.50
2007	48.49	85.17	12.81	65.60	5.20	1.56	53.33	0.50

①本表数据由市教育委员会提供。
②本表普通中等学校在校学生数中不包括工读学校在校学生。
❶Data in this table are provided by Shanghai Municipal Education Commission.
❷Quantity of students enrollment of secondary school in this table doesn't include those of reformatory schools.

表 20.4 主要年份各阶段教育实施情况
BASIC STATISTICS OF VARIOUS PHASES EDUCATION IN MAIN YEARS

单位:%

指 标	Indicators	2000	2006	2007
小 学	**Primary School**			
小学学龄儿童净入学率	Enrollment Rate of Schoolage Children	99.9	99.9	99.9
初 中	**Junior School**			
初中学生净入学率	Enrollment Rate of Students in Junior Secondary School Phase	99.9	99.9	99.9
高 中	**Senior School**			
高中阶段教育入学率	Enrollment Quotas of Senior Graduates School Phase	97.0	99.0	98.0
普通高中招生比例	Recruit Students Rate of Regular Senior Secondary Schools	51.0	55.0	54.0
高 校	**Institutions of Higher Education**			
普通高等学校录取率	Admission Rate of Students in Regular Institution of Higher Education	67.4	81.7	82.1

表 20.5 主要年份各级民办学校基本情况
BASIC STATISTICS OF CIVIL SCHOOLS IN MAIN YEARS

类 别	Types	2000	2006	2007
民办高等学校	**Civil Institutions of Higher Education**			
学校数(所)	Schools (unit)	3	16	16
在校学生(万人)	Students Enrollment(10 000 persons)	0.67	7.86	8.61
专任教师(人)	Full-time Teachers(persons)	304	3 422	3 521
民办中等专业学校	**Civil Specialized Secondary Schools**			
学校数(所)	Schools (unit)		3	3
在校学生(万人)	Students Enrollment(10 000 persons)		2 561	2 247
专任教师(人)	Full-time Teachers(person)		107	106
民办职业高中学校	**Civil Vocational Schools**			
学校数(所)	Schools (unit)	1	3	3
在校学生(万人)	Students Enrollment(10 000 persons)	0.08	0.14	0.13
专任教师(人)	Full-time Teachers(person)	30	95	50
民办中学	**Civil Secondary Schools**			
学校数(所)	Schools (unit)	155	126	124
班级数(个)	Class(unit)	1 842	2 331	2 334
在校学生(万人)	Students Enrollment(10 000 persons)	8.48	9.30	9.11
高 中	Senior	4.54	3.56	2.95
初 中	Junior	3.94	5.74	6.16
专任教师(人)	Full-time Teachers(person)	2 400	3 616	3 785
民办小学	**Civil Primary Schools**			
学校数(所)	Schools (unit)	35	22	24
班级数(个)	Class(unit)	987	950	1 115
在校学生(万人)	Students Enrollment(10 000 persons)	3.95	2.94	3.52
专任教师(人)	Full-time Teachers(person)	831	1 271	1 746
民办幼儿园	**Civil Kindergarten**			
学校数(所)	Schools (unit)	92	288	312
班级数(个)	Class(unit)	636	1 999	2 324
在校学生(万人)	Students Enrollment(10 000 persons)	1.77	4.80	5.68
专任教师(人)	Full-time Teachers(person)	1 056	3 840	4 637

注：本页数据由市教育委员会提供。
Note: Data on this page are provided by Shanghai Municipal Education Commission.

表 20.6　民办学校(园)基本情况(2007)
BASIC STATISTICS OF CIVIL SCHOOLS

单位:人(person)

指　标	Indicators	学校数(所) School	毕业生数 Graduate	招生数 Students Recruited	在校生数 Students Enrollment	专任教师数 Full-time Teacher
普通高等学校	Institutions of Higher Education	16	21 784	30 452	86 062	3 521
普通中等专业学校	Specialized Secondary School	3	850	578	2 247	106
职业高中学校	Secondary Vocational School	3	491	426	1 263	50
普通中学	Regular Secondary School	124	28 285	22 503	91 056	3 785
高　中	Senior School	82	13 990	6 866	29 504	1 195
初　中	Junior School	42	14 295	15 637	61 552	2 590
普通小学	Primary School	24	6 309	7 635	35 180	1 746
幼儿园	Kindergarten	312	13 375	21 737	56 824	4 637

注：根据《民办教育促进法》的新规定，民办中、小学统计口径中扣除了公立转制学校。
Note: According to New Provision of Civil Education Advance Law, the Scope of Civil Secondary and Primary School excluded public schools transformed.

表 20.7　外国留学生情况(2005～2007)
STATISTICS OF STUDENT ABROAD

指　标	Indicators	2005	2006	2007
外国留学生人数(人)	**Number of Foreign Students(person)**	**13 691**	**14 100**	**13 121**
按费用来源分	By Tuition Resource			
中国政府资助	Chinese Government Sustentation	934	815	1 050
本国政府资助	Homeland Government Sustentation	15	153	140
学校间交换	Inter-school Communion	463	2 255	960
自　费	Commoners	12 279	10 741	10 971
按地区来源分	By District			
亚　洲	Aisa	10 490	10 207	9 287
非　洲	Africa	289	353	512
欧　洲	Europe	1 927	2 253	1 999
北美洲	North America	766	984	1 057
南美洲	South America	129	191	166
大洋洲	Oceania	90	112	100

注：本页数据由市教育委员会提供
Note: Data on this page are provided by Shanghai Municipal Education Commission.

表 20.8 主要年份研究生人数 NUMBER OF GRADUATE STUDENTS IN MAIN YEARS

单位:人(person)

年份 Year	获博士学位人数 Number of Doctor's Degrees Obtained	获硕士学位人数 Number of Master's Degrees Obtained	研究生 Postgraduates 毕业生数 Graduates 普通高等学校 Institutions of Higher Education	研究所(院) Research Institutions (Academies)	招生数 New Students Enrollment 普通高等学校 Institutions of Higher Education	研究所(院) Research Institutions (Academies)	在读人数 Students Enrollment 普通高等学校 Institutions of Higher Education	研究所(院) Research Institutions (Academies)
1978			9		1 072		1 253	
1980			6		410		2 696	
1985	57	1 371	1 543	37	4 264	83	8 163	170
1990	300	2 746	2 953	369	2 803	324	8 533	1 035
1991	342	2 739	2 936	320	2 717	302	8 020	949
1992	343	2 124	2 262	264	3 323	345	8 858	997
1993	368	2 489	2 569	315	3 919	363	10 037	1 008
1994	442	2 363	2 608	251	4 665	465	11 905	1 185
1995	606	2 742	3 038	317	4 776	525	13 378	1 335
1996	627	3 233	3 537	323	5 915	592	15 307	1 528
1997	890	3 585	4 117	358	6 163	562	16 841	1 619
1998	1 090	3 552	4 253	389	7 281	593	19 499	1 663
1999	1 323	4 288	5 196	415	8 758	655	22 656	1 764
2000	1 307	4 546	5 435	433	11 796	856	28 582	2 032
2001	1 487	5 330	6 380	437	14 751	1 075	36 528	2 515
2002	1 655	6 067	7 481	445	17 848	1 363	45 713	3 183
2003	1 994	7 683	9 501	578	20 767	1 757	55 092	3 998
2004	2 678	10 580	12 788	681	23 545	1 789	64 747	4 690
2005	3 119	13 245	15 857	884	25 845	1 847	73 557	5 171
2006	3 772	15 957	18 833	1 098	28 250	1 849	81 487	5 419
2007	4 355	19 250	22 691	1 235	28 748	1 862	86 177	5 586

①本表数据由市教育委员会提供。

②2001 年前的获博士学位和获硕士学位的人数为当年毕业生人数。

❶Data in this table are provided by Shanghai Municipal Education Commission.

❷Number of Doctor's and Master's Degrees obtained refer to number of graduates in this year before 2001.

表 20.9　普通高等学校基本情况(2007)
BASIC STATISTICS OF INSTITUTIONS OF HIGHER EDUCATION

类　别 Types		学校(所) Institutions (unit)	毕业生数(人) Graduates (person)	招生数(人) New Students Enrollment (person)	在校学生人数(人) Students Enrollment (person)	教职员工(人) Staff and Workers (person)	其中 of which #专任教师 Full-time Teacher	其中 of which #正、副高级 Senior and Associate Title
总　计	**Total**	**60**	**118 512**	**144 577**	**484 873**	**71 838**	**35 480**	**15 804**
#综合大学	Comprehensive Universities	3	16 999	16 883	68 158	19 179	7 883	4 379
理工院校	Science and Engineering	24	49 318	61 764	198 956	28 100	13 583	5 733
农林院校	Agriculture and Forestry	2	4 093	4 715	15 983	1 509	1 050	465
医药院校	Medical	2	843	2 434	7 408	1 210	656	189
师范院校	Teacher Training	2	8 160	9 904	36 911	6 936	3 428	1 820
语言院校	Linguistics and Literacy	3	4 458	5 883	17 134	1 949	1 073	340
财经院校	Economics and Finance	16	24 339	32 263	101 338	7 961	4 996	1 879
政法院校	Politics and Law	3	3 926	5 782	18 255	2 509	1 396	537
体育院校	Physical Culture	1	951	1 014	3 933	729	400	168
艺术院校	Art Schools	4	2 315	3 935	11 480	1 756	1 015	294

注：学生数中未包括在读研究生人数，在分类院校学生数中未包括成人高等学校中的普通本专科学生。
Note: Post-graduates do not included in the students enrollment. Undergraduates and junior college students in adult education schools do not included in the students

表 20.10　普通高等学校分科专任教师数(2007)
FULL-TIME TEACHERS IN INSTITUTIONS OF HIGHER EDUCATION BY SUBJECTS

单位：人 (person)

类　别 Types		专任教师数 Full-time Teachers	其中 of which 正高级 Senior Title	副高级 Associate Title	中　级 Junior Title	初　级 Primary Title	无职称 Non-Title
总　计	**Total**	**35 480**	**5 461**	**10 343**	**13 641**	**4 434**	**1 601**
哲　学	Philosophy	872	140	267	334	99	32
经济学	Economics	2 315	354	735	929	212	85
法　学	Law	2 263	293	598	934	348	90
教育学	Education	2 990	222	621	1 208	708	231
文　学	Literature	8 376	824	1 953	3 441	1 589	569
历史学	History	390	125	106	119	18	22
理　学	Science	3 401	841	1 160	1 137	182	81
工　学	Engineering	10 555	1 968	3 669	3 831	767	320
农　学	Agriculture	320	76	129	85	24	6
医　学	Medical	1 658	254	375	717	236	76
管理学	Administrotion	2 340	364	730	906	251	89

注：本页数据由市教育委员会提供。
Note: Data on this page are provided by Shanghai Municipal Education Commission.

表 20.11 普通高等学校分科学生数(2007)
STUDENTS IN INSTITUTIONS OF HIGHER EDUCATION BY SUBJECTS

单位:人 (person)

类别	Types	毕业生人数 Graduates 本科 Undergraduate	专科 Junior College	招生人数 New Students Enrollment 本科 Undergraduate	专科 Junior College	在校学生人数 Students Enrollment 本科 Undergraduate	专科 Junior College
总 计	**Total**	**60 485**	**58 027**	**87 021**	**57 556**	**314 578**	**170 295**
哲 学	Philosophy	103		180		585	
经济学	Economics	5 147	4 709	8 489	3 783	31 860	11 582
法 学	Law	4 360	2 597	5 354	1 722	19 349	5 229
教育学	Education	1 448	420	1 782	784	6 592	2 467
文 学	Literature	9 202	13 177	14 957	12 690	51 589	38 373
历史学	History	190		234		817	
理 学	Science	5 448	50	7 418		26 624	84
工 学	Engineering	20 924	22 176	28 700	21 987	102 321	64 241
农 学	Agriculture	309	547	668	434	1 951	1 646
医 学	Medical	2 125	2 611	2 176	3 705	10 580	10 375
管理学	Administrotion	11 229	11 740	17 063	12 451	62 310	36 298

表 20.12 中等专业学校基本情况(2007)
BASIC STATISTICS OF SPECIALIZED SECONDARY SCHOOLS

单位:人 (person)

类别	Types	毕业生数 Graduates	招生数 New Students Enrollment	在校学生 Students Enrollment	专业课专任教师 Full-time Teachers in professional course	其中 of which #正副高级 Senior and Associate Title	#中级 Junior Title
总 计	**Total**	**38 577**	**32 324**	**128 081**	**2 769**	**623**	**1 415**
农业、林业	Agriculture, Forestry	601	458	2 027	37	9	23
资源与环境	Resource and Environment	923	510	3 372	15	4	5
能 源	Power	245	572	2 409	42	18	23
土木水利工程	Construction and Water Conservancy Engineering	2 250	2 158	7 245	117	30	61
加工制造	Machining and Manufacture	6 959	6 445	22 922	504	142	251
交通运输	Transport	2 385	3 209	11 390	249	52	123
信息技术	Information Technology	5 169	3 132	12 237	386	70	190
医药卫生	Health	3 234	3 615	14 832	296	76	172
商贸与旅游	Trade and Tour	7 641	6 033	26 408	151	33	72
财 经	Finance and Economics	3 656	2 816	10 744	227	49	116
文化艺术与体育	Arts and Physical Culture	3 731	1 707	9 494	556	116	267
社会公共事务	Society Commonality Business	1 698	992	3 786	41	7	22
其 他	Others	85	677	1 215	148	17	90

注：本页数据由市教育委员会提供。
Note: Data on this page are provided by Shanghai Municipal Education Commission.

表 20.13　各区、县普通中学基本情况(2007)
BASIC STATISTICS OF REGULAR SECONDARY SCHOOLS BY DISTRICTS AND COUNTIES

地　区 District		学校（所） Schools (unit)	毕业生数 （万人） Graduates (10 000 person)	招生数 （万人） New Students Enrollment (10 000 persons)	在校学生 （万人） Students Enrollment (10 000 persons)	教职员工 （万人） Staff and Workers (10 000 persons)	其中 of which 专任教师 Full-time Teachers
总　计	**Total**	**786**	**21.22**	**16.72**	**65.60**	**7.11**	**5.13**
浦东新区	Pudong New Area	107	3.26	2.70	10.47	1.02	0.78
黄 浦 区	Huangpu	25	0.87	0.59	2.46	0.30	0.18
卢 湾 区	Luwan	15	0.37	0.23	0.99	0.13	0.09
徐 汇 区	Xuhui	44	1.41	1.09	4.22	0.44	0.31
长 宁 区	Changning	29	0.93	0.62	2.52	0.28	0.19
静 安 区	Jing'an	15	0.54	0.39	1.56	0.18	0.12
普 陀 区	Putuo	52	1.31	0.85	3.63	0.42	0.27
闸 北 区	Zhabei	40	1.18	0.77	3.21	0.38	0.26
虹 口 区	Hongkou	46	1.14	0.81	3.25	0.30	0.21
杨 浦 区	Yangpu	59	1.57	1.05	4.31	0.49	0.37
宝 山 区	Baoshan	53	1.13	1.03	3.89	0.39	0.31
闵 行 区	Minhang	59	1.22	1.15	4.27	0.53	0.39
嘉 定 区	Jiading	31	0.72	0.63	2.48	0.28	0.22
金 山 区	Jinshan	30	0.86	0.69	2.73	0.30	0.21
松 江 区	Songjiang	33	0.89	0.77	2.94	0.33	0.23
青 浦 区	Qingpu	27	0.74	0.69	2.48	0.25	0.19
南 汇 区	Nanhui	41	1.19	1.04	4.05	0.41	0.32
奉 贤 区	Fengxian	38	0.76	0.80	2.81	0.30	0.21
崇 明 县	Chongming	38	1.10	0.77	3.20	0.37	0.26
农　场	Farm	4	0.03	0.05	0.13	0.01	0.01

注：本表数据由市教育委员会提供。
Note: Data in this table are provided by Shanghai Municipal Education Commission.

表 20.14 各区、县普通中学初、高中学生基本情况(2007)
BASIC STATISTICS OF REGULAR JUNIOR AND SENIOR SCHOOLS' STUDENTS BY DISTRICTS AND COUNTIES

单位:万人 (10 000 persons)

地区	District	毕业生数 Graduates		招生数 New Students Enrollment		在校学生 Students Enrollment	
		初中 Junior	高中 Senior	初中 Junior	高中 Senior	初中 Junior	高中 Senior
总计	**Total**	**10.98**	**10.24**	**10.57**	**6.15**	**42.70**	**22.90**
浦东新区	Pudong New Area	1.71	1.55	1.83	0.87	7.22	3.25
黄浦区	Huangpu	0.38	0.49	0.31	0.28	1.32	1.14
卢湾区	Luwan	0.18	0.19	0.14	0.09	0.60	0.39
徐汇区	Xuhui	0.68	0.73	0.68	0.41	2.64	1.58
长宁区	Changning	0.43	0.50	0.39	0.23	1.56	0.96
静安区	Jing'an	0.25	0.29	0.22	0.17	0.92	0.64
普陀区	Putuo	0.58	0.73	0.51	0.34	2.14	1.49
闸北区	Zhabei	0.62	0.56	0.46	0.31	2.02	1.19
虹口区	Hongkou	0.52	0.62	0.45	0.36	1.83	1.42
杨浦区	Yangpu	0.70	0.87	0.58	0.47	2.49	1.82
宝山区	Baoshan	0.61	0.52	0.69	0.34	2.69	1.20
闵行区	Minhang	0.65	0.57	0.77	0.38	2.92	1.35
嘉定区	Jiading	0.41	0.31	0.43	0.20	1.76	0.72
金山区	Jinshan	0.53	0.33	0.44	0.25	1.91	0.82
松江区	Songjiang	0.50	0.39	0.52	0.25	2.02	0.92
青浦区	Qingpu	0.45	0.29	0.45	0.24	1.73	0.75
南汇区	Nanhui	0.71	0.48	0.65	0.39	2.73	1.32
奉贤区	Fengxian	0.45	0.31	0.57	0.23	2.05	0.76
崇明县	Chongming	0.60	0.50	0.44	0.33	2.04	1.16
农场	Farm	0.02	0.01	0.04	0.01	0.11	0.02

注：本表数据由市教育委员会提供。
Note: Data in this table are provided by Shanghai Municipal Education Commission.

表 20.15　各区、县职业高中基本情况(2007)
BASIC STATISTICS OF SECONDARY VOCATIONAL SCHOOLS BY DISTRICTS AND COUNTIES

地　区	District	学校(所) Schools (unit)	毕业生数 (人) Graduates (person)	招生数 (人) New Students Enrollment (person)	在校学生 (人) Students Enrollment (person)	教职员工 (人) Staff and Workers (person)	其中 of which #专任教师 Full-time Teachers
总　计	**Total**	**31**	**15 071**	**15 236**	**51 580**	**4 655**	**2 941**
浦东新区	Pudong New Area	5	2 220	4 482	13 428	694	518
黄 浦 区	Huangpu	3	1 636	615	2 558	522	267
卢 湾 区	Luwan	2	587	630	2 169	187	137
徐 汇 区	Xuhui	2	709	1 259	3 293	353	225
长 宁 区	Changning	2	849	468	2 158	288	154
静 安 区	Jing'an	1	566	469	2 274	275	181
普 陀 区	Putuo	1	659	511	2 006	235	166
闸 北 区	Zhabei	1	730	243	1 163	206	137
虹 口 区	Hongkou	1	1 644	1 870	6 912	389	223
杨 浦 区	Yangpu	1	847	633	2 377	226	149
宝 山 区	Baoshan	2	1 342	754	2 644	272	118
闵 行 区	Minhang	4	558	891	2 692	229	141
嘉 定 区	Jiading	1	132	62	221	71	53
金 山 区	Jinshan				33		
松 江 区	Songjiang	2	799	931	3 026	353	236
青 浦 区	Qingpu	1	848	187	745	85	47
南 汇 区	Nanhui				61	12	8
奉 贤 区	Fengxian		80	61	154		
崇 明 县	Chongming	1	786	1 170	3 492	245	172
农　　场	Farm	1	79		174	13	9

注：本表数据由市教育委员会提供。
Note: Data in this table are provided by Shanghai Municipal Education Commission.

表20.16 各区、县普通小学基本情况(2007)
BASIC STATISTICS OF REGULAR PRIMARY SCHOOLS BY DISTRICTS AND COUNTIES

地 区	District	学校(所) Schools (unit)	毕业生数(万人) Graduates (10 000 persons)	招生数(万人) New Students Enrollment (10 000 persons)	在校学生(万人) Students Enrollment (10 000 persons)	教职员工(万人) Staff and Workers (10 000 persons)	其中 of which #专任教师 Full-time Teachers
总 计	**Total**	**615**	**10.55**	**11.00**	**53.33**	**4.84**	**3.85**
浦东新区	Pudong New Area	101	1.74	2.10	9.84	0.78	0.67
黄浦区	Huangpu	21	0.27	0.23	1.18	0.16	0.11
卢湾区	Luwan	14	0.14	0.13	0.65	0.09	0.06
徐汇区	Xuhui	43	0.69	0.62	3.25	0.26	0.21
长宁区	Changning	26	0.41	0.38	1.89	0.19	0.15
静安区	Jing'an	12	0.18	0.19	0.92	0.12	0.07
普陀区	Putuo	28	0.57	0.54	2.80	0.22	0.16
闸北区	Zhabei	36	0.44	0.42	2.15	0.22	0.17
虹口区	Hongkou	36	0.43	0.42	2.07	0.21	0.16
杨浦区	Yangpu	47	0.61	0.51	2.77	0.29	0.24
宝山区	Baoshan	58	0.76	0.86	4.08	0.35	0.30
闵行区	Minhang	42	0.73	0.95	4.22	0.38	0.31
嘉定区	Jiading	23	0.45	0.50	2.34	0.20	0.17
金山区	Jinshan	21	0.44	0.42	2.04	0.21	0.15
松江区	Songjiang	13	0.51	0.61	2.74	0.22	0.18
青浦区	Qingpu	22	0.47	0.48	2.30	0.21	0.16
南汇区	Nanhui	23	0.65	0.65	3.21	0.28	0.23
奉贤区	Fengxian	16	0.58	0.64	3.02	0.22	0.18
崇明县	Chongming	32	0.44	0.32	1.69	0.21	0.16
农 场	Farm	1	0.04	0.03	0.17	0.02	0.01

注：本表数据由市教育委员会提供。
Note: Data in this table are provided by Shanghai Municipal Education Commission.

表 20.17　主要年份实验性示范性中学基本情况
BASIC STATISTICS OF SECONDARY CAMPUS SCHOOL IN MAIN YEARS

指　标	Indicators	2000	2006	2007
学　校(所)	Schools (unit)	84	88	89
班级数(个)	Classes (unit)	2 584	3 098	3 035
在校学生(万人)	Students Enrollment(10 000 persons)	12.10	13.07	12.04
教职员工(万人)	Staff and Workers (10 000 persons)	1.40	1.49	1.46
#专任教师	Full-time Teachers	0.88	1.03	1.05

注：实验性示范性中学包括重点中学和寄宿制高级中学。
Note: Secondary campus school includs important secondary school and boarding high school.

表 20.18　主要年份幼儿园基本情况
BASIC STATISTICS OF KINDERGARTENS IN MAIN YEARS

指　标	Indicators	2000	2006	2007
幼儿园(所)	Kindergartens (unit)	958	1 057	1 058
幼儿数(万人)	Children Enrollment (10 000 persons)	24.12	29.98	31.32
教职员工(万人)	Staff and Workers(10 000 persons)	2.52	3.04	3.19
#教　师	Teachers	1.50	1.88	2.02

表 20.19　主要年份特殊教育基本情况
BASIC STATISTICS OF SPECIAL EDUCATION IN MAIN YEARS

指　标	Indicators	2000	2006	2007
学校(所)	Schools (unit)	34	28	28
毕业生数(人)	Graduates(person)	868	869	886
招生数(人)	New Students Enrollment(person)	1 141	675	741
在校学生(人)	Students Enrollment(person)	5 407	5 043	5 043
教职员工(人)	Staff and Workers(person)	1 584	1 614	1 603
#专任教师	Full-time Teachers	943	1 047	1 092

注：本页数据由市教育委员会提供。
Note: Data on this page are provided by Shanghai Municipal Education Commission.

表 20.20 网络教育基本情况(2005 ~ 2007)
BASIC STATISTICS OF NETWORK EDUCATION

单位:人(person)

指 标	Indicators	2005	2006	2007
网络教育毕业生数	**Graduates of Network Education**	**27 844**	**41 893**	**46 217**
普通生	Regular Students	7 467	18 583	22 250
成人生	Adult Students	20 377	23 310	23 967
网络教育招生数	**Network Education New Student Enrollment**	**50 635**	**58 115**	**76 568**
普通生	Regular Students	22 498	27 127	30 554
成人生	Adult Students	28 137	30 988	46 014
网络教育在校生数	**Network Education Student Enrollment**	**135 445**	**142 173**	**160 757**
普通生	Regular Students	58 161	65 265	66 766
成人生	Adult Students	77 284	76 908	93 991

表 20.21 分学科网络教育学生情况(2007)
BASIC STATISTICS OF NETWORK EDUCATION STUDENTS BY SUBJECT

单位:人(person)

类 别	Types	毕业生人数 Graduates		招生人数 New Students Enrollment		在校学生人数 Student Enrollment	
		本 科 Undergraduate	专 科 Junior College	本 科 Undergraduate	专 科 Junior College	本 科 Undergraduate	专 科 Junior College
总 计	**Total**	**16 428**	**29 789**	**27 878**	**48 690**	**54 986**	**105 771**
经济学	Economics	2 444	321	2 861	890	8 105	1 449
法 学	Law	573	252	524	82	1 638	337
教育学	Education	1 937	581	2 740	2 170	4 772	3 448
文 学	Literature	2 095	2 436	3 878	2 743	8 562	5 893
历史学	History	54		66		134	
理 学	Science	406		1 138		2 244	
工 学	Engineering	1 844	1 704	4 128	4 285	6 889	7 294
医 学	Medical	771	1 301	1 102	1 423	2 436	4 361
管理学	Administration	6 300	23 194	11 373	37 097	20 071	82 989

注:本页数据由市教育委员会提供。
Note: Data on this page are provided by Shanghai Municipal Education Commission.

表 20.22　主要年份成人教育基本情况
BASIC STATISTICS OF ADULT EDUCATION IN MAIN YEARS

类　别	Types	2000	2005	2006	2007
成人高等教育	**Special Education**				
学校（所）	Schools (unit)	37	21	21	21
毕业生数(万人)	Graduates(10 000 persons)	3.10	5.64	1.50	5.20
招生数(万人)	New Students Enrollment(10 000 persons)	4.22	6.50	6.78	7.25
在校学生(万人)	Students Enrollment(10 000 persons)	11.49	14.72	19.46	20.68
专任教师(万人)	Full-time Teachers(10 000 persons)	0.30	0.15	0.16	0.15
成人中等教育	**Adult Secondary Education**				
学校（所）	Schools (unit)	459	65	52	46
毕业生数(万人)	Graduates(10 000persons)	13.65	2.78	2.01	1.75
招生数(万人)	New Students Enrollment(10 000 persons)	20.53	0.37	0.45	0.31
在校学生(万人)	Students Enrollment(10 000 persons)	18.22	4.11	3.32	2.58
专任教师(万人)	Full-time Teachers(10 000 persons)	0.46	0.09	0.06	0.05
成人职业技术培训	**Adult Technical Training**				
学校（所）	Schools (unit)	917	901	827	781
毕业生数(万人)	Graduates(10 000 persons)	81.42	19.82	29.66	17.45
在校学生(万人)	Students Enrollment(10 000 persons)	18.00	35.43	41.12	25.08
专任教师(万人)	Full-time Teachers(10 000 persons)	0.48	0.74	0.65	0.55

表 20.23　各级各类成人学校基本情况(2007)
BASIC STATISTICS OF ADULT SCHOOLS AT VARIOUS LEVELS

类　别	Types	学校数（所） Schools (unit)	毕业生人数（万人） Graduates (10 000 persons)	招生数（万人） New Students Enrollment (10 000 persons)	在校学生人数（万人） Students Enrollment (10 000 persons)	教职员工人数（万人） Staff and Workers (10 000 persons)	其中 of which 专任教师 Full-time Teachers
成人高等教育	**Adult Higher Education**	**21**	**5.20**	**7.25**	**20.68**	**0.30**	**0.15**
广播电视大学	Broadcasting and TV Universities	1	0.02		…	0.03	0.01
职工高等学校	Staff Higher Education Schools	16	0.53	0.79	2.33	0.23	0.12
管理干部学院	Institutes for Administrative Officials	4	0.09	0.14	0.33	0.04	0.02
普通高等学校办	Run by Regular High Education Institutions	(81)	4.56	6.33	18.02		
函　授	Correspondence Programs	(14)	0.75	0.57	2.03		
业　余	Spare Time	(43)	3.48	5.33	14.72		
脱　产	Full Time	(24)	0.33	0.42	1.27		
成人中等教育	**Adult Secondary Education**	**46**	**1.75**	**0.31**	**2.58**	**0.10**	**0.05**
成人中等专业学校	Specialized Secondary Schools	35	0.45	0.31	0.93	0.08	0.04
成人中学	Adult Spare-time Secondary Schools	11	1.30		1.65	0.02	0.01
成人职业技术学校	**Adult Technical Secondary Schools**	**781**	**20.33**		**25.08**	**1.36**	**0.55**

①"( )"指高等院校举办的各类成人教学点数据。成人中学、成人初等学校在校学生数均为在校注册学生数；成人技术培训在校学生数为培训期超过半年的累计注册学生数。

②本页数据由市教育委员会提供。

❶The figures with"( )" refer to the number of the adult education places conducted by higher education institutions. Students enrollment of adult spare-time secondary schools and adult junior schools refer to the number of students registered at school. Students Enrollment of adult technical secondary schools refers to accumulative total number of students registered at schools who have been trained more than half a year.

❷Data on this page are provided by Shanghai Municipal Education Commission.

表 20.24 上海国际学校一览(2007) SHANGHAI INTERNATIONAL SCHOOLS

学校名称	Name of School	地 址	Address
上海美国学校	Shanghai American School	闵行区金丰路 258 号	No. 258 Jinfeng Road, Minhang District
上海日本人学校	Shanghai Japanese School	闵行区虹梅路 3185 号	No. 3185 Hongmei Road
耀中上海国际学校	Yaozhong Shanghai International School	长宁区水城路 11 号	No. 11 Shuicheng Road, Changning District
宋庆龄幼儿园国际部	International Section of Songqingling Kindergarten	长宁区虹梅路 3908 号	No. 3908 Hongmei Road N.
上海德国学校	Shanghai German School	青浦区诸光路 399 弄 30 号	Lane 399, 30 Zhuguang Road, Qingpu District
上海法国学校	Shanghai French School	青浦区诸光路 399 弄 30 号	Lane 399, 30 Zhuguang Road, Qingpu District
上海英国学校	Shanghai British School	沪南公路 2729 弄 600 号（康桥半岛）	Lane 2729, 600 Hunan Highway (Cambridge Peninsula)
上海协和国际学校	Shanghai Xiehe International School	浦东金桥明月路 999 号	No 345, Huangyang Road, Jingqiao Pudong
上海长宁国际学校	Shanghai Changning International School	长宁区虹桥路 1161 号	No. 1161, Hongqiao Road, Changning District
上海新加坡国际学校	Shanghai Singapore International School	闵行区纪翟路 288 号	No. 288 Jizhai Road, Minhang District
上海虹桥国际学校	Shanghai Hongqiao International School	长宁区虹桥路 2381 号	No. 2381 Hongqiao Road , Changning District
上海韩国学校	Shanghai Korea School	闵行区华漕镇联友路 355 号	No. 355, Lianyou Road, Caohua Town, Minhang District
上海美丘第一幼儿园	Shanghai Meiqiu No. 1 Kindergarten	闵行区虹许路 788 号(名都城)	No. 788, Hongxu Road, Minhang District (Mingdu City)
奥伊斯嘉上海日本语幼儿园	Shanghai Japanese Kindergarten	长宁区茅台路 715 弄 20 号	No. 20 Lane 715 Maotai Road
东进上海日本人幼儿园	Shanghai Dongjin Japanese Kindergarten	长宁区虹梅路 3081 号虹桥别墅内	Hongqiao Villa, No. 3081 Hongmei Road
上海恩吉尔幼儿园	Shanghai Angel Kindergarten	闵行区吴中路 2358 号	No. 2358 Wuzhong Road Minhang District
上海泰宁国际幼儿园	Taining International Kindergarten	徐汇区复兴西路 43 号	No. 43 Fuxing Road W.
上海瑞金国际学校	Shanghai Ruijin International School	莘庄镇东闸路 189 号	No. 189 Dongzha Road, Xinzhuang Town
上海李文斯顿美国学校	Shanghai Livingston America School	长宁区甘溪路 580 号	No. 580 Ganxi Road Changning District
上海德威英国国际学校	Shanghai Sulwich College	浦东金桥蓝桉路 222 号	No. 222, Lanan Road, Jinqiao, Pudong District
上海中学国际部	International Section of Shanghai Middle School	徐汇区上中路 400 号	No. 400 Shangzhong Road
华东师范大学二附中国际部	The International Section of the No. 2 Middle School Attached to East China Normal University	浦东晨晖路 555 号	No. 555, Chenhui Road, Pudong
上海外国语大学附中国际部	The International Section of the Middle School Attached to Shanghai International Studies University	中山北一路 295 号	No. 295 Zhongshan Road N1
进才中学国际部	The International Section of Jincai High School	丁香路 129 号	No. 129 Dingxiang Road
上海西华国际学校	Shanghai Xihua International School	青浦区联名路 555 号	No. 555, Lianming Road, Qingpu District

注：本表数据由市教育委员会提供。
Note: Data in this table are provided by Shanghai Municipal Education Commission.

上 / 海 / 统 / 计 / 年 / 鉴

主要统计指标解释

学　校

指按国家规定的设置标准和审批程序批准设立的，招收适龄人口实施各级各类教育活动的教育机构。

普通高等学校

指按照国家规定的设置标准和审批程序批准举办的，通过全国普通高等学校统一招生考试，招收高中毕业生为主要培养对象，实施高等教育的全日制大学、独立设置的学院和高等专科学校、高等职业学校和其他机构。

大学、独立设置的学院主要实施本科层次以上教育，高等专科学校、高等职业学校实施专科层次教育，其他机构是承担国家普通招生计划任务不计校数的机构。包括普通高等学校分校和批准筹建的普通高等学校等。

成人高等学校

指按国家规定的设置标准和审批程序举办的，通过全国成人高等教育统一招生考试，招收高中毕业或同等学历的人员为主要培养对象，利用函授、业余、脱产的多种形式对其实施高等学历教育的学校。包括：职工高等学校、农民高等学校、管理干部学院、教育学院、独立函授学院、广播电视大学、其他机构等。

中等专业学校

指经县或县以上教育行政部门批准设立，招收初中毕业生实施中等专业课程教育的教学机构。

职业中学（职业高中、职业初中）

指经县或县以上教育行政部门批准设立，招收小学或初中毕业生实施中等职业技术教育的教学机构。按学校性质类别可分为：独立设置的职业中学（包括：职业初中、职业高中、职业初高中合设学校）；附设有普通中学班的职业中学。

普通中学（普通高中、普通初中）

普通中学分为普通高级中学和普通初级中学两个阶段。普通初级中学是指独立设置的招收小学毕业的适龄人口进行初级中等基础教育的机构；普通高级中学是指独立设置的招收初中毕业的适龄人口进行高级中等基础教育的机构；完全中学是指普通初、高中合设的教育机构；一贯制学校是指在一所学校连续实施中小学教育的机构。其中包括实施九年义务教育的九年一贯制学校和实施高中教育的十二年一贯制学校。（说明：一贯制学校的办学条件如能划分为小学、初中、高中，则分开填报；如不能划分清楚，可按就高不就低的方法填入初中、高中报表中，不能重复填写。）

普通小学

指由区或区以上教育行政部门批准，招收学龄儿童实施初等教育的教学机构。

幼儿园

指招收三周岁以上（含三周岁）学龄前幼儿，对其进行保育和教育的单位。

特殊教育学校

指本市独立设置的招收盲聋哑和智残儿童，以及其他特殊需要的儿童、青少年进行普通或职业初、中等教育的教学机构。

小学学龄儿童净入学率

小学学龄人口中正在接受小学教育人数所占比重。

初中学生净入学率

是指初级中学（普通初中和职业初中）在校学生总数占初中学龄人口数的比重。

费，包括教育事业拨款、科研经费拨款、基建拨款和其他经费拨款。

SHANGHAI STATISTICAL YEARBOOK

EXPLANATORY NOTES TO MAJOR STATISTICAL INDICATORS

□ School Institutions

School Institutions refer to education establishment set up according to the government evaluation and approval procedures, enrolling population of the right age, providing various phase education activity.

□ Regular Institutions of Higher Education

Regular Institutions of Higher Learning refer to educational establishments set up according to the government evaluation and approval procedures, enrolling graduates from senior secondary schools and providing higher education courses and training for senior professionals. They include full-time universities, colleges, high professional schools, high professional vocational schools and others.

Universities and colleges are mainly providing undergraduate courses; those high professional schools and high professional vocational schools are mainly providing professional trainings; and others refer to educational establishments, which are responsible for enrolling students but not covered in the total number of schools, including: branch schools of universities and colleges, and universities and colleges that have been proved and prepared to construct.

□ Institutions of Higher Education for Adults

Institution of Higher Learning for Adults refer to educational establishments, set up in line with relevant rules approved by the government, enrolling personnel with senior secondary schools or equivalent education, and providing higher education courses in many forms of correspondence, spare time, or full time for adults. Institutions of higher schools for adults include schools of higher educations for staff and workers, schools of higher education for peasants, colleges for management cadres, pedagogical colleges, independent correspondence colleges, Radio and TV universities and other educational establishment, etc.

□ Specialized Secondary schools

Specialized Secondary schools refer to educational establishment set up according to approval and permission by educational administration department of district and above government, enrolling graduates from junior secondary schools and providing secondary professional education courses.

□ Vocational Secondary Schools (senior secondary schools and junior secondary schools)

Vocational Secondary Schools (senior secondary schools and junior secondary schools) refer to educational establishment set up according to approval and permission by educational administration department of district and above government, enrolling graduates from primary schools and junior secondary schools and providing secondary vocational education courses.

□ Regular Secondary Schools (senior secondary schools and junior secondary schools)

Regular Secondary Schools (senior secondary schools and junior secondary schools) are classified as senior secondary schools and junior secondary schools. Junior Secondary Schools refer to educational establishment enrolling graduates from primary schools and providing junior secondary educational courses. Senior Secondary Schools refer to educational establishment enrolling graduates from junior secondary schools and providing higher secondary educational courses.

□ Regular Primary Schools

Regular Primary Schools refer to educational establishment set up according to approval and permission by educational administration department of district and above government, enrolling graduates from children of school age and providing primary educational courses.

□ Kindergartens

Kindergartens refer to nursery and education establishment, enrolling children in 3 years old and above.

□ Special Education Schools

Special Education Schools refer to educational establishments set up independently, enrolling blind, deaf, dumb, amentia or other special children, and educational establishment, providing regular or vocational junior and senior secondary education for hobbledehoy.

EXPLANATORY NOTES TO MAJOR STATISTICAL INDICATORS

□ Enrollment Rate of School-age Children

Enrollment Rate of School-age Children refers to the proportion of school age children enrolled at schools to the total number of school age children both in and outside schools.

□ Enrollment Rate of Students in Junior Secondary School Phase

Enrollment rate of Students in Junior Secondary School Phase refers to the proportion of students in junior secondary schools to the total number of junior school age students.

第二十一篇

CHAPTER 21

卫生、社会保障和社会福利业

HEALTH, SOCIAL SECURITY AND SOCIAL WELFARE

表21.1 卫生事业基本情况(1978～2007)
BASIC STATISTICS OF PUBLIC HEALTH

年 份 Year	卫生机构数(个) Health Care Institutions (unit)	其中 of which #医 院 Hospital	卫 生 技术人员(万人) Medical Professionals (10 000 persons)	其中 of which #医 生 Doctors	卫生机构床位数(万张) Hospital Beds (10 000 beds)	其中 of which #医 院 Hospital	每万人口医生数(人) Doctors per 10 000 Persons (person)	每万人口医院床位数(张) Hospital Beds per 10 000 Persons (bed)
1978	4 823	388	8.50	3.35	5.47	4.68	31	43
1979	5 627	394	8.88	3.58	5.56	4.78	32	42
1980	6 067	399	9.41	3.92	5.80	4.94	34	43
1981	6 337	403	9.57	4.37	5.84	4.99	38	43
1982	6 445	408	9.88	4.72	5.93	5.11	40	43
1983	6 451	415	10.09	4.87	6.00	5.20	41	44
1984	6 318	420	10.24	4.84	6.16	5.34	40	44
1985	7 245	405	10.42	4.85	6.02	5.32	40	44
1986	7 306	419	10.71	4.91	6.22	5.47	40	44
1987	7 330	431	11.00	5.05	6.38	5.60	40	45
1988	7 471	444	11.46	5.40	6.79	5.89	43	47
1989	7 550	460	11.65	5.73	6.87	6.04	45	47
1990	7 690	462	11.84	5.82	6.96	6.21	45	48
1991	7 554	463	11.92	5.89	7.01	6.31	46	49
1992	7 363	454	11.82	5.88	7.07	6.42	46	50
1993	6 077	486	11.53	5.75	7.12	6.75	44	52
1994	5 606	497	11.20	5.52	7.20	6.81	43	53
1995	5 286	485	11.06	5.37	7.10	6.69	41	52
1996	5 200	477	10.95	5.24	7.00	6.73	40	52
1997	5 028	474	10.89	5.13	7.00	6.78	34	52
1998	4 637	473	10.84	5.03	7.02	6.83	39	52
1999	4 620	465	10.81	5.06	7.24	7.06	39	54
2000	4 400	459	10.71	4.99	7.53	7.31	38	55
2001	3 813	432	10.51	4.85	7.88	7.63	37	58
2002	2 422	436	10.16	4.38	8.15	8.13	33	61
2003	2 319	452	10.22	4.41	8.44	8.11	33	60
2004	2 577	489	10.17	4.38	8.64	8.50	32	63
2005	2 527	487	10.35	4.40	9.08	8.93	32	66
2006	2 519	505	10.90	4.55	9.44	9.28	33	68
2007	2 646	288	12.24	4.88	9.59	7.54	35	55

① 本表由市卫生局提供。
② 2002 年开始，卫生指标按照新的《中国卫生统计调查制度》统计。其中，医生为执业医师和执业、助理医师；护师、护士为注册护士。
③ 2007 年开始，医院统计范围按照新的《2007 国家卫生统计调查制度》统计，不再包括社区卫生服务中心、妇幼保健院和专科防治院。
❶ Data in this table are provided by Shanghai Municipal Health Bureau.
❷ Since 2002, statistics of health care has been based on "China Health Care Statistical Investigation System". Of which, Doctors refer to certified physicians and certified assistant physicians, senior and junior nurses refer to registered nurses.
❸ Since 2007, statistics of hospital has been based on "2007 National Health Care Statistical Investigation System", not including the community health care service center, maternity and child care hospital and special disease hospital (same to next table).

表 21.2 主要年份卫生事业基本情况
BASIC STATISTICS OF PUBLIC HEALTH IN MAIN YEARS

指标	Indicators	1990	2000	2006	2007
全市	**Total**				
机构数(个)	Institutions(unit)	7 690	4 400	2 519	2 646
#医院	Hospitals	462	459	505	288
门诊部、所、卫生所、医务室、护理站	Out-patient Departments, Clinics, Infirmaries and Nursing Stations	6 947	3 769	1 895	1 993
妇幼保健所	Maternity and Child Care Centers	23	10	13	13
专科疾病防治所	Special Disease Stations	41	16	14	13
急救中心(站)	First-aid Centers		12	12	12
疾病预防控制中心	Disease Prevention and Control Centers	33	28	22	22
床位数(万张)	Hospital Beds(10 000 beds)	6.96	7.53	9.44	9.59
#医院	Hospitals	6.21	7.31	9.28	7.54
工作人员(万人)	Personnel(10 000 persons)	15.85	14.67	13.80	15.55
#卫生技术人员	Medical Professionals	11.84	10.71	10.90	12.24
#医生	Doctors	5.82	4.99	4.55	4.88
护师、护士	Senior and Junior Nurses	3.66	3.83	4.22	4.67
药剂人员	Pharmacists	0.73	0.68	0.66	0.70
检验人员	Laboratory Technicians	0.54	0.50	0.53	0.56
县及县以上医院	**Hospitals at County Level and Above**				
机构数(个)	Hospitals(unit)	206	194	277	288
床位数(万张)	Hospital Beds(10 000 beds)	5.01	5.80	7.29	7.54
工作人员(万人)	Personnel(10 000 persons)	8.25	9.50	9.88	10.51
#卫生技术人员	Medical Professionals	6.04	7.03	7.79	8.31
#医生	Doctors	2.21	2.72	2.90	3.01
平均每万人口拥有	**Owned by Every 10 000 Persons**				
床位数(张)	Hospital Beds(bed)	54	57	69	70
#医院	Hospitals	48	55	68	55
#县及县以上医院	Hospitals at County Level and Above	39	44	53	55
卫生技术人员(人)	Medical Professionals(person)	92	81	80	89
#医生	Doctors	45	38	33	35
护师、护士	Senior and Junior Nurses	29	29	31	34

注：本表数据由市卫生局提供。
Note: Date in this table are provided by Shanghai Municipal Health Bureau.

表21.3 各区、县卫生机构基本情况(2007)
STATISTICS OF HEALTH CARE INSTITUTIONS BY DISTRICTS AND COUNTIES

地 区 District		机构数(个) Health Care Institutions(unit)	床位数(张) Hospital Beds (bed)	卫生技术人员(人) Medical Professionals (person)	其中 of which	
					#医 生 Doctors	#护师、护士 Senior and Junior Nurses
总 计	**Total**	**2 646**	**95 939**	**122 413**	**48 825**	**46 699**
浦东新区	Pudong New Area	376	7 747	12 227	5 405	4 678
黄 浦 区	Huangpu	99	5 236	8 782	3 489	3 383
卢 湾 区	Luwan	82	4 147	6 747	2 452	2 875
徐 汇 区	Xuhui	212	12 376	15 713	5 605	6 609
长 宁 区	Changning	117	3 893	7 960	2 529	2 481
静 安 区	Jing'an	98	4 652	7 843	2 872	3 183
普 陀 区	Putuo	139	4 830	5 992	2 539	2 270
闸 北 区	Zhabei	91	4 788	5 049	2 162	1 917
虹 口 区	Hongkou	94	6 562	8 275	3 273	3 249
杨 浦 区	Yangpu	174	6 195	7 355	2 918	2 974
宝 山 区	Baoshan	98	4 421	5 101	2 209	1 960
闵 行 区	Minhang	241	5 713	6 087	2 578	2 181
嘉 定 区	Jiading	182	2 695	3 894	1 696	1 398
金 山 区	Jinshan	98	3 759	4 360	1 709	1 665
松 江 区	Songjiang	177	3 886	3 807	1 662	1 347
青 浦 区	Qingpu	86	1 926	2 781	1 235	1 017
南 汇 区	Nanhui	115	4 954	4 151	1 719	1 353
奉 贤 区	Fengxian	61	4 540	3 224	1 421	1 115
崇 明 县	Chongming	106	3 619	3 065	1 352	1 044

注：本表数据由市卫生局提供。
Note: Date in this table are provided by Shanghai Municipal Health Bureau.

表21.4　各类卫生机构、床位及人员数(2007)
VARIOUS HEALTH CARE INSTITUTIONS,BEDS AND PERSONNEL

机构类别	Type of Institutions	机构数(个) Health Care Institutions (unit)	床位数(张) Beds (bed)	人员数(人) Personnel (person)
总　计	**Total**	**2 646**	**95 939**	**155 523**
医疗机构合计	Medical Institutions	2 571	95 746	149 307
医　院	Hospitals	288	75 433	105 877
综合医院	Comprehensive Hospitals	176	48 433	78 214
中医医院	Hospitals of Traditional Chinese Medicine	17	4 390	7 191
中西医结合医院	Hospitals of Combination of Chinese and Western Medicine	4	1 580	2 563
专科医院	Special Diseases Hospitals	79	18 517	16 897
老年护理院	Nursing Home for Aged Persons	12	2 513	1 012
社区卫生服务中心	Community Health Care Centers	232	18 857	26 817
专科疾病防治院、所	Special Disease Hospitals and Institutions	18	150	1 348
# 专科疾病防治院	Special Disease Hospital	5	150	570
妇幼保健院、所	Maternity and Child Care Hospital and Institutions	22	1 224	2 674
# 妇幼保健院	Maternity and Child Care Hospital	9	1 174	2 110
疗养院	Sanatoriums	2	62	184
门诊部	Policlinic	306	20	4 802
诊所、卫生所、医务室	Clinic, Health Center and Infirmary	1 687		5 999
急救中心(站)	First-aid Centers	12		1 400
其他医疗机构	Other Medical Institutions	4		206
疾病预防控制中心	Disease Prevention and Control Centers	22		3 186
卫生监督所	Health Supervision Centers	20		1 254
医学科学研究机构	Institutions of Medical Science	9		485
采供血机构	Blood Collection and Supply Institutions	9		576
其他卫生机构	Other Health Care Institutions	15	193	715

注：本表数据由市卫生局提供。
Note: Date in this table are provided by Shanghai Municipal Health Bureau.

表 21.4 续表 continued

机构类别	Type of Institutions	#卫生技术人员 Medical Professionals	#医生 Doctors	#护师、护士 Senior and Junior Nurses
总计	**Total**	**122 413**	**48 825**	**46 699**
医疗机构合计	Medical Institutions	118 431	47 323	46 408
医院	Hospitals	83 500	30 075	36 716
综合医院	Comprehensive Hospitals	62 445	23 010	27 402
中医医院	Hospitals of Traditional Chinese Medicine	5 918	2 314	2 264
中西医结合医院	Hospitals of Combination of Chinese and Western Medicine	1 956	702	749
专科医院	Special Diseases Hospitals	12 490	3 859	6 013
老年护理院	Nursing Home for Aged Persons	691	190	288
社区卫生服务中心	Community Health Care Centers	21 534	10 528	6 438
专科疾病防治院、所	Special Disease Hospitals and Institutions	1 010	579	258
#专科疾病防治院	Special Disease Hospital	389	196	126
妇幼保健院、所	Maternity and Child Care Hospital and Institutions	2 212	955	928
#妇幼保健院	Maternity and Child Care Hospital	1 761	647	856
疗养院	Sanatoriums	85	31	34
门诊部	Policlinic	3 474	1 701	1 091
诊所、卫生所、医务室	Clinic, Health Center and Infirmary	5 999	3 086	907
急救中心(站)	First-aid Centers	514	351	36
其他医疗机构	Other Medical Institutions	103	17	
疾病预防控制中心	Disease Prevention and Control Centers	2 249	1 280	86
卫生监督所	Health Supervision Centers	979		
医学科学研究机构	Institutions of Medical Science	200	122	7
采供血机构	Blood Collection and Supply Institutions	371	21	129
其他卫生机构	Other Health Care Institutions	183	79	69

表 21.5　医疗机构病床使用情况(2007)
STATISTICS OF HOSPITAL BED USAGE IN MEDICAL TREATMENT INSTITUTION

机构类别	Types	平均开放床位数(张) Average Beds Opened(bed)	病床周转次数(次) Turnover Times of Beds(times)	病床使用率(%) Usage Rate of Beds(%)	出院者平均住院日(日) Average Days to Inpatient in Hospital(day)
总　计	**Total**	**98 085**	**19.85**	**95.90**	**16.52**
卫生部门	Medical Institutions	81 640	20.71	98.50	16.48
#医　院	Hospital	61 238	23.36	103.17	15.27
#综合医院	Comprehensive Hospitals	40 047	28.98	102.07	12.79
中(西)医医院	Hospitals of Chinese and Western Medicine	5 908	21.22	102.07	17.00
护理院	Nursing Hospitals	864	5.28	108.41	72.17
社区卫生服务中心(站)	Community Health Care Centers	18 579	8.45	82.62	32.04
其他部门	Other Departments	16 445	15.55	83.02	16.72

表 21.6　家庭病床情况(2007)
FAMILY SICKBEDS

机构类别	Types	开展工作机构数(个) Running Institutions (unit)	上门诊疗总次数(次) Total Times of Family Call (time)	年底实有病床数(张) Year-end Sickbeds (bed)	年内开设总病床数(张) Sickbeds Set up in 2007 (bed)
总　计	**Total**	**161**	**1 038 331**	**22 600**	**42 614**
医　院	Hospitals	27	114 294	2 042	3 205
社区卫生服务中心	Community Health-care Centers	134	924 037	20 558	39 409

注：本页数据由市卫生局提供。
Note: Date on this page are provided by Shanghai Municipal Health Bureau.

表 21.7 医疗机构诊疗人次和入院人数(2007)
PATIENTS TREATED AND INPATIENTS IN MEDICAL TREATMENT INSTITUTION

机构类别	Types	诊疗人次（万人次）Total Patients Treated (10 000 person-times)	其中 of which #门、急诊 Outpatients and Emergency Patients	入院人数（万人）Inpatients (10 000 persons)	每百诊次的入院人数（人）Inpatients per 100 Patient-times (person)
总 计	**Total**	**13 217.93**	**13 026.38**	**194.81**	**1.5**
卫生部门	Public Health Sector	12 000.83	1 1821.69	169.30	1.4
医 院	Hospitals	6 844.21	6 804.66	143.75	2.1
综合医院	Comprehensive Hospitals	5 099.50	5 069.30	116.21	2.3
中(西)医医院	Hospitals of Chinese (Western) Medicine	985.80	983.62	12.56	1.3
传染病医院	Infectious Diseases Hospitals	25.80	25.80	1.07	4.1
精神病医院	Mental Hospitals	89.87	89.54	1.08	1.2
结核病医院	Tuberculosis Hospitals	47.30	47.30	2.47	5.2
肿瘤医院	Tumor Hospitals	51.01	51.01	1.80	3.5
儿童医院	Children's Hospitals	282.17	275.33	4.30	1.5
其他专科医院	Other Specialized Hospitals	245.84	245.84	3.81	1.5
护理院	Nurse Hospitals	16.92	16.92	0.45	2.7
社区卫生服务中心	Community Health-care Service Centers	4 739.53	4 616.86	15.59	0.3
妇幼保健院	Maternity and Child Care Hospitals	287.38	273.79	9.93	3.5
其他医疗机构	Other Medical Facilities	129.72	126.40	0.02	…
工业及其他部门	Industry and Other Sectors	1 217.10	1 204.69	25.51	2.1

表 21.8 主要年份公民献血、用血情况
BASIC STATISTICS OF BLOOD DONATION AND USE IN MAIN YEARS

指 标	Indicators	1995	2000	2006	2007
无偿(义务)献血（万人份）	Volunteer or Compulsory Blood Offer (10 000 person unit)	24.03	35.19	39.95	41.38
临床用血量(万人份)	Clinic Blood Use Volum (10 000 person unit)	52.20	34.70	37.32	39.22

①2006 年起，公民献血全部为无偿献血。
②本页数据由市卫生局提供。
❶Blood offer of citizens refers to volunteer blood offer since 2006.
❷Date on this page are provided by Shanghai Municipal Health Bureau.

表 21.9　前十位疾病死亡原因和构成(2007)
THE TOP 10 DEATH-CAUSING DISEASES AND COMPOSITION

死亡原因	Cause of Death	死亡专率(1/10 万) Death Rate(1/100 000)	占死亡总数(%) Percentage of Total Death(%)
循环系病	Circulation Diseases	257.43	34.62
肿　瘤	Tumor	227.52	30.60
呼吸系病	Respiratory System Diseases	86.73	11.66
损伤和中毒	Damage and Poisoning	41.71	5.61
内分泌营养代谢病	Endocrine-Immunity-Metabolic Diseases	30.59	4.11
消化系病	Digestive System Diseases	19.37	2.60
传染病及寄生虫病	Infectious & Parasitic Diseases	11.88	1.60
精神系病	Mental System Diseases	9.25	1.24
泌尿生殖系病	Genitourinary Diseases	8.21	1.10
神经系病	Nervous System Disease	7.13	0.96

表 21.10　婴儿前五位疾病死亡原因和构成(2007)
THE TOP 5 INFANT DEATH-CAUSING DISEASES AND COMPOSITION

死亡原因	Cause of Death	死亡专率(1/10 万) Death Rate(1/100 000)	占死亡总数(%) Percentage of Total Death(%)
先天异常	Born Abnormity	389.39	67.83
新生儿病	Newborn Diseases	117.93	20.54
呼吸系病	Respiratory System Diseases	14.46	2.52
损伤中毒	Damage and Poisoning	12.24	2.13
神经系病	Nervous System Disease	11.13	1.94

注：本页数据由市卫生局提供。
Note: Date on this page are provided by Shanghai Municipal Health Bureau.

表21.11 主要年份婴儿死亡率、新生儿死亡率、孕产妇死亡率
DEATH RATE OF INFANT,NEW BORN,PREGNANT AND LYING-IN WOMAN IN MAIN YEARS

指标	Indicators	1990	2000	2006	2007
婴儿死亡率(‰)	Death Rate of Infant(‰)	10.95	5.05	4.01	3.00
新生儿死亡率(‰)	Death Rate of New Born(‰)	7.17	3.09	2.60	1.88
孕产妇死亡率(1/10万)	Death Rate of Pregnant and Lying-in Woman(1/100 000)	23.76	9.61	8.31	6.68

表21.12 主要年份防病工作情况
BASIC STATISTICS OF DISEASE PREVENTION IN MAIN YEARS

指标	Indicators	1990	2000	2006	2007
传染病发病总例数(甲、乙)(万例)	**Cases of Contagious Diseases Reported (A,B)(10 000 cases)**	**4.56**	**3.58**	**2.78**	**2.51**
发病率(1/10万)	Disease Rate(1/100 000)	356.12	271.66	204.07	182.71
传染病死亡总人数(人)	Number of Deaths Caused by Contagious Diseases(person)	95	179	97	148
死亡率(1/10万)	Death Rate(1/100 000)	0.74	1.36	0.71	1.08
结核病登记病人数(千例)	T. B. Patients Registered(1 000 cases)	7.27	3.09	2.47	2.68
登记患病率(‰)	Registered Disease Rate(‰)	0.57	0.23	0.18	0.20
结核病新发病人数(千例)	Newly Reported T. B. Cases(1 000 cases)	5.67	5.18	3.70	3.79
登记新发病率(1/万)	Registered Newly Diseased Rate(1/10 000)	4.43	3.94	2.71	2.76
结核病死亡人数(人)	Number of Deaths Caused By T. B(person)	605	293	170	172
死亡率(1/10万)	Death Rate(1/100 000)	4.73	2.22	1.25	1.25
牙病受检人数(万人)	Number of People Undergoing Tooth Disease Check(10 000 persons)		51.89	58.26	53.27
龋牙患病率(%)	Rate of Caries Patients(%)		28.3	25.9	26.5
小学生视力不良率(%)	Rate of Nearsight In Primary School(%)	16.5	26.0	31.1	31.0
初中生视力不良率(%)	Rate of Nearsight In Junior High School(%)	39.8	55.0	63.6	63.9
高中生视力不良率(%)	Rate of Nearsight In Senior High School(%)	68.4	78.5	82.1	83.6
"五苗"接种率(%)	Rate of "Five Vaccines" Recipients(%)	98.6	99.7	99.3	99.2
乙肝疫苗全程接种率(%)	Rate of Hepatitis-B Inoculation(%)		99.9	99.8	99.8

注：本页数据由市卫生局提供。
Note: Date on this page are provided by Shanghai Municipal Health Bureau.

表21.13 主要年份妇幼卫生工作情况
BASIC STATISTICS OF GYNAECOLOGY AND PAEDIATRICS IN MAIN YEARS

指标	Indicators	1990	2000	2006	2007
妇女病普查人数(万人)	**Number of People Surveyed for Female Diseases(10 000 persons)**	**49.90**	**40.27**	**56.17**	**65.94**
患病率(%)	Rate of Sufferers(%)	42.9	35.0	25.0	28.4
治疗率(%)	Rate of Patients Treated(%)	80.1	91.1	96.5	97.2
胎儿娩出顺产数(万人)	Number of Smooth Delivery(10 000 persons)	8.04	4.05	7.16	8.57
顺产率(%)	Rate of Smooth Delivery(%)	59.4	47.5	49.2	47.2
出生低体重儿(人)	Number of Low-weight Newborns(person)		2 567	5 083	6 117
占活产总数(%)	Proportion in All Deliveries(%)		3.0	3.5	3.4
出生缺陷人数(人)	Number of Newborns With Innate Problems(person)		764	1 370	1 653
出生缺陷率(‰)	Rate of Disabled Among All Deliveries(‰)		8.96	9.40	9.10
0~6岁儿童保健管理率(%)	Rate of Children, 0~6 Years Old Under Health Programm(%)	78.3	94.3	95.8	96.2
0~6岁儿童眼保健率(%)	Rate of 0~6 Year-olds Under Eye-Health Program(%)		81.8	95.1	94.1
0~6岁儿童听力保健率(%)	Rate of 0~6 Year-olds Under Ear-Health Program(%)		83.7	91.3	94.9
0~6岁儿童口腔保健率(%)	Rate of 0~6 Year-olds Under Mouth-Health Program(%)		88.6	97.3	95.8
0~6岁儿童贫血患病率(%)	Rate of 0~6 Year-olds Suffering from Anemia(%)		6.0	4.2	3.7
婚前检查人数(万人)	Number of People Undergoing Pre-marriage Checkup(10 000 persons)	19.69	17.36	6.85	4.58
婚检率(%)	Rate of Pre-marriage Checkup Recipients(%)	97.4	98.4	22.4	20.7

注：本表数据由市卫生局提供。
Note: Date in this table are provided by Shanghai Municipal Health Bureau.

表21.14　主要年份社会保险参保人数
NUMBER OF PARTICIPANTS IN SOCIAL INSURANCE IN MAIN YEARS

单位:万人(10 000 persons)

指　标	Indicators	2000	2006	2007
城镇基本养老保险	**Urban Basic Pension Insurance**			
城镇职工	Urban Staff and Workers	431.27	460.75	467.45
个体工商户和自由职业人员	Individual Businessman	9.82	16.97	16.38
领取养老金的离退休人员	Retired Veteran Cadres and Retired Staff and Workers with Pensions	234.23	294.69	309.99
城镇基本医疗保险	**Urban Basic Medicare Insurance**			
城镇职工	Urban Staff and Workers	364.59	436.63	440.45
个体工商户和自由职业人员	Individual Businessman and Professionals		16.97	16.38
享受医保的离退休人员	Retired Veteran Cadres and Retired Staff and Workers with Medicare	202.14	294.04	309.30
城镇职工失业保险	**Unemployment Insurance of Urban Staff and Workers**	**434.86**	**476.41**	**491.54**
城镇职工生育保险	**Generational Insurance of Urban Staff and Workers**		**555.09**	**591.96**
城镇职工工伤保险	**Injured Insurance of Urban Staff and Workers**		**538.96**	**550.75**
农村社会养老保险	Rural Social Pension Insurance	121.00	83.71	74.16
小城镇社会保险	Town Social Insurance		139.80	138.61
#被征用土地农民参保人数	Land Expropriated Peasant Participated		94.71	92.72
来沪从业人员综合保险	General Insurance of Employment of Migratory Population		279.00	333.60
高龄无保障老人保险	Insurence of Old Ages Without Living Securing		6.28	6.13
普通高等院校学生基本医疗保险	Basic Medicare Insurance of Ordinary High Education Institutions Student			56.57
中小学生和婴幼儿住院门诊大病基本医疗保险	Basic Medicare Insurance of Serious Disease in Hospital or Clinic for Junior and Primary School Student and Infant		180.00	167.00
农村合作医疗	Cooperartion Medicare Insurance in Country		190.56	186.81
少儿住院基金	Medicare Fund of Children	212.47	180.13	181.29

注：本表数据由市劳动和社会保障局、市医疗保险局、市红十字会提供。
Note: Data in this table are provided by Shanghai Municipal Labour and Social Security Bureau, Shanghai Municipal Medicare and Insurance Bureau and Red Cross Society of China Shanghai Municipal Branch.

表21.15　主要年份社会保障标准
SOCIAL SECURITY STANDARD IN MAIN YEARS

单位:元(yuan)

指　标	Indicators	2000	2006	2007
职工工资最低标准	Minimum Standard of Wages of Staff and Workers	445	750	840
城镇基本养老金最低标准	Minimum Standard of Urban Basic Pension Insurance	460	460	460
城镇居民生活保障最低标准	Minimum Standard of Urban Living Security	280	320	350

注：本表数据由市劳动和社会保障局、市民政局提供。
Note: Data in this table are provided by Shanghai Municipal Labour and Social Security Bureau and Shanghai Civil Affairs Bureau.

表21.16 优抚、救济对象享受国家定期抚恤补助、救济情况(1980～2007)
PERSONS ENJOYING REGULAR SUBSIDIES AND COMMISERATION FROM THE STATE

单位:万人 (10 000 persons)

年 份 Year	合 计 Total	伤残抚恤 Pension for the Disabled	烈军属抚恤 Pension for Families of Martyr	复退军人定期补助 Subsidies for Ex-servicemen	享受国家定期救济人数 Number of People Receiving Regular Relief from the State	其中 of which			
						#社会困难户定期救助 Subsidies for Impoverished Residents	#精减退职老职工救济 Almsgiving for Retirees and Laid-off Workers	#城镇最低生活保障人数 People Under Urban Basic Provision Protection	#农村最低生活保障人数 People Under Rural Basic Provision Protection
1980	1.44	0.69			0.75	0.38	0.37		
1981	1.60	0.70			0.90	0.46	0.44		
1982	1.98	0.74	0.24	0.22	0.78	0.42	0.36		
1983	1.99	0.76	0.26	0.24	0.73	0.40	0.33		
1984	2.05	0.78	0.29	0.27	0.70	0.39	0.32		
1985	2.11	0.78	0.23	0.37	0.73	0.43	0.30		
1986	2.60	0.80	0.26	0.49	1.05	0.76	0.29		
1987	2.50	0.82	0.25	0.59	0.84	0.55	0.29		
1988	2.50	0.82	0.24	0.62	0.82	0.54	0.28		
1989	2.76	0.84	0.23	0.65	1.04	0.76	0.28		
1990	2.81	0.86	0.22	0.68	1.05	0.77	0.28		
1991	2.72	0.83	0.21	0.71	0.97	0.70	0.27		
1992	3.10	0.83	0.20	0.71	1.36	1.10	0.26		
1993	3.10	0.83	0.19	0.70	1.38	1.13	0.25		
1994	3.12	0.83	0.18	0.70	1.41	1.17	0.24		
1995	3.11	0.82	0.17	0.69	1.43	1.19	0.24		
1996	3.20	0.81	0.17	0.68	1.54	1.31	0.23		
1997	2.68	0.80	0.15	0.69	1.04	0.84	0.20		
1998	3.22	0.79	0.15	0.66	1.62	0.38		1.24	
1999	6.87	0.77	0.12	0.65	5.33	0.74	0.19	4.40	1.66
2000	22.26	0.76	0.12	0.66	20.72	0.94	0.18	19.60	2.26
2001	39.46	0.75	0.11	0.63	37.97	0.76	0.17	33.85	3.19
2002	51.47	0.74	0.11	0.59	50.03		0.17	43.16	6.71
2003	56.50	0.73	0.11	0.59	55.07			44.60	10.47
2004	50.87	0.72	0.12	0.57	49.46			40.36	9.10
2005	49.23	0.71	0.36	0.52	47.64			36.74	10.90
2006	49.58	0.71	0.73	0.47	47.67			35.14	12.53
2007	47.68	0.71	0.74	0.46	45.77			33.94	11.83

注：本表数据由市民政局提供。
Note: Date in this table are provided by Shanghai Civil Affairs Bureau.

表21.17 社会福利院、儿童福利院、社会福利医院和收养性老年福利机构情况(1980～2007)
INSTITUTIONS OF SOCIAL WELFARE, CHILDREN WELFARE,SOCIAL WELFARE HOSPITALS AND ADOPTIVE SENIORS WELFARE INSTITUTIONS

年 份 Year	社会福利院 Social Welfare Institutions			儿童福利院 Children Welfare Homes		
	单 位 (个) Units (unit)	床位数 (张) Beds (bed)	年末在院人数 (人) Year-end Papulation Housed(person)	单 位 (个) Units (unit)	床位数 (张) Beds (bed)	年末在院人数 (人) Year-end Papulation Housed(person)
1980	9	1 555	1 337	2	600	559
1981	9	1 621	1 313	2	650	634
1982	9	1 525	1 495	2	650	672
1983	9	1 644	1 491	2	600	676
1984	10	1 948	1 635	2	600	633
1985	10	1 727	1 630	2	580	625
1986	10	1 697	1 648	2	550	612
1987	10	1 991	1 770	2	378	449
1988	13	2 189	1 790	2	387	458
1989	14	2 418	2 012	2	538	481
1990	15	2 679	2 019	2	589	586
1991	14	2 687	2 138	2	611	592
1992	14	2 776	2 431	2	665	651
1993	14	2 874	2 554	2	708	690
1994	15	2 931	2 648	2	878	862
1995	15	3 006	2 722	2	988	919
1996	17	3 294	2 866	2	988	943
1997	21	4 012	3 441	2	988	946
1998	24	4 596	3 678	2	1 004	984
1999	20	4 215	3 498	2	981	958
2000	23	4 884	4 137	2	1 100	1 092
2001	26	5 570	4 410	2	1 221	1 221
2002	27	5 590	4 760	3	1 491	1 429
2003	26	5 818	4 779	2	1 087	1 512
2004	26	5 876	4 848	6	1 300	1 893
2005	23	5 999	4 809	6	2 016	1 986
2006	25	6 583	5 024	6	1 252	2 142
2007	24	6 499	5 068	6	1 252	2 341

注：本表数据由市民政局提供。
Note：Date in this table are provided by Shanghai Civil Affairs Bureau.

表 21.17 续表 continued

年　份 Year	社会福利医院 Social Welfare hospitals			收养性老年福利机构 Adoptive Seniors Welfare Institutions			
	单　位 （个） Units (unit)	床位数 （张） Beds (bed)	年末在院人数 （人） Year-end Papulation Housed(person)	机　构 （个） Institutions (unit)	床位数 （张） Beds (bed)	年末在院人数 （人） Year-end Papulation Housed(person)	其　中 of which #老　人 Elder
1980	3	1 475	1 424	42		630	
1981	3	1 460	1 430	53		762	
1982	3	1 490	1 422	58		1 022	
1983	3	1 490	1 432	90		1 402	
1984	3	1 460	1 380	135		2 328	
1985	3	1 480	1 360	199	3 870	3 038	2 786
1986	3	1 510	1 354	249	4 655	3 446	3 100
1987	3	1 497	1 342	277	5 520	4 262	3 893
1988	3	1 497	1 313	322	5 969	4 754	4 429
1989	3	1 433	1 324	349	6 281	5 129	4 835
1990	3	1 497	1 298	332	6 275	5 031	4 452
1991	3	1 391	1 285	341	6 731	5 763	5 642
1992	3	1 510	1 404	351	7 002	6 035	5 655
1993	3	1 510	1 394	331	7 143	6 365	5 934
1994	3	1 510	1 392	333	7 533	6 838	6 541
1995	3	1 510	1 409	330	8 576	7 405	6 633
1996	3	1 510	1 429	333	10 270	8 361	7 867
1997	3	1 500	1 452	323	11 253	9 295	8 647
1998	3	1 500	1 455	339	13 958	11 122	10 826
1999	3	1 710	1 703	331	16 526	12 698	12 013
2000	3	1 840	1 779	398	22 244	16 988	16 541
2001	3	1 894	1 894	378	23 627	17 363	16 923
2002	3	1 917	1 901	417	33 413	20 900	20 309
2003	3	1 680	1 881	422	36 791	23 451	22 682
2004	3	1 780	1 829	414	33 891	26 993	25 902
2005	3	1 811	1 811	450	43 131	31 301	30 181
2006	3	1 860	1 796	479	52 427	35 946	34 447
2007	3	1 852	1 806	536	64 115	42 665	40 731

表 21.18 主要年份社会福利事业机构数和职工人数
QUANTITY OF SOCIAL WELFARE INSTITUTIONS AND STAFF AND WORKERS IN MAIN YEARS

	指 标 Indicators	2000	2006	2007
机构数(个)	**Total Institutions(unit)**			
收养性福利单位	Adopting Social Welfare Institutions	427	515	570
优抚类	Subsidy	1	1	1
福利类	Welfare	426	514	569
社会福利企业	Social Welfare Enterprises	3 352	2 036	1 849
优抚安置单位	Subsidy and Arrangement Institution	45	42	41
救助类单位	Salvation Institution	16	22	22
婚姻登记服务单位	Marriage Rigister Service Institutions		10	12
殡仪服务单位	Funeral and Interment Service Institution	68	76	78
福利彩票发行单位	Issue Institution of Welfare Lottery	16	18	18
社区服务单位	Community Service Institutions	92	122	132
职工人数(人)	**Staff and Workers(person)**			
收养性福利单位	Adopting Social Welfare Institutions	7 793	13 738	15 248
优抚类	Subsidy	35	46	45
福利类	Welfare	7 758	13 692	15 203
社会福利企业	Social Welfare Enterprises	177 260	103 314	108 815
优抚安置单位	Subsidy and Anargment Institution	745	737	726
救助类单位	Salvation Institution	472	455	469
婚姻登记服务单位	Marriage Rigister Service Institutions		54	85
殡仪服务单位	Funeral and Interment Service Institution	2 577	2 999	3 350
福利彩票发行单位	Issue Institution of Welfare Lottery	86	77	72
社区服务单位	Community Service Institutions	1 014	1 696	2 008

表 21.19 民间组织和慈善团体情况(2005~2007)
STATISTICS OF CIVIL ORGANIZATIONS AND CHARITY

	指 标 Indicators	2005	2006	2007
民间组织数(个)	**Quantity of Civil Organization(unit)**	**7 556**	**7 975**	**8 396**
社会团体	Social Organizations	2 952	3 075	3 220
民办非企业	Civil Non-Enterprises	4 537	4 825	5 092
基金会	Foundations	67	75	84
慈善团体(个)	**Charity(unit)**	**14**	**14**	**14**

注：本页数据由市民政局提供。
Note: Date on this page are provided by Shanghai Civil Affairs Bureau.

表 21.20 收养类机构基本情况(2007)
BASIC FACTS ABOUT THE ADOPTIVE WELFARE INSTITUTIONS

福利机构名称	Name of Welfare Institutions	机构数(个) Institutions (unit)	年末职工人数(人) Staff and Workers (person)	床位数(张) Beds (bed)	年末在院人数(人) Year-end Papulation Housed(person)	其中 of which #老年人 Elder
总 计	**Total**	**570**	**15 248**	**73 768**	**51 897**	**45 452**
政府办	**By Governments**					
社会福利院	Social Welfare Homes	24	2 005	6 499	5 068	4 246
市 级	Prefectural Level	4	710	1 626	1 450	773
浦东新区	Pudong New Area	1	88	200	200	200
黄浦区	Huangpu	2	158	370	367	342
徐汇区	Xuhui	2	220	492	425	415
长宁区	Changning	2	87	244	116	116
普陀区	Putuo	1	93	234	234	230
闸北区	Zhabei	1	26	317	252	246
虹口区	Hongkou	2	163	420	380	380
杨浦区	Yangpu	1	109	330	306	306
宝山区	Baoshan	1	50	200	136	38
闵行区	Minhang	2	68	690	583	583
松江区	Songjiang	1	97	300	250	250
青浦区	Qingpu	3	78	874	214	212
奉贤区	Fengxian	1	58	202	155	155
儿童福利院	Children's Welfare Homes	6	646	1 252	2 341	
市儿童福利院	Shanghai Children's Welfare Home	1	426	1 000	2 118	
徐汇区儿童福利院	Capibility Rehabilitation Institution of Xuhui	3	105	102	92	
虹口区儿童福利院	Capibility Rehabilitation Institution of Hongkou	2	115	150	131	
社会福利医院	Social Welfare Hospitals Homes	3	617	1 852	1 806	458
荣誉军人康复院	Convalescent Homes for Honored Ex-servicemen	1	45	50	17	17
社会办	**By Social**					
城镇老年福利机构	Urban Senile Welfare Homes	284	6 849	29 912	20 829	20 587
农村老年福利机构	Rural Senile Welfare Homes	252	5 086	34 203	21 836	20 144

注：本表数据由市民政局提供。
Note: Date in this table are provided by Shanghai Civil Affairs Bureau.

表21.21 养老服务(2005～2007)
ENDOWMENT SERVICE

指标	Indicators	2005	2006	2007
一、机构养老服务	Endowment Service of Institutions			
机构数(家)	Quantity of Institutions(unit)	474	505	560
床位数(张)	Quantity of Beds(bed)	49 529	59 735	69 785
#新增养老床位	Newly Added Endowmet Beds	10 094	10 206	10 050
养老床位占60周岁及以上老年人口比例(%)	Ratio of Endowment Bed in Population above 60(%)	1.9	2.2	2.5
二、居家养老服务	Household Endowment Service			
社区老年人日间服务机构机构数(家)	Community Service Institutions for Aged People Daytime Quantity of Institutions(unit)	83	108	128
日托老年人数数(人)	Population of Daytime Service Aged People(person)	2 108	3 500	3 302
社区助老服务社(个)	Community Service Center for Assisting Aged People(unit)	233	233	234
社区居家养老服务月服务人数(人)	Monthly Population of Community Household Endowment Service(person)	54 776	105 000	135 000
获得政府补贴的老年人(人)	Population of Aged People Gained Governmental Subsidy(person)	39 355	59 600	68 413

注：本表数据由市民政局提供。
Note: Date in this table are provided by Shanghai Civil Affairs Bureau.

表21.22 老年医疗服务(2005～2007)
MEDICARE SERVICE FOR AGED PEOPLE

指标	Indicators	2005	2006	2007
一、老年护理院	Nursing Home for Aged People			
独立老年护理院	Independent Nursing Home for Aged People			
机构数(所)	Quantity of Institutions(unit)	13	13	12
建筑面积(平方米)	Structure Area(sq·m)	59 742	57 758	81 863
床位数(张)	Beds(bed)	2 353	2 499	2 513
住院人次(人次)	Person-time in Hospital(person-time)	4 346	4 663	6 533
非独立老年护理院(机构数)(所)	Dependent Nursing Home for Aged People(unit)	56	56	56
二、老年医院	Hospital for Aged People			
机构数(所)	Quantity of Institutions(unit)	3	3	4
住院人次(人次)	Person-time in Hospital(person-time)	9 124	8 698	10 255
三、家庭病床总数(张)	Total Quantity of bed in home(bed)	40 745	41 026	42 614

注：本表数据由市卫生局提供。
Note: Date in this table are provided by Shanghai Municipal Health Bureau.

表21.23　红十字会基本情况(2005～2007)
BASIC STATISICS ON RED CROSS SOCIETY OF CHINA SHANGHAI MUNICIPAL BRANCH

指　标	Indicators	2005	2006	2007
红十字会组织机构	**Institutions**			
红十字会各级组织机构(个)	Organizing Instituntions(unit)	2 934	3 341	3 419
红十字会医疗机构(个)	Medical Institutions(unit)	67	70	70
志愿工作管理机构(个)	Administrative Institutions on Voluntary Work(unit)	20	20	20
红十字会会员人数(万人)	**Number of Member(10 000 persons)**	**61.62**	**54.61**	**70.50**
#青少年会员(万人)	Hobbledehoy Member(10 000 persons)	37.16	37.3	46.16
团体会员单位(个)	Team Member(unit)	970	3 485	1 062
社区服务工作	**Community Service**			
社区公益服务站点(个)	Community Commonweal Service Station(unit)	1 589	2 293	3 698
社区志愿者人数(万人)	Number of Volunteer(10 000 persons)	1.75	2.56	2.23
组织各种宣传活动	**Times of Publicizing Activity(time)**			
在报刊登载宣传文章(篇)	Articles on Newspaper and Periodical(piece)	831	647	507
电视台播报宣传节目(条/次)	Programs on Television(piece/time)	459	313	261
参加艾滋病预防宣传救助活动人次数(万人次)	Person-time Attended AIDS Prevention Activities (10 000 person-times)	9.86	6.56	14.69
参加普及宣传无偿献血活动人次数(万人次)	Person-time Attended Publicizing Volunteer Blood Donation Activiies(10 000 person-times)		4.45	23.22
卫生救护工作	**Sanitation Rescue**			
救护普及培训(万人次)	Rescue Popularization Training(10 000 person-times)	24.72	29.76	38.57
救护师资培训(人次)	Rescue Teachers Training(person-time)	304	1 534	194
造血干细胞捐献工作	**Contributing Trunk Cell**			
当年参加造血干细胞捐献库人数(万人)	Number of Subscribers(10 000 persons)	5.60	6.41	7.63
配型相合人数(人)	Matching(person)	316	70	606
累计移植人数(人)	Transplanting(person)	68	87	114
遗体捐献工作	**Contributing Reliquiae**			
遗体捐献登记站(个)	Register Center(unit)	27	27	27
遗体捐献接收站(个)	Accepting Center(unit)	8	8	8
全年接受捐献遗体登记(人)	Number of Contributing Reliquiae(Person)	1 284	1 492	1 613
全年接受角膜捐献登记(人)	Number of Contributing Cornea(Person)	133	146	168
社会赈济和社区救助工作	**Working on Social Relieving**			
社会赈济救济投入(万元)	Social Relieve Devotion(10 000 yuan)	10 635.36	5 877.42	4 145.06
受益人数(万人)	Number of Beneficiaries(10 000 persons)	3.04	3.03	3.62
社区救助款物投入(万元)	Community Salvation Devotion(10 000 yuan)	1 538.12	3 010.10	3 052.81
受益人数(万人)	Number of Beneficiaries(10 000 persons)	2.87	4.29	3.63

注：本表数据由市红十字会提供。
Note: Data in this table are provided by Red Cross Society of China Shanghai Municipal Branch.

上 / 海 / 统 / 计 / 年 / 鉴

主要统计指标解释

■ 卫生机构

是指从卫生行政部门取得《医疗机构执业许可证》，或从民政、工商行政、机构编制管理部门取得法人单位登记证书，为社会提供医疗保健、疾病控制、卫生监督服务或从事医学研究、医学教育等卫生单位和卫生社会团体。

■ 医疗机构

是指根据《医疗机构管理条例》的规定，经登记取得《医疗机构执业许可证》的机构。包括医院、社区卫生服务中心(站)、卫生院、门诊部、诊疗所、医务室、村卫生室、妇幼保健院(所、站)、专科疾病防治院(所、站)、急救中心、临床检验中心。

■ 医　院

指设有固定床位，能收容病人住院并能为病人提供医疗、护理服务的医疗机构，包括县及县以上医院、农村乡卫生院和其他医院三部分。县及县以上医院按业务性质不同分为综合医院和专科医院。

■ 卫生技术人员

指从事卫生技术工作并在卫生事业机构领取劳动报酬的专业人员。包括中医师、西医师、中西医结合高级医师、护师、中药师、西药师、检验师、其他技师、中医士、西医士、护士、助产士、中药剂士、西药剂士、检验士、其他技士、其他中医、护理员、中药剂员、西药剂员、检验员、其他初级卫生技术人员。

■ 医　生

指在医疗、预防保健机构工作且取得《执业医师证书》的执业医师和执业助理医师。

■ 优抚对象

优抚指政府对革命烈士家庭、病故残疾工作人员以及参战负伤致残的民兵、民工的抚恤和人民群众对其的优待。优抚对象包括革命烈士家属、因公牺牲和病故军人家属、革命伤残人员、现役军属、退伍红军老战士、红军失散人员、复员军人、退伍军人、在职退役军人、在乡退役军人、带病回乡退伍军人、复退军人精神病员、孤老优抚对象等。

■ 社会福利事业单位

指集中收养社会孤老、残、幼的机构。包括由民政部门管理的社会福利院、儿童福利院、精神病人福利院和城镇集体办的福利院，以及农村集体办的敬老院。

■ 基本养老保险

1.(参保)职工人数：指报告期末按照国家法律、法规和有关政策规定参加基本养老保险并在社保经办机构已建立缴费记录档案的职工人数，包括中断缴费但未终止养老保险关系的职工人数，不包括只登记未建立缴费记录档案的人数。

2.(参保)离退休人员人数：指报告期末参加基本养老保险的离休、退休和退职人员的人数。

3. 基本养老保险基金收入：指根据国家有关规定，由纳入基本养老保险范围的缴费单位和个人按国家规定的缴费基数和缴费比例缴纳的养老保险基金，以及通过其他方式取得的形成基金来源的收入。包括单位和职工个人缴纳的基本养老保险费、基本养老保险基金利息收入、上级补助收入、下级上解收入、转移收入、财政补贴和其他收入。

4. 基本养老保险基金支出：指按照国家政策规定的开支范围和开支标准从养老保险基金中支付给参加基本养老保险的离休、退休、退职人员个人的养老金、丧葬抚恤补助，以及由于保险关系转移、上下级之间调剂资金等原因而发生的支出。包括离休金、退休金、退职金、各种补贴、医疗费、死亡丧葬补助费、抚恤救济费、社会保险经办机构管理费、补助下级支出、上解上级支出、转移支出、其他支出等。

5. 基本养老保险基金累计结余：指截止报告期末基本养老保险基金收支相抵后的累计余额。

■ 基本医疗保险

1. 参保人数：指报告期末按国家有关规定参加基本医疗保险的人数。包括参加保险的职工人数和退休人员人数。

2. 基金收入：指根据国家有关规定，由纳入基本医疗保险范围的缴费单位和个人，按国家规定的缴费基数和缴费比例缴纳的基金，以及通过其他方式取得的形成基金来源的款项，包括：单位缴纳的社会统筹基金收入、个

主要统计指标解释

人缴纳的个人账户基金收入、财政补贴收入、利息收入、其他收入。

3. 基金支出：指按照国家政策规定的开支范围和开支标准从社会统筹基金中支付给参加基本医疗保险的职工和退休人员的医疗保险待遇支出，和从个人帐户基金中支付给参加基本医疗保险的职工和退休人员的医疗费用支出，以及其他支出。包括：住院医疗费用支出、门急诊医疗费用支出、个人账户基金支出、其他支出。

4. 基金累计结余：指截止报告期末基本医疗保险的社会统筹和个人帐户基金累计结余金额。包括银行存款、财政专户、债券投资和其他。

失业保险

1. 参保人数：指报告期末按照国家法律、法规和有关政策规定参加了失业保险的城镇企业事业单位的职工及地方政府规定参加失业保险的其他人员的人数。

2. 失业保险基金收入：指按照规定从企业、事业及其他单位筹集的失业保险费及其他并入失业保险基金收入的总额。包括单位和个人缴纳的失业保险费、失业保险基金利息收入、上级补助收入、下级上解收入、转移收入、财政补贴和其他收入。

3. 失业保险基金支出：指报告期内为保障失业人员和下岗职工基本生活、促进其再就业等支出的基金总额。包括失业救济金、医疗费、死亡丧葬补助费、抚恤救济费、转业训练费支出、失业保险经办机构管理费、补助下级支出、上解上级支出、转移支出和其他支出。

4. 基金累计结余：指截止报告期末失业保险基金收支相抵后的累计余额。

工伤保险

1. 参加保险人数：指报告期末依据国家有关规定参加工伤保险的职工人数。

2. 享受保险待遇人数：指劳动者因工负伤致残、死亡或因患职业病致残，根据有关规定享受工伤保险待遇职工或供养直系亲属人数。包括伤残人数、职业病人数、因工死亡人数、供养直系亲属人数。

3. 基金收入：指根据国家有关规定，由参加工伤保险的单位按国家规定的缴费基数和缴费比例缴纳的工伤保险基金，以及通过其他形式取得的形成基金来源的款项。包括：单位缴纳的社会统筹基金收入、财政补贴收入、利息收入、其他收入。

4. 基金支出：指按照国家政策规定的开支范围和开支标准从工伤保险基金中支付给参加工伤保险的人员及供养直系亲属工伤保险待遇支出及其他支出。包括工伤医疗费、伤残补助金、工亡补助金、护理费、丧葬补助费、工伤预防费用、职业康复费用和其他支出。

5.基金累计结余：指截止报告期末工伤保险基金累计结余金额。包括银行存款、财政专户、债券投资和其他。

生育保险

1. 参保人数：指报告期末依据有关规定参加生育保险的职工人数。

2. 基金收入：指根据国家有关规定，由参加生育保险的单位按照国家规定的缴费基数和缴费比例缴纳的生育保险基金，以及通过其他方式取得的形成基金来源的款项，包括：单位缴纳的基金收入、利息收入和其他收入。

3. 基金支出：指按照国家政策规定的开支范围和开支标准，从生育保险基金中支付给参加生育保险的职工，因妊娠、分娩和计划生育手术而享受的待遇及其他支出。包括：生育津贴、医疗费用支出及其他支出。

4. 基金累计结余：指截止报告期末生育保险基金累计结余金额。包括银行存款、财政专户、债券投资和其他。

SHANGHAI STATISTICAL YEARBOOK

EXPLANATORY NOTES TO MAJOR STATISTICAL INDICATORS

□ Health Care Institutions

Health Care Institution refers to medical institutions and corporations providing health care, disease control and medical supervision service or engaged in medical research and medical education, which obtain Medical Institution Practice License from Medical Administration or Corporative Registration Certificate from Civil Administration, Commercial Administration or Organizational Management Administration.

□ Medical Organizations

Medical Institution refers to institutions which register Medical Institution Practice License according to Medical Institution Management Regulation, including hospitals, community medical service centers, medical house, clinics, dispensaries, medicine rooms, village medicine rooms, hospitals for maternity and kids care, special disease cure hospitals, first-aid center, clinical inspection centers.

□ Hospitals

Hospitals refer to medical institutions with permanent hospital beds, which are able to take in patients and provide them with medical and nursing services. Hospitals are classified into three categories: hospitals at or above the county level, hospitals of rural townships, and other hospitals. Hospitals at or above county level are divided into comprehensive and specialized hospitals.

□ Medical Professionals

Medical Professionals refers to those professionals engaged in medical work and receive salaries from medical institutions, including doctors of Chinese and Western medicine, senior doctors of integrated Chinese-Western medicine, head nurses, pharmacists of Chinese and Western medicine, laboratory specialists , other specialists, junior doctors of Chinese and Western medicine, nurses, midwives, druggists of Chinese and Western medicine, laboratory technicians, other technicians, other practitioners of Chinese medicine, nursing attendants, pharmacological workers of Chinese and Western medicine, laboratory workers and other primary medical personnel.

□ Doctors

Doctors refer to certified physicians and certified assistant physicians with certifications working in medical and health care and prevention agencies.

□ Special Care

Special Care is offered by the government to the family member of the martyrs, disabled or demobilized servicemen or laborers who were injured on duty. Entitled to the special care are family members of the revolutionary martyrs, family members of servicemen who dies on duty or died of an illness, disabled servicemen, family members of servicemen on active service, retired veteran Red Army soldiers, scattered Red Army soldiers, demobilized servicemen, ex-servicemen, servicemen who were demobilized while on duty, ex-servicemen back to their rural homes, ex-servicemen who were demobilized because of an illness and have gone back to their rural homes, ex-servicemen who suffer from mental illness and elderly persons with no family.

□ Social Welfare Institutions

Social Welfare Institutions refer to institutions taking care of old people without children, handicapped people and orphans. They include social welfare institutions run by civil affairs departments, children's welfare institutions, welfare institutions for mental patients, and collectively-run old people's homes in rural areas.

□ Basic Pension Insurance

1. Number of staff and workers covered refer to staff and workers participating in basic pension insurance programme in line with national laws, regulations and related policies by the end of reference period, who have already had payment records in social security management agencies, including those who interrupt payment without terminating the insurance programme. Those who have registered in the programme with no payment records are not included.

2. Number of retirees participating in basic pension insurance programme refer to number of retirees participating in basic pension insurance programme by the end of reference period.

3. Revenue of basic pension insurance refer to payments

EXPLANATORY NOTES TO MAJOR STATISTICAL INDICATORS

made by employers and individuals participating in pension insurance programs in accordance with the basis and proportion stipulated in state regulations, and income from other sources that become source of pension insurance fund, including the premium paid by employers and staff and works, interest income, subsidies from higher level agencies, income as transfer from subordinate agencies, transferred income, government financial subsidies and other income.

4. Expenses of basic pension insurance refer to payment made to those retired and resigned people covered in pension insurance program in terms of pension or compensation within the scope and standards of expenditure according to related national policies, and expenditure occurred due to shift of the insurance relationship or adjustment of funds among agencies, including pension for resigned people, pension for retired people, pension for people quitting jobs, various subsidies, medical fees, funeral subsidies, compensation pension, management fees for social security agencies, expenses on subsidies to lower subordinates, expenses as transfer to agencies at higher level, transferred expenditure and other expenditure.

5. Balance of basic pension insurance refers to the balance of basic pension insurance at the end of the reference period after deducting expenses from revenue

□ Basic Medical Care Insurance

1. Number of people participating in the insurance programme refers to people participating in the basic medical care insurance programme according to related regulations by the end of reference period, including number of staff and workers and retirees participating in this insurance programme.

2. Revenue of insurance programme refer to payments made by employers and individuals participating in medical care insurance programs in accordance with the basis and proportion stipulated in state regulations, and income from other sources that become source of medical insurance fund, including income of social comprehensive funds paid by employers, income from individual accounts, government financial subsidies, interest income and other income.

3. Expenses of insurance programme refer to payment made from social comprehensive funds to those retired and resigned people covered in basic medical care insurance within the scope and standards of expenditure according to related national policies, and medical care payment made from individual accounts to staff and workers and retirees, and other expenses, including medical expenses of hospital inpatients, medical expenses for outpatients and emergency patients, payment from individual accounts and other expenditure.

4. Balance of basic medical care insurance refer to the balance of medical care insurance of social comprehensive funds and individual accounts at the end of the reference period, including bank savings, special fiscal accounts, investment in bonds and others.

□ Unemployment Insurance

1. Number of people covered refers to staff and workers in urban enterprises or institutions who have participated in unemployment insurance programme in line relevant policies and regulations, and other people who have participated according to local government regulations, by the end of reference period.

2. Revenue of unemployment insurance refer to payments made by employers and individuals participating in unemployment insurance programme in accordance with relevant regulations and other income contributed to this programme, including unemployment insurance premium made by employers and individuals, interest income, subsidies from higher level agencies, income as transfer from subordinate agencies, transferred income, government financial subsidies and other income.

3. Expenses of unemployment insurance refer to total expenses during the reference period to guarantee the basic livelihood of unemployed people and laid-off staff and workers and to encourage their re-employment. Included are unemployment relief, medical fees, funeral subsidies, compensation pension, training expenses, management fees for unemployment insurance agencies, subsidies to lower level agencies, expenses as transfer to higher level agencies, transferred expenditure and other expenditure.

4. Balance of unemployment insurance refer to the balance of unemployment revenue deducting unemployment expenses at the end of the reference period.

□ Work Injury Insurance

1. Number of people covered refers to staff and workers who have participated in work injury insurance programme in line with relevant national regulations.

2. Number of beneficiaries refers to staff and workers and their direct dependents who can, in line with relevant regulations, benefit from work injury insurance, as a result of work injury leading to disability or death of the staff/worker, or occupational

EXPLANATORY NOTES TO MAJOR STATISTICAL INDICATORS

disease leading to disability. Included in this category are number of injured and disabled people, number of people with occupational diseases, number of deaths at work places, and number of direct dependents.

3. Revenue of work injury insurance refer to payments made by employers participating in work injury insurance programs in accordance with the basis and proportion stipulated in state regulations, and income from other sources that become source of work injury insurance fund, including income of social comprehensive funds paid by employers, government financial subsidies, interest income and other income.

4. Expenses of work injury insurance refer to payments made from work injury insurance funds to those who participated in the work injury insurance programme and their direct dependents within the scope and standards of expenditure according to related national policies, and other expenditure, including medical fees for work injury, injury and disability subsidies, death subsidies, nursing fees, funeral subsidies, injury prevention fees, rehabilitation fees for occupational diseases and other expenditure.

5.Balance of work injury insurance refer to the balance of the work injury funds at the end of the reference period, including bank savings, special fiscal account, investment in bonds and others.

□ Maternity Insurance

1. Number of people covered refers to staff and workers who have participated in maternity insurance programme according to relevant regulation at the end of the reporting period.

2. Revenue of maternity insurance refers to payments made by employers participating in maternity insurance programs in accordance with the basis and proportion stipulated in state regulations, and income from other sources that become source of maternity insurance fund, including income of funds paid by employers, interest income and other income.

3. Expenses of maternity insurance refer to payments made from maternity insurance funds to staff and workers who participated in maternity insurance programme within the scope and standards of expenditure according to related national policies, expenses paid for pregnancy, child delivery or surgeries related to family planning, and other expenditure, including allowance for child bearing, medical fees and other expenditure.

4. Balance of the maternity insurance refers to the balance of the maternity insurance funds at the end of reference period, including bank savings, special fiscal account, investment in funds and others.

第二十二篇

CHAPTER 22

文化和体育

CULTURE, SPORTS

表 22.1 主要年份文化机构数
QUANTITY OF CULTURAL INSTITUTIONS IN MAIN YEARS

单位:个(unit)

年 份 Year	图书馆 Libraries	群众文化活动机构 Mass Culture	艺术教育事 业 Art Education	文艺科研 Art Research	文物保护机构 Agency of Historic Relics Preservation	档案机构 Archives Institutions
1978	23	364	3		7	
1980	21	367	2	2	8	
1985	46	369	3	2	9	
1986	49	403	3	2	11	
1987	50	407	3	2	13	127
1988	54	416	3	2	16	125
1989	52	405	3	2	19	134
1990	51	410	3	2	18	137
1991	31	397	3	2	18	671
1992	31	394	3	2	20	745
1993	31	376	3	2	21	720
1994	31	371	3	2	23	
1995	31	332	3	2	23	768
1996	32	348	4	2	24	674
1997	32	352	4	2	24	681
1998	32	355	4	2	23	643
1999	32	349	4	2	24	994
2000	31	340	4	2	24	792
2001	32	276	3	2	23	614
2002	32	270	1	2	26	652
2003	35	261	1	2	26	656
2004	28	251	1	2	99	513
2005	28	248	1	2	106	545
2006	28	250	1	2	106	466
2007	30	247	1	2	111	524

①本表数据由市文化广播影视管理局、市文物管理委员会、市档案局提供。
②自 2004 年始文物保护机构中包括系统外的机构数。
❶Data in this table are provided by Shanghai Municipal Culture, Radio, Film and TV Administration, Shanghai Municipal Committee of Culture Heritage and Shanghai Municipal Archives.
❷Agency of Historic Relics Preservation refers to total number of Agency Bureau since 2004.

表 22.2 影剧院、艺术表演场所、艺术表演团体数(1978~2007)
QUANTITY OF CINEMAS,THEATRES AND ART PERFORMANCE TROUPES

单位:个(unit)

年 份 Year	电影放映单位 Film Projection Units	其 中 of which #影、剧院 Cinemas and Theatres	艺术表演场所 Art Performance Places	其 中 of which #剧 院 Theatres	#书 场 Storytelling Places	艺术表演团体 Art Performance Troupes
1978	803	109	31	26	4	17
1979	799	115	46	32	5	45
1980	770	119	47	43	6	48
1981	804	127	60	56	6	49
1982	815	134	31	48	6	46
1983	822	140	54	49	8	46
1984	815	146	54	48	8	44
1985	847	156	52	47	8	44
1986	859	169	53	49	9	42
1987	890	199	51	48	8	42
1988	734	215	53	50	8	40
1989	579	213	52	49	8	37
1990	577	211	49	46	8	38
1991	548	229	51	47	9	38
1992	530	249	51	47	9	37
1993	462	254	49	40	9	34
1994	462	254	47	39	8	35
1995	452	249	43	35	7	31
1996	488	280	45	38	7	31
1997	466	263	45	38	7	31
1998	445	242	44	39	5	29
1999	445	242	44	41	4	29
2000	445	242	44	39	5	29
2001	370	273	41	35	3	28
2002	370	273	37	31	2	28
2003	328	238	180	174	4	72
2004	311	225	177	163	7	75
2005	236	193	160	150	5	85
2006	245	186	148	137	2	97
2007	233	175	150	140	6	103

①本表数据由市文化广播影视管理局提供。
②2003 年起文化统计范围扩大到全行业。
❶Data in this table are provided by Shanghai Municipal Culture, Radio, Film and TV Administration.
❷The scope of statistics to culture expands to total sectors in 2003.

表 22.3 主要年份主要文化机构从业人员数
QUANTITY OF EMPLOYEES IN MAJOR CULTURAL INSTITUTIONSS IN MAIN YAERS

单位:人(person)

机构类别	Category of Institution	2000	2006	2007
总 计	**Total**	**217 572**	**245 296**	**229 699**
艺术机构	Art	4 759	6 145	6 245
图书馆	Libraries	2 513	2 425	2 456
档案机构	Archives Institution	2 330	2 418	2 581
群众文化活动机构	Mass Culture	3 874	3 756	4 164
文物保护机构	History Relic	1 136	2 278	2 340
文化娱乐机构	Cultural and recreational Institutions	63 297	62 992	57 240
新闻出版机构	Institutions Engaged in News and Publishing	138 492	164 659	153 150
其他文化机构	Other Cultural Institutions	1 171	623	1 523

注：2007 年艺术机构从业人员口径有变化，部分人员划归为其他文化机构人员。
Note: There are some changes in the quantity of employees of culture and recreational institutions in 2007, some of them have been changed into other culture institutions.

表 22.4 主要文化机构和人员数(2007)
MAJOR CULTURAL INSTITUTIONS AND PERSONNEL

机构类别	Category of Institution	机构数（个） Institutions(unit)	从业人数(人) Employees(person)
艺术机构	**Art**	**261**	**6 245**
艺术表演团体	Art Performance Troupes	103	3 877
艺术表演场所	Art Centers	150	1 990
艺术创作机构	Art Inditing	3	99
艺术展览机构	Art Exhibition	2	172
艺术教育机构	Art Education	1	50
文艺科研机构	Art Research	2	57
图书馆	**Libraries**	**30**	**2 456**
#少儿图书馆	Libraries for Children	5	117
档案机构	**Archives Institution**	**524**	**2 581**
群众文化活动机构	**Mass Culture**	**247**	**4 164**
群众艺术馆	Mass Art Centers	1	67
文化馆	Cultural Centers	29	1 153
文化站	Cultural Stations	217	2 944
文物保护机构	**Historical Relic**	**111**	**2 340**
文物保护管理机构	Agency of Historical Relics Protection	4	57
博物馆	Museums	106	2 174
文物商店	Cultural Relic Shop	1	109
文化娱乐机构	**Cultural and Recreational Institutions**	**4 164**	**57 240**
新闻出版机构	**Institutions Engaged in News and Publishing**	**12 828**	**153 150**

注：本页数据由市文化广播影视管理局、市文物管理委员会、市档案局、市新闻出版局提供。
Note: Data on this page are provided by Shanghai Municipal Culture, Radio, Film and TV Administration, Shanghai Municipal Committee of Culture Heritage, Shanghai Municipal Archives Bureau and Shanghai Municipal Press and Publication Bureau.

表 22.5　群众艺术馆和文化馆(站)情况（2007）
MASS ART AND CULTURAL CENTERS

指　标	Indicators	合　计 Total	群众艺术馆 Mass Art Centers	文化馆 Cultural Centers	文化站 Cultural Stations
单位数（个）	Number of Units（unit）	247	1	29	217
从业人员(人)	Employees（person）	4 164	67	1 153	2 944
组织活动	Organizing Activity				
文艺活动（次）	Literary Activity(time)	55 937	19	7 454	48 464
各类理论研讨和	Theoretics Conference and				
各类讲座（次）	Chair(time)	178	37	141	
举办训练班	Conducting Training Courses				
班　次（次）	Number of Classes（time）	25 195	57	2 799	22 339
结业人次（万人次）	Persons Completing the Courses（10 000 person-times）	57.85	1.50	4.49	51.86
举办展览个数（个）	Exhibitions Conducted（unit）	2 178	12	279	1 887

表 22.6　艺术表演团体情况（2007）
BASIC STATISTICS OF ART TROUPES

类　别	Types	剧团数（个）Troupes（unit）	从业人员（人）Employees（person）	国内演出场次(场) Times of Domestic Performance（time）	观众人数（万人次）Spectators（10 000 person-times）
总　计	**Total**	**103**	**3 877**	**19 727**	**7 877**
按隶属关系分	**By Administrative Relationship**				
市　级	Perfectural level	29	2 876	8 628	4 046
区　级	District level	73	985	10 961	3 641
县　级	County level	1	16	138	190
按剧种分	**By Type of Drama**				
话剧、儿童剧、滑稽剧团	Drama, Childrens Play & Comedy Troupes	16	626	1 800	829
歌剧、舞剧、歌舞剧团	Opera and Dance Troupes	10	636	750	947
乐团、歌舞团、轻音乐团	Philharmonic, Song & Dance, Light Music Troupes	17	480	1 600	838
戏曲剧团	Local Opera Troupes	27	1 266	8 827	1 928
曲艺、杂技、木偶、皮影团	Recitation & Ballad, Acrobatics & Cirus, Puppet Show, Shadow Puttet	14	679	6 600	2 857
综合性艺术表演团体	Comprehensive Art Troupe	19	190	150	478

注：本页数据由市文化广播影视管理局提供。
Note: Data on this page are provided by Shanghai Municipal Culture, Radio, Film and TV Administration.

表22.7 艺术表演场所基本情况(2007)
ART PERFORMANCE PLACES

类别 Types		机构数(个) Institutions (unit)	从业人员(人) Employees (person)	座席数(个) Seats (unit)	演(映)出场次(场) Number of Art Projections & Performances (time)	其中 of which #艺术演出场次 Number of Art Performances	观众人次(万人次) Spectators (10 000 person-times)	其中 of which #艺术演出场次 Number of Art Performances
总　计	**Total**	**150**	**1 990**	**123 613**	**38 871**	**10 759**	**985.4**	**637.6**
市　级	Municipal Level	20	941	31 626	3 903	3 885	391.1	389.6
#上海大剧院	Shanghai Grand Theater	1	190	2 664	549	549	131.6	131.6
上海音乐厅	Shanghai Concert Hall	1	68	1 149	173	173	19.4	19.4
贺绿汀音乐厅	He Luting Concert Hall	1	11	744	157	157	10.5	10.5
上海商城剧院	Shanghai Center Theater	1	15	991	260	245	23.4	22.1
上海话剧艺术中心	Shanghai Dramatic Arts Center	1	50	652	604	604	14.0	14.0
上海美琪大戏院	Shanghai Majestic Theater	1	52	1 328	181	181	19.6	19.6
逸夫舞台	Yifu Theater	1	33	928	338	338	24.3	24.3
兰心大戏院	Lyceum Theater	1	34	681	282	280	15.3	15.2
上海艺海剧院	Shanghai Yihai Theater	1	21	999	218	218	19.5	19.5
上海马戏城	Shanghai Circus World	1	75	2 252	543	543	46.4	46.4
上海体育馆	Shanghai Stadium	1	131	12 216	54	53	3.8	3.7
区　级	District Level	120	1 018	81 631	33 693	6 678	560.4	241.2
#中国大戏院	China Theater	1	19	400	128	128	5.6	5.6
县　级	County Level	10	31	9 356	1 275	196	33.9	6.8

注：本表数据由市文化广播影视管理局提供。
Note: Data in this table are provided by Shanghai Municipal Culture, Radio, Film and TV Administration.

表 22.8 博物馆、纪念馆情况(2007)
STATISTICS OF MUSEUMS AND MEMORIALS

指 标 Indicators		机构数（个）Quantity (unit)	馆内藏品实际数量 Real Quantity of Collections（万件）(10 000 pieces)	#一至三级藏品 Collections of Class One to Three	展览活动（个）Exhibit Activity (unit)	参观人次（万人次）Visiting Person-times (10 000 person-times)
总 计	**Total**	**106**	**154.98**	**18.08**	**279**	**1 056.5**
综合性	Comprehensive	14	5.96	0.62	73	179.7
历史类	Historical	14	4.16	2.34	40	233.8
艺术类	Art	6	13.43	13.27	82	125.3
科学类	Scientific	3	1.90		9	375.6
人物类	Character	18	11.00	1.83	29	55.2
行业类	Industrial	39	114.15	0.02	35	71.5
高校类	University	12	4.38		11	15.4

表 22.9 文物保护维修情况(2005～2007)
PRESERVATION AND MAINTAIN OF HISTORICAL RELICS

指 标	Indicators	2005	2006	2007
保护维修项目数(个)	Items of Preservation and Maintaining (item)	44	63	42
#国家级	National	4	10	7
市 级	Municipal	18	23	16
维修面积(万平方米)	Areas of Maintaining (10 000 sq. m.)	2.3	17.4	13.6
项目总预算(万元)	Aggregate Budget of Items (10 000 yuan)	19 650	44 702	16 727
#专项补助	Special Assistance	934	765	545
已拨入专项补助(万元)	Special Assiatance Appropriated(10 000 yuan)	1 209	520	452
当年保护维修支出(万元)	Expend on Preservation and Maintaining (10 000 yuan)	19 571	30 145	9 652

注：本页数据由市文物管理委员会提供。
Note: Data on this page are provided by Municipal Historical Relic Administrative Committee.

表 22.10 电视台和广播电台情况(2007)
TELEVISION STATIONS AND BROADCASTING STATIONS

类别 Types		节目套数(套) Programs(set)	公共节目播出时间(小时) Playing Hours of Public Program (hour)	其中 of which #自办节目 Self-produced Programs	全年制作节目时间(小时) Annual Production of Programs(hour)
电视台	**Television Stations**	**25**	**172 278**	**92 654**	**61 275**
市级电视台	Municipal Level	16	122 875	78 333	56 079
#上海教育电视台	Shanghai Educational Television Station	1	6 935	2 238	973
区县级电视台	District Level	9	49 403	14 321	5 196
广播电台	**Broadcasting Stations**	**21**	**130 511**	**97 290**	**86 733**
市级广播电台	Municipal Level	11	76 806	69 236	74 432
区县级广播电台	District Level	10	53 705	28 054	12 301

表 22.11 电视和广播公共节目播出时间(2007)
PLAYING HOURS OF TELEVISION AND BROADCASTING PUBLIC PROGRAMS

单位:小时(hour)

类别 Types		电视台 Television Stations 合计 Total	市级 Municipal Level	区县级 District Level	广播电台 Broadcasting Stations 合计 Total	市级 Municipal Level	区县级 District Level
总计	**Total**	**172 278**	**122 875**	**49 403**	**130 511**	**76 806**	**53 705**
新闻资讯类节目	News Program	24 716	19 385	5 331	32 056	20 640	11 416
专题服务类节目	Subject Service Program	31 640	26 043	5 597	20 149	12 899	7 250
综艺类节目	Recreational and Artistic Program	16 758	15 844	914	34 620	23 179	11 441
影视剧类节目	Film and TV Program	63 005	37 347	25 658			
广播剧类节目	Broadcasting Drama Program				16 968	9 001	7 967
广告类节目	Advertising Program	20 949	12 877	8 072	16 766	11 087	5 679
其他类节目	Others	15 210	11 379	3 831	9 952		9 952

表 22.12 主要年份有线电视基本情况
BASIC STATISTICS ON CABLE TELEVISION IN MAIN YEARS

指标 Indicators		2000	2006	2007
有线电视总用户数(万户)	Subscribers(10 000households)	303.00	477.20	499.30
有线电视入户率(%)	Popularity Rate(%)	64.5	96.1	99.94
有线广播电视传输网络干线总长(公里)	Lines Total (kilometer)	604	28 551	30 201

注:本页数据由市文化广播影视管理局提供。
Note: Data on this page are provided by Shanghai Municipal Administration of Culture, Radio, Film & TV.

表 22.13 电影摄制、译制和放映情况(1978～2007)
PRODUCTION, DUBBING AND SHOWING OF FILMS

年份 Year	摄制和译制电影片 Production and Dubbing 故事片(部) Feature Films (film)	美术片(本) Cartoons (reel)	科学教育片(本) Popular Science Films (reel)	译制片(本) Dubbed Films (reel)	电影放映 Film Showing 放映场次(万场) Showing (10 000 times)	其中 of which #影、剧院 Cinemas and Theatres	观众人次(万人次) Spectators (10 000 person-times)	其中 of which #影、剧院 Cinemas and Theatres
1978	10	24	84	275	35	17	27 405	15 291
1979	14	25	95	315	40	20	32 763	29 743
1980	17	30	105	382	39	20	29 304	18 039
1981	17	32	109	289	38	19	26 823	16 203
1982	19	35	112	604	38	20	25 828	15 586
1983	19	34	116	666	37	20	25 204	15 124
1984	19	40	117	633	36	21	24 149	15 539
1985	15	43	140	426	34	21	21 885	14 748
1986	19	38	150	450	36	24	23 220	16 720
1987	17	38	151	378	37	28	21 985	17 067
1988	13	29	156	501	38	30	20 461	16 742
1989	17	29	140	398	37	32	20 776	18 216
1990	16	47	142	340	38	33	19 351	17 021
1991	17	37	146	272	36	31	15 766	13 615
1992	17	42	146	325	29	25	9 145	8 089
1993	16	35	91	251	16	14	3 862	3 332
1994	14	13	69	162	22	20	4 001	3 617
1995	17	37	22	266	23	20	4 419	3 913
1996	10	58	6	283	27	25	4 420	3 783
1997	11	17	8	312	25	23	3 670	3 023
1998	4	16	6	271	23	21	2 924	2 451
1999	17	10	14	372	20	19	2 055	1 678
2000	10	500	12	438	18	17	1 794	1 452
2001	12	2	8	237	18	17	1 553	1 315
2002	10	2	11	204	20	17	1 198	921
2003	9	10	2	216	20	19	971	870
2004	12	1		18	24	23	1 364	1 183
2005	13			15	28	26	1 509	1 323
2006	9			24	27	26	1 254	1 173
2007	9			24	33	32	1 385	1 277

注：本表数据由市文化广播影视管理局提供。
Note: Data in this table are provided by Shanghai Municipal Administration of Culture, Radio, Film & TV.

表 22.14 各区、县文化娱乐机构情况(2007)
CULTURE AND ENTERTAINMENT UNDERTAKINGS BY DISTRICTS AND COUNTIES

单位:个(unit)

地 区	District	合 计 Total	其中 of which #歌舞娱乐场所 Singing & Dancing Rooms	#游戏电子游艺经营场所 Video Games Rooms	#其他娱乐场所 Other Places	#网 吧 Internet Bar
总 计	**Total**	**4 164**	**1 733**	**425**	**479**	**1 453**
市 级	Prefectural Level	591			60	457
浦东新区	Pudong New Area	615	282	91	67	175
黄 浦 区	Huangpu	91	41	5	17	28
卢 湾 区	Luwan	97	40	8	38	11
徐 汇 区	Xuhui	194	77	12	42	63
长 宁 区	Changning	170	111	5	18	36
静 安 区	Jing'an	103	60	10	8	25
普 陀 区	Putuo	171	59	32	13	67
闸 北 区	Zhabei	145	62	16	11	56
虹 口 区	Hongkou	154	61	27	13	53
杨 浦 区	Yangpu	171	56	29	13	73
宝 山 区	Baoshan	255	95	41	41	78
闵 行 区	Minhang	357	221	40	9	87
嘉 定 区	Jiading	212	113	19	11	69
金 山 区	Jinshan	118	59	22	19	18
松 江 区	Songjiang	221	124	18	30	49
青 浦 区	Qingpu	127	75	4	21	27
南 汇 区	Nanhui	182	100	21	25	36
奉 贤 区	Fengxian	116	46	19	19	32
崇 明 县	Chongming	74	51	6	4	13

注:本表数据由市文化广播影视管理局提供。
Note: Data in this table are provided by Shanghai Municipal Administration of Culture, Radio, Film & TV.

表 22.15 各区、县艺术表演场所、图书馆、群艺馆、文化馆基本情况(2007)
ART PERFORMANCE PLACES,LIBRARIES, MASS ART CENTERS AND CULTURE CENTERS BY DISTRICS AND COUNTIES

地 区	District	艺术表演场所 Art Performance Place		公共图书馆 Libraries		群艺馆、文化馆(个) Mass Art Centers and Culture Centers (unit)
		个 数 (个) Quantity (unit)	座席数 (个) Seat (unit)	个 数 (个) Quantity (unit)	读者人数 (万人次) Readers (10 000 person-times)	
总 计	**Total**	**150**	**123 613**	**30**	**1 323.27**	**30**
市 级	Municipal Level	20	31 626	2	167.47	1
浦东新区	Pudong New Area	11	7 585	3	179.90	5
黄 浦 区	Huangpu	5	3 438	1	103.35	1
卢 湾 区	Luwan	2	737	1	48.26	1
徐 汇 区	Xuhui	3	2 490	1	85.03	2
长 宁 区	Changning	3	1 110	2	36.84	2
静 安 区	Jing'an			1	62.08	1
普 陀 区	Putuo	1	445	2	119.42	3
闸 北 区	Zhabei	3	1 975	2	10.12	1
虹 口 区	Hongkou	1	861	2	41.37	2
杨 浦 区	Yangpu	2	2 117	3	106.89	1
宝 山 区	Baoshan	8	4 891	1	90.51	2
闵 行 区	Minhang	12	6 861	1	24.23	1
嘉 定 区	Jiading	4	3 107	1	33.67	1
金 山 区	Jinshan	5	3 349	1	11.96	1
松 江 区	Songjiang	6	3 940	1	49.53	1
青 浦 区	Qingpu	19	13 875	2	27.18	1
奉 贤 区	Fengxian	15	11 093	1	34.56	1
南 汇 区	Nanhui	20	14 757	1	52.90	1
崇 明 县	Chongming	10	9 356	1	38.00	1

注：本表数据由市文化广播影视管理局提供。
Note: Data in this table are provided by Shanghai Municipal Administration of Culture, Radio, Film & TV.

表 22.16 文化娱乐机构基本情况(2007) BASIC STATISTICS OF CULTURE AND ENTERTAINMENT INSTITUTIONS

类别	Types	从业人员（人）Employees (person)	主营营业收入（万元）Major Business Revenue (10 000 yuan)	主营业务利润（万元）Major Business Profits (10 000 yuan)	房屋建筑面积（万平方米）Floor Space of Buildings (10 000 sq. m)
总　计	**Total**	**57 240**	**924 690**	**371 811**	**223.10**
歌舞娱乐场所	Singing & Dancing Rooms	30 222	130 355	107 910	130.60
游戏电子游艺经营场所	Gaming Rooms	2 814	9 187	10 180	17.10
其他娱乐场所	Other Places	10 638	130 355	74 063	24.90
网　吧	Internet Bar	8 930	41 741	11 283	48.30
经营性互联网文化单位	Internet-Cultural Business Unit	4 636	613 051	168 376	2.20

表 22.17 公共图书馆情况(2007) PUBLIC LIBRARIES

指标	Indicators	合计 Total	市级 Municipal Level	区级 District Level	县级 County Level
机构数(个)	Quantity(unit)	30	2	27	1
从业人员（人）	Employees (person)	2 456	1 236	1 176	44
总藏量（万册、件）	Collection (10 000 copies)	6 253.94	5 224.26	985.91	43.77
#图　书	Books	2 319.69	1 365.61	910.52	43.56
报　刊	Newspaper and Magzines	315.16	296.74	18.41	0.01
本年新购藏量（万册、件）	Publications Newly Bought (10 000 copies)	146.11	53.35	90.26	2.50
#图　书	Books	128.95	46.16	80.42	2.37
建筑面积（万平方米）	Floor Space of Buildings (10 000 sq · m)	26.32	12.50	13.11	0.71
#书　库	Stack Room	7.99	5.84	1.99	0.16
阅览室	Reading Room	5.17	1.32	3.70	0.15
阅览座位（个）	Seats in Reading Room (unit)	16 136	2 634	13 002	500
图书借阅情况	Books Lending				
人　次（万人次）	Readers (10 000 person-times)	1 323.27	167.46	1 117.81	38.00
册　数（万册次）	Books (10 000 copy-times)	1 224.98	250.97	949.01	25.00
信息化装备	Information Equipment				
计算机（台）	Computer(unit)	5 434	2 665	2 689	80
#电子阅览室终端数	E-reading Room Terminals	1 548	150	1 340	58
为读者举办各种活动	Activities Held for Readers				
次　数（次）	Times(time)	3 965	681	3 249	35
参加人次（万人次）	Participants (10 000 person-times)	138.70	53.89	74.81	10.00

注：本页数据由市文化广播影视管理局提供。
Note: Data on this page are provided by Shanghai Municipal Administration of Culture, Radio, Film & TV.

表22.18 图书出版数量(1978～2007)
BOOKS PUBLISHED

年 份 Years	种 数 (种) Quantity of Publications (type)	其中 of which #新出版 Newly Published	总印数 (亿册) Total Printed (100 million copies)	总印张数 (亿印张) Total Ptrinted Signatures (100 million signatures)
1978	1 666	1 332	3.92	12.19
1979	2 040	1 563	4.58	15.54
1980	2 338	1 804	5.62	17.73
1981	2 801	1 949	6.01	22.89
1982	3 395	2 057	6.07	21.76
1983	3 653	2 254	4.65	21.31
1984	3 848	2 328	5.37	25.58
1985	4 176	2 634	4.96	23.95
1986	4 531	3 045	3.66	17.81
1987	5 103	3 151	4.26	19.84
1988	5 538	3 658	4.33	19.04
1989	6 765	4 960	3.28	14.52
1990	7 767	4 887	2.98	14.66
1991	8 141	4 756	3.11	17.30
1992	8 095	4 179	2.75	17.19
1993	7 721	4 272	2.26	15.34
1994	7 812	4 382	2.35	17.01
1995	8 338	4 185	2.44	17.92
1996	9 234	4 445	2.79	20.1
1997	9 928	4 844	2.70	18.00
1998	10 718	5 083	2.83	18.69
1999	11 381	5 880	2.68	18.69
2000	12 682	6 936	2.54	19.05
2001	14 000	7 947	2.68	21.24
2002	14 537	8 156	2.59	21.38
2003	15 636	8 726	2.74	23.27
2004	16 449	9 391	2.67	23.54
2005	16 504	9 286	2.59	23.65
2006	17 283	9 338	2.54	24.86
2007	16 958	9 085	2.40	24.05

注：本表数据由市新闻出版局提供。
Note: Data in this table are provided by Shanghai Municipal Press and Publication Bureau.

表 22.19 期刊出版数量(1978～2007)
PERIODICALS PUBLISHED

年 份 Years	种 数 (种) Quantity of Publications (type)	每期平均印数 (万册、份) Average Publications Issued (10 000 copies)	总印数 (亿册) Total Printed (100 million copies)	总印张数 (亿印张) Total Printed Signatures (100 million signatures)
1978	42	459	0.47	1.12
1979	90	721	0.73	2.08
1980	126	1 061	1.22	3.37
1981	266	1 873	2.03	5.95
1982	308	2 203	2.31	6.37
1983	349	2 572	2.51	7.07
1984	402	3 502	3.1	8.56
1985	491	3 424	3.45	9.21
1986	541	3 073	3.03	8.17
1987	546	3 058	3.13	8.05
1988	535	2 624	2.66	6.63
1989	527	1 793	1.86	4.58
1990	522	1 735	1.73	4.24
1991	504	1 749	1.79	4.44
1992	527	1 794	1.84	4.59
1993	535	1 668	1.82	4.95
1994	556	1 569	1.72	4.87
1995	565	1 583	1.78	5.3
1996	582	1 530	1.66	5.14
1997	587	1 513	1.66	5.35
1998	591	1 503	1.65	5.81
1999	606	1 493	1.78	6.87
2000	613	1 489	1.85	7.38
2001	616	1 413	1.85	7.58
2002	621	1 332	1.80	7.77
2003	626	1 335	1.83	8.51
2004	612	1 184	1.93	8.94
2005	612	1 130	1.90	8.96
2006	616	1 125	1.83	8.76
2007	624	1 117	1.83	8.75

注：本表数据由市新闻出版局提供。
Note: Data in this table are provided by Shanghai Municipal Press and Publication Bureau.

表 22.20 报纸出版数量(1978~2007)
NEWSPAPER PUBLISHED

年 份 Years	种 数 (种) Quantity of Publications (type)	每期平均印数 (万份) Average Publication Issued (10 000 copies)	总印数 (亿册) Total Printed (100 million copies)	总印张数 (亿印张) Total Printed Signatures (100 million signatures)
1978	5	257	6.41	6.20
1979	8	349	7.32	7.08
1980	12	464	8.55	8.20
1981	15	640	10.28	9.77
1982	31	936	14.93	13.13
1983	34	1 185	18.13	15.49
1984	41	1 429	19.63	16.57
1985	89	1 656	19.54	17.07
1986	93	1 750	19.94	18.37
1987	90	2 003	22.45	20.49
1988	83	1 958	21.38	22.07
1989	81	1 477	15.85	16.25
1990	81	1 510	16.16	16.76
1991	75	1 506	18.48	19.16
1992	77	1 506	24.76	24.76
1993	81	1 506	32.27	32.27
1994	87	1 369	30.43	30.43
1995	86	1 358	19.04	34.00
1996	87	1 357	18.93	36.96
1997	87	1 397	19.34	43.19
1998	80	1 441	19.73	49.84
1999	75	1 311	18.42	46.26
2000	103	1 135	16.77	44.57
2001	101	1 060	16.98	47.67
2002	101	983	16.46	51.42
2003	101	886	17.05	66.13
2004	103	939	19.71	83.66
2005	102	903	19.06	89.94
2006	101	850	17.89	87.33
2007	101	815	17.04	86.75

注：本表数据由市新闻出版局提供。
Note: Data in this table are provided by Shanghai Municipal Press and Publication Bureau.

表 22.21 主要年份新闻出版机构和人员数
NUMBER OF INSTITUTIONS AND EMPLOYEES ENGAGED IN NEWS AND PUBLISHING IN MAIN YEARS

指 标	Indicators	2000	2006	2007
图书出版机构	**Publishing Houses**			
机构数（个）	Institutions (unit)	37	39	39
从业人员（人）	Employee (person)	3 666	3 874	3 999
书刊印刷机构	**Printing Houses**			
机构数（个）	Institutions (unit)	4 543	5 281	4 950
从业人员（万人）	Employee (10 000 persons)	11.54	13.62	12.31
发行机构	**Issuing Houses**			
机构数（个）	Institutions (unit)	6 743	7 754	7 839
从业人员（万人）	Employee (10 000 persons)	1.94	2.46	2.61

注：发行机构数中包括发行网点数。
Note: Issuing Houses include quantity of net places.

表 22.22 图书出版数量(2007)
BOOKS PUBLISHED

类 别	types	种 数（种）Number of Publications (type)	其中 of which #新出版 Newly Published	总印数（万册）Total Printed (10 000 copies)	总印张数（万印张）Total Printed Signatures (10 000 signatures)
总 计	**Total**	**16 958**	**9 085**	**23 968**	**240 479**
书 籍	**Books**	**14 230**	**8 149**	**14 912**	**168 193**
哲学、社会科学	Philosophy and Social Science	3 511	2 388	2 484	38 872
文化教育	Culture and Education	5 395	2 453	7 673	79 738
文学艺术	Literature and Art	2 478	1 567	1 812	25 164
自然科学技术	Natural Science and Technology	2 183	1 316	1 160	17 762
少年儿童读物	Children's Reading Materials	663	425	1 783	6 657
课 本	**Textbooks**	**2 557**	**811**	**8 715**	**71 578**
#大专课本	University and College	769	318	1 683	27 641
中专技校教材	Specialized Secondary and Technical Worker School	64	24	116	1 234
中学课本	Secondary School	537	102	3 600	25 258
小学课本	Primary School	442	58	2 800	11 292
业余教育课本	Spare-time Education	65	18	54	573
教学用书	Teaching References	680	291	461	5 580
图 片	**Pictures**	**171**	**125**	**341**	**661**

注：本页数据由市新闻出版局提供。
Note: Data on this page are provided by Shanghai Municipal Press and Publication Bureau.

表 22.23 期刊出版数量(2007) PERIODICALS PUBLISHED

类别	Types	种数(种) Quantity of Publications (type)	出版期数(期) Quantity of Issue (issue)	总印数(万册、份) Total Printed (10 000 copies)	总印张数(万印张) Total Printed Signatures (10 000 signatures)
总　计	**Total**	**624**	**5 540**	**18 266**	**87 524**
综　合	Comprehensive	11	72	156	1 630
哲学、社会科学	Philosophy and Social Science	124	1 275	3 802	18 486
自然科学技术	Natural Science and Technology	359	2 756	2 798	21 613
文化教育	Culture and Education	78	827	1 991	13 152
文学艺术	Literature and Art	33	352	8 237	29 291
少年儿童读物	Children's Reading Materials	18	256	1 281	3 346
画　刊	Pictorial	1	2	1	6

表 22.24 报纸出版数量(2007) NEWSPAPER PUBLISHED

类别	Types	种数(种) Quantity of Publications (type)	期数(期) Issue (issue)	每期平均印数(万份) Average Publication Per Issue (10 000 copies)	总印数(万份) Total Printed (10 000 copies)	总印张数(万印张) Total Printed Signatures (10 000 signatures)
总　计	**Total**	**101**	**10 894**	**815**	**170 372**	**867 467**
综合报	Comprehensive	18	4 574	431	128 647	708 654
专业报	Specialized	83	6 320	385	41 725	158 813

表 22.25 音像电子出版数量 (2007) AUDIO, VIDEO AND ELECTRON PUBLISHED

类别	Types	种数(种) Quantity of Publications (type)	出版数量(万张、万盒) Quantity of Publications (10 000 piece box)	发行数量(万张、万盒) Quantity of Issued (10 000 piece box)	发行总金额(万元) Total Values (10 000 yuan)
总　计	**Total**	**3 569**	**5 282.91**	**4 448.82**	**33 096.49**
电子出版物	Electronic Publication	465	2 525.87	1 793.16	13 224.06
数码激光视盘	DVD	392	257.32	264.25	2 100.70
高密度激光视盘	VCD	221	157.24	97.98	1 038.15
录像带	Video	5	1.10	1.10	18.46
激光唱盘	CD	1 100	601.73	473.11	6 622.04
录音带	Tape	1 264	1 634.43	1 752.40	9 437.56
其　他	Others	122	105.22	66.82	655.52

注：本页数据由市新闻出版局提供。
Note: Data on this page are provided by Shanghai Municipal Press and Publication Bureau.

表 22.26 档案机构基本情况(2007)
BASIC STATISTICS OF ARCHIVE INSTITUTIONS

指 标	Indicators	合 计 Total	档案馆 Archives Library	其中 of which 综 合 Comprehensive	档案室(处、科) Archives
机构数(个)	**Number of Institutions(unit)**	**504**	**41**	**20**	**463**
从业人员(人)	**Employees(person)**	**2 231**	**674**	**380**	**1 557**
专 职	Full-time	1 291	674	380	617
兼 职	Part-time	940			940
馆藏档案	**Archives Collected**				
全 宗(个)	Overall Rolls(unit)	6150	5 380	5 280	770
案 卷(万卷)	Rolls(10 000 rolls)	1 368.42	930.59	752.47	437.83
以件为保管单位档案(万件)	Archives(Piece as Unit)	130.91	44.52	3.96	86.39
录音、录像、影片档案(万盘)	Recprd,Video and Film (10 000 disks)	6.08	1.56	0.86	4.52
照片档案(万张)	Photo Records(10 000 pieces)	109.75	56.83	43.28	52.92
底图(万张)	Base Maps(10 000 pieces)	1 133.32	203.36	2.03	929.96
电子档案(万张)	Electronic Records(10 000 disks)				
磁 盘	Disks	2.43	0.10	0.01	2.33
光 盘	Compact Discs	4.14	1.79	0.70	2.35
微缩胶片	Microfilm				
平 片(万张)	Flat Film(10 000 pieces)	10.19	8.78	7.88	1.41
开窗卡(万张)	Open Window Card(10 000 pieces)	67.36	43.32	22.82	24.04
档案利用	**Records Utilized**				
已开放档案	Records Opened				
案 卷(万卷)	Rolls(10 000 rolls)	164.08	164.08	117.83	
开放档案目录(万条)	Catalog of Records Opened(10 000 pieces)				
案卷级	Roll Grade	121.53	121.53	110.23	
文件级	Document Grade	147.80	147.80	118.21	
本年利用档案	Records Utilized This Year				
卷次(万卷次)	Roll-times(10 000 roll-times)	68.36	44.12	36.61	24.24
件次(万件次)	Piece-times(10 000 piece-times)	33.77	27.52	25.08	6.25
人次(万人次)	Person-times(10 000 person-times)	31.39	20.93	15.46	10.46

注：本表数据由市档案局提供。
Note: Data in this table are provided by Shanghai Municipal Archives Bureau.

表 22.27 等级裁判员、运动员人数和运动员破纪录情况(1978～2007)
CERTIFIED REFEREES,ATHLETES AND RECORD-BREAKING

单位：人（person）

年 份 Year	等级裁判员 Certified Referees	其 中 of which 国际裁判 International Referees	等级运动员 Certified Athletes	其 中 of which 国际运动健将 International Master Athletes	打破上年全国最高纪录 Break the Highest National Record of the Preceding Year 人 Person	队 Team	次 Time	项 Item
1978	268	5	1 957		25	4	77	20
1979	2 423		1 899		8	4	38	25
1980	1 610		1 871		51		164	50
1981	1 949	2	1 447		27	4	76	36
1982	1 250	3	1 367		13		19	11
1983	733	2	1 056		14		36	21
1984	1 244		2 635	4	15	2	33	16
1985	1 558		1 231	10	17	4	46	19
1986	980	4	1 412	17	21	7	47	31
1987	1 265	3	1 217	8	24		64	23
1988	828	5	1 100	7	15	2	41	25
1989	1 116	3	1 319		6		9	8
1990	1 110	4	1 455	4	13		18	18
1991	904	1	1 601	8	4		7	7
1992	805		782		58	8	99	82
1993	358	3	1 078	8	60	8	102	86
1994	520		1 570	12	20	2	34	21
1995	523	2	960	11	16	1	74	34
1996	1 310		1 159	12	20	2	8	8
1997	699	1	1 235	8	31	8	75	59
1998	1 175	2	1 996	15	12	10	30	29
1999	1 127		1 903		15	3	6	6
2000	880				3		4	3
2001	968		1 338	8	2	1	5	3
2002	459	2	991	7				
2003	535		1 189	18				
2004	301		524	12				
2005	357		793	5				
2006	274	5	699	18				
2007	659		841	23				

注：本表数据由市体育局提供。
Note：Data in this table are provided by Shanghai Municipal Sports Bureau.

表 22.28 主要年份优秀运动员、教练员情况
BASIC STATISTICS ON EXCELLENT ATHLETES AND COACHES IN MAIN YEARS

指 标	Indicators	2000	2006	2007
优秀运动员(人)	Excellent Athletes(person)	899	1 036	841
#女运动员	Women	402	498	450
优秀运动队专职教练员(人)	Full-time Coaches(person)	196	179	147
#女专职教练员	Women	30	40	44

表 22.29 体育系统职工人数(2007)
STAFF AND WORKERS IN SPORTS SECTORS

单位:人(person)

指 标	Indicators	总 计 Total	其中 of which #优秀运动队 Excellent Sports Teams	#体育运动学校 Physical Education and Sports Schools	#普通业余体校 Popular Sparetime Sports School	#公共体育场(馆) Public Stadiums and Gymnasiums
总 计	**Total**	**7 150**	**1 528**	**411**	**763**	**1 617**
#专职教练员	Full-time Coaches	336	147	23	73	93
运动员	Athletes	841	803		29	9
管理干部	Administraive Staff	3 230	262	84	260	546
专职教师	Full-time Teachers	272	45	67	160	
科技人员	Scientific and Technical Personnel	78	1	1	19	2
医务人员	Medical Personnel	75	54	10	8	3

表 22.30 主要年份群众体育健身活动场所情况
MASS PHYSICAL ACTIVITIES IN MAIN YEARS

指 标	Indicators	2000	2006	2007
社区体育健身设施数(个)	Quantity of Community Fitness Facilities (unit)	1 354	4 796	4 845
#健身点	Fitness Centers	1 271	4 537	4 586
社区健身场地面积(万平方米)	Area of Communtiy Fitness Space (10 000 sq. m)	65	300	301
社区公共运动场(个)	Quantity of Community Public Playground(unit)		130	176
社区公共运动场面积(万平方米)	Area of Community Public Playground(10 000 sq. m)		199	229

表 22.31 主要年份上海与国外体育活动交流情况
SPORTS EXCHANGES WITH FOREIGN COUNTRIES IN MAIN YEARS

指 标	Indicators	2000	2006	2007
来上海的外国体育团体	**Sports Groups From Foreign Countries**			
次数(次)	Times (time)	112	95	106
人数(人次)	Persons (person time)	4 623	6 775	8 910
上海派出的体育团体	**Sports Groups Sent By Shanghai**			
次数(次)	Times (time)	108	110	113
人数(人次)	Persons (person time)	981	1 005	1 060

注：本页数据由市体育局提供。
Note: Data on this page are provided by Shanghai Municipal Sports Bureau.

表 22.32 举办运动会(比赛)和全民健身活动情况(2007)
BASIC STATISTICS IN ATHLETIC MEETINGS AND MASS PHYSICAL ACTIVITIES

地区	District	运动会和比赛次数(次) Quantity of Sports Meetings (time)	其中 of which 综合运动会 Comprehensive Sports Meetings	单项比赛 Single Game	举办全民健身活动情况 Mass Physical Activities 活动次数(次) Quantity of Activities (time)	其中 of which 千人以上活动 above 1000 Persons	参加活动人次(万人) Person Time of Activities (10 000 persons)
总计	**Total**	**5 199**	**59**	**5 140**	**2 378**	**447**	**173.59**
市直属	Municipal Level	370	2	368	36	36	7.90
浦东新区	Pudong New Area	18	1	17	405	12	1.88
黄浦区	Huangpu	9		9	174	63	37.52
卢湾区	Luwan	9		9	8	3	3.50
徐汇区	Xuhui				220	12	8.00
长宁区	Changning	12	2	10	4	4	0.40
静安区	Jing'an	15	1	14	22	10	5.00
普陀区	Putuo	4 188		4 188	13	9	1.96
闸北区	Zhabei	3	1	2	31	4	20.00
虹口区	Hongkou	16	1	15	85	5	23.00
杨浦区	Yangpu	23		23			
宝山区	Baoshan	358	41	317	220	20	3.00
闵行区	Minhang	41	1	40	274	1	4.95
嘉定区	Jiading	15	2	13	78	1	8.21
金山区	Jinshan	9	2	7	320	250	25.00
松江区	Songjiang	26	1	25	257	2	9.80
青浦区	Qingpu	29	1	28	124	5	3.60
南汇区	Nanhui	27	2	25	19	5	8.67
崇明县	Chongming	31	1	30	88	5	1.20

注：本表数据由市体育局提供。
Note: Data in this table are provided by Shanghai Municipal Sports Bureau.

上 / 海 / 统 / 计 / 年 / 鉴

主要统计指标解释

文化机构

是指专门从事文化工作具有法人资格，独立核算的事业，企业单位，以及单独核算，附属于事业单位的经营性专业文化活动单位。包括从事艺术、图书馆、档案馆、群众文化、文物保护、艺术教育、艺术研究、文化娱乐、新闻出版等机构，以及其他文化机构。

电影放映单位

指具有放映机器设备、固定或不固定的放映场所与专职或兼职的放映技术人员，经有关部门登记批准，经常为一定的观众对象放映电影的机构。包括电影院、影剧院、开放礼堂、俱乐部、放映队、对内礼堂俱乐部。

艺术表演团体

指从事戏曲、音乐、舞蹈、杂技等专业艺术表演，有独立账户的单位，不包括半工半艺、半农半艺和民间职业剧团。该指标主要反映上海专业艺术表演团体发展规模水平。

艺术表演观众人次

指售票、包场演出或民族地区免费演出的艺术表演观众人次数，不包括彩排审查和内部观摩演出的观看人次数。该指标主要反映上海观看专业艺术表演团体演出的效益规模。

等级运动员人数

指经考核正式批准授予等级运动员称号的人数。运动员等级分为国际级运动健将、运动健将、一级运动员、二级运动员、三级运动员、少年级运动员。该指标主要反映运动员队伍的技术质量水平。

等级裁判员人数

指经考核正式批准授予等级裁判员称号的人数。裁判员等级分为国际裁判、国家级裁判、一级裁判、二级裁判、三级裁判。该指标主要反映裁判员队伍的技术质量水平。

SHANGHAI STATISTICAL YEARBOOK

EXPLANATORY NOTES TO MAJOR STATISTICAL INDICATORS

□ Cultural Institutions

Cultural Institution refers to undertaking and business institutions which specialize in cultural work and have legal personality and independent accounting system, and those professional cultural institutions attached to undertaking institutions and have independent accounting system. It includes institutions specialize in art, library, archives, mass culture, historical relic protection, art education, art research, entertainment, news and publication and other cultural institutions.

□ Film Projection Units

Film Projection Units refer to units with film projection equipments, full or part-time projectionists, permanent or non-permanent places, approved by related administrative departments to show films regularly for certain groups of audience, including cinemas, theaters, public auditoriums, clubs, film projection teams, and interior auditorium clubs.

□ Art Troupe

Art Troupe refers to the troupe which is engaged in drama, opera, music, dance, acrobatics or other art performance, opens independent accounts with banks and has self-supporting accounting system; excluding the troupes which are engaged partly in industrial or agricultural activities, partly in art performance and the professional troupes organized by the people. This indicator reflects the development of Shanghai's professional art troupes.

□ Number of Spectators at Art Performance

Number of Spectators at Art Performance refers to the number of attendants at commercial shows, completely booked shows or free shows given in minority national areas, and does not include the number of spectators at rehearsals for examination and internal shows for study. This indicator reflects beneficial results of spectators at Professional Art Performance.

□ Number of Athletes in Grades

Number of Athletes in Grades refers to the number of athletes who have been given titles through examination. The titles of athletes include international masters of sports, masters of sports, first-grade, second-grade and third-grade sportsmen and young athletes. This indicator reflects skill of the athletes.

□ Number of Referees in Grades

Number of Referees in Grades refers to the number of referees who have been given titles after examination. They are classified as international referees, national referees and referees of the first, second and third grades. This indicator reflects the skill of referees.

第二十三篇

CHAPTER 23

法律、公证和其他

LAWS, NOTARY AND OTHERS

表23.1 主要年份律师、公证及调解工作基本情况
BASIC STATISTICS OF LAWYERS, NOTARIZATIONS AND MEDIATIONS IN MAIN YEARS

指 标	Indicators	2000	2006	2007
律师工作	**Lawyers**			
法律律师事务所（个）	Law Offices (unit)	415	741	791
专职工作人员（人）	Full-time Staff (person)	5 127	11 141	8 830
#专职律师	Full-time Lawyers	3 522	7 366	8 143
取得法律职业资格（人）	Qualified Law Occupation (person)	4 642	7 896	8 676
#专职律师	Full-time Lawyers	3 522	7 366	8 143
兼职律师	Part-time Lawyers	731	530	533
全年办理	**Total Transacted**			
民事案件诉讼代理（万件）	Civil Lawsuit(10 000 cases)	7.05	8.95	8.72
刑事诉讼辩护及代理（万件）	Criminal Lawsuit and Vindication(10 000 cases)	1.13	1.47	1.90
非诉讼法律事务（万件）	Non-litigation Action(10 000 cases)	2.65	4.65	3.66
解答法律询问(万人次)	Legal Advisory Services (10 000 person times)	10.36	12.56	7.64
代写法律事务文书（万件）	Legal Documents Written on Behalf of Clients(10 000 cases)	1.92	2.56	2.84
行政案件诉讼代理（万件）	Administrative Lawsuit(10 000 cases)	0.12	0.16	0.20
公证工作	**Notarizations**			
公证处（个）	Notarial Offices (unit)	22	22	22
公证人员（人）	Notarial Personnel (person)	366	528	602
#公证员	Notaries	243	283	297
办理公证文书（万件）	Documents Notarized (10 000 cases)	47.72	40.41	44.27
#国内经济合同公证	Domestic Economic Contracts Notarized	18.73	9.69	10.30
在办理公证文书中	Documents Notarizing			
涉外公证（万件）	Foreign (10 000 cases)	19.93	22.26	23.40
国内公证（万件）	Domestic (10 000 cases)	27.79	17.16	19.69
公证费收入（亿元）	Revenue of Notarial Fees (100 million yuan)	1.13	3.11	3.34
人民调解工作	**People's Mediation**			
专职司法助理员（人）	Full-time Judicial Assistants (person)	416	736	734
人民调解委员会（万个）	People's Mediation Committees(10 000 units)	0.89	0.59	0.60
调解人员（万人）	Mediators (10 000 persons)	3.55	3.13	2.99
调解民间纠纷（万件）	Civil Disputes Mediated (10 000 cases)	6.37	9.09	12.89
#婚姻家庭	Family Disputes	1.97	2.22	2.24
邻 里	Neighbor Disputes	2.51	3.5	4.06
赔 偿	Compensation	0.25	0.56	0.93
房屋宅基地	Housing and Housing Sites	1.04	1.16	1.11

①本表数据由市司法局提供。
②办理公证文件中包括涉及港、澳、台公证文件。
❶Data in this table are provided by Shanghai Municipal Justice Bureau.
❷The number of notarized documents handled included Hong Kong, Macao, and Taiwan's.

表 23.2 主要年份国内公证文书分类情况
DOMESTIC NOTARIAL DOCUMENTS BY TYPE IN MAIN YEARS

单位:件(case)

指标	Indicators	2000	2006	2007
总计	**Total**	**277 949**	**171 598**	**196 929**
经济公证	**Business Notarized**	**187 304**	**96 867**	**103 040**
#贷款合同	Loans Contracts	80 980	30 484	39 152
招标、投标	Bidding	55	103	288
劳务合同	Labour Contracts	4 982	103	9
财产租赁	Property Leases	22	35	753
法人资格	Legal Person Identification	109	109	96
法人委托书	Legal Person Certificate of Entrustment	227	6 795	8 465
民事公证	**Civil Legal Relations Notarized**	**90 645**	**74 731**	**93 889**
#继承权	Rights of Inheritance	5 217	11 281	15 361
遗　嘱	Testaments	1 709	3 759	4 616
委托书	Certificate of Entrustment	4 520	29 977	40 809
赠与书	Presentation Documents	5 196	1 832	1 998
声明书	Declarations	10 424	5 092	5 170
其他民事协议	Other Civil Agreements	15 552	2 839	4 916
涉外公证	**Foreign Notarized**	**199 323**	**222 624**	**233 973**
#出　生	Births	28 535	25 187	29 140
学　历	Schoolihg	21 644	9 370	7 696
亲属关系	Kinship	22 488	18 096	22 042
婚姻状况	Marriages	20 274	9 371	5 584
受、未受刑事处分	Criminal Records & Uncriminal Records	20 669	14 597	15 363
文本相符	Confirmation of Copies and Photo-Offset Copies to Originals	23 645	29 291	33 196

注：本表数据由市司法局提供。
Note: Data in this table are provided by Shanghai Municipal Justice Bureau.

表 23.3 主要年份公安机关立案的刑事案件情况
CRIMINAL CASES REGISTERED IN PUBLIC SECURITY ORGANS IN MAIN YEARS

单位:起(times)

类 别	Types	2000	2006	2007
总 计	**Total**	**104 946**	**139 060**	**137 391**
杀 人	Homicide	252	229	214
伤 害	Injury	1 553	2 166	2 232
抢 劫	Robbery	3 033	2 698	2 591
强 奸	Rape	396	391	398
诈 骗	Fraud	8 425	11 975	13 626
盗 窃	Larceny	77 912	101 817	97 077
其 他	Others	13 375	19 784	21 253

表 23.4 主要年份公安机关查处治安案件情况
OFTENSE CASES AGAINST PUBLIC ORDER HANDLED BY PUBLIC SECURITY ORGANS IN MAIN YEARS

单位:起(times)

类 别	Types	2000	2006	2007
总 计	**Total**	**194 141**	**572 280**	**567 277**
#扰乱工作、公共秩序	Disturbing Work and Public Order	23 568	30 731	27 019
结伙斗殴、寻衅滋事	Gang Fighting or Picking Quarrels and Making Trouble	3 373	6 098	5 237
阻碍国家工作人员执行职务	Obstructing the Goverment Workers to Perform Their Duty	1 029	1 400	1 138
殴打他人	Beating Other Body	16 973	86 768	81 828
骗取、抢夺、敲诈勒索财物	Defrauding, Snatching or Extoring and Racketeering Valuables	2 936	21 954	21 651
故意损坏公私财物	Intentionally Damaging Public or Private Valuables	681	2 519	1 868
伪造倒卖票券、证件	Forging and Fraudulently Selling Bills or Certificates	5 551	604	706
卖淫、嫖娼	Prostitution or Going Whoring	4 631	9 929	6 592
赌 博	Gambling	17 464	51 861	30 211

注：本页数据由市公安局提供。
Note: Data on this page are provided by Shanghai Municipal Public Security Bureau.

表23.5　交通事故和火灾情况 (1980 ~ 2007)
BASIC STATISTICS OF TRAFFIC ACCIDENTS AND FIRES

年份 Year	交通事故 Traffic Accidents 次数 (万次) Number (10 000 times)	死亡人数 (人) Death (person)	受伤人数 (万人) Injuries (10 000 persons)	损失折款 (万元) Losses Converted -into Cash (10 000 yuan)	火灾 Fires 次数 (万次) Number (10 000 times)	死亡人数 (人) Death (person)	受伤人数 (人) Injuries (person)	损失折款 (万元) Losses Converted -into Cash (10 000 yuan)
1980	1.10	445	1.01	96	0.08	17	126	457
1981	1.18	507	1.06	119	0.09	33	81	202
1982	0.83	434	0.77	98	0.07	33	76	255
1983	0.73	443	0.70	99	0.06	24	67	533
1984	0.83	503	0.75	123	0.05	21	71	177
1985	0.71	687	0.57	318	0.05	30	74	374
1986	0.84	678	0.62	576	0.06	25	54	790
1987	1.01	811	0.67	959	0.06	51	56	575
1988	0.84	707	0.56	1 117	0.06	58	53	460
1989	0.75	652	0.49	1 137	0.03	30	30	394
1990	0.76	608	0.47	1 345	0.21	45	137	1 868
1991	0.75	594	0.45	1 530	0.17	38	112	937
1992	0.45	591	0.18	2 029	0.17	40	57	2 742
1993	0.81	699	0.29	4 652	0.14	73	128	2 252
1994	1.26	722	0.33	8 337	0.11	51	95	2 378
1995	1.67	788	0.38	12 077	0.11	47	86	2 100
1996	2.01	783	0.44	13 462	0.09	87	96	2 206
1997	2.16	780	0.58	13 682	0.74	51	138	2 639
1998	2.40	781	0.65	15 186	0.72	42	114	2 205
1999	2.61	726	0.78	15 924	0.66	43	90	1 487
2000	4.13	1 492	1.61	20 391	0.52	40	57	1 919
2001	4.21	1 503	1.57	23 883	0.32	31	65	966
2002	4.71	1 400	1.57	30 052	0.60	39	58	1 313
2003	5.42	1 406	1.12	39 721	0.58	47	85	1 724
2004	2.71	1 543	1.13	19 149	0.51	30	47	1 681
2005	0.92	1 393	0.88	7 961	0.43	54	84	1 731
2006	0.66	1 231	0.67	3 292	0.45	45	54	2 292
2007	0.40	1 171	0.38	1 943	0.42	50	45	2 650

注：本页数据由市公安局提供。
Note: Data on this page are provided by Shanghai Municipal Public Security Bureau.

表 23.6 交通事故情况(2007) BASIC STATISTICS OF TRAFFIC ACCIDENTS

类 别	Types	发生数(起) Number (case)	死亡人数(人) Death (person)	受伤人数(人) Injuries (person)	损失折款(万元) Losses Converted -into Cash (10 000 yuan)
总 计	**Total**	**3 952**	**1 171**	**3 771**	**1 943**
#死亡事故	Death Accident	1 094	1 171	371	724
伤人事故	Injury Accident	2 748		3 400	913
机动车	Motor-driven Vehicles	2 811	905	2 749	1 806
#汽 车	Automobiles	2 197	729	2 102	1 600
摩托车	Motorcycles	533	136	581	102
非机动车	Non-motor-driven Vehicles	847	151	816	105
#自行车	Bicycles	354	82	299	38
行人乘车人	Pedestrians and Passengers	234	79	169	24
其 他	Other	60	36	32	8

表 23.7 火灾事故情况(2007) BASIC STATISTICS OF FIRES

指 标	Indicators	合 计 Total	按事故发生程度分 By Serious Degree of Fires	
			重 大 Serious	一 般 Ordinary
次 数(起)	Number (case)	4 233	2	4 231
死亡人数(人)	Deaths (person)	50	10	40
受伤人数(人)	Injuries (person)	45	5	40
损失折款(万元)	Losses Converted into Cash (10 000 yuan)	2 650.04	7.21	2 642.83
平均每起事故损失(万元)	Average Loss per Fire (10 000 yuan)	0.63	3.60	0.62

注：本页数据由市公安局提供。
Note: Data on this page are provided by Shanghai Municipal Public Security Bureau.

表 23.8 检察院直接立案侦查案件情况(2007) CASES UNDER DIRECT INVESTIGATION BY PROCURATOR'S OFFICES

类别 Types		受案(件) Cases Accepted (case)	立案件数(件) Number of Cases Registered (case)	立案人数(人) Person of Cases Registered (person)	侦查终结件数(件) Number of Cases Settled (case)	侦查终结人数(人) Person of Cases Settled (person)
总 计	**Total**	**1 935**	**444**	**502**	**414**	**487**
贪污贿赂案件	**Number of Cases on Corruption and Bribery**	**1 708**	**408**	**464**	**373**	**443**
贪 污	Corruption	656	108	127	97	117
贿 赂	Bribery	932	260	289	243	285
挪用公款	Misappropriation of Public Funds	82	35	42	28	33
集体私分	Collective Illegal Possession of Publice Funds	13	3	3	3	3
巨额财产来源不明	Unstated Source of Large Properties	22	1	1		
其 他	Others	3	1	2	2	5
渎职侵权案件	**Number of Cases on Abuse and Dereliction of Duty**	**227**	**36**	**38**	**41**	**44**
滥用职权	Abuse of Power	111	25	25	26	26
玩忽职守	Dereliction of Duty	30	6	6	6	6
徇私舞弊	Fraudulent Practice	67	4	6	8	11
侵犯公民权利	Offences Against Citizens' Rights	17	1	1	1	1
其 他	Others	2				

表 23.9 检察院民事、行政案件办理情况(2007) CIVIL CASES AND ADMINISTRATIVE CASES HANDLED BY PROCURATOR'S OFFICES

单位:件(case)

类别 Types		受案 Cases Accepted	审查处理 Cases Investigated	其中 of which: 立案 Cases Registered	结案处理 Cases Settled	其中 of which: 抗诉 Appeals Rejected
总 计	**Total**	**1 425**	**1 361**	**508**	**470**	**63**
民事案	**Civil Cases**	**1 291**	**1 229**	**487**	**447**	**62**
#合同纠纷案	Contract Disputes	451	389	177	160	24
权益纠纷案	Rights and Interests Disputes	248	236	102	70	6
劳动争议	Labour Disputes	135	134	45	42	1
婚姻家庭、继承纠纷案	Marriages and Inheritance Disputes	74	73	21	23	4
行政案	**Administrative Cases**	**134**	**132**	**21**	**23**	**1**

注：本页数据由市检察院提供。
Note: Data on this page are provided by Shanghai Municipal People's Procurator's Offices.

表 23.10 检察院申诉案件处理情况(2007)
APPEALS HANDLED BY PROCURATOR'S OFFICES

单位:件(case)

类别	Types	受案 Cases Accepted	审查处理 Cases Investigated	其中 of which: 分送本院其他部门 Dilivering to Other Department of Such Procurator's Offices
总计	**Total**	**10 744**	**10 692**	**2 203**
首次申诉	**Appeals First Time**	**5 330**	**5 284**	**1 821**
#不服不立案	Appeals Against Rejection of the Case	265	264	207
不服刑事拘留	Appeals Against Criminal Detention	8	8	2
不服逮捕	Appeals Against Arrest	4	4	
不服刑事判决	Appeals Against Judgment of Criminal Case	272	274	25
不服民事行政裁决	Appeals Against Aadminnistration Arbitrament of Civil Case	1 885	1 842	1 329
不服劳教	Appeals Against Judgment of Reeducation Through Labor	7	7	
重复申诉	**Appeals Repeated**	**5 414**	**5 408**	**382**

注:本表数据由市检察院提供。
Note: Data in this table are provided by Shanghai Municipal People's Procurator's offices.

表 23.10 续表 continued

单位:件(case)

类别	Types	其中 of which: 移送其他检查院 Removing to Other Procurator's Offices	移送公安机关 Removing to Public Security Organs	移送其他机关 Removing to Other Organs	直接答复 Direct Reply
总计	**Total**	**3 066**	**557**	**3 401**	**772**
首次申诉	**Appeals First Time**	**1 143**	**275**	**1 194**	**553**
#不服不立案	Appeals Against Rejection of the Case	21	2		10
不服刑事拘留	Appeals Against Criminal Detention	1	5		
不服逮捕	Appeals Against Arrest	3			
不服刑事判决	Appeals Against Judgment of Criminal Case	69	1	28	21
不服民事行政裁决	Appeals Against Aadminnistration Arbitrament of Civil Case	313	1	43	146
不服劳教	Appeals Against Judgment of Reeducation Through Labor		4		2
重复申诉	**Appeals Repeated**	**1 923**	**282**	**2 207**	**219**

表23.11　法院各类案件办理情况(2007)
CASES HANDLED BY COURTS

单位:件(case)

类别	Types	收案 Cases Accepted	结案 Cases Settled	其中 of which 判决 Judgement	裁定 Arbitration	调解 Mediation
一审刑事案件	**First Trial Criminal Cases**	**20 086**	**20 113**	**19 934**	**167**	**12**
#侵犯公民人身权利、民主权利罪	Offences Against Citizens' Personal and Democratic Rights	2 464	2 488	2 346	130	12
侵犯财产罪	Offences Against Properties	10 697	10 699	10 676	23	
妨碍社会管理秩序罪	Offences Against Social Management of Order	4 100	4 107	4 101	6	
一审民事案件	**First Trial Civil Cases**	**197 695**	**197 785**	**75 457**	**72 093**	**50 235**
婚姻家庭、继承案件	Marriages and Inheritance Cases	26 837	27 003	8 788	6 209	12 006
婚姻家庭案件	Marriages and Fimily Cases	25 012	25 225	8 212	5 918	11 095
继承案件	Inheritance Cases	1 825	1 778	576	291	911
合同纠纷案件	Contract Disputes Cases	139 398	139 487	52 499	56 481	30 507
#买卖合同纠纷	Trade Contracts	22 190	22 276	7 673	6 430	8 173
房地产开发经营合同纠纷	Real Estate Development Contracts	6 056	6 103	4 131	1 218	754
借款合同纠纷	Loan Contracts	18 567	18 549	9 610	3 877	5 062
租赁合同纠纷	Lease Contract	8 205	8 200	3 399	3 104	1 697
劳动争议	Labor Disputes	10 901	10 898	5 367	2 803	2 728
劳务合同	Labor Contracts	1 316	1 359	555	307	497
权属、侵犯纠纷及其他民事案件	Disputes of Right Infringement of Right and Other Civil Affaires	31 460	31 295	14 170	9 403	7 722
#所有权及与所有权相关权力纠纷	Ownership and Related Rights	12 892	12 776	5 250	4 174	3 352
票据、证券权益纠纷	Disputes of Bill and Securities Disputes	28	20	12	7	1
股东权纠纷	Shareholder Rights	996	1 046	447	454	145
人身权纠纷	Personal Rights	12 604	12 440	6 678	1 853	3 909
其他民事案件	Other Civil Cases	4 940	5 013	1 783	2 915	315
一审行政案件	**First Trial Administrative Cases**	**1 929**	**1 952**	**897**	**1 054**	**1**

注:本表数据由市高级人民法院提供。
Note: Data in this table are provided by Shanghai Municipal Senior Court.

表23.12 法院执行案件情况(2007)
CASES EXECUTED BY COURTS

单位:件(case)

类别	Types	收案 Cases Accepted	结案 Cases Settled	其中 of which 自动履行 Automatic Performance	和解 Mediation	强制执行 Compellent Execution
总计	**Total**	**91 442**	**91 520**	**27 971**	**12 506**	**20 071**
刑事	Criminal Cases	6 064	6 250	536	25	345
民事	Civil Cases	76 130	75 877	24 027	11 472	17 473
行政	Administrative Cases	59	56	19	1	10
行政非诉审查与执行	Non-litigious Investigation and Execution of Administration	2 994	2 986	1 105	257	167
仲裁	Arbitration	5 699	5 831	2 201	610	1 989
公证债权文书	Notary Creditor's Rights	493	517	83	140	86
其他	Others	3	3		1	1

表23.13 法院各类案件结案情况(2005~2007)
CASES ENDED BY COURTS

单位:起(time)

类别	Types	2005	2006	2007
总计	**Total**	**283 230**	**311 493**	**338 726**
刑事案件	Criminal Cases	17 353	19 579	22 091
婚姻家庭、继承案件	Marriages and Inheritance Cases	28 563	29 111	28 173
合同纠纷案件	Contract Disputes Cases	128 118	138 130	154 936
权属、侵犯纠纷及其他民事案件	Disputes of Right Infringement of Right and Other Civil Affairs	31 153	32 455	35 244
行政案件	Administrative Cases	3 016	2 961	3 032
申诉、申请再审	Second Trial on Appeals and Requisition	4 023	4 145	3 726
司法赔偿	Justice Compensation	6	2	4
执行案件	Executed Cases	70 998	85 110	91 520

注：本表数据由市高级人民法院提供。
Note: Data in this table are provided by Shanghai Municipal Senior Court.

表 23.14 查处广告违法情况(2006 ~ 2007)
ILLEGAL ADVERTISEMENT PUNISHED

指 标	Indicators	2006 查处案件数(件) Case Punished (case)	2006 罚没款(万元) Amercement (10 000 yuan)	2007 查处案件数(件) Case Punished (case)	2007 罚没款(万元) Amercement (10 000 yuan)
总 计	**Total**	**1 471**	**1 185**	**1 615**	**1 915**
药 品	Leechdom	89	92	46	116
食 品	Foodstuff	302	105	319	341
化妆品	Cosmetic	93	33	121	78
医疗服务	Medical Service	255	93	162	120
房地产	Real Estate	136	297	152	393
家 电	Household Appliance	21	61	29	140
其 他	Others	575	504	786	727

表 23.15 商标认定情况 (2005 ~ 2007)
TRADEMARK CONFIRMED

单位:个(unit)

指 标	Indicators	2005	2006	2007
经认定的上海市著名商标数	Quantity of Confirmed Shanghai Famous Trademarks	126	178	174
上海市著名商标累计有效数	Accumulative Quantity of Shanghai Famous Trademarks	318	440	498

表 23.16 查处商标违法情况(2005 ~ 2007)
ILLEGAL TRADEMARK PUNISHED

指 标	Indicators	2005	2006	2007
查处商标违法案件(件)	Illegal Trademark Punished (case)	1 227	2 217	3 031
#商标侵权案件	Trademark Tort Case	1 108	2 076	2 946
处罚款(万元)	Amercement (10 000 yuan)	1 088	1 488	1 678
收缴和消除侵权商标标识(万件)	Confiscated and Eliminated Tortious Trademark Signs (10 000 cases)	162	160	138
移送司法机关案件(件)	Case Removed to Judicial Organ (case)	11	9	3

注：本页数据由市工商行政管理局提供。
Note: Data on this page are provided by Shanghai Administration of Industry and Commerce.

上/海/统/计/年/鉴

主要统计指标解释

律　师

指依法取得律师执业证书，担任法律顾问，民事(刑事、行政)案件代理人、刑事案件辩护人、办理非诉讼业务，解答法律询问，代写法律事务文书等，为社会提供法律服务的人员。

公证人员

指在国家机关依法办理公证事务的司法人员。包括公证员、助理公证员和在公证处工作的其他人员。

公证文书

指公证处根据当事人申请，依照事实和法律，按照法定程序制作的，具有法律效力的司法证明文书。根据公证书用途和使用地，公证书分为国内公证书、国内经济公证书、涉外民事公证书、涉外经济公证书四类。

调解民间纠纷

指调解委员会按照法律规定，根据自愿原则，用说服教育的方法调解民间发生的有关民事权利和义务争执的件数，包括调解成功数和调解未成功数。该指标主要反映人民调解委员会的工作量。

立　案

指人民检察院对受理的报案、控告、举报或自首及自行发现的犯罪线索、犯罪嫌疑人进行初步调查后，认为存在职务犯罪事实和应追究刑事责任，并决定作为刑事案件进行侦查的诉讼活动，是追究犯罪的开始。该指标主要反映人民检察院依法将职务犯罪线索作为刑事案件进行侦查的诉讼活动。

申　诉

指经检察机关信访部门审查处理后，移送到检察机关申诉部门的申诉案件，包括不服检察机关处理决定和不服法院刑事判决和裁定的申诉的案件。

EXPLANATORY NOTES TO MAJOR STATISTICAL INDICATORS

□ Lawyers

Lawyers are certified legal workers according to law, and who are employed by legal counseling firms to act as legal advisers, agents in criminal or civil lawsuits, or defenders in criminal lawsuits, or to handle non-litigious legal affairs, to advise on matters of law or to write legal papers for others, and provide service to the public.

□ Notary Personnel

Notary Personnel are judicial workers of the state notary organs handling notarization work according to law. They include notaries, assistant notaries, and other people working in notary firms.

□ Notary Documents

Notary Documents refer to the judicatory notary documents drawn up by the request of the party and are in accordance with facts and laws and following certain legal proceedings. According to usage and locality, the notary documents are divided into following 4 types: domestic notary documents, domestic economic notary documents, foreign-related civil notary documents and foreign-related economic notary documents.

□ Mediation of Civil Disputes

Mediation of Civil Disputes refers to number of cases made by mediation committees in mediating in civil disputes concerning civil rights and duties through persuasion and education in accordance with the provisions of law on a voluntary basis, so as to solve disputes by helping the parties involved come to an agreement and understanding, including those unsuccessful ones. This indicator reflects the workload of the mediation committees.

□ Acceptance of Case

Acceptance of Case refers to the decision made by the people's procuratorate office on reported cases, prosecution, impeachment, surrender, self-found criminal clues or suspects after initial investigation to confirm the act of crime and to start legal proceedings of the case as criminal case.

□ Appeals

Appeals refer to cases transferred to the appeal departments of procurator's offices after initial review by departments dealing with complaint letters and calls of the public. Included are appeals against decisions made by procurator's offices and appeals against court rules and verdicts.

第二十四篇

CHAPTER 24

浦东新区

PUDONG NEW AREA

表 24.1 主要年份人口、从业人员、工资和婚姻情况
POPULATION, EMPLOYMENT, WAGES AND MARRIAGE IN MAIN YEARS

指 标	Indicators	2000	2006	2007
年末总人口（万人）	**Year-end Population (10 000 persons)**	**164.87**	**187.56**	**191.16**
按性别分	Grouped by Sex			
男 性	Male	82.75	94.45	96.13
女 性	Female	82.12	93.11	95.03
按农业、非农业分	Grouped by Agriculture and Non-agriculture			
农业人口	Agriculture	30.30	12.32	11.26
非农业人口	Non-agriculture	134.57	175.24	179.90
人口密度（人/平方公里）	Density of Population (person/sq. km)	3 091	3 293	3 356
总户数（万户）	Total Households (10 000 households)	60.52	70.11	71.35
每户平均人口（人）	Average Persons Per Household (person)	2.72	2.68	2.68
人口自然变动	Natural Change of Population			
出生人口（人）	Number of Birth (person)	8 229	12 708	16 710
出生率（‰）	Birth Rate (‰)	5.07	6.83	8.82
死亡人口（人）	Number of Death (person)	11 007	12 910	13 718
死亡率（‰）	Death Rate (‰)	6.78	6.93	7.24
自然增长率（‰）	Natural Growth Rate (‰)	-1.71	-0.10	1.58
人口迁移变动	Migration			
迁入人口（人）	Inflows (person)	160 975	106 408	101 619
迁入率(‰)	Rate of Inflows (‰)	99.10	57.20	53.66
迁出人口（人）	Outflows (person)	103 486	78 638	68 683
迁出率（‰）	Rate of Outflows (‰)	63.70	42.20	36.27
净迁移率（‰）	Net Migration Rate (‰)	35.40	14.90	17.39
从业人员（万人）	Employees(10 000 persons)	104.05	146.71	149.08
职工人数（万人）	Staff and Workers (10 000 persons)	67.75	66.57	62.30
职工工资总额（亿元）	Wages of Staff and Workers (100 million yuan)	120.59	278.91	354.32
职工平均工资（元）	Average Annual Wages of Staff and Workers (yuan)	17 607	41 725	56 878
婚姻登记	Marriages			
准予登记结婚（对）	Marriage Registration Permitted (couples)	11 083	24 361	16 890
离婚登记（对）	Divorces (couples)	2 102	5 378	5 165

注：本表数据由浦东新区统计局提供。
Note: Data in this table are provided by Shanghai Pudong New Area Statistical Bureau. .

表 24.2 主要年份增加值和指数
VALUE ADDED AND INDEX IN MAIN YEARS

指 标	Indicators	2000	2006	2007
增加值（亿元）	**Value Added (100 million yuan)**	**920.63**	**2 365.33**	**2 750.76**
第一产业	Primary Industry	5.72	5.88	6.06
第二产业	Secondary Industry	488.60	1 194.47	1 306.49
工 业	Industry	445.43	1 133.76	1 237.36
建筑业	Construction	43.17	60.71	69.13
第三产业	Tertiary Industry	426.31	1 164.98	1 438.21
构成（%）	**Composition (%)**	**100**	**100**	**100**
第一产业	Primary Industry	0.6	0.2	0.2
第二产业	Secondary Industry	53.1	50.5	47.5
工 业	Industry	48.4	47.9	45
建筑业	Construction	4.7	2.6	2.5
第三产业	Tertiary Industry	46.3	49.3	52.3
增加值指数（以 1990 年为 100）	**Index of Value Added (1990 = 100)**	**633.5**	**1 492.2**	**1 707.1**
第一产业	Primary Industry	139.1	132.9	125.7
第二产业	Secondary Industry	506.5	1 187.6	1 307.5
第三产业	Tertiary Industry	1 084.9	2 591.0	3 057.4
增加值指数（以上年为 100）	**Index of Value Added (preceding year = 100)**	**116.5**	**113.4**	**114.4**
第一产业	Primary Industry	104.9	94.9	94.6
第二产业	Secondary Industry	115.2	112.1	110.1
第三产业	Tertiary Industry	119.6	115.0	118.8

注：本表数据由浦东新区统计局提供。
Note: Data in this table are provided by Pudong New Area Statistical Bureau. .

表 24.3 主要年份城市基础设施投资额和公用事业情况
INVESTMENT IN URBAN INFRASTRUCTURE AND PUBLIC UTILITIES IN MAIN YEARS

指标	Indicators	2000	2006	2007
城市基础设施投资额（万元）	**Investment in Urban Infrastructure (10 000 yuan)**	**545 081**	**1 560 384**	**2 345 407**
电力建设	Power Generation Facilities Construction	43 043	278 704	586 967
交通邮电	TranspOtation and Post	233 014	905 210	1 488 125
公用设施	Public Facilities	269 024	376 470	270 315
自来水	**Tap Water**			
自来水管道长度（公里）	Length of Tap Water Pipelines (km)	2 636	3 617	4 090
自来水生产能力（万吨/日）	Tap Water Supply Capacity (10 000 tons/day)	171.98	189.60	183.20
售水量（万吨）	Sales of Tap Water (10 000 tons)	33 014	44 475	46 882
#生活用水	Residential Use	17 655	29 689	25 690
液化石油气	**Liquefied Petroleum Gas**			
销售量（万吨）	Sales (10 000 tons)	3.58	4.69	4.10
#家庭用	Family Use	2.80	3.36	2.97
家庭用液化气户数（万户）	Liquefied Petroleum Gas Users(10 000 households)	45.55	46.30	38.85
道　路	**Road**			
铺装道路长度（公里）	Length of Paved Road (km)	835	962	619
铺装道路面积（万平方米）	Area of Paved Road (10 000 sq. m)	1 180	1 710	1 356
交　通	**Traffic**			
年末实有公交线路条数（条）	Length of Public Traffic (year-end) (route)	169	177	186
年末实有公交线路长度（公里）	Lines of Public Traffic Routes (year-end) (km)	4 030	4 402	4 480
年末运营公共车辆（辆）	Public Transportation Vehicles (year-end) (vehicle)	3 025	3 453	3 389
客运总量（亿人次）	Passengers Volume (100 million person-times)	5.0	6.4	6.3
城市绿化	**Urban Greenbelt**			
园林绿地面积（公顷）	Area of Parks and Green Areas (hectare)	3 830	8 739	8 300
人均公共绿地面积（平方米）	Per Capita Public Green Area (sq. m)	11.00	24.21	24.29
绿化覆盖率（%）	Green Area Coverage (%)	30.2	37.4	37.3
公园数（个）	Number of Parks (nuit)	12	17	18

①自来水管道长度包括系统外单位。
②本表数据由浦东新区统计局提供。
❶Lengths of tap water pipelines include which are outside the system.
❷Data in this table are provided by Shanghai Pudong New Area Statistical Bureau.

表 24.4 主要年份全社会固定资产投资主要指标
MAJOR INDICATORS OF TOTAL INVESTMENT IN FIXED ASSETS IN MAIN YEARS

指 标	Indicators	2000	2006	2007
投资总额（亿元）	**Total Investment (100 million yuan)**	**351.06**	**659.97**	**784.10**
#房地产	Real Estate	111.18	257.81	247.46
在投资总额中	**In Total Investment**			
按构成分	Grouped by Use of Funds			
#建筑安装工程	Construction and Installation	165.70	345.12	356.52
设备、工具、器具购置	Purchase of Equipment and Instruments	92.21	121.39	247.26
按建设性质分	Grouped by Type of Construction			
#新　建	New Construction	174.55	313.35	347.81
改　建	Reconstruction	22.35	42.14	95.91
扩　建	Expansion	19.66	28.76	71.45
按三次产业分	Grouped by Type of Industry			
#第二产业	Secondary Industry	143.62	139.65	224.59
第三产业	Tertiary Industry	206.77	520.32	559.51
按经济类型分	Grouped by Economic Types			
#国有经济	State-owned	118.90	238.93	275.35
集体经济	Collective-owned	20.24	30.91	11.97
联营经济	Joint Owned	9.68	8.06	5.06
股份制经济	Shareholding	56.85	174.38	237.78
外商投资经济	Foreign Funded	104.75	113.18	127.48
港澳台商投资经济	Hong Kong, Macau and Taiwan Funded	26.98	37.40	54.40
房屋建筑面积（万平方米）	**Floor Space of Buildings (10 000 sq. m)**			
施工面积	Floor Space of Construction	1 576.48	2 555.22	2 269.61
#住　宅	Residential Housing	735.93	1 521.58	1 267.03
竣工面积	Floor Space Completed	570.36	879.26	567.70
#住　宅	Residential Housing	278.93	597.93	379.02
房屋建筑面积竣工率（%）	Rate of Floor Space Completed of Buildings(%)	36.2	34.4	25.0
资金来源合计（亿元）	**Total Capital Source(100 million yuan)**	**407.97**	**1 015.33**	**1 098.90**
上年末结余资金	Balance at End of Previous Year	67.81	162.50	163.55
本年资金来源小计	Sub-total Capital Source of the Year	340.16	852.83	935.35
#国家预算内资金	State Budgetarg Funds	4.21	18.85	6.27
国内贷款	Domestic Loans	94.78	256.66	318.43
利用外资	Foreign Capital Absorbed	41.38	48.45	41.79
自筹资金	Self-financial Capital	148.87	301.98	285.69
其他资金	Other Capital	50.92	226.89	264.38

表 24.5 主要年份财政、金融和保险情况
MAJOR FACT OF FINANCE AND INSURANCE IN MAIN YEARS

指 标	Indicators	2000	2006	2007
全部财政收入（亿元）	**Total Fiscal Revenue(100 million yuan)**	**103.21**	**587.49**	**854.49**
地方财政收入(亿元)	**Local Fiscal Revenue(100 million yuan)**	**56.40**	**178.31**	**260.80**
#区级财政收入	Fiscal Revenue at District Level	35.59	179.52	287.06
#增值税	Value-added Tax	4.43	33.46	40.24
营业税	Business Tax	12.22	62.71	91.42
个人所得税	Personal Income Tax	7.77	24.14	32.05
城市维护建设税	Tax on Urban Construction and Maintenance	1.16	2.62	3.73
房产税	Tax on Real Estate	1.34	4.52	7.34
企业所得税	Enterprise Income Tax	7.27	30.46	51.48
契 税	Contract Tax	0.71	14.43	22.78
地方财政支出(亿元)	**Local Government Expenditures(100 million yuan)**	**69.60**	**222.58**	**287.24**
#一般公共服务	Common Pubic Service			15.60
公共安全	Pubic Security			11.70
教 育	Education			26.94
社会保障和就业	Social Security and Jobs			30.62
城乡社区事务	Urban and Country Community Affairs			111.14
工业商业金融等事务	Industrial,Commercial and Financial Affairs			44.59
中资银行存款余额（亿元）	Saving Deposit Balance of Chinese Financial Institutions (100 million yuan)	1 046.81	3 293.70	3 945.50
中资银行贷款余额（亿元）	Loan Balance of Chinese Financial Institutions (100 million yuan)	891.59	3 060.26	3 413.98
中资保险费收入(亿元)	Premium Income(100 million yuan)	63.31	171.47	182.33
赔 款(亿元)	Indemnite Expenditure and Payment(100 million yuan)	7.06	26.17	29.29
赔款率（%）	Indemnitey and Premium Ratio(%)	11.2	15.3	16.1

①2007 年财政支出启用新会计科目。
②本表数据由浦东新区统计局提供。
❶Fiscal expenditure start to use new accounting subjects in 2007.
❷Data in this table are provided by Shanghai Pudong New Area Statistical Bureau..

表 24.6 主要年份农业主要指标
MAJOR INDICATORS OF AGRICULTURE IN MAIN YEARS

指标	Indicators	2000	2006	2007
户　数（万户）	Households (10 000 households)	13.67	12.52	11.19
人　口（万人）	Population (10 000 persons)	36.82	35.21	32.45
劳动力（万人）	Labour Force (10 000 persons)	19.86	19.51	16.99
外省市流入劳动力（人）	Labour Move in from Outside Shanghai (person)	91 268	314 539	443 912
第一产业	Primary Industry	14 743	15 006	20 233
第二产业	Secondary Industry	52 715	211 823	285 187
第三产业	Tertiary Industry	23 810	87 710	138 492
农业总产值（亿元）	**Gross Output Value of Agriculture (100 million yuan)**	**12.57**	**11.50**	**11.65**
种植业	Planting	5.96	6.74	6.83
林　业	Forestry	0.13	2.28	2.03
牧　业	Animal Husbandry	6.08	2.07	2.37
渔　业	Fishery	0.40	0.42	0.42
上年末耕地面积（公顷）	Area of Cultivated Land (last year-end) (hectare)	12 799	8 849	8 287
当年减少耕地面积（公顷）	Decrease in Cultivated Area (hectare)	133	562	272
年末耕地面积（公顷）	Cultivated Areas (year-end) (hectare)	12 666	8 287	8 029
#水　田	Paddy Fields	11 239	7 570	7 374
旱　田	Dry Fields	1 427	718	655
主要农副产品产量	Output of Major Farm and Sideline Products			
粮　食（万吨）	Grain (10 000 tons)	6.83	1.35	1.25
蔬　菜（万吨）	Vegetables (10 000 tons)	32.17	27.08	23.38
水　果（万吨）	Fruit (10 000 tons)	0.21	0.53	0.46
生猪饲养量（万头）	Hogs Raised (10 000 heads)	55.83	21.18	8.28
猪肉产量（万吨）	Pork (10 000 tons)	3.13	1.26	0.72
牛奶产量（万吨）	Cow Milk (10 000 tons)	3.06	1.05	0.85
鲜蛋产量（万吨）	Poulty Eggs (10 000 tons)	1.27	0.09	0.05
水产品（万吨）	Aquatic Products (10 000 tons)	0.31	0.24	0.26
#淡水产品	Freshwater Aquatic Products	0.25	0.24	0.26
农业机械总动力（万千瓦）	Total Power of Agricultural Machinery (10 000 kw)	6.39	1.61	1.56
机电排灌面积（万公顷）	Drainage and Irrigation Area Used by Machinery and Electricity (10 000 hectares)	1.08	0.14	0.42

注：本表数据由浦东新区统计局提供。
Note: Data in this table are provided by Shanghai Pudong New Area Statistical Bureau..

表 24.7 主要年份工业企业主要指标
MAJOR INDICATORS OF INDUSTRIAL ENTERPRISES IN MAIN YEARS

指 标	Indicators	2000	2006	2007
工业总产值(亿元)	**Gross Output Value of Industry (100 million yuan)**	**1 793.14**	**4 306.13**	**4 649.41**
按轻、重工业分	Grouped by Light and Heavy Industry			
轻工业	Light Industry	439.02	805.77	926.74
重工业	Heavy Industry	1 354.12	3 500.36	3 722.67
按登记注册类型分	Grouped by Registration Categories			
国有经济	State-owned	300.12	134.04	94.15
集体经济	Collective-owned	56.84	33.71	32.06
其他经济	Others	1 436.18	4 138.38	4 523.20
#外商投资企业	Foreign Funded Units	795.43	2 361.97	2 951.46
按企业规模分	Grouped by Size of Enterprises			
大型企业	Large Enterprise	1 365.18	1 497.65	1 817.12
中型企业	Medium Enterprise	181.01	1 730.57	1 834.75
小型企业	Small Enterprise	246.95	1 077.91	997.54
出口交货值(亿元)	**Delivery Value of Industry Exports (100 million yuan)**	**436.61**	**1 347.43**	**1 339.4**
按轻、重工业分	Grouped by Light and Heavy Industry			
轻工业	Light Industry	122.42	272.31	277.76
重工业	Heavy Industry	314.18	1 075.12	1 061.64
按登记注册类型分	Grouped by Registration Categories			
国有经济	State-owned	44.94	37.30	5.89
集体经济	Collective-owned	4.49	1.24	1.49
其他经济	Others	387.18	1 308.89	1 332.03
#外商投资企业	Foreign Funded Units	270.44	867.88	820.09
按企业规模分	Grouped by Size of Enterprises			
大型企业	Large Enterprise	349.27	382.09	485.80
中型企业	Medium Enterprise	45.86	729.19	669.90
小型企业	Small Enterprise	41.48	236.15	183.70
工业企业经济指标	**Economic Indicators of Industrial Enterprises**			
年末资产总计(亿元)	Year-end Total Assets (100 million yuan)	3 028.13	4 432.93	4 827.87
年末负债合计(亿元)	Year-end Liability (100 million yuan)	1 354.44	2 332.94	2 632.40
主营业务收入(亿元)	Prime Operating Revenue(100 million yuan)	1 853.22	4 623.49	5 108.47
利润总额(亿元)	Pre-tax Profits (100 million yuan)	128.65	267.8	325.52
税金总额(亿元)	Tax and Duty (100 million yuan)	86.7	138.88	163.78
资金利税率(%)	Profits and Tax Total Assets (%)	7.1	9.2	10.1
成本费用利润率(%)	Profits/Cost and Expenses (%)	7.4	6.1	6.8
流动资产周转次数(次)	Turnover of Current Assets (time)	1.64	2.04	2.00

表 24.8　主要年份国内外贸易主要指标
MAJOR INDICATORS OF DOMESTIC AND FOREIGN TRADE IN MAIN YEARS

指　标	Indicators	2000	2006	2007
社会消费品零售总额（亿元）	**Total Retail Sales of Consumer Goods (100 million yuan)**	**215.17**	**400.02**	**456.04**
吃的商品	Food	81.55	125.88	128.65
穿的商品	Clothing	13.65	32.24	35.63
用的商品	Articles	117.94	240.83	283.44
烧的商品	Fuels	2.03	1.07	8.30
外商直接投资签约项目数（个）	**Contracted Projects of Foreign Direct Investment (unit)**	**693**	**1 446**	**1 254**
#中外合资	Joint Venture	109	143	112
中外合作	Cooperative Operation	21	7	3
外商独资	Foreign Enterprise	563	1 292	1 138
外商直接投资合同金额(亿美元)	**Contracted Foreign Capital of Foreign Direct Investment (100 million USD)**	**28.84**	**48.42**	**49.49**
#中外合资	Joint Venture	2.73	7.67	5.08
中外合作	Cooperative Operation	0.47	0.32	0.39
外商独资	Foreign Enterprise	25.63	39.56	41.30
进出口商品总额(亿美元)	**Total Value of Imports and Exports (100 million USD)**	**254.86**	**1 073.10**	**1 280.52**
出口总额	**Total Value of Exports**	**95.80**	**444.71**	**528.10**
#一般贸易	Originary Trade	44.21	212.50	257.50
来料加工装配贸易	Processing and Assembly Trade with Customer Materials	11.37	32.35	47.81
进料加工贸易	Processing Trade with Imported Material	37.32	146.32	135.96
进口总额	**Total Value of Imports**	**159.06**	**628.39**	**752.42**
一般贸易	Originary Trade	71.91	198.72	248.66
来料加工装配贸易	Processing and Assembly Trade with Customer Materials	9.03	10.80	25.77
进料加工贸易	Processing Trade with Imported Material	22.85	95.92	80.70
外商投资企业作为投资进口的设备物品	Imported Equipment and Materials as Investment of Foreign Investment Enterprises	10.19	11.41	13.04

注：本表数据由浦东新区统计局提供。
Note: Data in this table are provided by Shanghai Pudong New Area Statistical Bureau..

表 24.9 主要年份教育、卫生事业情况
STATISTICS OF EDUCATION AND HEALTH CARE IN MAIN YEARS

指 标	Indicators	2000	2006	2007
学 校（所）	**Schools（umit）**			
高等学校	Institutions of Higher Education	3	6	6
中等专业学校	Specialized Secondary Schools	8	7	7
职业中学	Vocational Secondany Schools	8	5	5
普通中学	Regular Secondary Schools	100	105	107
小 学	Primary Schools	136	104	101
特殊教育学校	Special Education Schools	3	2	2
在校学生数（人）	**Student Enrollment（person）**			
高等学校	Institutions of Higher Education	11 940	43 435	46 991
中等专业学校	Specialized Secondary Schools	12 070	18 774	15 843
职业中学	Vocational Secondany Schools	18 423	15 379	17 457
普通中学	Regular Secondary Schools	108 448	109 193	104 669
小 学	Primary Schools	110 573	95 281	98 391
特殊教育学校	Special Education Schools	532	571	618
教职员工（人）	**Staff and Workers（person）**			
高等学校	Institutions of Higher Education	1 828	4 532	4 555
中等专业学校	Specialized Secondary Schools	1 207	1 278	1 222
职业中学	Vocational Secondany Schools	1 058	849	868
普通中学	Regular Secondary Schools	9 816	10 405	10 182
小 学	Primary Schools	8 826	7 820	7 753
特殊教育学校	Special Education Schools	125	153	158
卫生机构数（个）	**Health Care Institutions（unit）**	**586**	**651**	**693**
医院床位数（张）	**Hospital Beds（bed）**	**5 157**	**7 652**	**8 098**
卫生技术人员（人）	**Medical Technical Personnel（person）**	**6 900**	**10 427**	**12 467**
#医 生	Medical Practitioners	3 238	4 792	5 582
护师、护士	Senior and Junior Nurses	2 388	3 999	4 725
医院治疗人次（万人次）	**Total Patients Treated（10 000 person-times）**	**922.22**	**1 433.61**	**1 668.26**
#门、急诊	Out-patients and Emergency Patients	888.80	1 400.50	1 629.05
医院入院人数（万人次）	**In Patients（10 000 person-times）**	**17.02**	**16.12**	**16.01**
医院每百诊次的入院人数（人）	**In-patients/Per 100 Patient-times（person）**	**1.90**	**1.12**	**0.96**
医院病床使用率（%）	Utilization Rate of Hospital Beds（%）	101.5	102.3	104.3

注：本表数据由浦东新区统计局提供。
Note：Data in this table are provided by Shanghai Pudong New Area Statistical Bureau..

中国统计出版社最新资料书简目

（仅供参考，以最后出书为准）

中国统计年鉴-2008
中国统计摘要-2008
国际统计年鉴-2008
2008中国发展报告
中国区域经济统计年鉴-2008
长江和珠江三角洲及港澳特别行政区统计年鉴-2008
中国社会统计年鉴-2008
中国第三产业统计年鉴-2008
中国城市统计年鉴-2007
中国劳动统计年鉴-2008
中国人口和就业统计年鉴-2008
中国工业经济统计年鉴-2008
中国建筑业统计年鉴-2008
中国房地产统计年鉴-2008
中国城市（镇）生活与价格年鉴-2008
中国商品交易市场统计年鉴-2008
中国零售和餐饮业连锁经营统计年鉴-2008
中国能源统计年鉴-2008
全国农产品成本收益资料汇编-2008
中国贸易外经统计年鉴-2008
中国基本单位统计年鉴-2008
中国民政统计年鉴-2008
中国农村统计年鉴-2008
中国农村住户调查年鉴-2008（中文）
中国农村住户调查年鉴-2008（英文）
中国县（市）社会经济调查年鉴-2008
中国农产品价格调查年鉴-2008
中国经济普查年鉴-2004
中国百强县（市）发展年鉴-2008
中国教育经费统计年鉴-2007
中国农村全面建设小康监测报告-2008
中国农村贫困监测报告-2008
中国国内生产总值核算历史资料(1952-2004)
中国季度国内生产总值核算历史资料(1992-2005)
中国高技术产业统计年鉴-2008
中国科学技术协会统计年鉴-2008
工业企业科技活动资料-2008
中国棉花年鉴-2006/2007
2004年经济普查年鉴系列
2005年中国1%人口抽样调查系列资料
第二次全国残疾人抽样调查资料系列
北京统计年鉴-2008
天津统计年鉴-2008
河北经济年鉴-2008
山西统计年鉴-2008
内蒙古统计年鉴-2008
辽宁统计年鉴-2008
吉林统计年鉴-2008
黑龙江统计年鉴-2008
上海统计年鉴-2008
江苏统计年鉴-2008
浙江统计年鉴-2008
安徽统计年鉴-2008
福建统计年鉴-2008
江西统计年鉴-2008
山东统计年鉴-2008
河南统计年鉴-2008
湖北统计年鉴-2008
湖南统计年鉴-2008
广东统计年鉴-2008
广西统计年鉴-2008
海南统计年鉴-2008
重庆统计年鉴-2008
四川统计年鉴-2008
贵州统计年鉴-2008
云南统计年鉴-2008
西藏统计年鉴-2008
陕西统计年鉴-2008
甘肃年鉴-2008
青海统计年鉴-2008
宁夏统计年鉴-2008
新疆统计年鉴-2008
新疆生产建设兵团统计年鉴-2008
石家庄统计年鉴-2008
唐山统计年鉴-2008
邯郸统计年鉴-2008
呼和浩特经济统计年鉴-2008
包头统计年鉴-2008
沈阳年鉴-2008
大连统计年鉴-2008
长春统计年鉴-2008
吉林市社会经济统计年鉴-2008
四平统计年鉴-2008
延吉统计年鉴-2008
哈尔滨统计年鉴-2008
齐齐哈尔经济统计年鉴-2008
黑龙江垦区统计年鉴-2008
上海浦东新区统计年鉴-2008
苏州统计年鉴-2008
无锡统计年鉴-2008
常州统计年鉴-2008
徐州统计年鉴-2008
南通统计年鉴-2008
盐城统计年鉴-2008
镇江统计年鉴-2008
江阴统计年鉴-2008
丹阳统计年鉴-2008
杭州统计年鉴-2008
宁波统计年鉴-2008
绍兴统计年鉴-2008
台州统计年鉴-2008
舟山统计年鉴-2008
温州统计年鉴-2008
金华统计年鉴-2008
嘉兴统计年鉴-2008
湖州统计年鉴-2008
衢州统计年鉴-2008
安庆统计年鉴-2008
福州统计年鉴-2008
福州经济技术开发区年鉴-2008
厦门经济特区年鉴-2008
南昌统计年鉴-2008
上饶经济社会统计年鉴-2008
九江统计年鉴-2008
济南统计年鉴-2008
青岛统计年鉴-2008
潍坊统计年鉴-2008
东营统计年鉴-2008
郑州统计年鉴-2008
洛阳统计年鉴-2008
三门峡统计年鉴-2008
南阳统计年鉴-2008
武汉统计年鉴-2008
宜昌统计年鉴-2008
十堰统计年鉴-2008
荆州统计年鉴-2008
黄冈统计年鉴-2008
长沙统计年鉴-2008
广州统计年鉴-2008
东莞统计年鉴-2008
惠州统计年鉴-2008
深圳统计年鉴-2008
桂林经济社会统计年鉴-2008
南宁统计年鉴-2008
柳州经济统计年鉴-2008
来宾市统计年鉴-2008
河池统计年鉴-2008
海口统计年鉴-2008
成都统计年鉴-2008
贵阳统计年鉴-2008
昆明统计年鉴-2008
西安统计年鉴-2008
庆阳年鉴-2008
银川统计年鉴-2008
乌鲁木齐统计年鉴-2008
吐鲁番统计年鉴-2008

（京）新登字041号

图书在版编目（CIP）数据

上海统计年鉴．2008／上海市统计局编．
——北京：中国统计出版社， 2008.6
ISBN 978-7-5037-5386-2

Ⅰ．上…
Ⅱ．上…
Ⅲ．统计资料-上海市-2008-年鉴
Ⅳ．C832.51-54

中国版本图书馆CIP数据核字(2008)第052469号

上海统计年鉴—2008

作　　者／上海市统计局
责任编辑／郑淼淼　王立群
E-mail／yearbook@stats.gov.cn
执行编辑／钱文瑛　曹美芳
封面设计／蔡旭洲
出版发行／中国统计出版社
通信地址／北京市西城区三里河月坛南街57号　中国统计出版社
邮　　编／100826
电　　话／(010) 63376907
印　　刷／深圳宝峰印刷有限公司
经　　销／新华书店
开　　本／889×1240毫米1/16
字　　数／144.56万字
印　　张／34.75
印　　数／1～4000册
版　　别／2008年6月第1版
版　　次／2008年6月第1次印刷
书　　号／ISBN 978-7-5037-5386-2/F・2626
定　　价／360.00元